Contents

Preface   ix

PART I   *FRAMEWORK FOR ANALYSIS*   1

CHAPTER 1   Explaining democratization   1
David Potter
  1.1   About this book   1
  1.2   What is being explained? Some democratization terminology   3
  1.3   Three theoretical approaches   10
  1.4   Explanatory factors   24
  1.5   Comparative methods   31
  1.6   So what?   36
  Appendix   37

PART II   *EUROPE AND THE USA*   41

Introduction   41

**CHAPTER 2   Democracy in the 'long nineteenth century':
             1760–1919**   46
David Goldblatt
  2.1   Patterns of democratization in the long nineteenth century   48
  2.2   Political routes to the modern world: Barrington Moore   54
  2.3   Moving on from Moore: Göran Therborn   58
  2.4   Michael Mann: a new synthesis   61
  2.5   Comparing theories and societies   65

CHAPTER 3   The crisis of modern democracy, 1919–45   71
Richard Bessel
  3.1   The consequences of the First World War   74
  3.2   The effects of economic crisis   77
  3.3   The effect of social and class divisions   82
  3.4   The challenge of conflicting nationalisms   86
  3.5   Explaining the exceptions: the USA, the UK, and France   89

CHAPTER 4   Democracy in Europe: 1939–89   95
David Goldblatt
  4.1   The course of European democratization   95
  4.2   European democracy in an international context: the
      Second World War and the Cold War   96
  4.3   Democratization in the West: victors, victims and vanquished   100
  4.4   The democratic revolutions in Southern Europe   107
  4.5   An exceptional half century? The quality of
      European democracy   115

CHAPTER 5   **Democracy in the USA since 1945**   **118**
Richard Maidment
5.1   Explanatory factors and US democratization   120
5.2   The politics of race   125
5.3   A democratic crisis   133

Afterword   **139**

PART III   *LATIN AMERICA AND ASIA*   145

Introduction   **145**

CHAPTER 6   **Democracy and dictatorship in Latin America,
               1930–80**   **152**
Paul Cammack
6.1   Competing approaches   152
6.2   The fragility of liberal democracy: 1930–80   156
6.3   Politics in the wake of the economic Depression   160
6.4   A new political project: Latin American populism   163
6.5   The Cuban revolution and its political consequences 166

CHAPTER 7   **Democratization in Latin America, 1980–95**   **174**
Walter Little
7.1   The 'third wave'   174
7.2   Explaining the 'third wave': transition factors   178
7.3   Problems of democratic consolidation   183

CHAPTER 8   **Why have the political trajectories of India
               and China been different?**   **195**
Vicky Randall
8.1   Contrasting experiences   196
8.2   Explaining the difference: modernization and
       structural approaches outlined   200
8.3   The emergence of India's parliamentary
       democracy: four explanatory factors   204
8.4   The road to China's communist rule: four
       explanatory factors   208
8.5   Does democratization matter?   214

CHAPTER 9   **Democratization at the same time in South Korea
               and Taiwan**   **219**
David Potter
9.1   Legacies of Japanese colonial rule   220
9.2   Democratization denied or snuffed out: 1945 to the 1980s 223
9.3   The turn towards democratization   228
9.4   A brief comment on the explanation   237

Democratization

edited by DAVID POTTER, DAVID GOLDBLATT,
MARGARET KILOH, PAUL LEWIS

POLITY PRESS

in association with

The Open
University

Cover illustration: F.V.E. Delacroix: *'Liberty leading the people'* (1831); *President Nelson Mandela of South Africa at a Workers' Day rally at Umlazi stadium.*

The Open University, Walton Hall, Milton Keynes, MK7 6AA
First published in 1997. Reprinted 2000, 2001 and 2005

© The Open University 1997

Published by Polity Press in association with The Open University.

Polity Press,
65 Bridge Street,
Cambridge, CB2 1UR.

Published in the USA by
Blackwell Publishers Inc.,
Commerce Place,
350 Main Street,
Malden, MA 02148
USA.

A CIP catalogue record for this book is available from the British Library and from the Library of Congress.
ISBN 0 7456 1814 6
ISBN 0 7456 1815 4 (pbk)

Edited, designed and typeset by the Open University.
Printed and bound in Great Britain by Athenaeum Press Ltd., Gateshead

This publication forms part of the Open University course D316 *Democracy: From Classical Times to the Present.* Details of this and other Open University courses can be obtained from the Course Reservations Centre, PO Box 724, The Open University, Milton Keynes, MK7 6ZS, United Kingdom: tel. +44 (0)1908 653231; e-mail ces-gen@open.ac.uk

Alternatively, you may visit the Open University website at http://www.open.ac.uk, where you can learn more about the wide range of courses and packs offered at all levels by The Open University.

To purchase this publication or other components of Open University courses, contact Open University Worldwide Ltd, The Berrill Building, Walton Hall, Milton Keynes, MK7 6AA, United Kingdom: tel. +44 (0)1908 858785; fax +44 (0)1908 858787; e-mail ouwenq@open.ac.uk; website http://www.ouw.co.uk

1.3

22779B/d316b2i1.2

**CHAPTER 10 Why has democratization been a weaker impulse
        in Indonesia and Malaysia than in the Philippines? 240**
James Putzel
10.1 Fledgling post-war democracies   242
10.2 The shift to authoritarian rule   250
10.3 Democratic restoration in the Philippines   257
10.4 Reflections on the process of democratization   260

Afterword   264

PART IV *AFRICA AND THE MIDDLE EAST*   **269**

Introduction   269

**CHAPTER 11 The rise and fall and rise (and fall?) of
        democracy in sub-Saharan Africa   272**
John A. Wiseman
11.1 The problems of cultural heterogeneity and economic
     underdevelopment   273
11.2 Ideology, state and class   275
11.3 Fluctuation and change: a periodization of African democracy 277

CHAPTER 12 South Africa: democracy delayed   294
Margaret Kiloh
12.1 The breakdown of authoritarian rule   295
12.2 Explaining the breakdown of authoritarian rule   304
12.3 The transition to liberal democracy   312

CHAPTER 13 Middle East exceptionalism – myth or reality? 321
Simon Bromley
13.1 Patterns of political development   321
13.2 The fortunes of democratic politics   325
13.3 Explaining the absence of liberal democracy   329
13.4 Structural and historical approaches   336

CHAPTER 14 Islam and democracy   345
Nazih N. Ayubi
14.1 Islamic doctrine and democracy   346
14.2 Islamic practice and democracy   351
14.3 Islam in opposition   358
14.4 Towards an explanation   362

CHAPTER 15 Israel: constraints on consolidation   367
Michael Dumper
15.1 State building and democratization   369
15.2 The consolidation of Israeli democracy   374
15.3 Ethnicity and nationalism: twin challenges to
     Israeli democracy   381

Afterword   387

PART V COMMUNIST AND POST-COMMUNIST COUNTRIES   393

Introduction   393

CHAPTER 16 Democratization in Eastern Europe   399
Paul Lewis
16.1 The end of communism in Eastern Europe   400
16.2 Patterns of democratization in Eastern Europe   405
16.3 Democratization and socio-economic development   410
16.4 Elite strategy and leadership choice in the democratization process   414

CHAPTER 17 Russia's troubled transition   421
Stephen White
17.1 Russia and democratic transition   422
17.2 Social science, communism and transition   429
17.3 The friends and foes of democratization   434

CHAPTER 18 Political participation in post-communist democracies   443
Paul Lewis
18.1 Participation and democratization   444
18.2 Participation and political change under communist rule   446
18.3 Participation in post-communist states   450
18.4 Institutional dimensions of participation and democratic change   455
18.5 Gender difference in participation   460

CHAPTER 19 Nationalism, community and democratic transition in Czechoslovakia and Yugoslavia   466
Peter Ferdinand
19.1 The legacy of history and the neurosis of national survival   468
19.2 The first attempt at political communities: Czechoslovakia and Yugoslavia between 1919 and 1945   470
19.3 Czechoslovakia and Yugoslavia under communist rule   475
19.4 The distintegration of Czechoslovakia   484

CHAPTER 20 Political change in Vietnam   490
Martin Gainsborough
20.1 Political liberalization and its limits   492
20.2 Explaining liberalization   498
20.3 How far can political change go?   504

Afterword   513

PART VI *CONCLUSION*   517

**CHAPTER 21 From democratization to democratic
                consolidation**   517

Adrian Leftwich

21.1 Evidence and explanation in the analysis of
      democratization   518
21.2 From democratic transition to democratic
      consolidation   524

Acknowledgements   537

Index   538

Democracy: From Classical Times to the Present

Open University Course Team

David Held, *Faculty of Social Sciences and Course Team Chair*
Mandy Anton, *Designer*
Richard Bessel, *Faculty of Arts*
Stephen Clift, *Editor*
Lene Connolly, *Print Buying Controller*
Jeremy Cooper, *Producer, BBC*
Jonathan Davies, *Graphic Designer*
Michael Dawson, *Course Manager, Faculty of Social Sciences*
Margaret Dickens, *Print Buying Co-ordinator*
Donna Dickenson, *School of Health and Social Welfare*
Mary Dicker, *Secretary, Faculty of Social Sciences*
Bram Gieben, *Staff Tutor, Faculty of Social Sciences*
David Goldblatt, *Faculty of Social Sciences*
Anne Hunt, *Secretary, Faculty of Social Sciences*
Tom Hunter, *Editor*
Margaret Kiloh, *Staff Tutor, Faculty of Social Sciences*
Valerie Kirby, *Secretary, Faculty of Social Sciences*
Simon Lawson, *Producer, BBC*
Paul Lewis, *Faculty of Social Sciences*
Richard Maidment, *Faculty of Social Sciences*
Anthony McGrew, *Faculty of Social Sciences*
Eleanor Morris, *Producer, BBC*
Ray Munns, *Cartographer*
David Potter, *Faculty of Social Sciences*
Paul Smith, *Media Librarian*

External Academic Consultants for this book

Nazih N. Ayubi, *University of Exeter*
Simon Bromley, *University of Leeds*
Paul Cammack, *University of Manchester*
Michael Dumper, *University of Exeter*
Peter Ferdinand, *University of Warwick*
Martin Gainsborough, *School of Oriental and African Studies, University of London*
Adrian Leftwich, *University of York*
Walter Little, *University of Liverpool*
James Putzel, *London School of Economics and Political Science*
Vicky Randall, *University of Essex*
Stephen White, *University of Glasgow*
John A. Wiseman, *University of Newcastle upon Tyne*

Preface

The purpose of this book is to provide an introduction to different ways in which patterns of democratization throughout the world may be explained. The struggle of nation-states to move in a democratic direction and to sustain and entrench democratic political systems is one of the central narratives of the nineteenth and twentieth centuries. *Democratization* is the first textbook to engage systematically in a major way with this story.

The book is one of three produced for the Open University course, *Democracy: From Classical Times to the Present*. The other two books are David Held's *Models of Democracy* (second edition) and *The Transformation of Democracy?* edited by Anthony McGrew. All three are published by Polity Press. Open University courses are put together by a course team consisting of academic authors and experienced tutors, editors and designers, BBC producers, academic administrators and secretaries, and an external academic assessor. The course team and the external academic consultants who helped to write this book are listed on the opposite page.

To produce a book like *Democratization* required bringing together a wide range of academic talent, so the Open University course team sought help from a group of academics who teach comparative politics and related subjects in various British universities. This large team met initially at a two-day workshop in early 1995 when agreement was reached on a common framework and a set of detailed chapter outlines. Both first and second drafts of each chapter subsequently received critical evaluation by the course team during 1995 and early 1996. We like to think these procedures helped to produce a book with an overall coherence not normally found in collaborative volumes.

We want to thank all our external contributors for the splendid way in which they responded so patiently, during a long collaborative process, to our numerous criticisms and suggestions for improvement. They took on board a lot while preserving the integrity of their initial conception of their chapter. We also acknowledge the excellent work of Adrian Leftwich, our external assessor, for his careful reading and constructive criticism of all the chapters. We were also saddened, during the latter stages of producing this book, by the death of one of our collaborators, Nazih Ayubi, a valued academic colleague. We are honoured to include in this book one of his last scholarly writings.

A large book like this can appear to claim comprehensiveness in relation to its subject matter; but although the book ranges widely throughout the world, it is inevitably quite selective in that the explanations of democratization based on comparative analyses are grounded in evidence from only certain countries. We would have liked, of course, to provide more, involving additional countries, but there are always limits imposed by publishers and limits to what students can absorb during a given period of study. Also, democratization is an ongoing process and books on such subjects require a cut-off date; ours is the end of 1995.

Many people within the Open University helped to produce this book and we are grateful to them all. We wish in particular to express our appreciation to Mary Dicker, Anne Hunt and Valerie Kirby for typing speedily and cheerfully all the various and quite different drafts that were involved; Michael Dawson who as course manager kept us on schedule and sustained the essential links with others in the Open University; Anthony McGrew for some brilliant suggestions on how to handle various intellectual problems posed by certain drafts; and David Held who profoundly shaped the entire contents of the book by virtue of his intellectual guidance, stimulus and encouragement at every stage of the proceedings.

The Editors

PART I
Framework for analysis

CHAPTER 1

Explaining democratization

David Potter

1.1 About this book

Democratization has been a major global phenomenon during the twentieth century. It has spread with particular vigour since the 1970s. In 1975 at least 68 per cent of countries throughout the world were authoritarian; by the end of 1995 only about 26 per cent were authoritarian, all the rest having held some sort of competitive elections and adopted at least formal guarantees of political and civil rights (Table 1.2 below). This rapid political transformation began in Southern Europe in the mid 1970s, spread to Latin America and parts of Asia in the 1980s, and then moved on to parts of sub-Saharan Africa, Eastern Europe and the Soviet Union in the late 1980s and early 1990s.

    Why has democratization been a strong impulse in some countries, a weaker or non-existent impulse in others? Why have democratic forms of government and politics at certain historical points in time been more prevalent in certain regions of the world, less prevalent in others? This book is primarily concerned with these two types of questions. To answer or deal with such questions requires having some working definitions; it requires engaging in relevant comparative analysis; and it requires having a set of ideas that directs attention to a manageable number of phenomena common to the countries being compared, together with certain generalizations that suggest answers to the questions about more or less democratization. Such a set of ideas and explanatory generalizations related to them can be referred to as a theoretical approach. There are several different theoretical approaches in the literature on democratization. In this chapter we[1] set out democratization terminology, theoretical approaches and comparative methods used in this book.

    All the other chapters are organized into four main parts, plus a short concluding part, as set out in the book's table of contents. There are two organizing principles. First, each main part considers one or two regions of the world and contains country comparisons within those regions. We do that because much of the empirical comparative analysis in the literature aimed at

---

[1] I use 'we' throughout this chapter to acknowledge the fact that the explanatory framework set out here is the fruit of collaborative effort by members of the course team indicated in the Preface.

explaining democratization is, for the most part, region-specific. Second, the sequential order of the four main parts relates roughly to the historical sequence of democratization impulses in different regions of the world.

Part II, therefore, starts where the democratization of nation states began, in Western Europe and North America. (Strictly speaking, New Zealand can claim to be the first liberal democracy; it was the first country to introduce universal adult suffrage – male and female – in 1907.) The four chapters in this section aim to explain the development of and challenges to liberal democratic politics in the West from roughly the French Revolution to the present day. The explanations are based primarily on historical comparisons of the UK, USA, France and Germany; political experiences of others are also referred to, for example Spain and Portugal.

Some of the 'new nations' that broke free from colonial or imperial rule in Latin America in the nineteenth century and Asia in the twentieth century formed restricted or very partial democracies. In most instances, however, these were subsequently replaced by more authoritarian regimes; partial democracies reappeared later in some countries but not others; then, in the 1980s, shortly after democratizations in Southern Europe, a major surge towards democratization occurred in Latin America and, to a lesser extent, in Asia. In short, liberal democracy did not flourish in Latin America and Asia until quite recently. Why? The chapters in Part III consider this question by engaging in comparative analyses of different countries in these two regions.

Sub-Saharan Africa and the Middle East have been perhaps the least fertile ground for liberal democracy. What have been the main barriers to democratization in Africa? Why did fledgling post-colonial democracies collapse so quickly there? Why did democratization suddenly commence again in Africa in the early 1990s? Why has democratization continued to be largely absent in the Middle East? Part IV suggests answers to these types of questions through comparative analyses of different countries in these two regions. South Africa and Israel receive special attention.

The states of Eastern Europe and the former Soviet Union were the latest to commence democratization, although the condition of post-communism has by no means provided a solid base for steady democratic development or the peaceful transition to a new political order. Explanations of post-communist democratization in Eastern Europe and Russia based on comparative analyses are set out in Part V. The development of effective political parties, a key institutional indicator of liberal democracy, and problems of nationalism and ethnic conflict in Eastern Europe receive special attention. Democratization pressures that build up in communist regimes as a consequence of economic liberalization are also considered by examining the case of Vietnam in the mid 1990s.

The four main parts of the book contain chapters each asking a different question about democratization in different countries. Each main part is briefly introduced; there is also a short 'Afterword' to each part drawing attention to themes that cut across those chapters. The book closes with a reflection on problems of consolidating democratic politics drawing on ideas and evidence in the text as a whole.

The book has been written mainly for students at a fairly early stage in their study of comparative politics. It concentrates on processes of democratization, perhaps the liveliest and most prominent 'growth point' in the current literature of comparative politics. All the chapters have a strong empirical base; they are quite specific about certain details of political life in the particular countries being compared for purposes of analysis. In consequence the book as a whole illustrates through such comparisons the rich diversity of political experience found throughout the world. The book is also fundamentally about different historical trajectories and different ways of explaining them. As a study of democratization in the modern world it could hardly fail to be otherwise.

Most introductory texts in comparative politics do not actually get around to doing comparative analysis aimed at answering a question about politics; they are preoccupied with approaching the subject in a general way – defining political terminology, discussing the nature of theories and types of (and problems with) comparative political methodology, and so on. Although these subjects are certainly important, such general introductory texts tend to remind us of A.G. Keller's jibe about the person who is endlessly packing a suitcase for a journey that never takes place. Our approach is very different. The authors of the chapters in this book go on journeys. The essential luggage for these trips is set out briefly in the rest of this chapter.

1.2   What is being explained? Some democratization terminology

The word 'democratization' refers to political changes moving in a democratic direction. The chapters that follow aim to explain why some political regimes move in a democratic direction and others do not, and why some are more democratic than others. But what does 'moving in a democratic direction' mean and how does one identify actual political regimes throughout the world as more or less democratic? The various answers to these definitional questions in the literature are far from simple or straightforward. Our own particular formulation of democratization terminology rests on a set of seven concepts grounded for the most part in David Held's (1996) *Models of Democracy* and Robert Dahl's (1989) *Democracy and Its Critics*.

We distinguish five types of political regime. Three main types are *liberal democracy, partial democracy* and *authoritarianism;* the other two are 'markers' (explained in a moment) – *direct democracy* and *participatory democracy*. The main distinctions between these five regime types relate to different attributes of *the state* and *civil society*. In this section we shall first give working definitions of these seven concepts, then comment on their meaning and significance as a whole, then show how actual political regimes can be identified as more or less democratic using this terminology.

A *state*, following Max Weber (1972), is characterized by an ensemble of institutional patterns and political organizations – coercive, administrative, legal – distinguished from other organizations in society by having the capacity to monopolize the legitimate use of violence within a given territory (see also Held, 1996, Chapter 5). Each state also aims to provide security from foreign intervention for people within its boundaries by conducting relations, both peaceful and warlike, with other states. Most states also seek continually to promote a sense of national identity and common citizenship in order to have their rule accepted by the people (or at least some of the people), and in doing so to define away, or suppress, competing ideologies subversive of the state's rule and what the state defines as 'the national interest'. Notice that the state's power is conditional. The state *seeks* predominance and *aims* to institute binding rules. What this underlines is that the state's predominance may be strong or weak, so weak indeed that the state's power may be of little consequence beyond the walls of a political leader's compound. States are relatively durable parts of the global political landscape; the concept of political regime (liberal democracy is one form) refers to the way that basic political relationships are constituted within the state; governments, on the other hand, are composed of individual leaders who come and go more frequently as a result of periodic elections or for other reasons.

The concept of *civil society* is distinct from the state and can be said to 'name the space of uncoerced human association and also the set of relational networks – formed for the sake of family, faith, interests and ideology – that fill this space' (Walzer, 1995, p.7). Examples of relational networks distinct from the state include unions, social movements, co-operatives, neighbour-hoods, societies for promoting particular interests. Political parties also occupy this space while also, in some respects, being part of the state. Civil society can be lush or sparse in terms of the number and vitality of associations and relational networks within state boundaries. Some social forces in civil society can facilitate democratization while others can obstruct it.

It is important not to see the state as totally 'separate' or 'impartial' with respect to the associations of everyday life in civil society. As Held (1996, Chapter 7) remarks, the state is involved in the reproduction of everyday life, and accordingly there is a 'meshing' of state and civil society.

The main distinctions between liberal democracy, partial democracy and authoritarianism relate to two broad attributes of the state – accountable government and free/fair elections – and two broad aspects of civil society – civil/political rights and associational autonomy. These distinctions provide the basis for the 'shorthand' characterizations set out in Table 1.1. The characterizations are grounded mainly in Dahl's (1989) classic formulation of the institutional features of liberal democracy (Dahl called it polyarchy).

A *liberal democracy* is a type of political regime in which binding rules and policy decisions are made not by the entire community but by representatives accountable to the community. This accountability is secured primarily through free, fair and competitive elections in which virtually all adult men and women have the right to vote and stand for elective office. Citizens within a liberal democracy have the right: 'to express themselves without the danger of severe punishment on political matters broadly defined, including criticism of officials, the government, the regime, the socioeconomic order, the prevailing ideology' and 'to form relatively independent associations of organizations including independent political parties and interest groups' (Dahl, 1989, p.221).

Authoritarianism is a type of political regime characterized by state leaders who direct and regulate society without being accountable to citizens. There are no competitive elections. Citizens are denied the right 'to

Table 1.1 Liberal democracy, partial democracy, authoritarianism

	Liberal democracy	Partial democracy	Authoritarianism
state	accountable government	limited accountability of government to citizens through elections	dominant state and government not accountable through elections to citizens
	free and fair competitive elections	unfree and unfair competitive elections	no competitive elections
civil society	civil and political rights	rights to freedom of expression curtailed	severe restrictions on individual civil and political rights
	associational autonomy	associational autonomy more or less compromised	autonomous associations and organizations critical of the state virtually nonexistent

Source: for liberal democratic criteria: Dahl (1989, p.221)

criticize officials, the government, the regime, the socioeconomic order, the prevailing ideology'; citizens who express such political views run the risk of severe punishment by the security forces of the state. Alternative sources of information for citizens do not exist or are not officially allowed; secrecy in the affairs of state is routine. Independent associations or organizations critical of the state are not allowed to form and develop, and if those that exist speak or act contrary to the wishes of the state they are suppressed.

Partial democracy is a 'mixed' type of political regime in which the accountability of government to citizens is more or less qualified; military, traditional or other non-elected establishments within the state restrict the effect of elections and compromise the authority of elected government. Elections are held, but organized to ensure that only certain candidates can be elected; opposition political parties may exist and even make some impact but the electoral system is organized to ensure that normally they would neither win an election nor form a government. There are restrictions on the rights to freedom of expression and access to alternative information. Some independent associations and organizations critical of the state exist but are carefully monitored by the state.

It is important not to equate liberal democracy with democracy as such. Liberal democracy is in some respects a limited form of democracy, although not as limited as partial democracy. For this reason we include in our democratization terminology two 'markers' which note the existence of forms of democracy which, in principle, go beyond liberal democracy.

Participatory democracy has figured in the programmes of some modern social movements but there has not (yet) been a participatory democratic regime at the level of the nation-state. Its advocates argue that in liberal democracy political participation by citizens in policy decisions that directly affect their lives amounts to little more than casting their vote from time to time. Participatory democracy extends and deepens liberal democracy in terms of both state and civil society by involving the majority of people in political life. Its advocates, for example, suggest that the sphere of democratic accountability can be extended beyond government and the state to economic enterprises, the workplace, local communities and the household.

Forms of *direct democracy* have also been advocated. Local communities have control over and administer important affairs that directly affect their lives and elect representatives to larger units of administration and control (for example, districts, regions) and these in turn elect representatives to national institutions; and a single political party could operate at all these levels, linking them while representing the larger interests of society as a whole. At election time, the choice is between the party's candidates and other candidates approved by the party. The status of such a model of democracy as more advanced than liberal democracy is controversial. Some argue that there are a few regimes that have approached this model, for example, Vietnam in the 1980s (see Gough, 1990); but as Held (1996) remarks, such an arrangement 'is a recipe, in principle, for the democratiza- tion of organizations in the state and civil society, but its association with single-party polities has led many critics to doubt whether it is a form of democracy at all'.

Participatory and direct democracy 'mark' the fact that liberal democracy is in some respects fairly limited and is only one of several models of democracy. It is important to be clear that liberal democracy, partial democracy and authoritarianism are also 'models'. Each one identifies abstractly key features of a type of political regime. An actual historical or existing political regime is then identified as one or the other type by making a judgement regarding the extent to which its features approximate the working definition of that model.

It is also important to be clear that there is no continuum built into our democratization terminology. A political regime, if it moves, does not have to move continuously from authoritarianism through partial democracy in order to get to liberal democracy and beyond. Some regimes have moved in that way. Many others have 'jumped' from authoritarianism to liberal democracy without passing through partial democracy. Regimes can 'jump' in this way towards liberal democracy; they can also 'jump' back, reverting directly to authoritarianism.

We said earlier that the word democratization refers to 'political changes moving in a democratic direction'. It is now clear from our democracy terminology that the character of such movement over time is from less accountable to more accountable government, from less competitive (or non-existent) elections to freer and fairer competitive elections, from severely restricted to better protected civil and political rights, from weak (or non-existent) autonomous associations in civil society to more autonomous and more numerous associations.

Judgements are required when using any working definitions to identify actual historical or political regimes at any one time as more or less democratic. We underline this important point by considering a few examples using our own working definitions. Britain in the 1980s is identified in Chapter 4 as a liberal democracy. There was ample evidence of accountable government, reasonably fair and free elections, civil and political rights (including the right of citizens to express themselves freely on the ideology of the state and the policies of Margaret Thatcher's government), and a plethora of autonomous associations and organizations. Some would query whether the electoral system was fair when a majority of citizens voted against the Thatcher government at general elections, but an overall judgement would still place Britain in the 1980s as reasonably close to the liberal democratic model. Spain and Portugal in the 1980s were also liberal democratic, having 'jumped' there from authoritarianism in the mid 1970s.

Iraq in the early 1990s is characterized in Chapter 13 as an authoritarian regime. The government was not accountable to citizens, there were no competitive elections, civil and political rights for citizens were profoundly insecure and independent association and organizations critical of the state were virtually non-existent. El Salvador and North Korea in the early 1990s were authoritarian regimes for the same reasons.

Mexico in 1975 and 1995 is characterized in Chapters 6 and 7 as a partial democracy. The main reason is that the governing political party, founded in 1929 and known as the PRI (the Institutionalized Party of the Revolution) never allowed free and fair elections (as of 1995). In this way they ensured that the opposition could not gain access to power. There were also restrictions on the right to freedom of expression and on access to alternative information.

India in the 1980s is one of those problem cases that tests the boundary between liberal democracy and partial democracy. Certain states in India's federal union – notably Punjab, Assam, Jammu and Kashmir – were essentially authoritarian for most or all of that decade; the central government took over the administration of those states, elections were suspended, citizens in these states were denied basic civil and political rights, and independent associations and organizations were carefully watched and in some cases brutally suppressed. However, in the other seventeen states of India and at the all-India level, control of government policy was vested in elected officials, there were normally fair and free elections, civil and political rights were not substantially compromised (and criticism of government officials, the socioeconomic order and so on was freely exercised), and there was evidence of associational autonomy more or less. For these reasons, India as a whole in the 1980s is characterized in Chapter 8 as a liberal democracy, closer to that working definition than to the one for partial democracy.

Characterizing Indonesia between, say, 1980 and 1995 tests the boundary between partial democracy and authoritarianism. Parts of Indonesia were thoroughly authoritarian; the most extreme case was East Timor where independent groupings were not allowed, elections were inconceivable, and perhaps as many as 200,000 inhabitants were killed by the Indonesian army during the period. At national government level, state direction and regulation by President Suharto and his government took place with minimal accountability to its citizens. There were elections to the People's Consultative Assembly, which formally elected President Suharto and a Vice-President for five-year terms, but the electoral system was organized to ensure that the government's Golkar party dominated. The military intervened pervasively in politics at all levels of the Indonesian state. Criticism of the President, the government, the regime, the socioeconomic

*Supporters of Fretelin freedom fighters,
East Timor*

order and the prevailing ideology of *pancasila* (see Chapter 10) was either
not allowed or heavily discouraged. Alternative sources of information for
citizens were meagre and independent associations and organizations were
carefully monitored and frequently suppressed. For these reasons Indonesia
is characterized in Chapter 10 as basically an authoritarian regime.

The authors of this book have agreed a categorization of 147 countries in
1975 and 164 countries in 1995 based on judgements in terms of our working
definitions of the democratization terminology. (Most of the countries
excluded are small island states in the Pacific and the Caribbean.) Table 1.2
shows the summary totals, broken down in terms of major regions of the
world. The names of the actual countries that make up the numbers in Table
1.2, together with one or two explanatory notes, are provided in theAppendix
to this chapter (pp.37–8).

Table 1.2 confirms what was said earlier – that patterns of democratization
(moving in a democratic direction) are different in different regions of the
world. Between 1975 and 1995 there was little regime change in Western
Europe, North America and Australasia, apart from Spain and Portugal moving
to liberal democracy. The main democratization story in this region occurred
for the most part well before 1975, during what has been referred to by some
scholars as the first and second 'waves' of democratization historically (see
Box 1.1). The reasons for this will be elaborated in Part II.

The 'third wave' commenced in 1974 and was still rolling in 1995. Table
1.2 shows striking democratization in Latin America during this period, with

Table 1.2 Evidence of democratization, 1975 and 1995

	1975			1995		
	Authori-tarian	Partial democracy	Liberal democracy	Authori-tarian	Partial democracy	Liberal democracy
Western Europe, North America and Australasia	2	0	22	0	0	24
Latin America	15	2	5	2	5	15
Asia	18	4	3	11	5	9
Sub-Saharan Africa	43	2	3	12	16	20
Middle East and North Africa	14	3	2	13	3	2
Eastern Europe and the USSR/former USSR	9	0	0	5	14	8
Totals	101	11	35	43	43	78
Percentages						
1975 N = 147	68.7%	7.5%	23.8%			
1995 N = 164				26.2%	26.2%	47.6%

Box 1.1 Waves of democratization according to Samuel Huntington (1991)

First, long wave 1828–1926
  Examples: USA, Britain, France, Italy, Argentina, the overseas British dominions.

First, reverse wave 1922–42
  Examples: Italy, Germany, Argentina.

Second, short wave 1943–62
  Examples: West Germany, Italy, Japan, India, Israel.

Second, reverse wave 1958–75
  Examples: Brazil, Argentina, Chile.

Third wave 1974-
  Examples: Portugal, Spain, numerous others in Latin America, Asia, Africa, Eastern Europe.

---

68 per cent of regimes being authoritarian in 1975 and only 10 per cent in 1995. The other 90 per cent in 1995 were either partial democracies or liberal democracies. The Latin American patterns suggested by the data are the subject of two chapters in Part III. The data for Asia in Table 1.2 show quite a lot of democratization but not as much as in Latin America, a trend that frames the analyses in the three Asia chapters in Part III.

The data in Table 1.2 show that authoritarianism was the overwhelmingly dominant regime type in sub-Saharan Africa in 1975. By 1995, the 'third wave' had swept through the region, such that nearly 67 per cent were either partial or liberal democracies. The reasons for this are examined in Part IV of this book. The data also show virtually no change in the Middle East and North Africa between 1975 and 1995, authoritarianism was by far the dominant political regime type in 1975 and remained so in 1995. An explanation of this unusual pattern is given in Part IV.

The data for Eastern Europe and the USSR/former USSR in Table 1.2 reflect the momentous political changes that occurred there during the period. All nine regimes were authoritarian in 1975; by 1995 the Soviet Union had broken up (also Yugoslavia and Czechoslovakia), the number of regimes in the region had nearly tripled, and democratization was underway in 81 per cent of them. Chapters in Part V help us to understand these patterns.

The democratization terminology has enabled us to identify various patterns of democratization set out in Table 1.2. The global totals in the table are also noteworthy. Authoritarianism was the predominant political regime type in 1975, whereas only 20 years later 74 per cent of regimes were partial or liberal democracies. However, the data also show that, despite widespread democratization during the 'third wave', less than 50 per cent were liberal democratic regimes by 1995. Having identified the patterns, we now face the challenge of explaining them.

1.3   Three theoretical approaches

To explain patterns of democratization we need a set of ideas and explanatory generalizations related to them. A large number of such explanations exists. Most of them can be said to relate to or be part of one of three general types of theoretical approach:

1   The *modernization approach* emphasizing a number of *social and economic requisites* either associated with existing liberal democracies or necessary for successful democratization.

2   The *transition approach* emphasizing *political processes* and *elite initiatives and choices* that account for moves from authoritarian rule to liberal democracy.

3   The *structural approach* emphasizing *changing structures of power* favourable to democratization.

We use the word 'emphasizing' deliberately, for two reasons. First, in each of these theoretical approaches there are a large number of different explanations by authors between whom there can be important theoretical differences. But it is possible to group them within a general approach because they tend to share certain ideas and analytic procedures not characteristic of the other two.

Second, between these three general approaches are certain shared interests. All three, for example, bring into their explanations ideas about the changing nature of the state and the effect of that on the prospects for democratization, but they do so in different ways. Each approach, then, does not offer a totally different type of explanation from the other two, but the emphasis of each one is certainly different.

The modernization approach

Perhaps the classic starting point for a set of ideas that has been used to approach the explanation of democratization is the essay 'Economic development and democracy' by Seymour Martin Lipset in his (1960) work, *Political Man*. Democracy, said Lipset, is related to a country's socioeconomic development or level of modernization. To demonstrate this relationship he classified the European countries and English speaking countries in North America and Australasia as stable democracies, unstable democracies and dictatorships; and he classified the countries of Latin America as democracies, unstable dictatorships and stable dictatorships. He then compared these countries in terms of their wealth, extent of industrialization, degree of urbanization and level of education. For each of these four he used various indices for purposes of measurement. Table 1.3 indicates what Lipset found for five of his fifteen indices.

What Lipset found for the five indices of economic development shown in Table 1.3 he found also for his other indices. That is, he found that, within each of the two regions, the more democratic countries had consistently higher mean levels of socioeconomic development on his indicators than the more authoritarian countries. Based on this evidence, Lipset concluded that 'the more well-to-do a nation, the greater the chances that it will sustain democracy' (Lipset, 1960, p.31).

Table 1.3 Five of Lipset's indices of development

	Per capita income	Telephones per 1,000 persons	Per cent males in agriculture	Per cent in metropolitan areas	Per cent literate
European and English speaking stable democracies	$695	205	21	38	96
European and English speaking unstable democracies and dictatorships	$308	58	21	23	85
Latin American democracies and unstable dictatorships	$171	25	52	26	74
Latin American stable dictatorships	$119	10	67	15	46

Source: Lipset (1960) pp.51–4. The data relate to the early 1950s.

It is important to notice right away distinctive features of this type of explanation. Clearly, the explanatory focus is on '*modernization*' variables or how 'well-to-do' a nation is, although as we shall see other related factors are also brought into the explanation. The extent of modernization, or levels of socioeconomic development, is the key. There is also a preoccupation with indicators that can be measured. *Quantitative evidence* is essential to explanations in the modernization approach. Also, each indicator or 'requisite' of democracy is expressed as a *variable,* as are indicators of more or less democracy. The *explanatory procedure* consists of identifying significant *correlations* between a number of discrete socioeconomic variables each of which is associated with a democracy variable. The explanation establishes correlations, not actual causal mechanisms.

There are two things about these correlations. First, each one is expressed in '*universal*' form. The relationships have a law-like quality; they apply to all countries. Indeed, explanations within the modernization approach characteristically are based upon comparisons of many, and in some cases all, countries. For example, take the Lipset-type correlation or proposition about the number of telephones in a country as one indicator of level of development; the greater the number of telephones, the more the democracy. The proposition is universal in the sense that it can be used to examine any and every country. That proposition, or a set of such propositions, can also in principle both explain the past and predict the future. Second, each correlational statement also assumes *linearity,* for example, no telephones, no democracy; some telephones, some democracy; many telephones, much democracy. The statement of a relationship between two variables assumes that the variation can be plotted on a single line or continuum, up or down. The assumption ignores various other possibilities, for example, that increasing levels of socioeconomic development may have an unsettling effect on the political regime and a negative impact on democracy (see for example Huntington and Nelson, 1976). Such propositions also assume that what explains moving from authoritarianism to partial democracy also explains the maintenance of liberal democracy. The transition approach (as we shall see) takes a different line on this.

Lipset was well aware that establishing correlation was not the same thing as establishing that democracy is caused by socioeconomic development. Therefore he spent considerable time in his famous essay discussing various causal mechanisms which might link the two. Much of this discussion is in the section called 'Economic development and the class struggle' (Lipset, 1960, pp.45–53). He said, for example: 'economic development ... and widespread higher education actually determines the form of the "class struggle" by permitting those in the lower strata to develop longer time perspectives and more complex and gradualist views of politics' (ibid., p.45). Also, 'the lower the absolute standard of living of the lower classes, the greater the pressure on the upper strata to treat the lower as vulgar, innately inferior' and hence unworthy of political rights and democracy (ibid., p.51). Socioeconomic development in a country can also strengthen the middle class and 'a large middle class' is good for democracy because it 'tempers conflict by rewarding moderate and democratic parties and penalising extremist groups' (ibid., p.51).

The causal mechanisms related to increased education also receive attention. Education, says Lipset, 'presumably broadens man's [sic] outlook, enables him to understand the need for norms of tolerance, restrains him from adhering to extremist doctrines, and increases his capacity to make rational electoral choices' (ibid., p.39). Notice the word 'presumably' here. Lipset's causal mechanisms were presumptions, suggestions of what might explain the correlations based on his quantitative analysis. The presumed causal mechanisms were not linked systematically to his correlations.

There have been literally hundreds of studies since Lipset which approached the explanation of democracy and democratization in a broadly similar way. More recent studies have considered not just the causative effect of socioeconomic development itself but also its impact in association with a range of additional variables like varieties of political culture, ethnic cleavage and conflict, political institutions and party systems, colonial legacies, international relations. There was little attempt, however, to show how all these variables combined to explain democratization.

Various chapters in this book draw at least in part on more recent modernization explanations, in some cases primarily to critique them; examples are Chapters 3, 8, 10, 11, 16 and 18.

—————————— *Summary of the modernization approach* ——————————

- *Focus on socioeconomic development.* Many other variables are also considered, but the level of development is central. Diamond (1992, p.468), one of many scholars working on democratization who uses this approach, sums it up as 'the more well-to-do the people of a country, on average, the more likely they will favour, achieve, and maintain a democratic system for their country'.

- *Quantitative evidence.* This preoccupation is still there, although the statistical techniques have become more sophisticated since Lipset's day.

- *Correlations.* This explanatory procedure remains paramount. However, there is now more attention given to trying to link correlations empirically to causal mechanisms.

- *Universal* and *unilinear* correlations. These features in Lipset's early work have been substantially modified. It is accepted that certain correlations may not hold for all countries due to important regional differences in the world. Also, there are democratization 'waves' in world history; democratization can be more likely during some periods, less likely in others.

The transition approach

An early, influential challenge to Lipset's thesis and the modernization approach more generally was Dankwart Rustow's (1970) article 'Transitions to democracy'. Rustow drew attention to the fact that the correlations of Lipset and others using that approach 'are couched in the present tense', and are fundamentally motivated by a 'functional curiosity' which leads them to ask a functional question: what factors can best preserve or enhance the health and stability of a democracy? Rustow and others interested in developing countries 'naturally enough have a somewhat different curiosity about democracy', leading them to ask the quite different question of 'how a democracy comes into being in the first place' (Rustow, 1970, p.340).

To cope with that kind of question, Rustow argued that a historical approach, marked by holistic consideration of different countries as case studies, provided a sounder basis for analysis than looking for functional requisites. In his article, he sketched, on the basis of a comparative analysis of the histories of Turkey and Sweden, a general 'route' that all countries travel during democratization. The route has four main phases.

First, there is a phase when *national unity* within a given territory is being established. Rustow does not mean consensus here, simply that the vast majority start to share a political identity, for example we are British, we are French.

Second, this national community goes through a preparatory phase marked by a prolonged and *inconclusive political struggle*. A typical example is a new manufacturing elite coming to prominence during the process of industrialization and demanding a significant place in the polity from older elites who want to retain the status quo. Each country goes through a different struggle; the historical details differ in each case, but there is always major conflict between opposed groups rather than some bland pluralism of group conflict. Rustow calls it 'not a lukewarm struggle but a hot family feud' (ibid., p.355). Democracy, in short, is born of conflict, even violence, never as a result of simply peaceful evolution. That helps to explain why democracy can be so fragile in the early stages, and why so many countries do not make it through the preparatory phase to the first transition. The struggle can be so intense that it tears the national unity apart, or one group can become so powerful that it overwhelms the opposition, concludes the (inconclusive) political struggle, and closes off the route toward democracy.

Third, there is the first transition or *decision* phase, a 'historical moment' when the parties to the inconclusive political struggle decide to compromise and adopt democratic rules which gives each some share in the polity. In Rustow's theory there is always a conscious decision by political elites to adopt democratic rules, for a country never becomes a democracy 'in a fit of absentmindedness'.

Fourth, there is the second transition or *habituation* phase. The conscious adoption of democratic rules during the 'historical moment' may have been seen by the parties to the inconclusive struggle as necessary rather than desirable due to compromises that had to be made; gradually, however, such rules, once made, become a habit. Some of the political elites who were party to the compromise decision to establish democracy may only grudgingly have put up with it in the early years, but they are eventually succeeded by a new generation of elites who have become habituated to democratic rules and who sincerely believe in them. With that, a democratic regime may be said to be firmly established.

This type of approach clearly differs from the modernization approach. The explanatory focus is on *historical political processes* marked by *social conflict*. Rustow remarks that historically 'a people who are not in conflict about some rather fundamental matters would have little need to devise democracy's elaborate rules for conflict resolution' (ibid., p.362).

Action, struggle, 'hot family feuds', and eventual conciliation historically in particular countries is what democratization is about, not inexorable movement on the comparatively bland terrain of timeless social requisites. What drives these historical processes is the agency of *political elites* in conflict. *Democracy is produced by the initiatives of human beings.*

Rustow's preliminary sketch of phases 3 and 4 (not 1 and 2) subsequently became elaborated into the transition approach now used by many social scientists interested in explaining democratization. Notable contributions include Guillermo O'Donnell and his colleagues (1986) *Transitions from Authoritarian Rule* (4 volumes), Scott Mainwaring *et al.* (1992) *Issues in Democratic Consolidation* and Yossi Shain and Juan Linz (1995) *Between States: Interim Governments and Democratic Transition.* They make a clear distinction, as did Rustow, between the initial *transition* from authoritarian rule or preliminary political liberalization and the *consolidation* of liberal democracy. The reason for this is that initial transitions sometimes succeed (get consolidated), but they also sometimes fail, or get stalled.

Political liberalization within an authoritarian regime begins with the easing of repression and the creation of certain civil liberties. These moves do not necessarily lead to democratization; such liberalization can abort, repressive rule can return. Once liberalization starts in earnest, however, various political actors begin to get involved in the historical interplay between regime and opposition forces. These include 'hardliners' and 'softliners' within the authoritarian coalition, and 'opportunists', 'moderates' and 'extremists' within the opposition (see Table 1.4). Certain scenarios involving particular links between some of the five categories and divisions between others are more favourable to a turn towards democracy than others. For example, comparative evidence from Latin America suggests that transitions are more likely to be successful if they are controlled by a coalition of 'softliners' and 'moderates', with 'radicals' kept out (see Chapter 7). Various processes or events can trigger political liberalization. One is the failure of the authoritarian regime due to military failure or economic problems. Another is the 'paradox of success', for example when a major success convinces an authoritarian regime that it has nothing to lose and international legitimacy to gain from political liberation. The move toward democratization can start with an assessment by the authoritarian regime that the costs of staying in

Table 1.4 Political actors during transitions

Within the authoritarian coalition		Within the opposition		
'hardliners'	'softliners'	'opportunists'	'moderates'	'radicals'
Firmly committed to maintaining authoritarian rule	Willing to negotiate with the opposition about possible political liberalization or democratization	Former regime supporters with no serious commitment to democratization but hoping to gain something from it	In favour of democratization while respecting the position of traditional elites (including the military)	Demand major democratic transformation, and unwilling to compromise with the authoritarian coalition

power are increasing because there is a forthcoming succession crisis, declining military cohesion, or declining domestic legitimacy. These perceptions can be reinforced by an assessment that the economic order from which they benefit will persist anyway despite democratization.

'Crucial to the outcome of democratic transitions', say Shain and Linz, is 'the question of who governs in the interim period and the way they use their power' (Shain and Linz, 1995, p.21). Based on comparative analyses of many democratic transitions in the latter part of the twentieth century, and on detailed case studies of the first transition in particular countries, they formulate four 'ideal types of interim government' (there are other types also, like transitions from colonial rule).

First, there are *opposition-led provisional governments*. These typically include a new ruling elite claiming to have broken completely from the old order following a revolutionary struggle or a *coup d'état*. The elite 'usually declares itself a provisional government, thereby indicating its intention to lead a democratic transition via free elections within a short period of time' (ibid., p.28). But such provisional governments face a number of tremendous challenges. For example, 'the total rejection of old forms of legality and/or the lack of any credible state institution raises the critical question regarding the provisional government's responsibility to honour public obligations and constraints made by their predecessors' (ibid., p.30). Many such provisional governments promising democracy are overthrown eventually by another revolution or coup. However, such regimes do sometimes move in a democratic direction. Portugal in 1974–76 is an example where a revolutionary provisional government dominated initially by radical elements replaced an authoritarian regime, yet more moderate elements eventually prevailed. The main reasons for this democratic transition were the rapid emergence of political parties to the right of the Portuguese Communist Party, sustained commitment to elections, the reduction in power of the armed forces and the heavy involvement of a wide variety of foreign actors, including foreign governments, NATO, the EC and the World Bank. This explanation emphasizes the 'political will and actions of domestic and international actors' committed to liberal democracy in Portugal who 'took advantage of opportunities, created them, and negotiated to achieve the desired outcome' (Bruneau, 1995, p.151). The case of democratization in Portugal is elaborated in Chapter 4.

Second, there are *power sharing* interim governments. These result either from a temporary coalition between representatives of the previous authoritarian regime and people from the democratic opposition or from an incumbent administration acting as a 'caretaker' until a democratically elected government can take over. Such governments 'are generally formed when the incumbents, though their power is severely weakened, remain strong enough to exercise control' and agree to share power 'in expectation of retaining some positions of power in the future democracy' (Shain and Linz, p.42). Democratic transition in Poland (1989–91) is an example discussed in Chapter 16.

Third, there are *incumbent-led caretaker governments*. Such governments 'are the product of transitions in which the outgoing authoritarian regime ... initiates a transition in the face of growing economic deterioration, or a severe rupture within the ruling elite, or a threat of opposition and even revolt' (ibid., p.52). Spain is an example (see Chapter 4); so is South Africa (Chapter 12) where the incumbent de Klerk government acted as a caretaker administration and then, from September 1993, as the main incumbent in a power-sharing coalition on the way to the election of a national government and a constituent assembly in April 1994.

Fourth, there are *international interim governments set up by the United Nations*. Such governments are 'especially appropriate in situations where the prospects for power-sharing are minimal because of historical and brutal rivalries and total distrust among the indigenous contestants, as well as the deep involvement of foreign states, and where none of the contestants, in power or opposition, can claim, or nearly claim, total victory' (Shain and Linz, p.68). Namibia (1989–90) and Cambodia (1989–93) are examples where such UN sponsored interim governments succeeded in overseeing democratic transition; Afghanistan in the early 1990s is an example where such intervention failed.

The second transition from interim government or preliminary political liberalization to the *consolidation* of liberal or partial democracy involves historical paths that are complex and uncertain (Chapter 7 gives examples). But here again, in this transition the actors who are committed to democracy are crucial to its success. Such democratic actors are always in a minority but certain factors work to their advantage. One is that an electoral majority in the country, although not necessarily committed to democracy, does 'not want the return of *that* authoritarian regime or military regime ... which it recently had to endure' (O'Donnell, 1992, p.20). Another is that authoritarian political discourse is ideologically much weaker on a global scale than democracy discourse. With such advantages, the minority of democratic actors can advance a polity toward democratic consolidation if they: (a) 'neutralize actors who are unconditionally authoritarian' (b) 'promote preferences and practices compatible with the functioning of democracy' (c) 'increase the number of democratic actors' and (d) 'agree to subordinate their strategies (including competition among themselves) to the imperative of not facilitating a return to authoritarianism'; this last is 'the great accord or pact of the second transition' (O'Donnell, 1992, p.22).

Chapter 21 provides a more extended discussion of the conditions for democratic consolidation. Other chapters draw at least in part on transition theories, for example, Chapters 3, 6, 7, 9, 12 and 16.

───────────── *Summary of the transition approach* ─────────────

- *Focus on political elites.* The focus is on 'hardliners', 'softliners', 'opportunists', 'moderates' and 'radicals', not on 'the people'.

- *Certain actions, choices and strategies of political elites are beneficial to democratic transition, others are not.* Democratization is largely contingent on what elites and individuals do when, where and how.

- A clear distinction is made between initial democratic transition and democratic consolidation (following Rustow's phases 3 and 4).

- *The historical route to liberal democracy is determined fundamentally by the agency of elite initiatives and actions, not by changing structures.* Elite initiatives and choices never take place in a complete vacuum; they are shaped to some extent at least by structures – a set of physical and social constraints, a set of changing opportunities, a set of norms or values that can influence the content of elite choices.

The structural approach

The explanatory focus here is on *long-term processes* of *historical change*. Unlike the transition approach, however, democratization processes are explained not by the agency of political elites but primarily by *changing structures of power*. The abstract idea of 'changing structures of power' is a tough one and needs a word of clarification before brief summaries of two democratization explanations using the structural approach are provided.

There are many structures of power that constrain the behaviour and shape the thinking of individuals and elites in society. The monetary system, for example, is a structure of power for Anthony Giddens (see Box 1.2).

Notice that this structure of power exists independently of Giddens, constrains his activities while offering him certain opportunities; yet he is also part of that structure and, with others, contributes to its persistence through time. An individual is born into structures, inherits them from the past, so to speak; the life of that individual is then shaped by structures which are more or less enduring although gradually changing through time as individuals 'use' them in practice and as each structure is influenced by those structures and by events.

> ### Box 1.2 The monetary system as a structure of power for Anthony Giddens (adapted from Giddens, 1993, pp.720–1)
>
> I did not invent the monetary system in Britain. Nor do I have a choice about whether I want to use it or not if I wish to have the goods and services which money can buy. The system of money, like other structures of power, exists independently of me and constrains my activities. It does not wholly determine what I do. I could choose to live without using money, should I firmly resolve to do so, even if it might prove very difficult to eke out an existence from day to day.
>
> At the same time, while the monetary system as a structure of power exists independently of me as an individual, it cannot be independent of all individuals in society taken together. All of us actively make and remake this structure during the course of our everyday activities. Indeed, the fact that I use the monetary system contributes in a minor, but necessary, way to the very existence of that system. If everyone, or even the majority of people, at some point decided to avoid using money, the monetary system would disintegrate.

The basic premise of the structural approach to democratization is that the particular interrelationships of certain structures of power – economic, social, political – as they gradually change through history provide constraints and opportunities that drive political elites and others along a historical trajectory leading towards liberal democracy. Other such structural interrelationships lead historically in other political directions. Since structures of power normally change gradually through history, explanations using this approach are *long term*, sometimes involving centuries.

A classic starting point here is Barrington Moore's (1966) *Social Origins of Dictatorship and Democracy: Lord and Peasant in the Making of the Modern World*. Moore's main question essentially was this; why was it that during the gradual historical transformation between the seventeenth century and the mid-twentieth century, when agrarian societies (where a majority of the population lived off the land) were changing to modern industrial ones, England and France and the USA moved towards the political form of liberal democracy, Japan and Germany moved towards fascism, Russia and China moved towards communist revolution and India moved in yet another political direction? Moore's approach to the question was to compare the histories of these eight countries (Germany and Russia to a lesser extent than the others) during this historical period not in terms of pattern variables or elite initiatives but in terms of changed interrelationships between four changing structures of power. Three were social classes – the peasantry, the landed upper class, the urban bourgeoisie; the other was the state.

Moore comes to the conclusion that, generally speaking, a common pattern of changing relationships between peasants, lords, urban bourgeoisie and state led towards the political form of liberal democracy (see Box 1.3).

Box 1.3 Barrington Moore's (1966) route to liberal democracy

– The surplus produced by the peasantry during the historical process was extracted by lords, other dominant classes and the state and directed towards industrial growth in the towns.
– The landed upper class turned increasingly towards commercial agriculture while setting the peasants 'free'.
– The peasantry was gradually transformed by the commercialization of agriculture and/or eventually eliminated as a political factor of consequence.
– A rough balance of power emerged between the landed upper classes and the state, a balance maintained during the historical process.
– A vigorous bourgeoisie with its own economic base emerged in opposition to the state, and eventually went on to become the dominant class in society.
– An inconclusive political struggle developed between the bourgeoisie and the older landed classes.
– Important sections of the landed upper classes were able to develop bourgeois economic habits at a fairly early stage and were able to maintain a fairly firm economic footing historically.
– There was a revolutionary break from the past led by the bourgeoisie.
– The route to liberal democracy was marked by violence and human suffering.

From this, Moore arrived at five general conditions for democratic development (Moore, 1966, pp.430–1). There was:

- 'The development of a balance to avoid too strong a state or too independent a landed aristocracy'.
- 'A turn towards an appropriate form of commercial agriculture'.
- 'The weakening of the landed aristocracy'.
- 'The prevention of an aristocratic-bourgeois coalition against the peasants and workers'.
- 'A revolutionary break from the past' led by the bourgeoisie.

By contrast, fascism emerged in conditions where the urban bourgeoisie was comparatively weak and relied on the dominant upper classes to sponsor commercialization of agriculture through their domination of the state, which enforced labour discipline among the peasantry. Communist revolution occurred in conditions where the urban bourgeoisie was weak and dominated by the state, the link between the landlord and the peasantry was weak, the landlords failed to commercialize agriculture, and the peasantry was cohesive and found allies with organizational skills.

India, for Moore, was a rather special case. Some of the conditions on the democracy route were there, but others were not, for example, there was no commercialization of agriculture or transformation of the peasantry, and no vigorous dominant bourgeoisie. That is why Moore believed (in 1966) that India's new liberal democracy was rather precarious.

Moore's approach is elaborated in several chapters in this book, notably Chapter 2. The role of international and transnational relationships, including war, hardly figured in Moore's analysis, nor was much attention given to the growth of the working class or industrial proletariat. The more recent structural explanation by Dietrich Rueschemeyer *et al.* (1992) builds these features in. Aspects of their approach are used in various chapters, notably Chapter 9. Rueschemeyer *et al.* engage in a comparative history analysis of advanced capitalist countries and countries in Latin America, Central America and the Caribbean. They argue on this basis that whether or not a society moves towards liberal democracy is 'fundamentally shaped by the balance of class power', and ' it is the struggle between the dominant and subordinate classes over their right to rule that – more than any other factor – puts democracy on the historical agenda and decides its prospects' (ibid., p.47).

Historically, democratization has been both resisted and pushed forward by the changing dynamics of *class power.* Five classes are singled out by Rueschemeyer *et al.,* distinctions between their different interests made, and their different orientations to democratization identified on the basis of the authors' comparative history analysis. *Large landlords* as a class have historically been the most anti-democratic force in society (a confirmation of Barrington Moore's finding). One reason for this is that they have been dependent on a large supply of cheap labour, and since democratization has tended to improve the position of rural workers (making their labour no longer cheap) landlords have perceived democracy as incompatible with their interests in making adequate profits from their land. Democratization has been resisted where large landlords have been powerful, particularly when they have been closely allied with the state apparatus; democratic prospects have been improved when landlords were weak. The *peasantry* as a class, including rural workers and independent farmers, have had an interest in democratization but have acted rarely on their own in support of it. They have not always been passive spectators, however. Peasant rebellions have occurred and some plantation proletariats have been well organized and powerful. On the whole, though, the peasantry have been disorganized and comparatively weak as a force for democratization. The *urban working class* has historically been an important force pushing for extension of the suffrage, union rights and other aspects of democratic advance. Capitalist industrialization can strengthen the working class and weaken the landed class, such developments being structurally favourable to the development of democracy. In this way, democracy can be said to emerge out of the contradictions of capitalism. The role of the urban *bourgeoisie* (owners or employers of enterprises engaged in industry, trade and commerce) has been less clear. They have not been as anti-democratic as the large landlords, but neither have they been known to press for liberal democracy. Indeed, there are plenty of cases where the bourgeoisie have supported the crushing of democracy. Their role has varied a lot depending on the alignment of other classes, the position and power of the state, and transnational forces. The ambiguous position of the *salaried* and *professional middle classes* on democratization has been similar. It depends on the context. Where the working class has been comparatively weak, the middle classes have pushed for democratization to improve their own position. Where the working class has been strong, the middle classes may or may not have been as energetic in pursuing democratization. The main general points are that the position of any one class on democratization cannot be considered in isolation from others; various class alliances can occur in different countries which can be more or less favourable to democratization; and capitalist development changes class alignments and therefore can be fundamentally important for democratic prospects.

The changing structure and form of *state power* has been fundamental to democratization. For example, the state apparatus separated at least to some extent from the array of classes in society has been a prerequisite for democratization demands from subordinate classes being successfully accommodated and implemented in the society generally. A very powerful and almost entirely autonomous state in relation to social classes and groups has provided a most uncongenial setting for democratization. This has been especially so where the military and the police have been strong within the state apparatus. Democratization has had more chance of success in the middle ground between not enough and too much state power. Also, capitalist development has historically led to the emergence of a denser civil society and the growth of political parties as counterweights to state power. As for parties, dominant classes are more likely to accommodate democracy where the party system includes a strong party of the right; where such a party is lacking or no longer able to protect their interests, such classes have been readier to appeal to the military to end democratic rule.

Rueschemeyer *et al.* show that changing configurations of *transnational power* can affect class alignments and the changing nature of the state. For example, the economic dependence of one country on another can delay industrialization and keep the urban working class small, thereby weakening pro-democracy forces. Geo-political dependence can be unfavourable to democratic consolidation if massive military and economic aid strengthens the state apparatus unduly in relation to the balance of class forces. The relaxation of international tension may improve the democratic prospect. The relation between war and liberal democracy, however, has not been straightforward, and has varied depending on other factors. Military defeat by a foreign power has led to the imposition of liberal democracy. The national mobilization of many men and women for war or in the face of external threat has also historically led to extensions of the franchise and other democratic advance. Yet war also has strengthened the military in society and within the state, and in the absence of other countervailing forces severely threatened the democratic prospect. Transnational ideological and cultural flows can also enhance democratization. Liberal democracy as a 'good idea', particularly following the end of communism in Eastern Europe and the breakup of the Soviet Union, has through improved communication networks percolated everywhere, even into societies dominated by repressive states and reactionary classes.

What tends to unite all explanations within the structural approach, including Moore and Rueschemeyer *et al.,* is that, whatever the particular circumstances, a country's historical trajectory towards liberal democracy or some other political form is finally shaped by changing structures of class, state and transnational power driven by a particular history of capitalist development. Such structured historical trajectories need not be 'smooth' or linear; wars are broad structural processes that can affect democratization in particular countries and are built into structural explanations (for example, Therborn, 1978), a subject given special attention in Chapters 2, 3 and 4.

───────────── *Summary of the structural approach* ─────────────

- *A focus on changing structures of class, state and transnational power.* Certain changing structural patterns have led in a democratic direction, others have led to authoritarianism.

- *Long-term processes of historical change are paramount.* The explanatory procedure is comparative historical analysis of whole countries aimed at discerning historical causes of democratization.

- *The historical route to liberal democracy is determined fundamentally by changing structures, not by elite initiatives and choices.* There are political leaders and elites who make choices, but those choices can only be explained by reference to the structural constraints and opportunities in which they find themselves.

───

Theoretical convergence?

It is possible to object that all such theoretical generalizations about democratization are a waste of time because they can never do justice to the immensely complex reality of a country's particular history and experience. The objection is pertinent to the extent that no theoretical generalization does that, but to ignore theory and engage only in endless descriptions of a particular set of events and processes can never produce answers to questions about why democracy is here and not there, or why democratization is taking place. Each of the forthcoming chapters of this book, in addressing such questions, rightly has a strong empirical base and gets quite specific about certain details of political life in particular countries. You will find, however, that the author cannot answer the question in the chapter about democratization except by engaging in comparative analysis of empirical details using a set of categories or concepts to do so and drawing on certain generalizations relating to the concepts. That is why theoretical approaches to democratization have been introduced here.

Most chapters actually draw on aspects of more than one theoretical approach; some, like Chapter 10, draw on all three. That scholars in the 1990s do this in their work on democratization is a sign of some theoretical convergence not characteristic of the founders. Moore in 1966 made no reference to Lipset in 1960. Rustow in 1970 referred a lot to Lipset 1960 but made only one glancing reference to Moore. Most strikingly, Lipset in the second edition of *Political Man* (1983) in which he added a chapter 'Second thoughts and recent findings related to the social requisites of democracy' (Lipset, 1983, pp.460–9) in effect dismissed Rustow's analysis in a paragraph and made no reference at all to Moore. That these scholars for the most part barely took notice of each other's work was symptomatic of the radically different explanatory focus and research strategy each employed. Over the years, however, scholars working with these different theoretical approaches have found that the empirical evidence related to democratization in any country is so complex and multi-faceted that no one theoretical approach completely captures that complexity and explains it satisfactorily. Certain ideas and modes of analysis from one approach may work well on aspects of the story; other aspects may be captured more effectively by using another approach. A recent symposium on 'the role of theory in comparative politics' concluded that 'contemporary theoretical controversies are not deeply divisive' (Kohli *et al.*, 1995, p.49).

This experience also has meant that scholars using different approaches have engaged critically with each other more than the founders did. Such critical engagement has resulted in modifications of certain features of each approach. For example, we saw how the 1990s summary of modernization theory is an amended version of Lipset's original formulation; the modifications were made in response to the criticisms Lipset had received. O'Donnell, Mainwaring, Shain and Linz and others have moved along while sharpening up Rustow's work; it has even been proposed, in light of criticism from structural theorists, that transition theories must incorporate 'the simple yet theoretically complex notion that actors make choices but not in circumstances of their own choosing' (Munck, 1994, p.371). Likewise, Rueschemeyer *et al.* have moved on from Moore and, in doing so, accept, for example, that the statistical association between modernization and democracy is an important finding.

Despite some convergence of this kind, the basic differences of explanatory focus and methodological strategy summarized in this section are still there. The work of most scholars, including the authors in this book, is primarily framed by one of these three theoretical approaches.

1.4   Explanatory factors

Within modernization, transition and structural approaches are various theories of democratization, each of which draws upon a set of interrelated factors to explain why democratization occurs in some countries and not others. An explanatory factor is a condition, structure or process that comparative analysis suggests is associated with, or causes, democratization. Many such factors receive attention in different theories. Here we set out six explanatory factors to which theories in all three theoretical approaches refer, but in different ways. These factors recur repeatedly in the chapters of this book.

Economic development

All explanations of democratization direct our attention to economic development as an important explanatory factor. For Lipset, Diamond and many others working within a broadly modernization approach, positive correlations between economic development (defined in terms of rising per capita income, growing per capita energy consumption, etc.) and democratization are profoundly significant. For Moore, Rueschemeyer and others, economic development is more exactly *capitalist* development which structures fundamentally the historical route that countries take toward liberal democracy or some other political form. For Rustow, O'Donnell, Linz and others who approach the explanation of democratization in terms of transition processes, economic development helps to trigger the actions of competing elites busy crafting the democratic compromise. The different approaches also recognize that economic crises, as in Europe between the world wars (Chapter 3), can destroy liberal democracy and that severe underdevelopment, as in much of sub-Saharan Africa (Chapter 11), has not been a promising context for democratization.

The puzzle that confronts all theorists is this: What exactly is it about economic development that produces democratization? On this question different theoretical approaches have moved in different directions. Those using a modernization approach look for 'intervening variables' – variables that mediate between economic development and democratization. Lipset, as we know, presumed that economic development determined the form of the 'class struggle' by reducing the inequalities between the higher and lower classes and strengthening the middle class; and he believed that such developments in turn tempered conflict, moderated extremist views and favoured the development of democratic parties. Others (for example Hadenius, 1992) have subsequently found it difficult to substantiate statistically the fact that reductions in class inequality sustain liberal democracy but have found strong positive correlations between high literacy rates (as a consequence of economic development) and liberal democracy. Others are interested in how economic development and the growth of a market economy generate democratic ideas among the whole society; for example, the experience of being a 'sovereign' consumer can begin to generate ideas of voter sovereignty, and the gradual separation of economic and political power into distinct spheres during economic development can strengthen civil society, the existence of which is intrinsic to the very definition of democratization. Throughout all the modernization studies one notices the assumption that economic development is a fairly universal, uniform process; despite the existence of historical 'waves' of democratization, countries becoming more 'well-to-do' are likely in due course to become more democratic, and countries that already are 'well-to-do' are likely to remain liberal democratic.

Structural theories approach the puzzle rather differently. Economic development is not a uniform process. Detailed historical analyses of case studies show that each country's economy has distinctive and unusual features, including the specific character of its relations with transnational economic processes. Close attention to the detail of economic processes and their historical consequences in each case would appear to lend itself more readily than the modernization approach to the identification of causal mechanisms linking economic development and democracy. Even here, however, there are difficulties. Direct historical links between the two are not always easily identified. One needs usually to trace the 'chains-of-causation' (not intervening variables) from, say, a particular form of capitalist development to a particular class structure and then from a changing class structure and set of class interests to democratization. Causal mechanisms are frequently tighter for some links in the 'chain' than others. Another difference is that economic development in the structural approach is definitely not a uniform process leading inexorably towards democracy. As countries become more 'well-to-do', they can be propelled, as Barrington Moore showed, toward democracy or toward fascism or some other authoritarian political form (see also Chapter 3). Furthermore, although economic development and 'free markets' can generate democratic ideas in society, such development can also retard or undermine democracy or provide support for authoritarianism. For example, 'the experience of being treated as a dispensable commodity in the labour market contradicts the publicly proclaimed idea of a democratic citizen as the bearer of rights in a context of social reciprocity' and 'the widespread unemployment and rapid fluctuations in market economies render voters vulnerable to demagogic mobilisation in support of authoritarian and exclusivist forms of politics' (Beetham 1994b, p.165). In short, the political consequences of economic development are ambiguous.

Social divisions

We have seen how, in both modernization and structural approaches, economic/capitalist development produces changing *class divisions* in society (divisions based on wealth and life-chances) which are important in explaining why some countries move towards liberal democracy and others do not. Socioeconomic modernization, said Lipset, leads to the growth of the middle class whose values can be essentially pro-democratic. Capitalist development, said Rueschemeyer *et al.*, produces social classes some of which (like the urban working class) develop an interest in democratization.

The inconclusive political struggle between classes and groups on the road to liberal democracy is also of central importance in transition theories.

No one class is going to have the same interest in democratization everywhere. For example, middle classes have not always been pro-democratic; some have either acquiesced in authoritarianism (as in South Korea in the 1970s and early 1980s – see Chapter 9) or actively supported it (as in Brazil in the late 1960s and early 1970s – see Chapter 6). This underlines the importance of appreciating that any one class's position on democratization in a country may be affected by its particular relations with other classes – hence the need to analyse the changing class structure as a whole, not just an individual class.

Class divisions are not the only forms of social inequality. Explanations of democratization also refer to *group divisions* defined in terms of ethnicity, race, tribe, language, religion or other cultural criteria. Democratic forms of politics are grounded in the principle of popular sovereignty or consent by the people and thus the question of who are 'the people' is profoundly important. Where 'the people' become so divided by group antagonisms that there is no sense of shared political identity, then democratization is impossible. As Rustow pointed out, a country cannot even start on the road to liberal democracy until there is some sense of at least minimal national identity.

The theoretical approaches agree on the relevance of these types of social divisions for democratization but weigh their significance differently. For example, modernization and transition theorists have argued that 'artificial' state boundaries were imposed on African society by colonialists resulting in either centralized or dispersed ethnic divisions in those countries (see Chapter 11). Where social conflict between two or several major ethnic groupings is a constant theme of politics nationally (as in Nigeria), the sense of shared political identity can be undermined leading to democratic instability or breakdown. Where there are dispersed ethnic divisions, with a multiplicity of cultural groups (as in India – see Chapter 8), inter-ethnic co-operation is more likely and can be a force for political pluralism and democratization. Structural theorists do not reject such arguments, but insist that class divisions in most social contexts have over-ridden ethnic divisions. For example, democratization in Belgium or Switzerland was not rendered impossible by deep ethnic division.

Another form of social division about which all theories of democratization so far have been essentially blind is *gender divisions*. For example, the political significance of the household, a crucial site of women's work and experience, is rarely considered in explanations of democratization. In those instances where structural theorists have referred explicitly to the subject, gender relations are marginalized on the grounds that they 'may well be of critical importance for future developments in democracy, but they were far less important [than class and other structural forces] in the known histories of democratization' (Rueschemeyer *et al.,* 1992, p.48). Chapters 2, 8, 14 and 18 in particular take a different position, arguing that gender divisions are important to an explanation of democratization.

State and political institutions

The state (defined on pp.3-4) is part of the ground on which our definitions of both different forms of democracy and democratization rest. The nature of the state that defines democratization cannot also explain it. However, the extent of its general power *in relation to* class divisions and/or civil society is an important explanatory factor in all theoretical approaches to democratization. We saw this earlier for state and class in the summaries of Barrington Moore and Rueschemeyer *et al.;* democratization routes, they say, are marked by rough balances of power between the state and relatively independent classes, not by excessively powerful states and dependent classes or states dependent on more powerful landed classes. Similarly, in modernization theories, overwhelming dominance of the state in relation to civil society is bad news for democratization. Such statism, says Diamond (1992, p.482), has led to democratic breakdown in Africa, Asia and elsewhere because in countries with 'low levels of development, swollen states control a vastly greater share of the most valued economic opportunities (jobs, contracts, licences, scholarships and development largesse) than they do at higher levels of development'; in consequence (as suggested in Chapter 11 on sub-Saharan Africa) economic growth is obstructed because economic competition from the private sector is crowded out, pervasive fraud and violence during elections occurs because of the enormous advantages that accrue to individuals who win them, political corruption and rent seeking are entrenched as the chief instruments of upward mobility, virtually all developmental activity is subject to state mediation and control, making community and individual advancement dependent on control of the state (therefore heightening inequality and tension between ethnic and regional groups) and so on. Modernization theorists argue, in short, that democratization involves moving away from statism and all it entails toward leaner states and vigorous capitalist development.

State and class as explanatory factors are very generalized, abstract categories. They can take us only so far in explaining democratization. They have difficulty explaining *variation* in democratization experiences of countries with similar state/class relationships. Most authors in this book therefore also pay attention to *intermediate-level political institutions* as explanatory factors (notably in Chapters 3, 5, 8 and 18). Institutions have been defined as 'enduring regularities of human interaction in frequently occurring or repetitive situations structured by rules, norms and shared strategies, as well as by the physical world' (Crawford and Ostrom, 1995, p.582). The British House of Commons is a political institution in this sense, but so is the military (where it is a separate political entity within the state), a particular system of competitive elections, the structure of a party system, the particular relations between different government departments, and relations between trade unions and political parties. Political parties are unusual in being located in both state and civil society, and their nature can help to explain different patterns of democratization (as in Chapters 8 and 20). 'Institutional analyses do not deny the broad political forces that animate various theories of politics', say Thelen and Steinmo (1992, p.3); what such analyses do is to explain how institutions shape more particularly the political

outcomes of broadly similar state–class relationships in different countries
(see also Held, 1996, Chapter 6).

Civil society

Civil society (defined p.4) enters explanations of democratization in terms of
its *relationships* with state and class divisions.

For modernization and transition theorists, a vibrant and pluralistic civil
society balances the power of the state. A robust civil society provides an
essential bulwark against the return of authoritarianism and is vital to the
consolidation and maintenance of liberal democracy. Also, the 'resurgence'
of civil society is crucial to explanations of transitions from authoritarianism
to liberal democracy in Southern Europe and Latin America (O'Donnell *et al.*,
1986). Democratization being stimulated by the growth and vitality of civil
society is also a constant theme in other contexts. Democratization in parts of
Asia, Africa and the former Eastern Europe and Soviet Union has been
stimulated by the development of a proliferation of autonomous groups and
social movements – students, women, trade unions, church groups,
consumers, the environmentally concerned, tribals, farmers, lawyers and
other professionals, and so on. Such growth of civil society frequently
involves the mobilization of independent media which can bring pressure to
bear on authoritarian states. The growth of civil society is discussed in
Chapters 5, 8, 16, 20 and elsewhere. For Diamond (1992, p.484), as a
modernization theorist, it is '*one* factor – socioeconomic development' that
contributes to the growth of civil society throughout the world by 'physically
concentrating people into more populous areas of residence while at the
same time dispersing them into wider, more diverse networks of interaction',
'decentralizing control over information and increasing alternative sources of
information', and 'dispersing literacy, knowledge, income and other
organizational resources across wider segments of the population' thereby
increasing the potential for protests that can challenge authoritarian regimes.

Rueschemeyer *et al.* and other structural theorists also refer to the
importance of the growth of civil society as an important counterweight to the
state apparatus. They go on, however, to consider how a dense civil society as
a by-product of capitalist development can also strengthen the organizational
capacity of the lower classes, thereby changing the balance of class power.
They also draw attention usefully to the point that a dense civil society is not
necessarily pro-democratic. Important groups in civil society can be hostile to
democracy. Furthermore, where an urban working class is weak, civil society
provides a convenient means for maintaining the authority of dominant
classes. That the growth of civil society itself is less important than its effects
on class relations is underlined by Rueschemeyer *et al.* (1992, p.50) when
they state that 'it is not primarily the density of civil society *per se*, but the
empowerment of previously excluded classes aided by this density that
improves the chances of democratization...'

Political culture and ideas

It would appear to be self evident that democratization is more likely in
countries where political cultures – peoples' values, attitudes and beliefs – are
pro-democratic. Actually, there is probably more theoretical dispute about

the role of political culture and ideas in explaining democratization than about the other explanatory factors considered here. For modernization theorists, it is a central explanatory factor: numerous studies have been conducted, based on survey data, that show a strong statistical association between a population's level of education (an outcome of modernization) and its commitment to democracy, participation, moderation, tolerance of opposition, etc. Structural theorists dispute that such correlations explain democratization at all, arguing that democratic political cultures (whatever they are) are likely to be a consequence of democratization, not a cause. Transition theorists have tended to ignore political culture; transitions to liberal democracy are caused by the calculations of political elites in conflict some of whom eventually recognize a common interest (not shared values) in a democratic compromise.

There has been more widespread acceptance of the political importance of values, attitudes and beliefs that are institutionally grounded, the main example being organized religions. A religious institution together with its adherents is politically significant because it is socially powerful. Religions also have the advantage over very generalized descriptions of cultures of being easier to identify for purposes of comparative analysis. In Lipset's day, all religions except Protestantism were regarded by political scientists as incompatible with liberal democracy. More recently, this view has been substantially modified by events. First, there were the transitions of Spain and Portugal to democracy in Europe, and widespread democratization in Latin America fuelled in part by grassroots Catholicism. Next, democratization in Asian countries threw question marks around the arguments of Pye (1985) and others that Confucianism and other Asian religious and cultural beliefs made democratization an unlikely prospect there. Next, there was the argument in the mid 1990s that the Middle East was authoritarian because this was the land of Islam. The trouble with all such 'negative' hypotheses about religion and democratization, as Beetham (1994b, p.168) remarks, is that they treat 'religions as monolithic, when their core doctrines are typically subject to a variety of schools of interpretation; and as immutable, when they are notoriously revisionist in the face of changing circumstances and political currents'. The hypothesis about Islam and democratization is considered in Chapters 13 and 14.

Transnational and international engagements including war

All explanations of democratization refer to what is going on in the world order beyond the boundaries of particular countries. These include 'international' interactions such as military alliances, war, diplomatic relations, the work of intergovernmental institutions like the United Nations, the World Bank and so on. Distinct from all that are 'transnational' interactions, global society-to-society relations more or less beyond state control. These can involve global, regional, national and local relations in *different kinds of political spaces*. These include global economic and financial processes, the global division of labour, global media, global communications networks. As the *Journal of Business Strategy* (May/June 1995) remarked: 'thanks to space age technology, borderless companies are spawning a borderless economy. In the process, the global cybermarket is becoming ... a virtual reality'. Such linkages also involve global coalitions or alliances of NGOs (non governmental organizations). There is an incredible array of such NGO global groupings like Greenpeace, Amnesty, Oxfam, the Red Cross, the International Confederation of Free Trade Unions, the World Council of Churches. There is indeed what can be called a global politics that involves both international and transnational behaviour. Explaining democratization requires paying attention to both.

Greenpeace protest in Kiev on the eighth anniversary of the Chernobyl nuclear power plant accident

We have seen how Rueschemeyer *et al.'s* structural explanation gives special emphasis to changing configurations of transnational and international power relations as they affect class relations and the state in a country. Chapter 6 suggests that transnational economic relations between advanced capitalist countries and dependent Latin American countries delayed industrialization in the latter and kept the urban working class small, thereby weakening pro-democracy forces. Chapters 2, 3, 4 and 9 indicate how international war can lead to the imposition of democracy on the vanquished in some cases, yet war can also have the consequence of strengthening the state apparatus unduly in relation to the balance of class forces, thereby threatening democratization. For modernization theorists, 'the nature of socioeconomic development in the 1960s and 1970s both required and promoted the opening of societies to foreign trade, investment, technology, tourism and communications' (Huntington, 1991, p.66), and these transnational processes began to undermine authoritarianism in many countries. International influence that is pro-democratic is also seen as important; powerful external agencies like the US government or the World Bank began to promote liberal democracy in Asia in the 1980s (after noticeably failing to do so in previous decades – see Chapter 10) and this put pressure on authoritarian regimes dependent on these external agencies for loans, aid and trade.

1.5 Comparative methods

Why has democratization been a strong impulse in some countries, a weaker or non-existent one in others? This is the general question that informs the content of this book. The question invites comparison between more democratic and less democratic countries. Why compare? Answer: only through comparative methods can social scientists try to identify the particular causes or conditions that propel some countries in a democratic direction and other countries in other directions. There are several ways to compare. One goes roughly like this:

1   identify democratizing countries;
2   seek to find the common factor A, or factors A/B/C, that preceded or are associated with democratization in those countries;
3   then identify countries that are not democratizing and make sure that A or A/B/C is not associated with them;
4   if that is so then explore the possibility that A or A/B/C is the condition or cause of democratization.

Another way to compare goes roughly like this:

1   identify a group of countries with some common characteristic (for example, they are Asian);
2   distinguish countries in that group which are democratizing from those that are not;
3   seek to find factors A or A/B/C that are common to the democratizing countries but not characteristic of the others;
4   explore the possibility that A or A/B/C is the condition or cause of democratization.

The comparative method is not that simple, of course. There is indeed a large literature on the problems involved in doing comparative analysis well, or the folly of attempting it at all. For example, can we be sure that there is a necessary link between cause and effect, between A or A/B/C and democratization? We shall touch on some of these problems in a moment.

One can see how such a method can be used to generate, or at least suggest, explanations of democratization grounded in empirical evidence.

Sometimes, when using comparative methods, social scientists will 'discover' a condition or cause apparently associated with democratization. Usually, however, social scientists come to comparative analysis equipped with a theory or at least some rough ideas about where to look for democratization conditions or causes. The six explanatory factors summarized in the previous section provide such pointers. Comparative analysis provides a method for testing or falsifying, with empirical evidence, such provisional explanatory ideas or hypotheses about democratization. For instance, the simple hypothesis that democratization is a consequence of international war can be falsified on grounds of evidence by comparing different countries that emerged from the Second World War in Asia (1941–45), for example democracy for Japan, but authoritarianism for Taiwan and Vietnam.

Explanations of democratization need to be both grounded in evidence related to the complex realities of the real world and general enough to be relevant to a number (or all) of the cases of the phenomenon being explained. There is a genuine tension between empirical complexity and generality. The quest for generalized explanation can lead to neglect of a very complex reality; a deep appreciation of such complexity can lead to explanations that appear to travel no further than a particular case being examined. The two main types of comparative method divide precisely in relation to this tension. The *variable-oriented approach* goes primarily for generalized explanations; the *case-oriented approach* is grounded more firmly in the complex reality (the two terms are from Ragin, 1987).

A classic example of a comparative analysis of democratization using the variable-oriented approach is Lipset's (1960) study. He started out, as has been indicated, with the very general idea that democracy is related to a country's level of modernization. This was then tested by disaggregating 'modernization' into fifteen measures of it, each expressed as a variable (more or less per capita income, more or less telephones, etc.) and then comparing many democratic and authoritarian countries in Europe and Latin America (and elsewhere) in terms of each of these variables. He found that more democratic countries consistently scored 'better' on these variables. He then reaggregated all the variables and concluded very generally from his comparative statistical analysis that more modernized nations are more likely to sustain liberal democracy. Many have subsequently used this type of approach based on comparisons based on many or all countries, aided by the development of computers able to store and manipulate vast quantities of socioeconomic and political data. The drive for generalized explanations of democratization based on evidence from all countries is impressive, but it does mean that one learns little about the complex realities of each country.

A clear example of a comparative analysis of democratization using the case-oriented approach is Barrington Moore's (1966) study. As you know, he set out with the idea that the changing ways that lords, peasants, the urban bourgeoisie and the state related to each other historically might explain why some countries in Europe and Asia moved to liberal democracy, others to authoritarianism. Moore spent nearly 80 per cent of his very large book on complex historical details of England, France, the USA, China, Japan and India, treating each case as a whole entity rather than as a collection of scores on universal variables. Only at the end of his book did he more briefly suggest, on the basis of comparisons of the six case histories (plus references to Germany and Russia), certain general conditions in his route to liberal democracy not found in the route to dictatorship. Furthermore, he essentially declined to generalize beyond his historical cases. The main emphasis was on the complex historical reality in each country, less on universal political generalizations. Moore gave the classic rationale for engaging in comparative history as a method for seeking an explanation of democratization (see Box 1.4). Many other social scientists use this method of historical comparison in their work. Rustow, for example, suggested his general route to democracy on the basis of a comparison of just two countries.

> ### Box 1.4 Barrington Moore (1966, pp.x–xi) on the value of comparison in generating explanations of democratization
>
> Comparisons can serve as a rough negative check on accepted historical explanations. And a comparative approach may lead to new historical generalizations. In practice these features constitute a single intellectual process and make such a study more than a disparate collection of interesting cases. For example, after noticing that Indian peasants have suffered in a material way just about as much as Chinese peasants during the nineteenth and twentieth centuries without generating a massive revolutionary movement, one begins to wonder about traditional explanations of what took place in both societies and becomes alert to factors affecting peasant outbreaks in other countries, in the hope of discerning general causes. Or after learning about the disastrous consequences for democracy of a coalition between agrarian and industrial elites in nineteenth and early twentieth century Germany, the much discussed marriage of iron and rye – one wonders why a similar marriage between iron and cotton did not prevent the coming of the Civil War in the United States; and so one has taken a step towards specifying configurations favourable and unfavourable to the establishment of modern Western democracy.

Many social scientists now in effect supplement their case-oriented comparisons with some variable-oriented generalizations, or buttress their essentially variable-oriented approach with case studies. These take what amounts to a *combined approach*. Such methodological 'convergence' reminds us of what was said earlier about theoretical convergence. Rueschemeyer *et al.* is an example. Much of their explanation of democratization is grounded in a case-oriented, comparative history approach to twelve countries in Europe plus the four (former) British settler colonies in North America and Australasia, and to 22 countries in Latin America, Central America and the Caribbean. Clearly it was not possible in their book to give detailed histories of all 38 countries of the sort provided by Barrington Moore. So they rely on a combination of some case studies and variable-oriented generalizations.

Examples of such combined approaches to comparative political analysis are found in Chapters 3, 4, 6, 7, 11, 13, 16 and 18. Chapter 14 on Islam and democracy is another (unusual) example of a combined approach, where a single complex variable (Islam) is examined in a number of cases. Some chapters illustrate case-oriented comparative analysis involving only two or several countries, for example Chapters 2, 8, 9, 10 and 19. There are also case-oriented comparisons involving detailed study of a single 'case' pursued over time and set in a comparative context in the sense that the case critically tests or otherwise throws light on explanatory factors or generalizations about democratization. Examples in this book are Chapter 5 on the USA, Chapter 11 on South Africa, Chapter 15 on Israel, Chapter 17 on Russia and Chapter 20 on Vietnam. There is no example in this book of a purely variable-oriented comparative approach to explaining democratization (apart from the summary of Lipset in this chapter).

Table 1.5 Summary of three approaches to comparative method

Variable-oriented	*Case-oriented*	*Combined*
Comparison using many variables, involving many or all countries, aimed at very generalized explanations of democratization	Comparison of a few countries, or detailed study of one country, aimed at a less generalized explanation of democratization based more firmly on detailed evidence	Comparison which relies to some extent on both variable-oriented and case-oriented methods

In all of the chapters the explanations of democratization based on comparative methods are stated somewhat tentatively. The main reason for this is that tightly controlled experiments as in a scientific laboratory are not possible when it comes to explaining a large social phenomenon like democratization; hence looser methods of comparative analysis are employed to try to identify causes or conditions, and these methods deliver explanations that are necessarily inexact and incomplete. Three problems that contribute to such inexactitude are briefly mentioned here as illustration.

Causal complexity. Democratization of whole countries is a very large-scale political change caused by aspects of the six explanatory factors indicated earlier and other causes and conditions. It is not the separate or independent effect of each condition that explains democratization. What matters is their *combination or intersection in time and space.* Democratization occurs as a result of 'the intersection of appropriate conditions – the right ingredients for change' at the right time(s) (Ragin, 1987, p.25). That the causes of democratization are both multiple and conjunctural (combined in time and space) makes for causal complexity. Identification of such causal complexes through comparative analysis is demanding, and perhaps the identification of all relevant causes-in-combination is impossible. For case-oriented comparative methods, detailed consideration of one or several particular cases historically is a promising method for identifying a combination of at least some important conditions or causes. Critics can charge that such explanations are not wholly reliable because they are less than complete. Variable-oriented methods largely avoid such causal complexity by making some simplifying assumption (Ragin, 1987, pp.32–3). For example, they assume that each cause as a variable is discrete and can simply be added to others. This assumes that any one cause is the same in all countries regardless of the character of other causes. But this procedure contradicts the idea that historical causation is multiple and conjunctural; if used alone, this method reduces the plausibility of such explanations.

Faulty data. Explanations of democratization are only as convincing as the data or evidence on which they rest. Problems of measurement and interpretation of evidence are the staple diet of comparativists. Concepts which 'catch' the data can be unclear and even when they are clear the data may be of poor quality. For example, quantitative comparisons of more and less democratic countries in terms of their economic development tend to rely on indicators like GNP (gross national product) and GDP (gross domestic product). Such data are compiled in official statistics and are readily available. All countries, however, also 'have "a black economy" not measured in official statistics because citizens conceal economic activity from the government to avoid taxes' and for other reasons; the size of black economies varies a lot from country to country and is impossible to measure, but it is pretty certain that, taking the black economy into account, Italy's GNP in the mid 1990s was greater than Britain's but according to the official statistics the reverse was the case (Mackie and Marsh, 1995, p.182). Despite such problems, quantitative comparative analyses still rely on GNP or GDP as measures of economic activity, the accuracy of which can be questioned.

Comparability. Convincing comparative analysis is in danger unless the units of analysis are comparable. Clearly, there is a great variety of important levels and forms of politics, including non-state forms. However, most explanations of democratization are based on comparing *countries,* and we follow that practice in this book. But countries also are remarkably different in all sorts of ways. Are China and Singapore comparable? Ideally, the units of analysis to be explained – more and less democratic countries – should be identical except for their variation in extent of democracy and in one explanatory factor that also varies; a comparison could then establish how that factor causes or is a condition of more or less democracy. But the real world is not like that. Even to identify several countries as sharing a characteristic of being a liberal democracy obscures considerable variation; they may be liberal democratic at the national level but vary a lot in terms of the extent to which organizations *within* the country are democratic. There is even more variation regarding what can be called explanatory units of analysis. Some explanatory factors are transnational, others are local or involve individuals. It is hard to ensure sufficient comparability necessary to the identification of a set of factors explaining democratization.

The danger here, to which variable-oriented quantitative research is particularly prone, is that comparability is 'forced' by using concepts like liberal democracy or economic development *as if* they had universal application. But 'economic development is a social construct having different meanings in different societies' and liberal democracy 'does not exist independently of the way it is experienced, or the meaning that individuals and groups attach to it' (Mackie and Marsh, 1995, pp.182–3). The problem of coping with variable social constructions of reality is shared by all comparative methods involving attempts to explain democratization in different countries. Once again, however, case-oriented comparative methods are more likely to cope better with such difficulties.

———————————— *Summary of Section 1.5* ————————————

- Comparing more democratic and less democratic countries is a method of analysis which can identify causes or conditions of democratization.

- Comparative political analysis provides a method for testing, on the basis of empirical evidence, provisional explanations for democratization.

- There are variable-oriented and case-oriented approaches to comparative method, and an approach combining these two.

- Problems of causal complexity, faulty data and comparability make comparative political analysis aimed at explaining democratization an inexact science.

1.6 So what?

Democratization terminology has been introduced in this chapter to enable us to identify the phenomena to be explained. Theoretical approaches and explanatory factors used to explain the phenomena have been outlined. Methods and problems of comparative analysis have been indicated. All of this is brought together and elaborated repeatedly in the chapters of this book.

So what? Does knowing about democratization throughout the world and how one might try to explain it actually matter to anyone besides academic people who write books? It matters to many people who want or need to improve their understanding of political life; such increased understanding throughout society can enhance political life, and the quality of life generally. It also matters, says Peter Evans (1995, pp.3, 9), to 'the consumers and patrons of social science who want help in figuring out what is likely to happen if they take one course of action rather than another' and 'how they might be able to improve perspective outcomes' through wise policies. It matters also, says David Beetham (1994a, p.172), in 'the ongoing struggle for democratization' in which 'social science can have a modest accessory role in helping political actors to be more intelligent, through a systematic awareness of comparative experience elsewhere'. That 'ongoing struggle' is premised in the belief that authoritarianism can wreck human lives, democratization can improve them. Contributing to the understanding of democratization throughout the world may in due course make a difference for people whose lives are profoundly affected by the political regime with which they have to contend.

Appendix: notes on Table 1.2

The purpose of Table 1.2 is to indicate patterns of democratization in different regions of the world by classifying political regimes for 1975 and 1995. The classifications have been made by authors of this book on the basis of characteristics of the three regime types as defined in this chapter. The need to place political regimes throughout the world into three neat types for purposes of comparative analysis has required some rough judgements (a spectrum would be more accurate than clear distinctions between only three types). For example, in a few countries classified as liberal democracies in 1995 there was heavy state repression or civil war in a portion of the territory, e.g. India, Sri Lanka and Turkey; our judgement is that the classification is acceptable because liberal democratic characteristics obtained more or less in most of the country at the time, including the government having been formed on the basis of competitive elections that were reasonably free and fair (in most of the country). As for partial democracy, a few regimes were very partial indeed, for example Egypt. Also, several states were in a virtual state of anarchy at the time, with no central government of any sort, for example Liberia and Somalia; but for convenience we have called them 'authoritarian' because they certainly cannot be classified as liberal or partial democracies.

The following classifications provide the basis for the data in Table 1.2:

1975

Authoritarian:
Portugal, Spain, Chile, Uruguay, Bolivia, Brazil, Ecuador, Peru, Cuba, Guatemala, Honduras, Paraguay, Haiti, Panama, El Salvador, Dominican Republic, Nicaragua, Afghanistan, India, Bangladesh, Nepal, Bhutan, Maldives, Burma, Laos, Kampuchea, Vietnam, Indonesia, Brunei, Philippines, Taiwan, South Korea, China, Mongolia, North Korea, Angola, Benin, Burkina Faso (then called Upper Volta), Burundi, Cameroon, Cape Verde, Central African Republic, Chad, Comoros, Congo, Côte d'Ivoire, Djibouti (still under colonial rule), Equatorial Guinea, Eritrea (still part of Ethiopia), Ethiopia, Gabon, Ghana, Guinea, Guinea-Bissau, Kenya, Lesotho, Madagascar, Malawi, Mali, Mauritania, Mozambique, Namibia, Niger, Nigeria, Rwanda, Soa Tome and Principe, Seychelles, Sierra Leone, Somalia, South Africa, Sudan, Swaziland, Tanzania, Togo, Uganda, Zaire, Zambia, Zimbabwe, Morocco, Algeria, Libya, Tunisia, Syria, Iraq, Saudi Arabia, North Yemen, South Yemen, Oman, United Arab Emirates, Bahrain, Qatar, Kuwait, USSR, Poland, East Germany, Czechoslovakia, Hungary, Romania, Yugoslavia, Bulgaria, Albania.

Partial democracy:
Mexico, Colombia, Thailand, Malaysia, Pakistan, Singapore, Liberia, Senegal, Egypt, Jordan, Iran.

Liberal democracy:
Finland, Norway, Sweden, Denmark, Iceland, Ireland, Britain, Netherlands, West Germany, Belgium, Luxemburg, Austria, Switzerland, France, Italy, Greece, Malta, Canada, USA, Australia, New Zealand, Greenland, Costa Rica,

Venezuela, Jamaica, Trinidad, Argentina, Sri Lanka, Papua New Guinea, Japan, Botswana, The Gambia, Mauritius, Israel, Turkey.

1995

Authoritarian:
Cuba, El Salvador, Afghanistan, Bhutan, Maldives, Myanmar, Laos, Cambodia, Vietnam, Indonesia, Brunei, China, North Korea, Burundi, Chad, Equatorial Guinea, Eritrea, The Gambia, Liberia, Nigeria, Rwanda, Sierra Leone, Somalia, Sudan, Swaziland, Morocco, Algeria, Libya, Tunisia, Syria, Iraq, Saudi Arabia, Yemen, Oman, United Arab Emirates, Bahrain, Qatar, Kuwait, Azerbaijan, Kazakhstan, Tajikistan, Turkmenistan, Uzbekistan.

Partial democracy:
Mexico; Peru, Guatemala, Honduras, Panama, Nepal, Thailand, Malaysia, Taiwan, Singapore, Angola, Burkina Faso, Cameroon, Central African Republic, Comoros, Côte d'Ivoire, Djibouti, Ethiopia, Gabon, Guinea, Guinea-Bissau, Kenya, Mauritania, Togo, Uganda, Zaire, Egypt, Jordan, Iran, Albania, Armenia, Belarus, Bosnia, Croatia, Georgia, Kirgizistan, Macedonia, Moldova, Romania, Russia, Serbia-Montenegro, Slovakia, Ukraine.

Liberal democracy:
Finland, Norway, Sweden, Denmark, Iceland, Ireland, Britain, Netherlands, Germany, Belgium, Luxemburg, Austria, Switzerland, France, Italy, Greece, Malta, Canada, USA, Australia, New Zealand, Greenland, Spain, Portugal, Costa Rica, Venezuela, Argentina, Columbia, Chile, Uruguay, Bolivia, Ecuador, Brazil, Paraguay, Haiti, Dominican Republic, Nicaragua, Jamaica, Trinidad, India, Pakistan, Bangladesh, Sri Lanka, South Korea, Papua New Guinea, Philippines, Japan, Mongolia, Benin, Botswana, Cape Verde, Congo, Ghana, Lesotho, Madagascar, Malawi, Mali, Mauritius, Mozambique, Namibia, Niger, Sao Tome and Principe, Senegal, Seychelles, South Africa, Tanzania, Zambia, Zimbabwe, Israel, Turkey, Bulgaria, Czech Republic, Estonia, Hungary, Latvia, Lithuania, Poland, Slovenia.

References

Beetham, D. (1994a) 'Key principles and indices for a democratic audit' in Beetham, D. (ed.) *Defining and Measuring Democracy*, London, Sage.

Beetham, D. (1994b) 'Conditions for democratic consolidation', *Review of African Political Economy*, no.60, pp.157–72.

Bruneau, T. (1995) 'From revolution to democracy in Portugal' in Shain, Y. and Linz, J. (eds) pp.144–59.

Crawford, S. and Ostrom, E. (1995) 'A grammar of institutions', *American Political Science Review*, vol.89, no.3, pp.582–600.

Dahl, R. (1989) *Democracy and Its Critics*, New Haven, Yale University Press.

Diamond, L. (1992) 'Economic development and democracy reconsidered', *American Behavioral Scientist*, vol.35, no.4/5, pp.450–99.

Evans, P. (1995) in Kohli, A. *et al.*

Giddens, A. (1993) *Sociology* (2nd edn), Cambridge, Polity Press.

Gough, K. (1990) *Political Economy in Vietnam*, Berkeley, Folklore Institute.

Hadenius, A. (1992) *Democracy and Development*, Cambridge, Cambridge University Press.

Held, D. (1996) *Models of Democracy* (2nd edn), Cambridge, Polity Press.

Huntington, S.P. (1991) *The Third Wave: Democratization in the Late Twentieth Century*, Norman, University of Oklahoma Press.

Huntington, S.P. and Nelson, J.M. (1976) *No Easy Choice: Political Participation in Developing Countries*, Cambridge, Harvard University Press.

Kohli, A., Evans, P., Katzenstein, P., Przeworski, A., Rudolph, S., Scott, J. and Skocpol, T. (1995) 'The role of theory in comparative politics: a symposium', *World Politics*, vol.48, pp.1–49.

Lipset, S.M. (1960) *Political Man*, London, Heinemann.

Lipset, S.M. (1983) *Political Man* (2nd edn), London, Heinemann.

Mackie, T. and Marsh, D. (1995) 'The comparative method' in Marsh, D. and Stoker, G. (eds) *Theory and Methods in Political Science*, London, Macmillan.

Mainwaring, S., O'Donnell, G. and Valenzuela, J. (eds) (1992) *Issues in Democratic Consolidation*, South Bend, University of Notre Dame Press.

Moore, B. (1966) *Social Origins of Dictatorship and Democracy: Lord and Peasant in the Making of the Modern World*, Boston, Beacon Press.

Munck, G.L. (1994) 'Democratic transitions in comparative perspective', *Comparative Politics*, vol.26, no.3, pp.355–75.

O'Donnell, G. (1992) 'Transitions, continuities, and paradoxes' in Mainwaring, S. *et al.*, (eds) pp.24–52

O'Donnell, G., Schmitter, P. and Whitehead, L. (eds) (1986) *Transitions from Authoritarian Rule* (4 vols), Baltimore, Johns Hopkins University Press.

Pye, L. (1985) *Asian Power and Politics: the Cultural Dimensions of Authority*, Cambridge, Harvard University Press.

Ragin, C.C. (1987) *The Comparative Method: Moving Beyond Qualitative and Quantitative Strategies*, Berkeley, University of California Press.

Rueschemeyer, D., Stephens, E. and Stephens, J. (1992) *Capitalist Development and Democracy*, Cambridge, Polity Press.

Rustow, D. (1970) 'Transitions to democracy', *Comparative Politics*, vol.2, pp.337–63.

Shain, Y. and Linz, J. (eds) (1995) *Between States: Interim Governments and Democratic Transitions,* Cambridge, Cambridge University Press.

Thelen, K. and Steinmo, S. (1992) 'Historical institutionalism in comparative politics' in Steinmo, S., Thelen, K. and Longstreth, F. (eds) *Structuring Politics: Historical Institutionalism in Comparative Analysis,* Cambridge, Cambridge University Press.

Therborn, G. (1978) 'The rule of capital and the rise of democracy', *New Left Review,* no.103 (May–June), pp.3–41.

Walzer, M. (1995) 'The concept of civil society' in Walzer, M. (ed.) *Towards a Global Civil Society,* Oxford, Berghahn Books.

Weber, M. (1972) 'Politics as a vocation' in Gerth, H.H. and Mills, C.W. (eds) *From Max Weber,* New York, Oxford University Press.

PART II
Europe and the USA

Introduction   41

CHAPTER 2 **Democracy in the 'long nineteenth**   46
           century', 1760–1919

CHAPTER 3 **The crisis of modern democracy,**   71
           1919–39

CHAPTER 4 **Democracy in Europe, 1939–89**   95

CHAPTER 5 **Democracy in the USA since 1945**   118

Afterword   139

Introduction

David Goldblatt

Part II of this book explores the uneven and often tortuous history of democratization in Europe and the USA. It was here that both the ideas of representative, parliamentary and liberal democracy were first articulated and their institutional forms began to emerge during the English Revolution of the seventeenth century and the French and American Revolutions of the eighteenth. Yet, even at these moments of historical breakthrough the course of democratization was not smooth. Indeed it would take until the last quarter of the twentieth century for liberal democratic government to be entrenched across all these societies.

Chapter 2 begins by asking why the issue of democracy became a central element of political discourse and political struggle in this era. It describes an epoch characterized by intense debates and battles over the relationship between state and civil society and the proper distribution of political power between and within both. It asks why was it that the old regimes of these states – monarchy, church, aristocracies and landlords – found themselves challenged and forced to contemplate the expansion of the suffrage, the accountability of the executive and the entrenchment of civil and political rights? It broadly argues that the cluster of institutions that emerged in these societies – capitalist economies, diffuse literacy, bureaucratic nation-states, industrialized warfare – were responsible for these conflicts. Capitalism generated new and powerful economic classes – bourgeoisie, urban working classes – who demanded inclusion within the polity. Diffuse literacy, communications and transport technologies provided them with the means to effectively organize political protest. The immense financial costs of fighting industrialized warfare made it imperative that elites could mobilize their populations through consent rather than force. The immense human costs of this new type of warfare meant that popular control of state power had become a matter of life and death. The First World War which ends the long nineteenth century underlined this.

However, over the long nineteenth century the course of democratization was neither universal nor inevitable. Chapter 2 focuses on Britain, the USA, France and Germany examining how the general patterns of social change played themselves out under specific national conditions. This gives rise to particular questions: Why did the USA produce the earliest liberal democratic polity in the 1780s, but maintain a restricted suffrage for the longest? Why was France, the first European society to experience a popular democratic revolution, unable to consolidate the democratic gains of 1791 until the last quarter of the nineteenth century? Why was Britain able to maintain the longest record of peaceful inter-elite electoral competition and parliamentary government accompanied by a significantly slower expansion of the suffrage? Why did Germany, until the cataclysm of the First World War, develop a highly partial democracy that is better described as a semi-authoritarian monarchy? Chapter 2 seeks to answer these questions by focusing on patterns of class formation, alliance and organization and the impact of industrialized warfare. It also touches on the reasons for the late or very late achievement of female suffrage, the role of religious and regional social movements, and the importance of strategic decisions and alliances made by key social forces.

Chapter 3 begins where Chapter 2 finishes, with the First World War. Its central questions are: Why did some democracies survive the tumult of the inter-war era? and Why did so many democracies succumb to variants of authoritarianism? However a number of contrasts appear between the chapters. First, in Chapter 2 the main consequence of the war was to accelerate processes of democratization by forcing the pace of social mobilization, dismembering the multinational empires of old Europe and destroying defeated authoritarian elites. In Chapter 3 the longer-term consequences of the war serve primarily as an explanation of democratic retreat. Second, while Chapter 2 seeks to explain the emergence of democracies and the endurance of authoritarian polities, Chapter 3 reverses this. It seeks to explain the emergence of authoritarian politics and the survival of democracies. Third, Chapter 2 explores the development of momentous social forces over almost a century-and-a-half, while Chapter 3 covers a period of intense and generalized turmoil. In the 20 years it covers, democratic states had to contend with the economic and social dislocation of the most destructive war in human history, the political polarization and conflict that emanated from the Russian Revolution and the formation of new states across Europe, and then the Great Depression of the 1930s. The prize for survival was a further war of unparalleled destructiveness. The collapse of democratic politics in Germany provides the main case study. In addition Chapter 3 examines the fate of the new democracies of Italy, Austria, Poland, Yugoslavia and Czechoslovakia which progressively fell to internally generated or externally imposed authoritarianism. Fourth, while Chapter 2 seeks to ask what were the facilitators and preconditions of democratic politics, Chapter 3 examines what was absent and what was missing. What made enduring agreement on the distribution of economic resources and political power between classes and ethnic and national groups impossible to achieve? In the later sections of the chapter the cases of France, Britain and the USA re-emerge, for it was only here (as well as in Scandinavia and the Low Countries) that liberal democracies were able to endure the turmoil of the era. The question that the chapter addresses in this section is: What made those conflicts solvable within a democratic framework in these states? In answer, the chapter emphasizes the importance of political parties and parliamentary institutions in the survival of democratic politics.

Once again, the narrative of democratization in Europe and the USA is punctuated by total war. Chapter 3 seeks to explain the distribution of democratic and authoritarian polities on the eve of the Second World War. Chapter 4 explores the impact of the war on democratization. By 1942 the entire European continent outside of Sweden and Switzerland had fallen to authoritarian forces. While defeat of the Axis powers was not to prove a guarantee of liberal democratic politics in Europe it was a necessary condition for some. The chapter describes the democratic experience on post-war Europe as a trifurcation. In Eastern and Central Europe, communist states emerged on the basis of either external Soviet imposition or national revolutions, as in Yugoslavia. This consigned the area to over four decades of authoritarian rule. In Western and Southern Europe both the victors and the vanquished of the war established entrenched liberal democratic polities. Democracy was revived in France, the Low Countries and Scandinavia and as with Britain infused with a momentous wave of social reform. In Germany and Italy liberal democratic politics was externally imposed and successfully maintained domestically. In Southern Europe the pre-war dictatorships of the Iberian peninsula were shielded by neutrality from the democratic impact of the Second World War. Without the shock of war it would require another three decades for domestic social forces to generate the democratic revolutions of the mid 1970s. Chapter 4 focuses on the last two of these three European paths, asking the question: What accounts for the successful entrenchment of liberal democracy in post-war Europe and its late but successful development in Southern Europe? We return to the fate of Eastern and Central European democratization in Part V. In Western and Northern Europe, Chapter 4 focuses on Germany, Italy, Britain and France, in the South on Spain and Portugal. It highlights the enduring importance of military and geo-political factors in European democratization. The Cold War and East–West conflict define the chapter's end date and provide an important explanatory factor both in the creation of Western democracies and the lateness of Southern European democratization. The account of democratic successes and consolidations is complemented in the final section of the chapter by a short review of some of the enduring problems of European democracy.

The temporal scope of Chapter 5 parallels Chapter 4. But the sole focus on the USA denotes America's very different experience of democratization and points to a wider set of social, economic and political differences between US and European histories. Above all America emerged from the

Second World War economically and geo-politically invigorated and dominant. Chapter 5 returns to the question first asked in Chapter 2: Why did the USA produce the earliest liberal democratic polity in the 1780s, but maintain a restricted suffrage for the longest? In short the answer is race and ethnicity; for only the USA, amongst the states covered in this part, possessed a significant slave economy and a large population of African descent. It is hardly surprising that a society and culture that could tolerate and legitimize the permanent enslavement of part of its population would have difficulty according them equal political status. Chapter 5 seeks to explain this paradox of early and late democratization, a political culture that simultaneously embraced and enriched the language of democratic politics and harboured an enduring politics of authoritarian racism.

While Chapters 2, 3 and 4 have relied on war, geo-politics and class as the main explanatory factors of democratization, Chapter 5 pays particular attention to state structures and political institutions, for it is this that unlocks some of the USA's distinctive history. In short, it argues that the federal structure of the American state made political space for an authoritarian racist enclave in the South. The party structure of the USA allowed space for Southern elites to politically survive despite defeat in the Civil War and a more democratic political culture in the North. How was it then, that this authoritarian straitjacket was finally burst asunder? The answer is the Civil Rights Movement of the 1950s and 1960s. Chapter 5 explores the origins and success of this movement. It concludes, paralleling the critical assessment of European democracies in the final section of Chapter 4, by asking: Why, at the apparent moment of democratic success – with the passage of Civil Rights legislation in the 1960s – the US democratic political system should find itself faced with a massive decline in trust, legitimacy and effectiveness? How is it that a political and economic structure that can generate a liberal democracy can so effectively problematize its working?

Like any narrative, the story of democratization constructed in Part II is selective. First, its focus is consistently on either the creation and consolidation or the failure and dismemberment of *liberal democratic* polities. The many democratic experiments and challenges of the nineteenth and twentieth centuries that sought to democratize economic rather than political power go unrecorded as do the struggles and demands for a participatory politics that goes beyond the limits of parliamentary and representative institutions; the Paris Commune of 1871 and the popular movements of 1968 are not present. Second, the geographical coverage of Part II is selective. What unites the USA and Europe together is not that they constitute a geographical region but that they simultaneously experienced shared patterns of social change from the mid eighteenth century onwards. Their unity is sociological – the experience of modernity – of capitalism, bureaucratization, secular ideologies, unparalleled scientific and technological change, and the growth of nation-states. However, for reasons of space it has not been possible to cover other states that have followed a similar trajectory. In particular the experiences of Australia, Canada, New Zealand and Japan do not appear.

Third, its use of the three theoretical approaches outlined in Chapter 1 is uneven, modernization theory does not feature in any of the chapters of Part

II. One of the reasons for the limited applicability of modernization theories in this part is that its greatest empirical weakness is the case of Germany (see Chapters 2 and 3). For no more modern, advanced state and society can be found that proved such consistently infertile ground for democratic government. The outline of structural theories presented in Chapter 1 is developed and elaborated on in Chapter 2 which discusses the work of three writers: Moore, Therborn and Mann. Chapter 2 attempts to summarize and evaluate these positions. In Chapters 3 and 4, the role of structural theory is less explicit but it forms the explanatory backbone of each.

Amidst these clashes of titanic historical forces, it is clear that the choices and decisions, however framed, of key political actors and the leaders of social movements have proved decisive in tipping ambiguous situations towards democratic or authoritarian outcomes, for example: Chapter 3 highlights the importance of the tactical political decisions on both left and right in the rise of Hitler; Chapter 4 examines the conduct of negotiations and the complex trade-offs between former enemies in Italy, Germany and Spain; in Chapter 5 the essential role of the leadership of the Civil Rights Movements and the shift of position taken by key congressional actors in the passage of the Voting Rights Act are touched upon. In each case the description of the events can be illuminated by transition theories. There is no exploration of these theories in this part comparable to the discussion of structural theories. Rather the narrative and explanations of each chapter provide material for reflection on some of the key hypotheses of transition theories. While transition approaches to democratization usefully focus on the role of elites in political change all four of the chapters in Part II remind us that democratization requires the active and engaged struggle of millions of men and women – from the French sansculottes of the 1790s, to the British suffragettes of the 1900s, to the American Civil Rights protesters of the 1960s – who have demanded an equal role in their own rule from the elites and regimes that had withheld it.

CHAPTER 2

Democracy in the 'long nineteenth century', 1760–1919

David Goldblatt

Introduction

In 1760 no polity anywhere in the world was democratic in any sense that we would currently use. Indeed, no society in 1760 would have described itself as democratic. 159 years later, in 1919, liberal democratic regimes had been established in Britain, the United States of America, the white settler dominions of the British Empire (Canada, New Zealand, Australia) and across Western and Northern Europe (Scandinavia, the Low Countries, France, Switzerland, Germany, Austria and Italy). In this chapter I focus on the process of democratization in the four most powerful states of the era: Britain, France, Germany and the USA. The questions that this chapter engages with are very simply stated. Why did democratization occur in these polities? How can we explain the differential timing and character of democratization in these polities?

The period between 1760 and 1919 has been described by some historians as the *long nineteenth century*. They have done so because the nineteenth century itself forms the core of an epoch of social change during which the characteristic institutions of modernity came into being. The period starts with the Industrial Revolution which began in Britain in the mid eighteenth century and transformed the nature of economic power and social stratification in Western societies. The first stirrings of the Industrial Revolution were quickly followed by the American and French Revolutions (1776–87 and 1789–99 respectively) which transformed the political character of European and American societies. Military and cultural power were also changing. Wars lasted longer, became more expensive to wage, deployed greater levels of technology and destructive firepower, and required more intensive levels of social mobilization by the states that fought them. Literacy spread rapidly beyond the elites of these societies providing an important basis for political organization amongst other social classes and drawing more social groups into a denser civil society of regularized political interaction. The long century ended when these massively expanded forms of social power were turned against each other to devastating effect in the inferno of the First World War.

Although the pace of economic, military, cultural and political change varied amongst Western states, all were exposed to these interconnected trends which in different ways placed the question of democracy at the centre of politics, if not always successfully. Industrialization and capitalist development created new, more powerful social classes that demanded a stake in political power from the traditional elites. The middle classes, working classes and independent farmers were to prove more formidable adversaries of old regimes than isolated urban artisans and dependent peasants. The industrialization of war led states to intensify their levels of tax extraction and military conscription and recruitment as well as their control of economic life. This in turn forced more people to engage politically with states they had previously been able to avoid. Literacy, and new forms of transport and communication made political organization on these issues more feasible for previously ruled groups. Therefore, in the domain of politics a wider swathe of social groups, more powerful and organized than before, staked a claim for a share of power and control of the state. Thus the central political narrative of the long nineteenth century is the drive, sometimes successful, sometimes unsuccessful, almost always partial and limited, for democratization.

I will return to these very general conditions of, and pressures for, democratization in the conclusion to this chapter. Before doing so we need to examine the actual history of democratization in some key states. In Section 1, I will sketch the outlines of the process of democratization in Britain, France, Germany and the USA. In Sections 2–4, I will review three explanations of the patterns and pace of Western democratization: first, that of Barrington Moore in Section 2; second, that of Göran Therborn in Section 3; and third, that of Michael Mann in Section 4. All of these writers take a structural approach to explaining democratization and try to establish by comparative analysis which long-term processes of social change have predisposed these societies towards a democratic or authoritarian polity. That said, there are considerable variations between them. Each of them has chosen a different set of case study countries to compare. Where this effects their interpretation of democratization in our four central countries I will examine their arguments in some detail. All three writers differ in the weight they allot to different explanatory factors. Moore focuses on agrarian economic change, class formation and class alliances. Therborn takes more account of the social divisions of race and gender and the impact of war. Mann pays particular attention to the structure of pre-democratic states and the role of nations in processes of democratization. In Sections 2–4, I will try and unpack the relationship between these explanatory factors and the processes of democratization. In Section 5, I will compare and contrast the strengths and weaknesses of the different theoretical models

―――――――――――――― *Summary of Introduction* ――――――――――――――

- The 'long nineteenth century' runs from 1760 to 1919, starts with the Industrial Revolution and ends just after the First World War. At its beginning no Western state was democratic. By its conclusion nearly all had developed some form of liberal democracy.

- The emergence of industrial capitalism, industrialized warfare and mass literacy increased the power and mobilizing capacity of subaltern classes *vis-à-vis* ruling classes. This led to consistent, if rarely successful, pressures for a share in power and control of the state – democratization.

- The main theoretical explanations are structural. They vary according to their choice of case studies and dominant explanatory factors.

2.1 Patterns of democratization in the 'long nineteenth century'

The USA

In Britain's American colonies in the 1760s property qualifications for the vote were low and wealth, especially land, was much more evenly dispersed than in Europe, yet no more than 50–80 per cent of the adult male population was on the electoral register. Even less actually voted and this takes no account of the 20 per cent of the population who were totally disenfranchized slaves. Government was conducted by elected state assemblies, London-appointed governors and networks of patronage amongst large landowners and the urban middle classes. Actual parliamentary or representative control of state executives and legislation was minimal. The American Revolution, which ran from the beginning of the War of Independence in 1776 to the establishment of the new American constitution in 1787, changed all of this. What began as a predominantly anti-imperial struggle became entwined with a national struggle for democratization. One of the central slogans under which the American War of Independence was fought was 'no taxation without representation', for the imposition of British fiscal demands on the colonies – unrepresented at Westminster – had fuelled the conflict. Consequently, in the post-war era, when the new American political constitution was being discussed, there were strong calls for a suffrage of taxpayers at the very least. In many states there was a poll tax which made such a call equivalent to one for white male suffrage. The constitution of 1787 established a popularly elected federal (national) legislature and executive, alongside a powerful system of decentralized state (local) governments, a powerful and independent judiciary and entrenched a series of universal civil and political rights into the American polity.

However, property qualifications for the vote remained in the USA at a state level for another 60 years with only small advances in the post-constitutional era and in the 1830s. Women, native Americans, and black Americans remained overwhelmingly excluded from the democratic process. Indeed as literacy tests were introduced as part of the voting registration process, illiterate, poor immigrants to the Northern states also found themselves excluded. It was the American Civil War, 1861–65, that was the next crucial stage in American democratization. We will return to the origins and consequences of the war below. Here it will suffice to state that the war ended slavery in the South, politically broke the back of the Southern plantation aristocracy, maintained the territorial integrity of the nation and curtailed the development of an explicitly anti-democratic coalition of Northern and Southern elites. However, in the reconstruction period after the war enough space was left to Southern elites to maintain the exclusion of black Americans from the political process. It was not until after the First World War that women finally achieved the vote in all state and federal

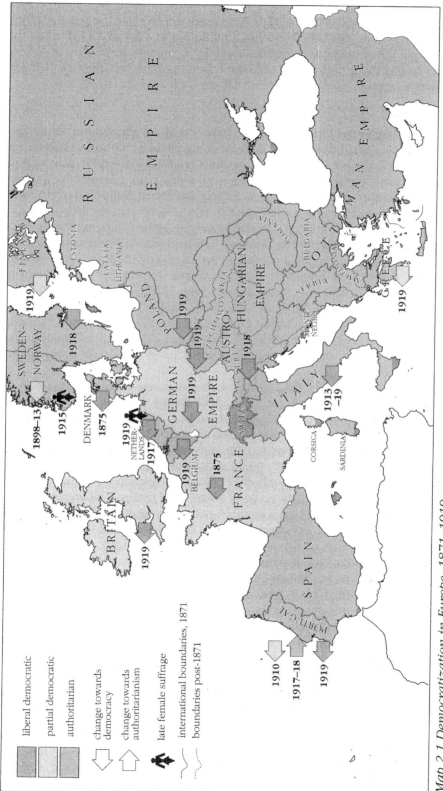

Map 2.1 Democratization in Europe, 1871–1919

elections. The inclusion of black Americans would await the passage of the
Civil Rights Act and the Voter Registration Act in 1964 and 1965 when the
federal government acquired the capacity to prevent Southern states from
excluding them. Only then could the USA reasonably be called a full liberal
democracy.

Britain

Britain began the long nineteenth century with an ambiguous democratic
inheritance. On the one hand, there is some truth to the claim that Britain was
the earliest modern democracy. Since the Civil War (1640–49) which put paid
to the establishment of an enduring royal absolutism, considerable powers
had been wrested from the monarchy and transferred to the elected House of
Commons and the unelected House of Lords. Control of the executive had
peaceably passed between different loosely organized factions of aristocracy
and bourgeoisie and peaceful inter-elite competition had been established as
the basic norm of political conflict in the eighteenth century. On the other
hand, the suffrage remained highly restricted by property and ownership
qualifications. The electoral system was invariably corrupt and the
boundaries of constituencies massively skewed towards rural areas.
During the Napoleonic Wars (1799–1815) and their turbulent aftermath,
many basic civil and political liberties were effectively suspended and
widespread state directed repression of the press and political opponents
was conducted.

In the course of the next century the suffrage was gradually expanded. In
1832 the upper segments of the middle classes were brought within the
British polity, effectively separating them from more radical demands from
below. Successive waves of radical and working-class protest in the shape of
the Chartist movement pressed for universal suffrage, initially including
women, and a reform of political institutions but were successively
repressed, conciliated and rebuffed before the movement collapsed in the
1850s. Only after this great wave of protest had declined did reform come.
First, in the 1867 Reform Act which enfranchised a substantial electorate in the
cities and boroughs and second, in the 1884 Reform Act which extended
suffrage expansion to the shires and the country. Third, in 1885 the first
equitable distribution of parliamentary constituencies was established. By
this time, around two-thirds of men could vote and about 40 per cent of all
workers. However it would take another three and a half decades before
something approaching a liberal democracy was established. The unelected
power of the House of Lords was first limited by the elected commons in 1911
in a raging dispute over taxation. The limits of even this reform were
demonstrated by the other enduring problem of British democracy, Ireland.
The inclusion of Irish parliamentary representatives at Westminster had
begun in 1801 but by the late nineteenth century this incorporation had given
way to persistent demands for Irish home rule. This was passed repeatedly by
the Commons from the 1880s onward and repeatedly rejected by the
permanent Unionist majority in the Lords until 1914, when the Home Rule Act
was passed but suspended for the duration of the First World War. Only after
the war in 1919 was something approaching universal adult suffrage
introduced. Indeed women did not achieve proper equality within the

suffrage until 1929 and plural voting was only abolished completely in 1948. Simultaneously, the democratic status of Ireland was ultimately secured by succession, independence and partition.

France

The course of French democratization is one of advances and reversals throughout the long nineteenth century, oscillating between republican democracies and authoritarian monarchies. The French Revolution began in 1789 and swept away the political and legal infrastructure of 200 years of royal absolutist rule and half a millenium of feudal economic relations. In the face of a fiscal crisis – the French state was bankrupted by the Seven Years War and the inability of the monarchy to extract any tax from the nobility or the church – Louis XVI summoned the *estates generale* to find a way out of the financial and social impasse. This essentially consultative body was drawn up on feudal lines and politically weighted towards the aristocracy and the Church. It was rapidly transformed under external popular and internal elite pressures into the *National Assembly* signalling the fundamental political equality of social groups and the existence of a singular popular nation. The first attempt to craft a post-revolutionary polity was the constitution of 1791 that proposed a constitutional monarchy and limited franchise. This solution was both too reactionary and too radical for key social groups. The opposition of the forces of both popular and counter-revolution as well as the intransigence of the king made such a resolution impossible. With the declaration of a republic and the execution of Louis XVI in 1793 hopes for an authoritarian constitutional monarchy were lost. Instead, a radical democratic programme of universal male suffrage, entrenched civil and political rights and representative government were declared in the constitution of the First Republic in 1793. However, this was never likely to be implemented under the Jacobin Terror of 1793–94. The combined impact of external war and internal counter-revolution in France led first to the creation of a more authoritarian Thermidorian directorate (1795) and eventually to the recreation of monarchy and empire under Napoleon Bonaparte (1799).

Defeated by Britain in the long Napoleonic Wars for supremacy in Europe, France reverted to an authoritarian constitutional monarchy in 1815. In 1830 the narrowly based Bourbon monarchy was displaced by the Orleanists who ruled on a narrow suffrage and authoritarian polity until the revolutionary uprisings of 1847–49. Radical republicans, urban artisans and peasants combined to displace the monarchy and declare a democratic Second Republic in 1848, only to be swamped by the authoritarian *coup d'état* of 1851 led by Louis Napoleon, later Napoleon III. A lasting democratic constitution entailing universal male suffrage was not achieved until the collapse of the old regime was precipitated by defeat in the Franco-Prussian War of 1870–71. Radical republicans and their allies achieved a democratic constitution in 1875, the Third Republic. After victory in the 1884 elections they managed to emasculate the unrepresentative upper house. However, the triumph of 1875 was preceded by the violent repression of an altogether more radical experiment of participatory democracy. This grew out of the Paris commune of 1870 when radical artisans and the Parisian working class took control of the capital. None of the three republics declared a suffrage that extended to French women. Indeed the precocious advance of universal male suffrage was paralleled by the very late arrival of a genuine universal suffrage in the 1946 elections.

Declaration of the French Third Republic on the steps of the Hôtel de Ville

Germany

To speak of the history of Germany's democratization over the long nineteenth century is an anachronism, for a unified German nation-state did not emerge until 1870. Germany was, before this, an idea and a rough geographical area in which German speakers were preponderant (including parts of the Austro-Hungarian empire and Switzerland). Politically it was fragmented into a multiplicity of separate states like Prussia and Bavaria, principalities and dukedoms, and free cities like Hamburg. The Europe-wide revolutions of 1848–49 found some democratic echoes in Germany where urban artisans and liberals forced political changes across the fragmented German political landscape, demanding and receiving universal suffrage in a number of states and cities. However, authoritarian government was restored when local elites called in the reliably reactionary Prussian army to impose order.

After 1870 a Prussian dominated Germany emerged in which universal male suffrage was granted in the constitution of 1871. However, the German polity was only very partially democratic. Despite such a broad suffrage, broader than that of either Britain or America at the time, power remained highly concentrated and unaccountable in the Second Reich. The powers and prerogatives of the monarch remained substantial. The executive and

Revolutionary soldiers and sailors, Berlin, 1918

chancellor continued to be appointed by the crown and were effectively uncontrollable by, and unaccountable to, the elected Reichstag which did not elect the chancellor. Local government remained in the hands of unelected local elites. Power was particularly concentrated in the Prussian Landtag or state government (including control of the army) which had one of the most unequal franchises in Germany, heavily weighted towards property owners. Civil liberties were fragile everywhere and both socialists and Catholics were ruthlessly pursued and politically marginalized until the First World War. Though never formally prevented from contesting elections, the party of organized German labour the SPD (*Sozialdemokratische Partei Deutschlands*) was banned from organizing (1879–90) and alongside labour unions was repressed by the courts, police and army. The Catholic Church and its main representative, the Centre (*Zentrum*) Party were subjected to Bismarck's *Kulturkampf* in the 1870s and 1880s. Under this policy the state attempted to secure control of the Catholic hierarchy and its assets, while actively limiting their ability to organize politically and socially. It was only in the wake of defeat in the First World War that the first full German democracy emerged. Amidst widespread military mutinies and civilian disorder, including the establishment of enclaves of radical people's democracies (in Bavaria and Berlin in late 1918 and early 1919) the monarchy abdicated and the Kaiser fled to the Netherlands. Under the auspices of the SPD in unholy alliance with the far right, these radical movements were repressed and the Weimar constitution was declared in 1919. This provided for universal suffrage, for both men and women, an accountable executive and representative legislature and the constitutional entrenchment of regular elections, changes of power and civil and political liberties. As we know, it was to last a mere fourteen years.

——————————————— *Summary of Section 2.1* ———————————————

- In the USA an early white male democracy was both entrenched and limited by the outcome of the Civil War and the reconstruction of the South. Women remained excluded from the polity until after the First World War, black Americans remained excluded.

- In Britain, the pattern of democratization stretches back to the creation of parliamentary government after the Civil War on a very narrow franchise. Gradual expansion of the suffrage and reform of core institutions gathered pace in the late nineteenth century but along with some kind of resolution to the Irish question were only completed after the First World War.

- French democratization was more volatile, moving back and forth between partially democratic republics and authoritarian monarchies. More radical democratic models were crushed in the counter-revolutions of 1795 and 1851 and the defeat of the Paris commune of 1870, while the democracy of the Third Republic continued to exclude women from the suffrage until much later than the other three cases.

- German democratization was closely bound up with the process of national unification. Unification and capitalist development were conducted under the auspices of an authoritarian Prussian monarchy and state that created a highly restricted democracy in the late nineteenth century. By contrast, the fragile Weimar republic declared in 1919 was more democratic, on paper, than any other polity.

2.2   Political routes to the modern world: Barrington Moore

One of the first attempts to try and explain the different patterns and paces of democratization that I have described was Barrington Moore's classic book, *Social Origins of Dictatorship and Democracy: Lord and Peasant in the Making of the Modern World*, published in 1966 (see Chapter 1). In the book, Moore argues, on the basis of comparative historical analysis, that there are three main political routes through modernity. Some societies achieve a form of democracy through a *bourgeois revolution* (France, Britain and the USA); others experience a conservative and reactionary *revolution from above* which ultimately leads to the creation of fascist authoritarian dictatorships (Germany and Japan); finally, some societies experience a radical *peasant revolution from below* led by communist parties which results in various forms of authoritarian state socialism (Russia and China). The task of Moore's work is to try and explain why these different paths are taken by different societies.

    The subtitle of the book – *Lord and Peasant in the Making of the Modern World* – gives a clue as to the main type of explanation pursued. In effect, Moore argues that we can primarily determine which political path a society will take on the basis of its agrarian social structure and economy. In terms of our explanatory factors outlined in Chapter 1, Moore's abiding concerns are changing class structures and class alliances. While Moore introduces both caveats and specific explanations for individual cases, three factors run through all of his case studies: the economic situation of the aristocracy and its response to the commercialization of agriculture; the relative strength and political organization of the bourgeoisie; the fate of the peasant class in the transition to modernity.

The importance of Moore, amongst other things, is that he attempted to link economic divisions and interests (class structures) with political strategies and interests (attitudes to democratization). The aristocracy has been, almost everywhere, anti-democratic in its political outlook. It is hardly surprising that a social class whose economic and political power rested on a fundamentally unegalitarian vision of human society and human nature should have difficulties with democracy. The beneficiaries of a hereditary distribution of economic resources, social status and positions of political and juridical power have few compelling reasons to accept the necessity of a popular mandate or widened access to economic and political power. Therefore, where the aristocracy remained the most powerful social class into the modern era, the conditions for democracy were poor. However, where the aristocratic response to the commercialization of agriculture has been to adapt to market-driven economics and rely on a formally free-wage laboured force, democracy has been possible. The commercialization of agriculture eradicates a dependant peasantry by converting them into landless labourers and circumvents a potential agrarian revolution. However, where landlords have relied on labour repressive agriculture – sharecropping, slavery, serfdom – they have required unimpeded access to the coercive force of the state to ensure labour discipline and economic survival. In such a context they have been extremely resistant to allowing either peasants or workers access to state power. They have been therefore anti-democratic.

Where the power of the aristocracy has been broken by economic or political change democratic prospects have been brighter. The key social force in effecting that change has been, according to Moore, the bourgeoisie – the industrial and commercial middle classes. Their significance is not just that they displace aristocratic domination but that they are the sociological vectors of liberal and democratic ideologies and the active creators of liberal democratic institutions. Capitalist economic relations recognize no enduring differences between human beings on the basis of rank, status or family. Indeed those social divisions act as restraints and fetters upon the rational application of economic resources and the smooth functioning of free markets. Thus on this reading the bourgeoisie's economic circumstances generated a set of economic and political beliefs that were conducive to democratization. Moreover, as a class they emerged within societies economically and politically dominated by the aristocracy. The promotion of their own class interests required control of the state so that feudal economic systems could be dismantled and trade and economic development initiated. This required that the state become accountable to them.

Where the bourgeoisie have been socially and politically powerful, aristocratic domination has been broken by bourgeois revolutions. The meaning of this term is a contested one. There are at least three senses in which Moore applies the term, though he does not always distinguish sharply between them. It can refer to a process of radical political change in which the key revolutionary agent is the bourgeoisie. Bourgeois revolution can refer to a similar process in which the bourgeoisie emerges as the most powerful political class, irrespective of who initially made the revolution. Or finally, it can refer to a process of political change in which, irrespective of the initial creators and beneficiaries of the revolution, a state structure is created and a set of public policies are implemented which provide the basis for the expansion of capitalism. This facilitates the economic dominance of the bourgeoisie and enhances their political power. Where the bourgeoisie has been weak they have capitulated to the political leadership of the aristocracy and formed part of a broader anti-democratic coalition that has in its effects, if not its personnel, conducted a bourgeois revolution from above.

It is perhaps easiest to start with Moore's authoritarian case, Germany. In this case Moore does not ask, how did democratization happen, but why the anti-democratic forces proved so strong? The key actors were the German Junkers, the class of Prussian aristocratic landowners. In the face of international competitive pressures in agriculture, the Junkers maintained their declining economic strength by using the coercive power of first the Prussian and later the German state to maintain labour-repressive practices on their agricultural estates. In the wake of unification and industrialization the coalition of aristocracy and state was expanded to encompass Germany rather than just Prussia as well as the emergent bourgeoisie. Rather than conducting their own bourgeois revolution, German capital 'exchange[d] the right to rule for the right to make money' (Moore, 1966, p.437). This coalition of *iron and rye* conducted the industrialization of Germany from above, simultaneously repressing dissent from peasants and workers, while maintaining a highly partial democracy. This secured the support of the middle classes, but left the state and conservative leadership sufficient autonomy to effect a transformation of the German economy without transforming its social structure or the locus of political power.

The democratic cases, as Moore calls them, are more varied in their origins. What unites them all is that at some point a violent break from the past destroyed the old order, excluded the possibility of an authoritarian route to modernity or a peasant revolution and constituted, in some sense, a form of bourgeois revolution. This laid the ground for the emergence of capitalism and the eventual triumph of bourgeoisie and democracy. In the case of England, the Civil War served to diminish the power of the monarchy and stimulated the commercialization of agriculture. The resultant process of enclosures (the transformation of common lands and peasant strip fields to single fields primarily for sheep grazing) led to a commercially-orientated aristocracy with close economic and social ties to an emergent urban bourgeoisie and the destruction of the peasantry. The English ruling classes, therefore, no longer required access to a repressive state to maintain their agricultural labour force while the possibility of a peasant revolution was effectively ended. Having established the conditions for capitalist growth in the seventeenth and eighteenth century and eroded significant differences of interest between rural and urban ruling elites, the nineteenth century gave way to peaceful political competition within the ruling class. Authoritarian options for modernization were not necessary.

When Moore examines the case of France the puzzle is why, given the massive differences in the agrarian social structure of France in comparison to England, did a democracy still emerge? The aristocracy remained highly subordinate to an absolutist monarchy, peasant agriculture was deeply entrenched and the extraction of a surplus from them required the use of coercive force. The answer to that puzzle is the French Revolution. Moore argues that the revolution effectively broke the back of both the absolutist monarchy and a politically powerful aristocracy. Although the subsequent counter-revolutions and monarchical restorations of the nineteenth century indicate the incompleteness of the revolution, it remains true that the events of 1789–99 destroyed French feudalism and laid the legal and social grounds for a process of capitalist development. Therefore, the authoritarian options exemplified by Germany could not happen. The aristocracy were broken if not eliminated. The need for labour-repressive agriculture and a repressive state was extinguished and capitalist development had been initiated without the need for a revolution from above. However, that process of development was the weakest of our four states, a fact evinced by the comparative weakness of the French bourgeoisie. This made the achievement of democracy more difficult than the English experience.

Finally, it is interesting to contrast Moore's account of Germany with that of the USA. Rather than focusing on the American Revolution and the establishment of a partial democracy in the eighteenth century, Moore is concerned with the fate of American democracy in the nineteenth century when processes of modernization and industrialization really gathered pace. In this context he poses the question, why did the USA not follow the German path? Why was there not an authoritarian alliance between the slave owning plantation aristocracy of the Southern states and the Northern industrial bourgeoisie, excluding blacks and workers alike from the American polity? Moore argues that the continued success of Northern capitalism could not be secured if the new states of the West were allowed to become slave states. The American Civil War functioned as a bourgeois revolution, politically decimating landowners in the South and establishing commercial capitalism all across the USA.

----------- *Summary of Section 2.2* -----------

- Moore argues that there are three main political routes through modernity: democratic bourgeois revolutions, authoritarian revolutions from above, and peasant revolutions from below.

- The route a society takes depends on the changing balance of economic power and interests amongst three key classes: the aristocracy, the bourgeoisie and the peasantry. This, in turn, is closely linked to their response to the commercialization of agriculture. The attitude of the different classes to democratization is strongly shaped by their economic interests and ideological outlooks.

- Authoritarian responses succeeded where the aristocracy remained dependent on labour coercion and non-democratic control of the state. This is facilitated where they can make an anti-democratic alliance with a politically weaker bourgeoisie repressing workers and peasants.

- Democratic routes are taken where: bourgeois revolutions break the political back of the aristocracy and block authoritarian options; the aristocracy go over to commercial agriculture and ally with the bourgeoisie; and where commercialization erodes a significant peasant class.

2.3   Moving on from Moore: Göran Therborn

Since its publication *Social Origins of Dictatorship and Democracy* has set the standard by which sociological investigations of democratization are judged. None the less, it remains a flawed classic and Moore has attracted considerable criticism for it. These include: his failure to examine the impact of international events on processes of democratization; his flawed account of bourgeois politics; his claim that bourgeois revolutions are central to the creation of democracies; and his inattention to the role of the working class. The small number of case studies covered has opened Moore up to further criticism because of the different paths to democracy in other countries. His focus on England, rather than Britain, indicates that he paid little attention to the complexities of national questions and the simultaneous struggles over territorial as well as representative issues. Finally, his equation of democracy with parliamentary democracy in *Social Origins* led Moore to ignore the extension of suffrage to workers and women. Some of these criticisms have been taken up by other authors such as Göran Therborn.

Göran Therborn's (1977) article, 'The rule of capital and the rise of democracy' differs from Moore's *Social Origins* in a number of important ways. First, he covers a much wider range of capitalist states, including all of the small states of Western Europe and the white dominions of the British Empire. Second, he examines the emergence of both representative and accountable government and full universal suffrage unhindered by exclusions of class, gender, race or ideology. Third, he is much more concerned with the international determinants of domestic politics, particularly war – one of our six explanatory factors. Finally, Therborn argues that contrary to Moore's claim, no bourgeois revolution has ever installed a functioning and sustainable liberal democracy. Whatever the long-term implications of the English and American Civil Wars and the French Revolution for patterns of democratization the actual achievement of representation and suffrage have more immediate and significant historical causes. Moore, in effect, establishes only some preconditions for democratization rather than the historical forces that actualize it: democracy by *defeat*, by *national mobilization*, and by *internal development*.

Democracy by defeat

Looking across many countries over a long historical time frame Therborn argues that processes of democratization received a decisive acceleration in the aftermath of both world wars. We will return to the impact of the Second World War in Chapter 4. Here it will suffice to note that in 1918 and 1919 a whole clutch of previously authoritarian monarchies became liberal democracies. These include not only Germany, but also Austria, Finland and Sweden. In all of these countries the pre-war balance of political forces did not favour democratization and, arguing counterfactually, Therborn claims that in the absence of war authoritarian regimes would have maintained their hold on power. Defeat in war destroyed the legitimacy of those regimes; directly in Central Europe and indirectly through example in Scandinavia. A similar case can be made for the collapse of authoritarian forces in France after their defeat in the Franco-Prussian War.

Democracy by national mobilization

The achievement of democracy through national mobilization has two sources. Democracy can either be introduced as a *means of* national mobilization or it can *result from* processes of national mobilization and integration. The idea of mobilization needs some clarification. Therborn is suggesting that under conditions of industrialized warfare the survival of states and regimes depends on the achievement of internal stability and consensus so that all available social energies can be directed towards the external threat. The conduct of industrialized warfare exacts an enormous toll on societies: it requires mass armies with high levels of conscription for periods of time unheard of in the past; production must be accelerated and transformed; work rates rise; control over the labour process increases; conditions and wages must invariably harshen. Consumption, too, must be redirected from individuals and families to armies. Thus increasing amounts of labour, military and civilian, are accompanied by decreasing consumption and security. Moreover, states become less and less likely to accept immediate challenges, threats and dissent. Yet they also become even more dependent on the co-operation of the societies they are mobilizing. It is not surprising, therefore, that democracy is the price paid by authoritarian regimes for their survival in war either as a carrot to encourage mobilization or as the inevitable pay-off for a mobilization conducted under the old regime. The former is exemplified by Canada and Italy where reforms of the suffrage in the midst of the the First World War helped diffuse internal protest against the war. In the cases of democracy as a result of national mobilization, war has speeded up processes of democratization already in train. In Britain the extension of suffrage to all men and some women, and in the USA to women, seems clearly related to the mobilization of men and women in mass citizen armies and a highly regulated industrial work force.

Democracy by internal development

Democracy by internal development alone can account for democratization in only three countries: Australia, New Zealand and Switzerland. However, alongside warfare it played a major role in our three democratic cases. Therborn argues that the most consistent domestic advocate for democratization has been the working class. The reason for this is not difficult to see. Excluded from power, but requiring state power to protect their interests and with increasing numbers of their side, labour movements have recognized that their interests would be best served by the irresistible logic of working-class numbers in a democratic polity. However, 'it was nowhere strong enough to achieve bourgeois democracy on its own, without the aid of victorious armies, domestic allies more powerful than itself, or splits in the ranks of its enemies' (Therborn, 1977, p.24). Labour movements systematically pressed the case for democracy in Western societies across the nineteenth century. However, in the absence of defeat in war and in addition to the impact of national mobilization, labour has only achieved that end under two further conditions: when the dominant classes have been politically divided and incapable of maintaining united support for authoritarian politics; and when the labour movement has forged an alliance with an economically significant and politically organized class of small or medium-sized farmers.

In Switzerland, New Zealand, the USA and Australia the inauguration of male democracies preceded the establishment of a powerful working class, and the role of small farmers demanding a share in power was even more significant. In Denmark and Sweden where authoritarian regimes lasted longer these classes proved powerful allies of emergent labour movements. However, Therborn does not note the occasions on which labour movements have pursued strategies other than the creation of liberal democracies, nor does he accurately specify why some labour movements have been able to forge effective cross-class alliances in pursuit of democratization and why others have failed.

The trajectory of democracy in France, Britain and the USA was closely tied to ruling-class divisions. Therborn expands upon this arguing of elite disunity, as long as there is no serious threat from below, division can lead to intense vying for popular support; and providing there exists an underlying unity 'they may help to promote institutional procedures securing peaceful coexistence and opposition' (Therborn, 1977, p.26). In France and Britain serious threats of disorder and radical democratization from below were violently quelled; in Britain during and after the Napoleonic Wars, and in France in 1848 and 1870. In France the ruling classes politically divided after the Franco-Prussian War over the return of the monarchy and the status of the Church. Consequently, they were unable to resist the democratic forces that inaugurated the Third Republic. In Britain, when more cautious demands for democratization were made it became the occasion for different fractions of the ruling class to compete for mass support. Thus the 1867 Reform Act, Therborn argues, was designed by the Conservative government under Disraeli to both placate popular demands for democracy and obtain a significant part of the new electorate for the Conservative Party. Further extension of the suffrage was intended to both control the process of political change and win a further block of worker support for the Liberal Party. In the USA, the role of elite division is more complex to assess. Along with Moore we can argue that ruling disunity led to both the Civil War and the eradication of an authoritarian political option. However, in the aftermath of the war the essential unity of the ruling groups ensured that the extension of the franchise to black ex-slaves would not be an option.

Summary of Section 2.3

- Therborn argues that there are three overlapping causes of democracy – democracy through defeat in war, democracy as the pay-off for national mobilization in war, and democracy through internal development.
- In all of these struggles the role of the working class was a key one, but it had to find allies in the shape of victorious foreign armies, divided elites and independent agrarians, to achieve lasting democratic reforms. Why the working class pursued this political strategy and the conditions under which it made those alliances successfully are less clear.

2.4   Michael Mann: a new synthesis

While Therborn clarifies and goes beyond some of the limits of Moore's original work a number of important questions remain unanswered. First, neither writer addresses at any length the ways in which transformations in the nature of the state affects struggles for democratization. Second, although Therborn notes the importance of national liberation struggles, neither looks at the way in which the national and the representative questions entwine with each other. Third, while Therborn gives some consideration to why certain social classes have been democratic or anti-democratic he does not generate a comprehensive set of explanations as to why different groups of workers and agrarians pursued either democratic or non-democratic political programmes and on what basis they allied with each other. Each of these themes – the changing character of the state; the impact of the national question; and, the connection between class structure and the political strategies of labour and agrarians – is investigated by Michael Mann in his book, *The Sources of Social Power* (1993).

State structures and democratization

Mann argues that the character of the state in the West underwent a profound set of transformations in the long nineteenth century. First, the size of states, measured in terms of their total revenues, expenditure and levels of employment massively expanded. The overwhelming importance of military expenditure and personnel in the eighteenth century state gave way to a predominantly civilian set of functions and activities in the late nineteenth century. Those developments equipped states with a much greater capacity to actively intervene in the organization and functioning of the societies they governed. States became much more important to their citizens and subjects. Mann makes the crucial point that prior to the long nineteenth century the small size and ineffective instruments of governance available to states ensured that most of the population, most of the time, could ignore them. There was no need to organize politically to obtain a share of state power. Once states became so large and so powerful that they penetrated into every-day life then social classes and nations were forced to engage with the struggle for state power on a regularized basis. In short, the growth of the state is an essential precondition of the mobilization of broader democratization struggles. Thus the old regime of aristocracy and allied classes was forced, in the course of the long nineteenth century, to develop strategies of political inclusion and political control that met the challenges from below without decisively yielding power to subaltern classes and nations.

Democratization and the national question

The role of nations and the territorial question need some unpacking. Simply put, Mann argues that struggles over state power were concerned with both how state power should be controlled (the representative question) and over what area and including which ethnic and national groups that power should legitimately be exercised (the territorial question). Democratization struggles are not only about *how the people should rule* but also *who are the people.* Thus essentially class-based struggles over state power were intertwined with struggles over the territorial extent and territorial distribution of power. In the Austro-Hungarian Empire, conflicts over representation were probably less important than establishing separate political arrangements for the many component nations and territories of the empire. In Germany, the Catholic minority of the South, Danes in the North and Poles in the East were as concerned with ensuring that state power would be exercised locally (in their regions) rather than centrally (from Berlin and Prussia) as they were with its representative quality. For the Irish, home rule was always more important than struggles for universal suffrage for the Westminster parliament.

Class structures, class alliances and democratization

The working classes of the late nineteenth century did not all pursue similar strategies of democratization. On the one hand, some elements of the organized working class pursued predominantly economic rather than political strategies using their strength in the labour market and at the core of the production process to extract rewards and concessions. The core of the American labour movement was committed to the systematic pursuit of increased wages and control at the work place through unions rather than actively supporting a socialist political party or an extension of the franchise to blacks and women. Important components of the French labour movement supported anarcho-syndicalist strategies of revolutionary economic action and bore a deep suspicion of all forms of centralized political power – democratic or otherwise. On the other hand, not all labour movements that pursued a political strategy orientated themselves towards a reformist achievement of universal suffrage. The leading elements of the Russian working class, under the aegis of the Bolshevik party, shifted in the years before the First World War towards revolutionary politics. This was also true at the level of rhetoric, if not practice, of the German SPD.

Amongst agrarian classes, Mann argues that large landowners and farmers were for the reasons I have already outlined, consistently anti-democratic. Landless labourers were invariably under the intense economic and political subordination of those landowners. This made their political organization exceptionally difficult and their support for programmes of democratization minimal. Only in those economies where landowners were predominantly absentee landlords were autonomous communities able to organize politically. Even then as in Spain, they were predominantly drawn to revolutionary and syndicalist programmes that emphasized land redistribution over political transformation. This leaves the political orientation of small independent farmers. The relationship between economic circumstance and political outlook is much more ambiguous and variable amongst this class. Their economic independence meant that they were not natural allies of either authoritarian or democratic coalitions. Their primary economic demands were for land security, access to and control of credit institutions and access to markets. This made them amenable to suitably reformist and interventionist programmes from either right or left. The direction in which they moved and their support for democratization turned on which coalition made the most effective pitch for their support. This entailed not only agricultural support policies but some acknowledgement of the regional and clerical sensitivities of these communities – often religious, suspicious of secular and atheist philosophies, and distrustful of overmighty centralized states and programmes of agricultural collectivization. Where labour movements were committed to a highly centralized vision of the state and overtly revolutionary ideologies and policy programmes, agrarians did not ally with the democratic coalitions.

Applying the theory

How do these arguments affect our accounts of democratization? In the case of the USA, the character of the state and its impact on the emergent working class helps explain the failure of any broad alliance of workers across racial and gender lines to emerge and thus the late arrival of a real universal suffrage in the USA. The strategy of rule adopted by the Northern elites of the USA was an aggressive liberal militarism in which the process of industrialization was conducted in the context of a partial liberal democracy and the ruthless suppression of collective rights and union organization. However, for white men of the nascent US working class the pre-industrial achievement of universal suffrage precluded the formation of a wider cross-class, race and gender alliance of the excluded. Independent agrarians in the Midwest had already been incorporated into the polity and provided no potential alliance for democratizing forces. The USA's reactionary judiciary legally emasculated workers' organizations. This was backed up by both public and private sources of armed coercion against workers. Aside from Russia, no other Western elite repressed its work force with the ferocity of US capital. Workers divided in the face of this onslaught and abandoned political strategies in a polity where the judiciary could not be controlled by elected representatives and the unity of the labour movement was fragmented by ethnicity, skill levels and geography. Those that were powerful enough to carve out a small defensible space in the labour market retreated into an apolitical and economically orientated strategy. Thus a combination of the character of the US state (partially democratic, with a politically independent judiciary) led to a fragmentation of the labour movement, political retreat and lasting divisions amongst the politically excluded. Democratization effectively stopped with the end of the Civil War.

Mann's model helps to account for the failure of a broad democratic coalition to come into being in Germany. The regime pursued a form of semi-authoritarian incorporation in which modernization would be conducted without either large-scale violent repression (as happened in Russia) or a transformation in the social structure. The granting of universal male suffrage in 1871 alongside a powerless legislature helped minimize demands for a broader alliance of the excluded. Alternate repression of workers and Catholics (the anti-socialist laws and the *Kulturkampf*) and their active pacification (Bismarck's pension schemes and welfare reforms and reversals of Catholic suppression) served to keep the main opponents of the regime divided. However, what really stymied the emergence of a broad cross-class alliance were the strategies and outlooks of these two excluded groups. The SPD remained a predominantly Lutheran protestant movement (in terms of its members' origins) concentrated in northern Germany and orientated towards a highly centralized and secular vision of the nation-state. Catholics, both workers and farmers in the South and West were alienated from the SPD by both its atheism and its centralism. By contrast, where labour movements were able to soften their centralism, bridge religious divides and construct political programmes that gave economic support to small farmers, cross-class and cross-regional alliances were achievable that made the democratic coalition infinitely more powerful (Sweden and France are good examples of this).

The nature of the British state made the authoritarian options pursued in Germany and the USA more difficult, for the weight of coercive force always lay with the Royal Navy and pointed outwards, rather than inwards. The late development and Christian reformism of British labour may have aided the process of democratization. Had the British workers' movements of the 1860s and 1870s been politically organized into a mass party, then the ruling elites would have been much less likely to extend the franchise in 1867 and 1884 in the knowledge that many of the votes would flow to such a party rather than themselves. The weakness of labour was compounded by the absence of potential allies. The Irish were focused on national rather than representative questions, no significant denominational minority provided a regional focus of popular discontent and the peasantry had long been extinguished. The final creation of a universal male suffrage in 1919 was linked to both the process of national mobilization and the rising political power of the recently formed Labour Party.

A similar moderation in the French labour movement – or rather its internal fragmentation and political marginalization – helps account for French democratization and the inclusion of agrarians in the democratic coalition. The drive for democracy under the Second Republic 1848–51 was rolled back by the authoritarian coup of Louis Napoleon yet it succeeded in 1875 with the creation of the Third Republic. In the early case radical working-class movements and a small urban intelligentsia remained isolated from broader political alliances, particularly from peasants and the provincial middle classes scared off by the radical social programmes that accompanied the calls for democratization. In the 1870s the role of the working class in the Republican coalition was diminished as urban liberals forged a broader and more moderate alliance with the provincial bourgeois and middle classes that was sufficiently robust to deny an already fragmented elite plausible allies.

—————————— *Summary of Section 2.4* ——————————

- The expansion in size and civilian importance of the modern state forced social groups to struggle more insistently for a share of, or control of, state power than had hitherto been necessary. Democratization struggles in the long nineteenth century entwined both the representative question and the territorial question and thus conflict and alliances between classes and nations.

- The outcome of these struggles rested partly on labour movements decisively opting for political rather than economic strategies and reformist rather than revolutionary strategies. They also depended on their capacity to forge alliances with farmers and ethnic and religious minority opponents of the old regime.

2.5   Comparing theories and societies

A proliferation of case studies and theoretical explanations can confuse as much as they clarify. In this section I will try and reduce the arguments of earlier sections into a number of key propositions about democratization in the West over the long nineteenth century (see Table 2.1). This will serve as a basis for clarifying the weaknesses and limits of these theories, some of which I will then try to address.

Class and democracy

All our structural theories argue that class is the key social force in democratization struggles. The special case of ethnicity and race in the USA is acknowledged. However, with the exception of Therborn, none of the theories tackles the question of gender divisions, the exclusion of women from the polity and the struggle for women's suffrage. This is the central failing of all of the work we have been considering and I return to it below.

Structural theories focus on the role of the four main classes in democratization struggles: the aristocracy, the bourgeoisie or commercial and industrial capital, the working class and agrarians, either peasants or small farmers. Aristocracies that have relied on labour-repressive agriculture have been the most consistent and strongest anti-democrats. Aristocracies that have adapted to commercial agriculture have socially and politically been prepared to share power with the bourgeoisie but have hardly been enthusiastic democrats. The bourgeoisie, contrary to what Moore says, have rarely been advocates of democratization beyond their own inclusion in a parliamentary system elected on a very narrow suffrage. In France and Britain fractions of that class have been limited advocates of democratization while in other states they have been active opponents (Germany, the USA).

Bourgeois revolutions have been important in France, Britain and the USA where they have broken the political dominance of aristocracies and opened the door to the commercialization of agriculture and capitalist development (weakening aristocracies and strengthening the working classes) but these have not been led or initiated by the commercial and industrial bourgeoisie nor did they create enduring liberal democracies. The working class had usually been the most consistent advocate of democracy

Table 2.1 Summary of explanations of democratization

	Britain	*France*	*Germany*	*USA*
Moore	Early bourgeois revolution (Civil War) initiates capitalist development and terminates Royal Absolutism Commercialized aristocracy and gentrified bourgeoisie maintain inter-elite competition in restricted parliamentary democracy	Early bourgeois revolution destroys aristocracy, initiates capitalist development and strengthens bourgeoisie Popular revolution prevents creation of authoritarian monarchy	Labour repressive landlords control state Weak bourgeoisie in subordinate anti-democratic alliance with aristocracy	Labour repressive landlords destroyed by Northern Bourgeoisie and Western farmers Post-Civil War reactionary alliance maintains capitalism in North and exclusion in the South
Therborn	Partial democratization through internal development: elite division unhindered by aggressive labour movement Full democratization by mobilization for First World War Balance of power shifts to labour-led democratic coalition leading to universal suffrage	Partial democratization through internal development Further democratization by defeat after Franco-Prussian War Full democratization through mobilization for war. Women obtain suffrage after Second World War	Full democratization by defeat in First World War Balance of power shifts to fragile labour-led democratic coalition after First World War Defeat in Second World War required for final destruction of authoritarian coalition	Partial democratization by internal development Democratization by internal mobilization for women after First World War Exclusion of blacks maintained until 1960s
Mann	Democratization aided by weak domestic repressive state Late political development and mild reformism of labour movement encouraged suffrage extension and intra-elite party competition	Democratization hindered by radicalism and fragmentation of labour movement Democratization aided by exclusion of radicals and incorporation of agrarians	Democratization hindered by radical atheist labour movement and failed alliances with minorities and agrarians	Extension of suffrage to women and blacks hindered by pre-industrial white male suffrage, economic orientation of core working class, aggressive repression and independent judiciary

for the basic logic of numbers in democratic systems favours the masses over elites. However, those labour movements that have pursued economic strategies (France, the USA) or revolutionary political strategies (Germany, Russia) have been less consistent advocates. Small farmers and peasants have proved a key swing vote in democratization struggles sometimes forming part of an authoritarian coalition (Southern Italy, Austria) sometimes allying with workers as part of a democratic coalition (Sweden, France).

The state and the national and representative questions

The general expansion of the size and governing capacity of the state in the long nineteenth century was a central factor in politically mobilizing classes and nations. However, the political aims and ends of democratization struggles vary amongst our theories. Moore focuses on the achievement of parliamentary government, but pays little attention to struggles for, or the timing of, universal suffrage. Therborn pays more attention to the achievement of suffrage alongside representative institutions and to the achievement of female suffrage, but focuses on the final push for suffrage at the expense of earlier struggles for democracy. Mann places the question of representation in a broader context of political changes of which the most important is the national question. He therefore asks not only how the people came to rule, but who are the people and how did they come to be defined in certain ways? Conflicts over democratization became entwined with struggles for national liberation and struggles between advocates of centralized and decentralized states.

Where landlords have had access to the repressive capacities of the state authoritarian coalitions have been possible and the prospects for democracy have been poor (Germany, *antebellum* Southern USA). Where labour-re-pressive landlords have failed to obtain that control they have succumbed to democratic forces (Australia, *post-bellum* Southern USA) as have those aristocracies that have not possessed a state with great repressive capacities (Sweden, Britain). Where states have been democratized in some form before industrialization (the USA, German suffrage without representative government) the pressures for a broad alliance of the excluded is dimin-ished and authoritarian coalitions are stronger, delaying the emergence of democracies. Where there have been significant struggles over the territorial extent of a state and the balance between central and local powers, minority ethnic groups and dominated national groups may provide allies for the democratic coalition. However, more often than not divisions between labour movements and their potential allies have occurred allowing authoritarian regimes to last longer (Britain, France, Germany, the USA).

War, alliances and strategies

Therborn demonstrates beyond doubt the importance of international factors in democratization, and war in particular. Where processes of democratiza-tion were already underway national mobilization speeded up and radicalized the process (Britain, France, the USA). Where authoritarian regimes remained stronger than democratic coalitions, defeat in the context of industrialized war destroyed their legitimacy and self-confidence (Germany). The price of victory was successful national mobilization which strengthened subordinate classes organizationally and morally. It became impossible to demand national sacrifice in war and exclude people from a share of power.

Therborn also demonstrates along with Mann that democratization struggles turn on the relative strength of class alliances. Democratization struggles are successful when the working class can secure allies from amongst disenfranchized nations, excluded minorities, women and independent farmers. This requires that they are neither too radical, centrist, patriarchal nor militantly anti-clerical in their outlook. It also requires that the differences that exist within the authoritarian coalition are so large and morale so low that they can be politically outflanked (France after 1870) or that the divisions are so small and morale so strong that democratization is an opportunity for more intensive political competition within the elite (Britain). The suddenness of post-war changes, particularly in defeated nations and the general significance of alliances and regime strategies points to a final limitation of all our theories. Strategies must be devised, alliances must be actively secured and renewed, crucial decisions at moments of great flux must be taken. Thus alongside broad structural, long-term changes, accounts of democratization must also examine the role of key individuals, leaders and short-term tactical decision making.

The struggle for female suffrage

I want to try and address one of the limits of the theories we have examined – the struggle for women's suffrage. The struggle for women's suffrage was only one, and often a late, component of the political struggles for women's inclusion in the polity in the West (Lovenduski, 1986). As with labour movements, the first wave of feminism often divided on economic–legal and political strategies. In the case of the former women demanded equal treatment before the law, the securing of women's property rights, access to the professions and education. The limits of such a strategy, in a polity dominated by men of all classes, led many to turn to political strategies and the achievement of universal suffrage as the best means to these ends as well as an end in itself. However, early feminism was further divided in its relationship to class. Most of the early organizations were established by middle-class women and represented the interests of middle-class women. Socialist feminists of this era were not only divided from middle-class women but were consistently thwarted by the male leaderships of unions and socialist parties who remained wedded to patriarchal models of gender and the family as well as seeking to exclude women from the workplace to protect the interests of men. As such the creation of broad alliances amongst women and between women and workers in pursuit of the suffrage were difficult to engineer.

In the majority of cases women's suffrage was ultimately achieved along with a universal male suffrage. In some cases this was primarily as a result of internal democratic developments (Australia in 1903, New Zealand in 1907), accelerated by the impact of the First World War (Denmark in 1915, Sweden in 1918). After the First World War, women's suffrage was achieved after shattering defeat (Germany in 1919, Austria in 1918) or as part of the pay-off for national mobilization in which women were drafted into the industrial work-force in record numbers (Britain partially in 1918, the USA in 1919). However in a number of countries none of these mechanisms proved sufficiently powerful to ensure the vote for women. It required a further round of upheavals during and after the Second World War to secure the vote in France (1946), Belgium and Italy (1948) and Switzerland (1971). A number of factors may help explain these variations. As with workers, women required internal unity and external allies to achieve the suffrage. In Germany, Britain and the USA, some co-operation was possible across class lines, much less so in France. Similarly, both the British Independent Labour Party and the German SPD were much less opposed to women's inclusion than their French and Italian counterparts, evidenced by the existence of distinct women's sections within the parties. Finally, the impact of Catholicism cannot be discounted. The four countries with the most recent women's suffrage were either overwhelmingly catholic or in the case of Switzerland with a very substantial and reactionary catholic minority. The impact of Catholicism operated at an ideological level, generating a widely accepted culture of women's moral superiority and political inferiority and institutionally through the creation of women's organizations opposed to suffrage.

Capitalist development and liberal democracy

The arguments above confirm the importance of widespread changes in political and military power in the development of democracy. Equally universal changes in cultural power had important effects. The spread of literacy and the development of new modes of communication was a significant factor in the development of political nations and minorities. For the first time it became possible for secular ideologies to cross class boundaries forging new political units based on a shared ethnicity and language, imagined and real shared histories. The emergence of Irish and Czech nationalism and the challenges to the British and Austrian old regimes would have been inconceivable without these kinds of change.

However, it is probably true to argue that economic change – capitalist industrialization – was the most important factor in stimulating democratic challenges to the old order in the West across the long nineteenth century. Commercial agriculture massively weakened peasants and labour-repressive landlords. Industrialization created a large working class concentrated in particular urban neighbourhoods and larger workplaces, free of segmental feudal control and networks of paternalism, patronage and clientelism. However, if capitalist development created the core class of a successful democratic coalition and weakened the core classes of authoritarian coalitions it was, by itself, no guarantee of success. Capitalist development, as we have seen, was able to thrive in the context of both authoritarian monarchies (Germany) and repressive, racist partial democracies (the USA). Power is rarely, if ever, democratized simply by the subterranean movements of social change or the benevolence of the powerful. At some point, whatever the preconditions, it must be actively taken by the excluded. However, where they have done so in pursuit of a democracy that exceeded the limits of liberal representative government they have been sharply checked. Capitalism accommodated liberal democracies. Its compatibility with more radical models was beyond the limits of political possibility in the long nineteenth century. It may still be.

—————————————— *Summary of Section 2.5* ——————————————

- The main explanatory factors of democratization in the long nineteenth century are: class, class alliances and the relative strength of authoritarian and democratic coalitions; the strength of the aristocracy and its dependence on labour repression; the nature of the state; the coalition preferences of labour movements, national minorities and agrarians; and the impact of war through defeat or mobilization.

- The main weaknesses of structural theories are their inattention to women's suffrage, the role of nations and the importance of leadership, tactics and human agency.

- Change in the character of economic, political, cultural, and military power have all shaped democratization struggles, but capitalist development was probably the most important democratizing force in the long nineteeth century.

References

Lovenduski, J. (1986) *Women and European Politics: Contemporary Feminism and Public Policy,* Brighton, Wheatsheaf.

Mann, M. (1993) *The Rise of Classes and Nation-states, 1760–1914: The Sources of Social Power, Volume II,* Cambridge, Cambridge University Press.

Moore, B. (1966) *Social Origins of Dictatorship and Democracy: Lord and Peasant in the Making of the Modern World,* Harmondsworth, Penguin.

Therborn, G. (1977) 'The rule of capital and the rise of democracy', *New Left Review,* no.103 pp.3–41.

CHAPTER 3

The crisis of modern democracy, 1919–39

Richard Bessel

Introduction

After the First World War liberal democracy appeared to have triumphed in Europe. The great crusade articulated by the American President Woodrow Wilson to make the world 'safe for democracy' had been fought and won. The German, Austro-Hungarian and Ottoman Empires had been defeated and destroyed. Revolutionary movements had swept away dynastic rule. Tsarist autocracy had been overthrown. The Western democracies were able to dictate terms of the peace treaties signed at Versailles, St Germain and Trianon. The principle of national self-determination was accepted as the basis for drawing new state frontiers. Parliamentary governments with democratic constitutions were established in the successor states to the Habsburg and Hohenzollern Empires. Suffrage, the right of active partici-pation in the (democratic) polity and a central pillar of active citizenship which hitherto had been restricted largely to propertied males, was extended in some countries to include women and the poor. The end of the First World War spelled the triumph of national and popular sovereignty across the European continent.

Twenty years later the picture could hardly have been more different, or more depressing. Democratic government had collapsed and been super-seded by dictatorship and/or military rule in country after country, leaving only the British Isles, Scandinavia, the Benelux countries and Switzerland with viable democratic political systems in Europe. Across the continent, democratic government had proved itself to be weak, unworkable, disgraced, despised. From Portugal to Poland, from Germany to Greece, from Italy to Hungary, from Austria to Spain, democratic government was replaced by authoritarian rule. The milestones along the road from European democracy to European dictatorship were depressingly numerous: Mussolini's March on Rome in 1922, Pilsudski's military coup in Warsaw in 1926, King Alexander's royal coup in Yugoslavia in 1929, Salazar's assumption of power in Portugal in 1929, Hitler's arrival in the Berlin Reich Chancellery in 1933, Franco's victory in the Spanish Civil War in 1939 – to name but some.

What had gone wrong? Why did the triumph of national and popular sovereignty after the First World War, which appeared at the time to establish liberal democracy as the natural and secure form of government across the European continent, so quickly turn into defeat? Why did democratic government prove so fragile so soon after its apparent victory? Four general factors seem of central importance here, and will comprise the subject matter

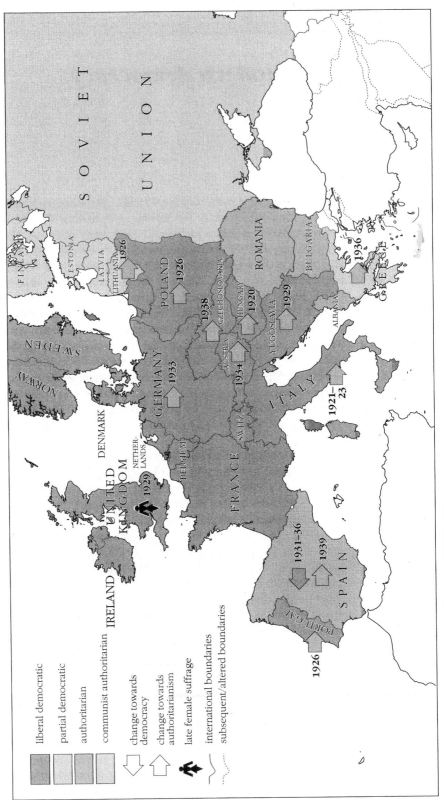

Map 3.1 Democratization in Europe, 1919–39

of this chapter: the enormously damaging effects of the First World War; economic crises of truly unprecedented proportions; and social and national divisions which could not be accommodated within a democratic frame-work. All four of these explanatory factors were new, not in their essence but in their scale. Europe, and the world, had known wars before, but never before had there been a *world* war, a war which had devoured so many human and material resources and which left so many deep scars as did the conflict of 1914–18. Europe, and the world, had known inflation, economic depression and unemployment before, but its people had never experienced anything on the scale of the hyperinflations of the early 1920s or the terrible economic contractions and mass unemployment of the 1930s – economic crises which appeared to call into question the very survival of the capitalist system. Europe, and the world, had known social and national divisions, but never had these erupted with such force as in the first half of the twentieth century. While this period may have begun with high hopes about the dawn of an age of democracy, it became what Eric Hobsbawm, in his recent history of 'the short twentieth century', has justly described as the 'age of catastrophe' (Hobsbawm, 1994).

The contrast between the 'long nineteenth century' (discussed in the previous chapter) and 'the short twentieth century' (the first, catastrophic decades of which are discussed in this chapter) is striking. The nineteenth century was regarded, in retrospect and by many at the time, as a century of political, social and economic improvement, of the development of civilized behaviour: the successful 'bourgeois century'. By twentieth century standards it was remarkably peaceful, and standards of public and political behaviour were remarkably civilized – characteristics which are vitally important for the successful development of democratic politics. Note Hobsbawm's comment about reactions to the widely reported anti-Jewish pogroms in the Russian Empire in 1881 and 1903: 'The handful of dead of 1881, to forty to fifty of the Kishinev pogrom of 1902, outraged the world – and justifiably – because in the days before the advance of barbarism, such a number of victims seemed intolerable to a world which expected civilization to advance' (Hobsbawm, 1994, p.120). Democracy depends as much on civilized behaviour as it does on organizational structure and economic developments.

The story told in this chapter is of the limits of liberal democratic politics, of liberal democracy at its moment of most spectacular and tragic failure. It is an extremely uncomfortable story, not only because of the horrors which were unleashed in the wake of democracy's failure in inter-war Europe but also because of the disturbing general implication that there may be some burdens which democratic government cannot bear. This suggestion presents itself with greatest force in the case of inter-war Germany. While one might be able to ascribe the failure of democratic government in inter-war Italy, Spain or Poland to a relative lack of social and economic modernization the same cannot be said of Germany. Indeed, when looking at inter-war Europe it would be difficult to find a country which had enjoyed greater socio-economic development or a higher level of modernization than did Germany in, say, 1928. In terms of wealth, extent of industrialization, degree of urbanization and level of education, Germany stood near the top of the table – just a few years before German democracy collapsed and was replaced by the most vicious and destructive dictatorship the world has ever known.

How can we explain this? I have identified four major areas of challenge to democratic government in inter-war Europe. Each of these involve the interplay of longer-term structural factors with short-term contingent factors.

1   The consequences of the First World War.

2   The effects of economic crisis.

3   The effect of social and class divisions.

4   The challenge of conflicting nationalisms.

3.1   The consequences of the First World War

There are two general areas where explanations for the collapse of democratic government in inter-war Europe have been sought: in the political, economic and social structures which developed over the nineteenth century; and in the cataclysm of the First World War, which brought the apparently stable world of nineteenth-century Europe crashing down. Structural explanations which have been highlighted in the previous chapters tend to concentrate on the mismatch of political structures on the one hand and social and economic structures on the other – for example, the persistence of the power of old landed ('feudal') interests within the context of a developed industrial economy and society. To stress the effects of the First World War, on the other hand, puts greater emphasis on contingent factors – on disruption and discontinuity as the source of the weakness of inter-war democracy rather than on longer-term structural continuities. Certainly the First World War marked a fundamental divide. The war, and the revolutions which followed, overturned not only economic and political structures; it also destroyed a sense of stability and security which is so necessary to stabile political formations. As Ernst Niekisch, a prominent left-wing journalist who was active in the council movement in Bavaria at the end of the war, wrote of Germany at this time:

> There are times in which all conditions which were thought to be unshakeable and eternal are called into question. The feeling spreads that the ground is being pulled out from under people's feet. Such a time descended upon Germany after 1918. Germany's great power status was gone; the social strata which had identified themselves with it found that there was no longer any air for them to breathe. One lived from hand to mouth and saw oneself time and again on the edge of precipices and catastrophes.

(Niekisch, 1958, pp.173–4)

This could be said not only of Germany, but of much of Europe. The war had pushed a self confident and apparently stable continent to 'the edge of precipices and catastrophes' – and this provided shaky foundations on which the new democratic structures of the inter-war period had to be built.

Thus the First World War left Europe a contradictory political legacy: it made democratic government both possible – by weakening old dynastic and authoritarian political structures – and difficult – by presenting new democratic states with enormous difficulties. Generally speaking, the First World War had two great, but contradictory, effects upon the history of democratization in Europe. On the one hand, the war fought to make the world 'safe for democracy' brought democratic forms of government to lands previously under (often foreign) dynastic rule. The collapse of the Habsburg and Hohenzollern Empires as a result of the war and the revolutionary unrest it provoked led to the creation of liberal parliamentary democracies where previously there had been authoritarian dynastic regimes with varying degrees of (or lack of) popular participation in the political process. The successor states in Central and Eastern Europe – (Weimar) Germany, Poland, Austria, Hungary, Czechoslovakia, Finland, Estonia, Latvia, Lithuania, Yugoslavia – all adopted essentially liberal democratic forms of government. Wilsonian ideals of democracy – often instrumentalized by nationalist politicians in order to gain Allied support at the peace conferences for statehood for their national group – and the concept of popular national sovereignty triumphed when the major authoritarian dynastic states collapsed in the final stages of the war.

On the other hand, the war left behind enormous problems for the parliamentary regimes of post-war Europe. The humiliating losses which followed from defeat in the cases of Germany and Austria, as well as the 'mutilated victory' which left Italians dissatisfied, created political difficulties which placed huge strains on parliamentary government. Perhaps the most prominent of these difficulties were those created by dissatisfied veterans of the conflict who found it difficult to readjust to civilian life – the groups of men who resisted demobilization – and by younger men who had missed out on their war – the men who joined the volunteer paramilitary organizations of the *Freikorps* (in post-war Germany) and the *arditi* and *fasci di combattimento* (in post-war Italy). Much has been made of the importance of such people for the rise of fascist movements, and certainly in the Italian case their involvement was crucial. As Adrian Lyttelton has observed: 'Fascism, as distinct from some other hypothetical form of reaction, simply could not have existed without these men. The *ardito* is the prototype, ideologically and symbolically, of the Fascist' (Lyttelton, 1996, pp.17–18). A particularly striking expression of this mentality can be found in the introduction to the *Diary 1922* (published in 1932) of Italo Balbo, the young ex-serviceman who became a radical Fascist leader in Ferrara:

> Fight, struggle, to come back to the country of Giolitti who put every ideal up for sale? No. Better to give up everything, destroy everything, if it meant that everything might be rebuilt from the foundations ... In my opinion, it is certain that without Mussolini three-quarters of the young Italians who returned from the trenches would have become bolsheviks; a revolution at any price!

(Quoted in Corner, 1975, p.61)

The radical rejection of the liberal parliamentary regime of Giolitti 'who put every ideal up for sale' left little room for the development of democratic politics in the turbulence of post-war Italy.

However, such attitudes formed only part of the damaging legacy of the First World War. The problems left behind by the need rapidly to demobilize millions of men, to dismantle the wartime economy, to repair war-damaged housing and factories, to supply food to populations which had been undernourished for years, and to cope with severe economic disruption combined with high popular expectations, would have been difficult enough for well-established parliamentary systems to deal with. For the new democracies created after 1918 the challenges they presented were all but impossible to master.

The extent to which the consequences of the war undermined democratic government is illustrated well by the German case, where the bitterness left behind by the Versailles Treaty poisoned the politics of the Weimar Republic. Rejection of the Versailles settlement comprised perhaps the only issue around which there were no bitter internal divisions and where there was a degree of consensus across the political spectrum; however, this consensus rested upon a refusal to face the narrow domestic and foreign-political constraints within which Germany now had to operate. Germans stubbornly refused to recognize that they had to pay for a lost war and that they had to acknowledge the security interests of a France which could, if it chose, easily march into Germany.

Perhaps even more important, in terms of the political climate of Weimar Germany, were the enormous human costs of the war which continued to be paid long after the Armistice had been signed. The war left behind millions of widows, orphans, and invalids, who now looked to the state for care and who felt betrayed when their expectations were not met. Not only did this overshadow the lives of millions of families; the resulting pensions also put enormous demands on government finances. In Germany, for example, it was claimed that 40 per cent of national government expenditure went towards paying war-related pensions (Whalen, 1984, p.157). Yet, for all the money which went to pay war widows and invalids, almost everyone involved was left dissatisfied: on the one side, war victims who felt that they were being inadequately compensated; on the other, finance ministers who saw government expenditure spinning out of control. Not surprisingly, attempts to control such expenditure provoked angry protest, particularly in the early 1930s when the economic crisis greatly reduced government revenues and vastly added to the pressures to cut government expenditure. In Germany, between 1928 and 1933 the budget for war victims' pensions was cut by one-third, leaving hundreds of thousands of people – who had been promised during the war that 'you can be sure of the thanks of the Fatherland' – embittered (Whalen, 1984, p.170). Yet there was no democratic way to square the circle: neither the funds nor the parliamentary majorities existed on which to base taxation and spending policies which might have satisfied impoverished war victims. As the leadership of the largely Social Democratic *Reichsbund der Kriegsbechädigten* (Reich Association of War Invalids) wrote to President Paul von Hindenburg: 'Nothing is won for the public good, and much is lost if the great majority of the war victims, as a result of these governmental measures, are radicalized to the left or to the right' (Whalen, 1984, p.170). This was hardly a recipe designed to promote support for democratic government.

―――――――――――――――― *Summary of Section 3.1* ――――――――――――

- The First World War opened the way for a tremendous spread of democratic government in Europe.

- At the same time, the social, economic and political destruction caused by the war undermined democratic government in inter-war Europe.

- The damaging effects of the First World War lasted well beyond the crises of the immediate post-war years, and this helped to undermine democratic government in the 1930s.

3.2   The effects of economic crisis

Politics involve setting priorities – deciding who gets what. Democratic politics involve popular participation – or at least the formal approval of the electorate – in the decisions about who gets what; and successful democratic politics involves the acceptance of decisions which do not favour one's own interests. Obviously this is easier done where levels of economic development and well-being are high and rising. Where that is not the case, and particularly where economic activity declines sharply, distributional struggles tend to become particularly bitter, and where these struggles occur within the framework of democratic political institutions they put great strain on those institutions. This is why, as Lipset noted (see Chapter 1) in his book, *Political Man*, 'the more well-to-do a nation, the greater the changes that it will sustain democracy' (Lipset, 1960, p.31). It is a lot easier to accept the legitimacy of other people's economic interests when you do not feel that your own back is to the wall!

The history of inter-war Europe provides some of the most depressing examples of what happens when economic crisis leads to bitter distributional conflict. The 1920s and 1930s witnessed the worst inflations and the most severe economic contractions that the world had ever seen. These economic catastrophes blighted millions of lives, and injected a bitterness into political life which proved deeply corrosive of democratic government. The problems of inflation and the problems of depression (which, in the early 1930s was accompanied by deflation) were not the same, but both posed fundamental challenges to the viability of democratic politics.

To begin with inflation: no European country emerged from the First World War with the value of its currency completely intact. The suspension of the gold standard and demands of wartime expenditure, the financing of the war and the post-war transition by recourse to massive borrowing and/or the printing presses left European currencies devalued against the US dollar. In the case of sterling, which had been the lynch-pin of the pre-1914 world financial system, the devaluation was relatively modest; in the case of France and Italy it was rather greater; in the case of Germany the old currency disappeared in the whirlwind of hyperinflation. Hyperinflation was a new phenomenon after the First World War; altogether, five European countries experienced it: Austria, Hungary, Poland, Russia and Germany. Leaving Russia out of the discussion here – because of the special circumstances created by revolution and civil war – 'the forces behind each inflation were very similar', as Derek Aldcroft has observed.

> The war had left all countries in a weak state, with large debts, balance of payments problems and inadequate taxation levels. Large fiscal requirements for reconstruction and other purposes were imposed on governments too weak to raise finance through the normal channels and the only option left was inflation through the printing press.
>
> (Aldcroft, 1977, p.138).

For our discussion the last point – namely that the governments in question were 'too weak to raise finance through the normal channels' – is of central importance. Why? Because this weakness was essentially an inability to settle difficult distributional conflicts within a democratic framework. Governments were unable to take difficult and unpopular economic decisions about taxation and expenditure and then to survive. Democratic government and difficult economic decisions were mutually incompatible, and so weak governments ducked the problem by resorting to the printing press rather than raising taxes. The results were disastrous, both for the economies of the countries in question and for parliamentary government. None of the countries which suffered hyperinflation at the beginning of the inter-war period were still parliamentary democracies by its end.

What is more, hyperinflation appears to have posed insurmountable problems for democratic government even in the short term: when it came, currency stabilization proved difficult to reconcile with democratic decision

Hyperinflation: laundry baskets are required to carry pay packets, Berlin, 1923

making. In Hungary and Austria the currencies were stabilized essentially through the League of Nations reconstruction schemes which involved a temporary surrender of economic sovereignty: international loans (for Austria in 1922 and for Hungary in 1924) followed by supervision of government finances by League of Nations staff. That way, no domestic political coalition had to take responsibility for necessarily tough economic measures. In Poland, where the new currency (the 'mark' created with the new state at the end of the First World War at a parity of 9.8 to the dollar), slipped to 17,800 to the dollar by 1922 and to over ten million to the dollar in December 1923 (Pease, 1986, pp.14, 22). Hyperinflation was accompanied by industrial unrest and political instability. In 1922 alone Poland had five successive governments, four of which were composed primarily of 'experts' without party affiliation and depended on shifting parliamentary majorities (the fifth, an attempt in July 1922 by Wojciech Korfanty to form a right-wing government with a majority in the *Sejm* – but rejected by Head of State Josef Pilsudski – collapsed in less than a month!). In December 1922 Poland lost its first President, Gabriel Narutowicz, through assassination in the wake of a nasty right-wing campaign in which Narutowicz was accused of selling Poland out to the Jews (Polonsky, 1972, pp.110–11). Not long thereafter, in 1926, Poland's discredited parliamentary system succumbed to another challenge – to the coup engineered by Pilsudski.

The classic example of how economic crisis undermined parliamentary democracy is that of Weimar Germany, which at the beginning of the 1920s suffered the world's worst inflation and at the beginning of the 1930s bore the brunt of the world's worst depression. Over the past few years historians have focused particularly sharply on the damaging consequences of the inflation which reached its terrible climax in 1923. It was, however, in fact 'a decade-long affair of considerable variation and complexity' (Feldman, 1993, p.5), beginning with the outbreak of war in 1914 (when 4.2 German marks could buy one US dollar) and ending with the complete collapse of the German currency in the autumn of 1923 (when one US dollar cost 4,200,000,000,000 marks). Inflationary financing of the war effort, when Germany financed a high proportion of its expenditure from borrowing rather than taxation, was followed not only by failure to secure reparations to pay off the war debt but also by huge new demands on government coffers. The democratic regime which assumed power after the Kaiser abdicated in November 1918 faced not only the enormous debts which had arisen from prosecuting the war and which gobbled up three-fifths of the national budget; it also faced huge expenditures for the demobilization, for keeping people at work during the post-war transition (opting, for understandable political reasons, for policies aimed at securing full employment), for war-related pensions, and for social and economic reforms and, of course, for reparations to the allies (Bessel, 1993; Borchardt, 1991). It was also weak: confronted with revolutionary unrest on the left and coup attempts from the right, able to count on the support of only a minority of the electorate from Reichstag elections of 6 June 1920 onward, Weimar governments were in a poor position to impose the tax increases which would have allowed the budget to be balanced and the currency to be stabilized.

The inflation proved profoundly destabilizing for German society and German democracy. It was accompanied by industrial conflict on a scale never before seen in Germany, food riots, ugly anti-semitic outbursts (against Jewish shopkeepers), political violence which claimed the lives of numerous leading politicians (including in 1922, the Foreign Minister and architect of Germany's war economy, Walther Rathenau) and hundreds of others, and huge increases in crime. This comprised more than a series of interrelated public-order problems; it pointed to the undermining of the values of a civilized society, values which are essential to the functioning of a viable democracy (Weisbrod, 1996). In an important recent study which stresses the harmful effects of the inflation, Niall Ferguson has pointed out:

> The 'silent bourgeois revolution' of the nineteenth century had inculcated an intricate set of values – the virtue of industry and thrift, the sanctity of property and contract, the importance of *Bildung* and *Kultur*. In wiping out the assets of savings banks, private schools and all kinds of voluntary associations, the inflation effectively undermined the institutions on which those values were based, and thus the values themselves.

> (Ferguson, 1995, p.18)

Not only that: the inflation conflicts undermined the political parties of the bourgeois middle, which saw their support diminish as interest groups abandoned political projects which transcended narrow economic concerns. This, in turn, made it difficult if not impossible for political parties to bridge the interests and retain the support of different groups; for example, the left-liberal German Democratic Party (one of the three parties of the original democratic Weimar coalition) found it increasingly difficult simultaneously to hold the allegiance of the independent middle class (which resisted tax increases) and the civil service (whose salaries came from tax revenue), both of which initially had been among that party's main sources of electoral support; at the same time, the inflation created enormous financial difficulties for the party itself, which found it difficult to meet its own operating expenses (Jones, 1988, p.166). The result was the degeneration of German politics into a Hobbsian war of all against all.

When it finally came, stabilization could not be achieved within a strictly democratic framework. During his short period as Chancellor from August to November 1923 (when agreement was reached with the French about reversing the occupation of the Ruhr and the necessary fiscal measures put in place to stabilize the currency, against a background of threatened coups from left and right), Gustav Stresemann had to operate repeatedly on the basis of emergency decrees, bypassing parliament. There simply was no popular democratic basis, as represented in the Reichstag, for the painful measures necessary to end the inflation and to restore financial stability. Germany's democratic government was given a stay of execution, but only through the partial suspension of democratic government. Furthermore, conflict did not suddenly evaporate once the currency was stabilized. Currency stabilization brought mass unemployment in 1924, and left in its wake hundreds of thousands of creditors who felt they had been cheated of what they had been owed and who became alienated from a democratic political system which they believed had failed them.

German democracy emerged battered from the political unrest which accompanied the inflation, but it did survive. The economic crisis which accompanied its downfall was of a different sort: of the severe depression and *de*flation which followed the New York stock market crash of 1929. Once again, distributional conflicts could not be resolved democratically, and in order to enact painful but economically necessary legislation – involving deep cuts in expenditure as tax revenues plummeted – it became necessary once again to bypass the Reichstag as governments resorted to emergency legislation. Why was economic crisis accompanied by the collapse of Weimar democracy in the early 1930s when it had not succumbed in the early 1920s? Three factors seem particularly important: first, particularly in the late 1920s, support for the 'middle ground' of German politics (parties representing special economic interests, such as The Economics Party of the German *Mittelstand,* and the two liberal parties) as well as for the conservative German National People's Party was disintegrating – as a result partly of the nasty residue left behind by the inflation and partly of dissatisfaction with the performance of parties once they participated in government. This left an opening for the Nazi Party, hitherto rather isolated on the right-wing racialist fringe, to attract the votes of the many people, from across the political and economic spectrum, disenchanted with their former political home. Second, the use of emergency legislation by Chancellor Heinrich Brüning between 1930 and 1932, and by his successor Franz von Papen during the spring and summer of 1932, signified not so much a temporary use of emergency powers to get over temporary difficulties (as had been the case under Stresemann in 1923) but an attempt to reshape the German state in a more authoritarian mould. By the early 1930s, there existed a fairly broad conviction that democratic government had become unworkable and that a more authoritarian form of government was necessary to deal with the enormous economic and social problems facing the country. And third the foreign-political constraints on German domestic politics were considerably less in the early 1930s than they had been in the early 1920s, when the French had been prepared to send their army into the Ruhr in order to secure reparations payments. Once French troops had left the Rhineland in 1930 and the reparations issue had been shelved in 1931, there was little likelihood that the establishment of a right-wing dictatorship in Germany would provoke foreign intervention.

The discussion thus far suggests that democratic government may not be able to withstand economic crisis. Yet, before we conclude that economic crisis necessarily leads to political instability and undermines democratic government, we should consider some important cases where economic crisis did not, or did not immediately, lead to the collapse 'of democratic politics. The most important of the exceptions is the United States of America, whose economy contracted no less than did that of Germany during the early 1930s but whose political system remained intact. I will return to the USA below, but here will consider another intriguing case: that of Spain. The political history of Spain constitutes one of the great disasters of inter-war Europe, where democratic government ended in a terrible civil war. However, perhaps paradoxically, the Depression itself was accompanied in Spain by the establishment in 1931 of the 'Second Republic', the country's first real democratic system. To be sure, Spain had suffered significant economic dislocation at the end of the First World War (from which, as a neutral power, she had profited), and political unrest followed with the *trienno bolchevique* of 1918–20, which saw strikes (particularly in the countryside), civil disorder, arson and the destruction of property. In September 1923 Spain experienced a bloodless military coup led by General Miguel Primo de Rivera, whose initial success was due more to dissatisfaction with the old inept political oligarchy than with radicalization born of economic crisis. Primo de Rivera's military dictatorship, which initially enjoyed fairly wide support, eventually succumbed as underlying political problems remained unsolved and economic problems mounted in the late 1920s (depression in agriculture, severe budget deficits, a decline in the value of the peseta). When, in January 1930, the King requested Primo de Rivera's resignation, the tired and diabetic general quietly left the political stage, setting in motion a transition which was to give Spain its first, short-lived democratic government. Thus in Spain, it was the transition not to dictatorship but to democracy in 1930–31 which occurred as the world plunged into depression. The collapse of Spanish democracy occurred later, in the face of social unrest, military uprising and foreign intervention.

This suggests that economic instability does not so much undermine democratic government as it undermines the legitimacy of any government which cannot satisfy popular expectations because of economic constraints. Economic instability is not an automatic recipe for dictatorship, as the examples of Spain and the USA in the early 1930s suggest; however, it certainly is not just circumstance that the fragility of parliamentary democracy in inter-war Europe developed against the background of tremendous economic instability.

––––––––––––––––––––– *Summary of Section 3.2* –––––––––––––––––––

- Economic instability is not conducive to political stability, makes democratic governance considerably more difficult and threatens the survival of democratic government.

- Economic instability undermines democratic government by making it more difficult to set social and economic priorities, which is the fundamental task of government.

- Nevertheless, there is no easy economic explanation for the success or failure of democratic government. Economic problems damage the popularity and legitimacy of governments whether they are democratic or dictatorial, and can occasion a transition from dictatorship to democracy as well as vice versa.

3.3   The effect of social and class divisions

Deep social and class divisions are no more conducive to the smooth functioning of democratic government than are severe economic problems, and the two are interrelated. Economic tensions heighten social divisions, fuel subversive and militant political traditions, and make difficult the sorts of compromises and accommodations which are necessary for stable demo-

The March on Rome, October 1922: Mussolini and military supporters

cratic government. In this regard, the history of inter-war Europe often reads like a textbook case of social divisions and economic tensions combining to topple one parliamentary regime after another.

Of course, social and economic divisions were nothing new in 1918. The extreme social and economic inequalities and distress which arose with industrialization, the growth of organizations representing the interests of labour, patterns of protest and industrial militancy were products of the long nineteenth century and conditioned how Europeans reacted to the situations in which they found themselves after 1914 (Geary, 1981). Yet here too the First World War was a watershed; in its aftermath there was an upsurge across Europe of what may be termed 'class conflict'. The example of the Bolshevik Revolution in Russia provided inspiration for many working people and militant labour activists, but the causes of the upsurge in labour militancy also had other immediate causes. War economy both reduced the living standards of Europe's industrial workers and increased their political leverage. The need for labour to produce the arms, dig the coal, operate the railways, etc., while millions of soldiers were at the front, led to severe labour shortages. Furthermore, post-war political changes in many countries made it far easier for workers to organize collectively, as legal restrictions on trade union activity were removed. Consequently there were huge increases in trade union membership (not just in former combatant countries but in neutral countries such as the Netherlands as well), huge increases in the numbers of workers covered by collective agreements, and huge increases in industrial unrest. (See for example the tables in Kendall, 1975, pp.336–7, 364–78.) Italy experienced its *bienno rosso* (two red years) of strikes and factory occupations; Spain experienced its *trienno bolchevique* with its upsurge of labour unrest on the land; demobilization and the 'German revolution' of 1918 and 1919 were accompanied by an enormous increase in industrial conflict.

This upsurge in post-war left wing militancy and industrial unrest did not necessarily directly undermine democratic government. Left-wing dictatorships were conspicuous by their absence in inter-war Europe west of the Soviet border. In Hungary the Soviet regime set up (against the background of riots in Budapest, widespread food shortages and major territorial losses) under the leadership of Béla Kun in March 1919, survived but a few months; the authoritarian right-wing regime which followed, under Admiral Nicholas Horthy, proved far more durable. The Italian liberal state survived the *bienno rosso;* what it did not survive was the vicious Fascist reaction in 1921 and 1922 to the temporary successes which the left had achieved immediately after the war. Much of Mussolini's appeal, both to the political elites who caved in to the Fascist leader at the time of the March on Rome in 1922 as well as to the Italian population in general, was that his movement offered a bulwark against a left which had appeared so dangerous immediately after the First World War. The Weimar Republic survived the waves of labour militancy in 1919 and 1920; what it did not survive was a depression during which the bargaining power of organized labour was effectively destroyed by mass unemployment which left two-fifths of the industrial work-force unemployed and another fifth on short time. The unrest of the immediate post-war period shocked many Germans who previously had regarded their country as a place of order and hierarchy; and no doubt the spectre of a growing German Communist Party which attracted roughly six million votes in the Reichstag elections of November 1932, frightened many. However, in retrospect we can see that there was little chance that the extreme Left could capture state power and overthrow the Weimar Republic – after all, most of the communists' supporters in 1932 and 1933 were unemployed, which took the wind out of the sails of a party calling for a general strike in response to the formation of the Hitler government.

The social and class divisions which erupted with such force during and after the First World War did not exclusively, or even necessarily primarily, involve urban dwellers or the industrial working class. In many countries, conflicts on the land and conflicts of interest between rural agricultural producers and urban consumers of food – against a background of a worldwide decline in agricultural commodity prices – was even more important. In Italy the Fascist movement made its decisive breakthrough in 1921 and 1922 in the northern and central Italian countryside, where it mobilized local landowners, sharecroppers, leaseholders and smallholders and broke the power of socialist organizations of agricultural workers (Lyttelton, 1973, pp.61–4, 70–1). In Spain, the Second Republic (1931–36) was shaken not just by the severe industrial unrest among the Asturian miners (which erupted in open rebellion in 1934) but also the exacerbation of long standing rural conflicts, in a country where large latifundia dominated economic and political life and where landless labourers were driven to desperation by grinding poverty and political powerlessness.

Social and political divisions in the countryside undermined parliamentary government not only in the less developed countries where the majority of the population lived on the land. In continental Europe's most developed major industrial state, in Germany, family farmers who comprised the largest group of voters in rural regions reacted to their increasingly desperate economic plight by turning their backs on Weimar democracy: already in 1928, before the rise of the Nazi Party as a mass party, there were violent mass protests among farmers in northern Germany; and in the early 1930s support for the Nazis had grown among the rural population (particularly of Protestants in northern and eastern Germany) to such an extent that Nazi supporters had largely removed the representatives of the old landed elites from local agricultural associations and obtained huge majorities among the voters of isolated farm villages. By the late 1920s, German democracy found little support in the countryside.

In the previous chapter, the emphasis is upon class as the key social force in democratization struggles over the period 1789–1919. In this chapter, we may be looking at phenomena which comprise just the opposite: the collapse of democratic government in the context of a retreat from class politics. While it is true that the end of the First World War was followed by a huge upsurge of labour militancy and class conflict and that these were the years which saw the rise of communist parties, class politics was not generally a recipe for success. Indeed, the most successful political movements which we have been discussing – in particular Italian Fascism and German National Socialism – explicitly denied the validity of social and class divisions. Although established interests certainly were able to profit from the Fascist and Nazi regimes, their ideologies posited national communities which transcended social and class divisions. This message proved attractive not only for middle-class people who felt threatened by left-wing radicalism but for people across the social and economic spectrum: both the Fascist and Nazi movements were able to draw support – both active (members) and passive (voters) – from across the social and economic divides which had characterized Italian and German society (Schieder, 1976). It is symptomatic of the weakness of parliamentary democracy in inter-war Italy and Germany that the politics which transcended narrow social or economic interests were explicitly anti-democratic. Left-wing class-based politics largely failed in inter-war Europe, either to provide a sturdy prop for parliamentary democracy or to offer a viable alternative. And in the Italian and German case, traditional liberal and conservative politics also failed to transcend their class base and to hold onto their support in the face of the attractions of Fascism and Nazism.

Finally, a word about gender divisions. In the previous chapter, it was noted that one of the main weaknesses of the structural theories used to explain Western democratisation lies in their inattention to women's suffrage. It may appear that this weakness has been replicated in this chapter, for such concerns have not been prominent here either. This omission may seem especially remarkable since the period under discussion here saw great strides in extending the franchise to women. Yet the main reasons for the crumbling of liberal Italy in the face of the Fascist advance, the inability of Poland to sustain parliamentary democracy in the mid 1920s, the collapse of the Weimar Republic, or the bloody destruction of the Spanish Second

Republic through civil war, had little to do with whether or not women were prominent or even represented in the public sphere.

But this is perhaps more a consequence of how the 'story' is framed than it is an assessment of the viability of democratic government. It might be argued that a political system which ignores gender divisions and fails to allow representation of women's interests is not truly democratic. Certainly women were nowhere to be found at the head of government in inter-war Europe, and in some countries (France and Italy, for example), they did not even have the vote. Indeed, the drawing of women into political and public life is one of the most important long-term changes in the social and political life of twentieth-century Europe. In her recent study of 'how [Italian] Fascism ruled women', Victoria de Grazia (1992) suggested that the twentieth century has seen a 'nationalization of women', which is a counterpart to the nineteenth century nationalization of men ('the creation of hardened soldiers, dutiful taxpayers, disciplined workers, thrifty consumers, and, ultimately, of course, predictable voters') which accompanied the rise of liberal parliamentary government. However, the 'nationalization of women' – their mobilization as paid workers, their participation as voters, public recognition as citizens, and the active intervention of the state in matters of reproduction – did not necessarily occur within a democratic framework (de Grazia, 1992). One of the unhappy lessons of the history of inter-war Europe is that achieving citizenship is not necessarily accompanied by achieving democracy.

_____ *Summary of Section 3.3* _____

- The First World War was followed by a huge upsurge in class and national divisions. The power of labour rose, left-wing and labour militancy grew and bitter social conflict developed.

- The increase in the power of labour was in large measure a consequence of the democratization of European politics after the war, which gave the left added political leverage and legal protection.

- The militancy of the post-war years was only temporary, helped to undermine the popular legitimacy of democratic, parliamentary government, and in many cases was followed by authoritarian reaction.

- The most successful destroyers of democratic government in inter-war Europe, the Fascists and the Nazis, were successful in transcending social and class divisions in the popular support they attracted.

- Whereas the inter-war years saw considerable advances with regard to extending the franchise to women and expanding the role of women in the public sphere, this appears to have played little part in the success or failure of democratic government in inter-war Europe.

3.4   The challenge of conflicting nationalisms

The establishment of democratic government, of government of and by the people, makes it necessary to define who are 'the people'. In this regard, the triumph of popular sovereignty and national sovereignty with which the First World War ended paralleled one another. Popular sovereignty and national sovereignty were viewed widely as being one and the same thing: democracy was the proper form of government, the people should rule themselves, and the unit of organization for such democratic governance was to be the 'nation'. That these assumptions were given additional force with the triumph of popular and national sovereignty after the First World War was in large measure the flip-side of the demise of multinational dynastic empires – most obviously of the Habsburg (Austro-Hungarian) Empire. For a brief moment, the triumph of the nationality principle in Europe could be regarded as a triumph for democracy.

However, translating principle into practice was extremely complicated, not least due to patterns of settlement which left various ethnic and cultural groups intermingled among one another. Drawing neat national boundaries proved impossible after the First World War; and Europeans had not yet plumbed the depths of depravity to which they were to sink a quarter of a century later, when millions of people were brutally uprooted from their homes because by virtue of their nationality they were deemed to be living on the wrong side of a state border. Consequently, after 1918 Europe witnessed a succession of border conflicts and the establishment of new multinational republics, the most important of which were Poland, Yugoslavia and Czechoslovakia. In none of these major multinational successor states did democratic government survive until the Second World War. It is to this sorry aspect of political failure in inter-war Europe that we now turn.

Poland, the largest of the multinational successor states, provides perhaps the most ambiguous example of how national conflict affected democratic government. Unlike in either Yugoslavia or Czechoslovakia, in Poland one nationality – the Poles – was, by far, in the majority. However, unlike the Polish state which was to emerge from the ashes of the Second World War, the inter-war Polish Republic contained large national minorities; roughly 30 per cent of the Polish Republic's population consisted of non-Polish groups, the most important of which were Byelorussians, Ukrainians, Jews, and Germans. The tendency of these national groups to seek their own political representation to promote their own particular interests certainly did not add to the stability of a parliamentary system plagued by a multitude of parties and a succession of weak governments. Politics in inter-war Poland was coloured by mutual suspicions among the various nationalities, and by a strong streak of anti-semitism. However, the main reasons for the collapse of democratic government were not to be found in the tensions among the nationalities. Rather, the extraordinary economic difficulties, social conflict, and multiplicity of political parties representing sectional interests ultimately made stable parliamentary government impossible.

In Yugoslavia, however, things were a little different. Yugoslavia – or, more properly, the Kingdom of the Serbs, Croats and Slovenes which was proclaimed on 1 December 1918 – was a complex mix of nationalities, reflected in a plethora of parties represented in parliament, concerned to defend the interests of the national groups which had sent them there. There were many national groups, ranging from the Slovenes in the north to the Albanians and Macedonians in the south, with ethnic Germans, Magyars and Romanians as well as the largest national groups, the Serbs and Croats. The new, centralized parliamentary constitutional monarchy, outlined in the constitution which was ratified by the Constituent Assembly in June 1921, did not last long. Short-lived governments and political conflict proved the hallmarks of the new state, culminating in the shooting of five Croatian deputies (three of whom died) during a violent dispute in parliament in June 1928 and the suspension of parliamentary government by the monarch, King Alexander, in January 1929. In Alexander's eyes, party divisions, which largely reflected national divisions, had made parliamentary government impossible: 'My sacred duty', he proclaimed, 'is to preserve by every means within my power the unity of the nation and the state' (quoted in Pavlovich, 1971, p.74). There was no real protest at the royal coup of January 1929, as anti-communist legislation was strengthened, parties based on regional, ethnic and religious sectionalism were banned, and Yugoslavia joined the growing number of European states which turned their backs on parliamentary government.

Whereas national divisions clearly undermined parliamentary government in Yugoslavia, in Czechoslovakia developments took a rather different turn. This multinational state – containing Czechs, Slovaks, Hungarians and the German speakers who lived largely in the Sudeten regions along the German and Austrian borders – managed to maintain not only economic and (relative) currency stability during the turbulent years after the First World War, but also a parliamentary system. The problem of nationalities was not life-threatening until it became entwined with great-power politics and pressures from across the border, when in the late 1930s the German minority acted as the gravedigger of inter-war Czechoslovakia. During the first decade and a half of the new, multinational Czechoslovak state, the majority of its ethnic Germans were supporters of the democratic process. In 1920 the German Social Democrats emerged as the strongest German political party, and they remained so until 1935 (Bruegel, 1973, pp.178–9). German political parties participated in government in Prague during the 1920s and German-speaking politicians held government ministries, while the nationalist German vote declined. It was not really until the mid 1930s, when the dubious attractions of the (militantly anti-democratic, nationalist, racist) Nazi regime across the border radically altered political opinion among the Sudeten Germans, that things changed. In 1935 the new, pro-Nazi *Sudetendeutsche Partei*, under the leadership of an obscure gymnastics teacher named Konrad Henlein, captured the vast majority of the German votes. However, although the Nazis took advantage of the national divisions within the country, both the catalyst and the engine for the destruction of parliamentary government in Czechoslovakia in 1938 and 1939 was external. The real destroyer of Czechoslovak parliamentary democracy was Adolf Hitler.

What conclusions are we to draw from this? It may be tempting to conclude that national divisions were fatal for parliamentary democratic regimes. Yet in the multinational United Kingdom the parliamentary system survived; and when one looks across the sorry political landscape of inter-war Europe, it is not the countries which contained national conflicts within their borders which present the most striking cases of the collapse of democratic government. Although they contained relatively small national minorities, in neither Italy (which had an Austrian-German minority in the

Alto Adige/Südtirol) nor Germany (which contained a Polish minority living primarily along the Eastern border regions) nor Spain (where the Basques and Catalans tended to be among the supporters of Republic against Franco, who subsequently imposed a centralist regime in which regional political and cultural autonomy was crushed) were national conflicts of primary importance in the decline of democratic government. So, it would appear that internal conflict among nationalities is not a necessary component of democratic collapse, nor is ethnic homogeneity a patent recipe for democratic stability. But deep national divisions certainly do not help!

—————————————— *Summary of Section 3.4* ——————————————

- The First World War was a turning point which thrust nationality onto the political agenda of Europe as never before – by establishing the principle of nationality as the basis for states and by causing the demise of multinational dynastic states.

- In the multinational successor states of continental Europe, tensions among the nationalities put parliamentary government under considerable strain.

- However, conflict among nationalities was not necessarily incompatible with viable parliamentary government, nor was it a necessary ingredient for the collapse of democratic government in inter-war Europe.

3.5   Explaining the exceptions: the USA, the UK, and France

The message and tone of this chapter is, so far, negative and pessimistic. Whereas the story of the previous chapter is essentially one of the advance of democracy, here it largely is one of retreat. Nevertheless, before concluding that democratic government was everywhere in retreat during the inter-war years, we should remember that there were significant exceptions: the United Kingdom, France, the Benelux and Scandinavian countries, and – perhaps most significantly – the USA. Certainly it can hardly be pure coincidence that none of these exceptions were among the losers of the First World War. However, the challenges to their political systems were not inconsiderable.

Of all the world's major industrialized countries, only in the USA did the economy contract as sharply during the inter-war Depression as in Germany. Millions were thrown out of work; 'Hoovervilles' – shantytowns of unemployed homeless men – blighted the American urban landscape; hundreds of banks closed their doors, leaving their depositors penniless. And yet for all the desperation felt by millions of Americans, the political structure emerged virtually unchanged; the two-party, four-year rhythm of American politics survived; and a smiling new President was able to pull off the amazing confidence trick of convincing the electorate that 'the only thing to fear is fear itself'. The contrast with Germany was quite striking. Hardly less striking was the contrast between the UK and Germany. Although far less severe than what occurred in Germany, Britain too faced an economic slump in the early 1930s, and the ways in which the economic crisis rocked the political system had some interesting parallels in the two countries. Specifically, the rock on which the Labour government smashed in 1931 – the problem of how to deal with the financial consequences of rising unemployment – was precisely the same as that on which the last Weimar government with a parliamentary majority (and led by the Social Democrats) was broken in 1930. Whereas in Britain, members of the Labour Party could not stomach accepting that unemployment benefits would have to be cut, in Germany Social Democrats could not stomach accepting that workers' contributions would have to be raised. Yet, whereas after the demise of the SPD-led coalition German governments increasingly bypassed parliament, in Britain an essentially Conservative 'National Government' was formed which enjoyed a substantial parliamentary majority. In Britain, parliament remained the accepted forum of legitimate government and politics; in Germany, it did not.

So, how are we to explain that while Germany got Adolf Hitler, America got Franklin Roosevelt, Britain (after a few more years of Ramsay MacDonald) got Stanley Baldwin? What – in addition, of course, to Baldwin and Roosevelt – did the United Kingdom and the USA possess that Germany lacked? Certainly both the UK and USA benefited from the fact that they had been among the victors of 1918, while Germany had to cope with the political as well as economic and social fall-out of defeat in the First World War. However, perhaps more important was the fact that both the USA and UK displayed remarkable *political* stability. The parliamentary and democratic political institutions of Britain and the USA had long histories and had developed over decades; it was taken largely for granted that politics was to be carried out within parliamentary and/or democratic institutions. Consequently, these institutions were not called into question in the way they were in Germany. There were no calls to do away with parliamentary government in the UK or with the Constitution and Congress in the USA which carried the force or attracted the support as did calls to do away with the Weimar 'system' in Germany. No less significant was the fact that the mainstream political parties in the UK and the USA were able to hold on to their electoral supporters, and thereby to keep them within the frame of parliamentary and democratic politics, in a way which their liberal and conservative counterparts in Germany proved singularly unable to do. Whereas in the UK the supporters of the Liberals and Conservatives largely continued to vote liberal and conservative, and in the USA the supporters of the Republican and Democratic Parties continued to vote for republicans and democrats, in Germany support for conservatives and liberals declined precipitously, leaving an opening for the advance of the militantly anti-democratic Nazi Party. Perhaps the most important thing which Britain possessed which Germany lacked was a strong Conservative Party capable of holding its constituency within the frame of parliamentary politics.

The other great exception – inter-war France – provides further clues as to why democratic government collapsed or survived. Although the French Third Republic came under strain during the inter-war years, it survived more or less intact until the disaster of 1940. Despite deep political cleavages between left and right, the Third Republic enjoyed a number of advantages that the Weimar Republic did not. First, France emerged from the First World War as a victor; while France had endured far greater losses of men and material than did either the USA or the UK, the legacy of a victorious war was not so damaging as the legacy of a lost one. Second, France's economy was not hit so hard by crisis either in the 1920s or in the 1930s as was the German: French post-war inflation was mild compared with the German inflationary nightmare, and the 1930s slump affected France less sharply, more gradually and later (reaching its worst point in 1935) than it had in Germany. Third, France had a long tradition of republican government, so that the French Republic enjoyed a greater degree of popular legitimacy than did the German; even in February 1934, when right-wing groups of *anciens combattants* and others marched on the French parliament building and attempted to storm it, they remained essentially republicans (Prost, 1977, pp.159–68). As in Britain and the USA, but unlike in Weimar Germany, in France the legitimacy of the political constitution was not really questioned.

——————————————— *Summary of Section 3.5* ———————————————

- Economic crisis did not necessarily undermine democratic government. Given the right conditions, it was possible for parliamentary and democratic government to survive.

- The durability of democratic political systems in the face of economic crisis may be explained in large measure by the long-term stability and perceived legitimacy of political institutions and the ability of established political elites to retain popular support.

- As the fact that no country where democratic government survived was among the losers in 1918 suggests, the legacy of the First World War was of enormous importance in determining the durability of such government in the face of political and economic crisis.

Conclusion

In Chapter 1, three basic theoretical approaches are used to explain democratization; the modernization approach, the transition approach, and the structural approach. The emphasis there is on the positive. The question which these theoretical approaches are used to answer is: how do we explain success? The ways to do this are to list the social and economic requisites necessary for successful democratization; to list the political processes and choices which account for the transition from authoritarian to democratic rule; or to list the changing structures of power which are favourable to democratization. Whereas Chapter 2 applied these approaches in a positive sense, this chapter has a different character. Its story is essentially one of failure; the tests it offers of the approaches outlined in Chapter 1 are essentially negative. The question here is not what essential pieces of the jigsaw were in place but what pieces were undermined, missing or destroyed – not what went right but what went wrong.

In conclusion and to help set you thinking about how you might apply these approaches to the dark side of the democratization story, let me summarize some of the important explanatory factors which the failures had in common:

1   *Effects of war.*

War, particularly major wars, particularly for countries which have been defeated, poses enormous challenges for any political system – all the more so for a political system in which the people are effectively represented. War breaks political systems and leaves behind an enormous residue of bitterness, broken lives, huge costs, massive obligations on the state that the state is not necessarily able to meet. This was never more true than in the case of Europe in the wake of the First World War, which profoundly interrupted the long-term evolution of democratization and determined how democratic government fared in the first half of the twentieth century.

2   *Severity of economic difficulties.*

Economic crises need not always condemn democratic government, but economic health and stability do not provide an environment in which parliamentary democracies tend to collapse. While not all countries which suffered severe economic contraction saw democratic political structures destroyed, it cannot be ignored that the failures of democratic government in Europe took place against a background of the most violent economic storms which the world has ever seen.

3   *Social divisions.*

Divided societies do not make for successful democratic polities. This is true whether the perceived divisions are of class, nationality, social group or region. Of course, all societies are divided to some extent, but for democratic government to function well there must be agreement at some level that the general interest overrides the particular interest, that what unites a polity is ultimately more important than what divides it.

4   *Political institutions I: multiplicity of parties.*

The presence of a great number of political parties no doubt makes forming stable parliamentary government difficult. This may speak for the wisdom of having electoral systems which militate against large numbers of parties; however, it may be that large numbers of parties are the symptom rather than the cause of instability, and that the real cause lies in the divisions which the parties represent.

5   *Political institutions II: absence of a long tradition of parliamentary or democratic government.*

The countries of inter-war Europe where democratic government did not crumble tended to be those in which political institutions had developed gradually (for example, the UK, the Netherlands, the Scandinavian countries) and where, as a consequence, parliament's central political role was not really questioned. In countries with more abrupt or violent changes of constitutional system or where parliamentary democracy came about suddenly as a consequence of revolutionary unrest (for example, Germany, Austria, Hungary, Spain), the new form of government was bitterly contested. In conditions of economic crisis and against the background of deep divisions, democratic government never became accepted as the natural framework within which politics are exercised.

There is, of course, no single factor which provides the explanation of why democracies either survived or crumbled. Neither economic crisis, nor social division, nor national conflict, nor defeat in war provide by themselves a sufficient explanation of why democratic government collapsed in inter-war Europe. Explanations, if they are to be satisfactory, need to be found in the interplay of the developments outlined above, all of which contributed to undermining the legitimacy of democratic government. If there is a common thread to this catalogue of failure, it is in a crisis of the legitimacy of democratic systems; and if there is a lesson to be found in the sorry history of inter-war Europe, it is that there are no easy answers.

References

Aldcroft, D.H. (1977) *From Versailles to Wall Street,* London, Allen Lane.

Bessel, R. (1993) *Germany After the First World War,* Oxford, Oxford University Press.

Bessel, R. (ed.) (1996) *Fascist Italy and Nazi Germany. Comparisons and Contrasts,* Cambridge, Cambridge University Press.

Borchardt, K. (1991) 'Germany's Experience of Inflation' in *Perspectives on Modern German Economic History and Policy,* Cambridge, Cambridge University Press.

Bruegel, J.W. (1973) 'The Germans in pre-war Czechoslovakia' in Mamatay, V.S. and Luza, R. (eds), *A History of the Czechoslovak Republic 1918–1948,* Princeton, Princeton University Press.

Corner, P. (1975) *Fascism in Ferrara 1915–1925,* Oxford, Oxford University Press.

de Grazia, V. (1992) *How Fascism Ruled Women, Italy, 1922–1945,* Berkeley, University of California Press.

Feldman, G.D. (1993) *The Great Disorder, Politics, Economics, and Society in the German Inflation 1914–1924,* New York, Oxford University Press.

Ferguson, N. (1995) *Paper and Iron. Hamburg Business and German Politics in the Era of Inflation, 1897–1927,* Cambridge, Cambridge University Press.

Geary, D. (1981) *European Labour Protest 1848–1939,* London, Croom Helm.

Hobsbawm, E. (1994) *Age of Extremes. The Short Twentieth Century 1914–1995,* London, Michael Joseph.

Kendall, W. (1975) *The Labour Movement in Europe,* London, Allen Lane.

Jones, L.E. (1988) *German Liberalism and the Dissolution of the Weimar Party System, 1918–1933,* Chapel Hill, University of North Carolina Press.

Leslie, R.F. (ed.) (1980) *The History of Poland Since 1863,* Cambridge, Cambridge University Press.

Lipset, S.M. (1960) *Political Man. The Social Bases of Politics,* London, Heinemann.

Lyttelton, A. (1973) *The Seizure of Power. Fascism in Italy, 1919–1929,* London, Weidenfeld and Nicolson.

Lyttelton, A. (1982) 'Fascism and violence in post-war Italy; political strategy and social conflict' in Mommsen, W.J. and Hirschfeld, G. (eds) *Social Protest, Violence and Terror in Nineteenth- and Twentieth-century Europe,* London, Macmillan.

Lyttelton, A. (1996) 'The crisis of bourgeois society and the origins of Fascism' in Bessel, R. (ed.).

Moore, B. (1969) *Social Origins of Dictatorship and Democracy. Lord and Peasant in the Making of the Modern World,* Harmondsworth, Penguin.

Niekisch, E. (1958) *Gewagtes Leben. Begegnungen und Begebnisse,* Cologne, Kiepenheuer & Witsch.

Pavlovich, S.K. (1971) *Yugoslavia,* London, Ernest Benn.

Pease, N. (1986) *Poland, the United States and the Stabilization of Europe, 1919-1933,* New York, Oxford University Press.

Polonsky, A. (1972) *Politics in Independent Poland 1921–1939. The Crisis of Constitutional Government,* Oxford, Oxford University Press.

Prost, A. (1977) *Les anciens combattants et la société Française 1914–1939, vol.I, Histoire,* Paris, Presses de la Fondation Nationale des Sciences Politiques.

Schieder, W. (ed.) (1976) *Faschismus als soziale Bewegung. Deutschland und Italien im Vergleich,* Hamburg, Hoffmann and Campe.

Weisbrod, B. (1996) 'The crisis of bourgeois society in interwar Germany' in Bessel, R. (ed.).

Whalen, R.W. (1984) *Bitter Wounds. German Victims of the Great War, 1914–1939,* Ithica, Cornell University Press.

CHAPTER 4

Democracy in Europe, 1939–89

David Goldblatt

4.1   The course of European democratization

The 50 years covered by this chapter are defined by two epochal moments in world history: the beginning of the Second World War in 1939 and the effective end of the Cold War in 1989 with the collapse of Eastern European communism. What are the democratic resonances of these events and the character of the democratic experience in Europe in the short half-century between them? It is difficult to overestimate the importance of the Second World War to the course of European democratization. As we have already seen, the inter-war period saw the defeat of democratic forces and the establishment of authoritarian or totalitarian regimes in Germany, Austria, Italy, Spain and Greece, and the entrenchment of already established authoritarian regimes of the left and the right in Eastern Europe, the Soviet Union and Portugal. In the first three years of the Second World War, authoritarian governments of occupation and collaboration were established wherever Axis armies were victorious. The fate of European democracy, or what was left of it, hung on the outcome of the war. Whatever else accounts for the trajectory of European democracy in the post-war era, its starting point was the military destruction of fascism by that strange alliance of Soviet communism, American liberal capitalism and the British Empire.

The Second World War also confirmed a new global distribution of power. Europe, exhausted and devastated by the two great wars of the first half of the twentieth century found itself shaped and constrained by two opposing continental powers of ambiguous European heritage; the Western colonial outpost across the Atlantic and the Eurasian giant: the USA and the Soviet Union. The Cold War that they subsequently conducted in Europe and elsewhere was the defining feature of this era and the rhetoric of that conflict, if not always its substance, was of both capitalism against socialism, and democracy against dictatorship. It ended with the internal disintegration of communist regimes in Eastern Europe and apart from Yugoslavia and Romania, their faltering transition towards liberal democratic polities.

The configuration of European democracy in an era defined by the defeat of fascism and the global struggle between East and West was three-fold.

1   Under American economic and political hegemony liberal democracies were established in Western Europe, amongst the victors, the victims and the vanquished of the Second World War. This included the establishment of relatively stable democracies in Germany, Italy and Austria for the first time.

2   However, membership of the Western camp was no guarantee of democ-
     racy. In Southern Europe the post-war period saw the entrenchment of
     authoritarian regimes in Iberia before the democratic revolutions of the
     mid 1970s.

3   The experience of Eastern Europe was less ambiguous. The final battle
     lines of the Second World War found the Red Army firmly encamped in
     the Baltic States, Eastern and Central Europe. The Soviet presence and the
     course of the Cold War extinguished democratic possibilities in Eastern
     Europe until the events of 1989.

In Section 4.2 I outline the political history of Europe between 1942 and
the early 1950s, examining the immediate impact of the Second World War
and the Cold War on democratization in Europe. In Section 4.3 I examine the
democratic transitions in Britain, France, Italy and Germany. In Section 4.4 I
examine the differential course of Portugal and Spain where dictatorships
survived until their collapse and the transition to democracy in the mid
1970s. In both Sections 4.3 and 4.4 I try and establish the long-term structural
factors that brought these societies to the brink of democratization and the
short-term decisions and strategies that allowed for relatively successful
transitions to democracy. In Section 4.5 I take a more critical look at the
quality of democracy in Western Europe since 1945 for the evident
triumphalism of the period is underscored by the limits and deficiencies
of the liberal democracies created.

─────────────── *Summary of Section 4.1* ───────────────

• The course of European democratization has been profoundly
  shaped by the Second World War and the Cold War.

• The trajectory of democracy in Europe since 1945 has been three-
  fold: democratization and consolidation in the West; authoritarianism
  and late democratization in the South; authoritarian socialism in the
  East until 1989.

• These events can be explained by a combination of structural and
  transitional approaches.

4.2   European democracy in international context: the Second World War and the Cold War

In early 1942 German military power had reached its greatest extent in
Europe. Hitler's armies stretched from the Atlantic coast of France to the
southern steppes of Russia, from Norway in the north to the Balkans and the
North African coastline in the south. Europe had not possessed so few
democracies since before the First World War. At the heart of Europe stood
the totalitarian German Empire encompassing the Germany of the Versailles
treaty, Germanic Austria, Northern and Western Czechoslovakia, much of
Poland and Alsace-Lorraine in the West. In the south a string of notionally
independent allies of the Third Reich ruled by satellite fascist dictatorships:
the Vichy Republic in southern France and Mussolini's Italy in the west;

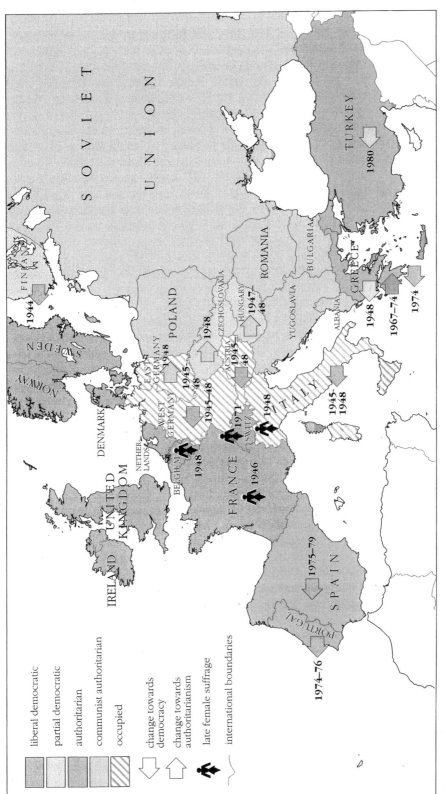

Map 4.1 Democractization in Europe, 1945-88

Hungary, Croatia, Slovakia, Romania and Bulgaria in the south and east. Harsh regimes of authoritarian military occupation, with varying degrees of local collaboration and indigenous fascist support, governed western Russia including the Ukraine and the Baltic States, Greece, the dismembered Yugoslavia, Denmark and Norway, the Low Countries and northern France. In Iberia, the pre-war fascist dictatorships of Salazar in Portugal and Franco in Spain remained outside of the war and firmly in place. In the unoccupied parts of the Soviet Union Stalin's rule remained as totalitarian as ever. The only states to escape occupation, dictatorship and terror were three neutrals – Sweden, Switzerland and the Republic of Ireland – and two combatant but peripheral states – Britain and Iceland. Even here the pre-war character of democracy had been warped by the exigencies of war. Elections had been suspended in Sweden and Britain, very broad coalition governments of national unity had been formed, civil liberties were curtailed everywhere.

The course of the war had already turned in 1941 with the entry of the USA decisively shifting the long-term balance of industrial and military might from Axis to Allies, while the failure of the German armies to capture Moscow in the winter of 1941 signalled the initial limits of German expansion. In 1942–43 defeat at Stalingrad heralded the beginning of the Germans' long retreat in the East; defeat at Kursk in 1943 put the outcome of the German–Soviet conflict beyond doubt. Through 1943 and 1944 the Red Army cleared the Axis forces from Soviet territory and began to push into Eastern and Southern Europe. Simultaneously, the tide began to turn in North Africa and the Pacific. The Allied armies first checked the Germans at El Alamein then swept across North Africa in late 1942, invaded Sicily and Italy in mid 1943 and southern France and Normandy in 1944. The relative speeds of these advances as well as the agreements between the USA, the Soviet Union and Britain on post-war spheres of influence in Europe helped determine the democratic fate of regimes. The Soviets reached Berlin first in May 1945. The Red Army occupied much of Eastern Germany, Czechoslovakia, Poland, Hungary and the Eastern Balkans. Indigenous partisan armies had liberated Yugoslavia and Albania. Allied armies had swept across France, the Low Countries, Greece, Italy and Western Germany.

The elite coup of court, army and senior fascists against Mussolini and the subsequent Italian surrender in 1943 had allowed for the establishment of an anti-fascist but unelected government of national unity (and minimal powers) alongside the Allied military government. In German-occupied Northern Italy partisans had begun to establish enclaves of self-government through the Committees of National Liberation that sprang up in the course of 1944 and 1945. In France, De Gaulle led the Free French armies under the auspices of the Americans and British into Paris in August 1944, disbanding the Vichy regime and establishing a provisional government. Governments of national unity and liberation were established from amongst the relatively uncompromised pre-war parties in occupied Scandinavia and the Low Countries. The forces of both left and right were committed to the establishment of democratic constitutions and free elections. Pre-war authoritarian political forces had been irredeemably tarnished by the experience of fascist occupation or the democratic populism required to mobilize nations for the inferno of industrialized total war. There were limits to consensus, an alliance of the domestic right and US military and economic support squeezed communists out of government in France and Italy in 1947.

In Eastern Europe the presence of the Red Army and the direction of Soviet foreign policy allowed for no more than a brief flirtation with democratic constitutions and elections. Communist regimes were established by the Soviets in Poland, Romania and Bulgaria under cover of governments of people's democracy and national unity. Pre-war communists returned from Moscow to staff the remnants of these states, pre-war parties of the gentry and bourgeoisie were banned. Peasant parties were either disbanded, harassed or incorporated. By contrast, the indigenous communist-led partisan armies of Yugoslavia and Albania liberated themselves and established their own peculiar variants of communist authoritarianism. In Hungary free elections were held in late 1945 delivering a victory for the smallholders party – the communists received only 17 per cent of the vote. However, by 1947 the Hungarian communists had established themselves deeply enough within state institutions and had sufficient support from the Soviets to remove their opponents from the government and declare the creation of a People's Republic. In Czechoslovakia the non-communist forces held out somewhat longer and a non-communist government was established after elections in 1946 only to fall on its own internal divisions and a Soviet backed *coup d'état*.

Thus in both East and West the developing dynamic of the Cold War had a decisive impact on the course of democratization. The division of Europe had already been prefigured in the negotiations at Yalta and Potsdam in which distinct spheres of influence for the Soviets in the East and the Americans and British in the South and West were acknowledged. In retrospect it is clear that only the mutual threat of fascism could have held the Soviets, British and Americans together. With the defeat of fascism and the division of Europe this strange alliance quickly descended into a permanent state of armed opposition, political conflict and ideological hostility. The key events of the period began with the withdrawal of the British from Greece in early 1947 where they had been supporting the monarchist right in the civil war against communist partisans. Exhausted by war and preoccupied by decolonization and domestic reform the British did not posses the means to pursue such a policy. The USA stepped in. In the Truman Doctrine, the President of the USA pledged the nation to a unremitting global war of containment against communism. The economic reconstruction of Western Europe through the loans and grants of the Marshall plan and the exclusion of communist parties from governments of national unity in Italy and France confirmed anti-communism as the central purpose of US foreign policy in the West. The establishment of communist regimes and the destruction of opposition forces demonstrated Soviet dominance in the East. The establishment of the North Atlantic Treaty Organization (NATO) in 1949 and the Warsaw Pact soon afterwards confirmed the division of Europe into two hostile military camps.

The course of the Cold War was most closely reflected by the course of German democratization. The country was divided into four zones of military occupation – Soviet, French, British and American – with Berlin, deep inside the Soviet sector being divided up in the same manner. The differential democratic trajectory of the Eastern and Western halves of Germany and the subsequent division of the country cannot, of course be understood without reference to the escalating conflict and confrontation between East and West. After the occupying powers had failed to come to an agreement on the political future of Germany, economic and political integration began in the west while the German Communist Party in the east (KPD) and its Soviet patrons first extinguished the opposition and then blockaded Berlin in late 1948. By mid 1949 the Western zones had fused and a democratic, if provisional, constitution had been established in the Federal Republic.

By 1950 the political map of Europe had been set into a pattern by the combined forces of international politics and occupation and domestic conflict and consensus: in the west and the north the entrenchment of capitalist liberal democracies of varying quality; in the south authoritarian capitalist regimes; in the east authoritarian socialist regimes. That map would not be disturbed until the democratic revolutions of Southern Europe in the mid 1970s and those of Eastern Europe in 1989–90.

─────────────── *Summary of Section 4.2* ───────────────

• The Second World War had a profound effect on democracies in Europe. Under German domination only a handful of European democracies survived the war years. The experience and defeat of fascism destroyed the legitimacy of right-wing authoritarian politics amongst the victors, victims and vanquished of the war.

• The dynamic of the Cold War and the direction of US foreign policy in the West reinforced this trend and gave it an anti-communist slant. In the East, the Cold War and Soviet foreign policy resulted in the active repression of communism's opponents and the closure of democratic options.

4.3   Democratization in the West: victors, victims and vanquished

Britain

The course of British democracy in the post-war years was never sharply contested. The war had been fought under a grand national coalition of Labour and Conservative parties and normal electoral competition had been suspended for the duration of the war. In early 1945, as final victory approached, the coalition was disbanded and general elections were arranged for the summer of 1945. Despite the enormous prestige of Churchill as a wartime leader, the Conservatives were thrown out of office by the single greatest victory for the left in British electoral history. The 1945 Labour government was elected on a radical manifesto of economic and social reform with a clear parliamentary majority and political mandate from the country. While the Attlee government set about a series of major transformations in British economic life – nationalizing the Bank of England, the rail and coal industries, for example – and established and institutionalized the key components of the post-war British welfare state, these reforms were not accompanied by any significant changes in the political constitution of Britain. Around the margins a number of changes were made with the abolition of plural voting in local elections and the bizarre university constituencies. Similarly, outside of Britain the long process of decolonization began with the establishment of an independent and democratic India in 1947. The irony of this era is that Britain's most radical and reforming government of the century was quite content to live with the archaic structures and institutions of the British state, untouched since the introduction of universal suffrage, and ideologically embalmed in the sanctifying myths of the post-Civil War settlements. What was at the time the most left-wing elected government in a major European state was quite content to maintain the power of an unelected, aristocratic second parliamentary chamber, nor felt any need to establish a codified bill of rights. Indeed, the self-image of British democracy was stronger than ever in the aftermath of the war. It would take another three decades of economic decline, an upsurge in Celtic nationalism and the systematic abuse of the unwritten constitution for the efficacy and legitimacy of British democracy to be called into question.

France

While Britain was unambiguously a victor and liberator of the Second World War, France's position was more ambiguous, and the course of its post-war democratization more tortuous (Williams, 1972; Rioux, 1987). In the shape of Vichy France it was a defeated country, in the shape of the occupation it was a liberated country and in the shape of De Gaulle's Free French movement and the Resistance it was a victor. The independent recreation of a democratic polity in France, rather than one conducted under the auspices of US occupying forces turned on the success of De Gaulle in establishing his Free French movement as the legitimate representative of anti-Axis France. He thus led French armies, under Allied cover, through France in late 1944, establishing the authority of his provisional government in every liberated department.

Alongside De Gaulle the other legitimate political forces of the moment were those that had participated in the resistance movement – communists, socialists and radical Catholics. Together, in both Paris and the regions, they formed a provisional government of national unity. De Gaulle had already clearly declared for the establishment of a democratic fourth French republic. He had, by decree, ensured that its suffrage would, for the first time in French history, be genuinely universal through its extension to women. However, beyond this, there was considerable disagreement between the parties and De Gaulle over the precise shape of the democratic constitution. The disagreement essentially turned on the relative roles and powers of executive and legislature in the new France; above all, would it be a presidential or a parliamentary system? Indeed, such was the rancour of the disagreement that De Gaulle resigned from office in early 1946 arguing that the parliamentarianism of the parties would create a polity plagued by the same political disorder and weakness as the last years of the Third Republic. He was not entirely wrong. The government of national unity that ruled France in mid 1946 consisted of members of the Communist Party (PCF), the Socialist Party (SFIO) and the Christian Democrat Party. The constituent assembly that they dominated proposed a constitution that was rejected in the referendum of May 1946 and accepted in modified form in a national referendum in October. General elections followed in November establishing the first democratically elected government of the Fourth Republic. However, the course of French democracy was not smooth and the Fourth Republic was only to last another twelve years.

The limits of the Fourth Republic and the seeds of its decline are not difficult to chart. First, the extreme wings of French politics came to systematically oppose the Republic. The communists, under extensive US pressure, were expelled from government in 1947 and continued to oppose the regime for a decade, in an unholy alliance with the extreme right – Gaullists and Poujadists – who also opposed the Republic. Simultaneously the core parties of republican support – christian democrats and socialists – steadily lost ground over the 1950s. Most importantly, the capacity of the Republic to form stable governments, pursue politically rather than bureaucratically directed policy programmes and provide adequate political representation was, as De Gaulle had warned, minimal at best. Those weaknesses were sharply exposed in the mid 1950s under the pressures of decolonization and imperial revolt. The first cracks in the regime appeared in the mid 1950s as France fought a bitter and ultimately unsuccessful defence of its Indo-Chinese colonies culminating in the humiliating defeat of Dien Bin Phu at the hands of the Vietminh. But this was as nothing compared to the Algerian civil war between French colonists, settlers and the French army against Algerian nationalists. As the war became increasingly bitter and violent in the late 1950s it became clear that control of Algeria could only be maintained at an exceptionally high price. By 1958 the government, which was now wavering on the issue and contemplating negotiations with the nationalists, effectively lost control of the army in Algeria and in the outlying island of Corsica. The possibility of a military coup and the collapse of French democracy seemed possible. It was at this moment that the course of French democratization and De Gaulle intertwined again. The national assembly voted to install De Gaulle as Prime Minister, who reasserted civilian control over the army in return for the legal right to construct a new constitutional settlement that would avoid the limitations of the Fourth Republic, and the right to present it to the French people in a referendum. The constitution of the Fifth Republic, which reversed the balance of power between legislature and executive, was passed by referendum in September 1958 and De Gaulle was elected President of the Fifth Republic. This centralized but democratic polity has subsequently endured.

Italy

Like France, Italy's status at the end of the war was ambiguous: defeated protagonist in 1943, occupied victim of the Germans in 1944, liberator and victor in 1945. The course of Italian democratization after fascism is closely linked to the twists and turns of Italy's international status and its intersection with the broad conflicts of the Second World War and the Cold War (Ginsborg, 1990, Pasquino, 1986; Woolf, 1972). The authoritarian dictatorship and failed totalitarianism of Mussolini came to a close on 25 July 1943. With the Allied armies already in Sicily, it was starkly apparent to the Italian ruling elites which way the winds of war were blowing. Mussolini was deposed by an alliance of the army, court and king and leading figures in the Fascist Grand Council that had ruled the country. Within a few months political power and sovereignty in Italy had fragmented. In the south of the country a new Italian government had been formed, headed by the conservative monarchist Marshall Badoglio, which existed in a subordinate and uneasy relationship to the Allied military government that accompanied British and US forces up the Italian peninsula. The Badoglio government signed an armistice in September 1943 and declared war on Germany. In the north, the Germans had invaded and occupied Italy establishing Mussolini's short lived fascist *Republic of Salo* alongside their own organs of military government. Both were challenged by the emergence of a radicalized and organized armed resistance in the North principally staffed by the Italian Communist Party (PCI), but built around newly formed inter-party alliances, the Committees for National Liberation (CNL). These formed the germs of self-government and a radical democratic politics in the North for the rest of the war.

The ambiguity of Italian government was resolved by the liberation of the north and the end of the war. Power passed to the Parri civilian government of national unity in April 1945. The left-dominated CNL's of the north (which had governed many cities in the north after liberation) were effectively marginalized, absorbed and demobilized. The dominant forces in Italian domestic politics could now square up to each other. On the left stood the PCI led by Togliatti, returned from Moscow in 1943. The PCI had effectively abandoned a revolutionary political strategy in 1943 announced in a speech by Togliatti christened, the *Svolta de Salerno*. The PCI would join the government of national unity and support the establishment of a democratic polity. Whether this reflected a profound departure from communist norms, specific to the Italian case, or whether it merely reflected a shrewd assessment of the balance of domestic and international forces in Italy by Togliatti remains uncertain. The presence of US and British armies and the example of the allied-backed destruction of the communists in the Greek Civil War could not be ignored. On the right, stood the Christian Democrats or DC led by De Gasperi. Drawing together the disparate elements of the pre-Mussolini democratic right and centre, systematically backed by the Catholic church and the US government, De Gasperi created a political coalition of north and south, middle and upper classes united by the ideological cement of Catholicism and militant anti-communism. These two forces, and their allies (the Socialists (PSI) on the left, the Liberals and Republicans on the right) shared power under De Gasperi's premiership from December 1945. In 1946 a referendum rejected the monarchy and established an Italian Republic, while elections to the constitutional assembly in the same year delivered 35 per cent of the vote to the DC, 21 per cent to the PSI and a mere 19 per cent to the PCI. Under the pressures of the Cold War and emboldened by a clear shift to the right domestically, De Gasperi was able to exclude the communists from government in 1947. The constitutional draft of late 1947 reflected the strength of the right and the fragmentation of the left as Italy created and ratified (in early 1948) a liberal democratic constitution in which the social and economic rights demanded by the left were legally extolled and practically ignored. In 1948 the first general election of the Italian Republic, in which women voted for the first time, confirmed the drift to the right, delivering a massive victory for De Gasperi and the DC. They were to remain in power for over four decades until the polity they had created and prospered by was shaken to its foundations by the end of the Cold War and the public display of its internal corruption.

Germany

More than any other nation, the course of German democracy was determined externally rather than internally in the post-war era (Bark and Gress, 1993; Gimbel, 1968). As final victory came into sight the basic outlines of the future German polity were being drawn up by the Allied governments at the Yalta and Potsdam conferences in early and mid 1945. It was agreed that Germany would be split into four zones of military occupation. Berlin, inside the Soviet zone, would also be quartered and a central Allied occupational committee would be established. The purposes of occupation would be denazification, democratization, demilitarization and possibly the deindustrialization of Germany so that its capacity to wage war would be terminated. However the unity of purpose established at Potsdam began to fragment almost immediately the occupation began and served as both a major cause and central outcome of the Cold War that followed.

In the Soviet occupied zone in the East control was quickly established in the hands of the recreated German Communist Party (KPD) and the administration of Soviet military occupation. Germany, like Eastern Europe was to be made safe for authoritarian socialism not liberal democracy or capitalist economics. Political authority was swiftly vested in a government of national unity which consisted of re-established pre-war parties like the German Socialist Party (SPD) and the reconstituted KPD. Over the following year the KPD installed itself and its cadres in key positions within the governing apparatus, especially in the Berlin and provincial police forces which served as the main instruments of repression and control. By mid 1946 the KPD was powerful enough to force through an inequitable unification of the left-of-centre forces, diluting the previously independent SPD into the German Socialist Unity Party (SED). From this moment, all organized political opposition to the communists effectively ceased. This was eloquently demonstrated in the rigged elections of 1946 which returned an overwhelming if highly questionable vote to the SED. By 1947 all pretence of a democratic constitution, organized opposition and conventional liberal civil and political rights had been abandoned.

The divergence of the East helped confirm the reality of East–West conflict in the post-war era and triggered a series of shifts in policy and practice in the Western occupied zones. Allied policy turned from creating a unified, disarmed, neutral Germany to a recognition that a divided Germany was becoming a reality and that the western part of the country should be rebuilt and integrated into the West. The formation of political parties and the establishment of self-government at local and länder (regional) level had already begun in West Germany in 1946. Although small extremist parties were established on the left and right, the centre of political gravity lay with the reconstituted SPD, the newly formed Christian Democrats (CDU) and centre-liberals (FDP). Thus Germany, for perhaps the first time, had major parties of the right that appeared unequivocally committed to liberal democratic norms.

The shape of the new German polity began to emerge in early 1947 with the formation of the bizonal economic council integrating the US and British zones and establishing a unified economic council in Frankfurt. The process of territorial integration and the creation of a centralized administration gathered pace with the currency reform of 1948 which, in effect, created a single and separate West German economy. The response from the East was the systematic blockade of the Western zones of Berlin in an effort to forestall the creation of a Western-orientated German state. The Western response was the continuous supply of Berlin by airlift, which continued for almost a year, and the creation of a constitutional convention of the major Western parties which drew up the *Grundgesetz* (Basic Law). This served as the interim constitution of the Federal German Republic while leaving open the question of the final constitutional and territorial status of the now divided Germany. If the territorial and legal standing of the *Grundgesetz* was ambiguous, its democratic orientation and its conscious attempt to remedy the limitations of Weimar's democracy were not. The law was confirmed and supported by all of the new German parties, with the exception of the communist representatives who abstained. The law came into force in 1949 followed by the first national elections for the Federal Republic, over-whelmingly won by the CDU under the leadership of Konrad Adenauer. Simultaneously sovereignty over domestic affairs passed from the military authorities to the new civilian government. More complete sovereignty over military and external affairs passed to the Federal Republic in 1955.

Comparisons and explanations

The democratization of Western Europe after the Second World War can be accounted for in terms of the continuation of long-term trends and the short-term but overwhelming impact of the war itself and the Cold War that followed. The defeat of fascism and the recognition of its appalling crimes placed authoritarianism of any hue ideologically and politically beyond the pale. The non-democratic reconstruction of Western and Northern European polities was simply not an option contemplated by the political elites of the victorious or defeated nations of the war. Moreover, it was not an option contemplated by the subaltern classes that had once again been mobilized for and fought an industrialized total war. All across Western Europe expectations of the post-war world were running high: neither authoritarianism nor the brutal capitalism of the inter-war era would prove acceptable social models. The popular mood was unequivically in favour of social reform.

In France and Britain, the end of the war simply extended and entrenched the developments of the pre-war era. Democracy was reactivated in Britain and recreated in France. In both cases the working class and its political representatives were strengthened institutionally and morally by the course of the war; French communists through their leadership of the resistance, British Labour through its commanding role in the governance of the Home Front. In France, the most reactionary elements of the old aristocracy and bourgeoisie had been terminally disgraced by their collusion with the Vichy government. The debate in these countries, as in the Low Countries and Scandinavia, was not between democracy or authoritarianism but what kind of democracy. In Britain, Fabian caution left the structures of the British state untouched. In France, women finally achieved the suffrage but entered a polity in which communists were excluded from government (if not electoral participation) and prone to fragmentation and indecision. It would take another twelve years for France to generate a democracy of sufficient resilience that it could accommodate both a fragmented party system and the turmoils of imperial retreat.

In Italy and Germany a more complex set of explanations are required to account for both the creation and entrenchment of democratic regimes. After all, neither polity had proved very accommodating in the past. In both cases, the defeat of fascism and the dominant role of US foreign policy made authoritarian solutions unacceptable. The longer-term prospects for democracy were improved by the effective elimination of key components of old authoritarian and fascist coalitions. In Italy the 1946 referendum dispensed with the monarchy. In Germany, the loss of its eastern regions, and the dismemberment of the army cut the remnants of the junker class off from the territory and institutional core of the new Federal Republic.

However, despite the overwhelming importance of these *structural* explanations some attention to the dynamics of the *transition* to democracy is required for the political strategies of both left and right ensured that new democracies would be effectively established. In both Germany and Italy, for the first time, the majority party of the centre-right was liberal democratic in its outlook. The creation of Christian Democratic parties in these states heralded an ideological and institutional transformation in the politics of the right, bringing bourgeoisie and middle classes together in a pro-democratic anti-communist coalition shorn of their militant clericalism and imperial nationalism. Similarly the key parties of the left opted for democracy rather than revolution. Liberalism became liberal democratic, socialism became social democratic – in intentions if not in name. In Germany, this was to be expected as the SPD drew upon pre-war democratic traditions shorn of their disastrous Marxist expectations. The KPD, which might have pushed for a less democratic route had been decimated by fascism and was politically overshadowed by the antics of its Eastern compatriots. It was banned in the 1950s. In Italy, the size and power of the PCI could have presented an altogether more significant challenge to democratization had it chosen to pursue a revolutionary road to power. The decision of Togliatti to pursue a democratic route was perhaps the most decisive reason for a successful democratic transition. However, in both Germany and Italy a price was to be paid for the creation of a notionally liberal democratic polity. In the Federal Republic democratic transition was accompanied by national fragmentation and authoritarian socialism in the East. In Italy, the transition was effected at the price of the systematic exclusion of the left from government and the effective establishment of a one-party state in which the DC dominated. The price of anti-communism was to be pervasive and systemic corruption.

─────────────────── *Summary of Section 4.3* ───────────────────

- The democratization of Western and Northern Europe in the post-war era can be explained in terms of: long-term structural trends towards democratization; the immediate ideological and institutional impact of the defeat of fascism; the pressures of the Cold War and US foreign policy in Europe; and, widespread popular demands for a change in the social order.

- The post-war struggle therefore rotated around what kind of democracy rather than democracy or authoritarianism. Radical models of democratization were rejected and communist exclusion from power was a central component of post-war politics.

- The decisions of key actors on the left and right in Germany and Italy was of great importance in ensuring a smooth democratic transition, but this was bought at a certain price.

4.4   The democratic revolutions in Southern Europe

Authoritarianism in Southern Europe

While the Second World War had swept like a tidal wave across the political landscapes of Western and Eastern Europe it only lapped against the authoritarian shores of Europe's southern periphery. In Portugal and Spain, the authoritarian dictatorships established in the inter-war period remained neutral and survived the war intact. Neutrality in the Second World War and isolation afterwards helped consolidate support for regimes in Iberia and keep the opposition quiescent. The Cold War helps account for US support. The need to protect NATO's southern flank with stable anti-communist states ensured the democratizing consequences of the Cold War on West Germany and Italy were not extended southwards.

Portugal

The perceptible decline of the Portuguese dictatorship began with the death of Antonio Salazar in 1970, although the structural roots of the regime's weakness extended backwards over a decade (Birmingham, 1993; Gallagher, 1982; Graham and Wheeler, 1983; Maxwell, 1986; Pridham, 1984, 1991). Power passed to Caetano who attempted a series of minor domestic liberalizations, caustically described as 'fascism with a human face'.

What ultimately hollowed out the regime was the endless and futile prosecution of colonial wars in the Portuguese African Empire. For over a decade the Portuguese army fought a rearguard action against movements of national liberation in Mozambique, Guinea and Angola. While the infinitely more powerful colonial states of Western Europe had long abandoned imperial pretensions, the weak and impoverished Portuguese state clung tenaciously to the preservation of empire. The costs were enormous. Portuguese spending on defence outstripped its richer neighbours, the level of conscription was so high that one in four men of military age were serving in the early 1970s. The loss of life and injury in the wars was high while within the army discipline, loyalty and morale were fractured by conflicts of interest between regulars and conscripts, poor pay and strategic disagreements on the prosecution of the war. By late 1972 the Army Forces Movement (MFA) of junior officers was already mobilizing and organizing discontent within the army. In late 1973 as the wave of discontent grew the Caetano government, preoccupied with a rise in domestic labour agitation, bungled a series of army reforms. It only required discrete promptings from the senior officer corps for the MFA to organize and execute a fully fledged coup in both metropolitan Portugal and the colonies. Beginning on 25 April 1974 the Portuguese Revolution, decisively led and executed by the military, toppled the Caetano regime. It fell like a house of cards. No resistance was effectively made and the MFA found itself as the provisional government of a new Portuguese Republic.

The course of the democratic transition that followed, culminating in the new constitution and democratic general election of early 1976 are immensely complicated. (See Chapter 1 for a model of transition.) We can simplify the transition by breaking it into two periods. Between April 1974 and March 1975 the centre of political power moved towards key fractions of a radicalized left-wing armed forces movement and the

Lisboners celebrate the coup, Lisbon, May 1974

remergent Portuguese Communist Party (PCP). These forces had committed themselves to the establishment of democracy, though by no means a conventional liberal democracy. Both sought to radically diminish the capacity of political opponents to participate in the political process and looked forward to a new constitutional order in which their superior power would be institutionally entrenched. From March 1975 to Autumn 1975 that coalition was divided and displaced by a process of counter revolution from the right and from the countryside and by the more centrist urban alliance of senior military officers, the Portuguese Socialist Party (PSP) and Catholic Christian Democrats (PSD) who effectively settled on a more conventional model of Western European liberal democracy.

In early 1974 the MFA established the first provisional government, promised a new constitution within a year and a general election a year after that. They made General Spinola, a key figure in the senior officer corps who had encouraged and supported the junior officers coup, president and head of state. With almost no political experience available to them the MFA turned to the cadres of the long-established but clandestine political parties – Catholic radicals, republicans, communists and socialists – to organize and run the state centrally and locally. In the following nine months the African wars were terminated, a rapid and chaotic programme of decolonization was executed, counter-coups from the die-hard right easily snuffed out and radical programmes of political liberalization and economic redistribution begun. Large-scale land seizures swept the south of the country and the central civilian props of the old regime – large landowners and industrial monopolists – were dispossessed. In an atmosphere of mounting radicalism, popular mobilization and local democratic experiments in economic and municipal politics, the MFA was reconstituted as a Council for the Revolution and allied with the PCP, easily the largest and best organized of the old political parties. Together they dominated the provisional government and declared an even more radical programme of constitutional change and economic socialization.

The MFA itself was increasingly divided over this period, discipline and organization within the army completely collapsed. The PCP, although monolithically centrist under Antonio Cuhnal newly returned from Moscow, suffered debilitating divisions between older pre-revolutionary members and the massive wave of post-revolutionary members. Alongside internal division the communist's central mistake was to profoundly alienate both the rest of the left as well as the peasants and small farmers of the north and centre of the country threatening both a limited democracy (evidenced by attempts to actively dominate the media and institutionalize the revolutionary council as a centre of power) and agricultural collectivization. Peasant riots in the summer of 1975 destroyed much of the communist's organizational infrastructure in the north and centre while the organizational capacity of the PSP (funded by the German SPD and US government) proved more than a match for the communists. The leverage of the Germans and Americans rose over the spring and summer of 1975 as Salazar's hoard of foreign currency was rapidly spent and the Portuguese economy went into tailspin. Above all, the basic inclination of the Portuguese people was for the moderate settlement of the PSP and its allies. In the April 1975 election for the Constitutional Assembly the communists only managed 12.5 per cent of the vote. The PSP took 38 per cent and its main centrist allies the PSD 26.4 per cent. By autumn 1975 the sixth provisional government was headed by the PSP's Soares which crushed an officerless coup of radical left-wing paratroopers in Lisbon, marginalized the PCP, halted the process of radical economic reform and saw through the creation of the eminently liberal democratic constitution of 1976. In 1979 the Portuguese revolution was consummated by the democratic election of a right-wing government.

Spain

In Spain, Franco's dictatorship had established deeper and more solid ideological and institutional roots than its counterpart in Portugal. In the end, Franco died in power and in his bed (Carr and Fusi, 1982; Maravall, 1982; Maravall and Santamaria, 1986; Pridham, 1984, 1991). Therefore the seeds of authoritarianism's decline had been germinating longest, for they needed to be more powerful than elsewhere. Indeed, we can realistically trace the process of democratization as far back as the mid 1950s when the autarchic and austere economic polices of Francoist Spain took another turn for the worse. In a Spain made safe for authoritarian Catholicism through exhaustion in civil war, starvation and repression, economic liberalization was deemed necessary, possible and politically unthreatening. Indeed key groups within the Francoist coalition argued that economic well-being would prove the most powerful anti-democratic sedative. As leadership of the Francoist coalition passed from its most reactionary elements to a new generation of Catholic technocrats and the financial and industrial bourgeoisie, a process of state directed industrialization was begun. This was accompanied by an end to protectionism, internal liberalization of economic policy, openings to foreign capital, the expansion of the tourist industry, and the active pursuit of emigration to reduce social and economic pressures. The results were spectacular. Spain experienced its greatest ever period of concentrated economic growth and radical structural change. In the 1960s and early 1970s, Spain was transformed from a rural to an urban society and from a closed, agrarian to an open, industrial economy. Demographically the ranks of the working class and professional and commercial middle classes swelled. The liberalization of economic policy required some slackening of the repressive system of labour relations, expanding the legal space for worker protests. Simultaneously the dominant economic power of repressive landlords was eclipsed by the new managerial bourgeoisie and the financial and industrial aristocracies that sat at the apex of Spain's massively concentrated banking and manufacturing sectors. How did these long-term structural changes to the balance of economic and political power in Spain play themselves out?

Prior to Franco's death the organizational capacity and political unity of the opposition forces had been growing for ten years while the internal cohesion of the ruling alliance had been diminishing, the repressive capacity of the state had regressed and broad popular support had waned. The challenge from below came simultaneously from a number of directions in the late 1960s and early 1970s. Fuelled by demographic expansion, legal relaxations, urban concentration and the inevitable tide of rising economic expectations, working-class protest reached new heights in Spain. The number and the length of strikes steadily progressed and acquired an increasingly political dimension. The separatist nationalisms of Catalonia and the Basque country revived, acquiring solid middle class support in Catalonia and taking a violent turn towards organized terrorism under the Basque Separatist Organization (ETA) in the Basque country. The rise of the urban middle classes, funnelled through the expanded but deeply reactionary university system generated persistent student organization and protest, culminating in the sacking of liberal professors, the repression of student organizations, and the closure or occupation of campuses. In all three cases, repression maintained the status quo but failed to break oppositional organizations. Moreover, the regime's claim to guarantee stability, peace and cohesion, looked increasingly threadbare to its traditional middle-class constituencies.

The ruling-class response was to divide. The power and influence of the old fascist falangist movement was marginalized in the late 1960s when Franco sacked the entire cabinet, installed his preferred successor – the impeccably reactionary Admiral Carrero de Blanco – as Prime Minster and turned to the reformist Catholic technocrats of Opus Dei to run the government. De Blanco's strategy was overwhelmingly repressive. In four years there were three states of emergency, widespread arrests of union organizers, and tighter controls on the press. Divisions increased as the falangists were joined on the margins of the old Francoist coalition by the Catholic church. The church signalled its opposition to the regime in 1971 by criticizing the course and the outcome of the civil war. The medium-term continuation of authoritarianism was probably forestalled by ETA's assassination of De Blanco in 1973 in the midst of a further huge wave of strikes. Franco declared King Juan Carlos as his appointed successor as head of state while the new Prime Minister Arias Navarro remained becalmed between a policy of limited political liberalization and the authoritarian die-hards of the Franco coalition in the Cortes and in the country ('the Bunker'). In the dying days of Franco's rule the opposition within and outside of Spain finally managed to achieve a semblance of unity, coalescing around the communist-led *Junta Democrática* and the socialist-led *Plataforma de Convergencia Democrática*. However, when Franco finally died in November 1975 the state that he had created remained authoritatively in power.

With Franco's death the structural pressures of the last decade were finally unleashed in a process of negotiated democratic transition. Both the new head of state, King Juan Carlos, and the new conservative Prime Minister, Adolfo Suárez (who replaced Navarro in mid 1976), declared themselves for some kind of managed democratic transition, though one in which the communists would still be excluded from the polity. The process of transition was greatly aided by the achievement of unity amongst the pro-democratic forces within the old regime and the unity of opposition forces around a minimalist democratic platform and organization – *Coordinacion*

Democrática – in early 1976. Suárez secured support for a democratic opening from the financial and industrial elites, the Catholic church and crucially from the army. Popular support for the democratic transition was secured in the referendum of December 1976 and the Francoist Bunker was effectively marginalized. In the final transitional talks of 1977 Suárez and the right agreed to the dissolution of the Francoist falange and the legalization of the Spanish Communist Party (PCE) in the new Spanish polity. The opposition conceded the maintenance of the monarchy, the non-prosecution of Francoist functionaries and an electoral system heavily skewed towards the rural bastions of electoral conservatism. In the general elections that followed the political and constitutional edge of the right was underscored, Suárez's newly formed Union of the Democratic Centre (UCD) achieving 46 per cent of the vote and a majority of seats. The significance of these elections was in part to demonstrate that two of the oldest Spanish political cleavages – which had made peaceful democratic coexistence so impossible in the early Spanish republics – had passed away. Neither clericalism nor monarchism were significant issues. Spanish politics had come to rotate around class divisions between left and right, and centre–periphery divisions between opponents of devolution and the nationalists of Catalonia and the Basque Country. The success and stability of Spanish democracy since has rested in part on the construction of a new constitution that embedded the agreements on church and monarchy and found a satisfactory (to most) solution of the regional and national question with considerable devolution to the old nations as well as other regions of Spain. Even the class division in the new Spain proved capable of accommodating the peaceful victory of the Spanish Socialist Party (PSOE) in the 1982 elections.

Comparisons and explanations

Despite their considerable differences, the transitions to democracy in Southern Europe are sufficiently similar for more general arguments about the relative merits of *structural and transition* theoretical approaches to be made. First, both processes of democratization were triggered by a short-term crisis which became unmanageable. In the case of Portugal this stemmed from excessive military commitments which undermined the legitimacy and capacity of the authoritarian regime, while in Spain the death of Franco brought simmering internal discontent to a head. However, none of these short-term problems would have initiated a process of democratization if there had not been a substantial series of structural changes in these societies which weakened authoritarian coalitions and institutions and strengthened the potentially pro-democratic forces.

In Spain, a process of rapid economic growth and structural economic change had been shifting the balance of forces for over a decade. Economic growth demographically and organizationally strengthened the urban working classes, middle-class students and the professional middle classes. All three of these groups found their own economic interests checked by the Francoist state and the arrangements for political representation unacceptable. Simultaneously the core classes of authoritarian rule in both societies were weakened by both economic and cultural changes – authoritarian landlords, conservative peasants, the Catholic church. The decline in structural power was matched by the declining purchase of authoritarianism's ideological legitimation. In a Spain rent by protest and violence Franco's peace looked unpersuasive. In increasingly secular societies, the preservation of the church seemed less urgent than in the inter-war years. As the memories of civil war receded, the threat from communists and socialists seemed to diminish. What ultimately sealed the fate of authoritarian regimes was the emergence of major divisions within their ruling coalitions. At the moment of crisis the Portuguese state found itself bereft of any significant allies in civil society. In Spain, the authoritarian core of Francoism found itself progressively abandoned by the church, the bourgeoisie and eventually even the army. In Portugal, however, where the pace of economic change was slowest it actually required the early phase of the revolution to liquidate the economic and political power of the most reactionary landlords and industrial bourgeoisie.

Once the crisis had broken and the new balance of forces had begun to align, the usefulness of structural theories of democratization diminishes. The outcome of the Portuguese revolution could have gone in a number of directions, liberal democracy or a communist–army dominated restricted democracy. Similarly it was by no means clear in early 1975 that Spain would become a democracy or if it did that it would be more structurally sound than the ill-fated Second Republic. Transition theory's contribution to these questions is less a fully formed body of explanations, rather it offers a series of partial hypotheses and claims about the preconditions for successful democratic transitions (see DiPalma, 1990). These include:

1   Democratic transitions are successful where there are minimal divisions within the forces of old regime and the opposition. This ensures that a clear dialogue can be conducted and extremists can be marginalized.

2   Democratic transitions are successful where the vital interests of all participants are guaranteed in the transition period and the new constitution. Thus previously recalcitrant forces come to believe that a change in government will not threaten them. Opposition forces accept that they have a better chance of sustained political power in an electoral rather a than a revolutionary situation.

3   Democratic transitions are successful where the balance of international forces and support favour democratizing forces over authoritarian forces and where incentives are made available to all participants to compromise.

All three points are illustrated by the post-crisis transitions in Southern Europe. In Spain the capacity of Suárez and Juan Carlos to obtain elite support for a democratic opening, prior to transitional talks, was essential in calming ruling-class fears and marginalizing extremists. Similarly, the capacity of the opposition to create a unified platform made political agreement easier and the prospects of democracy seem less threatening. Both sides, gave the democratic impulse a boost by being prepared to compromise on key questions in the transitional negotiations (for example the right on legalizing the communists, the left on accepting the monarchy). The process of transition was eased by the agreement of left and right on the limited prosecution of functionaries of the old regime and the maintenance of legal continuity from the authoritarian era. In neither case were international pressures central to the transitional process, though there is good reason to believe that the promise of European Community membership exercised a powerful attraction for the commercial elites and solidified their acceptance of democratic change.

In Portugal the process of transition was altogether more complex, violent, uncertain and internationally determined. While the right remained in the driving seat throughout the transition in Spain, the Portuguese revolution was made and swiftly dominated by force of the far left – the PCP and the MFA. It was under their auspices that the economic base of the old regime was liquidated in 1974 and early 1975. However, it is probably true to say that the emergence of stable liberal democracy was predicated on their eventual defeat and marginalization. The rather restricted model of democracy that the constituent assembly was drawing up in 1975 was defeated by an alliance of moderate socialists, the senior military corps and small farmers and peasants fearful of agriculture collectivization. Quite simply, the PCP overplayed its hand, narrowed its base of support, underestimated its opponents and paid the price of its miscalculations. In this struggle international factors were important. The economic constraints that were applied to the Portuguese revolution by the exhaustion of foreign reserves and a collapse in production, gave the US and German governments important leverage over the provisional Portuguese governments and helped squeeze the communists out of office. Simultaneously, Moscow's financial support for the PCP was matched by Western aid to the PSP.

--------------------------------- *Summary of Section 4.4* ---------------------------------

- The crisis of authoritarianism in Southern Europe arrived in the mid 1960s and led to democratic revolutions in the mid 1970s. These shifts were brought about by long-term structural changes and short-term crises. The key structural changes were: capitalist development which strengthened the democratic forces and weakened the authoritarian coalition; a decline in the potency of authoritarianism's ideological arsenal and division within the ruling class. The crises were externally imposed in Portugal and domestically generated in Spain.

- The success of the subsequent transitions to democracy rested on the capacity of both the old authoritarian coalition and the new democratic forces to achieve unity amongst themselves and marginalize or defeat extremists in their ranks. This allowed them to strike significant compromises over the shape of the new democratic polity which demonstrated the mutual worth of negotiated agreements and power sharing. Democratically negotiated transitions helped consolidate democratic polities.

4.5   An exceptional half century? The quality of European democracy

The short half century between 1945 and 1989 proved to be an exceptional era in the history of European democratization. Stable democracies had been created in the persistently authoritarian German, Italian and Austrian polities. The suffrage was extended to women in all Western European states, although it took until 1970 for the Swiss to do so. Democracies emerged and were consolidated in Southern Europe. In 1989 the collapse of authoritarian socialism in the East brought the prospect of an even greater extension of European democracy. Indeed such was the momentousness of 1989 that Fukuyama declared that the 'end of history' had arrived (Fukuyama, 1989). The West had won the Cold War, capitalism had no meaningful economic competitor and liberal democracy had no meaningful political competitor. The titanic struggles that had marked the course of Western democratization were at an end. Is this the final word on democracy and democratization in Europe?

First, while it is true that liberal democracy has outlasted and defeated its authoritarian competitors it is not clear that it has done so on the basis of its political and normative legitimacy alone. The success and consolidation of democracy in post-war Europe has been closely tied to its economic and military performance. The apparent quality of post-war European democracy has rested on the absence of any genuinely popular and powerful challenges to the democratic order from authoritarian political projects of the left or right. There can be little doubt that liberal democracy's capacity to peaceably resolve social and political conflicts and accommodate different interests has made a major contribution to its legitimacy and the marginalization of extremist politics. However, its task has been made infinitely easier by the emollient solvent of economic growth. In the context of rapid increasing overall economic wealth, the creation of welfare states, expanding levels of consumption and some increases in social mobility, the sharpness of class conflict, the demand for repressive politics on the right and revolutionary strategies on the left has been diminished. Thus capitalist development has been both a long-term structural cause of democratization and a central feature of its entrenchment and consolidation. Furthermore, the dominance of liberal democracy in the West is a martial achievement. The fall out of the First World War had already put paid to the authoritarian monarchist alternatives to liberal democracies. The Second World War destroyed the fascist alternative in the heart of Europe and created the authoritarian state socialism of the East. The Cold War saw off the communist route to modernity. Liberal democracy was left standing, it would seem, because it has prosecuted industrialized warfare more effectively than any other form of modern state.

The question remains as to whether military and economic superiority can be equated with political legitimacy. Liberal democracies may have no serious competitors left other than the normative benchmark of their own democratic rhetoric. It is not entirely clear as to whether they have met this as effectively as they have met military and economic challenges. First, in a number of European countries where the tight labour markets of the post-war boom were relieved by mass immigration, the economic contribution of immigrants had been rewarded by social and political exclusion. For example, millions of Turks in Germany, many second-generation German, have yet to acquire the most minimal social and civil rights or an extension of the suffrage. Second, the legitimacy of any democracy rests not only on representative issues but territorial issues as well. In a number of European countries significant national minorities have found rule from the centre, of what is perceived to be an alien nation, morally unacceptable. What is the point of voting for the government of a state that one does not recognize in the first place? Perhaps the sharpest examples of this territorial disenfranchisement has been the situation of the Catholic minority in Northern Ireland and the Basques in Spain. In Belgium, the national division between Waloon and Flemish communities has placed the legitimacy of the hybrid Belgian state in question.

Third, the representative quality of parliaments and legislatures across Europe have been undermined by excessive centralization of powers within centralized bureaucracies and the political executive, be it the French Presidency or the British Prime Minister and Cabinet. In these instances there is a good case for arguing that the influence of the public outside of rarely contested general elections is nugatory. Their parliamentary representatives and legislatures have minimal powers of control and investigation over the executive and are inevitably corralled by party loyalty into rubber stamping the decisions of the executive. Nor does local government provide a strong and entrenched set of political checks and balances on central power.

Normative deficits aside it is becoming increasingly obvious that the rate of economic expansion of the post-war era will not return. Instead, European democracies face increasing competition from the newly industrializing countries of the east and south, the diminished capacity of national governments to steer economic policy and a rising mountain of long-term structural unemployment and social exclusion. It is more likely than not that, economic and political inequalities will increase, economic discontent will rise and the mainstream political organizations of Europe will have a looser and shallower hold over the polity. The possibility of authoritarian alternatives acquiring even greater support than the contemporary popularity of the far right in Western Europe demonstrates, while by no means certain, cannot be excluded.

––––––––––––––––––––– *Summary of Section 4.5* –––––––––––––––––––––

- The consolidation of European democracy can be accounted for in terms of economic growth and military capacity as much as political legitimacy.

- The quality of that democracy has been limited by exclusion, territorial disagreements and centralization.

References

Bark, D. and Gress, D. (1993) *A History of West Germany, Volume 1: From Shadow to Substance, 1945–1963* (2nd edn), Oxford, Blackwell.

Birmingham, D. (1993) *A Concise History of Portugal*, Cambridge, Cambridge University Press.

Carr, R. and Fusi, J. (1981) *Spain: Dictatorship to Democracy* (2nd edn), London, Allen and Unwin.

Di Palma, G. (1990) *To Craft Democracies*, Berkeley, University of California Press.

Fukuyama, F. (1989) 'The end of history?', *The National Interest*, no.16.

Gallagher, T. (1982) *Portugal: a Twentieth Century Perspective*, Manchester, Manchester University Press.

Gimbel, J. (1968) *The American Occupation of Germany: Politics and the Military, 1945–1949*, Stanford, Stanford University Press.

Ginsborg, P. (1990) *A History of Contemporary Italy: Society and Politics, 1943–1988*, Harmondsworth, Penguin.

Graham, L. and Wheeler, D. (eds) (1983) *In Search of Modern Portugal: the Revolution and its Consequences*, Madison, University of Wisconsin Press.

Maravall, J.-M., and Santamaria, J. (1986) 'Political change in Spain and the prospects for democracy' in O'Donnell, G. *et al.* (eds).

Maravall, J.-M. (1982) *The Transition to Democracy in Spain*, London, Croom Helm.

Maxwell, K. (1986) 'Regime overthrow and the prospects for democratic transition in Portugal' in O'Donnell, G. *et al.* (eds)

O'Donnell, G., Schmitter, P. and Whitehead, L. (eds) (1986) *Transitions from Authoritarian Rule: Southern Europe*, Baltimore, Johns Hopkins University Press.

Pasquino, G. (1986) 'The demise of the first fascist regime and Italy's transition to democracy: 1943–1948' in O'Donnell, G. *et al.* (eds).

Pridham, G. (ed.) (1984) *The New Mediterranean Democracies: Regime Transition in Spain, Portugal and Greece*, London, Frank Cass.

Pridham, G. (ed.) (1991) *Encouraging Democracy: the International Context of Regime Transition in Southern Europe*, London, Leicester University Press.

Rioux, J.-P. (1987) *The Fourth Republic, 1944–1958*, Cambridge, Cambridge University Press.

Williams, P. (1972) *Crisis and Compromise: Politics in the Fourth Republic*, London, Longman.

Woolf, S. (ed.) (1972) *The Rebirth of Italy, 1943–1950*, New York, Humanities Press.

CHAPTER 5

Democracy in the USA since 1945

Richard Maidment

Introduction

This chapter addresses two issues. The first of these is: Why did the United States of America finally achieve universal suffrage, perhaps the most fundamental prerequisite for a democracy, only in the latter half of the twentieth century and much later than in most other liberal democracies? As we saw in Chapter 2, the USA was, at its inception, the most democratic modern polity with something approaching universal suffrage for white men. Suffrage for women however was not obtained until the aftermath of the First World War. And it took until the late 1960s for the suffrage to be meaningfully extended to African-Americans in the Southern states. In Section 5.1 I will look briefly at the historical background to this in the light of five of the six explanatory factors outlined in Chapter 1.

The integration of African-Americans into the mainstream of US life has been the dominant domestic problem of the USA. It has also been the most striking failure of the political system since the creation of the Republic. While slavery and *de jure* segregation had been abolished, the full integration of African-Americans remained the most difficult issue on the political agenda. The presence of a black underclass in the large urban areas, the continuing existence of widespread racial discrimination and a powerful and growing backlash at some of the remedies that were put into place to deal with this discrimination, provide a clear indication of the continuing dimensions of the problem. This should not be taken to suggest that the legislation passed and reforms that were instituted, during the 1950s and 1960s, were unimportant, but that the condition and treatment of African-Americans remains the most profound unresolved domestic issue.

Those decades brought about, in the view of many observers, the culmination of the journey to a complete and full democracy in the USA. The enfranchisement of millions of African-Americans in the states of the South finally ended a process of exclusion that had, at certain points, also included women and some other minority ethnic groups. The passage of the Civil Rights Act of 1964 and the Voting Rights Act of 1965 appeared at the time to be a watershed. It was a remarkable achievement for the Civil Rights Movement and it also offers an instructive insight into the state of US democracy. In Section 5.2 I examine the forces that brought about the passage of the legislation and wrought a substantial change in attitudes and consider what it tells us about the processes of democratization in the USA.

The second issue addressed in this chapter turns on the fact that, for most of their history, Americans have seen themselves as democrats and the USA as the pre-eminent liberal democracy. They have done so, on the whole, in a remarkably unproblematic manner even when behaviour and practice in the USA did not apparently conform with the canons of democratic belief. But intriguingly at the time of writing, this sense of conviction in the democratic destiny of the USA has diminished. There is a crisis of confidence over the democratic credentials of the US polity and the ability of institutions and processes to deal with the concerns and aspirations of the electorate.

There has been a significant loss of belief in political institutions and perhaps politics itself as an instrument of reform. Bluntly, the political system no longer has the confidence of a clear majority of Americans because it no longer appears to function satisfactorily. Opinion polls from the 1970s onwards have consistently recorded a growing level of disenchantment with all the federal institutions, as well as parties and politicians. Even more persuasive indicators have been the decline in electoral participation rates, the sharp reduction in identification with the Democratic and Republican parties, the quite striking volatility in the behaviour of the US electorate, and broadly a loss of trust in the entire democratic political process. In Section 5.3 I ask why has this set of conditions appeared, and again what does it suggest about the state of US democracy?

In the Conclusion I will consider the view that the USA is a society apart, where the historical experience as well as the social and economic conditions that have prevailed, have been singular and unique. The US experience, it is often argued, has been so distinctive that comparisons with other societies and polities are not particularly useful. So does US exceptionalism, as this doctrine is called, also imply that the processes of democratization in the USA are equally specific with no essential point of useful and informative comparison with the experience of other liberal democracies?

To conduct such a comparison we need to bring the post-war history of US democracy within a comparable framework. We therefore begin this chapter by seeing which, if any, of the six explanatory factors introduced in Chapter 1 are useful in explaining the course of US democratization.

5.1   Explanatory factors and US democratization

Chapter 1 describes six explanatory factors. At least five are relevant to the post-war USA. The nature of *social divisions*, particularly ethnic divisions between black and white have provided one of the defining issues of US democratization. I shall explore this in more detail in Section 5.2. Two factors – (1) *economic development* and *economic structure*, and (2) *international enmeshment* – provide the broad backdrop to both the successes and failures of US democratization. I consider these below. Two further factors – (1) *political culture*, and (2) *the structure of the US state and political institutions* – are probably decisive in explaining both the lateness of universal suffrage in the USA and the consequent paralysis and crisis of contemporary US democracy. The last two, of course, are related for the US constitution has both defined the institutional parameters of the US state and provided the central reference text of US political discourse and culture. Given the importance of these factors, I explore their history and democratic credentials in some detail later in this section. While the constitutional structure of the USA was determined in the eighteenth century, contemporary forms and patterns of political party have a more recent genesis. In Section 5.2 I examine the role of party affiliations and coalitions in initially retarding the emergence of universal suffrage and institutionalizing African-American exclusion in the South. However, shifts in the character of political coalitions within the US party system, beginning with the New Deal Democratic Party of the 1930s are a significant factor in explaining the final success of the Civil Rights Movement. In Section 5.3, the nature of US political parties continues to help explain the current difficulties of US democracy.

Economic development and international enmeshment

The particular character of capitalist development in the USA has shaped the course of democratization in a number of ways. As we have already seen in Chapter 2, the comparatively favourable economic conditions in the eighteenth and nineteenth centuries, provided fertile ground for democratization in the USA. The availability of land created a widely dispersed propertied class and a mass political system at an earlier point than virtually any other nation in the North Atlantic. The tension between the industrial capitalism of the Northern states and the slavery and semi-feudalism of the South was one of the central reasons for the Civil War. The victory of the North was a democratic milestone. The emergence of the Civil Rights Movement is partly linked to the mass migration of African-Americans from the rural South to satisfy the labour needs of the industrial North.

The second explanatory factor is international enmeshment. War, in particular, has had an enormous impact on democratization in the USA and on the politics of race. The Civil War and the First and Second World Wars had an all but transforming impact on US democracy. The First World War ended isolationism and brought the nation and its citizens into contact with the rest of the world. It ended an innocence about US democracy and race relations. It also hastened the emergence of the female suffrage. Similarly, the Second World War, with the deployment of African-Americans in all the major theatres of that war, was a defining moment in black consciousness. The rhetorical justification for US involvement in the war, the experience of societies which did not racially separate its citizens combined to create a watershed in the African-American experience. The returning soldiers were key players in the rejection of segregation, institutionalized discrimination and in the mobilization of black opinion after 1945.

Political culture and state structure

The third factor is *political culture*. The dominant US political culture has from the outset embraced equality and liberty and within a few decades after 1776, it also embraced populism. In other words it was a culture that was familiar with and supportive of liberal democracy. The discourse of US politics, for some considerable time, has been essentially a democratic discourse. The problem, however, has been the very real gap between these dominant values and beliefs on the one hand and the reality of political behaviour on the other. The gap has been the greatest in the realm of race relations and this chapter will attempt to account for the pattern of racial politics within a political culture that has been instrumental to the process of democratization. In short, the basic language of US political culture has seen human beings as fundamentally equal, bearing natural rights and liberties. In such a context it has required considerable effort and tortuous justifications to maintain that women and African-Americans should not be included within the polity. One of the central reasons that this has been possible is that the structure of the US state and the nature of US political parties has provided sufficient space for the survival of an entrenched local politics of racism and exclusion. To explain this we must return to the original formation and characteristics of the US constitution and the US state.

The US government, unlike the governments of virtually every other Western liberal democracy, operates within a constitutional structure that was created at the end of the eighteenth century and which remains essentially intact. The objectives and the concerns of those who framed the Constitution at the Federal Convention of 1787 were not those of democrats. They were strongly influenced by the liberal writings of John Locke, David Hume and Montesquieu. But they were not wedded to notions of democracy. They endorsed the principles of consent, liberty, political and property rights but not the other key ideas and practices that are central to modern democratic beliefs. The American colonists used the language of liberalism to make their case against the manner in which successive British governments had behaved towards the colonies. Thomas Jefferson in 1776 documented these grievances against Britain and George III in the Declaration of Independence in 1776. He and his fellow colonists attributed these problems to the corruption of British political institutions that allowed both the Crown and politicians at Westminster to behave in a tyrannical and autocratic manner. But the solutions that the colonists sought to prevent a recurrence of such behaviour in a newly independent America were not democratic solutions but essentially liberal ones. There was little demand for even universal white male suffrage and no sense that the new constitutional and political arrangements should enshrine majority rule. Indeed, the tenor and thrust of the debate in the Federal Convention was directed towards the creation of a set of governmental institutions and a political process that controlled and limited the influence and power of the simple majority. The primary concern of the delegates was to protect the individual rights of speech, press, religion as well as property and to protect them against the will of the majority.

The strategy deployed to control the majority faction revolves around three elements. The first element is that certain crucial matters are removed from the arena of everyday politics. A good example is the first ten amendments to the Constitution, also known as the Bill of Rights, where particularly important civil liberties are guaranteed. These constitutional guarantees can only be modified or rescinded by a process of constitutional amendment, and cannot be tampered with by either the President or by legislation of a traditional kind. Furthermore, the process of constitutional amendment is long and elaborate and has only been used successfully on sixteen occasions since 1787, bar the Bill of Rights. The second element was the adoption of a federal structure which created two principal levels of government, one at state level, the other nationally. Moreover, the national or federal government was given very specific and limited responsibilities and powers. The final element of the strategy established that the powers designated to the federal government were allocated in such a manner that the institutions of the federal government would be profoundly suspicious of each other and consequently find it extremely difficult to act in concert.

The delegates very deliberately established each of the three branches of the federal government with a degree of constitutional independence from each other. The presidency, Congress and the federal judiciary were endowed with designated and limited powers, which could not be modified by the other branches. Nevertheless, the Constitution also built in a degree of interdependence, which was intended to heighten the friction between the institutions. The presidency was not designed solely as an executive institution, it was given a legislative role through the power of veto over legislation passed by the Congress. Similarly, the Congress was authorized to intervene in matters traditionally within the domain of the executive. Moreover, all of the political institutions of the government had different constituencies with differing methods of election, which the Convention assumed would result in members of the House of Representatives, the Senate as well as the occupant of the White House having a very different perspective and agenda. The clear intention behind this very elaborate and complex governmental structure was to produce a political process that did not act easily and smoothly. Indeed the overriding desire was to create a system that functioned only when an overwhelming majority of Americans were in agreement. In the absence of such agreement the conflict designed and built into the political process would prevent any faction, but particularly the faction of a majority of 50 per cent plus 1, from controlling the government and making policy which would put in jeopardy the liberty and property of their fellow citizens. There was one final element of this structure which was also the final safeguard in the event that Congress and the President did manage to co-operate in infringing constitutionally guaranteed rights, the federal judiciary. The judiciary were the guardians of the Constitution. Federal judges possess the authority to declare unconstitutional actions of the President as well as federal and state legislation. If the political institutions either failed to protect civil liberties or property rights or themselves were the source of threat, then the courts had the power to intervene. Moreover, federal judges were appointed, not elected, and could only be removed by the process of impeachment, a difficult and very rarely used procedure. So the protectors, in the last resort, of the Constitution were unelected judges, which is the most telling indicator of the Constitution's profound suspicion of politics, politicians and the dangerous instincts and tendencies of majority opinion.

However, by the third decade of the nineteenth century the fear of majorities, and mass opinion had receded sharply. The political culture was imbued with a populist impulse. The period identified with the presidency of

Andrew Jackson (1829–37) was a watershed in US political history. At about this point, the political process was irrevocably transformed into a mass political system. Even property qualifications, which were still in place in several states, were no longer a significant barrier to a broad spectrum of participation. Almost 80 per cent of white males exercised their right to vote in presidential elections and the political system, by no stretch of the imagination, could any longer be described as elite, even if it could not be described as democratic. Increasingly, US political culture was in the sway of a majoritarian impulse. The expansion of the electorate resulted in a striking change in political discourse. Concerns about majorities were no longer electorally productive. This majority was now required to provide an election victory. The electoral connection between the rulers and the ruled ensured that politicians sought to identify, rather than distance themselves from the views and aspirations of their constituents and sought to represent their values and beliefs in the full range of political institutions. The language of US politics now paid homage to mass opinion.

This transformation reflected the substantial changes that were occurring in US society. Waves of immigration, westward expansion, and the growing industrialization of the economy were altering the social structure. The elites that dominated colonial society were primarily based in agriculture and the traditional professions. They now found their position challenged. The rapid expansion of commerce and industry provided new sources of economic power and they required and demanded political representation. The map of political influence in the USA was being redrawn. It was difficult, if not impossible, to resist the claims and demands of the newly arrived and the newly propertied to participate, at the very least, in the political process.

Thus the legacy of US political culture and the US state for democratization in the twentieth century has been ambiguous. On the one hand, the USA began the twentieth century with the most securely entrenched democratic constitution of any state and a universal suffrage for white men. Moreover, the dominant cultural values which had made the exclusion of the poor and new immigrants difficult to justify continued to make the exclusion of women and African-Americans ideologically problematic. However, the same state structure also provided entrenched and untouchable power for the enduringly racist elites of the South. In Section 5.2 I go on to examine how that entrenched power was finally overcome. In Section 5.3 I examine how the same problems of blocking minorities and high democratic expectations have combined to produce a form of democratic crisis and paralysis at the very moment that the exclusion of African-Americans was overcome.

———————————— *Summary of Section 5.1* ————————————

- The five useful explanatory factors in dealing with the USA are: economic development; social divisions; state and political institutions; political culture and ideas; and transnational and international enmeshment.

- The USA, unlike other liberal democracies, operates within a constitutional system that was devised in 1787 but is essentially intact. The US Constitution was not devised by democrats.

- The concerns over majorities evaporated considerably during the early decades of the nineteenth century as the USA succumbed to a populist impulse, but the constitutional structure remained essentially unchanged.

- The principal concern of those who framed the Constitution was to control the majority faction. In order to achieve this objective, power was dispersed between the individual states and the federal government as well as between the institutions of the federal government.

5.2   The politics of race

If there is a case to be made for the exceptionalism of the USA, the racial composition of the US population would certainly be one of the most persuasive elements in the argument. The extraordinary racial and ethnic heterogeneity of the population does indeed distinguish it from virtually every other society. Nor has the composition of this racial mosaic in the USA stablized. There has been, in recent decades, a very substantial wave of immigration from Latin America, the Caribbean, and East and South Asia that is transforming the population, society and politics of every major conurbation. The importance of this ethnic and racial diversity, as far as it is germane to the concerns of this chapter, is twofold. First, traditionally race and ethnicity has provided the social cement, the ties that bind, the sense of community in the USA. The connection provided by the link of a shared racial or ethnic past has proved durable. The ideology of the melting pot did not work, at least to the extent that an American all but divorced from the past, has not emerged out of this varied and disparate heritage. Racial and ethnic ancestry have been resistant to the overt attempts, particularly in the nineteenth and early twentieth centuries, to shed the past and produce a new and uniform American identity. The emergence of multiculturalism, in recent decades, is a testament to the importance and resilience of personal racial and ethnic histories. The significance, to this discussion, of the critical role of race and ethnicity is that class has played a less important role in the construction of US society.

The second point about race specifically concerns African-Americans. They, of course, were never supposed to be a part of the melting pot. Those who were in positions of power and influence in a society which had been overwhelmingly European in ancestry until the late twentieth century, did not see a place for African-Americans within the mainstream. But they also did not know quite what location they wanted African-Americans to have.

The reason it has been such a source of tension is that the dominant cohort of ideas and beliefs has always seemed to be at variance with the treatment of African-Americans. 'We hold these truths to be self-evident, that all men are created equal', wrote Thomas Jefferson in the Declaration of

Independence. Yet at the point that he was writing those words in 1776 there were a million black slaves, some of whom were owned by Jefferson. Slaves had no rights and indeed each slave only counted as two-thirds of a person. The paradox and tension between these words and the institution of slavery were also self-evident even in 1776 and increasingly in a society that was in the throes of change. The property qualifications to exercise the franchise were of diminishing importance in restricting the size of the electorate. The appeal of the USA was the availability of land and the development of the frontier. This created a large cohort of small farmers and landowners who had little time for slavery.

Politics, unlike in Europe, was not the exclusive property of elites, parliamentary or otherwise. The US polity, by the 1830s, was already a mass polity. Politicians stressed their commitment to equality and held privilege and rank to ridicule and contempt. The discourse of US politics in the states of the North and the West at least was almost exclusively, if not democratic, then certainly populist and egalitarian. The institution of slavery could not be easily reconciled with this style of politics. The gap between the Northern states and the slave owning states of the South became a chasm which could not be resolved through the normal operation of the political process. There were innumerable attempts to achieve a compromise, all of which failed in part because it was an issue which did not appear to be amenable to compromise as it raised the most fundamental questions over societal values. It is no coincidence that the only complete breakdown in the political process occurred over the issue of race. The Civil War, of course, was not only fought over slavery, there were other significant reasons which divided the two sides. However, the issue of slavery undoubtedly was the key factor why a satisfactory compromise could not be fashioned.

Racial politics after the Civil War: segregation

The Civil War not only ended slavery and constitutionally established the rights of the former slaves to be citizens and to exercise the rights of citizenship, it was a watershed in the US polity. The political allegiances forged during the war proved to be remarkably durable. The South's almost monolithic allegiance to the Democratic Party lasted over a century and has not entirely disappeared. The Republican Party, which emerged during the conflict over slavery, gained the loyalty of voters in the North and West which allowed it to dominate the federal government until the onset of the Great Depression in the 1930s.

The victory of the North was far from complete. Militarily the triumph was total; politically it was far more limited. The apparent triumph of a political culture which was populist and egalitarian was limited by the re-emergence of the former slave owners as the political leaders of the South, after the end of the Reconstruction (the period, 1865–77, after the Civil War when the South was reorganized and reintegrated into the Union). The South, for several decades after Reconstruction, resisted the impulses and forces that were dominating the politics of the North. Industrialization and heavy immigration from Eastern and Southern Europe which were reinforcing the process of democratizion in the North were, to a striking extent absent, from the South. The passage of the Thirteenth, Fourteenth and Fifteenth Amendments to the Constitution, which did abolish slavery but were designed also to guarantee the rights of former slaves, were effectively nullified soon after the end of the war. They were nullified because the North and the Republican Party, apart from the years of Reconstruction, were not interested in enforcing the amendments. The division between the regions and the parties allowed a *de facto* compromise to be fashioned over the issue of race. Apart from Reconstruction, when there was a concerted attempt to bring former slaves into the political process, the Northern Republicans acquiesced in the restoration of the pre-Civil War political class in the South.

The position of African-Americans effectively disappeared from the national political agenda. The abolition of slavery ended the involvement of the Republicans with the interests of African-Americans. Slavery was the transparent and fundamental contradiction. The electorate and their representatives were not interested in the new circumstances. The white South used a variety of devices to restore the subordination of the former slaves. A series of laws (the notorious jim-crow laws) were passed introducing legal segregation and the disenfranchisement of African-Americans. Interestingly, all of these laws claimed that they operated within the mandates of the Civil War amendments. They did not confront, as over slavery, the political culture and values of equality and liberty. Segregation, it was claimed, allowed services both public and private to be provided which were separate but were equal. It was a fictive claim which allowed the reality of the practices to be shielded from public view, if that was the desire of the viewers. Several states introduced literacy tests which had to be passed before a citizen could be registered as a voter. The rationale for these tests was that the right to vote was far too valuable to be automatic. Citizens, it was argued, needed to show at least a minimal level of education before they could exercise such a privilege. Of course the true intent was to disenfranchise African-Americans and these tests achieved their objective. There were virtually no black voters throughout the South. Few if any sat on juries.

The structure of the US state and the character of US political institutions reinforced the marginalization of African-Americans. Even the most flagrantly illegal practices, notably lynching, were not addressed by either the presidency or the Congress. There were several reasons for this. First, both the Republican and Democratic parties are and have always been substantial coalitions held together less by programmatic beliefs than by the desire for power. Accordingly, they have been unusually tolerant, at least by the standards of most other countries, of virtually all shades of opinion in order to construct a winning coalition. The Democrats' only hope of winning the presidency for the half century after Reconstruction rested on their Southern base. Without the South the party could not begin to construct a majority in the electoral college. Accordingly, Northern Democrats simply accepted the price of party harmony, which was to acknowledge the legitimacy of Southern views and not to challenge them. Second, the hegemony of the Democratic Party in the South helped to ensure that

Southern Democrats were particularly influential in the Congress. The seniority rules that rewarded length of service and which operated in both the House of Representatives and the Senate gave them a disproportionately influential position within the Congress. Third, the rules in the Senate allowed unlimited debate, unless a two-thirds majority of Senators voted to curtail the debate. This allowed Southern senators to 'filibuster' any attempt to legislate on issues related to race, including lynching. They were almost invariably successful because senators from the North in their broad desire to conciliate the South were unwilling to close debate. African-Americans could not enter the political process in the South and they had no allies outside of it. The result was a political system that handed control over public policy on race to white Southerners, a position which would continue until the Second World War.

However, in the inter-war years, a number of structural demographic and political changes began to undermine the capacity of the white South to maintain a veto on the politics of race. Southerners could only maintain that veto if most African-Americans continued to live in the South. However, from the end of the First World War a vast and historic migration began, which took black Americans from the rural South to the major urban conurbations of the North. A black electorate began to emerge. A growing cohort of politicians in the North began to be receptive to African-American interests. Politicians who campaigned and sought African-American votes, also began to represent their interests. During the 1930s, Franklin D. Roosevelt's New Deal Democrats radically altered the landscape of government and politics in the USA; for example, the era saw the growth of the labour movement and the use of the institutions of the federal government to support the interests of the disadvantaged. A powerful coalition of liberal interests was developed in the 1930s; a coalition which was suspicious of the South and on the whole supportive of African-American interests, at least up to a point. However, this Democratic Party was not in thrall to the South. Labour unions, liberal groups, urban interests now drove the national Democratic Party and they controlled the presidential nomination process. Southern Democrats still retained their importance within the Congress and their interests continued to be seen as legitimate although not sacrosanct. They had to be consulted and conciliated but their position was not invulnerable.

Racial politics after 1945: civil rights

The period from the end of the Second World War to the passage of the Civil Rights Act of 1964, the Twenty Fourth Amendment to the Constitution also in 1964, which abolished the poll tax, and the Voting Rights Act of 1965, saw the completion of a key aspect of the democratic project in the USA. With the enactment of the Voting Rights Act, in particular, the last substantial restrictions on the franchise were removed. It was the final step of a long journey. During this period, as in the years before the Civil War, Southern practices of race relations became increasingly difficult to justify with the national polity. There were several factors which led to this.

The first and the most important was the emergence of the Civil Rights Movement, which altered the balance of racial politics. Scholars who write

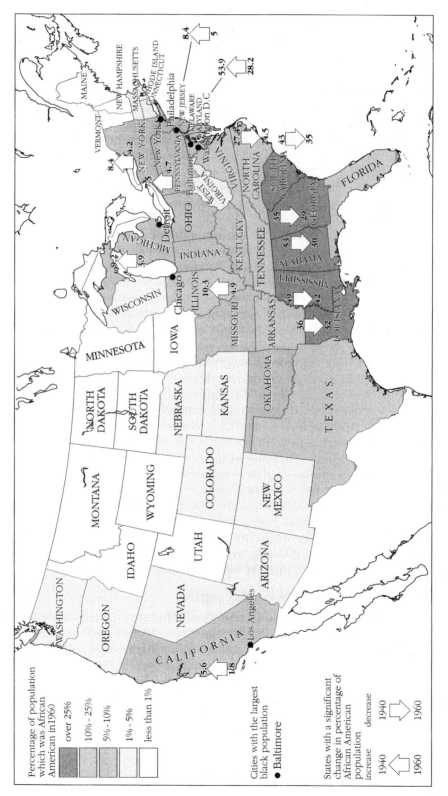

Map 5.1 African-Americans in the USA, 1940–60

on civil rights point to numerous reasons for the emergence of the movement during the 1950s and 1960s. Among the more significant was the Second World War itself, which was fought in part to defeat doctrines of racial superiority. Moreover, African-Americans who served overseas, even though all the branches of the US Armed Forces operated a version of racial segregation, became aware that discrimination and segregation were not inevitable. The experience of the war certainly fuelled dissatisfaction. Within a few years the dissatisfaction became visible and it was given an effective political voice because by 1960 over 40 per cent of the black population lived in the North. There was a politically significant black electorate which wanted to end racial segregation and their views were represented.

A further reason was the emergence of an effective black leadership, whose appeal transcended the African-American community. This leadership came overwhelmingly from the black churches of the South who provided the initial funding, organizational infrastructure and personnel of the umbrella group the Southern Christian Leadership Conference. The most important of these leaders was Dr Martin Luther King Jr., a charismatic figure who preached non-violence and civil disobedience. The chemistry of this particular combination of personality and doctrine was enormously attractive and persuasive other than to those who believed in white supremacy. King was a particularly effective advocate with Northern whites. The discourse and language of King and the Civil Rights Movement was that of the political mainstream, embedded in a value and belief system that was both endorsed and supported by a substantial majority of the electorate. King and the movement were asking for those entitlements which were constitutionally protected rights. They wanted legal equality extended to blacks. It was a claim that could not be defended by the South within the discourse of US politics. The South, however, could avoid the debate as it had done since Reconstruction, and it could continue to believe it could defuse the issue by parading the formal position of separate but equal and the arguments about citizenship that lay behind the literacy tests. The problem for the white South was that the Civil Rights Movement controlled the terms of the debate, partly because the debate was no longer conducted within the confines of a narrowly drawn political class. It was no longer only the concern of politicians and legislatures. The acts of civil disobedience against segregated facilities at lunch counters or on buses plus the Freedom Marches were compelling and absorbing political theatre, that were reported extensively by television which, by 1960, was received by most households. In many respects this was the first major domestic issue that was defined by television. Civil rights became an issue of mass concern. All of these events forced civil rights onto the national political agenda and in a manner that produced sympathy and support for the civil rights.

The broad national sympathy for the position and interests of black Americans was due in part to the response of the Civil Rights Movement by those in control in the South. On the whole the response was repressive and visibly so. The police in several cities on numerous occasions were brutal in their attempts to control the protests and acts of civil disobedience. The

Birmingham, Alabama, 3 May 1963

brutality was displayed on television and could not be concealed from a large audience. The behaviour of the police, notably in Selma and Birmingham both cities in Alabama, was so extreme that it was etched into the national consciousness and is now part of the national memory. The political implication of the behaviour of Southern police forces was profound. Essentially it fatally damaged the legitimacy of the Southern position. It became impossible to conceal the reality of Southern race relations from the rest of the world. The rhetorical veneer was removed and the practice exposed. The most significant impact was on the white electorate, particularly in those states, which did not have a substantial black population. On the whole these voters in the Farm Belt, the Mountain States and the Pacific North West had ignored the issue. In turn their members of Congress had been unwilling to legislate on civil rights and most importantly the Senators from these states had not supported the attempts to stop the Southern filibusters over civil rights legislation. The majority of these Senators were Republican and they accepted, implicitly or otherwise, some aspects of the Southern position. Certainly, they had endorsed the view that this was not an issue for the federal government, but was a matter for the states, which was a central element of the Southern doctrine of States' Rights. Until the 1960s, they framed discussion of civil rights within broad constitutional arguments of federal powers versus those of the individual states. This cohort of Republicans were the key political allies of the white South. Without them, the Congress would have passed civil rights legislation. After Selma and Birmingham the alliance crumbled.

A further reason for the South's move to beyond the margin of political respectability lies in the particular characteristics of the USA's political process. The judicial branch of government has a far greater impact on the public policy-making process than in any other liberal democracy, and the rulings of the Federal Courts and in particular the US Supreme Court were increasingly unhelpful to the maintenance of the status quo in the South. Some two decades before the Congress passed the Civil Rights Act of 1964, a number of Supreme Court decisions were undermining the legal and constitutional basis of segregation and black disfranchisement. Initially the court made it clear that if the South wanted to operate a system of separate and equal then the services provided or regulated by the state had to be equal. The economic implications, of course, were profound and the consequent financial burden almost certainly could not have been borne by the poorest section of the nation. However before the South could begin to grapple with this difficulty, the Supreme Court ruled in 1954 in one of the most important cases in the judicial history of the USA, *Brown v. Board of Education of Topeka*, that legally enforced segregation was unconstitutional. Separate was inherently unequal. Furthermore, the court was gradually removing the legal authority for many of the transparent devices which were used to exclude African-Americans from the political process. A favoured device was to let blacks register to vote in the general election, but exclude them from the primary elections of the Democratic Party on the grounds that the party was a private organization and consequently could regulate the terms of its membership. However, the Supreme Court recognized the reality of politics in the South and outlawed the use of this procedure and several others. Although the court's decisions were not universally accepted and there was fierce resistance in the South to implementing the judgement on segregation, the cumulative impact of successive rulings was to delegitimize the racial practices of the South.

The Civil Rights Act of 1964 and the Voting Rights Act of 1965 were both enacted after the US Senate voted to impose a limitation on debate. It was the first time since the end of Reconstruction that effective civil rights legislation was passed, because it was the first time that the white South had been politically isolated. The structure, dynamic and coalitional politics of the political process, which had allowed the South to maintain a discordant political culture as well as social, political and legal regimes which were distinctively different, were altered fundamentally in the years after 1945. The change occurred rapidly and it was difficult for the participants and the political actors to realize fully the dimensions of the sea change. The key element was the emergence of a black electorate in the North and with it the representational dynamic of the political system ensured that equation of racial politics was going to be re-configured. In that sense the political process worked but at an astonishingly slow pace. However the passage of the Voting Rights Act resulted in the creation of a large black electorate in the South. The politics of the South, and indeed of the nation, since then has been altered dramatically. There are now several thousand black politicians in elective office. African-American interests are represented at all levels of the political system. Nevertheless race continues to be the central fault line that runs through US society and many of the problems associated remain unaddressed. Full representation has not solved these problems. The Acts of 1964 and 1965 removed legal restrictions and completed the process of democractization but the removal of restrictions has not resolved the racial divide in US society. In some respects the difficulties appear to have worsened. The belief that fair representation of African-Americans was the answer has not been borne out. The political system has not delivered. The reason lies with a political system that sits uneasily with a democratic and majoritarian political culture.

--------------------- *Summary of Section 5.2* ---------------------

- The position of African-Americans in the USA has been the central domestic issue of US politics since the creation of the Republic. The political process has found the issue of race relations extremely difficult to deal with. The only complete breakdown of the political system took place over slavery.

- After the Civil War, African-Americans were effectively excluded from the political process. The elites who controlled the South, before the war, reasserted their control and new forms of legal subordination were introduced. The federal government ignored what was taking place in the South.

- From the end of the First World War, African-Americans began to migrate in vast numbers from the South to the states of the North and the West. This started to alter the dynamics of the politics of race. However, the power of the white South continued to be disproportionate given the institutional structure and practices of US government.

- After 1945, the Civil Rights Movement was able to mobilize a very broad spectrum of public opinion. The response of the governing class in the South alienated the vast majority of opinion outside the South. The political isolation of the South led to the passage of the 1964 Civil Rights Act and the 1965 Voting Rights Act.

- Despite the passage of the two Acts, the issue of race continues to be among the most intractable of domestic problems.

5.3   A democratic crisis

The achievement of universal suffrage in the 1960s was not the completion or even the near completion of the democratic project in the USA. The concern is frequently expressed that the political process does not work and that its democratic credentials are increasingly suspect. Despite universal suffrage, the political process has ceased to be representative; or rather it represents 'special interests', rather than the wider electorate. Access is reserved for the powerful and the wealthy, the average voter has effectively lost the franchise because both politicians and government do not respond to their desires and worries. What kind of democracy has emerged in the USA? These are concerns that have the patina of truth.

The most striking characteristic of policy making during this period has been the apparent inability of the political process to address some of the most pressing problems confronting the USA: a phenomenon known as gridlock. The institutions, for instance, have grappled with the question of the federal budget deficit for well over a decade but the issue continues to be at the centre of political debate without any definitive resolution in sight. Health policy, similarly, has also exercised the electorate for several years. There is all but universal dissatisfaction with the current system of health care. No significant element of opinion and no major interest endorses the health system that has evolved. It has no support and yet significant reform appears very unlikely because any possible reform alienates one or more of the significant participants within the industry.

It is no exaggeration that there has been a collapse of trust in the political system. Opinion polls regularly record the electorate's distaste for the institutions of government, politicians of all parties, and the very activity of politics. There is an extraordinary cynicism about politics which manifests itself in the volatility of the electorate, the decline in voter identification with either of the major parties and a level of voter participation that is the lowest amongst liberal democracies. In the presidential election of 1992, barely 50 per cent of the electorate voted and in the congressional elections of 1994 it hardly reached 40 per cent. The voters who do go to the polls appear to change their minds with a bewildering frequency. Only one President between 1961 and 1995, Ronald Reagan, has served two full terms in office. Virtually every other administration, regardless of party, has ended with the smell of failure. The presidencies of Lyndon Johnson, Gerald Ford, Jimmy Carter, George Bush and, above all, Richard Nixon culminated in defeat or resignation. In 1992, the victory of Bill Clinton was due in large part to a sense that it was time for a change, only for the electorate to establish Republican majorities in both houses of Congress in 1994. The electorate appears to have lost confidence in politics and politicians to represent their values, beliefs or aspirations. They have lost their trust in the key and central mechanism of a democratic political process. The key reasons for this have been the failure of the USA's democratic system to effectively deal with enduring and systematic problems in US society; and the mutation of US democracy from one in which mass opinion and a universal suffrage shaped political outcomes to one in which only the strongest of organized interests can effectively shape policy decisions.

Why is the political system apparently unable to provide coherent policy responses to the most important issues and concerns that confront the electorate? The fundamental reasons for this are historical and systemic, which were established in Section 5.1. The division of power between the three branches of government, the different systems of election and representation each is founded on, and the significant devolution of power to the states help ensure that decision making is protracted, minority voices can be heard and agreement is difficult. This was the way that the US government was supposed to function. However, there have been some new developments over the last three decades that have exacerbated the problem of governance in the USA and made gridlock all the more severe and dissatisfaction with democratic politics more widespread. These developments are: party fragmentation, the hyper-pluralization of the policy process; a shift in power from mass opinion to organized interests; and the exclusion in policy making and electoral contests of the interests of the poor.

The first of these is the continuing decline of the Democratic and Republican parties. Parties have provided a degree of cement in this divided and fragmented political system, even though by the standards of most other liberal democracies, US parties have never possessed similar levels of organizational and programmatic cohesion. They have always been large coalitions of diverse interests and beliefs. During the early decades of the twentieth century, the parties were able to act in concert on a sufficient number of occasions, notably during the New Deal in the 1930s for a substantial legislative programme to be passed. However, since the end of the Second World War there has been a decline in the ability of parties to put together a legislative programme and enact it.

Parties have lost control over the nomination process for presidential and other candidates. The widespread use of primary elections has transferred control over the process from party organizations to the electorate. The key players are no longer party officials but candidates and those who are expert at winning-elections, the political, financial and media consultants as well as' opinion pollsters. Individual candidates construct their own organizations, raise their own finance in order to contest both primary and general election campaigns. Parties in a meaningful sense have been replaced by individual campaign organizations. Politics, in this respect, has been privatized. The consequences of this development for governance are profound. Candidates if elected owe few if any debts or obligations to their parties. Their success is due to their own efforts. Party discipline in the Congress has diminished substantially and is vastly lower than in the legislatures of other Western democracies. More importantly there has been a sharp decline in a shared political identity of a common purpose and set of objectives. The combination has resulted in a Congress that finds it very difficult to pass a substantive legislative programme.

Second, the decline of party has been mirrored by an explosion of interest group activity over the last few decades. The US political system is now characterized by hyper-pluralism and the range of interests, their demands and their ability to influence government, appears to overload or deadlock the political process. To some extent this has occurred because the parties are no longer able to develop and implement coherent legislative programmes. The two major parties as corporate national organizations are not the prime focus for attention. They are no longer that important. Groups now feel that it is necessary for them to operate extensively in Washington at all levels of government to protect their interests and it is the case that the divided system of government does allow them both far greater access and influence than in any other Western democracy. Over 30,000 interests are registered in Washington with a significant number who are important 'players' in the governmental process. In addition the US legislative process has more built-in hurdles which have to be successfully negotiated than in any comparable system with a far larger number of opportunities to obstruct and hinder the development and passage of legislation. Health care illustrates this. Most voters have wanted to put in place a health care system that had universal coverage but where costs were controlled and were roughly in line with other Western countries. It has not been possible to achieve these objectives, because of the vast range of interests involved and because of their individual and collective power to prevent the passage of legislation. Politicians have been unable to impose a settlement. Between the years 1993 and 1995 a Democratic President with a Democratically controlled Congress was unable to do so.

It is notable that the power of interests is primarily exercised in a negative manner. They are more able to prevent reforms rather than sponsor and put into place new and innovative legislation. The balance of power, by and large, favours those interests that are established and have been players in Washington for some considerable time. So while hyper-pluralism does mean that the process is open, accessible and that there are a host of players capable of influencing policy outcomes, it does not mean that the playing field is level. Interests which are well organized, well funded with long established networks and a record to defend are better placed. These include producer groups, professional associations, those who are focused on a single interest (of which abortion is a good example), labour unions, plus a host of associational groups, such as the National Rifle Association (NRA). They work through the Democratic and Republican parties in both Washington and in the electoral districts. Consequently, politicians, of both parties, are very reluctant, for instance, to oppose the NRA. The NRA has a large, active and a strongly motivated membership. It is well funded and organized and able to mobilize supporters. Moreover, it makes substantial financial contributions during elections. The laws regulating the funding of elections in the USA vary, but in all elections money is a critical factor for success. A generous supporter is assiduously cultivated and accordingly no politician alienates the NRA, or comparable interests with equanimity.

Gun control provides another example where the opinion of the electorate has been clear and *consistent*. A considerable majority of Americans over a substantial period of time have been in favour of a degree of regulation over the possession of firearms. Yet no substantial regulatory legislation has been passed, due to the influence of the NRA. Majority opinion is not channelled to have the greatest impact. Nor is it well funded or organized. It simply is politically ineffective. The NRA has been able to frustrate and obstruct proposals for gun control.

By contrast those who are on the periphery of economic life are not as effective in participating in the political system, which heightens their sense of alienation from politics. That part of the population which depends on their income from welfare are the urban dispossessed, of whom a disproportionate percentage are African-Americans and Hispanics. They make up a substantial element of the population, approximately 25 per cent, but are marginalized politically. They vote less frequently and they are not organized with the inevitable result that the political process does not respond to their concerns. It is no coincidence the agenda of US politics in the late 1990s includes welfare reform, a sharp reduction in governmental social expenditure, the ending of affirmative action programmes, etc. All of these issues are ones that work to the disadvantage of the poor and some minority ethnic groups. The entry cost to be an effective participant in the political process is high and a significant percentage of the electorate and their representatives are unable to cross this barrier, which is a profoundly serious problem for a political culture that views itself as the epitome of the democratic tradition.

───────────────── *Summary of Section 5.3* ─────────────────

- All the indicators suggest that US voters are profoundly disenchanted with politicians, government and the very activity of politics.
- The US political system appears to be in a state of gridlock, unable to resolve issues and problems that have been pressing for a very considerable time.
- The vast number of interest groups and their access to the governmental process is responsible, to a considerable extent, for gridlock.
- There is a very considerable disparity in both access and influence. The disparity causes increasing disquiet about the credentials of US democracy.

Conclusion

In the years since the end of the Second World War, US democracy has been transformed by the final and long overdue inclusion of African-Americans within the suffrage. It has also been marked by a collapse in public confidence, as pressure groups have dominated over mass public opinion and policy making has succumbed to inertia and fragmentation. Do these processes suggest that the US experience of democratization has been in some profound sense exceptional or are there useful and meaningful points of comparison between the USA and the European states examined in Chapters 2–4?

The timing of US democratization is certainly different from that of much of Europe. As we have seen, the USA created the first enduring democratic polity in the eighteenth century but it was one that was founded as much on a suspicion of democratic politics as a celebration of its values. It was also the first Western state to move towards a mass politics albeit one reserved for white men. The timing of women's suffrage in 1919 suggests that in this domain at any rate, US experience has been unexceptional. Women gained the suffrage across much of Northern Europe just before or after the First World War. However, the inclusion of African-Americans would have to wait until the 1960s. In this regard, the USA is exceptional both in possessing from its inception such a large non-European population and in excluding any significant part of the adult electorate for so long. (Although in its treatment of Native Americans there are parallels between the USA and Australasian treatment of indigenous peoples.) It is not surprising therefore, that there are very significant and important causal differences which distinguish the democratization in the USA from virtually every other Western liberal democracy. Its sense of identity emerged out of an anti-colonial struggle, but without a social revolution. It did not have the experience of feudalism. There were no lords and peasants, a relative abundance of land, and as a result a sense of class identity which is less than most comparable nations.

These factors help explain the early character of democratization in the USA and the very limited political constituency for authoritarian politics. But the late arrival of universal suffrage requires a different set of explanatory factors. Obviously enough the USA is the only Western state which possessed a significant slave economy and slave population. While other states have had to grapple with the complexities of multinational populations nowhere have they assumed the historical character of the African-American experience in the USA. The record of dehumanization, racism and oppression underscores the fierce resistance of the South to their inclusion in the electorate. But the success of the South in discriminating against African-Americans, despite defeat in the Civil War, relied on the fragmented and localized nature of political power in the USA. While other federal states have existed and divisions of power are common in constitutions, the degree of dispersion and the potential for powerful minorities to maintain a veto on core interests is unparalleled in the USA.

The success of the Civil Rights Movement, while clearly unique in its ethnic dimensions, bears many similarities to processes of democratization outside the USA. Capitalist development has, in nearly all the cases examined so far, empowered subaltern classes or groups by allowing them to escape from old relations of patronage and clientalism and providing them with employment and organizational skills. The movement of African-Americans from the South to the North allowed them to escape the relations of domination that existed in the South and register their political voice in the North. Again, like other excluded groups they were able to force the issue of democratization but victory was only possible when they gained sufficiently powerful allies – in this case Northern liberal Democrats and Western Republicans. Where the experience is perhaps different from many others is that victory turned on questions of legitimacy and ideology. Skilfully deploying the egalitarian and democratic rhetoric of mainstream political culture, the Civil Rights Movement aided by the tactical incompetence of the white South, destroyed the legitimacy of openly racist politics.

Is the fate of US democracy exceptional? It is certainly not easy to be sanguine over the state of US democracy as the twentieth century draws to a close. The problems are both substantial and systemic. Moreover there is no indication that the source of many of these difficulties which derive from an eighteenth century Constitution are going to be modified. Frustration and alienation are evident but the desire for constitutional reform is muted. The electorate makes its disenchantment with politics and politicians evident, but continues to hold the Constitution in high regard. Individuals rather than the constitutional structures are the source of the problem. The Constitution is not going to be amended in the near future. To some extent this view is understandable. The electorate of the USA is not the only one to register frustration. Electorates in several Western democracies have shown that they similarly are dissatisfied. Voters in Italy, and to some extent the United

Kingdom share the sense that politics does not appear to deal with their concerns. The political system does not deliver. Indeed in Italy the problems in many respects appear to be far more severe. So is the USA merely caught up in a democratic malaise that extends far beyond its borders?

The answer in part is yes, because the USA is no longer quite as exceptional as it has conceived of itself. It has to confront a very similar list of concerns to other states. Inflation, unemployment, a decline in manufacturing, urban decay, crime, etc., are all problems which are as intractable in the USA as elsewhere. US political institutions also have to confront the reality that control of the nation-state over global economic forces is difficult and diminishing. What, perhaps, does distinguish the USA are three factors. First, given the paucity of the US welfare system and the fragmented nature of its labour market, the poor are more sharply excluded from political influence than in comparable countries. There is, after all, no significant socialist tradition or political party which might represent those interests. Second, the degree of party fragmentation and the privatization of politics is greater in the USA than in other countries. Third, the depth and density of US civil society, reflected in the hyper-pluralization of US politics is greater than elsewhere. As noted in Chapter 1, democratization can be retarded and democratic politics made problematic either where the state is so powerful that civil society is extinguished or where the state is so weak that meaningful democratic decision making cannot be affected. Most cases of problematic democracy fall into the former category. US exceptionalism may rest on its occupation of the latter.

References

Wofford, H. (1980) *Of Kennedys and Kings*, New York, Strauss and Giroux.

Peters, B. (1993) *American Public Policy* (3rd edn), Chatham, Chatham House.

Mayhew, D. (1991) *Divided We Govern*, New Haven, Yale University Press.

Afterword

David Goldblatt

The tasks of this afterword are: (a) to review the main theoretical approaches used in Part II; (b) to review the main explanatory factors used in Part II; and (c) to examine the types of comparison conducted across the case studies in Part II.

Theoretical approaches

The four chapters in Part II drew on both structural and transitional approaches to democratization. Chapter 2 did so by explicitly building on the account of structural approaches in Chapter 1. It also acknowledged that strategic and tactical decisions taken by the leaders of social movements as well as the agency of millions of people were key components of democratization struggles. Chapters 3, 4 and 5 all combined these two approaches. The shifting balance of class and national forces alongside party structures and the impact of wars formed key components of the arguments in Chapters 3 and 4. Chapter 5 cast the emergence of the Civil Rights Movement against the backdrop of structural shifts in the geography of the African-American labour force in the post-Second World War USA. The ways in which these structural approaches deployed explanatory factors is dealt with in the next section. Here it is worth noting some key elements of structural approaches to democratization.

First, structural theories provide reasons as to why democratization becomes an issue at all. By casting the last two hundred years of political struggle in Europe and the USA against the backdrop of industrialized warfare, capitalist development, diffuse literacy and expanded states it explains why more social groups have been forced to stake a claim on state power and why, in contrast to earlier eras, subaltern classes and nations have found sufficient means to be serious challengers to old regimes. Second, democratization struggles can often be viewed as a conflict between a democratic coalition and an authoritarian coalition of social classes and groups. Structural theories provide the tools to explain why different social classes are members of different alliances; how much political power each member of a coalition can bring to bear; how united or divided those coalitions prove in the heat of battle. Third, structural theories have been used to explain why large-scale social processes, like war or economic crises, can both force the pace of democratization struggles and make their democratic resolution difficult or impossible. Chapter 3 in particular looked at the way in which the structural pressures of hyperinflation, mass unemployment and international economic dislocation present political actors with conflicts and differences of interest that become insoluble within democratic decision-making frameworks.

Transition approaches informed the chapters in different ways. Chapter 3 moved beyond the long processes of historical change described in Chapter 2 that brought about the initial breakthroughs to democracy in Europe and the USA. Its focus, like that of transitional approaches, was the *consolidation* or *habituation* of these democracies in the face of international and national economic and political crises. Chapter 4 drew on transitional approaches in two ways. In relation to Western Europe the focus was again on consolidation, though more successful consolidations than those that followed the First World War. Transitional approaches have argued that consolidation is most likely to be successful where the political extremes in a society are weakened. Thus one of the reasons for the successful consolidation of democracy in West Germany and Italy was the marginalization, ideologically and organizationally, of both the far right and the far left. In relation to Southern Europe, transition theories provided the framework for explaining the successful shift from authoritarianism to liberal democracy. The vocabulary of structural theory could explain why authoritarianism came under such fierce attack and give us a picture of the political balance of forces, but it could not explain how and why the various coalitions involved in the democratic transitions were able to successfully consolidate a liberal democratic polity. Transitional approaches to the role of elite agents, their classification as hardliners, softliners, etc., the importance of bargains and trade-offs over the form of the new regime and the status of the old, and the form of transitional authorities, all proved useful in exploring the Iberian cases.

Chapter 5 on the USA also drew on the vocabulary and perspectives of transitional approaches to explain the precise form and timing of the civil rights legislation of the 1960s. Chapter 5 argues that the victory of the Civil Rights Movement in terms of legitimacy, public support and votes in Congress, turned on short-term tactical decisions by key actors in the struggle. For example, the extent and viciousness of repression in the South was publicly exposed by the tactical blunders of Southern elites and their police forces. Meeting peaceful protest with water canon and dogs in an age of television helped shatter any lingering invisibility or legitimacy for the politics of segregation and exclusion. At that point the silent coalition of Midwestern Republicans and Southern Democrats fragmented making federal legislation on civil rights possible.

Explanatory factors

All four chapters in Part II try and answer their main questions by drawing heavily on the role of *geopolitics and war* and the interconnections between *economic development and structures* and *social divisions* and *alliances*. In all of these cases the explanatory factors are revealed as dual-edged; they can provide explanations of both the successes and failures of democratization. War can both accelerate democratization by destroying old elites and facilitate the rise of authoritarianism by leaving a legacy of economic catastrophe to new democracies. Economic change can increase the size and political weight of pro-democratic classes and economic growth can reconcile old adversaries to a collective negotiated politics. On the other hand, economic development can reinforce the power of anti-democratic classes and economic crises can make democratic consolidation impossible. These dualities are explored below. In addition the importance of *state structures, political institutions* and *political culture* has been highlighted in Part II. Chapter 5, in particular, drew upon these factors, but they have formed an important sub-plot in the narrative of Part II. Once again their impact is variable: demilitarized state structures can facilitate democratization and overbearing militaries can retard it; cultural movements and institutions can form part of democratic or authoritarian coalitions. Below I try and summarize the way in which Part II has used these explanatory factors. A final note: Chapter 5 on the USA argued that the density of US *civil society* relative to the organizing powers of the US state was part of the reason for the hyper-pluralism and political gridlock that characterize contemporary US politics. That apart the concept of *civil society* is rarely used in Part II.

Geo-politics and war. The structural implications of preparation for industrialized warfare and the fighting of total war are central to the narrative and explanation of democratization in Europe and the USA. The demands of fighting more expensive wars meant that states became bigger and more intrusive relative to the societies they ruled. It also meant that they needed to mobilize the active support and co-operation of producers, consumers and mass citizen armies. The first of these demands made popular control over the state more pressing, the second made popular exclusion more difficult to justify. While these structural pressures were building up across the long nineteenth century, they were only fully unleashed by the First World War. The price of victory in that war was to decisively strengthen democratic coalitions and hasten processes of democratization (Britain, the USA in Chapter 2). The cost of defeat was the collapse of authoritarian regimes (Germany in Chapter 2).

However, Chapter 3 demonstrated that the impact of the First World War on democratization was ambiguous. For while the war unleashed a process of continental democratization it also established conditions of economic and social dislocation that contributed to the eclipse of those democracies in the inter-war years (Germany, Italy, Austria, Yugoslavia and Poland in Chapter 3). The consequences of the Second World War appeared initially, even worse. By 1942 German authoritarian military power had apparently triumphed all over mainland Europe. Thus the outcome of the Second World War appears even more decisive in the history of European democratization than that of the First World War. It required both total defeat and armed occupation of the Axis powers for the impact of the war to turn decisively in favour of democratization in Western and Northern Europe. The end of the Second World War did not mean that military imperatives and power ceased to impact upon processes of democratization. Chapter 4 argued that the impact of the Cold War on democratization was broadly positive in Western Europe and negative in Southern Europe. Chapter 5 argued that the rhetoric of the Cold War and growing African-American participation in the US army helped delegitimize the exclusion of African-Americans from the suffrage.

Economic development and social divisions. For the most part these two factors are conceptually tied to each other in Part II. Chapter 2 argued that the character of economic development in Europe and the USA is best thought of as a process of capitalist industrialization. The social classes, groups and divisions generated by capitalist industrialization are central to democratization struggles. A struggle between authoritarian and democratic coalitions lies at the heart of all processes of democratization. The nature of economic development helps explain the relative size, potential strength and democratic alignment of different social classes within those coalitions. Capitalist industrialization tends to diminish the economic power of aristocracies, increase the power of the bourgeoisie and in its later stages creates a substantial white collar middle class. It tends to eradicate and marginalize peasants, expand and solidify the urban working classes and can either squeeze small independent farmers or leave space for their economic survival.

Aristocracies have been anti-democratic and will if reliant on coercive labour and state employment be very anti-democratic, commercialized aristocracies may be more pliable. Business, bourgeoisie and middle classes have been enthusiastic supporters of their own inclusion and the creation of parliamentary governments but on restricted franchises. The key component of democratic coalitions since the American Revolution have been working-class movements. The lateness of capitalist industrialization in Southern Europe and the correspondingly small size of the Iberian working classes is an important reason for the lateness of successful democratic revolutions there. The capacity of the organized working class to attract allies from amongst small farmers, and regional and linguistic minorities has been a key factor in explaining the success or failure of those coalitions. Across Chapters 2–5 the specific character of national economic change, linguistic and regional cleavages can be combined with these broad propositions about social divisions and democratic politics to generate explanations for why different states democratized successfully or not at different times.

Part II has also suggested that the term economic development may be too neutral to describe the full range of impacts that economic affairs can have on democratization. Development can appear to suggest a smooth process of uninterrupted reliable change. However, the economic circumstances of Europe and the USA have been uneven alternating between long periods of growth, change and expansion punctuated by phases of economic recession, stagnation and crisis. Chapter 3 in particular argued that the long-term structural effects of economic change cannot be understood separately from contingent economic conditions. Hyperinflation is a profoundly problematic experience for any liberal democracy and particularly so where the legitimacy of the governing institutions is fragile. The costs of imposing currency stabilization are invariably large and harsh and difficult to agree upon. Similarly, the difficulty of conducting a politics of negotiated consensus is made more difficult under conditions of fiscal crisis where state expenditures must be cut or taxes raised significantly or both (see Germany in Chapter 2, the USA in Chapter 5). Mass unemployment and economic recession do much the same. By contrast, in the post-war era at any rate, long periods of sustained economic growth allied to welfare expenditure have provided fertile ground for democratic politics in states that had previously proved infertile. However, the Spanish experience of the 1960s and 1970s suggests that there are limits to the emollient effect of economic growth on authoritarian states.

States structures and political institutions. If the first three explanatory factors helped explain who has been supportive of democratization, who its opponents have been and how their capacity to organize and mobilize political power has changed, they do not tell us how those interests have been politically organized. No social or economic force can effectively shape struggles over the character of state power without means of organization, communication, propaganda, public and electoral mobilization. Similarly no *ancien regime* can resist such pressures without political control over state institutions, political networks and military resources. Some types of state and some types of political party have favoured democratization struggles and some have hindered them. For example, in Chapters 2 and 5 the role of the independent judiciary and the impact of a federal system of government are important components of explaining the lateness of American democratization. In Britain the predominantly naval character of the British military is part of the explanation as to why authoritarian options were so rarely pursued in Britain. The politicization of the military behind authoritarian political and social projects provided an important component of the explanation for the defeat of democratic transitions (Spain and Germany in Chapter 3) and the endurance of authoritarian regimes (Spain and Portugal in Chapter 4). The role of encompassing parties of the right and long-established parliaments in surviving inter-war democracies was explored in Chapters 3 and 4. In the inter-war years the absence of strong parties of the right that could coherently represent powerful economic interests in a parliamentary arena substantially contributed to the rise of authoritarian movements who appeared to secure those interests more effectively. After the Second World War the emergence of popular Christian Democratic parties in Italy and Germany with external support helped consolidate the democratic transitions.

Political culture and ideas. The role of cultural power appeared in Part II in a number of guises. First, the chapters touched upon Christianity both as a body of belief and practice and as a set of cultural and political institutions. The record is ambiguous. On the one hand, negative: the role of the church in opposing women's suffrage (Chapter 2); its support for authoritarian regimes and counter-revolutions (Spain and Portugal in Chapter 4); denomination as a point of fatal cleavage within democratic coalitions (Germany in Chapters 2 and 3). On the other hand, the Christian Church has played some part in democratizing the right (Christian Democrats in Germany and Italy, Chapter 4). In the South of the USA churches provided the core institutions, resources and personnel of the Civil Rights Movement (Chapter 5). The impact of literacy and the means of communication and culture are also examined as factors in democratization struggles. Chapter 2 pointed to the importance of widespread literacy in enabling subaltern classes to organize and the subaltern nations of the old European empires to articulate their history and national political agendas. Chapter 3 demonstrated how these forces could, once mobilized be captured by an authoritarian and exclusivist nationalism (Italy, Germany and Yugoslavia in Chapter 3). By contrast, in Chapter 5, the appallingly low literacy rates of African-Americans in the South of the USA provided the perfect instrument for denying them the vote.

Comparisons within Part II

Chapter 2 argued that there are common factors of social and economic change across all Western countries that place democratization on the agenda and set up a struggle over state power between the excluded and the dominant social groups; bigger, more intrusive states; better organized, literate, subaltern classes. There are also common international factors like wars and economic cycles that transnationally effect processes of democratization. But explaining the success and failure of those struggles and the consolidation or retrenchment of democracies created by them requires us to understand how those common factors have been filtered and received by national and regional economic and political structures. Chapter 2 focuses on their interrelationship with the First World War, Chapter 3 with the First World War and the international economic depression of the 1930s, Chapter 4 with the Second World War and the Cold War.

Against this backdrop of shared historical experiences, the main mode of comparison between states in Part II has been to contrast those states that experienced early and successful industrialization and democratization with those states that industrialized later and underwent democratization late or unsuccessfully. In the former group, with various reservations, fall France, Britain and the USA with Germany and Italy in the latter. Spain and Portugal as even later industrializers and successful democratizers provide a further point of comparison. Three problems immediately arise from these simple comparisons. First, the correlation of industrialization and democratization suggested by these comparisons fails to account for early democratizers, but late industrializers like Switzerland, Denmark and New Zealand. Therefore, more detailed and specific comparisons are required. Second, there is failure to account for the lack of success in early breakthroughs to democracy, the rise of authoritarianism, the success or consolidation of later democratic revolutions or the passage and timing of female suffrage. Third this mode of comparison, looking to match the presence of explanatory factors with the advent or success of democratization, needs to be complemented by strategies of comparison which look for absences and failures. Female suffrage is touched upon in Chapter 2 and a negative mode of comparison – searching for differences rather than similarities – is used in Chapter 3.

The use of more detailed and specific use of explanatory factors as an instrument of comparison runs throughout Part II. Three examples suggest the diversity and utility of these comparisons. First, comparisons of Britain and the USA with Spain and Germany suggest that moderate and fragmented labour movements are more likely to achieve successful democratization than radicalized and revolutionary labour movements. Comparison of Spain in the 1970s with Germany after the First World War suggests that democratic consolidation can be successful where moderates and softliners dominate politics and is jeopardized where radicals and the far right are strong. Comparison of inter-war Britain and Germany suggests that the far right is strong where more mainstream liberal and conservative parties are weak and fragmented. There are of course many more comparisons both within Part II and, as you will see, between Part II and the rest of this book.

PART III
Latin America and Asia

Introduction   145

CHAPTER 6   Democracy and dictatorship in Latin   152
              America, 1930–80

CHAPTER 7   Democratization in Latin America,   174
              1980–95

CHAPTER 8   Why have the political trajectories of   195
              India and China been different?

CHAPTER 9   Democratization at the same time in   219
              South Korea and Taiwan

CHAPTER 10   Why has democratization been a   240
              weaker impulse in Indonesia and
              Malaysia than in the Philippines?

Afterword   264

Introduction

David Potter

This part moves from Europe and the USA to Latin America and Asia. In doing so, it draws again on the explanatory framework set out in Chapter 1 to explain democratization patterns. Latin American countries come first because they were the first of the 'new nations' (after the USA) to break free from European colonial rule. Asian countries began seriously to disengage from imperial or colonial controls only in the mid twentieth century, following the Second World War in Asia (1941–45).

Maps of Latin America in the Introductions to Chapters 6 and 7 in this part show that the region includes the countries of South and Central America. Most of these countries shared, to some extent at least, a cultural heritage in the sense that they experienced Iberian colonial rule (Brazil was Portuguese, the rest were Spanish) and moved to independence by 1830 under Creole, culturally Spanish or Portuguese, elites. Indigenous Indian peoples and black slave populations played almost no part in the political activity of what were largely Iberian settler colonies. This common Spanish heritage (Brazil is the main exception) is still important, not least in the common literary language of the region; but it has been substantially modified over the years due to racial mixing and immigrants from other European nationalities moving in. Such processes have affected the composition of political elites and of society more generally in the twentieth century. Nevertheless, one can still refer to Latin America as a region with a fairly distinct identity.

During the nineteenth and early twentieth centuries, Latin America was marked by political turmoil. Independence from Spain was rather abruptly seized by elites throughout most of the subcontinent in the 1820s, and this was followed by civil wars or wars between these new nations whose boundaries were at first ill-defined. Armies were prominent in the political histories of these countries, and civilian political institutions only gradually began to be established. Such conflicts also made it impossible initially to form a confederation of Latin American states similar to what had formed in the United States in North America. Nevertheless, during the nineteenth century competitive and representative political institutions began to figure in the political life of some Latin American countries, notably Chile, Uruguay, Argentina and Costa Rica. These were very partial democracies in which competition and representation were confined to a narrow elite; only later was room gradually made for at least some mass political participation. But such limited elitist democratization in the nineteenth and early twentieth centuries, partial as it was, distinguished Latin America from Asia and Africa. Democratization may have been placed on Latin America's political agenda, but one should not overestimate its significance. Broadly speaking, between 1830 and the mid twentieth century much of Latin America was more or less under some form of authoritarian rule, military or civilian. The establishment of liberal democracy in Costa Rica (1948) and Venezuela (1958) was exceptional.

Bearing this historical context in mind, Chapters 6 and 7 in this part concentrate on the most striking features of the democratization story in Latin America in the twentieth century. Chapter 6, covering the period 1930–80, asks: why was there no clear trend towards liberal democracy in Latin America before 1980? And why did the most promising democratic opening of the early 1960s collapse in the 1970s into the most authoritarian period the region had ever known? These questions are approached in terms of structural and transition theories. Major attention is therefore given to the structures of class relations and their political consequences in particular countries, and to the character of both the global economy and international relations between states and their specific regional dynamics at particular times in history. Within this structural context, differences between Latin American countries are explained by the different transition processes through which conflicts were fought out and choices made by the men and women involved.

Chapter 7, covering the period 1980–95, concentrates on an equally striking development: why, in the 1980s and early 1990s, did Latin America suddenly swing politically towards more sustained democratic transitions, such that by 1995 liberal democracy had become the norm rather than the exception? In addressing this question, a broadly transition approach is found useful. In consequence, the chapter examines the behaviour of softliner and moderate elites (see Chapter 1 on transition theories); questions are asked as to whether these elites were broadly agreed on future policy and how they handled radicals and hardliners (including the military). Certain contextual factors affecting the success of these elite transitions are also considered, including (a) the maintenance of political order and institutional unity by the authoritarian regime, together with (b) successful economic performance undermining authoritarian legitimacy, and (c) pro-democracy international pressures.

The two chapter titles suggest a rigid separation before and after the year 1980, but there is inevitably some overlap between the two chapters. Also, the comparative analyses in these two chapters are grounded mostly in the fourteen major Latin American countries shown in Figure III.1, which indicates the swing towards democratization throughout the region between 1975 and 1995.

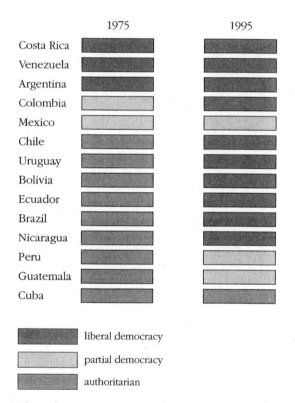

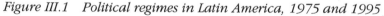

Figure III.1   Political regimes in Latin America, 1975 and 1995

Asia, unlike Latin America, is not really a region at all, for there is virtually no way to delimit it clearly in terms of geography, history or culture. The point is underlined by the existence of many very different Asian languages written in different scripts and the juxtaposition of diverse and profoundly different religious traditions in different Asian countries. Also, unlike Latin America, Asian countries did not share a common colonial history prior to independence. The British were in India, Ceylon, Burma, Malaya and Hong Kong; the Dutch in the Netherlands East Indies; the French in French Indo-China; the Portuguese in Goa, Portuguese Timor and Macau; the Americans in the Philippines; the Japanese in Korea and Formosa; and there were also non-

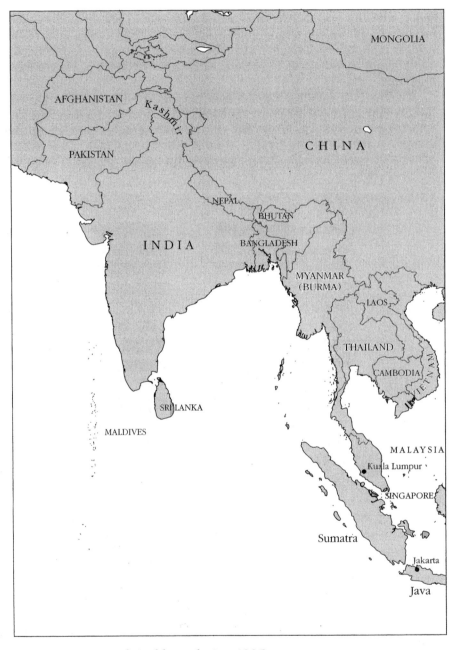

Map III.1   Asia: political boundaries, 1995

colonial forms of authoritarian rule, e.g. one party bureaucratic rule (with some foreign powers also influential) in China, fascism in Japan, royal absolutism in Thailand and Nepal. The political trajectories of these countries in the latter part of the twentieth century have also been extremely varied. There may be no single Asian entity but there are 25 different countries shown

on the map which are conventionally identified as Asian by scholars, and this part of the book talks about some of these countries.

Liberal democracy has not flourished in Asia either. There was virtually no such polity anywhere until after the Second World War in Asia. From 1945 to the 1980s democratization struggled or was thwarted throughout Asia. A few countries became liberal democracies and remained so; others went communist, blocking democratization; others, buttressed by support from the USA and other capitalist countries, made initial moves towards liberal democracy, then succumbed to military intervention and authoritarian rule; yet others just remained authoritarian. From the mid 1980s to the mid 1990s, however, 'the third wave' of democratization began to register in Asia, although not to the same extent as in Latin America. This is indicated by the comparative classifications for 25 Asian countries in Figure III.2.

	1975	1995
Japan		
Papua New Guinea		
Sri Lanka		
Singapore		
Malaysia		
Thailand		
India		
Pakistan		
Bangladesh		
South Korea		
Mongolia		
Philippines		
Taiwan		
Nepal		
China		
North Korea		
Vietnam		
Indonesia		
Burma/Myanmar		
Afghanistan		
Maldives		
Bhutan		
Brunei		
Kampuchea/Cambodia		
Laos		

liberal democracy

partial democracy

authoritarian

Figure III.2   Political regimes in Asia, 1975 and 1995

Chapters 8, 9 and 10 examine aspects of these diverse political patterns by engaging in case-oriented historical comparisons of seven Asian countries from 1945 to the mid 1990s: India – sustained liberal democracy more or less; China – sustained communist authoritarian rule; Malaysia – sustained partial democracy more or less; South Korea and Taiwan – moved from capitalist authoritarianism to democratization; Indonesia – moved from partial democratization to capitalist authoritarianism; the Philippines – moved from partial democratization to capitalist authoritarianism to democratization.

Chapter 8 asks: why have the political trajectories of the two 'giants' of Asia, India and China, been so different? The question is approached in terms of aspects of recent modernization and structural approaches. The author compares these two countries in terms of political culture, the character of civil society, political institutions (especially the political party system), and experience of transnational imperial or colonial powers.

The main question for Chapter 9 is: why did two of the economic 'tigers' in Asia, South Korea and Taiwan, commence sustained democratization at the same time in the late 1980s? The comparative analysis is framed by structural and transition theories. Particular prominence is given to similar changes in class structures resulting from rapid economic development, similar changes in state power, and similar changes experienced by both countries in relation to transnational/geo-political power; and it is argued that these structural factors shaped the choices and actions of the political elites involved in driving these democratic transitions.

Chapter 10 asks: why has democratization been a stronger impulse in the Philippines and Malaysia, a weaker impulse in Indonesia? The analysis is framed more or less by aspects of all three theoretical approaches. Use is accordingly made of a wide range of explanatory factors, including different structures of state and class power, different ethnic and religious and national identities, different patterns of economic change, different ideas about democracy, the contradictory influence of international factors, and the degree to which the political system is generally accepted as legitimate by its citizens.

So, each chapter in Part III is quite distinctive in terms of the questions asked, the theoretical approach taken, the array of explanatory factors used, and the particular countries compared. As you move through the chapters you will gradually begin to notice some general themes that cut across them. Some of these will be drawn to your attention at the end of this part in the Afterword.

CHAPTER 6

Democracy and dictatorship in Latin America, 1930–80

Paul Cammack

Introduction

Latin America presents the student of comparative politics with a puzzle. As late as the mid 1970s, by which time the great majority of states in the region had experienced around 150 years of political independence, it appeared that there was no clear trend among them towards liberal democratic government. Most were under military or dictatorial rule, or under civilian regimes which placed severe limits on political competition. Cases such as Costa Rica and Venezuela, where stable and genuinely competitive liberal democracy could be found, were highly exceptional, and even there its establishment was recent (dating from 1948 and 1958 respectively). The political map of Latin America (Map 6.1) indicates the position in 1975 (when Argentina was briefly and unusually between dictatorships).

Against this background the puzzle is that a general process of democratization took off in the late 1970s, and by the mid 1990s liberal democracy had become the norm rather than the exception: every military regime in mainland Central and South America had disappeared, and partially or fully democratic systems dominated the region. In this and the following chapter we reflect upon this record. In view of the transformation of the region since 1979–80 this chapter focuses on liberal democracy's mixed fortunes over the first eight decades of the twentieth century (primarily from 1930), while the next takes up the story of recent democratization. Why was there no clear trend towards liberal democracy before 1980? And why did the apparently promising democratic opening of the early 1960s fail, leading to the worst and in comparative terms the most distinctive period of dictatorship the region had ever known?

6.1   Competing approaches

The modernization approach does not help to explain either the spread of dictatorship from the 1960s onwards, or the burst of democratization that followed. The countries which experienced the longest and most repressive dictatorships were among the most developed in the region, with the largest and most politically active middle classes; among them, Chile and Uruguay in particular had the longest previous experience of unbroken liberal democracy in the region. What is more, the wave of democratization, when it came, affected not only these relatively wealthy and developed countries, but also the poorest and least developed – Ecuador, Peru and Bolivia were among the earliest to experience democratization. Not surprisingly,

Map 6.1   Political map of Latin America, 1975

modernization theories have not been influential in recent studies on Latin America.

In the substantial literature produced on the region since the mid 1960s emphasis has shifted from the structural approach to the transition approach. The approaches dominant in the 1960s, largely influenced by the *dependency* perspective, tended to place the emphasis on the structural context in which politics took place. In the dependency perspective, the economies and societies of Latin America were seen as dependent upon the advanced capitalist states of Western Europe and the USA for capital, markets, technology and sophisticated industrial goods, and therefore unable to complete the process of modernization. A large part of the analysis that resulted focused not so much on international economic relationships as on the consequences of dependency for the class structure of Latin American societies, and its negative implications for progressive political change. In terms which tie in with Barrington Moore's approach (summarized in Chapters 1 and 2), writers stressed the limited development of commercial agriculture, the strength of landed elites and their ability to control or resist the state, the tendency for the weaker urban bourgeoisie to side with the landed elites against workers and peasants, and the resulting difficulty of effecting any revolutionary break with the past. They argued that these internal obstacles to change were reinforced by the direct support Latin American elites received from foreign capital and Western governments, and they were generally pessimistic about the prospects for liberal democracy.

In recent years emphasis has shifted from structural obstacles to political process and the possibilities for transition to democracy, with renewed interest shown in leadership and choice, and the potential for political creativity to overcome structural constraints. Faith in alternatives to liberal democracy has waned, and analysts within and outside the region are much more likely to express a preference for liberal democracy than either a commitment to revolutionary transformation or a lingering belief in the need for authoritarian rule.

This change of perspective was announced by Linz and Stepan at the end of the 1970s. Their four-volume collection on *The Breakdown of Democratic Regimes* sought 'to analyze the behaviour of those committed to democracy, especially the behaviour of the incumbent democratic leaders, and to ask in what ways the actions of the incumbents contributed to the breakdown under analysis' (Linz and Stepan, 1978, p.ix). At the same time, it looked to the future, calling for further analysis of 'the conditions that lead to the breakdown of authoritarian regimes, to the process of transition from authoritarian to democratic regimes, and especially to the political dynamics of the consolidation of post-authoritarian democracies' (ibid., p.xii). Thus examination of the processes by which democracies broke down led directly to reflection upon the means by which they could be reconstructed, and to a focus upon the *procedural* and *institutional* requirements for redemocratization.

Linz acknowledged the importance of structural factors, but treated them as 'a series of opportunities and constraints for the social and political actors, both men and institutions, that can lead to one or another outcome', and started from 'the assumption that those actors have certain choices that can increase or decrease the probability of the persistence and stability of a regime' (Linz, 1978, p.4). Within this framework, he stressed the importance of leadership, and the need for leaders to value and defend democracy for itself. In this spirit, Stepan's account of the breakdown of democracy in Brazil in 1964 stressed errors of judgement and wrong choices made by the ousted President Goulart, while parallel accounts of the restoration of democracy in Colombia and Venezuela in the late 1950s emphasized pacts made between elite political actors in order to limit the extent of political competition and control its effects. This approach was a direct challenge to the structural determinism of earlier work, and it marks a significant turning point. However, it did not reject structural approaches altogether, but sought to shift the *balance* of explanation towards institutional and procedural issues, and leadership and choice.

It is indeed vital to retain the insights the structural approach provides. Along with the attention it directs to class relations and their political consequences in particular countries, it points to the significance of the international political and economic conjuncture: the state of the global political economy (in other words, the state of the global economy, and the character of international relations between states), and its specific regional dynamics, at a particular moment in time. As we shall see, a large part of the explanation for the changing political fortunes of Latin America over the last 40 years lies in the contrasting circumstances, both global and domestic, of the 1960s and the 1980s.

Within this structural context, however, the processes through which conflicts were fought out and choices were made varied widely from country to country, and had their own political and institutional logic. They cannot be explained by reference to structures alone, because they were in the end the outcomes of political agency – the actions of men and women engaged in purposive political activity. For this reason, the emphasis on political process and choice in the transition approach is helpful. At the same time, in accepting that structural context does not explain everything, it is important to avoid falling into the trap of leaping straight from 'structure' as an explanation at one extreme to 'choice' at the other. We ought instead to consider how we might bridge the gap between structural constraint and choice.

Attention in this chapter to two 'intervening variables' – the *interests* which political actors represent, and the *political projects* (programmes for the achievement of power and the orientation of government) they adopt in order to pursue them – will bring out the reciprocal relationship between structure and choice, and make the nature of the connections clear. After all, political actors seek to advance particular interests. They do so by promoting political projects which identify and seek to overcome the obstacles to advancing those interests. Their choices reflect the interests they seek to further and the projects that emerge from their understanding of the structural constraints on political action. Without attention to the goals particular political leaders or groups were seeking to pursue, and the assessment they made of the structural context in which they were operating – in terms of national and global structures of political and economic power – we cannot understand why particular choices were made, and why, for example, liberal democracy was more or less favoured by one group or another, or from one period to another. Attention to choices is not an alternative to attention to constraints, as each can only be understood in terms of the other.

Throughout the period considered here, severe structural constraints provided political actors of all kinds with immense challenges. If they provoked widespread political instability, they also prompted substantial political creativity, as innovatory political regimes were devised and introduced in order to respond to the challenges faced. The introduction into the picture of interests and political projects makes it possible to understand the different political options observed in Latin America in the period as competing responses to broadly common structural challenges. All the contending forces were seeking to advance particular interests, and to win support for versions of the 'national interest' which favoured some groups and worked to the disadvantage of others. As a result, they were often seriously at odds with each other, locked into exactly the kinds of fundamental conflicts which Rustow (see Chapter 1) identifies as intrinsic to politics, and only with difficulty resolved through the creation of democratic institutions. In addition, even those who shared similar goals often took different views of the circumstances in which they found themselves – the conjuncture, as I described it above – with the result that they could often differ over the best way to achieve those goals. In pursuing the question of how much structural factors can explain we need to be aware of the space between structure and choice, for it is in this space – the realm of interests and resulting political projects – that politics takes place.

—————————————— *Summary of Section 6.1* ——————————————

- The recent history of Latin America is not easily understood in terms of the modernization approach.
- Structural accounts were dominant in the 1960s, but have since been displaced by a focus on transition and political process.
- Attention to structure remains an essential starting point.
- A focus on interests and political projects clarifies the connections between 'structure' and 'choice'.

6.2   The fragility of liberal democracy: 1930–80

Liberal democracy has not prospered in twentieth-century Latin America. The region has an understandable reputation for high levels of instability, marked by frequent episodes of social revolution, military intervention and dictatorship. The first of the world's great twentieth-century revolutions began in Mexico in 1910, leading to the overthrow of the dictator Porfirio Diaz and a decade of intense armed conflict; revolutionary tin miners overthrew the old regime of Mamerto Urriolagoitia in Bolivia in 1952; Fidel Castro and his band of guerrilla fighters came to power in Cuba at the beginning of 1959, after chasing the corrupt dictator Fulgencio Batista from power in the unlikeliest of campaigns; and between 1979 and 1990 the FSLN (Sandinista National Liberation Front) in Nicaragua sought to build socialism on the ruins left by the dictatorship of Anastasio Somoza.

Striking as this record is, it has been overshadowed by an even more persistent pattern of military intervention and dictatorship. The Venezuelan Gomez, installed in power just before the fall of Porfirio Diaz, survived until 1935; Cuba's Batista was only one, and by no means the-worst, of the many dictators who dominated politics in much of Central America and the Caribbean in the first half of the century; and Anastasio Somoza himself was preceded in power by his father (also Anastasio) and his elder brother Luis in over 40 years of family rule. Paraguay's Alfredo Stroessner, the last of the old-style dictators, held out until 1989.

As the century advanced, however, military intervention and rule tended to displace personal dictatorship and revolution as the most significant challenge to liberal democracy. The military intervened in Chile and Ecuador in the 1920s, and in Argentina, Brazil and Peru in 1930 alone. From that point on intervention became a common occurrence in the region. Between 1930 and 1960 periods of military intervention tended to be short, generally giving rise to new civilian regimes, but during the 1960s a widespread phenomenon of long-term military rule emerged. Such long-term military rule is a recent development in Latin America, not a mere hangover from earlier traditions.

In 1964 General Humberto Castelo Branco seized power in Brazil, giving rise to 21 years of military rule under successive military presidents. Two years later the military seized power in Argentina, and retained power for fourteen of the next seventeen years. Enduring military dictatorships were then installed in Peru (1968), Ecuador (1971) and Bolivia (1971). In 1973 the generals seized power in Uruguay, and in the same year General Augusto Pinochet seized power in Chile, putting himself at the head of a regime which would stay in power until 1990.

Against this background, the record of liberal democracy in the region has been poor. Mexico emerged from the revolutionary period with a stable civilian regime, but it must be classified as a partial democracy since the governing party (founded in 1929 and known from 1946 as the PRI – the Institutionalized Party of the Revolution) never allowed the free and fair competition which could enable the opposition access to power. Both Chile and Uruguay sustained increasingly unstable liberal democracies between the 1930s and 1973, and civilians ruled in Brazil between 1945 and 1964, although the military intervened three times – in 1954, 1955 and 1961 – to attempt to influence the course of politics. Colombia's competitive civilian regime – dominated by the contending Liberal and Conservative parties – collapsed into violent civil war in the 1940s, and military intervention in 1953. It was restored four years later in conditions of such restricted political competition that it too was at best a partial democracy. Against this background the two outstanding successes – Costa Rica and Venezuela – are all the more surprising in that each emerged from unpromising circumstances. Costa Rica's enduring democracy emerged in 1948 out of a civil war, while Venezuela had previously known only three years of civilian rule (1945–48), themselves inaugurated and ended by military intervention, before setting up what proved to be a stable and competitive liberal democracy in 1958.

At first sight, the complexity of the politics of the region in the period between 1930 and 1979 (summarized in Figure 6.1) is bewildering, as this brief summary may suggest. However, some preliminary points can be made before we enter into a detailed discussion.

First, the fragility of democracy in the middle decades of the twentieth century does not simply represent a continuation of an unbroken record of instability and authoritarian rule in the region since independence. Despite the instability that affected most of the region in the first decades after independence (secured by 1830, if not before, in mainland Central and South America), the last quarter of the nineteenth century saw a boom in economic development based on mineral, agricultural and pastoral exports, and the

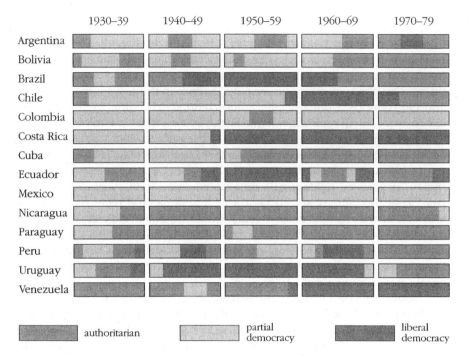

Figure 6.1   Political regimes in Latin America, 1930–79

beginnings of what seemed to be a process of transition to stable civilian and increasingly competitive political regimes. In the early years of this century limited parliamentary regimes were commonplace, dictatorships such as those of Mexico and Venezuela were if anything exceptional, and significant extensions of the franchise were taking place in such countries as Argentina, Chile and Uruguay. Across the region, leaders looked upon civilian rule, and liberal democracy as it was beginning to emerge in Europe and the USA, as the appropriate form of government for well-established and independent states. Both in terms of actual political practice and of prevailing political values, it seemed that the region's future lay increasingly in the direction of democratization.

Second, there is such a degree of variety in the experience of the countries of the region that no simple explanation can cover all the cases to be observed. It is necessary, therefore, to be mindful of the limits of comparative analysis – in suggesting possible broad patterns and generalizations – and to give due weight to the specific historical experience of each country. Comparative analysis should aim to illuminate the variety – the exceptional cases such as Costa Rica, with its sustained democracy, and Mexico, with its sustained single-party civilian rule – as much as the uniformity that appears elsewhere.

Third, specific regional factors have shaped and defined the general structural context in which Latin American politics has taken place since 1930: reaction against export-oriented development; the search for developmentalist alternatives; and willingness to experiment with novel and innovatory political regime forms. These were in turn regional forms of three broader structural features of the period: the transition to a genuinely global capitalist economy; the ascendancy during that protracted transition of commitments to active state intervention; and the limited appeal of liberal democracy in comparison with other available forms of politics. These global and regional factors defined the context in which Latin American politics took place. The transition to a genuinely global capitalist economy was experienced through the shift from British to US ascendancy, and the shift of foreign capital from primary export production to manufacturing (from the 1950s) and then to finance (from the 1970s). State intervention first sought to respond to the immediate crisis caused by the collapse of export markets in 1929–30, then moved towards the promotion of alternative models of development along with the reorganization of social and political participation; and in the absence of any strong global consensus on the virtues of liberal democracy, state corporatist, revolutionary socialist, and authoritarian political options exerted a powerful appeal. In the period as a whole, the late 1940s marked a significant turning point, as it saw the inauguration of the Cold War, and the reinterpretation of conflicts around alternative paths of development in terms of a supposed global conflict between capitalism and communism.

Fourth, the modern period is fundamentally shaped by two cycles of instability and dictatorship – the first around 1930 and the second from the mid 1960s to the mid 1970s. The first betrayed the hopes that late-nineteenth and early-twentieth century development might lead to the emergence of a family of stable democracies in the Americas. The second, accompanied by repression and official terror on a quite horrific and unprecedented scale, was the most tragic episode in the history of the region. It was all the more shocking because it was preceded by a brief wave of optimism regarding the prospects for democracy – ironically, it had briefly seemed in the late 1950s and early 1960s that in South America at least the prospects for democracy were improving fast. This widespread descent into repressive dictatorship from the mid 1960s onwards, with the installation of long-lasting military regimes in the most developed countries of the region, was quite unexpected, and still poses a challenge to the comparative analyst.

In sum, then, the twentieth century pattern has been one of the persistent influence and early promise of liberal democracy as a model, the marked variety of experiences from country to country, the shifting character of the regional political economy, and the broadly cyclical movement between democracy and authoritarian dictatorship. Its central feature is not slow and steady progress towards democracy, but the more pronounced character of the cycle since the 1960s, with the descent into long-term military rule. The current revival of democracy, the strongest the region has ever experienced, was preceded by the worst period of dictatorship it had known. Equally, the descent into dictatorship from the 1960s represented, in comparative historical terms, the period of sharpest contrast to the pattern of politics elsewhere.

This highlights a crucial point in relation to Latin America's experience of democratic politics. The highly elitist oligarchic republics of the early twentieth century were not so dissimilar to their counterparts in much of Western Europe, and both the general breakdown of these regimes in the 1930s (see Chapter 3) and the restoration of democracy after the Second World War ran parallel in some respects to the European experience. It is only

in the recent period that there has been such an extreme divergence between
Europe and Latin America. While we may look further into the past for the
reasons, it is the post-war record, dominated by the descent into protracted
dictatorship, which most requires explanation.

In order to analyse these issues further, the following sections examine
the changing character of structural constraints and political responses in
three successive periods: following the Depression and the end of export-
oriented development in 1929–30, following the end of the Second World
War in 1945, and after the Cuban Revolution in 1959 and the intensification of
Cold War conflict in the region.

Summary of Section 6.2

- In the early twentieth century constitutional civilian rule was
  widespread, and the prospects for democratization seemed fair.

- Constitutional rule became increasingly unstable after the First World
  War, and was plunged into crisis after 1930.

- In a minority of cases (Mexico, 1911; Bolivia, 1952; Cuba, 1959;
  Nicaragua, 1979) personal dictatorship or oligarchic rule gave way to
  social revolution.

- After 1930, intervention by the military became the main threat to
  democracy.

- After 1960, military intervention spread to the largest and most
  developed countries in the region, and led to long-term military rule.

6.3   Politics in the wake of the economic Depression

In the five decades before the crash of 1929, export-oriented development
transformed Latin America, generating political stability and considerable
wealth. In this period growing foreign demand for Latin American products
and new techniques of production and transport gave rise to transformed
economies based upon the export of primary commodities. In turn, the
income generated by rising exports paid for manufactured goods from
Europe and the USA, while governments across the region enjoyed new flows
of revenue derived from taxes on rapidly increasing foreign trade. It was in
this period that Latin American states became identified around the world
with the particular commodities in which they specialized: coffee for Brazil
and Colombia, sugar for Cuba, tin for Bolivia, copper for Chile and Peru, beef
and wheat for Argentina, and coffee again, rather than bananas (despite the
term 'banana republic') for most of Central America.

Despite the palpable sense of progress, the new ascendancy of elite-
dominated civilian regimes, and the emergence of competitive party politics
in this period, these developments proved to be a weak foundation for liberal
democracy. Throughout the region, the regimes which emerged were closely
identified with the export-oriented economies they ran, and the economic
interests at the centre of them. Export-oriented development tended to
strengthen landed and mine-owning elites, providing them with significant
influence or direct control over the state. In the countryside, peasants often

found themselves tied to the land in quasi-feudal tenancy arrangements or forms of debt slavery. In the towns, rapid development revolved around the interests of the export sector; there was little industrialization; workers were politically isolated; and when urban middle classes appeared and began to play a role in politics, they were generally themselves directly dependent upon the export economy and the elites who controlled it. Where party politics began to engage the attention of the urban population, as in Argentina, Chile and Uruguay, it was generally on the basis of export-dependent patronage and political machines which were funded by the surplus resources extracted from export industries. In short, Barrington Moore's conditions for democratic development (Chapter 1, Box 1.3) were not met: no vigorous new bourgeoisie emerged, the state barely escaped the control of the landed upper class, there was no general development of commercial agriculture to free the peasantry from landlord control, and no revolutionary break from the past took place. Factors not considered by Moore may also be relevant; for example, the urban working class was weak, and Latin America did not experience international war that might have produced democratizing consequences.

In these circumstances, power remained in the hands of narrow elites. Landowners played a dominant role in politics virtually everywhere, and where the broadening of the political system occurred, it generally involved the mobilization of peasants under landlord control, or the incorporation of a part of the urban middle class which depended on the export sector or on state employment. At the same time the success of export-oriented development, while it continued, produced new social forces and social problems – a growing working class, for example, and the tensions associated with rapid urbanization. In the wake of the First World War the political systems of the region were showing the strains generated by these narrowly based civilian regimes, as clashes took place between workers and the state, and anti-elite movements emerged in newly professionalized armies.

Coming against this background of rising tension, the crash of 1929 (see Chapter 3) revealed the fundamental fragility of the economies of the region and provoked a general political crisis. Demand for exports slumped, foreign exchange earnings fell away, unemployment increased, and government revenues dropped sharply. These unexpected developments undermined the project of elite-controlled export-oriented development, and governments collapsed in one country after another. In conditions of social unrest and political turmoil military interventions and the establishment of personal dictatorships became commonplace.

The collapse of export-oriented development in the region gave rise to a long period of political instability. Old elites who had preached for decades that prosperity depended upon accepting Latin America's role as an exporter of primary commodities lost their credibility, and new counter-elites rose to challenge them. New forms of politics emerged, and fierce debate ensued over alternative paths of development. The basic source of instability in the period between 1930 and 1945 was that the conditions for export-oriented development in a world of steadily expanding and relatively free trade no longer existed, but that no clear alternative project proved able to win the consent of active political forces. In political terms, the key feature of the period was a negative one – rejection of liberal democracy as a form of politics both because of its association with a model of economic development and international alliances which had proved vulnerable, and because of mutual mistrust between elites and masses: the elites doubted that the majority of their fellow citizens would respect their privileges and act with moderation, while the masses doubted that the dominant elites would listen to their demands for sweeping social reform. In Cuba in 1933 a strongly nationalist revolution briefly produced soviets (workers' councils) in the country's ubiquitous sugar mills. In Argentina, Bolivia and Brazil, European fascism – interpreted as a potent weapon against communism and a developmental response to economic backwardness – enjoyed considerable appeal in the 1930s among junior army officers, and inspired a wave of interventions. In general, elites across the region had lost their ability to govern with the consent of the people, in pursuit of a form of economic development which seemed to offer benefits to all, and command general assent.

The one outstanding exception to this general trend was the case of Mexico, where the tensions generated by rapid export-oriented development and the concurrent beginnings of industrialization around steel and textiles had prompted peasant, working-class and middle-class opposition to the long-running dictatorship of Porfirio Diaz (1876–1911). Here a social revolution developed out of an initially liberal democratic challenge to Diaz's continued dictatorship, costing a million lives between 1910 and 1920. One by one the revolution consumed its leaders, as Francisco Madero, Emiliano Zapata and Francisco 'Pancho' Villa were assassinated in turn. The result of protracted social conflict, however, was the weakening of the old oligarchy, and the establishment during the 1920s of a state which enjoyed more authority, and more autonomy, than others in the region. A new ruling party, the National Revolutionary Party, was set up at the end of the decade. Under the reforming President Lazaro Cardenas (1934–40) it proved able both to organize workers and peasants on a massive scale, and to incorporate them into the regime behind a project for national development, the centrepiece of which was the nationalization of foreign oil companies in 1938. Now known as the Institutionalized Party of the Revolution (PRI), the same party went on to win eleven successive presidential elections between 1934 and 1994. The exceptional social and political consequences of the revolution had freed the state from direct dependence on landed elites and their allies, and created the conditions for a new regime to emerge, able to pursue both economic development and social reform.

The new regime that emerged in Mexico was far from being a liberal democracy. The PRI, as it became, was essentially a 'party of the state' – constructed by successive Presidents through the use of executive power, dependent upon its monopoly of both official patronage and official means of repression to retain its ascendancy, and neither able nor willing to compete on equal terms with potential rivals. Neither in Mexico nor anywhere else in the region was there any substantial faith in the ability of liberal democracy to resolve the problems thrown up by export-oriented development and its crisis after 1929.

────────────────── *Summary of Section 6.3* ──────────────────

- The crash of 1929 revealed the vulnerability of the export-oriented economies of the region, and provoked a general disenchantment with liberal democracy.

- Outside Mexico, the state lacked the capacity to neutralize landed elites and incorporate the peasantry and working class, resulting in increasingly severe economic crisis, social tension and political instability.

- In the Mexican case, political stability was achieved after 1930 on the basis of a dominant party of the state, rather than through competitive liberal democracy.

6.4   A new political project: Latin American populism

In the inter-war period, industrialization came to be seen as an alternative to renewed reliance on primary exports in the larger and more urbanized economies of the region. In view of the general loss of faith in *laissez-faire* economics as a result of the Depression, and the relative backwardness of industrial development across the region, it was taken for granted from the start that successful industrialization would require the organized support of the state and of the social groups – mostly workers and new entrepreneurs – who might be expected to benefit from it. The stage was thus set for a lengthy battle between these new proponents of state-led development, and the older exporting elites who would be required to surrender their previous social, economic and political privileges as the emphasis shifted to urban and industrial growth. As described by Skidmore and Smith (1992, pp.55–6) the political regimes which emerged took one of two forms: either what in this book would be called partial democracies – such as Chile – in which industrialists and workers gained some limited access to power through relatively open electoral competition, or 'populist regimes' – such as Argentina and Brazil – in which more authoritarian leaders put together multi-class alliances through corporatist organization and strictly controlled mobilization of political participation. Of the two, it was the 'populist regime' which had the greatest regional and international impact, and which best reflects an innovative political response to some of the structural constraints of the period. Consideration of the cases of Argentina and Brazil reveals the difficulties attending democratic politics in the period.

In Argentina, the Depression had brought about the narrowing of a political regime which had expanded under the Radical Party after 1916 to incorporate a large proportion of the (male) urban middle class. The oligarchy returned to power in 1930 in the wake of a military coup, and governed through 'repression and fraud' until another military intervention (1943–46) led to a decade of populist rule by Colonel Juan Domingo Perón. Perón built up a following among workers in Buenos Aires while Vice-President and Minister of Labour under the military regime, then used labour support to force his adoption as the official candidate for election to the presidency in 1946. Once in power, he organized labour through a

*Juan and Eva Perón on the balcony at the Plaza de Mayo, Buenos Aires,
8 May 1951. Eva Perón receives a message from the crowd*

corporatist system of official trade unions, pushed up wages, and set about
the pursuit of industrialization, taxing exports heavily to raise resources, and
buying up the British-owned railways.

In Brazil, political participation had not expanded before 1930, and the
onset of the Depression brought about the collapse of the old regime
(brought about by a military coup in 1930), and made way for the entry of
new forces into politics. A brief intervention by the military hierarchy was
swiftly followed by the assumption of power by Getulio Vargas, the defeated
candidate in the election of 1930. A Constituent Assembly called in 1933 gave
rise in 1934 to a new constitutional order, but Vargas himself broke with the
constitution in 1937, producing a dictatorship over which he presided until he
was ousted from power, again by the military, in 1945. From 1942 onwards
Vargas too organized working-class support through official trade unions
orchestrated by the Ministry of Labour. After 1945 these unions, and the
Brazilian Labour Party (PTB) organized around them, became the means by
which workers were mobilized behind Brazilian populism.

Cárdenas in Mexico, Perón in Argentina and Vargas in Brazil are generally
grouped together as populists who promoted state-led industrialization, and
incorporated the working class (and the peasantry in Mexico) into state-
controlled trade unions in order to establish a political base for themselves.
For comparative purposes, four common features of their regimes stand out.
First, each revolved to a significant extent around an individual leader.
Second, each was developmentalist. Third, although each had progressive
elements, none was committed to or observant of the principles of liberal

democracy. In fact, all abused the civil and political rights of their citizens in order to establish their supremacy. Fourth, the liberal or liberal democratic opposition which each faced was generally politically impotent, and often the least progressive grouping on the political scene. Even after Perón was sent into exile in 1955 the formerly powerful Radical Party was unable to achieve victory at the polls without the aid of the proscription of Peronist candidates, and it split into two long-irreconcilable rival groupings. To their right, Argentinian liberals represented the interests of landowning elites, and bitterly opposed the intrusion of popular forces into politics. In Brazil the liberal democratic National Democratic Union (UDN), created in 1945, proved hostile to social reform, and was unable to defeat Vargas's chosen candidate (General Dutra, his former Minister of War) even in the immediate aftermath of his expulsion from power. Mexico's opposition National Action Party (PAN), was marginalized for decades after it was allegedly cheated of electoral victory by fraud in 1940, and became a by-word for conservative reaction against all the revolution stood for.

In each case, these populist regimes gained a political advantage by mobilizing the working class under state control behind a project for state-led development based upon industrialization. Beyond that, differences between the regimes can largely be explained by the status of the peasantry. In Mexico it was a subordinate part of the regime, and hence a source of its greater stability and longevity. In Brazil it was a major resource outside the populist coalition, still mobilized by landowners for electoral purposes, and hence a key element in conservative opposition to reform. Argentina, in contrast to both, had virtually no traditional peasant class at all, with the result that Perón enjoyed national majority support in which the urban working class alone was the decisive social force.

There is no great mystery about the weakness of liberal democracy in Latin America in this period. It was associated with export-oriented development, elite ascendancy, and social and economic conservatism. The elites refused to surrender enough of their privileges to make their continued rule acceptable to the majority of the population. At the same time, they lacked a plausible *economic* project to advance in place of export-oriented development. The 'populists' proved more able than the old elites to advance such a project, largely because they were prepared, at least within the limits of state-led industrial development, to incorporate elements of the working class into their political alliances. In sum, in the two decades after the Depression swept export-oriented development and rule by civilian elites away, it was Latin America's new populists who showed political creativity.

However, although populism was the most successful political strategy attempted in Latin America after 1930, it had weaknesses which limited its ability to provide economic development and stable government over the long term. Its proponents needed to maintain the confidence of business sectors (with many traditional elites alienated from the start) while preserving the loyalty of the working classes and keeping control of the political organizations (usually state-backed trade unions) created to mobilize them. These conflicting political demands continually threatened to become unmanageable, particularly when their economic strategy began to run into difficulties. This depended heavily upon protected production of a limited range of consumer goods for limited national markets, and discouraged exports while still relying on them to generate foreign exchange and tax revenues. Such policies centred on economic nationalism and the expansion of purely national markets; but this focus was inconsistent with the demand from business interests for new technologies from abroad. It was also inconsistent with the general development of production on a global scale and the growth of multinationals in the global economy, processes which quickened after the Second World War. Only Mexico, with its modernized state and multiple means of social and political control, would manage to adapt its regime to meet these new challenges. Perón was overthrown and exiled in 1955, while in Brazil escalating conflicts in the early 1950s which centred on economic nationalism and the role of labour in the populist regime led to the deposition of Vargas by the military and his suicide in 1954. In retrospect, it can be argued that populism contained but did not resolve fundamental social tensions arising out of the character of Latin American development before 1930 and the consequences of its collapse. Those tensions were to surface in the 1960s across the region as a whole, and the catalyst was the Cuban revolution of 1958–59.

───────────────── *Summary of Section 6.4* ─────────────────

- In the wake of the Depression, state-led developmentalism emerged as the alternative to export-oriented development.

- It was most successful when supported by the politics of populism, in which governments organized workers in trade unions controlled by the state.

- Liberal democrats, generally locked into conservative social and political alliances and lacking an alternative political project, could not compete with populists in electoral terms.

- Populism, although progressive in some respects, was undemocratic in that it was hostile to political competition.

6.5 The Cuban revolution and its political consequences

The Cuban revolution transformed political calculations in the whole of Latin America. It took place at a time when liberal democrats were giving little sign of commitment to much-needed social reform, and when the model of national developmentalism espoused by the populists was already showing signs of political and economic weakness. As we have seen, this was in part because of internal tensions, and in part because it was ill-suited to a new global economy increasingly dominated by transnational corporations seeking not only local markets but also globally-oriented production sites around the world. The Cuban revolution added a new and explosive element to the situation, by posing the choice in terms of socialist revolution or acquiescence to the dictates of US imperialism. In its wake, three broad political options were pursued by various political forces around the region:

Fidel Castro supporters on the move towards Havana, January 1959

socialist revolution, democratic reform and authoritarian reaction. The first of these centred on attempts to emulate the Cuban revolution, supported by a new theory of revolution developed by Castro and his Argentine comrade-in-arms Ernesto 'Che' Guevara. This approach, popularized by the French student activist and intellectual Régis Debray, was called the foco theory because it claimed that revolutions could be started by a nucleus (*foco* in Spanish) of revolutionary activists in the countryside. It abandoned the standard Marxist–Leninist strategy of building a revolutionary party based on the urban proletariat in favour of rural revolution led by a committed vanguard, and prompted substantial guerrilla movements across the region, with lasting consequences in Colombia, El Salvador, Guatemala, and Nicaragua in particular (Wickham-Crowley, 1989).

The appearance of these movements, reflecting the radicalization of politics on the left across the region, is crucial to understanding the significance of the brief opening towards liberal democracy in the period and its early obliteration as a new wave of authoritarian regimes spread across the region. The 'democratic openings' of the 1960s were not the products of a steady process of positive social and economic change imagined by theorists of modernization, nor of a fundamental commitment either to progressive social reform or to liberal democratic values. Rather, they were tactical responses by political elites to the failure of populist methods of social and political control, and the threat of social revolution. These changes intersected with pressure for greater democratization from below, from social and political actors who did look to liberal democracy to set in motion an often long overdue process of fundamental social reform. Where liberal democratic regimes failed to prosper, it was because the political elites who sponsored them were at best lukewarm about such social change, while the majority of social and political elites were adamantly opposed to it. With other mobilized groups unwilling to abandon the goal of fundamental reform, there was no basis for a consensus between contending social and political forces as to the policies newly democratic regimes should pursue. In other words, there were fundamentally opposed interests behind the project of democratization, and consensus between such fundamentally opposed interests could not be achieved. These internal tensions were overlaid by further pressures arising from the intervention of the USA, which briefly threw its weight behind liberal democracy and reform in a bid to reduce the appeal of more radical alternatives. However, this pressure for democratic reform from the USA went hand in hand with a focus on national security – that is, a focus on the development of military forces in order to combat communism. This focus rapidly brought the military throughout the region to the centre of the political stage. There was no contradiction here: for the USA, liberal democracy in Latin America, however welcome it might be for itself, was principally a counter-revolutionary political project.

In these circumstances, the liberal democratic regimes which flourished briefly in the early 1960s were never soundly based. They were reflections of the state of extreme flux and political instability in the region rather than effective responses to it, and far from resolving the tensions out of which they arose, they provided a political framework within which they could mature to a point of crisis. Their almost universal collapse confirmed the view, general at the time as I noted earlier, that the conditions for a lasting transition to liberal democracy in the region were generally lacking.

In both Argentina and Brazil, fragile democracy gave way to authoritarian rule as populism weakened and new pressures mounted. In Argentina, the departure of Perón into exile in 1955 had led to three years of military rule. In its wake, successive attempts were made to restore democracy while blocking the return of Perón. The military were determined to keep the Peronist forces at bay, but the arithmetic of political competition in the country (the unshakeable Peronist majority) made it inevitable that contenders for power would either seek the support of the Peronists, or be condemned to governing with minority support. As a result, there was no basis for a stable electoral regime. Between 1958 and 1966 two rival wings of the once dominant Radical Party sought to govern the country, under Frondizi (1958–62), and Illia (1963–66), with a brief military intervention in between. Illia, elected in a multi-candidate competition with less than a third of the vote, proved unable to establish his authority, and was eventually overthrown by a junta which handed the presidency to General Onganía, a convert to the doctrine of 'national security' (excluding 'subversives' from domestic politics) intensively propagated from Washington and West Point in the period.

In Brazil, politics entered an equally destabilizing cycle from 1960 onwards, when the briefly successful centrist developmentalist Kubitschek left power. Kubitschek was replaced by Quadros, a maverick independent who had made a name as a flamboyant reformer in state and São Paulo politics, and was then chosen as presidential candidate by the UDN,

desperate to break the hold on power of Vargas and his heirs. But Quadros
was elected on a reform programme which the UDN proved unwilling to
support once he took office and he resigned dramatically in April 1961. After a
stand-off which split the military, the presidency passed to Vice-President
João Goulart, the radical leader of the PTB, the Brazilian Labour Party (under
an electoral system in which presidential and vice-presidential elections were
separate, and could be won by the candidates from different parties). Goulart
was at first obliged to govern under a parliamentary system hastily introduced
in order to limit his independence, but succeeded in restoring the presidential
system after overwhelming victory in a referendum called in 1963. Thereafter,
he moved towards the adoption of a programme of structural reform whose
central features were land reform and the mobilization of support among
rank-and-file soldiers and sailors. In a situation of increasing polarization, he
was overthrown by a military coup which triumphed on 1 April 1964, and
power passed within days to General Castelo Branco.

In these cases, as we have seen earlier, political problems had arisen from
the attempt to pursue policies of nationally-oriented economic development
under 'populist' regimes which sought the backing of workers organized
through the state. In both cases 'official' trade union movements and other
associated political organizations were escaping the control of national
leaders in the period prior to military intervention. In Argentina, Peronist
trade unions formed the backbone of opposition to the Frondizi and Illia
regimes, while in Brazil the internal radicalization of the union movement
and the Brazilian Labour Party placed Goulart between increasingly assertive
leftist forces on one side, and the conservative military on the other. In each
case, the unstable political compromise achieved by populism was coming
undone under a variety of pressures: problems internal to the chosen strategy
of economic development, national security concerns exacerbated by the
Cuban revolution, and the changing balance of forces within contending
political coalitions. Liberal democracy was brought down by a combination
of circumstances coming together at a particular point in time, rather than by a
single factor which could be isolated from the rest.

It is this perspective – the unravelling of existing political arrangements
under pressure from a number of destabilizing forces which came together at
a particular historical moment – which best explains the catastrophic failure
of civilian rule in Latin America in the 1960s and 1970s, and the onset of
prolonged and repressive dictatorship. As the record of political change in the
region shows, this is a much broader question than a concentration on the
breakdown of populist politics in the largest and most developed states in the
region alone would suggest. The crisis and collapse of existing civilian
political regimes was all but universal across the region, whether the
countries concerned were large or small, or more or less developed, and
whether or not they had a significant history of populism. Among the
wealthier and more developed countries, the case of Chile shows that non-
populist civilian regimes were equally vulnerable.

Chile, unlike most of its neighbours, had preserved civilian rule
throughout the period from 1931, after authoritarian interventions arising
out of instability in the 1920s. However, civilian rule in this period did not
equate with stability. First, it was never characterized by the alternation of

deeply-rooted political parties in power. In fact, throughout the whole period, no party or combination of parties ever succeeded in returning to power once it had gone into opposition. In addition, the whole party system in Chile was unstable, particularly at the centre, as witnessed by the fact that over the period one centre party – the Radicals – all but disappeared, to be replaced by another — the Christian Democrats. Second, the succession of governments entered into a particularly destabilizing phase from the 1950s onwards, suggesting that the absence of a basis for a populist regime was a source of instability in itself. The 1952 elections were won by a political independent, General Ibañez (formerly President 1927–31). He tried and failed to put together a populist coalition modelled on that of Perón in neighbouring Argentina, and was followed in office by conservative, reformist (Christian Democrat) and socialist (Popular Unity) Presidents in turn. From the mid 1960s, when it became clear that Eduardo Frei's Christian Democratic regime was too deeply infiltrated by conservative forces to carry out the reform programme it had promised (a 'Revolution in Liberty' to contrast with the presumed tyranny offered by the left), a process of rapid polarization and destabilization took place. Its final phase came with the election of the Socialist leader Salvador Allende in 1970, at the head of a weak coalition dominated by the Socialist and Communist parties. Elected with only minority support, Allende faced the unremitting hostility of the right and of the USA, proved unable to hold his fractious coalition to a consistent course, and was overthrown by General Pinochet in 1973.

Thus the weakness of civilian and democratic regimes in Latin America in the 1960s was not confined to those in which populism had been the dominant form of politics after 1930. One way of looking at the Chilean experience is to note that workers were generally loyal either to the Communist Party or the Socialist Party, and to suggest that it was the absence of any political initiative capable of winning working-class support for capitalist economic development either orchestrated by the state (the classic recipe for populism) or sustained by the market (the liberal option) which lay at the root of destabilization in the period. By and large, as my earlier discussion suggests, the conditions for such initiatives were far worse in the 1960s than they had been in the earlier post-war decades. It is true that the populist regimes of Argentina and Brazil collapsed under the strain, but collapse was just as frequent where a populist regime did not prosper. As we have seen, a common feature in all cases was the absolute refusal of the elites, whether formally enrolled in democratic parties or not, to contemplate any loss of privilege as part of a broader process of social reform.

Finally, we may test these ideas against the apparently exceptional cases of Costa Rica and Venezuela. These show that the structural pressures against civilian rule and liberal democracy in the period were not irresistible, and in doing so they offer support for the arguments made above. As we have seen, democracy collapsed because almost everywhere social and economic conditions were not conducive to it, elites were not committed to making it work, and the majority of the population had little faith in its efficacy as a solution to their problems. In Costa Rica and Venezuela there were good reasons why this was not the case. In Costa Rica coffee, the major export crop, developed on the basis of merchant dominance, a substantial class of smallholding farmers, and free wage labour. Inter-elite political competition led to a significant expansion of the (male) franchise before the First World War, and elite-led groups with working-class support clashed in the 1940s over proposals for social reform. Not only were landowners relatively weak, but with industrial development little advanced (in contrast to the cases of Argentina, Brazil *and* Chile) the working class itself was neither so organized nor so sizeable as to appear as a significant threat to elites. The outcome, after a short civil war, was the establishment in 1949 of a liberal democratic system in which the capitalist orientation of economic development, the rights of the opposition and the legitimacy of social reform were accepted.

In Venezuela, a different combination of circumstances had the same broad effect. The collapse of the system into crisis occurred early – in the 1940s – allowing an early response which prompted the establishment of a liberal democratic regime in the 1950s, prior to the Cuban revolution. The weakness of landowners in the country, along with the revenues provided by oil, gave the political elites the freedom of movement and the material resources to back liberal democracy with social and economic reform. Here too, the urban working class was relatively small, and the new elites remained confident that they could control the consequences of limited reform. In both Costa Rica and Venezuela, anti-communist pro-democratic alliances undertook reformist projects where elsewhere such reforms would prove impossible.

In each case, structural features strongly favoured democratization, but in neither did the presence of such features make the process easy, or guarantee success. In this important respect the broad pattern observed – in which contending forces first engaged in significant conflict over issues of substance, then entered into a process of negotiation which led to their common acceptance of liberal-democratic procedures – recalls Rustow's model of the process of transition. The two cases, therefore, bear out the general arguments developed here, and confirm the merit of an approach which begins with an examination of structural constraints, but proceeds to examine the choices made within those constraints, and the interests and political projects they reflect. They also point to the folly of focusing on 'choice' without a close examination of the structural contexts in which choices are made, the interests at stake, and the capacity of the political projects which emerge to achieve consensus between those interests.

––––––––––––––––––– *Summary of Section 6.5* –––––––––––––––––––

- The Cuban revolution generated a regional concern with national security, and greatly heightened existing internal conflicts and tensions.

- In combination, these circumstances led to widespread military intervention and long-term military rule across the region.

- Democracy proved sustainable (in Costa Rica and Venezuela) only where rural elites and the urban working class were relatively weak, and a reform-oriented state was able to secure consensus for its policies before the Cuban revolution took place.

Conclusion

These various examples all demonstrate in different ways a vitally important fact about Latin American politics in the 1960s. In one way or another, the great majority of electoral regimes in the region were either in terminal decline in this period, or fragile because they were introduced as expedients 'for fear of something worse', without an underlying commitment to the social and economic reforms which would have made for stability. The first of these cases recalls the argument of Rueschemeyer *et al.* (1992) that *institutions* introduced in response to particular 'structural' and political circumstances may develop a life and a logic of their own. It follows that they may persist after their useful life is over, and become a problem in themselves rather than a means to a solution. This confirms the need to examine both the structural context in which political institutions originate, and the internal dynamics through which they evolve. The second directs attention to the *context* in which liberal democratic institutions are promoted, and the political project to which they are linked, emphasizing the need to take account of the political and economic circumstances prevailing at the time, both domestically and at an international level.

In all the cases examined, the emphasis attached by Linz and Stepan and others to political creativity, 'leadership', and procedural issues in general is of vital significance. But three comments suggest themselves. First, the regimes in twentieth-century Latin America which have given most evidence of leadership and political creativity are not for the most part democratic. If the region has contributed anything truly original to the universe of political regimes, it is economically developmentalist, socially progressive, but politically authoritarian populism. Second, the broad contrast between the 1960s and the 1990s is still best explained by the diametrically opposed character of the prevailing structural constraints, which were equally powerful in each case, but were hostile to liberal democracy in the first case, and supportive of it in the second. In 1930 and in 1960 an external shock (the onset of the Depression in the first place, and the Cuban revolution in the second) exacerbated existing internal tensions and rendered liberal democracy not viable as a project. It is this broad contrast which explains why it was possible to enact the pacts and understandings which made widespread transitions possible in the particular historical conjuncture of the 1990s, where it had been virtually impossible at each of these previous turning points.

These conditions, which dominated the period from 1930 until the debt crisis hit the region in the mid 1970s, no longer applied in the mid 1990s. In global terms, the world capitalist economy became a reality, not only because of the demise of the Soviet Union and its Eastern European allies, but also because of the global reach of capital, and the emergence of multiple national sites of capitalist competition both among advanced states (Japan, the USA and Western Europe) and throughout what was once called the Third World. With the global ascendancy of neo-liberalism, itself a consequence of the global crisis of welfare capitalism, the idea of developmental alternatives to market-oriented capitalism gave way, for the time being at least, to a concern with alternative alliances and means of incorporation into the new world capitalist economy. At the same time, it placed substantial obstacles in the way of state intervention, whether to resist international market forces or to promote the economic and social welfare of disadvantaged groups. Meanwhile, at the level of regime types, alternatives to liberal democracy no longer appeared as viable as in the past, or to many as desirable.

All this means that the structural context in which politics was conducted in Latin America had become quite different, in its overall character, to that which prevailed either before or after 1945. But this does not mean that structural constraints have been removed. Political options are always structurally constrained. The objective of analysis should be to identify the *particular* constraints operating at any moment in time, and the *particular* political processes which they favour or hinder. What has happened in Latin America since the mid 1970s is that the character of the dominant constraints has changed, so that by 1995 it was extremely difficult to pursue any alternative to market-oriented capitalist development within liberal-democratic political regimes. Political development is in many ways *more* structurally constrained at the end of the twentieth century, with *fewer* alternatives available, than at any time in the past. However welcome the general advance of liberal democracy may be in Latin America, we should not fall into the trap of thinking that it alone reflects the triumph of human creativity over structural constraint.

References

Linz, J. (1978) *The Breakdown of Democratic Regimes: Crisis, Breakdown and Re-equilibration*, Baltimore, Johns Hopkins University Press.

Linz, J. and Stepan, A. (eds) (1978) *The Breakdown of Democratic Regimes: Latin America*, Baltimore, Johns Hopkins University Press.

Rueschemeyer, D., Stephens, E. and Stephens, J. (1992) *Capitalist Development and Democracy*, Cambridge, Polity Press.

Skidmore, T. and Smith, P. (1992) *Modern Latin America* (3rd edn), New York, Oxford University Press.

Wickham-Crowley, T. (1989) 'Winners, losers, and also-rans: toward a comparative sociology of Latin American guerrilla movements' in Eckstein, S. (ed.) *Power and Popular Protest: Latin American Social Movements*, Berkeley, University of California Press, pp.132–81.

CHAPTER 7

Democratization in Latin America, 1980–95

Walter Little

Introduction

In 1980 only a handful of countries in Latin America were liberal democracies in the sense that governments were accountable to the people via broadly free and fair elections. The rest were authoritarian in one way or another. By 1995, only 15 years later, at least half of the region was more or less liberal democratic or partially democratic (see Map 7.1). Cuba in 1995 was the only example of unequivocal authoritarianism. This striking political trend was part of the 'third wave' of democratization (see Chapter 1) that occurred in many parts of the world during this period. This trend may not, of course, be sustained in the future and it has not been a uniform process but it does appear that liberal democracy has become both more widespread and more deeply rooted.

This chapter is primarily about the 'third wave' in Latin America during the period from 1980 to 1995. It considers two main questions: (a) why did these democratic transitions take place? and (b) what problems have attended the attempts to consolidate these 'new' democracies? In coping with this agenda, the chapter first describes the character of the 'third wave' in Latin America (Section 7.1), then suggests some reasons why democratic transitions took place (Section 7.2), and then discusses some of the problems and tensions involved in democratic consolidation (Section 7.3).

7.1   The 'third wave'

Figure 7.1 categorizes sixteen major Latin American countries in terms of their regime types for 1970, 1980 and 1990. Indicators of the 'third wave' are found in the categorizations for 1980 and 1990 and in Map 7.1 for 1995. Figure 7.1 suggests that there have been three broad trends: redemocratization, liberalization, and democratic deepening. As usual the devil lies in the detail but, provided individual countries are viewed comparatively and not singly, this becomes less of a problem. For example, one can debate how real or otherwise Chilean democracy was in 1970 but no one would deny that it was more democratic than, say, that of Brazil at that time. Similarly, the fact that Bolivia's experience of democracy during the whole period has been different from that of Argentina's does not mean that they do not have more in common with each other than they do with, for example, Costa Rica.

The categories of liberal democracy, partial democracy and authoritarianism in Figure 7.1 are as defined in Chapter 1. Authoritarian regimes can be either military or civilian dominated. The category 'authoritarian (liberalizing)' refers to a situation when a country is in the

Map 7.1   Political map of Latin America, 1995

first stages of authoritarian relaxation. I also distinguish a 'partial democracy (hybrid)', of the sort found in Brazil in 1990, from other partial democracies. All these categories are intuitive and of course somewhat date-arbitrary but overall would not differ greatly from less judgemental indices (e.g. Johnson, 1977). Panama, the Dominican Republic, El Salvador and Nicaragua variously experienced civil war, revolution and US intervention in this period and are excluded from Figure 7.1.

As previously noted, those countries which have undergone redemocratization (Argentina, Chile, Uruguay, Brazil, Bolivia, Ecuador and Peru) have done so in different ways (Baloyra, 1987, pp.15–18). By any reasonable standards Uruguay was a liberal democracy in 1970 and remained so in the mid 1990s. Argentina – fully liberal democratic in the 1990s – was only partially democratic in 1960 since the largest political movement

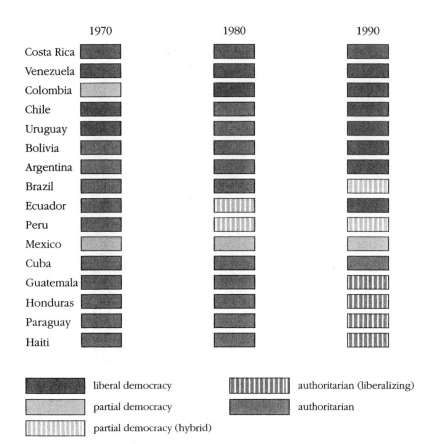

Figure 7.1   Political regimes in Latin America, 1970–90

(Peronism) had been prevented from contesting the 1958 elections. Even so, for ordinary citizens it was probably a good deal more democratic in terms of everyday rights than Ecuador, Bolivia and Peru. The picture in the early 1990s was similarly mixed.

Brazil was a case in point. From 1989 to the mid 1990s Brazilian governments were accountable via largely but not completely free elections. In the cities voters were offered a wide choice of political parties and their votes were, in general, counted honestly. In the countryside it was a different matter. There, radical groups often found it prudent not to put forward candidates; intimidation of voters was widespread and electoral fraud was common. Brazil also presented a mixed picture in respect of associational autonomy. Pressure groups abounded at every level from employers' associations to shanty town credit co-operatives and most were free to organize without hindrance. However, it was a different matter when such associations sought to alter significantly the prevailing order as the violence meted out to rural trade unionists and indigenous leaders illustrated. The problem was not that the state directly intruded on the autonomy of society. Rather it was that the state was either too weak to prevent or collaborated in the infringement of one group's rights by another. The murder with impunity of street children by off-duty policemen was an example.

How then are we to determine whether or not Brazil was a liberal democracy given that rights and freedoms were enjoyed to the full by some and hardly at all by others? The answer would seem to be that Brazil was a partial democracy but not in the sense implied in Chapter 1. It was not in an intermediate state between authoritarianism and democracy but was simultaneously authoritarian and democratic. Much the same could be said of Peru and Ecuador.

Figure 7.1 also illustrates that a number of countries (Costa Rica, Venezuela and, more debatably, Colombia) succeeded in establishing broadly democratic forms of government in the 1940s and 1950s and did not succumb to military takeover in later decades. Indeed, all three have survived major crises, suggesting that their democratic institutions have become deeply rooted. If they have problems (and Colombia and Venezuela certainly do) then they are problems to do with the deepening of democracy rather than its creation or recreation.

The final pattern comprises those states which have scarcely known democracy and which have only begun tentatively to democratize over the last few years. Cuba and Mexico are civilian-led authoritarian regimes which have survived largely intact during a very turbulent era. In each one revolution led to a single-party dominant system which did not brook opposition but which, at the same time, was not wholly indifferent to public opinion. Each was relaxing central control in the mid 1990s to some degree (though only in the economic sphere in the case of Cuba) but neither could yet be described as democratic. The other cases of recent democratization are more varied in so far as some have been highly unstable (notably El Salvador and Nicaragua) while others (Paraguay and Honduras) have faced relatively few challenges. They too could be said to be liberalizing rather than democratizing their systems of rule.

Even employing multiple categories in this way presents difficulties because Latin American political development has rarely proceeded in a linear way. On the contrary, it has been characterized by unexpected ruptures, and interference from outside. This is illustrated by the case of Guatemala. Before 1944 it was dictatorial and oligarchic. Between 1944 and 1954 it was democratic and reformist. From 1954 until the mid 1980s it was run by military regimes infamous for their human rights record. Only in the last few years has it moved tentatively towards a highly restricted form of democratic government. Throughout, it has been dominated by the USA.

Thus the Latin American experience of democracy has been a very varied one. Some countries have never known it. Others' experience of it has been unfortunate. Only a few have passed the acid test of survival in a crisis. So far as democratization is concerned, the tasks are accordingly different. For countries like Paraguay it involves elementary measures such as drawing up proper electoral registers, preventing coercion at the polling stations, and allowing greater diversity of the media. For others, like Peru, it means creating a more effective legislature, a more obedient military and a more accountable executive. For the most democratic states such as Venezuela or Costa Rica democratization is about issues such as devolution of power, citizen redress, and minority rights.

However, many people in Latin American countries do have in common a *desire* for democracy. From the time of independence onwards the ideal of representative government has been a constant and in the course of this century it has come to be fused with the ideal of popular sovereignty. Frequently betrayed in practice and often vitiated by an alternative culture of hierarchy and authoritarianism, it has nevertheless inspired one political generation after another.

―――――――――――――― *Summary of Section 7.1* ――――――――――――――

- Complex patterns of regime change in Latin America were evident between 1970 and 1995.

- The dominant patterns from 1980 to 1995 were redemocratization, liberalization and democratic deepening, all aspects of Latin America's experience of the 'third wave' of democratization.

7.2   Explaining the 'third wave': transition factors

Theoretical approaches

If Figure 7.1 were to include data of the sort often found in modernization approaches to the explanation of democratization (GDP per head, literacy rates, levels of urbanization and so on), then this complex picture would not become any simpler. Latin American experience suggests that if there is a relationship between economic and political development it is not a straightforward one. This may be because highly aggregated data say little about distribution (for example, Brazil has one of the largest economies in the world but also one of the most unequal distributions of income), but even if more nuanced information on income or class structure were added it is unlikely that any clear relationship would emerge.

Argentina exemplifies the difficulty of applying modernization approaches to democratization. For the last 50 years at least it has been highly literate, urbanized and industrialized. It has a large middle class, a well-organized working class and a plethora of secondary social organizations. It has no ethnic or racial cleavages to speak of, has a long tradition of party political activity, and held its first democratic elections as early as 1916. Yet during the latter part of the twentieth century it has been highly unstable with recurrent military intervention, Caesaristic leadership, and high levels of partisan political violence. 1989 was the first occasion in Argentina's entire history that an election led to the peaceful transfer of power to an opposition party.

However, absolute levels of economic and social development may not be wholly irrelevant. It would seem that extreme levels of poverty and economic underdevelopment are inconsistent with democratic institutions (Seligson, 1987, pp.6–9). If this is so then there is no reason in principle why the current cycle of democratization should not prove more durable than earlier ones. For all the vicissitudes of the last 50 years every country in Latin America (Haiti aside) has become more literate, more prosperous, and more socially complex. Whatever the thresholds might be, if economic and social evolution is a necessary though *not* sufficient condition for democracy then most of Latin America would appear to have met it. That said, this does not explain actual processes of recent democratization.

Structural theoretical approaches would seem to be even less relevant. In their more extreme form structural theories suggest that, as a consequence of Latin America's subordinate integration into the capitalist world economy, local class structures had been created which made genuine democracy impossible. Logically, it followed that those democracies which did exist in Latin America (and perhaps outside as well) were in some sense fraudulent. If democracy were to be established it would therefore have to be via some sort of revolution and would not be bourgeois or liberal in form. Other structuralists were less doctrinaire and acknowledged that economic dependency on global capitalism did not necessarily preclude some degree of economic development but they were not much interested in or optimistic about politics as an autonomous activity. At that time democracy seemed to be collapsing in much of the region so this pessimism was understandable, but it does limit the usefulness of structural approaches.

Recent structuralist theorists – via their stress upon specific, local class structures – might seem to offer the possibility of some sort of synthesis between the givens of the international economy and the uncertainties of local politics. Certainly in the longer historical sense structural theories have some utility. For example, the suggestion that entrenched landed power, a powerful state, and a relatively weak national bourgeoisie have impeded the development of democracy in Latin America (Rueschemeyer *et al.*, 1992, Chapters 5, 6) is persuasive. However, when it comes to analysing the third, contemporary, wave of democratization recent structural theories are less useful and it is interesting that the explanations offered by them are as much political as they are structural.

This suggests that *transition* approaches which stress the primacy of politics over international or local structural factors are the most appropriate means of analysing the 'third wave'. Indeed this is precisely the approach taken by most of the recent literature. This does imply considerable stress upon elite behaviour but not to the complete exclusion of consideration of pressure from mass popular action.

The process of transition

Analysts of the transition process (e.g. Share and Mainwaring, 1986; Huntington, 1991; O'Donnell, 1989) have used different vocabularies but agree that there have been four main forms: concession, negotiation, retreat, and intervention.

– *Concession* refers to a situation where a dominant regime decides that it is in its own interests to move towards democracy. In such cases pressure from the wider society is fairly muted, the process is long drawn-out, and the end product only partially democratic. Latin American examples would include Mexico, Brazil, Guatemala and Honduras.

– *Negotiation* comprises situations where regimes decide to withdraw from office but where they are obliged to consult with a broad range of civil opinion. The process is thus more fluid and less elite controlled

than in cases of concession. Uruguay, Peru, Chile and El Salvador more
or less fit this pattern.

– *Retreat* describes those cases where authoritarian regimes are unable to
stabilize their power and are basically driven out of office by the weight
of opposition and their own internal divisions. Argentina, Ecuador and,
to a lesser extent, Bolivia are examples.

– *Intervention* refers to situations where democracy is introduced
essentially at the instigation of some external power. In the cases of
Panama and Haiti this involved military action by the USA.

These categories are not watertight. One could argue, for example, that
Chile was really a case of concession and that US intervention was the major
factor in the Honduran case. The central fact is that in almost all cases (apart,
perhaps, from Argentina) there was extensive negotiation between the
regime and its opponents (and allies) in the wider civil society.

Nor was the process a predetermined one. In each case major struggles
occurred between hardliners and softliners within the government and the
opposition. Alliances were created, fell apart, and were replaced by others.
Moreover the very process had its own internal dynamic in that liberalization
(preliminary relaxation of authoritarianism) itself generated raised
expectations and provided political space for civil society to organize
(Gillespie, 1991, Chapter 7). Thus what might have begun as concession
could turn into negotiation, as seems to have been the case in Peru. Finally the
speed with which transition occurred varied widely from over ten years in the
case of Brazil to less than a year in Argentina.

However, for all the variation from country to country there were some
common elements. One was for *softliners* to become *dominant within
government* and *moderates* within the *opposition*. If compromise were to
be reached *radicals* on the left and *hardliners* on the right had to be
excluded from the negotiating process. Second, the parties had to agree
to *draw a veil over the past* and over the many abuses that had been
committed. The dead were to be left to bury the dead. Finally, there had
to be *broad agreement* that *future policy* would be *consensual* in character
and that the *position of traditional power holders*, especially the *military*,
would *not be jeopardized* (see also Chapter 4).

For the centrist opposition this was a price well worth paying. Many of
them had in any case at one time actually supported authoritarian
government, few had been grievously persecuted, and the exclusion of
the left was clearly in their interest. Democratization, above all, meant the
chance to rebuild interrupted political careers. For those who had suffered
rather more from authoritarianism (the radical clergy, trade union activists,
liberal-minded professionals), democratization based on a pact agreed
between elites offered rather less but even for them the promise of some
personal and organizational freedom was clearly better than nothing.

The form which democratization took does not, however, explain its
basic dynamics. Here there are various explanatory factors involved.
Important ones in the Latin American context include the maintenance of
political order and institutional unity by the authoritarian regime, combined
with continuing successful economic performance undermining the

legitimacy of the regime and, to a lesser extent, international pressures in favour of democratization.

Political order was crucial in a number of cases. In Argentina, Uruguay and Chile the justification for authoritarian rule was made in large part on grounds of restoring a political order that appeared to be under major threat from the left. Here political groups on the centre and right had tacitly condoned military intervention and had mostly kept quiet about subsequent human rights violations in the expectation that once the crisis had subsided, they would be restored to office. When it became clear that the military had other plans and intended to stay in power for a long period they withdrew their covert support and so helped to isolate the regime. Increasingly, majority opinion began to feel that the military had done their job and, suitably thanked, should return to barracks.

The military as an independent social force and institution had more grandiose ideas of reforming society root and branch over as long a period as was necessary but even they never went so far as to claim that they were a permanent alternative to electoral politics. They were in fact acutely aware of the fact that their legitimacy was conditional as is shown by their frustrated attempts to create their own political movements and obtain popular endorsement through referenda, packed assemblies and the like. In this respect their very success in restoring order was a source of subsequent weakness.

Legitimacy also depended upon *successful economic performance* and military failings in this arena further eroded their standing. Even in those cases where there had been some initial success (Brazil from 1968 to 1973, Argentina from 1977 to 1979, Chile from 1977 to 1982) the military found that sustained improvement was beyond them. Not only did this prevent them from reaching out into civil society to 'buy' support but it also led to disenchantment with their rule on the part of their natural allies among the property-owning classes. In the cases of Peru and Ecuador where reform-minded regimes had come to power in 1968 and 1972 this hostility from the business sector was a key factor in their eventual demise.

This bears on the argument noted earlier that economic and democratic development are in some way linked. In aggregate terms Latin America did develop in the 1960s and 1970s, as Chapter 6 suggests, but the growing perception of the political classes was that authoritarian economic policies were no more successful than democratic ones.

Pressure from below, however, was only rarely a factor in the democratization process. Where it took radical form (as in Guatemala and El Salvador) it led to a tightening of authoritarian control and only in Nicaragua in 1979 did popular protest succeed in overthrowing authoritarianism. The fact that the Somoza regime in Nicaragua prior to 1979 was a personal dictatorship of Neronic dimensions is surely relevant. Elsewhere the closing down of normal party politics by the military was accompanied by an upsurge in community level activity but though this was occasionally an irritant for governments (particularly church-led activity in the human rights arena) it was for the most part tolerated. It may prove to be a vital element in the future consolidation of democratization but it was not critical to the process of transition.

Only one regime succumbed because of military defeat. The Argentine defeat in the Falklands/Malvinas conflict with the UK in the early 1980s would have probably signalled the end of any government because the immense symbolic importance of the islands and human rights abuses on a grand scale had stripped the military regime of every claim to legitimacy (Pion-Berlin, 1987, pp.220–3).

Such *international influence* more generally does seem to have been a factor in the demise of authoritarianism but, for most countries, as a second order one. International pressure, particularly from the USA, over human rights was a constant embarrassment – especially for Argentina and Chile – but was not decisive. Similarly, the 'snowball' effect whereby Uruguay, for example, was inspired by what had happened to Argentina or Spain was no doubt important but it cannot have been critically so. However, in the case of the highly dependent micro-states of Central America it is clear that US military and economic pressure in favour of greater democratization was crucial. Without it, it is inconceivable that Panama, Honduras or Guatemala should have moved in this direction (Arnson and Forman, 1992, pp.250–6).

One element which seems to have been widely present in the move towards democratization was the perception in military circles that holding power inevitably meant the politicization of the military institution as different factions split over policy issues. In the case of Peru, Ecuador and Bolivia these splits were extremely deep but even in highly institutionalized regimes like Brazil's they were present. Since military power and autonomy rested above all on *institutional unity* the longer they stayed in power the greater became the internal pressures to withdraw.

No single cause explains transition. External pressure was crucial for the smaller countries for example but less so in the case of Brazil or Chile. If a single cause *had* to be identified it would be that the authoritarian interlude had broadly served its purpose and hence was no longer needed.

─────────────── *Summary of Section 7.2* ───────────────

- The transition theoretical approach has been found useful by many Latin Americanists attempting to explain recent democratizations in the region.

- Democratic transitions have taken more or less elite-controlled forms: concession, negotiations, retreat, and intervention (by an external power).

- Such elite-controlled forms of transition are more likely to be successful if: (a) they are controlled by reformers and moderates within both government and opposition groups, not by radicals, (b) the parties agree to respect the position of traditional power holders, and (c) there is broad agreement on future policy.

- Important *explanatory factors* in transition processes include (a) the maintenance of political order and institutional unity by the authoritarian regime, together with (b) successful economic performance undermining authoritarian legitimacy, and (c) pro-democracy international pressures.

7.3   Problems of democratic consolidation

Latin America provides historical examples of countries that started processes of democratic transition and then reverted to authoritarianism. Partly for this reason, Latin Americanists distinguish clearly between explanations of initial democratic transitions and (different) explanations of democratic *consolidation*. There are various reasons why such consolidation in Latin America has been a difficult achievement. Four major problems in this connection are discussed in this section.

Demilitarization

In 1979 there were military governments in Brazil, Uruguay, Chile, Argentina, Paraguay, Bolivia, Peru, Ecuador, Guatemala, El Salvador and Honduras. By a decade later they had all been replaced by elected, civilian governments. On the face of it, this represents a turnaround as dramatic as it was welcome.

On closer examination the picture is more complex. First, in all cases (even in Chile where the military regime was particularly isolated from civil society) those military governments had ruled in alliance with a range of civilian interests and all had civilian Cabinet appointees. Indeed, all had come to power at least in part because of the prompting of disenchanted civilians. Second, the extent to which the exercise of political power has been subsequently demilitarized in the sense that the military exercise no kind of veto is very far from clear.

Women's groups and human rights in Argentina. Members of the Mothers of the Plaza de Mayo weep during a protest in front of the Navy's School of Mechanics, one of the military institutions where hundreds of people were tortured and killed in the 1970s. Buenos Aires, 23 March 1995

Three criteria can be used to evaluate the extent of effective demilitarization: the issue of human rights trials, military budgets, and the question of constitutional prerogatives and organizational autonomy. Within the latter are subsumed a series of sub-criteria among which are parliamentary oversight, promotions, military justice, intelligence and security services, legal status, participation in government, and the role of commander-in-chief and those of service chiefs.

Whether or not (or how) the military were to be tried for human rights violations by their civilian successors has been a critical issue in several countries both during the actual disengagement from formal power and afterwards. In general the military have succeeded in obtaining immunity from prosecution.

Argentina represents the most difficult case. Partly this was because of the sheer scale of abuse (thousands of 'disappeared'), partly because a large proportion of the officer corps had been (quite intentionally) involved in one way or other, and partly because many of the victims have relatives with the financial and legal skills required to press a case. It is significant that the working-class victims of the period of the 'dirty war' from 1975 to 1978 have received less attention.

The Alfonsín government which came to power in 1983 tried to address the human rights question by distinguishing between those who had actually committed the crimes (mostly middle-rank officers and NCOs) and those who had ordered and organized them. Thus, service chiefs in the armed forces (e.g. Videla, Massera, Galtieri) who had ruled between 1976 and 1982 were tried, convicted and gaoled. This symbolic rebuke was acceptable to more junior officers but when the pressure to expand the scope of investigation increased, Alfonsín was faced with a series of military rebellions by hardliners. None of these aimed to topple the government but they did weaken it and ensure that deeper investigations could not be pursued. They also had the effect of ensuring that Alfonsín's hopes of institutional change (in military education, recruitment, civilian oversight) became bogged down.

Alfonsín's successor in 1989 – Carlos Menem – took a quite different line, inverting the Nuremberg principle in his law of Due Obedience which explicitly absolved those who might have carried out abuses on the grounds that they were 'only obeying orders'. He also pardoned the chiefs-of-staff indicted by his predecessor (along with a number of guerrilla leaders) in an attempt to close the issue once and for all. Despite revelations during the mid 1990s about what actually went on during the 'dirty war' the likelihood of anyone in the military being punished in the future is extremely remote.

In large part because of this stance Menem succeeded in putting civil–military relations in Argentina on a firmer footing. In return for what was effectively a blanket amnesty the military gave ground in a number of areas which were bones of contention for Alfonsín. These included the sale of military property, the rationalization of the military-run defence industries, cuts in staffing levels, more open recruitment and promotions policies, the abandonment of intermediate-range missile development programmes (a source of considerable worry for the USA), and the installation of civilian heads of military intelligence and security as well as at the Ministry of Defence. This possibility of modest progress in civilian control of the military has to be set against Argentina's very special circumstances. There the military failed to restructure the economy, waged an illegal war against their fellow citizens, and, finally, were proved during the Falklands/Malvinas debacle to be militarily incompetent. It would be odd if so comprehensive a failure were not followed by some restructuring of civil–military relations.

Elsewhere in Latin America the issue of human rights has arisen but has had relatively little political resonance. Chile – the next greatest offender after Argentina – is a case in point. Though in 1994 there was a challenge from the Appeals Court to the Chilean Supreme Court ruling of 1993 that the Geneva Convention did not apply to Chile between 1973 and 1978 as well as one or two high profile cases, the military has not been under serious threat on the human rights front. It has been clear that the government preferred not to have to deal with the issue at all and that there was little enthusiasm amongst the people for conjuring up demons from the past.

In Uruguay and Brazil attempts to raise the issue of human rights have been openly rebuffed not just by the military but by their civilian successors. Brazil's congressional amnesty of 1979 has been contested only a few times, on each occasion without result. In Uruguay the one occasion when the judiciary ordered former officers to appear in court triggered the passing of a general amnesty the day before the scheduled court appearance. This was widely criticized at the time but has not been seriously challenged since.

It is also interesting that some of the worst abuses of human rights by the military have occurred not under military governments but under civilians. Peru is an example. Throughout the 1980s in response to the armed threat from the Sendero Luminoso guerrilla movement the Peruvian military harassed, tortured and killed thousands of peasants along with a significant number of students, journalists and other members of the inconvenient classes. Despite intense pressure from international pressure groups almost nothing has been done to address these abuses. National security – as interpreted by the military – clearly takes precedence over constitutional guarantees not only in Peru but also under civilian governments in Colombia, Ecuador and much of Central America.

Clearly this reflects considerations of *realpolitik* (politics based on realities and material needs rather than on morals or ideals) but there were also technical reasons why the military throughout the continent should have succeeded in avoiding the human rights trap; for example, a good deal of time had passed, care was taken at the time to ensure deniability, witnesses were few or frightened and bodies could only be identified with difficulty. Even if governments and courts were not well disposed towards the military securing convictions under such circumstances would be very difficult.

There is also the deeper question of the extent to which society truly wants to have such matters investigated. Poll after poll in country after country show that respondents – when specifically asked – attach a high value to human rights. When asked open-ended questions about the salience of various issues, however, human rights is prioritized by only a few per cent. This reflects understandable concern about economic actuality but also the brutal truth that those currently in power in Latin America have a great deal to thank the military for. Their 'dirty wars' have – though none will openly acknowledge it – allowed the propertied classes to rest easy in their beds at night.

Spending on the military is a very difficult area about which very little is known. In part this is because much of it is secret and because much of it is swallowed under other categories of public spending. However, with the notable exceptions of Cuba, Nicaragua and El Salvador, military spending in Latin America is not particularly high by international standards. The image of a continent groaning under the weight of the generals' greed is far from the mark.

In principle, the return of elected governments should still have led to a fall in military spending. Civilian presidents are well aware that tension between countries legitimizes military demands for scarce money and they have gone out of their way to keep such tension within manageable bounds. Moreover, cuts in unproductive spending on the military releases money for more sensible ends, is consistent with the anti-statist mood, and is endorsed by the IMF and the World Bank.

However, the (negative) evidence to date is that the return of liberal democracy and its stress on demilitarization has produced little in the way of cutbacks. Argentina may be an exception but the rule seems to be that military spending continues much as before. Indeed, in Brazil and Chile undisturbed levels of funding were an explicit part of the negotiated transition to democracy. It is hard to avoid the conclusion that the price of military quiescence may be levels of military spending far beyond those justified by objective national security needs.

The final criterion encompasses the institutional and constitutional position of the military. On the institutional dimension the picture varies from considerable change (Argentina) to a modest diminution of military prerogatives (Uruguay), to little or no change (Brazil, Chile, Peru, Central America). In Argentina the security services are now under civilian direction, promotion to senior rank requires presidential endorsement, the police have been significantly demilitarized in command structure, few state enterprises remain under military direction and the Cabinet is entirely civilian in composition. However, congressional oversight of military affairs remains low and the jurisdiction of civilian courts is still limited. In Uruguay, the picture is much the same though Congress plays a more dominant role. In Brazil and Chile, however, the institutional prerogatives of the military remain extremely high: no congressional scrutiny, military representation at Cabinet level, legal autonomy, financial independence, military control of promotions, involvement in state enterprises, and autonomy in the intelligence arena.

In the constitutional as distinct from the institutional realm the position of the military throughout Latin America remains well protected. First, in a large number of countries the constitution provides for 'regimes of exception' involving, under certain circumstances (including threats to public order), the suspension of civil liberties, rule by decree and even martial law. Second, in many countries the military have succeeded in retaining a constitutionally defined mission which, as in Chile and Brazil, includes 'guaranteeing' the constitution itself. Third, in a number of countries national security legislation passed by military governments remains intact. Finally, though rarely implemented, the military in a number of countries (Peru and Ecuador, for example) retain legal jurisdiction over civilians, particularly those held to have impugned the honour and integrity of the military institution or charged with treason or sedition.

It would not be unreasonable to conclude that by most criteria the majority of Latin American countries have so far failed to depoliticize the military. The military are less active than they were in politics but this is largely because the conditions which brought them to power in the first place (economic volatility and political strife) are mainly absent. If these conditions were to return (as they have done in Venezuela, provoking two failed coup attempts in one of Latin America's most democratic countries) then the military would be likely to return to the political centre, threatening democratic consolidation. The military may, in short, be 'out' but they are very far from 'down'.

Party systems and representation

The variety of parties and systems in Latin America is very considerable. There are parties such as Uruguay's Colorados or Colombia's Conservatives which can be traced back to the period of Independence (1810–25). Others such as Venezuela's Causa Radical or Brazil's Workers' Party have only developed over the last decade or two. In some countries such as Costa Rica parties play a dominant role in politics whilst in Paraguay or Panama they are largely peripheral. Some, like Argentina's Peronists, enjoy mass support while others – particularly regional and ideologically radical ones – are highly exclusive in character. And of course they vary considerably in their internal organization and in their relations with each other.

By way of contrast Latin American electoral systems display a considerable degree of homogeneity. Presidentialism is the rule with most Presidents being elected by simple plurality or run off majorities (when no clear winner emerges in the first round). Conversely most legislatures in Latin America are elected on a proportional basis using closed party lists. Historically, executive–legislative relations have either been characterized by presidential domination (as in Mexico) or by deadlock as in the case of Peru.

Political parties are dominant actors in Costa Rica, Colombia, Venezuela, and Mexico. They are significant but non-dominant in Argentina, Brazil, Chile, Uruguay, Cuba, Nicaragua, and the Dominican Republic. They are of secondary importance in Peru, Ecuador, El Salvador, Honduras, Guatemala and Bolivia, and of little or no import in Paraguay, Panama and Haiti. Developments over the last few years suggest that in Chile, Uruguay and Bolivia parties may have increased their political salience.

These intra country differences reflect the levels of socio-political development of the various countries but in no very simple way. There is, in particular, no very clear link between levels of economic development and social mobilization on the one hand and systems of party politics on the other as the very different cases of Argentina and Costa Rica illustrate. Argentina, despite its industrial-urban character, has failed to develop stable party politics whilst the much less well-developed Costa Rica has succeeded in doing so. This suggests that the key lies in the particular political evolution of the different countries.

Some examples might serve to illustrate this point. Until very recently Mexican politics had been dominated since the early 1930s by the Institutionalized Party of the Revolution (PRI). Created *by* the state rather than emerging *from* civil society, it has been simultaneously corporatist, centralized, authoritarian, and inclusive. Corrupt yet reformist, intolerant of opposition but also open to talent, it has never been democratic but it ensured that Mexico has enjoyed a long period of political stability. Its durability is only understandable in terms of the memory of the extreme violence of the revolutionary period. Chile could hardly be more different. An oligarchic democracy in the late nineteenth century, it developed a multi-party system divided on left-centre-right lines which was both competitive and representative but which led ultimately to stalemate and political collapse.

One historic characteristic of Latin American party systems survives to this day: the tendency towards ideological borrowing in the formal sense and its adaptation to Latin American reality in the substantive sense. Successively, European liberalism, socialism, fascism, social democracy and Christian democracy have had an impact but one which became transformed into Latin American oligarchy, militarism, populism and paternalism. Today the same process seems to be occurring with the efforts of parties of the right to embrace neo-liberalism and those of the left to re-invent the language of social democracy. Like the rest of the world the region's political parties are finding such adjustment extremely difficult and while the language of adjustment sounds familiar its substantive results are likely to be idiosyncratically Latin American.

In functional terms political parties tend to be weaker than their European counterparts. Though many leaders (such as Menem in Argentina) have spent their lives working their way up through a party, political recruitment also takes non-party forms. Retired generals, leading intellectuals (such as the Peruvian novelist Vargas Llosa who stood for the presidency in 1990), and ambitious businessmen have as much of a chance as party hacks of reaching the top in many countries. Only in Uruguay, Chile and Mexico could parties be said to dominate the process of political recruitment.

This reflects the enduring institutional weakness of most political parties. Active membership is very low, party dues are insignificant in financial terms, internal decision making (less so on the left) tends to be undemocratic, and factionalism, personalism and localism are present. It is in part because of the uncertain articulation of parties in respect of mass electorates that they are so often prone to 'capture' by special interest groups such as labour organizations, wealthy individuals, and foreign interests. It may also account for their clientelistic and sometimes openly corrupt behaviour.

The period from 1980 to the mid 1990s has been one of considerable fluidity characterized by the decline of traditional populist parties such as Venezuela's Christian Democrats (COPEI) and Argentina's Peronist movement, a crisis on both the extreme and moderate left, a resurgence of presidentialism, and the emergence of *concertación* (coalition) politics based on pacts. Party politics remains contested but no longer in an ideological sense.

Venezuela's party system in the early 1990s illustrates the depth of the crisis. The old two-party duopoly of social democracy and Christian democracy was in tatters, challenged both from the centre-left (the Movement towards Socialism and Radical Cause) and internally. Levels of voter disenchantment (reflected in 60 per cent rates of abstention as well as in street protests) were exceptionally high largely because the government could no longer fund distribution of jobs and favours via the parties. The military remained a threat and the government – unable to abandon populism for electoral reasons yet unable to fund it – was paralysed. Venezuela pointed to a crucial weakness found elsewhere in Latin America: deadlock between congress and the presidency and the disarticulation between the electoral and policy role of the parties.

So far as the traditional left is concerned these were testing times. Outside of Chile they were never able to attract mass support (hence their flirtation with violence) but at least they had the comfort of an ideological position. They either virtually disappeared, became middle-of-the-road reformers (in the way of the once radical Chilean Socialist Party) or found themselves challenged by new but inchoate left-of-centre coalitions such as the Workers Party in Brazil or the PRD (Democratic Revolutionary Party) in Mexico. Nowhere were they able to win power through the ballot box and, even if they could, the political and economic costs of changing the dominant economic model were prohibitive.

The current marginality of once-powerful political movements was reflected in the emergence of political outsiders promising radical reform and in the growth of presidential power. In 1990, both Presidents Collor of Brazil and Fujimori of Peru came out of complete obscurity as self-proclaimed saviours of the nation and their promises of a clean sweep of the political stables clearly struck a chord with the electorate. Collor failed while Fujimori succeeded but they each symbolize a popular distaste for the old party politics.

Presidents Menem of Argentina and Fujimori of Peru epitomized the willingness of the electorate to see congress reduced to a simple rubber stamp. Indeed, Fujimori – with the backing of the army – closed congress and saw his popularity ratings go through the roof. President Menem with an in-built majority, did not need to go so far but like Fujimori he completely dominated the political scene. And in Venezuela there were plenty urging President Caldera in the early 1990s to follow suit, appeal directly to the people, and thus short-circuit the checks and balances of the representative system.

In the past political parties have been mainly concerned with occupying the state apparatus and using it for partisan ends. This may have made sense when the state was so preponderant, but as its powers are diminished political parties are faced with an acute crisis of adaptation. Institutionalization (that is, political order) requires that the parties must straddle the competing demands of representation on the one hand and responsibility in office on the other. Thus, they must somehow incorporate currently excluded groups (such as the poor who, if they participate at all, do so as ballot box fodder) *and* continue to play by the rules of the game.

The evidence so far is that they have made progress in the art of compromise but have a long way to go in the field of representation. Chile is a case in point. The left have abandoned the socialist project and have accepted the role of the right as a loyal opposition. Similarly, in Argentina all of the major political players have renounced the old practice of turning to the military when excluded from the political process. The problem is that this has had a representational price. That is, the democracy which the dominant parties now espouse is clearly elitist. Broadly speaking, democratic consolidation can be difficult where party systems are weak.

Political corruption and political reform

There is nothing new about political corruption in Latin America. Yet as a political issue it has a high resonance in Latin America. Four recent Presidents have been indicted (García of Peru, Lusinchi and Perez of Venezuela, and Collor of Brazil). Salinas of Mexico (1988–94) – facing charges not only of corruption but complicity in murder – went underground. Menem of Argentina, in the early 1990s, was also deeply tainted but survived. Such corruption can gnaw away at the credibility of political regimes and threaten the consolidation of regimes involved in the difficult business of democratic transition.

Partly this high resonance reflects the fact that the media – subject though it still is to censorship and self-censorship – has been relatively free. It still does not engage in much investigative journalism but it is fairly free to publish. Partly it is because partisan scores are being settled. The language of Latin American political debate is often intensely personal (indeed slanderous) and allegations of corruption are held to go down well with voters. They also have the virtue – from the point of view of those who feel vulnerable in this regard – of pre-empting possible attacks. In this sense the pattern of allegation and counter-allegation in so many countries has acquired a ritualized – almost comic opera – overtone.

Yet there are some grounds for believing that in quantitative terms political corruption has become a major problem for Latin America's evolving democracies. First, the sheer volume of cases (proven and alleged) is impressive. Second, those who allege that it now occurs on a massive scale are themselves credible witnesses. Third, the amount of money alleged to have been misappropriated during the period 1980–95 was of such proportion as to be macroeconomically destabilizing. Last, cases abound not at low political level but in the 'core' institutions of the state such as the Supreme Court, Central Bank and Ministry of Finance.

Nor is it impossible that corruption on this scale is somehow associated with democratization. In principle democratization – via competition – should have led to greater accountability and transparency. However, liberal democracy in Latin America remains seriously deficient on these counts. There are also positive reasons why corruption might have increased across the board. One is the parlous financial condition of the political parties and the very high cost of modern elections. There is abundant evidence that political parties exchange favours (contracts, insider information, exemptions from obligations) in return for cash, air-time, favourable print coverage, etc. Another is that as a result of years of exclusion in many countries a whole new generation now has the opportunity to build a capital stake; politics in Latin America, as elsewhere, is often an alternative to earning a living in the private sector. Finally, there is the problem of volume. With liberal democracy many more people have a piece of the action and to the extent to which decisions are decentralized throughout the political system so the number of potential 'corruptees' rises.

There are also two specific circumstances in recent years which may have increased the return on corrupt behaviour by politicians and civil servants. One is privatization of publicly owned companies which has involved the sale of billions of dollars worth of assets with virtually no scrutiny. The second is the narcotics trade which is no longer restricted to the producing and processing countries (Bolivia, Peru, Colombia) but includes the whole of Latin America in transhipment and money-laundering activities. Whilst some areas of government activity (notably the management of exchange rates) has become more honest – or at least more predictable – others remain highly discretionary and hence susceptible to corrupt administration.

Efforts have been made to tackle the problem with strengthened laws, greater co-ordination between regulatory agencies, and the creation of special task forces. However, such efforts will come to nothing if they are not accompanied by major structural changes. At a minimum these would include changes to party financing, judicial reform, greater decentralization, major civil service reform, and reform of the media. Even given the political will the likelihood of change on this scale seems slim.

The problem is that the political culture of Latin America remains heavily influenced by deeply-rooted traditions of nepotism, familism, and clientelism – the handmaidens of corruption. For so long as the absolute scarcities and extreme inequalities which underpin these traditional ways of behaving persist so will the issue of political corruption.

Social debt, social movements and democracy

It is an often noted paradox that democratization in Latin America has gone hand in hand with widening disparities in living standards and increases in absolute poverty. In brief, debt servicing, cuts in subsidies of basic consumption goods and reductions in spending on health and education have hit the old poor hard and have also created a new poor. As the extent of the social crisis became clearer opinion divided between (a) those (notably Latin America's creditors) who argued that such sacrifices were inevitable, that low inflation was in fact more advantageous to the poor than to the well-off, and that orthodox policies would ultimately lead to trickle-down and (b) those (in the aid agencies and academia in particular) who argued that orthodoxy was simply code for exploitation. Latin American governments themselves initially tried to straddle this divide by adopting heterodox macroeconomic policies which tried to combine fiscal orthodoxy with the maintenance of across-the-board social provision.

It was the failure of these experiments in heterodoxy (for example, in the 1980s under Alfonsín in Argentina, and Sarney in Brazil) which has created a new orthodoxy. Drawing upon the experiences of Chile in particular, this argues that the social costs of restructuring can be alleviated through targeted programmes of relief. Examples would include the Chilean public works programme initiated under Pinochet in the 1970s and the post-1985 Bolivian Emergency Social Funds.

This new orthodoxy argues that widespread poverty is economically damaging. It compounds the problem of low domestic demand, damages productivity, reduces the numbers who pay tax, contributes to crime, insecurity and political violence and encourages wasteful use of resources. It also argues that the resources to tackle poverty do exist and only need redirection. Thus, if provision is decentralized from federal ministries to local government, if spending on education is redirected away from tertiary to primary level, and if health care is reoriented towards preventative rather than curative strategies then many social needs can be met without increases in overall levels of public spending.

This sounds too good to be true and it probably is. First the problem of poverty has changed. The rural sector and the informal urban sector has always been poor but the last decade has seen the emergence of a new kind of poverty. With the deregulation of labour markets, the curtailing of the power of the trade unions, reductions in public sector jobs and the selling off of state companies many who were once in stable, if low-paid, jobs have become unemployed or informally self-employed. That is, the 'old' working class has shrunk and the informal sector has grown. At the same time the rich have become super-rich.

The problem with 'targeting' is that it involves diverting public spending from middle income to poor recipients, requires extremely authoritative policy making, and presupposes a reasonably efficient system of public administration. Though the Bolivian programmes did produce positive benefits for some they also became heavily contaminated with clientelistic politics and it is probably significant that the one seeming success story – Chile – had both an authoritarian government and a traditionally quite efficient public welfare system. Even there, and despite ten years of continuous high GDP growth, over a third of Chileans currently live below the poverty line.

In short the 'social debt' cannot be met by targeting existing resources more efficiently, desirable though this may be as an interim measure. It requires capital to be invested in high-employment sectors, wage rises in line with productivity, and greater equity in the collection of taxes. Such policies are not in the short-term interests of either local or foreign investors and consequently are most unlikely to be introduced on the scale necessary to seriously dent the problem of mass poverty. Even a modest 'targeting' strategy is likely to encounter political resistance from the lower middle income groups which would be adversely affected by any redirection of spending. In short, the problem of widespread poverty looks set to stay.

This raises the issue of the political response of the poor to their poverty. The last decade has seen some popular protest but on nothing like the scale that would be required to bring about fundamental political change. Supermarkets have been looted in Brazil, public employees have gone on strike in Argentina, and there have been extremely serious riots in Venezuela and local rebellion in Mexico. But compared to the scale of deprivation the popular reaction has been rather muted. Moreover, even when protest has been on a large scale (as it was in Venezuela) it has resulted only in temporary relaxation by government. Where it has involved ideologically organized violence (as in Mexico, Peru and Colombia) governments have resorted to force.

The relative absence of mass protest can be attributed to the fact that the poor may have learned to value low inflation and economic stability and to the fact that they have learned to value democracy and realize that it cannot deliver the impossible. This does not seem particularly plausible and it is worth recalling that reformers such as Menem, Fujimori and Perez got in precisely because they (fraudulently) promised a return to the old ways. More reasonable explanations for mass passivity could be found in lack of unity and leadership, the localized nature of deprivation, economic vulnerability, ignorance and apathy, fear of state repression, and traditional patrimonial politics.

This interpretation of the political behaviour of the poor would be disputed by many. The last decade has seen an explosion in the study of new social movements – human rights organizations, women's groups, indigenous movements, environmentalism, and neighbourhood associations. Some have claimed that this issue-oriented form of popular association amounts to the democratization of civil society in Latin America.

This is surely an exaggeration. It is true that grass-roots social movements have grown significantly both as a reaction to the authoritarianism of military rule and since then in the freer atmosphere of liberal democracy. It is also true that they have had their successes in a variety of forms of collective empowerment – credit unions, self-help housing, local infrastructure, preventative health care provision and so forth. But it is also true that, compared to the level of need, growth has been modest, issue specific, ideologically muted and externally influenced. Social movements have also been subject to 'capture' by governments and to traditional clientelistic practices. This is not to say that they have achieved nothing nor that they should be belittled but claims sometimes made that these movements have the potential to advance and consolidate democratization are exaggerated. From the point of view of a Menem or a Fujimori they are probably positively welcome and certainly to be preferred to a powerful trade union or guerrilla movement.

─────────────── *Summary of Section 7.3* ───────────────

- An important distinction in explanations of democratization in Latin America is between democratic *transitions* from authoritarianism and the *consolidation* of democracy.

- Factors explaining democratic transitions do not in the same way explain democratic consolidation.

- Democratic consolidation in Latin America is affected by many problems including ones related to the continuing importance of the military within the state, weaknesses in party and representation systems, political corruption, and widening social inequalities together with the disinclination of the poor to engage in popular protest.

Conclusion

This chapter has considered factors that explain the 'third wave' of democratization in Latin America. It has also examined four problems that make the consolidation of democracy a difficult political achievement. I have argued that the forms and dynamics of democratization processes have been largely elite controlled. Reference has been made to pressures from civil society and the role of social movements, but such actions from that direction have not had a major bearing so far on the outcome. For the traditionally poor, as well as those who have recently slipped into poverty, democratization has been a grievous disappointment. They are not nostalgic for authoritarian rule and not indifferent to the freedoms that democratization has brought with it, but their material circumstances have deteriorated significantly. They may not be able to do much about this but unless democratization does lead to improved life chances for the majority in Latin America then the process will continue to be tentative rather than consolidated.

References

Arnson, C.J. and Forman, J.M. (1992) 'Projecting democracy in Central America: old wine, new bottles?' in Goodman, L.W., Leogrande, W.M. and Forman, J.M. (eds) *Political Parties and Democracy in Central America*, Boulder, Westview.

Baloyra, E.A. (1987) 'Democratic transition in comparative perspective' in Baloyra, E.A. (ed.) *Comparing New Democracies. Transition and Consolidation in Mediterranean Europe and the Southern Cone*, Boulder, Westview.

Gillespie, C.G. (1991) *Negotiating Democracy. Politicians and Generals in Uruguay*, Cambridge, Cambridge University Press.

Huntington, S.P. (1991) *The Third Wave. Democratization in the Late Twentieth Century*, Norman, University of Oklahoma Press.

Johnson, K.F. (1977) 'Research perspectives on the revised Fitzgibbon–Johnson Index of the Image of Political Democracy in Latin America, 1945–1975' in Wilkie, J.W. and Ruddle, K. (eds) *Quantitative Latin American Studies: Methods and Findings*, Los Angeles, UCLA Latin American Centre Publications.

O'Donnell, G. (1989) 'Transitions to democracy: some navigational instruments' in Pastor, R. (ed.) *Democracy in the Americas. Stopping the Pendulum*, New York, Holmes and Meier.

Pion-Berlin, D. (1987) 'Military breakdown and redemocratization in Argentina' in Lopez, G.A. and Stohl, M. (eds) *Liberalization and Redemocratization in Latin America*, New York, Greenwood Press.

Rueschemeyer, D., Stephens, E. and Stephens, J. (1992) *Capitalist Development and Democracy*, Cambridge, Polity Press.

Seligson, M.A. (1987) 'Development, democratization, and decay: Central America at the crossroads' in Malloy, J.M. and Seligson, M.A. (eds) *Authoritarians and Democrats. Regime Transition in Latin America*, Pittsburgh, University of Pittsburgh Press.

Share, D. and Mainwaring, S. (1986) 'Transitions through transaction: democratization in Brazil and Spain' in Selcher, W.A. (ed.) *Political Liberalization in Brazil: Dynamics, Dilemmas, and Future Prospects*, Boulder, Westview Press.

CHAPTER 8

Why have the political trajectories of India and China been different?

Vicky Randall

Introduction

China and India are the two 'giants' of Asia: in the mid 1990s their combined population accounts for over one-third of the world's total. Each country is associated with a distinctive culture or civilization whose roots go back thousands of years. In addition, while each includes a significant and expanding industrial sector, their population remains overwhelmingly rural and agricultural. But while they have these important features in common, in many other respects China and India diverge, and in none perhaps so much as in their political history. India, arguably, has enjoyed a form of parliamentary democracy since it gained political independence in 1947; China has never come anywhere close to adopting a liberal democratic system of government and there is by no means agreement in the mid 1990s that political and economic developments formed a prelude to democratization.

How do we explain two such different political trajectories? In seeking to shed light on this question, this chapter will draw on some of the most relevant themes and interpretations in the country-based literatures and how these relate to the broader theoretical approach to democratization. On almost any reckoning, a satisfactory explanation for the difference requires one to examine developments over the medium to long term. For that reason, transition theories, whose central focus typically is the actions and decisions of key actors and institutions over a few critical years, are unlikely to be illuminating and will not be used here.

Both modernization and structural approaches have more to offer, though neither entirely fits the bill. The shortcomings of a simple modernization approach, which associates the emergence of democracy with indicators of social and economic development, are particularly apparent when dealing with the cases of India and China. Those revised versions of modernization theories which take into account a broader range of variables, including political culture, colonial legacy and political parties, are more pertinent. They still fail to identify any systematic interrelationship between the variables involved, though it is open to those who make use of them to suggest their own. Structural approaches, on the other hand, do point to interconnections between different structural factors. Their main limitation is that they tend to focus on specific kinds of structures, notably social class alignments and the state, whilst neglecting others. So formulated, they arguably shed more light on China than on India.

There can be no simple explanation for the differences between India and China examined here, but it will be argued that neither modernization theory nor structural theory in itself provides an adequate explanatory framework.

Rather, drawing on both, but also in some ways transcending their culture–structure split, we need to centre our analysis on a series of elements which have tended to take a different form in India and China, and which have interacted over time in a different way. These elements include, first, what can be summed up as indigenous political tradition, second, forces of imperialism, be it British (for India) or Japanese (for China), and, third, the precipitate of the encounter between the first two elements in terms of civil society and a distinctive political system institutionalized to an extent through the dominant political party.

8.1   Contrasting experiences

Before proceeding to issues of explanation it is necessary to set out more fully the strikingly divergent political experiences of the two countries since the mid nineteenth century. India is frequently described as 'the world's largest democracy'. Following independence from British rule in 1947, its constitution, adopted in 1950, declared India to be a 'sovereign, democratic republic' and set out the formal arrangements underpinning a parliamentary, federal system of government. The first competitive general election, with universal suffrage, was held in 1952. Since then there have been ten further general elections as well as elections regularly held at provincial or state level. While the Congress Party has tended to dominate the national assembly, it has never won an outright majority of the vote. In fact 57 parties have contested at least two national elections since 1952 (Sisson, 1993, p.38). Beginning in 1977, four national elections resulted in a defeat for the incumbent government. At state level too, since 1967, non-Congress Party governments have been numerous (although, as noted in Chapter 1, direct presidential rule from the centre has also been imposed over a long period in a number of states). In addition, India has a vibrant and, for a 'Third World' country, relatively independent press, together with a set of fundamental citizen rights that are set down in the constitution and largely defended by the courts.

Moreover these democratic traits did not emerge out of the blue at Independence. The British had already introduced liberal representative institutions, albeit with limited powers. The elective principle was first incorporated at local level in 1884 and at provincial level in 1892. The Morley–Minto reforms of 1909 extended this principle to the state legislative council, and expanded the franchise. The 1919 Montagu–Chelmsford reforms devolved responsibility for a number of domestic policy areas, including education and health, to the provincial councils. The 1935 Government of India Act consolidated these moves towards a federal and representative system of government and was in turn to provide much of the basis for independent India's constitution.

The Indian National Congress, the movement for national independence originating in the 1880s, was from the start heavily influenced by, and its leadership increasingly committed to, Western liberal notions of representative democracy. A key component of this movement were members of a 'new middle class', generated by the requirements of the expanding colonial bureaucracy and legal system but frustrated in their bid for political and economic advancement. Their Western-style education and occupational training brought them into contact with new liberal ideas. Later, with the openings for indigenous political representation in India, and despite misgivings, many of them had experience of participating in the new representative institutions.

To say that India is a parliamentary or liberal democracy ignores a large literature that has questioned the possibility of 'real' democracy in a country with such marked social inequality, depths of poverty and low rates of literacy. In these conditions, clientelism (the intrusion of patron–client relationships into the working of political institutions) has flourished, while corruption and even intimidation have been regularly reported. It also ignores questions raised about the future prospects for liberal democracy in India. India, in particular, experienced from the late 1960s a trend of 'creeping authoritarianism', culminating in the imposition of a state of national emergency from 1975 to 1977. Many observers have also pointed to a more protracted process of political 'deinstitutionalization', or decay, from the mid 1960s and a heightening of communal conflict.

There is another question that needs to be asked about liberal democracy in India, and that is about its consequences: to put it crudely, has democracy been good for India in the sense of hastening social reform and economic development? This, again, I shall return to. None the less, the main conclusion of this section must be that liberal democracy of a kind, and especially in comparison with other developing countries, took remarkable root in India and has persisted. The period of emergency rule was followed by a general election which threw out the offending Congress Party government. More recently elements of deinstitutionalization in some spheres have been offset by, for instance, the increasing assertiveness of the press, the Electoral Commission, civil rights organizations and local protest movements.

If India has been 'exceptional' within the developing world for the resilience of its liberal democratic institutions, China has been exceptional for its resistance to the world-wide waves of democratization. Just at the time India was adopting its new constitution, China was setting up a 'People's Democratic Republic', in which 'bourgeois' democracy was emphatically rejected and power and authority were rapidly concentrated in the ruling Communist Party. China's close identification with the Soviet Union in the early years of the emerging Cold War reinforced its mistrust of Western cultural and political influences, and specifically of bourgeois forms of democracy.

Successive Chinese constitutions have underlined the Communist Party's pre-eminent role in leading the proletariat (people) towards communism, by providing the correct ideological and political line. Although a number of other political parties survived the Communist Revolution these were suppressed during the 'Cultural Revolution' (1965–69), a period of bitter internal party struggle and upheaval in which all conceivable manifestations of bourgeois ideology were attacked. Although they resurfaced in the 1980s, they had 'ceased to be democratic or parties in any commonly understood sense of these words' and were best viewed as 'components of a corporate state' (Seymour, 1986, pp.991, 1003). The central organizing principle of the Chinese Communist Party (CCP) itself has been 'democratic centralism', according to which 'the individual is subordinate to the organization, the minority is subordinate to the majority, the lower level is subordinate to the central committee' (Saich, 1981, p.97). In practice, and for most of the time, this has meant extremely hierarchical, centralized decision making, with power above all concentrated in the supreme executive body, the Politburo. To this was added, during the 1960s and up to his death in 1976, the extraordinary personality cult of the Party Chairman, Mao Tse-tung.

The 1954 constitution established a corresponding state structure, which has remained essentially unchanged since. Modelled closely on the Soviet system it has provided for an elaborate pyramid of territorially-based assemblies, from commune or city-level upwards, elected either directly or indirectly, and with fixed terms of office. These have largely paralleled the structure of the CCP, thereby facilitating Party control. At the summit, the National People's Congress, indirectly elected every five years (except in the stormy aftermath of the 'Cultural Revolution') is, formally speaking, the highest organ of state power. But its unwieldy size and infrequent meetings, together with *de facto* domination by the CCP, have reduced its role to one of ratifying, usually by unanimous vote, decisions taken elsewhere. Nor in China can one find the kind of civil and political freedoms generally ident-ified as characteristic of liberal democracy. The Party has retained tight control over the mass media and public debate, except when disputes within the leadership have temporarily opened up some limited space as during the 'Hundred Flowers Campaign' of 1956 and the 'Democracy Wall Campaign' following Mao's death in 1976. Similarly, from the adoption of the 1954 constitution to 1958 and more consistently under Mao's successors there have been some moves towards less day-to-day interference with the workings of the lower courts and the growth of a specialist legal profession; but the CCP has rejected the notion of an independent judiciary as charac-teristic of class-divided society and the product of bourgeois ideology.

Again in contrast with India, by the 1940s, there was in China no significant democratic tradition or experience of working with democratic institutions. In the course of the nineteenth century, the Chinese imperial system was being steadily undermined by the combined pressures of internal demographic and economic changes and aggressive external imperial powers, including Britain, and it ended formally with the collapse of the Qing dynasty in 1911. In the surrounding political turmoil democratic ideas were a minor theme. Adherents of the Reform Movement (1895–98) and of the Revolutionary Alliance formed in 1905, particularly its leader Sun Yat-sen, admired Western institutions of political representation. In the wake of the Reform Movement, provincial assemblies and eventually in 1910 a national assembly were set up, though on a very limited franchise and with an advisory role only, but the disputes that arose within them only hastened the process of political disintegration and in the case of the provincial assemblies ultimately helped pave the way for warlordism. By the 1920s embryonic democratic ideas and practices were largely discredited and submerged by a rising tide of authoritarian nationalism.

Again, we must acknowledge differences over the meaning of 'democracy'. The Chinese communist leadership, like the Soviet leadership before it, has dismissed Western 'bourgeois' or liberal democracy as a fraud, designed to obscure the reality of class rule. It has argued that its own system is more truly democratic. Going back to the heroic, pre-revolutionary days when the embattled Party was consolidating its strength for the final advance in the northern stronghold of Yanan, a distinctively Maoist tenet was the importance of the 'mass line'. This means absorbing and systematizing ideas *from* the masses, as well as relaying them back. Communist leaders have also cited the extent of popular participation in the running of enterprises and through the system of elected assemblies. Indeed, in the case of the assemblies, in the early 1980s, state reforms expanded on their formal democratic elements by recognizing electors' rights to recall deputies, and requiring an element of competition for assembly seats. The CCP leader, Deng Xiaoping, exhorted China to create 'a democracy which is at a higher level and more substantial than that of the capitalist countries' (cited in Nathan, 1986, p.x), while communist China's fourth constitution, adopted in 1982, and incorporating these changes, referred to China as a 'socialist democracy'. From this perspective, China perhaps approximates the model of direct democracy outlined in Chapter 1 and elaborated in Held (1996).

None the less, to many, China's system of government remains steadfastly un-democratic or anti-democratic, corresponding rather to the authoritarian model. Mao Tse-tung's death in 1976 was part of the background to the emergence of the small but significant 'Democracy Wall' movement, which Deng Xiaoping briefly supported but then effectively crushed. There were further student protests in 1986. Then in April 1989, the death of Hu Yaobang, the former CCP General Secretary, who had resigned from that post following the 1986 student demonstrations, triggered a resurgence of the democratic student movement. Its moderate demands were met with brutal repression. The final confrontation in Tiananmen Square in

'Goddess of Democracy and Freedom' stands in Tiananmen Square, Beijing, 30 May 1989

the centre of China's capital, Beijing, was witnessed on television screens around the world. Authoritarianism still prevailed in the mid 1990s.

Since the late 1970s China has been undergoing a dramatic and far-reaching process of economic liberalization. It is argued that this has contributed to the expansion of Chinese civil society (discussed below), which generally is seen as a precondition for effective democratization. The youth- or student-led democracy campaigns since the 1970s are taken as symptoms of this development. Nevertheless, they made little headway against the communist leadership, nor was it clear by the mid 1990s that they had attained widespread popular support within China.

─────────────── *Summary of Section 8.1* ───────────────

- In India at Independence, liberal representative ideas and institutions had already taken some hold and subsequently developed into a kind of parliamentary democracy. This has persisted despite continuing social and economic inequality, authoritarian strains culminating in the mid 1970s in emergency rule, institutional decay and communal conflict.

- In contrast, by the 1940s in China ideas and institutions that could have sustained democratic development were only very weakly established. The communist system of rule then installed was explicitly opposed to 'bourgeois democracy'. Although described as socialist democracy, this system has been in essence authoritarian, despite reforms since Mao's death.

8.2 Explaining the difference: modernization and structural approaches outlined

All the perils of generalization and inference associated with the comparative method of studying politics are multiplied tenfold when seeking to compare two such vast, diverse and ancient societies as these. The status of any explanation or difference must be recognized as provisional in the extreme. It is also noteworthy that political scientists have reflected at some length on the reasons for liberal democracy in India, but the literature on China tends to approach the question of democracy more obliquely. What will be attempted here is to bring together insights from the existing literature on the two countries and more general theories of democratization.

The modernization approach

As noted in Chapter 1, the modernization approach in explaining the development of democracy is not a single, self-identified school and takes numerous forms. These tend to have in common a belief that economic (and generally it is assumed capitalist) development generates social change which in turn has consequences for the political sphere. Such an approach often entails the use of quantitative data, where selected indicators of modernization on the one hand and of liberal democratic politics on the other are systematically correlated. Although this type of approach tended to go into abeyance from the late 1960s with the apparent failure of ostensibly developing countries to democratize, during the 1990s, and in a more cautious and qualified vein, it has resurfaced. Thus Lipset and others reaffirmed in the early 1990s the positive relationship between economies and democracy which Lipset and others argued for back in the early 1960s. Responding to criticisms and modifications of their argument in the intervening period, more recent scholars have recognized the need to analyse this relationship over time and at different stages of economic development. Accordingly, Lipset's statistical reworking of existing cross-national data suggests that, up to average annual income levels of approximately $2,000 and beyond levels of approximately $4,000, there is a positive relationship between economic development and liberal democracy; but in the interim zone the relationship is more complex and can even go into reverse (Lipset *et al.*, 1993).

On its own, this observation is not particularly illuminating in the case of India and China. Both fall well within the first income band: in 1992 China's average annual income was estimated at $470 and India's at $310. Though both were, therefore, well within the range in which development and democracy are expected to grow concomitantly, they could not be expected to be far advanced in the process and their per capita income figures are so close that they could not help to explain the tremendous contrast in political trajectories.

Modernization theorists do not, of course, rely solely on the income per head indicator but examine a range of data, including indicators of urbanization and literacy (see Table 8.1). These data show, however, that the scores for the two countries were generally close and on several indicators – life expectancy, illiteracy, percentage of GDP attributable to agriculture, GDP per head – it was liberal democratic India that lagged behind.

While the emphasis of the modernization approach has been on the level of socio-economic development, it has more recently (with the wisdom of hindsight), sought to identify further requisites or conditions favourable to

Table 8.1 China and India: social and economic indicators (for 1992, except where otherwise stated)

	China	*India*
Population (million)	1,162.2	883.6
GDP per head ($)	470	310
Life expectancy (1980–85)	68	55
Urban population as percentage of total (1985)	20.6	25.5
% illiteracy (1990)	27	52
% labour force in agriculture (1988)	73.7	62.6
% GDP based on agriculture	24	29

Source: World Bank (1994); The Economist (1990)

democratization, thereby tacitly conceding that modernization in and of itself may not be sufficient. In this context, political culture, the legacy of colonial rule, civil society and political institutionalization – notably the role of political parties – are some of the aspects that have been singled out. These four are especially relevant to the cases of India and China and will provide key elements of the analysis which follows. However, they are insufficient by themselves and need at least to be supplemented by more structural considerations. In particular the notion of political culture requires some understanding of the 'structural' context.

Structural approaches

The explanatory focus of structural approaches to democratization is on the long-term processes of historical change shaped by changing structures of power, as is made clear in Chapter 1. There are various structures of power, but three are usually given prominence: state, class and transnational structures. Certain structural arrangements and changes are more favourable to democratization; others are less favourable.

A classic structural explanation of why India moved to liberal democracy and China to communist revolution at the same time (the 1940s) is found in Barrington Moore's (1966) *Social Origins of Dictatorship and Democracy* (see Chapters 1 and 2). India and China were two of the eight countries Moore used in his comparative analysis. His primary focus was on the different and changing structural relations between landed upper classes, peasants, urban bourgeoisie and state structures.

Why communist revolution in China? Moore found that the revolution occurred in structural conditions where the urban bourgeoisie was weak and dominated by the state, the links between landlords and peasants were weak, the landlords had failed to commercialize agriculture, and the peasants were cohesive and found (communist) allies with organizational skills. Why liberal democracy in India? Moore found that an Indian bourgeoisie was growing in opposition to the colonial state, the colonial state was linked closely to the landed upper classes, the landlords failed to commercialize agriculture leaving a huge non-cohesive peasantry on the land, and the Indian urban bourgeoisie was driven by this arrangement to link up with the peasantry in order to obtain a massive base for its struggle (with others) against foreign rule. As Moore remarks:

> By splitting the landed upper classes from the weak and rising urban leaders, the English presence prevented the formation of the characteristic reactionary coalition [where the urban bourgeoisie and the state were weak and dominated by the landed upper classes] on the German or Japanese model. This may be judged a decisive contribution toward the eventual establishment of parliamentary democracy on Indian soil, at least as important as the osmosis of English ideas through Indian professional classes. Without at least some favourable structural conditions, the ideas could scarcely have been more than literary playthings.

> (Moore, 1966, p.354)

The heart of Moore's general explanation of democratization is that, arising out of the historical development of classes and class alignments,

'favourable structural conditions' emerged which made a 'decisive contribution toward the eventual establishment of parliamentary democracy'. The
people in certain classes who made choices and acted to drive India toward a
liberal democracy independent from colonial rule were moved by ideas of
liberal democracy brought by the British to India, but their choices and
actions *were profoundly shaped by class structures*, and the democratic ideas
would have been no more than 'literary playthings' in the absence of such
favourable structural conditions.

To say that political cultures – ideas about politics – were of no political
significance until favourable structural conditions made them so is an
important consideration in explaining where such cultures come from. But I
suggest that this structural perspective fails to account for the *persistence* of
liberal democracy in India and the *persistence* of authoritarian rule in China
from the 1940s where the different political cultures have been very important to our understanding of these different political trajectories.

Likewise, Moore's emphasis on the character of the state and the different
ways in India and China that class structures related historically to the state is a
pertinent comparative point. But 'the state' is very abstract in this formulation;
we learn almost nothing about particular political institutions (e.g. the
military, the civil bureaucracy, political parties) or particular political
processes (e.g. electoral practices). I suggest that key aspects of an
explanation of the different political routes of India and China relate
precisely to differences in such practices (some competitive elections took
place in colonial India, no elections occurred in China). Also, there were
important differences in the nature of political institutions, especially
differences between the dominant political party in each country.

Similarly, Moore is cognizant of civil society as associations and
groupings within broad social classes as they relate to the state. But I
suggest that the striking differences between China, with a scanty civil
society, and India, with a comparatively lush one, is a factor of great
importance and requires independent consideration when explaining
political differences between India and China.

—————————————— *Summary of Section 8.2* ——————————————

- A modernization approach which focuses only on indices of social and
  economic development sheds little light on political differences
  between India and China.

- Different political cultures, colonial legacies, party developments and
  civil societies explain the differences better.

- Both more recent modernization approaches and structural approaches
  refer to these four factors, but in different ways.

- Both approaches are inadequate on their own.

8.3   The emergence of India's parliamentary democracy: four explanatory factors

Important ingredients in an explanation of India's democratization were a particularly propitious encounter between what may be termed the indigenous *political culture* or tradition and *British colonial rule*. This in turn contributed to the emergence of *civil society* and relatively effective representative institutions including *political parties*, foremost amongst them the Congress Party.

Political culture

This is a notoriously problematic concept (as has been emphasized in Chapter 5). Despite the considerable criticisms made of Almond and Verba's (1963) pioneering study, *The Civic Culture*, which first systematically developed the idea, the term has come back into mainstream use relatively unchanged (see Diamond, 1993a). Broadly it is seen as the totality of popular attitudes towards politics and political authorities in a society. Political culture cannot, however, be seen in suspension; it has to be situated in a specific historical and social context (the structural dimension).

India's traditional political culture was shaped by two influences in particular: Hinduism and social pluralism. Although Hinduism has by no means been the only religion – in the mid 1990s it accounts for around 83 per cent of the population, with Islam around 12 per cent and Buddhism, Sikhism and Christianity all represented – it goes back furthest in time and has been the faith of the large majority. Historically, Hinduism has been characterized by its lack of a centralized hierarchy and the diversity of its forms, both regionally and in terms of a 'great' (Brahminical) and a 'little' or local, vernacular tradition. It is argued that the Brahminical tradition and the authority it imparted to the Brahmin or priestly *varna* (or group of castes), first, helped to preserve the cultural unity of the sub-continent, second, encouraged a certain detachment from the secular, political sphere and, third, 'constructed formidable obstacles to the creation of a powerful centralized state ... through religious concepts of legitimation which embedded authority in the dominant clans, lineage's and castes of localized society rather than in the bureaucratic and military offices of the centralized state' (Frankel, 1989, p.2). At the same time the diversity of Hinduism, and of the caste system which it sanctioned, itself contributed to social pluralism.

India's social diversity – regional, linguistic, religious and caste-based – is legendary. However, partly because of the multiple and cross-cutting nature of these divisions, they have not generally given rise to political polarization or civil war. The obvious major exception has been the Muslim–Hindu conflict which culminated in political partition when the Indian sub-continent was divided into separate states, India and the largely Muslim Pakistan. Over a million lives were lost in the process of partition. Broadly speaking, the caste system has contributed to social cohesiveness. This is a long standing, complex system of social stratification, maintained through ascription (you are born into your caste), endogamy (you may not marry outside it) and Hindu notions of purity and pollution, and based, at least originally, on a social division of labour. Not only has the caste system held the different caste – and outcaste (Untouchable) – groups together in a single social system, it has incorporated social groupings originally outside the caste system. Barrington Moore has evoked eloquently the self-contained, cohesive nature of India's caste-infused social order: 'Indian society reminds one of the starfish whom fishermen used to shred angrily into bits, after which each fragment would grow into a new starfish' (Moore, 1966, p.458).

The contention is that India has traditionally been characterized not simply by extraordinary social diversity but by social pluralism or the *tolerance* of diversity. This, it is argued, helped to pave the way for subsequent accommodative politics. Here we need to be careful. In the first place it is clear that while Hinduism may have contributed to social pluralism, it has also included a less tolerant strain. Mentioned above were the communal clashes at the time of partition. More recently a militant Hindu fundamentalism, embodied in organizations like the VHP (Vishwa Hindu Parishad), and exploited by an increasingly influential national party, the BJP (Bharatiya Janata Party), claims to be reviving religious tradition – though to some extent this is the reinvention of tradition – and is threatening to undermine the very culture of tolerance that Hinduism helped to nurture. Second, it is important not to romanticize or idealize the traditional social system. Although plural in the sense of dispersing power from the centre, it was far from egalitarian. Local communities were microcosms of oppression, especially for women and for Untouchables. Caste was above all a mechanism of social control. None the less its effect was to diffuse rather than to concentrate power.

British colonial rule

This indigenous political tradition interacted with the experience of British rule. Weiner (1987), among others, has pointed out the powerful, though by no means perfect, correlation between the survival of liberal democracy in developing countries and colonization by the British. India's experience of British rule was unusually extended; it can be traced back to Clive's victory at Plassey in 1757, although Parliament and the Crown only acquired a significant regulatory role towards the end of the eighteenth century.

It is argued that the British fostered liberal democracy in two main and related ways. The requirements of an expanding administration together with associated educational reforms stimulated the growth of a professional middle class, which, when it found channels to further economic and political advancement blocked, was to become the backbone of the Indian national movement. Despite the authoritarian character of colonial rule, these partly Westernized groups were bound to encounter liberal democratic ideas steadily taking root in Britain. Second, the British introduced a system of independent courts, based on liberal judicial principles, and, as noted earlier, in the decades before independence began to introduce liberal representative institutions, in which many of India's future political leaders participated.

Box 8.1 India's political history: key dates

1757 – Battle of Plassey

1857 – Indian mutiny

1885 – Founding of Indian National Congress

1909 – Morley–Minto reforms

1919 – Montagu–Chelmsford reforms

1935 – Government of India Act

1947 – Independence and partition (into India and Pakistan)

1950 – Constitution adopted

1964 – Death of Nehru

1966 – Mrs Gandhi becomes leader of the Congress Party

1975–January 1977 – Emergency rule

1977 (March) – Congress Party defeated in a general election.

It is often suggested that liberal representative institutions could not have thrived so well in India had they not proved highly compatible with the society's traditional political culture. In fact the influence was not all one way. Manor (1990, p.24) argues that Indian culture, together with the size and complexity of its society, 'made it difficult for the British to avoid building a system which consisted in significant part of accommodative institutions ... The British protected social pluralism'.

On the other hand, Indian social values could be used to sustain liberal institutions. As the Rudolphs (1987, p.67) emphasize, indigenous Hinduism and imported liberal theory diverged widely: the former stressed family, caste and tribe, the latter the individual. Yet they converged with respect to the priority of societal values over state goals. Both saw society as preceding and limiting the state.

Civil society

The recent democratization literature, whether leaning towards a modern-ization, structural or indeed transition emphasis, has brought to the fore the concept of civil society. Perhaps modernization theorists concentrate more on the intrinsic character of civil society and structuralists on its strength and autonomy in relation to the state, but all regard it as an essential ingredient for democratization. In many ways a significant part of the process I have been describing in the preceding paragraphs could be understood as the emergence of Indian civil society. One difficulty here is the lack of agreement about definitions. Civil society is a term lifted from a particular European historical experience and applied to quite dissimilar contexts. Partly as a result, there is some inconsistency as to what it does or does not include. Rueschemeyer *et al.* (1992, p.6) define it as 'the totality of social institutions and associations, both formal and informal, that are not strictly production-related nor governmental nor familial in character'. However, some other usages would include such production-related institutions as trade unions but query the inclusion of groupings based on particularist and, especially, ethnic identities, which weaken rather than strengthen social cohesion.

Accordingly not all are agreed that by the time of Independence, India already possessed a vibrant and autonomous civil society (for a dissenting view, see for instance, Kaviraj, 1991). However, while he does not use the term civil society, Sisson, in his account of the emergence of a liberal democratic political culture in India, describes how the nineteenth century already witnessed the

> development of a rich associational life. These associations ranged from Westernized political discussion groups to reformist organizations that demanded the government use its resources to engineer social change; it included organizations of landed and commercial interests as well as cultural revivalist organizations and movements bent on resisting the encroachments of Western culture. Particularly after the Mutiny of 1857, numerous political associations were created for the purpose of petitioning government for reform.

> (Sisson, 1993, pp.40–1)

This emergent civil society can be seen as the product of traditional political culture together with the character of British rule, but also finally the gradual development of an indigenous business community. The consequences of British rule for India's economic development have been much debated, with the balance of opinion leaning towards a fairly negative assessment. Even so, infrastructural provisions such as the railways, a system of law, irrigation and access to international financial markets did facilitate the growth of commerce and, especially in the twentieth century, of industry. The existence of capitalism is no guarantee of liberal democracy. Moreover, following Independence the state played a prominent role in the Indian economy, creating complex chains of interdependence. None the less, to the extent that it was autonomous, the competitive ethos and organizational vitality of capitalist enterprise was bound to invigorate civil society.

The Congress Party

Both traditional political culture and extended exposure to liberal ideals and institutions are seen as having been important in shaping the character of the Congress nationalist movement and the Congress Party, which dominated Indian national party politics for many decades after Independence and has itself been vital to democratic institutionalization in India. The Indian National Congress was founded as long ago as 1885 and as it broadened into a national movement it needed to be decentralized and accommodating. After Independence there emerged what Kothari has called the 'Congress system'; that is, a party system in which Congress was the dominant 'party of consensus' but tolerated and interacted with 'parties of pressure' at the margin. The operation of factionalism within the Congress Party functioned in such a way as to make the Party and the system as a whole responsive to

The first Indian National Congress, 1885

external political pressures and concerns (Kothari, 1964). It was this Congress system which gave life to independent India's formal institutions of parliamentary democracy.

─────────────────── *Summary of Section 8.3* ───────────────────
This section has analysed India's political development in terms of the following.

- India's traditional political culture, as shaped by Hinduism, social diversity and, within limits, social pluralism.

- India's prolonged encounter with British colonial rule in the course of which liberal representative values and institutions began to take root, and capitalist market relations strengthened.

- The outcome of this process in a relatively dense and autonomous civil society.

- A party system, centred on the Congress Party, which has been important in helping to institutionalize democratic politics.

8.4 The road to China's communist rule: four explanatory factors

The contrasts with China could hardly be greater. In general, traditional Chinese *political culture*, and within it the doctrine of Confucianism, has been seen as antithetical to liberal democratic values or pluralism. China was *never colonized* as such and its encounter with Western and Japanese powers persuaded it of the priority to be attached to national unity and survival. Many studies have emphasized the striking continuities between the old imperial system of rule and rule by the CCP since 1949. That is, the collision of China's traditional political culture with modern imperialism helped to precipitate the system of communist rule, centred around the role of a single, Leninist, vanguard *political party*. That collision also hindered the development of *civil society*.

Political culture

It is in fact even more difficult for China than for India to separate out discussions of political culture from the structure of power itself. The feudal era in China ended as early as 221 BC with the founding of the Qin dynasty. Thereafter the basic pattern of rule which evolved and to which, however disrupted, the system reverted, was one in which an emperor reigned over the whole of China by means of centralized bureaucracy. Officials were recruited, for the most part, from a scholar–landlord class. That is, officials and landowners, though not always the same people, came from the same social stratum. Officials used their income from imperial service to acquire land for their family or clan. But these officials were selected by means of merit-based examination and their political authority derived from the centralized state system. This pattern of rule persisted, in principle at least, for over 2,000 years, to the ending of the last, Qing, dynasty in 1911.

According to the classic Chinese view, the emperor was the son of heaven, with a divine mandate to rule (Franke, 1970). Within the dominant political culture, the imperial system was further buttressed by the precepts of Confucianism, an essentially secular doctrine which soon came to be the official perspective of the bureaucracy. Confucius himself lived in the pre-Qin era (551–479 BC), when the feudal order was breaking down, and his teachings reflect a yearning for unified authority and social harmony (Zhengyan Fu, 1993). As taken up by the imperial regime, the teachings emphasized order, hierarchy, obedience and correct behaviour, in the relationship between ruler and ruled, husband and wife and parents and children. Considerable importance was attached to the role of education in instilling proper moral values, although formal education was confined to the scholar-gentry. Also relevant to the present discussion, while there was certainly an emphasis on propriety and virtuous rule, there was no notion of either individual rights or even the rights of social collectivities *vis-à-vis* the supreme authority. Within Confucianism, and especially within the teach-ings of his disciple Mencius, there was recognition that officials might need to warn their emperor of failings in the regime. In the words of Mencius, 'he who restrains his prince, loves his prince' (cited in Nathan, 1986). But such 'remonstration' was at the official's peril.

This account must at once be qualified. Imperial China (in striking contrast to pre-colonial India) had a long-standing tradition of peasant revolt. 'The tradition was a rich one not only in the sense that peasant rebellions were frequent and often on a large scale, but also because it remained very much alive in the minds of the peasants of China in the nineteenth and twentieth centuries' (Chesneaux, 1973, p.7). In these revolts, secret societies often played a crucial part; they also drew on dissident strains of Daoism and Buddhism. More than once, such revolts actually overthrew the reigning emperor and his ministers. None the less, in the first place, the frame of reference for such revolts remained the traditional conception of the divine mandate. The emperor was seen to have shown himself as unworthy of the mandate, but often it was the rebel leader himself 'who assumed imperial power and re-established Confucian legitimacy' (Chesneaux, 1973, p.9). In Chesneaux's words again, peasant revolts, 'never challenged more than the abuses of the traditional regime'. Second, it could be argued that such revolts precisely demonstrated the absence of any legitimate channels through which questions of social rights could be pursued.

Interpretations that stress the impact of traditional political culture on Chinese political development point to the elements of continuity between the ancient regime and the present (see, for example, Zhengyan Fu, 1993). China, from the mid nineteenth century, was in severe crisis. This can be explained (see Skocpol, 1979) in terms of the coincidence of two harmful processes. First was the regime's internal dynamic, the tendency for prosperity and stability to wax and wane with the rise and fall of each dynasty. In the downswing of the cycle corruption grew, inequalities widened, military efficiency declined and peasant revolt intensified. China was in such a period of dynastic decline in the nineteenth century that it left the country especially vulnerable to the second process, the onset of external pressures (discussed below). In this context, from the turn of the century, there were growing demands for reform. But it is argued that Confucian assumptions infused the new reformist thinking. A typical and influential thinker ·was Liang Qichao. Despite his extensive reading of the Western liberal classics, he continued to believe in the harmony of individual and collective interests. In his later years, he came to recognize that such harmony did not always exist but it remained his ideal and he stressed the need to educate people into the right frame of mind in order to achieve it (Nathan, 1986). Sun Yat-sen, founder of what was to become the Kuomintang Party (KMT), came to prominence later than Liang and was more radical; for instance, prior to the 1911 revolution, he wanted China to become a republic and to enjoy democratic institutions on the Western pattern. One of his three

Box 8.2 China's political history: key dates

1850–64 – Taiping Rebellion

1894–95 – China defeated in Sino-Japanese War

1895–98 – Reform Movement

1911 – Revolution

1937 – Japanese invasion

1949 – Communist Revolution

1958–60 – Great Leap Forward

1965–69 – Cultural Revolution

1976 – Death of Mao

1978 – Democracy Wall Movement

1989 – Tiananmen Square.

founding principles was the Principle of People's Rights. But in elaborating on this principle, he stressed he was not advocating individual liberty: 'If we apply it to a person, we shall become a sheet of loose sand; on no account must we give more liberty to the individual; let us secure liberty instead for the nation'. To cite Franke, 'The "Three People's Principles" already revealed ... tendencies towards a totalitarian state, which the KMT later exerted itself to translate into practice' (Franke, 1970, p.125).

It can even be argued that, while Marxist–Leninism was itself clearly an exogenous factor, China was particularly susceptible to its doctrine, especially as it was adopted by Mao. The tradition of peasant revolt, the deference towards enlightened intellectuals and the general assumption that there was one correct way of thinking and acting, for instance, could be seen as preparing the ground. However, it is difficult to take this argument very far: China, as the structural theories contend, surely did experience a major social revolution and historical rupture in 1949. Confucianism, bureaucratism and hierarchy were categorically repudiated. Even so, there is a significant contrast between the 'success' of communism in China and its fortunes in India. India has had a communist movement, dating back to the 1920s like the CCP, but it has struggled all along, building beachheads in certain states but basically caught in the mire of complexities of the caste system and its relationship with the Congress Party.

On many accounts the influence of traditional Chinese political culture survived the Communist Revolution of 1949, and affected the way in which communism was adapted to Chinese circumstances. Nathan argues that Mao himself had absorbed the teachings of Liang in his youth: 'the premised identity of personal and collective interests governed the meaning of the various democratic procedures that Mao invented or adapted from Lenin' (Nathan, 1986, p.64). On the other hand, many of China's own internal critics of the regime from the late 1970s have blamed the failure of communism on China's cultural backwardness. For instance, the relatively outspoken Enlightenment Group declared in the early 1980s that the 1911 Republican Revolution 'overthrew the emperor as a person only, but the concept of emperors remained in people's minds' (Nathan, 1986, p.xiii).

The colonial intrusion

Rather than simply emphasizing the continuity of Chinese political culture, it seems more plausible, as in the Indian case, to look at the intersection of culture with colonial intrusion. Traditionally, China had been wont to see itself as the centre of the world, the Middle Kingdom, to which the neighbouring peoples paid tribute. In the nineteenth century, China's isolation and complacency were first shaken by Russian expansionism, then by Western inroads. The Opium Wars of 1839–42 and 1856–60 ended in humiliating treaties, which formed part of the background to the major mid-century peasant revolt, the Taiping Rebellion (1850–64), whose long-term effect was further to weaken the Qing regime. From the 1860s, educated opinion increasingly looked to the West for lessons in how to make China stronger, but initially the focus was on Western technology. It was China's defeat in the Sino-Japanese War of 1894–95 which prompted the Reform Movement. Thus, from the start, interest in Western achievements, including liberal democracy, was bound up with the concern for national survival. This increasingly prompted the conclusion that the crumbling and corrupt imperial system would have to go. Though 1911 marks the formal end, the abolition in 1905 of the official examination system, and thus the basis of legitimation for rule through officials, was perhaps more practically and symbolically significant.

The collapse of the imperial system left China prey both to the centrifugal tendencies it had held in check and which ultimately degenerated into warlordism and to further encroachments by foreign powers. The ultimate consequence was the increased militarization of political life (a point emphasized in Skocpol, 1979) and the reinforcement of authoritarian political tendencies. Especially following the death in 1916 of the strongman, Yuan Shih-k'ai, who assumed the Presidency of the Republic in 1912, political control in China came largely to reside in 'warlord'-dominated regional military machines. The increasingly nationalistic KMT and the Chinese Communist Party emerged at roughly the same time, in the early 1920s, and both were committed to national unification. Initially in collaboration, later in mutual opposition, this effectively meant that each party had to mount a military as well as a political campaign, especially following the Japanese invasion in 1937. The KMT developed a National Revolutionary Army, headed by Chiang Kai-shek who soon became the effective leader. From 1927, as the limitations of an urban-based strategy and the treachery of the KMT were revealed, the CCP also developed its own campaign of peasant-based guerrilla warfare.

There are two related conclusions to underline here. First, the eventual victory of Mao's communist army was not only because, modifying the original Marxist–Leninist line, it concentrated its appeal on a deeply disaffected peasantry and took up the issue of land reform; but also, and partly for this reason, it was able to succeed – where the KMT had failed – in expelling the Japanese. That is, the perceived threat to post-Qing China from Western and Japanese imperial forces helped to ensure the persistence of authoritarian tendencies amongst the contenders for power and limit the influence of Western notions of liberal democracy. (The authoritarian character of subsequent KMT rule in Taiwan is discussed in Chapter 9.) Second, politics within the communist movement that came to power in 1949 had been significantly militarized. Not only the military itself but quasi-military approaches to popular mobilization were notable elements of the ensuing regime. The implications of such a militarization of party politics for democracy should be clear and contrast considerably with the experience of India's Congress movement, and the non-violent tactics advocated by its renowned leader, Mahatma Gandhi.

Japanese imperialism arguably had a further consequence for China's political development. Its bitter memory was a significant contributory factor in Mao's decision in 1949 that China should 'lean to the side' of the Soviet Union under the conditions of the emerging Cold War; also General McArthur's activities in Japan fuelled fears of a new American–Japanese axis. Subsequently, Chinese fears shifted more exclusively onto the USA, with the outbreak of the Korean War in 1950 and American support for the Kuomintang who, expelled from mainland China, were firmly ensconced in the island of Taiwan (see Chapter 9). Chinese fears of Japan and America meant that China's new communist regime became for a time closely identified with the Soviet Union, designing political and economic institutions to a considerable extent on the Soviet model and receiving Soviet material aid and advice. Although these ties weakened following Stalin's death in 1953 and Mao's disagreements with Stalin's successors, the Cold War legacy persisted in China's prolonged cultural and political isolation from the West.

The Communist Party

As a result of this particular pattern of interaction between indigenous political tradition and external pressure – and again in contrast to India – from 1949 China's political institutions were dominated by the single ruling Chinese Communist Party. As we have seen, though other small parties were allowed to exist they had no real political power, while internally the ruling party itself was run on the Leninist principle of democratic centralism. I have already noted the claims made that the CCP embodied a more authentic form of democracy. The fact remains that in itself it has constituted the chief institutional bulwark against what is currently understood as democratization. Its exclusive claim on political power and authority was reaffirmed in Deng Xiaoping's statement in 1980: 'The Party cannot be separated from the people and the people cannot be separated from the Party' (Nathan, 1986, p.36).

Civil society

Returning to the notion of civil society, and once more in contrast with India, this is often identified as the critical ingredient whose absence explains China's failure to democratize. The preceding analysis has shown how circumstances in China combined to place great obstacles in the way of its development. In imperial China, it was held in check by the structure of power and language of authority: 'The power of the traditional state rendered private associational activity both difficult and dangerous' (Perry and Fuller, 1991, p.666).

Qualifying this, however, Perry and Fuller argue that with the disintegration of the Qing empire, from the late nineteenth century, civil society 'Chinese-style' did begin to emerge and reached a high point under the Republic (1911 to 1949), though it tended to take the form of oppositional movements rather than social organizations. With the advent of communist rule, however, not only political repression but state direction of the economy arrested this process.

More recently, and especially following June 1989, a discussion has begun amongst sinologists as to whether we are witnessing the birth, or resurgence, of Chinese civil society. Both economic liberalization and restraints on central political control, following Mao's death, may have contributed. Under Deng, there was renewed emphasis on achieving the Four Modernizations: agriculture, industry, science and technology, and national defence. This in turn has been seen to require less direct supervision of the economy, so as (in the words of a popular slogan of 1986) to 'stimulate the initiative of the individual' (Gold, 1990). Partly as a consequence, China in the late 1980s and early 1990s enjoyed a phenomenal rate of economic growth, though this was concentrated in the eastern and coastal areas. With economic reforms have come increased contacts overseas and greater academic freedom.

Perry and Fuller sift the evidence from the Tiananmen uprising carefully. On the negative side, and lending support to the cultural continuity school of thought, they point to the exclusive elitism of the student activists concerned; they were 'bedevilled by the intellectuals' reluctance to foster close relations with other social groups'. Yet despite this rebuff, 'the extent of participation by workers and other citizens was quite remarkable' (Perry and Fuller, 1991, p.669). Entrepreneurs staged a sit-in in sympathy, and donated vital financial support and sophisticated technology, including faxes, motorcycles and the pedicabs which rescued student casualties. The Beijing Workers' Autonomous Federation, aiming to stimulate a nation-wide organization in emulation of Poland's Solidarity trade union, ran an underground printing press supplying handbills, organized factory pickets and encouraged the mushrooming of workers' federations in cities across the country. It is possible, then, that we may be witnessing the emergence of a denser and more autonomous civil society in China. The picture in the mid 1990s, however, was still uncertain and the broader point is that its relative absence both symptomatized and contributed to the inauspicious conditions for democratization in China.

─────────────── *Summary of Section 8.4* ───────────────

This section has analysed China's political development in terms of the following.

- Traditional Chinese political culture as antithetical to liberal democratic values.

- The coincidence of a downswing in the cycle of dynastic rule with increasing pressures from external imperial powers, which elevated in importance the maintenance of national unity and survival.

- The consequences of this for the militarized character of both communist and nationalist parties before 1949, and the CCP after 1949.

- The weakness of civil society.

8.5   Does democratization matter?

Has democratization delivered economic and social development for the people of India? Have the people of China lost out by not living in a liberal democratic polity? Such questions, of course, are not easily answered. One cannot say that development in India since 1947 is *because* of the liberal democratic political system any more than China's record is a consequence of authoritarian rule.

A place to start would be Barrington Moore's (1966) observation that liberal democracy in India was helping to obstruct the revolutionary break with the past needed to set the country on the road of thoroughgoing economic and social modernization. Liberal democracy's price was economic and social stagnation. Bardhan (1988) has also suggested that liberal democracy enabled the diverse dominant proprietary classes in India both to reconcile their conflicting interests in such a way as to ensure stability and their shared dominant position and to ensnare the Indian economy in a net of parasitic transactions – rents, regulations and licences, bribes and subsidies – sometimes summarized as the 'licence–permit raj', stifling economic growth.

Certainly economic growth in India since Independence has been steady but slow, only just keeping ahead of population growth, although with increasing economic liberalization this pattern may be beginning to change. But in addition, democratization in India has been accompanied by tremendous social and economic inequality. The eminent Indian economist Amartya Sen, has commented on the enduring elitism of Indian society and politics. Although the elite's conscience has been sufficiently tender to prompt steps to prevent any repetition of the last great famine, in Bengal in 1943, regular malnutrition, as distinct from acute starvation and famine, has survived; according to Sen, 'At least a third of the rural population seems to suffer from nutritional inadequacies' (Sen, 1986, p.32).

Life expectancy is low. Illiteracy is still widespread. Although women from elite social backgrounds have done relatively well in India, making inroads into the professions and the world of politics for instance, and despite the existence of a lively feminist movement, 'the general position of women in Indian society is nothing short of scandalous'. Their life expectancy has been lower than men's, they have been more prone to malnutrition, and their literacy rates have been lower (Sen, 1986, p.37).

For a time, at least, it seemed that China, however authoritarian its politics, had through the extreme egalitarianism of its policies, substantially reduced these kinds of social inequalities. With the revelations following the death of Mao it became increasingly clear, however, that official figures provided had been seriously inflated. The State Statistical Bureau had been hampered in its attempts to collect and publish reliable information. Subsequent attempts to trace the effects of the Great Leap Forward (1958–60) and then the Cultural Revolution (1965–69) suggested that while there had been further redistribution, production for consumption and thus overall living standards had if anything worsened (Field, 1986). It was also disclosed that during the Great Leap Forward, when peasants were forced to combine their holdings in huge people's communes, millions died in the great famine that resulted from such economic and political disruption. Experts are not entirely agreed on the numbers of deaths: estimates have ranged from 16.5 to around 30 million (Ashton et al., 1984), but as Sen writes of China, 'there cannot be any serious doubt that there was truly appalling extra mortality during the food crisis years' (Sen, 1986, p.40).

Sen also argues that India's political system would have made such a terrible famine inconceivable: 'even a fraction of the death toll would have immediately caused a storm in the newspapers and a turmoil in the Indian parliament, and the ruling government would almost certainly have had to resign' (Sen, 1986, p.40). Ashton et al. (1984, p.632) add that democracy 'may also play a role in alerting the *government* where normal reporting systems cannot be relied on to be objective'.

I can draw no simple conclusions about the benefits of democratization for the mass of people in developing countries, but the cases of India and China caution against any uncritical endorsement. It is possible that by conferring a degree of legitimacy on governments and contributing to political stability (though this is a complex question), liberal democracy in India may actually have reduced pressures for more far-reaching reforms. At any rate what is clear is that democratization provides no guarantee that substantive social and economic development will follow. On the other hand, without democratization, ambitious projects of social and economic development, especially when advanced in the name of the people, can go horribly awry and are open to all kinds of abuse.

———————————— *Summary of Section 8.5* ————————————

• Democratization may offer increasing protection against the most extreme forms of government mismanagement or abuse.

• Democratization in itself does not guarantee economic and social development.

Conclusion

The primary concern of this chapter has been to explain the very different encounters with liberal democracy in India and in China. It has drawn upon modernization theories, or their more recent, and revised, formulation that takes particular cultural, historical and political institutional features into account; and it draws on structural approaches, but has found it necessary to go beyond their implicit culture/structure divide. In doing so, it has focused on the intersection of two very broadly defined elements, political tradition or culture (within which structural components have been identified) and imperialist intervention. It has also focused on the role of political parties and the importance of civil society.

India's indigenous political tradition, it is suggested, was one in which, as a consequence in part of Hinduism and social diversity, central political authority was limited, and power and authority were widely dispersed between different communities (although often relatively concentrated within them), in a way that largely provided for both social cohesion and social control. In China, traditionally, the political authority of the emperor and his centralized bureaucracy were extensive, and buttressed by cultural values in Confucianism although peasant revolt, against the perceived abuses of the system not the system itself, was endemic. But these differences in themselves would be insufficient to explain later patterns of political change. India and China encountered the forces of modern imperialism in very different ways. India was conquered and then ruled for a considerable period by the British; the colonial regime found it necessary to accommodate the dispersed power structures of traditional India and it was instrumental in instilling liberal representative values in the nationalist elite and introducing the beginnings of representative government, which in turn proved remarkably compatible with Indian political culture. China, however, experienced extraneous imperialisms in the nineteenth century as threatening only, compounding disintegrative tendencies in the regime. Their effect was to reinforce traditional authoritarian elements in the new nationalist and communist political movements and to cut short any brief experiment with democratic ideas or forms. As a consequence of these different encounters, India emerged with a relatively strong and autonomous civil society (given problems with defining that entity), while China, especially before the onset of economic liberalization, had a comparatively weak civil society. India's party system, based around the Congress Party as the embodiment of the nationalist movement, was also to play a vital role in institutionalizing parliamentary democracy. Under the communists in China, the Party's monopolistic role and internal principle of democratic centralism ensured that formally representative institutions served largely as the trappings of authoritarian rule.

References

Almond, G. and Verba, S. (1963) *The Civic Culture*, Princeton, Princeton University Press.

Ashton, B. *et al.* (1984) 'Famine in China, 1958–61', *Population and Development Review*, vol.10, pp.613–45.

Bardhan, P. (1988) 'Dominant proprietary classes' in Kohli, A. (ed.) *India's Democracy: an Analysis of Changing State–Society Relations*, Princeton, Princeton University Press.

Chesneaux, J. (1973) *Peasant Revolts in China 1840–1949*, London, Thames and Hudson.

Diamond, L. (1993a) 'Introduction: political culture and democracy' in Diamond, L. (ed.).

Diamond, L. (ed.) (1993b) *Political Culture and Democracy in Developing Countries*, Boulder, Lynne Rienner.

The Economist (1990) *Economist Book of Vital World Statistics*, London, Hutchinson Business.

Field, R.M. (1986) 'The performance of industry during the Cultural Revolution', *China Quarterly*, December, no.108.

Franke, W. (1970) *A Century of Chinese Revolution*, Oxford, Blackwell.

Frankel, F. (1989) 'Introduction' in Frankel, F. and Rao, M.S.A. (eds) *Dominance and State Power in India*, Oxford, Oxford University Press.

Gold, T.B. (1990) 'The resurgence of civil society in China', *Journal of Democracy*, Winter, vol.1, no.1, pp.18–31.

Held, D. (1996) *Models of Democracy* (2nd edn), Cambridge, Polity Press.

Kaviraj, S. (1991) 'On state, society and discourse in India' in Manor, J. (ed.) *Rethinking Third World Politics*, London, Longman.

Kothari, R. (1964) 'The Congress system in India', *Asian Survey*, vol.4, no.12, pp.1161–73.

Lipset, S.M., Seong, K.-R. and Torres, J.C. (1993) 'A comparative analysis of the social requisites of democracy', *International Social Science Journal*, vol.45, no.2, pp.155–70.

Manor, J. (1990) 'How and why liberal and representative politics emerged in India', *Political Studies*, vol.38, no.1, March, pp.20–38.

Moore, B. (1966) *Social Origins of Dictatorship and Democracy*, Boston, Beacon Press.

Nathan, A.J. (1986) *Chinese Democracy*, London, I.B. Tauris.

Perry, E.J. and Fuller, E.V. (1991) 'China's Long March to democracy', *World Policy Journal*, vol.53, no.4, pp.663–85.

Rudolph, L.I. and Rudolph, S.H. (1987) *In Pursuit of Lakshmi: the Political Economy of the Indian State*, Chicago, University of Chicago Press.

Rueschemeyer, D., Stephens, E. and Stephens, J. (1992) *Capitalist Development and Democracy*, Cambridge, Polity Press.

Saich, T. (1981) *China: Politics and Government*, London, Macmillan.

Sen, A. (1986) 'How is India doing?' in Basu, D.K. and Sisson, R. (eds) *Social and Economic Development in India: a Reassessment*, New Delhi, Sage.

Seymour, J.D. (1986) 'China's satellite parties today', *Asian Survey*, vol.26, no.9, pp.991–1004.

Sisson, R. (1993) 'Culture and democratization in India' in Diamond, L. (ed.).

Skocpol, T. (1979) *States and Social Revolutions*, Cambridge, Cambridge University Press.

Weiner, M. (1987) 'Empirical democratic theory' in Weiner, M. and Ozbudun, E. (eds) *Competitive Elections in Developing Countries*, Durham, NC, Duke University Press.

World Bank (1994) *Social Indicators of Development*, Baltimore, Johns Hopkins University Press.

Zhengyan Fu (1993) *Autocratic Tradition and Chinese Politics*, Cambridge, Cambridge University Press.

Many people have commented helpfully on the first draft of this chapter but I should especially like to acknowledge the advice and encouragement of my father, Charles Madge, who sadly died in January 1996.

CHAPTER 9

Democratization at the same time in South Korea and Taiwan

David Potter

Introduction

The region of East and Southeast Asia has been widely known for strong states and phenomenal rates of economic growth. This is the land of Japan and the Asian 'tigers' (countries undergoing very rapid capitalist industrialization from the 1960s to the 1990s). Other political regimes with less dynamic growth rates are located there also, and you will learn about several of these in Chapter 10. Here we examine two of the tigers – South Korea and Taiwan. Their peoples speak different languages, have different cultures and social arrangements. Yet both, in the twentieth century, experienced authoritarian rule by the Japanese for 40 to 50 years, became two of Asia's best known economic 'tigers' under the auspices of authoritarian political regimes during the next 40 years, and finally commenced serious democratization at about the same time. How can these remarkably similar political trajectories be explained?

Addressing this large question is a hopeless exercise without a set of explanatory ideas which direct attention to a manageable number of phenomena common more or less to the two cases being compared. The comparative analysis in this chapter is guided primarily by four of the six explanatory factors set out in Chapter 1 of this book. First, *geopolitical* and *international* engagements including *wars* in Asia are central to explaining these two similar democratization experiences. Second, the extraordinary *economic/capitalist development* of these two 'tigers' during the latter part of the twentieth century had profound political and social consequences. Third, such economic developments changed *class divisions*, which shaped the drive toward democratization. Fourth, the changing nature of the *state* and *political institutions* had a major bearing on the outcome. These four factors, and the *interrelationships between them*, frame the explanation of democratization in this chapter. The other two explanatory factors – civil society and political culture – also figure in the analysis, although to a lesser extent.

Of the three theoretical approaches to explaining democratization (see Chapter 1), the modernization approach looks least promising as a mode of analysis for addressing the main question in this chapter. For one thing, the main hypothesis in this approach is that higher levels of socio-economic development are associated with more, or more stable, democratic forms of politics; yet the socio-economic indicators for South Korea and Taiwan during authoritarian rule were much higher than for liberal democratic India in the same period. Also, modernization theories presuppose a steady progression toward liberal democracy and therefore grapple poorly with the historical 'moments' when countries move from authoritarianism to some form of democracy; in South Korea and Taiwan democratization commenced quite suddenly in the late 1980s. The transition approach, therefore, seems more promising here, given its attention to the choices and actions of political elites in the short term. Also, it is clear that changing structures of class, state and transnational power driven by particular histories of capitalist development profoundly shaped these short-term choices and actions. For these reasons, I bear in mind ideas in both structural and transition approaches in what follows.

The chapter has four sections. The first two consider why South Korea and Taiwan were essentially authoritarian until the latter part of the 1980s. The third, building on the first two, suggests an explanation for why democratization occurred at the same time in both countries. The concluding section then comments briefly on what the explanation highlights about the strengths and weaknesses of transition and structural theories.

9.1   Legacies of Japanese colonial rule

South Korea and Taiwan were both authoritarian for 40 to 50 years as colonies of Japan, until the end of the Second World War in Asia (1945). It may seem a diversion to spend time on this historical period. However, colonialism did set in motion distinct social forces, economic practices and political arrangements that help us to understand patterns of democratization in the two countries after 1945.

Indeed, it is necessary to remark briefly on the states and societies that preceded colonial rule. The region which is now Korea has a history going back over 2,000 years, nearly all of it 'independent' of foreign control. Five centuries of Chosŏn rule prior to Japanese colonialism were marked by unusual political and social stability, making the dynasty one of the most durable in East Asian history. A major explanation for this stability was the deep penetration of both state and society by the *yangban* class (landed aristocracy), who controlled much of the land, the main form of wealth, and whose power over the Chosŏn state was considerable. The *yangban* class also articulated Confucian cultural and ideological norms (see Chapter 8) throughout society which buttressed their power. During this period also, Korea developed its own political identity, aided by the introduction of its own phonetic writing system in the fifteenth century.

The early history of Taiwan (Formosa) was very different. The Malay *yuan-chu min* (literally 'original dwellers'), the remnants of whom are collectively referred to today as 'aborigines', lived there before Chinese immigrants arrived and settled on the island in the early seventeenth century. Taiwan was conquered in 1683 by forces of the Qing dynasty, and representatives of the Chinese Court were stationed on the island. Taiwan had mostly an 'aboriginal' population until the eighteenth century. By the end of the nineteenth century more Chinese, mainly from the Fujian Province, had arrived and became the main group on the island.

Into these two very different situations stepped the Japanese. Taiwan was ceded to Japan following the Sino-Japanese War of 1894–95. Also part of Japanese expansionism at the end of the nineteenth century were its various interventions in Korea; following the Russo-Japanese War of 1904–5 Korea was finally annexed in 1910. Both countries then began rapidly to share a very similar economic and political trajectory as a consequence of Japanese colonial rule.

The main reason for this was that the central government of the two colonial states, under broad direction from Tokyo, quickly achieved a high degree of dominance over the economies, societies and polities of their new acquisitions. Such dominance was more or less characteristic of all colonial rules. Japan's took a particularly exaggerated form, especially in Korea. Japan arrived late to the imperial game: colonialism had been in existence for hundreds of years. As King Leopold of Belgium remarked in 1865, 'the world had been pretty well pillaged already' (cited in Cumings, 1984, p.8). Being late, Japan was in a hurry to shape its new colonies to the maximum advantage of the Japanese economy. Moreover, Korea and Taiwan were close to Japan, enabling particularly tight control to be established and maintained. For example, a land army could more easily be, and was, stationed in both countries as a coercive force. Tightly disciplined, coercive colonial states penetrating society everywhere replaced the previously comparatively weak states. No associations independent of the state were allowed to exist.

The advantages for the Japanese of Korea and Taiwan being close also had an economic dimension. Contiguousness facilitated tight integration of market relations between colony and metropolis. Japan quickly began to use this potential by opening ports, building railways and improving communications. The colonies were not only regarded as 'agriculture appendages' of Japan; they also were industrial adjuncts to the Japanese economy, with Japanese capitalists setting up industries in the colonies close to raw materials and cheap labour. These interventions were particularly marked in the 1930s during the preparations for war. These developments helped to account for the overall gross national product growth rates in Korea, Taiwan and Japan in the 3–4 per cent range, double the rates of inter-war Europe (Allen, 1980, p.1).

The 'sprout' of capitalism in Korea and Taiwan, although driven overwhelmingly by the state and Japanese capitalists, created small indigenous bourgeoisies in the two colonies. In Korea prior to Japanese colonization, a few enterprising Koreans had made fortunes as agents or middlemen in the international rice trade and imported manufacture. Even more important in the process of capital accumulation were the Korean *yangban* landlords who owned the rice fields; as the price of rice rose, so too did the profits of the landlords, some of whom had accumulated great wealth by the time the Japanese arrived in 1910. At first, these Korean entrepreneurs had great difficulty surviving; but

> in the 1930s and 1940s, as the Japanese army conquests in Manchuria, China proper, and finally Southeast Asia turned much of the contemporary continent of Asia into a single imperial market and the demand for military goods escalated, Korea rapidly developed into the most industrialized country in Asia after Japan itself, and many Koreans made money as traders and manufacturers.
>
> (Eckert, 1993, p.99)

For most of them the gains were modest, but a nascent bourgeoisie had emerged, dependent on the colonial state.

Similar trends occurred in Taiwan. During the 1930s, 'manufacturing grew at an annual average rate of about 8 per cent'; by 1941 'factory employment, including mining, stood at 181,000'; and 'by the end of the colonial period, Taiwan "had an industrial superstructure to provide a strong foundation for future industrialisation"' (Ho, 1978, cited in Cumings, 1984, p.13).

Agrarian structures were also affected by colonial rule. Immediately upon arrival, the Japanese conducted major land reforms in Taiwan (1898–1906) and Korea (1910–18). The consequences were not the same for both countries. In Taiwan the 'great' Chinese absentee landlords were expropriated, making the tenants the legal owners. Rice and sugar, the two main crops, were henceforth grown mostly by owner-operators for commercial markets which included Japan. The state set up 'an elaborate network of agricultural associations' to provide owner-occupiers and tenants with 'extension education, the cooperative purchase of fertilisers, warehousing, and other services' (Amsden, 1985, p.81). Although rural communities resisted these changes, police were employed to enforce them. The network brought scientific expertise to farming, improving production; it also enabled the colonial police to control the countryside. Broadly speaking, the Japanese in Taiwan 'fostered a class of entrepreneurial landowners, emerging "from below"', who 'had less land than their Korean counterparts and were far more productive' (Cumings, 1984, p.11). As for the peasantry generally, they were unorganized and not allowed to have any influence on the economic policies of the state.

In Korea, the upshot of the land reform was a decision to ground the centuries-old *yangban* class even more firmly in the agrarian structure, in order to discipline peasants producing rice for the Japanese market. This was agricultural development 'from above', by big landlords allied to the state, and it was tougher for those peasants who remained on the land. Many left for the factories in the cities, part of the huge population shift caused by the industrial dynamism of the imperial market.

——————————— *Summary of Section 9.1* ———————————

There were three main structural legacies of Japanese colonial rule that profoundly shaped the political trajectories of both Korea and Taiwan after 1945.

- *Authoritarianism.* There was not even a whiff of democracy. Korea and Taiwan were embedded in a transnational colonial structure of great power and ruthlessness that permitted no participation in government policy or affairs of state by Koreans or Taiwanese.

- *Late capitalist development.* Korea and Taiwan became an integral part of the East Asian imperial market; capitalist industrialization and the commercialization of agriculture occurred rapidly in both the metropolis and the colonies.

- *Dependent classes.* Small indigenous bourgeoisies and working classes emerged in both countries, but any attempt by them to form organizations to defend their interests was severely dealt with by the colonial state. The landed classes and the peasantry generally were unorganized.

In short, the Japanese left structural legacies in Korea and Taiwan making democratization an unlikely prospect in 1945.

9.2 Democratization denied or snuffed out: 1945 to the 1980s

The Second World War in Asia (1941–45) and its immediate aftermath profoundly affected Pacific Asia. It put an end to Japanese colonialism. It was a major contributory factor to the success of the communist revolution in China (Chapter 8). It also pulled both the USA and the USSR (the two new superpowers) into the Asia Pacific as major players. As Korea and Taiwan emerged from the Japanese colonial embrace they became almost immediately entangled in the geopolitical conflicts of the Cold War. Such structural entanglements had major political consequences in both countries.

In Korea, once the Japanese had surrendered on 15 August 1945, Soviet troops immediately crossed the border and moved south to the thirty-eighth parallel, as had been agreed with the USA. In the South, Koreans immediately formed 'peoples' committees' and a Korean 'People's Republic' but they were peremptorily swept aside by the American military commander, General Hodge, once he arrived in September. He was under instructions to set up a military government and deal severely with such indigenous developments. There was considerable Korean dissent, especially in 1946 and 1948. The first Republic of Korea was formed in 1948 with the election of Syngman Rhee as President. Rhee had spent decades in exile in the USA. He was in favour of parliamentary democracy in principle, but autocratic government in practice. He began almost immediately to use the sweeping National Security Law of 1948 to coerce the press, the educational establishment and political opponents. The army was built up as a major power within the state. The regime started to become highly centralized, repressive and corrupt even before the Korean War broke out.

On 25 June 1950 North Korean troops (with Soviet and Chinese support) crossed the thirty-eighth parallel and within two months had occupied nearly all of the South before the US-UN forces arrived to begin pushing them back. The Korean War went on until the armistice in July 1953 when the thirty-eighth parallel was recognized as the boundary between North and South Korea. South Korea was devastated by the war and the USA committed huge resources to building it up again.

Rhee's government lost a lot of political support during the summer of 1950 when the invading North Korean communists summarily dispossessed the landlords and gave land to the peasantry. Rhee needed to win back the confidence, or at least acquiescence, of the rural majority once the US-UN forces began to retake the countryside in late 1950. Partly for this reason, and because US advisers pressed for it, a radical land reform was implemented during 1951–52. Rhee needed 'the cooperation and backing of the wealthy' beholden to him, including landlords, but he reluctantly backed the reform 'while ensuring that some of the biggest former landlords ... were able to secure a position within a new emerging ruling class' (Putzel, 1992, p.104). The US advisers also backed the reform on the grounds that it would 'help cut the political ground from under the feet of the communists and aid the forces that make for a middle-of-the-road; stable rural society' (Ledijinsky, cited in Putzel, 1992, p.77). Landlords 'received state bonds convertible to industrial wealth' (Cumings, 1989, p.12). The Korean landlords were thus eliminated as a class, 'thereby removing one of the major social obstacles to full industrialisation and simultaneously enhancing the role of the bourgeoisie in South Korea's economy and society' (Eckert, 1993, p.100). For these and other reasons, capitalism in independent Korea grew dramatically after the war. Big business groups called *chaebols* were very prominent in this development, some of which date their origins from the colonial period, e.g. Samsung, Hyundai and Lucky-Goldstar. They were, however, subject to, and dependent on, the economic policies and practices maintained by the Korean state. Indeed, all social classes were weak in relation to the growing power of the state.

Taiwan in 1945 became a province of Chiang Kai-shek's China. A military government was quickly installed. Inept and corrupt leadership, misconduct by KMT (Kuomintang, or Nationalist Party) soldiers, and other irritants, 'soon soured the views of the residents of Taiwan towards their mainland cousins and reinforced whatever notions of Taiwanese identity already existed' (Wachman, 1994, p.96). These tensions were exacerbated during the 'Taiwan uprising' of 28 February 1947, when an incident turned Taiwanese frustration and hostility towards mainlanders into violence in the cities. This was followed by several months of terror imposed by the KMT, buttressed by troop reinforcements sent from the mainland who 'systematically wiped out the political and intellectual elite of Taiwan' (Wachman, 1994, p.99). Memories of this incident provided a rallying point for subsequent Taiwanese nationalism.

Chiang Kai-shek, the KMT and the remnants of Chiang's government and army retreated from the victorious communists on mainland China to Taiwan in 1949 (see Chapter 8). Their arrival added at a stroke nearly two million soldiers and civilians to the roughly six million Taiwanese already living on the island. The KMT saw themselves as the government of all China, temporarily resident in one part of China. Their fundamental mission was to build up strength and retake mainland China by force. Nothing, certainly not the interests of the Taiwanese, would be allowed to deflect them from that purpose. This wild scheme gradually dimmed as the communist regime on the mainland settled. What 'had begun as a fierce resolve ... became an aspiration, then a myth, then a liturgy' (Crozier, 1976). But the scheme helped to legitimize the authoritarian character of a regime bent on military preparations for war. The communist threat from mainland China served the same purpose.

While preparing for war, the KMT government set about streamlining the state and tightening party discipline. At the top of it all was Chiang – Party Chairman, President of the Republic, Commander of the Armed Forces. At the bottom were party cadres attached to the agricultural associations set up by the Japanese during colonial rule. No other party was allowed to exist. Local and provincial elections were gradually permitted and Taiwanese non-party candidates could compete. But all policy making of any consequence was highly centralized, out of their reach.

The KMT state was far less dependent on the political support of powerful classes and groups in society than Rhee's South Korean state. In particular the KMT were not dependent in Taiwan on land-owning elites as they had been on mainland China. They were therefore comparatively free to set a low ceiling on land holdings, abolish absentee ownership of land, reduce land rent, provide secure leases for tenants and extend credit and other facilities for the new owner-cultivators and leasehold tenants. US advisers urged the reforms for the same reasons as in South Korea. The result was a real transfer of power and wealth in the countryside, which 'succeeded in coopting grateful tenants into the existing political order' (Putzel, 1992, p.74). Together with a quiescent and carefully controlled peasantry there was an unorganized working class accustomed to state-imposed discipline and a weakly organized group of Taiwanese capitalists. The transnational power of the USA gave Chiang and his government an ironclad guarantee that they would not be overwhelmed by foreign aggression. The relationship also provided extraordinary economic and military aid in the 1950s critical for initial capital formation, although aid and investment from overseas Chinese also helped, as well as the fact that the KMT had brought China's gold reserves with them in 1949.

In the beginning of the 1960s both South Korea and Taiwan were moving towards an economic strategy of export-led capitalist development under the direction of what are broadly identified as developmental states. Leftwich (1995) defines a developmental state in terms of six main components, each of which found classic expression for the next two decades in the states of South Korea and Taiwan:

1 *A determined developmental elite.* A small core of elite politicians and bureaucrats (civilian and military) committed to development were instrumental in economic policy making. Although sharing that commitment, intra-elite policy conflicts could and did occur.

2 *A powerful, competent and insulated economic bureaucracy.* The strategic work of organizing the relations between state and economy was done by an extremely able set of technocrats in powerful economic organizations.

3 *The effective management of non-state economic interests.* 'By using a battery of policy instruments covering conditionality ... , screening and monitoring of foreign capital, these states have "given a virtuoso performance" (Johnson, 1987, p.163) in setting terms which have attracted foreign capital while making it serve the state's domestic economic development priorities'; and as for private internal economic institutions, 'the state has been active in promoting, pushing, persuading and bullying these interests in directions which conform to its development strategy' (Amsden, 1989, cited in Leftwich, 1995, p.417).

4   *Relative autonomy.* These developmental states, including the econom-
    ic elites within them, were largely independent of class and other inter-
    ests in society. Some of these interests benefited more from the
    economic policies of the state than others, but none controlled the state.

5   *A weak and subordinated civil society.* Organized interest groups were
    weak or non-existent in the early years of these developmental states,
    and distinct social classes were not yet well formed.

6   *Repression, legitimacy and performance.* Both these developmental
    states were non-democratic and suppressed, sometimes with great bru-
    tality, any dissent or attempts by individuals to exercise political and civil
    rights. At the same time, many people broadly accepted the legitimacy of
    these regimes most of the time because their performance resulted in
    high rates of growth and rising living standards.

Rates of growth, indeed, were phenomenal. From the 1960s to the 1990s,
the annual rates of growth (GNP per capita) on average of South Korea and
Taiwan were the highest in the world after Botswana (for elaboration on
Botswana see Chapter 11). Between 1962 and 1986 Taiwan leapt up the
economic hierarchy of nations from the eighty-fifth richest country in GNP
per capita to thirty-eighth; South Korea from ninety-ninth to forty-fourth. In
terms of the world's biggest exporter of manufactures, between 1965 and
1986 Taiwan rose from twenty-eighth to tenth; South Korea from thirty-third
to thirteenth. In 1986 Japan was number one supplier of manufactured goods
to the USA, Taiwan number four, Korea number five (Wade, 1990, p.3). Such
figures fully justified the growing reputation of these two countries as the
most remarkable of the Asian 'tigers', and the most extraordinary of the Asian
NICs (newly industrializing countries).

At the heart of these achievements, and broadly directing them, were
non-democratic developmental states. Their power was enhanced by the
military and economic aid lavished upon them by the USA. These two rather
small countries together received between 1946 and 1978 roughly $18.6
billion from the USA. To gauge just how huge this investment was,
comparative figures for the same period show that *all* of Latin America and
all of Africa *together* received $24.8 billion (Cumings, 1984, p.24). In return
South Korea and Taiwan maintained extraordinarily overdeveloped militaries within the state apparatus to defend themselves and help the
Americans 'defend the free world'. The military/civilian ratios in both countries were among the highest anywhere.

The overwhelming power of these two developmental states did not go
completely unchallenged. Periodic dissent in the early years later became
more major conflicts between the state and increasingly powerful social
classes.

In South Korea, following protests in 1960 by students and others hostile
to Rhee's corruption and rigged elections, a military coup in 1961 brought
General Park Chung Hee to power. Park's authoritarian regime was
'bolstered by military elites, upper bourgeoisie, state managers, technocrats
of the state and private sectors, and the omnipresence of US strategic and
economic interests' (Choi, 1993, p.35). Park had a 'vision' of a developmental
project; together with his supporters he moved in pursuit of it through the

agency of South Korea's developmental state. The economy grew quickly
during his rule. The rural population declined by half during this period as
huge numbers migrated to the cities to swell the growing mass of industrial
and service workers, miners, peddlers and the unemployed. There was also
considerable rural development which helped to make the countryside,
broadly speaking, an area of support for the regime. Large *chaebols*
(conglomerates) also grew in importance, but deferred to the state in light
of the communist threat.

Industrial workers had been receiving roughly one-fifth the wages of
white collar workers, state health insurance schemes were designed for the
middle class, social services were poorly developed or non-existent, 'and a
"development first" logic that had little regard for the plight of the workers ...
was the dominant ideology driving the state' (Choi, 1993, p.30). Industrial
workers began, with students and others, to press for democratization at the
workplace and in the polity generally; but they were suppressed by a forceful
state pressing for export-led growth requiring a disciplined labour force and
low wages. A middle class of white collar workers grew in importance; it
remained wary of the working class and hence not particularly keen on
democracy.

Park ruled until 1979 when he was assassinated by his own Security Chief.
As Choi remarks, the state, which was temporarily immobilized following
Park's assassination,

> allowed workers to demonstrate their class aspirations through collective
> action; however, in both relative and absolute terms, the strikes and other
> actions in 1980 were much more massive and intense [than in 1960],
> reflecting the tremendous expansion of the industrial workforce in the
> twenty-year period, as well as the depth of its accumulated discontent.

(Choi, 1993, p.30)

This massive demonstration of discontent was suppressed by force following
a military coup by a hardline military group led by General Chun Doo Hwan.
Martial law was imposed in May 1980. The actions of the military in Kwangju
City, Cholla Province, were particularly brutal and savage. The massacres
there excited widespread revulsion. The Chun regime quelled dissent and
kept it bottled up until 1987. Capitalist development roared on, attended by
political discontent amongst subordinate classes (Choi, 1993, pp.35–40).

In Taiwan, opposition to the non-democratic KMT state began to surface
seriously for the first time in the early 1970s, particularly following US
recognition of the People's Republic of China on the mainland and the
expulsion of the Republic of China on Taiwan from the United Nations. These
setbacks 'represented massive disturbances to the credibility of a regime that
had boasted at home and announced abroad that it would be the sole
legitimate government of China' (Wachman, 1994, p.135). These momentous
developments were perceived by the opposition as a clear signal that the
legitimacy of Chiang Kai-shek's KMT regime was fading, and they began to
set about trying to mobilize support for a successor. Chiang was about 85
years old at the time, and his leadership was passing to his son Chiang Ching-
kuo. The younger Chiang started during the 1970s to bring more Taiwanese
into political posts within the state alongside second-generation mainland

elites. Also, some supplementary seats in the National Assembly were opened up for election, although the Assembly remained 'frozen' by the preponderance of KMT legislators elected to it in mainland China in 1948 who were not required to stand for re-election. There were, by comparison, many seats available at provincial and local levels for opposition candidates to contest. For non-KMT politicians the electoral route provided an opportunity to accumulate political experience and gain political recognition. The main current of Taiwan opposition movements ran through the electoral route.

Such a route appealed to moderates, not radicals, and indeed the non-KMT candidates were mostly wealthy Taiwanese becoming successful in business and the professions. Wealth improved campaign efforts and 'security in professions enabled them to run the risk of political defeat' (Chu, 1993, p.174). By 1977 some non-KMT politicians declared themselves *tangwai* candidates (literally, candidates outside the KMT) in local elections, won about one-fifth of the seats, and became in effect a quasi political party.

In 1979 the *tangwai* organized a series of rallies. The one in Kaohsiung on 10 December to mark 'International Human Rights Day' became a riot which was crushed with considerable force. The leaders were jailed. Local expressions of dissent by *tangwai* leaders were then suppressed throughout Taiwan. The autonomous, non-democratic KMT state was still very much alive despite President Chiang Ching-kuo being more moderate in his political views than his more autocratic father. In both Taiwan and South Korea, when pro-democracy disruption occurred, the threat that it would bring external communist intervention was enough to silence opposition or prevent such opposition defining itself in politically relevant terms.

───────────────── *Summary of Section 9.2* ─────────────────
Why was there little or no democratization in Taiwan and South Korea between 1945 and the 1980s?

- *Powerful states*, in which the military was prominent and coercive force was used regularly to suppress democratization tendencies, dominated in both countries for most of the period. They also intervened massively in the economy and society to orchestrate rapid, late capitalist development.

- *Dependent classes*. The state in both countries remained largely autonomous in relation to social classes, which were either dependent on the state or weak in relation to it.

- *Geopolitical relationships*. The states in both countries received massive economic and military support from the USA. The presence of communist enemies nearby – China and North Korea – helped to legitimize authoritarian military rule.

9.3   The turn towards democratization

In June 1987 in South Korea, there was a mass uprising by workers and others against the Chun government. The streets in Seoul and elsewhere were alive with riot police and masses of demonstrators. This time, unlike 1960 and 1979–80, the ruling elites within the state were divided between *hardliners*, including Chun, who were bent on ending the uprising with force, and *softliners*, including Roh Tae Woo, who represented a faction in the military unwilling to repeat the bloody suppression of dissent as in 1980. Roh declared publicly on 29 June 1987 in favour of holding direct presidential elections, ensuring local autonomy, guarantees of basic rights for all citizens and an end to strict government control of many aspects of life. Roh's faction prevailed, and Roh was elected President in 1988. Roh's cause was helped by the fact that Chun was constrained to avoid using force with the 1988 Olympic Games, to be held in South Korea, hanging in the balance.

Riot police trapped by students and others demanding the fall of the government of President Chun, Seoul, 10 June 1987

In December 1992 Korean voters went to the polls again to elect a President. The three main candidates were civilians: Kim Young Sam of the DLP (Democratic Liberal Party), Kim Dae Jung of the DP (Democratic Party), and Chung Ju Yung the billionaire head of the Hyundai *chaebol* (conglomerate) and leader of the newly created UNP (Unification National Party). Kim Young Sam won, receiving 42 per cent of the total vote. There was a 77 per cent turnout. The two defeated candidates 'accepted the voters verdict with grace' (Scalapino, 1993, p.70). Kim Young Sam was still President in 1995.

Also in 1987, in Taiwan, martial law (under which Taiwan had been ruled by the KMT since the 1940s) was lifted and some freedom of speech, the press and assembly were also promised. This move did not occur on the occasion of a mass uprising, as in Korea. It emerged out of negotiations which had been going on for several years between KMT 'softliners' including President Chiang Ching-kuo, and opposition forces in the Democratic Progressive Party (DPP), which was formally recognized in 1986 as an opposition party able to contest parliamentary elections. In the KMT's political shift towards tolerating the DPP there was an understanding that the opposition would not use violence, not advocate Taiwanese 'independence' from the mainland and not support communism. It was a democratic beginning, although very qualified.

In December 1992, as in Korea (almost to the day), there was a general election for the National Assembly. Candidates of the KMT obtained 53 per cent of the vote (96 of the 161 contested by the Party), far below the Party's total in previous elections. The DPP took 31 per cent of the vote. There was a 72 per cent turnout. The elections were widely regarded as a major step forward in political openness; one of the candidates, for example, 'had spent 25 years in prison for advocating Taiwanese independence and other "subversive" activities, and had been released only two years earlier' (Scalapino, 1993, p.71). Furthermore, the unelected President and Vice President were by 1992 both KMT Taiwanese, not mainlanders.

Elections at the end of 1994 confirmed the prominent role of the KMT in democratization. For example, in the contest for the governor of Taiwan Province, which covers all the island except the independent cities of Taipei and Kaohsiung, the KMT incumbent, James Soong, won 56 per cent of the 8.4 million votes cast, winning in all but one of the 21 cities and counties in the province. The island's oldest independent newspaper, the *Independent Evening Post*, made the significant remark that the polls showed 'that no clear provincial differences are felt among the twenty million residents here – all are Taiwanese now' (cited in *Far Eastern Economic Review*, 15 December 1994, p.15).

How does one explain the turn towards democratization at the same time in these two Asian 'tigers'? The South Korea shift in 1987 was on the face of it more sudden and dramatic than the shift in Taiwan. For Taiwan, the KMT leadership was becoming more tolerant of *tangwai* leaders several years prior to lifting the ban on organizing new political parties in 1986 and lifting martial law in 1987. In South Korea, the state maintained its repressive, authoritarian stance right up to 1987, when the ruling elite within the state suddenly split in response to widespread demonstrations by workers, students and others.

Changing class alignments in South Korea profoundly shaped the split within the state and the democratic opening in 1987. These changes developed during the period following the military suppression of dissent, especially in Kwangju in 1980. They were accentuated by the policies of the Chun government (1981–87).

In the first place, the Chun government developed out of the breakdown of its predecessor and the draconian military suppressions in the 1980s required to contain dissent. To maintain its position it had to engage in direct military rule during its period of office, which was generally unpopular throughout society. Second, export growth had slowed at the end of the 1970s and inflation had increased, so the Chun government moved to restore macroeconomic stability with economic polices emphasizing monetary control, fiscal restraint and a freeze on wages. The short-term results were successful – inflation dropped, economic growth quickly resumed – but the political consequences were adverse. Tight credit controls hurt the *chaebols*;

their main umbrella organization, the Federation of Korean Industries, protested against the policies. Farmers were also alienated by fiscal restraints and import liberalization for foreign products which undercut the farm support structure, providing 'fertile ground for activist groups' and sporadic demonstrations against government policies (Haggard and Moon, 1993, p.87). These developments posed a real problem because farmers and big business were key forces upon which the Chun government depended. Third, Chun's 'highly repressive tax system, which taxed salary and wage incomes at much higher rates than income from capital and land, placed the burden of supporting the expanded state on the shoulders of the lower and middle classes' (Choi, 1993, p.36). Fourth, Chun presided over a vast network of corruption involving extortion of funds from business.

The more immediate political consequences of the Chun government's policies were framed by broader changes in class structure. Export oriented economic growth had linked the South Korean economy to the international capitalist economy for some time and by the early 1980s it was becoming clear that the Korean bourgeoisie had developed their knowledge and expertise to such an extent that they were 'now as – or more – capable of making sound economic decisions than the state, especially in the context of the growing complexity of both the South Korean and the world economies' (Eckert, 1993, p.106). This marked their increasing independence from the state. By 1987 their disgruntlement with the Chun government was buttressed by their chafing at what they increasingly perceived as excessive state control of business.

The middle classes, comprised broadly of white collar workers in the public and private sectors of the economy, including urban professionals, intellectuals and people in the media and the self employed had swelled in size and importance during the 1960s and 1970s with urbanization and the rapid growth of the economy. By 1980, probably about 30 per cent of the work-force in the urban sector of the economy were white collar workers (Ogle, 1990, p.149). Their political tendencies by the early 1980s were not all that clear. Disaffected sectors in 1987 included people in medium and small businesses who had been hurt financially by the Chun government's tax policies, parents who were upset by students being clubbed, people in cities outside Seoul who had been disadvantaged, and Christians (about 25 per cent of the population) who had been galvanized by church leaders in favour of democratization. However, being a comparatively new social formation, the middle classes tended to be 'far more interested in making money than contesting for power'; many held relatively secure jobs in large public organizations and offered little independent resistance to the state (Cumings, 1989, p.27).

Korean workers were comparatively (for Asia) well organized. Many of the most militant unions were in the larger industries run by the *chaebols*. Workers generally were brutally suppressed in 1980 and they were bottled up more or less until 1987, kept on low wages essential to Korean economic prosperity and badly treated. Many student activists and other dissidents, incensed by the Kwangju incident, began to move from the universities into the factories to link up with the labour movement. Pent-up frustrations boiled over in 1987 after Chun's declaration of opposition to any constitutional advance and the death of a student after police torture. Swiftly, '69 per cent of firms that hired a thousand or more workers were confronted with work stoppages, 38.5 per cent hiring less than a thousand had the same experience' (Ogle, 1990, p.116). The unions were far stronger and more militant than in 1980. Many of the demands were essentially political, 'focused on changing repressive labour laws and obtaining the right to organize independent unions free from state and company control' (Choi, 1993, p.39). Almost overnight, white collar unions began to be formed in insurance companies, brokerage houses, banks, government and private research laboratories, newspaper offices, hospitals and so on. The impetus for this whole campaign to move beyond Chun's repressive regime towards democratization came from the middle classes and the working class. Production began grinding to a halt, foreign investors became anxious. This was a political and economic crisis.

The 'soft' response of Roh Tae Woo and his military faction within the state offering some liberal democracy within a continuing capitalist order appealed to important sections of the bourgeoisie as a way forward. More importantly, the initiative succeeded in separating the middle classes from the working class by defining the crisis 'in terms of "bo-hyuk" (conservative–radical), that is, as conflicts between conservatives who uphold capitalist order and liberal democracy, on the one hand, and leftist revolutionaries who strive to overthrow the existing order through violent means, on the other' (Choi, 1993, p.39). The media framed the conflict in these terms and state repression of militant workers produced violence, thereby reinforcing the dominant definition of the conflict. Annexing the middle classes in this way weakened the pro-democracy movement, which was forced to compromise with the Roh government by accepting a more limited conception of democracy involving competitive elections and some civil rights. Workers and students had been speaking a different language of democracy in which the concepts of equality, social justice and community were paramount. But they were insufficiently powerful now to press this conception forward without the broad support of the middle classes.

In the countryside, the problem of a powerful landed class that might have put a break on any democratization had been 'solved' in the 1940s by the land reforms. The small-farm rural economy that remained had been focused mainly on rice production and was controlled by the state. In time the statist agriculture began to diversify; for example, by the 1980s a large-scale livestock-producing (and feed grain-importing) sector 'emerged as a well-organized interest group in its own right, and one well-represented in the various public agencies concerned with agricultural policy' (Moore, 1988, p.147). This was one indicator of what was a gradual shift by the 1980s from statism to pluralism as the private sector increasingly was allowed to move in to supply farm inputs, e.g. farm machinery and fertilizer. By 1987 most agriculturalists were not noticeably pro-democracy in the sense of sharing more radical conceptions of democracy being advanced by workers and students, but neither were they any longer a conservative structure of power blocking any democratization.

In Taiwan the position of agriculturalists was fundamentally similar by the mid 1980s: no powerful landed class, small peasant proprietors, a shift towards increasing pluralism as the private sector moved in, not a powerful force pressing for democratization (Moore, 1988). This was so despite certain differences; for example, 'individualism, familism and a sense of moral limits to state control or private behaviour are more in evidence in Taiwan' than Korea, and industrial development was more decentralized in Taiwan than in Korea (where it was concentrated around just two cities) thereby making 'the combination of industrial employment with agriculture much more frequent in Taiwan' (Moore, 1988, pp.118–19).

The prevalence in Taiwan of small-scale, spatially decentralized businesses producing for export meant that industrial development and the development of the working class was 'more embedded in traditional labour systems, mainly communal paternalism and patriarchal systems, in which labour was linked to employers through multi-stranded work and non-work relationships reaching into communities and covering major life-cycle events of the employee' (Douglass, 1993, p.155). An important consequence was that the working class was less well organized and less militant than in South Korea. It had a comparatively weak class identification and mild ideological orientation. When in the 1980s independent unions began to appear, and then a Labour Party (later Workers Party) in November 1987, characteristically they were initially 'organized by a handful of political activists' (Chu, 1993, p.180). During the 1980s, however, independent trade unions began actively to protest about aspects of development policy about which they had no voice. Some of these protests became violent (Bello and Rosenfeld, 1992).

Democratization for Taiwan was pushed in earnest in the 1980s by a loose alliance of independent trade unionists, Taiwanese politicians and intellectuals including students. This was stimulated by changes in civil society in the 1980s involving a host of social movements – of consumers, workers, women, aborigines, farmers, students, teachers and the environmentally concerned – breaking free of traditional deference and state intimidation to make various demands (Gold, 1990). The demand was in effect a nationalist demand: Taiwan for the Taiwanese, not for a small minority of mainlanders who ruled it as 'part of China'. The Taiwanese were in a substantial majority; democratization would mean Taiwanese empowered to decide their own destiny. Democratization was resisted by the KMT partly for the same reason.

The suppression of *tangwai* demonstrations in 1979 had resulted in the jailing of *tangwai* leaders in Kaohsiung and elsewhere. In elections at the end of 1980 relatives of and attorneys for these leaders were elected to office (Cohen, 1988, p.41). This incident appears to have 'made a deep impression on President Chiang, who realized that despite the effort to purge the opposition of its key leaders, voters were willing to support the purge victims – if only symbolically' (Wachman, 1994, pp.140–1). Chiang became receptive to the idea of political liberalization. By 1983 he allowed the *tangwai* opposition to form a support committee to co-ordinate an election campaign. In 1986 the *tangwai* declared the establishment of the Democratic Progressive Party on the eve of parliamentary elections in 1986. The government not only allowed it, they started formal discussions with *tangwai* leaders. A competitive election occurred, martial law was lifted, democratization commenced.

These choices and actions were shaped by changes in state, class and transnational structures of power. As for the state, bringing more Taiwanese into positions of power in the KMT and the state generally, which had been going on for decades, meant that by 1987 70 per cent of the KMT were Taiwanese (Chiang, 1989, cited in Chu, 1993, p.187). By the mid 1980s also, united and hardline state resistance to democratization had broken apart. In the National Assembly, mainland elected members had mostly died off, and for those that remained 'unification of China seemed so remote' (Chu, 1993, p.177). As for state officials, a large majority were now Taiwanese and for them also there was less interest in unification with China, and more in the advance of the interests of Taiwan. As for the ruling party, there were political and financial scandals in the mid 1980s which undermined their efficient and righteous image in the society. There was also an inter-party struggle going on between 'hardliners', including conservative military and security people opposed to change, and 'softliners', including a younger generation (many having received advanced education in the USA) inclined more towards tackling the political demands of opposition dissidents. By the mid 1980s President Chiang could be classified as a 'softliner'; and before his death in 1988 he had selected a 'softliner' as his Vice President and successor: Lee Teng-hui, a Taiwanese.

Dynamic capitalist development was also rapidly affecting the class structure of Taiwan. For example:

> The literacy rate increased; mass communication intensified; per capita income rose; and a differentiated urban sector – including labor, a professional middle class, and a business entrepreneurial class – came into being. The business class was remarkable for its independence. Although individual enterprises were small and unorganized, they were beyond the capture of the party-state. To prevent the formation of big capital, the KMT had avoided organizing business or picking out 'national champions'. As a result, small and medium enterprises dominated industrial production and exports. As major employers and foreign exchange earners, these small and medium businesses were quite independent of the KMT.

> (Cheng, 1989, p.481)

By the late 1980s more than 50 per cent of the electorate in Taiwan identified themselves as 'middle class' and their political attitudes 'ranged from moderately conservative to liberal, favouring gradual and stable change' (King, 1994, p.145). The main reasons for this fast-growing middle class were rapid industrialization and the dramatic expansion of higher education. Workers also, as we saw earlier, were becoming organized and mobilized. Political liberalization by the KMT state in the 1980s was shaped by the need to accommodate this changing structure of class power.

The KMT state had no control over events outside Taiwan. This was demonstrated when the USA decided to recognize the People's Republic of China in the early 1970s which, as I noted earlier, had the effects of both isolating Taiwan in the international community and energizing dissident forces in Taiwan. Similarly, the KMT had no influence on the collapse of authoritarian rule in the Philippines with the fall of Ferdinand Marcos in February 1986; this event appears to have had a major influence on the thinking of KMT leaders at that time, including the President, and contributed to the decision to seek an accommodation with *tangwai* leaders in 1986–87.

External events can help to trigger democratization. Even more important, changing geopolitical and international processes can profoundly affect domestic states and class structures in the longer term and propel them in a democratic direction. Both South Korea and Taiwan have been affected by such changes beyond their control. Five examples must suffice here.

First, it has frequently been remarked that the striking economic success of South Korea and Taiwan grounded in a clear and urgent ideology of capitalist industrialization owed much to the threat of external communist enemies – North Korea and mainland China respectively – who were very close, well-armed and dangerous. Such well-perceived external threats to national security cowed organized interests into submitting to the state, to an extent that was impossible in places where such threats were absent, e.g. the Philippines. These international tensions did not disappear in 1987. However, surveys of South Korean attitudes towards the end of the 1980s showed that the sense of physical danger was easing and this, together with greater economic security due to rises in living standards, meant that gradually the views of increasing numbers of people were shifting from security concerns to the 'importance of the quality of life, especially political life' (Park, 1991, p.759). Tensions between Taiwan and mainland China also began to ease at the end of the 1980s, although not to the same extent (and relations between the two became taut again at the beginning of 1996). The general relaxation of international tensions tended to weaken the power of authoritarian states and the military within them. These trends were reinforced at the end of the 1980s by the weakening of the world communist movement with the demise of communist regimes in Eastern Europe and the Soviet Union.

Second, and related to the first, the posture of the US government changed in the latter part of the 1980s from one consistently supporting anti-communist military regimes in Asia to one advocating limited democratization along Japanese lines. In 1987, for example, the American Embassy in Seoul was 'proffering to the men who rule South Korea' a model of democracy with 'one-party rule, with a legitimate but impotent opposition – a labour party of some sort to accommodate the urban working class and render it politically docile' (Cumings, 1989, p.32). Cumings explains this changed orientation in terms of the pressure of economic interests in the USA. Authoritarian governments in South Korea and Taiwan held wages down, making their exports to the USA very competitive; some democratization would mean (a) a rise in wages, (b) exports to the USA less threatening to American business interests, and (c) the opening up of Asian markets to American goods and service industries. Other major Western governments, and international organizations like the World Bank and OECD, were likewise leaning more heavily on Asian states to move toward some form of liberal democracy. Four main influences shaped these changing orientations: the experience of structural adjustment packages in the 1980s, the development of neo-liberal views in the West that democracy and free market economies would reinforce each other, problems in the communist world, and the rise of pro-democracy movements in Latin America, the Philippines and elsewhere (Leftwich, 1993).

Third, Japanese democratic conditionalities also put pressure on authoritarian states in Asia. This was particularly true for South Korea, which had operated since the Second World War as, in effect, a frontier defence in part for a Japanese state not permitted to rearm. The relaxation of global international tensions in the late 1980s eased that situation. At the same time, Japan became even more important than the USA (or any other country) in providing aid and loans to other Asian countries. Such assistance was provided by Japan taking into account 'the recipient country's military expenditure as well as their efforts towards democratization ... ' (*Japan*, 7 February 1995, p.3).

Fourth, the influence of democratic conditionalities and the changing international context meant that democratization also came to be seen by the mid 1980s by increasing numbers of important people in the bourgeoisie and the state as a necessary ticket for membership in the 'advanced' international club to which they aspired. This provided a strong incentive for economic and political liberalization which, once started, made subsequent democratization more likely.

Fifth, changes in the structure and processes of the global economy were beginning to make export-led growth less plausible as a basis for continuing economic development by the Asian 'tigers'. The global economy was marked by economic slowdown, protectionism in the West, increasingly flexible specialization and automation in Western production processes. Asian economies began switching from export-dependent economic strategies towards ones that were more inward looking, based mainly on domestic and Asian markets. Japan led the way. South Korea and Taiwan followed. The revised economic strategies meant increases in real income for workers (cheap labour being provided by workers in other Asian countries like Indonesia and Vietnam), more money put into research and development for domestic needs and so on. All this was not possible 'without legitimation of a political community outside of the state' (Douglass, 1993, p.163). Once again, one sees how changing structures of geopolitical and international power have domestic political consequences which can be favourable to democratization.

––––––––––––––––––––––––– *Summary of Section 9.3* –––––––––––––––––––––––––

Explaining democratization in South Korea and Taiwan.

- *Changing class power.* Dynamic capitalist development had the consequence of swelling the industrial working class, particularly well organized in South Korea; they made both reformist (e.g. better wages) and radical (e.g. democratization at the workplace) demands. They, together with students and other intelligentsia, pushed hardest for democracy. They were joined by a much enlarged middle class of white collar workers who were generally favourable to liberal democracy, but wary of the more radical demands of the workers. The power of bourgeois and professional people grew in relation to the state. They began to find state controls increasingly irksome. Also, there was no powerful landed class to stifle pro-democracy forces, as in Latin America.

- *Changing state power.* Changing class power weakened somewhat the social basis of authoritarian rule. The power of the military within the state also declined and international tensions fuelled by superpower conflict eased. Amongst the new generation of people moving into positions of power within the state apparatus were increasing numbers who were more disposed to accept some form of democratization as a sensible political strategy for defusing the mobilization of discontent.

- *Changing geopolitical power.* Domestic structural transformations driven by dynamic capitalist development were reinforced by changing geopolitical processes. The easing of international tension has already been mentioned. The 'wave' of democratization elsewhere also mattered; the fall of Marcos in 1986 seemed to have made a significant impact on the thinking of state leaders in Taiwan and South Korea. Democratic conditionalities also began to figure prominently in the 1980s in the 'advice' of intergovernmental organizations, the USA, Japan and others. Also, the movement of goods, labour and capital tended to be easier in liberal or partial democratic regimes.

9.4   A brief comment on the explanation

It has not been possible to go into much of the rich historical detail about South Korea and Taiwan on which the explanation summarized here is based. Nevertheless, a brief comparative analysis, grounded in historical evidence and framed primarily in terms of the four explanatory factors indicated at the outset, has been set out in this chapter and has produced an explanation of democratization in the two countries. The framing of the explanation in terms of changing structures of *class, state* and *transnational* power driven by the particular histories of *capitalist development* in the two countries is reminiscent of the structural theory of democratization by Rueschemeyer *et al.* (1992) summarized in Chapter 1. The growing importance of the industrial working class in relation to other classes, particularly in South Korea, is precisely what Rueschemeyer *et al.* would have looked for in their analysis of democratization. Within these changing structural contexts, however, the precise choices that were made and actions taken that led to democratization were also crucially important, and different in South Korea and Taiwan. The transition approach, which concentrates on the choices and actions of men and women in particular countries involved in the political process in the short term, is a necessary part of the explanation in this chapter. (For an explanation relying entirely on the transition approach, see Cheng and Kim, 1994.)

Indeed, the comparative analysis in this chapter shows how structural theories of democratization are *incomplete* without the inclusion of choice and action so central to the transition approach. Perhaps the most telling example relates to changes in rural class structures precipitated by land reforms in 1949–50 in South Korea and Taiwan. The reforms resulted in the virtual elimination of the landlord class. As Barrington Moore (1966) showed, and other structural theorists have broadly accepted, large landlords as a class have historically been the most anti-democratic force in society. One reason for this is that they have been dependent on a large supply of cheap labour, and since democratization has tended to improve the position of rural workers (making their labour no longer cheap), landlords have perceived democratization as incompatible with their interests in making adequate profits from their land. Democratization has been resisted where large landlords have been powerful, particularly when they have been closely allied with the state apparatus; democratic prospects have improved where landlords were weak or non-existent. So says part of structural theory. However, as we have seen, democratization did not commence in South Korea and Taiwan when the land reforms eliminated the large landlords. Instead, the reforms benefited the peasantry and stabilized the countryside, which helped to sustain authoritarian rule, not democratization, for the next 35 years. The vital point this underlines is that changes in rural class structure did not by themselves *cause* democratization; but the choices and actions that propelled these two countries in a particular political direction 35 years later were unlikely to have been democratic if there had existed a powerful landlord class closely allied to the state.

The general point is that explanations of democratization are grounded in choices and actions shaped by an array of structures of power which come together as particular historical conjunctures in time and place. The content of the choices made and the character of the actions taken would not be democratic without favourable structural conditions. It is for this reason that both structural and transition approaches need to be kept in mind when trying to explain why democratization occurs when it does.

References

Allen, G. (1980) *Japan's Economic Policy*, London, Macmillan.

Amsden, A. (1985) 'The state and Taiwan's economic development' in Evans, P. *et al.* (eds) *Bringing the State Back In*, Cambridge, Cambridge University Press, pp.78–106.

Amsden, A. (1989) *Asia's Next Giant: South Korea and Late Industrialization*, New York, Oxford University Press.

Bello, W. and Rosenfeld, S. (1992) *Dragons in Distress: Asia's Miracle Economies in Crisis*, Harmondsworth, Penguin.

Cheng, T. (1989) 'Democratizing the quasi-Leninist regime in Taiwan', *World Politics*, vol.41, pp.471–99.

Cheng, T. and Kim, E. (1994) 'Making democracy: generalizing the South Korean case' in Friedman, E. (ed.) *The Politics of Democratization: Generalizing East Asian Experience*, Boulder, Westview Press, pp.125–58.

Choi, J.J. (1993) 'Political cleavages in South Korea' in Koo, H. (ed.), pp.13–50.

Chu, J.J. (1993) 'Political liberalization and the rise of Taiwanese labour radicalism', *Journal of Contemporary Asia*, vol.23, no.2, pp.173–88.

Cohen, M. (1988) *Taiwan at the Crossroads: Human Rights, Political Development and Social Change on the Beautiful Island*, Washington, Asia Resource Center.

Crozier, B. (1976) *The Man who Lost China*, New York, Scribner.

Cumings, B. (1984) 'The origins and development of the Northeast Asian political economy: industrial sectors, product cycles, and political consequences', *International Organizations*, vol.38, no.1, pp.1–40.

Cumings, B. (1989) 'The abortive abertura: South Korea in the light of Latin American experience', *New Left Review*, vol.173, pp.5–32.

Douglass, M. (1993) 'Social, political and spatial dimensions of Korean industrial transformation', *Journal of Contemporary Asia*, vol.23, no.12, pp.149–72.

Eckert, C. (1993) 'The South Korean bourgeoisie: a class in search of hegemony' in Koo, H. (ed.) pp.95–130.

Gold, T. (1990) 'The resurgence of civil society in China', *Journal of Democracy*, vol.1, no.1, pp.18–31.

Haggard, S. and Moon, C. (1993) 'The state, politics, and economic development in post-war South Korea' in Koo, H. (ed.) pp.51–93.

Johnson, C. (1987) 'Political institutions and economic performance: the government–business relationship in Japan, South Korea and Taiwan' in Deyo, F. (ed.) *The Political Economy of the New Asian Industrialism*, Ithaca, Cornell University Press.

King, A.Y.C. (1994) 'A nonparadigmatic search for democracy in a post-Confucian culture: the case of Taiwan' in Diamond, L. (ed.) *Political Culture and Democracy in Developing Countries*, London, Lynne Rienner, pp.131–53.

Koo, H. (ed.) (1993) *State and Society in Contemporary Korea*, Ithaca, Cornell University Press.

Leftwich, A. (1993) 'Governance, democracy and development in the third world', *Third World Quarterly*, vol.14, no.3, pp.605–24.

Leftwich, A. (1995) 'Bringing politics back in: towards a model of the developmental state', *Journal of Development Studies*, vol.31, no.3, pp.400–27.

Moore, B. (1966) *Social Origins of Dictatorship and Democracy: Lord and Peasant in the Making of the Modern World*, Boston, Beacon Press.

Moore, M. (1988) 'Economic growth and the rise of civil society: agriculture in Taiwan and South Korea' in White, G. (ed.) *Developmental States in East Asia*, London, Macmillan, pp.113–52.

Ogle, G. (1990) *South Korea: Dissent Within the Economic Miracle*, London, Zed Books.

Park, Chong-Min (1991) 'Authoritarian rule in South Korea: political support and governmental performance', *Asian Survey*, no.31, August.

Putzel, J. (1992) *A Captive Land: the Politics of Agrarian Reform in the Philippines*, New York, Monthly Review Press.

Rueschemeyer, D., Stephens, E. and Stephens, J. (1992) *Capitalist Development and Democracy*, Cambridge, Polity Press.

Scalapino, R. (1993) 'Democratizing dragons: South Korea and Taiwan', *Journal of Democracy*, vol.4, no.3, pp.70–83.

Wachman, A. (1994) *Taiwan: National Identity and Democratization*, London, M.E. Sharpe.

Wade, R. (1990) *Governing the Market: Economic Theory and the Role of Government in East Asian Industrialization*, Princeton, Princeton University Press.

CHAPTER 10

Why has democratization been a weaker impulse in Indonesia and Malaysia than in the Philippines?

James Putzel

Introduction

The three countries of Southeast Asia to be examined in this chapter – Indonesia, Malaysia and the Philippines – have had markedly different experiences with democratic and authoritarian forms of government. Indonesia, with the world's fourth largest population and the largest Islamic community, can be counted among the most authoritarian regimes in the world. Malaysia is a small country with an impressive record of economic development often thought of as a borderline case between partial democracy and liberal democracy (see Chapter 1), but here shown to be better understood as a partial democracy close to the border of authoritarianism. The Philippines, once touted as 'Asia's first democracy', fell prey to the ravages of the Marcos regime but later experienced a spectacular restoration of liberal democratic government.

The three countries together constitute a rich terrain for comparative analysis of the possibilities of democratic transitions in developing countries. Their diversity of colonial rule, religious, ethnic and social composition and indigenous political traditions provide an ideal setting to evaluate competing theoretical explanations about democratization relevant to understanding the process far beyond the region itself.

This chapter draws on the insights of the three main theoretical approaches examined in this book to propose a new synthesis that highlights the importance of legitimacy to understanding regime change and prospects for democratization. In attempting to explain differential impulses in relation to liberal democracy, the chapter focuses on five interrelated explanatory factors, drawn from the three theoretical approaches.

The first factor, a preoccupation of structural theories, concerns the historically constituted structures of power within, and between, state and society that shape possibilities for political action. By 'structures of power' I mean the patterned relationships that reflect the relative capacity of actors to maintain or transform their social and physical environment, which emerge and endure over time (Lloyd, 1986, p.19; Held, 1989, p.1). This perspective allows us to examine the structural characteristics of the state (for instance, the role and relative power of the bureaucracy and the military), as well as those of society (for instance, the role and relative power of different classes or social groups), and how the spheres of the state and society interrelate. My proposition is that these structures of power constrain but do not in themselves determine political change.

The second explanatory factor, most discussed by modernization theorists, centres on patterns of national integration related to ethnic and religious identities that influence the basis on which politics is conducted. This concerns the extent to which a population of a given nation-state has come to share a common national identity even while holding diverse ethnic or religious identities (Anderson, 1991, pp.5–7). The chapter argues that a weak sense of national identity will act as a barrier to democratization for two reasons: (a) it provides leaders the chance to justify anti-democratic actions in ethnic and religious terms, and (b) if a nation-state lacks cohesion, democratic forms of government can quickly lead to national disintegration through separatism or violent confrontation.

The third factor, important to all three theoretical approaches, is concerned with the relationship between economic and political change, especially the extent to which capitalist development either requires or facilitates democratic forms of governance. Contradictory propositions abound concerning the causal relationship between economic development and political change. There is general consensus that economic growth and modernization lead to similar patterns of organization of production and exchange across remarkably different social and cultural situations. However, it is argued here that these patterns of economic change will not necessarily produce uniform political outcomes.

Fourth, a concern of both transition and modernization theorists, is the role of ideas, especially the idea of democracy, as the basis for choices and actions that determine political outcomes. In structural theories, ideas are generally seen as derivative of the basic structural characteristics of the state and society as discussed above. I am concerned with the extent to which political action inspired by ideas can transform structures of power while recognizing that these same structures influence the evolution of ideas in the state and society.

Fifth, dealt with in decidedly different ways by all three approaches to the study of democracy, is the contradictory influence of international factors in the determination of democratic possibilities in developing countries. Clearly, colonialism has had a major impact on all three countries studied in this chapter and the shape of post-colonial development has in part been determined by the role of international actors. I argue here that international factors constrain political action but do not determine outcomes in any absolute way.

These explanatory factors are tied together through a focus on the problem of 'regime legitimacy', traditionally a concern only of the modernization theorists. Legitimacy, or as Lipset (1963, p.22) defined it, 'the degree to which [a political system] is generally accepted by its citizens', is crucial to understanding transitions between one regime type and another. For any regime to survive – whether democratic or authoritarian – it must succeed in establishing a general acceptance of its right to rule. Placing emphasis on legitimacy as *acceptance* of the right to rule, rather than *belief* in the *moral* right of a regime to rule, distinguishes this analysis from an important recent book on political legitimacy in Southeast Asia (Alagappa, 1995).

A regime must establish its legitimacy, or acceptance of its right to rule, among the powerful in society and within the state itself (defined as those on whom the regime depends to retain its position), whether on pragmatic, instrumental or normative grounds. It must also establish at least 'passive legitimacy' within society as a whole. In other words, the majority within society will go along with the regime and not rebel. A regime that loses legitimacy among the powerful in society and the state, or loses passive legitimacy among the majority within society, cannot long remain in power.

Everywhere in the modern world a strong source of regime legitimacy rests on positive economic performance almost exclusively measured in terms of economic growth. However, at any given moment, other social issues may assume prime importance to regime legitimacy, such as problems of violence, economic or ethnic inequality, or national integrity. Much of what happens in politics is actually a battle over establishing the grounds of legitimacy. Therefore the shifting basis of legitimacy is crucial to understanding past and potential regime change in the three countries under study.

Like many countries in the developing world, Indonesia, Malaysia and the Philippines experimented with democratic forms of government after independence. The next section analyses the character of these new democracies and what led to their breakdown. Section 10.2 examines the emergence of authoritarian regimes, their claims to embody indigenous forms of democracy, and the relationship between economic and political change. Section 10.3 considers why liberal democracy gained more ground in the Philippines than in Indonesia or Malaysia in the 1980s and early 1990s. Finally, the last section attempts to sum up the theoretical insights emerging from this comparative study, placing particular emphasis on the shifting bases of regime legitimacy.

10.1 Fledgling post-war democracies

The regimes established in all three countries at independence were essentially liberal democratic in form, but were based on sharply divergent political, economic and social foundations. Liberal democracy proved to be most short lived in Indonesia, where the parliamentary system gave way to Sukarno's 'Guided Democracy' in 1959. In Malaysia, parliamentary rule within the new federation was briefly suspended and greatly curtailed after racial riots in 1969. Liberal democratic government lasted longest in the Philippine Republic, where the system, based on a US style separation of powers, endured until Marcos declared martial law in 1972. Changing patterns of state power, the extent of national integration, the challenge of managing economic development, the legacy of ideas inherited from colonialism and nationalist movements, and the geopolitics of the region all influenced the legitimacy and endurance of the democratic regimes.

Changing patterns of power

Before the Portuguese imposed the first European colonial outpost in Southeast Asia in Malacca in 1511, vibrant communities and centres of trade at various levels of economic development and political integration existed in the region (Hall, 1981, part 1). These communities had long been influenced by the spread of Buddhism and Hinduism from East and South Asia and the presence of Chinese merchants, and Islam began to influence the region from the end of the thirteenth century. However, the modern contours of power in the region began to be drawn only with the arrival of the European colonial forces.

Indonesia

The Dutch established their presence in Java in 1602 through the United East Indies Company and the Dutch state assumed control in 1799. Following the pattern of traditional Javanese political authority, Dutch direct rule through a Javanese bureaucracy predominated at the centre with increasing autonomy remaining with traditional elites toward the periphery (Anderson, 1983). By the end of colonial rule, the indigenous economic elite derived its wealth mainly from its connection to the emergent state bureaucracy rather than private economic activity. The plantation and commercial sectors were mainly in the hands of Dutch, British and US corporations, while smaller-scale business and agricultural trade were dominated by long-resident Chinese business interests (Robison, 1986, pp.5–22).

During their short-lived occupation of the colony (1942–45), the Japanese set up a home army to defend the islands from the Western allies, providing an important training ground for future Indonesian officers (Anderson, 1990, pp.109–10). The nationalists under Sukarno declared independence in 1945, but the Dutch refusal to recognize the Republic led to guerrilla warfare against the Royal Netherlands Indies Army over the next three years. By the time independence was secured at the end of 1949, the embryonic military had laid claim to a nationalist heritage within the fractious state.

After a brief experience with federalism foisted on Indonesia by the Dutch, a unitary parliamentary system was established in 1950, but over the next seven years failed to consolidate authority over the whole archipelago. The state was marked by conflict between socialist, communist and nationalist groupings within the independence movement as well as between those who had served on opposite sides during the four-year independence war. More important, as Anderson (1990, p.103) noted, was 'the penetration of the state by society', where officials and officers in the military were more loyal to particularist groups in society than to the state. Since no political party had a majority, government was marked by changing coalitions and cabinets, with the unelected President Sukarno as the only constant.

There were many small parties; the most important grew out of the independence movement – the Indonesian Nationalist Party (PNI), the Islamic parties (Masyumi and Nahdatul Ulama, NU) and the Communist Party of Indonesia (PKI). The parties themselves, especially the PNI, built what Robison (1986, pp.48–9) called 'politico-economic empires' using their influence within the state. Divisions between the parties were based as much on religious and regional identities as on competing class interests.

Malaysia

British rule over the territory of present day Malaysia evolved through a series of alliances, though not without employing force, with the traditional sultanates, or *negeri*, on the peninsula. The East India Company established its first foothold on the island of Penang in 1786 and the Crown assumed responsibility in 1867. While the British developed the extractive economy by a massive immigration of Chinese and South Asian labour, they allowed only Malays to join the colonial bureaucracy where they remained in a subordinate position to the British. Plantations were mainly established by British and Chinese business interests, with Malays virtually excluded from the burgeoning export economy and the commercial sector more generally (Jomo, 1988, Chapters 6 and 7).

During their occupation of the colony, the Japanese encouraged the collaboration of much of the colonial bureaucracy and the traditional rulers. However, their brutality toward the Chinese fuelled Chinese participation in the anti-Japanese guerrilla movement led by the Malaysian Communist Party (MCP). After the Second World War, the MCP engaged the British in armed conflict but the Party's support never reached far beyond the Chinese community. The use of British armed forces to put down the movement precluded any major role for an independent military in the new state.

The Federation of Malaya achieved independence only in 1957. Because it was secured through negotiation with the elite-dominated United Malays National Organisation (UMNO) rather than armed struggle, the new state was much more cohesive and the military much less prominent than in Indonesia. Under Tunku Abdul Rahman, the UMNO had constructed the Nationalist Alliance with the Malayan Chinese Association (which financed the Alliance election campaigns) and the Malayan Indian Congress and won an overwhelming parliamentary majority in pre-independence elections (Ahmad, 1989, p.354). The new regime also included the traditional royal houses, which brought legitimacy both in terms of traditional Malay custom and Islam.

Domestic business was almost entirely in the hands of the Chinese who were highly organized both professionally and politically. Malays dominated the political elite. This tended to channel the demographically dominant Malay peasantry toward support for the state and regime rather than radical opposition. Independent trade unions were all but destroyed during the pre-independence battle with the MCP and by repressive labour legislation enacted in the decade after independence (Jomo, 1988, pp.235–6).

Philippines

Colonial incursion in the Philippine islands, first by the Spanish from the 1570s and later by the USA in 1898, left a legacy distinctly different from the Dutch and British in Indonesia and Malaysia. Colonial conquest was a joint venture between the Spanish Crown and the Catholic Church, in a territory of much smaller and less organized communities than those found by the Dutch and British. The expansion of export agricultural production toward the end of the Spanish period and its acceleration under the USA consolidated the position of an emerging landed oligarchy. After crushing the Philippine independence movement with a brutality rivalling US continental conquest in North America (Francisco and Fast, 1985), the US colonial administration grafted an elitist partial democracy onto the existing system of patron–client relationships.

During the Second World War in Asia (1941–45), much of the elite collaborated with Japanese occupation forces, which gave rise to a significant expansion of communist influence in the rural areas of Central Luzon where a guerrilla war was maintained throughout the occupation. When the USA returned in 1945, they encouraged the disarming of the guerrillas and immediately began preparations for independence in 1946. Thus independence was achieved swiftly and peacefully. The new state was established as an elitist partial democracy under the security umbrella of the USA with a weak military force of its own.

The single party, the *Nacionalistas*, that had contained shifting clan alliances in the colonial government, split in 1945 when the USA supported Manuel Roxas in forming the Liberal Party and winning the presidency. Until 1969, elections every four years resulted in single-term Presidents, while Congressional elections resulted in long-term dynasties (Institute for Popular Democracy, 1992). Elections were generally marked by violence, intimidation and either outright vote-buying or the systematic 'delivery' of the vote by local political bosses. Like in Indonesia, a weak state was 'penetrated' by society, but unlike Indonesia the rules for political competition were largely accepted by elite politicians. The 'military' was weak, subordinated to politicians, and relied on the presence of US troops and military advisers who were pivotal in defeating the communist-led Huk revolution in the early 1950s.

While the Chinese were significant in the business community their position was not nearly as exclusive as in Malaysia or Indonesia. The wealth of the clans that dominated politics often originated in land ownership and was extended to other types of monopoly control in finance, transportation and import licences. This oligarchy was highly organized with professional and sectoral associations whose interests were represented through Congress and patronage relations with the presidency.

Patterns of national integration and identity

Modern boundaries between the three countries owe much more to the colonial division of territories than affinity by cultural, language or religious identities. The independent states that emerged from colonialism were imperfectly integrated, demonstrating the differing extent to which their populations shared what Anderson (1991, pp.6–7) called the 'imagined community' that underpins the modern nation-state.

Indonesia

In Indonesia, Dutch influence was concentrated on Java and fitful on the Outer Islands until after the 1870s. The process of incorporating the Outer Islands through conquest and treaties was accelerated over the next 40 years. The colony remained marked by tensions based on a diversity of linguistic and religious identities.

Indonesia achieved independence with little agreement among its component parts on the shape of the nation-state. A revolt broke out in West Java in the early 1950s and an Islamic rebellion in Aceh (North Sumatra) was not put down until 1962. In the 1955 election, the vote was evenly split between Islamic and secular parties, and the PNI, PKI and NU drew most of their support from the Javanese, while Masyumi was strongest in West Java and the Outer Islands.

Malaysia

In Malaysia, the British colonial administration created both a more sharply divided society along ethnic lines and more continuity within each ethnic community. The sharp ethnic divide, especially between Malays and Chinese, emerged as a result of the schism the British promoted between a better-off largely urban-based Chinese community and the rural-based Malay population left largely under the jurisdiction of traditional Malay rulers.

Efforts to develop a fully integrated polity in Malaysia were defeated even before independence. A consensus among the Malay political elite was achieved in peninsular Malaysia, though the more autonomous *negeri* have at times challenged the Kuala Lumpur capital. The Chinese, who make up almost a third of the population, were effectively made second-class citizens. The integration of Singapore, Sarawak and Sabah in 1963 led to a threat to both Malay dominance and UMNO supremacy within the fledgling democracy. Tension between the federal and state governments led to the forced expulsion of Singapore from the Federation in 1965.

Philippines

In the Philippines, the Spanish successfully achieved the conversion of most of the lowland population to Christianity. It was left to the USA to bring the Islamic areas of the south under colonial authority, and, through a process of resettlement, render them a minority in their own territory. An elite emerged in the colony that shared the language of the colonizer – first Spanish then English – but maintained important regional identities.

Strong regional linguistic identities persisted in the Philippines, but national integration was achieved based on a shared identity among the elite, with the strongest common bond in society being Catholicism. Indigenous 'tribal' peoples were marginalized offering only localized challenges to the authority of the state. The greatest challenge was posed by the Islamic 'Moro' peoples of Mindanao, though this became most acute only after the declaration of martial law.

Processes of economic change

During the colonial period in all three countries some of the basic institutions for a capitalist economic system had been established, including private property rights, contract law and basic principles and mechanisms of taxation. However, the development of indigenous entrepreneurs was limited by the dominant position of foreign capital, while access to new economic opportunities depended mainly on connections with the state.

In Indonesia, since both PNI- and Masyumi-led Cabinets were generally deferential to foreign and domestic private interests, the liberal democratic period saw the continued domination of Dutch and Chinese capital, which left a negative impression of both the market economy and liberal democracy (Robison, 1986, pp.38–48; Sundhaussen, 1989, p.465). Separatist feeling was fuelled by the well-founded perception that economic enterprise in the Outer Islands was serving Javanese interests. Access to state resources, especially licensing also favoured Javanese as the government attempted to promote *pribumi*, or indigenous capitalists, while foreign exchange policy did the same at the expense of business in the Outer Islands (Robison, 1986, pp.58–60; Sundhaussen, 1989, p.433).

In Malaysia, as in politics, ethnicity shaped the economy (Jomo, 1988, pp.244–5). The threat to Malay political supremacy once Singapore was incorporated into the Federation, inflamed resentment toward the economically privileged Chinese. During the first decade after independence foreign capital continued to dominate the industrial sector, and the government's 'pioneer industry' programme tended to reinforce the pre-eminence of Chinese over Malay capital (Jomo, 1988, p.234). Income inequality greatly increased over this period within all ethnic groups, but was most manifest between the poor Malay majority and the dominant position of Chinese business (ibid., pp.251–2).

In the late 1940s the Philippines appeared to have the best chances of stimulating economic growth and consolidating liberal democracy. However, inequality both within the rural sector and between rural and urban dwellers, and landlessness that increased with the impact of the advance of the market into rural areas, led to wide peasant support for the communist-linked Huk rebellion (Kerkvliet, 1977). While the movement was defeated by the early 1950s through military means and the promise of reform, its underlying causes remained unsolved and peasant armed struggle was reignited in the 1960s. Clan-based economic empires expanded through *rent-seeking activities* (like bribery to gain preferential access to income generated from licences, quotas or other government controlled economic instruments) and the protectionism linked to import-substituting production (Rivera, 1995). The transparently privileged place of these old families was increasingly associated with the democratic system.

The legacy of ideas

The nationalist movements that emerged in reaction to colonial rule, and the process through which independence was achieved, shaped the dominant political ideas in the post-colonial states. In the immediate post-independence period, democratic ideas were less influential among leaders and the population at large in Indonesia than in Malaysia or the Philippines.

Nationalism in Indonesia emerged in the 1920s against an increasingly intransigent and illiberal Dutch colonial authority (Steinberg, 1987, pp.336–8). This encouraged the development of a largely illiberal nationalist movement, inspired partly by an essentialist view of an Eastern society based on 'harmony and consensus' and the ideal of the Javanese bureaucracy based on 'order, authority and hierarchy' (Robison, 1993, p.42). In 1945, Sukarno promulgated the *pancasila*, or 'five pillars', as the official and secular ideology of the movement (the belief in one god, nationalism, international cooperation, democracy and social justice). Adopting a populist stance, President Sukarno, who had never been elected by universal suffrage, spoke against parliamentary democracy from the start (Legge, 1972, Chapter 10, especially p.270). Neither was there any commitment to liberal democracy among the major contestants for state power – the military, the Islamic parities and the PKI.

On the Malay peninsula, the incorporation of the traditional rulers under direct and indirect forms of British rule led to the development of an ethnically defined and much more tame nationalist movement than in Indonesia. Nationalist thinkers in the 1920s and 1930s failed to gain a mass following (Steinberg, 1987, pp.336–7). However, the attempt by the British to introduce the Malayan Union Scheme in 1946, calling for a unitary state with equal rights for Malays and non-Malays, met fierce opposition from the Malay elite who established the UMNO to represent their interests. While incorporating some of the Asian essentialism that characterized the Indonesian movement, the UMNO was more identified with moderate Islam sanctified by the tamed authority of the traditional rulers. Malaysia's first Prime Minister, Tunku Abdul Rahman, was a staunch advocate of parliamentary democracy (Ahmad, 1989, pp.352–3), but from the start ethnicity took primacy over the democratic principle of universal suffrage. The regime's legitimacy among the Malay elite depended more on securing Malay dominance than following democratic procedures.

In the Philippines, inspired by liberal political cultures of the West, nationalists founded the first republic in Asia in 1898, but it collapsed under the weight of the US invasion (Agoncillio, 1960). During the US period, the Filipino elite thoroughly imbibed an incrementalist approach to independence. While political competition in the independent republic was based more on clan alliances than programmatic politics, the elite shared a commitment to the procedures of partial democracy introduced by the US colonial government. Thus, democratic ideas were widely propagated and the shifting clan alliances that controlled the presidency and the legislature sought to legitimize their rule in democratic terms.

The ambivalence of US and Western support for democracy

In the aftermath of the Second World War, and especially after the victory of the Chinese revolution, Southeast Asia became increasingly important to the strategy of the Western powers to contain communism. The USA endorsed the decolonization drive in Southeast Asia and initially supported the establishment of democratic forms of governance in the new states (Colbert, 1977, pp.86–7). However, its strategic concerns soon led it to place almost exclusive emphasis on securing solid anti-communist allies often at the expense of democratic consolidation. The recent literature examining democratization and its failures in the region has tended to neglect the important role played by the USA in *weakening* democratic prospects in the region (especially the contributors to Diamond *et al.*, 1989).

In Indonesia, the revitalization of the PKI and the increasingly neutralist stance of Sukarno by the mid 1950s, led the USA to channel most of its assistance to the military and police and to support the large Islamic parties as a counter-weight to the PKI (Kolko, 1988, pp.174–5; Kahin and Kahin, 1995). In Malaysia, the British were determined to root out the Communist Party before granting independence and quickly backed down on demands for a non-ethnically determined political system to secure an alliance with the conservative Malay leadership. In the Philippines, the USA established its two biggest foreign military bases and was prepared to overtly endorse whatever political constellation was most favourable to maintaining US economic and military interests (Putzel, 1992, pp.82–101).

The legitimacy of the post-war democracies

An important aspect of legitimacy of any regime is the extent to which it can ensure political and social stability. This was central not only to securing legitimacy among elite actors and domestic and foreign investors, but also in securing 'passive legitimacy' among the population at large. The patterns of authority that emerged within and between the state and society affected both the legitimacy of the early liberal democratic regimes and the composition of actors prepared to intervene at the level of the state.

During the early periods of formal liberal democracy, there was much greater stability within the state in Malaysia and the Philippines than in Indonesia. The military emerged as an important actor in Indonesia, but not in the other two countries. In Indonesia, the state incorporated representatives of polar extremes that challenged the constitutional framework of the state and regime, while national level organizations played by the rules in the Philippines and Malaysia.

Society was in turmoil after Indonesia's independence, while in Malaysia and the Philippines long-established patterns of authority persisted as communist challengers were defeated. However, in Malaysia social division along ethnic lines, combined with the pre-eminence of Chinese among the wealthy, was potentially more explosive than in the Philippines, where class stratification was clearer but conflict was controlled through patronage politics.

Democratic government is more precarious where the very boundaries of the state are not seen as legitimate. Regional identities were bolstered by religious identities in both Indonesia and Malaysia, though these were more significant in the former. These divisions were used by opportunist leaders to challenge the viability of liberal democracy, but they represented a deeper problem for democracy since it was objectively more difficult to put democratic mechanisms into practice where the very parameters of the nation-state were not accepted.

The economic performance of the democratic regimes affected their legitimacy and therefore the possibilities for democratic consolidation. In all three countries, the initial democratic period was characterized by a combination of efforts to promote a market economy bolstered by state promotion of import-substitution industrialization. These measures proved insufficient to bring about the kind of radical break from the structure of the colonial economies hoped for after independence. On the other hand, they left plenty of room for the rent-seeking activities of newly powerful elites. These activities in varying degrees cast a shadow on the effectiveness of both the market economy and the liberal democratic political system with which it was associated.

The weaker legacy of democratic ideas in both Indonesia and Malaysia meant that the presence of democratic institutions and organizations was a less important criterion in the judgements made about the legitimacy of their regimes than in the Philippines. This was one reason why a democratic form of government endured longer in the Philippines than in the other two countries.

Finally, the readiness of international actors to favour the political forces most open to safeguarding both the strategic objectives and the private interests of the developed countries did little to promote the cause of democracy. The USA and Britain were more preoccupied with defeating communism than promoting democratic forces. This trend proved to be particularly important in the consolidation of authoritarian rule during the 1960s and 1970s.

─────────────── *Summary of Section 10.1* ───────────────

Democracies emerged and faltered for the following reasons.

- The strength of the military and fractious character of the state in Indonesia acted as barriers to democratic government whereas there were weaker military organizations and more elite consensus within the state in Malaysia and the Philippines.

- A weak national identity in Indonesia and an ethnically divided society in Malaysia made democratic politics more difficult than in the Philippines where the elite shared a 'Filipino identity'.

- Poor economic performance, rent-seeking behaviour of economic elites and the continuation of colonial economic patterns weakened the legitimacy of democratic forms of government in all three countries.

- Democratic ideas were much more embedded in the Philippines and thus more important to regime legitimacy than in either Indonesia or Malaysia.

- Western democracies were much more concerned with securing their own strategic interests in these countries than in promoting democratic forms of governance.

10.2 The shift to authoritarian rule

In all three countries, the rise of authoritarian rule reshaped the coalitions that controlled the state and transformed the relationship between state and society. Even the most repressive regimes claimed to be pursuing their own 'indigenous' forms of democracy distinct from and often at odds with models of liberal democracy that evolved in the West. Contradictory claims have been made about the relationship between economic change on the one hand, and the rise and decline of authoritarian and democratic regimes on the other. Western democracies tended to facilitate, and in some cases actively endorse, the new authoritarian regimes.

Establishment of authoritarian regimes

In Indonesia, Malaysia and the Philippines it was civilian authorities that initially turned away from democracy. However, the possibility of consolidating authoritarian rule depended on the position of the military within the state and the process invariably politicized the military. Leaders attempted to legitimize authoritarian rule by pointing to the 'threat of communism' or 'national disintegration' on the one hand, and the abuse of power and economic mismanagement by civilian elites on the other.

Indonesia

Sukarno took the first steps toward authoritarian rule in Indonesia when he declared martial law in 1957 in an effort to deal with widespread regional revolts in the Outer Islands. In 1959, with the military defeat of most of the rebellions, Sukarno restored the 1945 constitution based on presidential rule and ushered in the era of 'Guided Democracy'. Over the next five years, the military became more consolidated and profited from control over nationalized industries. The new government represented an uneasy alliance between Sukarno, the PKI and the military. Sukarno attempted to legitimize authoritarian rule in nationalist terms, launching a successful campaign to regain West Irian from the Dutch and later an unsuccessful drive to oppose the establishment of the Federation of Malaysia. Foreign firms were nationalized, but with huge government deficits and inflation reaching 1,000 per cent by 1965 (World Bank, 1993, p.171), the economy went into a tail-spin. In September 1965, factionalism within the military culminated in the kidnapping and execution of six members of the military high command. The move, which the supporters of Major General Suharto claimed was backed by the PKI and condoned by Sukarno, gave the Suharto group the opportunity to seize power. Hundreds of thousands of people even loosely identified with the PKI were massacred by mainly Muslim groups, encouraged and in places led by the armed forces (Sundhaussen, 1989, p.437; Kolko, 1988, pp.177–82).

General Suharto formally assumed the presidency in 1968 backed by the military and the state bureaucracy. The 'New Order' regime succeeded in 'pacifying' and uniting the whole Indonesian archipelago, greatly reducing inflation and the budget deficit, and presiding over a long period of economic growth. Economic growth was underpinned by the exploitation of petroleum, forest and agricultural resources, the promotion of manufacturing exports, a mixture of state enterprise and private and foreign investment, severe restrictions on the organization of urban and rural labour, and a system of patronage which has tied emerging Indonesian business groups and Chinese business to the bureaucracy and the President himself.

Malaysia

Malaysia's uneasy democracy was abruptly aborted in the wake of racial rioting after the UMNO's continued supremacy was put into doubt by elections in 1969. The government suspended the constitution and parliament, while effective power was transferred from Prime Minister Tunku Abdul Rahman to a new National Operations Council, led by Deputy Prime Minister Tun Abdul Razak bin Hussein. By the time emergency rule was lifted in 1971, Tun Razak had become Prime Minister and the UMNO-led Nationalist Alliance had restored its two-thirds majority in parliament. The constitution and the sedition ordinance were modified committing the state to redressing racial imbalances in the economy and banning any public discussion or criticism of Malay special rights, the status of Malay rulers, the pre-eminence of Malay language and the status of Islam. Politicians such as Dr Mahathir bin

Mohamad, who had been expelled from the UMNO for advocating Malay supremacy and a one-party UMNO state, were elevated to Cabinet posts. While the military, tied by patronage to the Prime Minister and often by affinity to the Malay rulers, assumed new importance, they remained subordinate to civilian politicians who relied on police forces to maintain order.

A 'New Economic Policy' (NEP) was proclaimed giving the state a greater role in economic affairs and *bumiputra* (Malay and indigenous peoples) preferential access to business opportunities, education and government-funded programmes. The UMNO enlarged its coalition forming the twelve-member *Barisan Nasional*, or National Front, effectively reducing the influence of non-Malay organizations, especially the Malayan Chinese Association, and increasing the influence of Islamic groups. The National Front succeeded in dominating parliament in every subsequent election with Dr Mahathir assuming the leadership of the UMNO and the government in 1981. The UMNO presided over a growing economy, and the importance of the state in economic management gave the Prime Minister and party leaders access to enormous resources of patronage (Means, 1991, pp.286–7).

Philippines

The elite democracy of the Philippines which saw the successful alternation of power between incumbents and challengers in six presidential elections between 1945 and 1965 was abandoned when President Ferdinand Marcos, elected to an unprecedented second term in office in 1969, declared martial law in 1972. Marcos was first elected as a 'modernizing' President committed to social reform, but even in his first term began to concentrate more power in the executive and brought the military into rural development work. The 1969 elections were marked by extensive corruption and violence as Marcos used unprecedented levels of government funds on his campaign and provincial private armies of Marcos allies expanded (Doronila, 1985, pp.111–15). In the aftermath of the election the nationalist, student, worker and peasant protest movements that had been growing over the decade began to influence Congress and even attitudes at the Supreme Court (Putzel, 1992, pp.120–1).

Marcos drew upon these sentiments to call a Constitutional Convention and attempted to push for amendments that would allow him to stay in office beyond the two-term limit. Convinced he could not win support in the Convention, and drawing on elite fears at the level of popular mobilization in society and a general public sentiment for change, Marcos declared martial law in 1972. He justified the suspension of Congress, government control over the media, and the arrest of opposition leaders by exaggerating a threat to the state posed by the relatively small Communist Party of the Philippines and its New People's Army formed in the late 1960s.

The alliance which assumed control of the state included the Marcos family, the military and selected members of the oligarchy drawn from both the business community and powerful provincial political clans (Putzel, 1992, pp.143–6). Marcos proclaimed a plan to build a 'New Society' based on social and economic reform and a programme of rapid industrialization, but his social reform turned into widespread repression with the exercise of arbitrary military power against both the militant communist opposition and all forms of popular organizing and protest.

An Asian form of 'democracy'?

In all three countries leaders defended their political systems by appeals against the 'universalism' of Western critics who did not understand and who berated 'Asian values'. The most articulate exponent of this point of view was Malaysian Prime Minister Dr Mahathir who argued for the particular merits of 'Malaysian democracy' distinct from, 'democracies where political leaders are afraid to do what they know is right ... [where] the people and their leaders live in fear ... of the free media which they so loudly proclaim as inviolable' (speech at Cambridge University, 15 March 1995). Mahathir gained much respect in his own country and throughout the developing world for his outspoken criticisms of Western chauvinism and arrogance.

However, his defence of 'Malaysian democracy' echoed past proclamations by President Suharto and his New Order generals that Indonesia was pursuing its own unique form of '*pancasila* democracy' based on consensus politics, and President Marcos's claim that his New Society was based on direct democracy with presidentially engineered referenda (the latter not to be discussed here, but see Wurfel, 1988). Some modernization theorists have been sympathetic to such benign interpretations of authoritarian rule (see the contributions to Diamond *et al.*, 1989, especially Sundhaussen, Chapter 11, and Jackson, Chapter 6).

Liberal democracies in the West are riddled with contradictions and remain in many domains entirely inadequate (systemic gender discrimination, widespread inequality, abuse of minorities, etc.). Nevertheless, examining the Indonesian and Malaysian political systems in relation to two of the defining characteristics of liberal democracy (as outlined in Chapter 1) demonstrates the extent to which claims for 'indigenous forms of democracy' appear to be no more than justifications for authoritarian rule.

Elections and universal suffrage

Indonesia's New Order constitution vested extraordinary power in the hands of the President effectively placing him at the pinnacle of a patrimonial network of patronage. The doctrine of *dwifungsi*, or 'dual function', guaranteed a place for the military at every level of the state. Elections, held every five years, were neither free nor based entirely on universal suffrage. The President was not only elected indirectly by the MPR (People's Deliberative Assembly), but the supposedly sovereign MPR itself was dominated by presidentially approved delegates from 'functional groups' and the military. The subordinate House of Representatives, whose members all sat in the MPR, was 'elected' every five years with 100 seats set aside for presidentially appointed military representatives. Elections were consistently won by the state-controlled party, Golkar (Golongan Karya – Functional Groups), in which the military held a dominant position. Officially sanctioned opposition parties were allowed to operate but only during the weeks leading up to an election and could do so only under strict state control.

In Malaysia, executive and legislative power was vested in the 177 member People's Council (*Dewan Rakyat*), led by the Prime Minister and elected every five years. A 69 member State Council (*Dewan Negara*) included two members elected by the legislative assemblies of each of the states and the balance appointed by the monarch. While elections at both the federal and state levels were based on universal suffrage the constituencies were overwhelmingly weighted in favour of rural Malay villages, thus ensuring the UMNO's continued dominance (Crouch, 1993, p.137). After 1971, the federal government's emergency powers have been used to overthrow state governments when they appeared to threaten separation or concerted opposition to the UMNO. Malay supremacy was constitutionally guaranteed even though the population was composed of approximately 51 per cent Malay, 10 per cent indigenous tribal peoples, 30 per cent Chinese and 9 per cent South Asians.

Freedom of expression and access to information

Freedom of expression within Indonesia's 'elected' bodies and in society at large was curtailed by the requirement that all political parties as well as non-governmental organizations adopt the state ideology of *pancasila* as their only ideological basis. Decisions in the MPR and the legislature were said to be taken by 'consensus' which, though sometimes allowing factions to block controversial measures, generally blurred debates and facilitated coercive control by the President and top state officials. Opposition parties were pledged to refrain from challenging the authoritarian basis of the state, to uphold 'consensus' policy making, and to refrain from claims to represent any particular religious, class or group aspirations or values. Access to information was curtailed by heavy press and media censorship and widespread intimidation and arrests of government critics.

Malaysian political leaders also proclaimed adherence to their own indigenous form of democracy, embodied in their 'national ideology', *Rukunegara*, introduced after parliamentary rule was suspended (Ahmad, 1989, p.362). Freedom of expression and information were severely limited by both direct and indirect government and ruling party intervention. The Sedition Act and Official Secrets Act were used to inhibit public debate, while the main newspapers were owned indirectly by the National Front parties. Radio and television were largely government owned with one station indirectly owned by the UMNO (Ahmad, 1989).

By referring to authoritarian political systems in terms of 'indigenous cultural values' and 'non-Western forms of democracy' both political actors and analysts have been able to abstract from the brutality of authoritarian rule. 'Asian democracy', defined in opposition to Western liberal democracy, has been used to legitimize the Suharto regime – one of the world's most oppressive political systems – and Malaysia's increasingly authoritarian regime. However, as Marcos discovered in the Philippines, positive economic performance is crucial to maintaining both an authoritarian regime's legitimacy in the eyes of the elite and its passive legitimacy among the people at large.

Economic change and regime change

Capitalism requires a basic institutional framework that guarantees property rights, a legal system capable of enforcing contracts, the presence of a labour force that needs and is willing to work, and a political regime that ensures a degree of predictability in regard to basic economic policy. While the development of capitalism everywhere gives rise to patterns of social diversification based on class it is extremely problematic to ascribe particular political inclinations to the business class (or bourgeoisie), the working class, or to that diverse group that emerges between the two alternately referred to as the 'petty bourgeoisie' or middle class.

Evidence from Indonesia, Malaysia and the Philippines suggests that, at different historical moments, both authoritarian and democratic regimes have been inimical to capitalist development. The arbitrary exercise of power and the predatory nature associated with authoritarian regimes has often inhibited the development of market capitalism, as during Sukarno's 'Guided Democracy' and the latter period of Marcos's rule. On the other hand, the fledgling democracies in Southeast Asia in the 1950s allowed cartels and monopoly interests to operate that undermined government efforts to stimulate market development.

As Hewison *et al.* (1993, p.3) argued, studies of the rise of new business classes in Southeast Asia (Anek, 1992; MacIntyre, 1990) that see in them an inevitable movement toward democracy suffer from 'crude instrumentalism'. Capitalists in Indonesia, Malaysia and the Philippines tended to regard authoritarian regimes as legitimate as long as they guaranteed the basic institutional framework and ensured the continued possibility of capital accumulation, investment and profit making.

It is also inaccurate to assume that the working class has uniformly favoured democratization. In fact, it is perhaps more instructive to consider the political stance of 'the poor' in developing countries rather than the 'working class', since the latter often form a small minority and are not necessarily the most exploited. However, even the larger category of the poor were not particularly staunch advocates of democratization in Indonesia, Malaysia or the Philippines. For the most part the poor were preoccupied with matters of economic survival and relatively receptive targets for the corporatist organizations parented by the Suharto, Marcos and UMNO governments.

In all three countries, maintaining legitimacy among the 'middle class', or the middle-income groups, was crucial to every regime. Their numbers expanded rapidly with capitalist development. Having access to education and command over small enterprises, they acted as a crucial bridge between the wealthiest in society and the poor majority. With a growing share of income they commanded resources crucial to expanding consumption or the size of domestic markets.

It is reasonable to expect that the middle-income groups would be the most prone to adopting the cause of democratization. Commanding a certain degree of wealth they invariably wish to enjoy the individual freedoms previously the preserve of the wealthiest. With education they become interested in a media that is not simply the mouthpiece of government and may well want to influence the elaboration of public policy. Student movements demanding political change in Malaysia in 1974, under Marcos between the mid 1970s and mid 1980s, and in Indonesia all emerged from this group. Many of the leaders of non-governmental organizations that mushroomed in the Philippines in the early 1980s and were expanding their influence in Indonesia in the 1990s came from this group.

Yet the participation of middle-income groups in movements for democratization has also depended on the regime's capacity to co-opt or intimidate them. In Malaysia student protests were met with the 1975 Amendment to the University College Act preventing them from engaging in political activity. In Indonesia, the regime was intent on co-opting or suppressing non-governmental organizations rather than allowing them to develop outside of government influence. In the Philippines, the middle-income groups initially mounted little opposition to the Marcos regime after martial law was declared.

It is clear that positive economic performance remains a key determinant of securing both the legitimacy of a regime among the wealthy and the growing middle-income groups, and at least passive legitimacy among the poor majority. The staying power of the Suharto regime and the UMNO's pre-eminence were underpinned by expanding economic performance and the Marcos regime was fatally wounded by the economic crisis of the early 1980s. However, it is not possible to argue that capitalist development or positive economic performance is linked to either authoritarian or capitalist regime types, nor is it possible to assume, *a priori*, that particular classes will act as agents of democratization.

The international community and authoritarian rule

In all these cases authoritarian rule was established with the complicity of the USA, most Western European countries and Japan. In the late 1960s and throughout the following two decades the World Bank actively supported these regimes.

In 1958, when military rebels against Sukarno declared independence in Sumatra they received covert support from the USA and its allies in the region including the Philippines government (Marchetti and Marks, 1974, pp.51–2, 128; Putzel, 1992, pp.95, 111; Kahin and Kahin, 1995). When Suharto and his generals declared the 'New Order' in 1968 the USA and its allies once again provided support. While a subject of international debate, Indonesian aggression and brutal suppression of the population of East Timor neither led to sanctions nor to a slow down in Western arms trade with the dictatorship.

The USA, eager to protect its military bases in the Philippines and significant private economic interests from growing nationalist sentiments, and worried about its imminent loss in Vietnam, was quick to support Marcos after the declaration of martial law in 1972. Japan actively courted the Marcos regime over the following decade, and Western European countries continued promoting business opportunities in the archipelago.

Anxious to have a share in the Malaysian economic success, Western countries followed the lead of Britain in turning a blind eye to the authoritarian tendencies of the Malaysian regime even as Mahathir promoted an anti-British 'Look East' policy. Japan profited from the policy as did South Korea whose anti-labour measures inspired the Malaysian regime.

—————————————— *Summary of Section 10.2* ——————————————

Authoritarian regimes sought legitimacy in all three countries by pointing to the threat of communism and/or national disintegration and the need for state intervention to curb the economic power of traditional elites.

- When measured against the standards of liberal democracy, claims made by these regimes to be promoting indigenous forms of democracy ring hollow.

- Evidence in these three countries suggests that there is no clear-cut functional relationship between the development of capitalism and either authoritarian or democratic forms of governance, nor are there any absolute proclivities of particular classes toward democracy.

- The developed countries did not hesitate to provide support for the authoritarian regimes in the region and this contributed to regime legitimacy.

10.3 Democratic restoration in the Philippines

During the late 1980s, the wave of democratization which swept over many parts of the developing world reached the Philippines. However, the authoritarian regime in Indonesia remained unshaken, underlining enduring differences between the two nations.

Liberal democracy restored

President Corazon Aquino came to power in 1986 following a military revolt against Marcos that was bolstered by a massive demonstration of what came to be known as 'people power'. After much hesitation, the USA abandoned their support for the ageing dictator and attempted to ensure the restoration of a liberal democratic regime friendly to Western interests (see Putzel, 1992, Chapter 9). Aquino presided over the restoration of basic liberal democratic institutions and organizations introducing a constitution modelled on the US-style 1935 charter abandoned by Marcos.

Elections of the President (limited to a single six-year term), the bicameral legislature (House of Representatives and Senate) and provincial and local governments once again became real contests based on universal suffrage. Elections in 1987, 1992 and 1995, while far from free of violence and money-driven clan politics, were seen as essentially fair. Retired general and former defence secretary Fidel Ramos was elected to the presidency in 1992 in a six-way race, reflecting the splintering of political parties, as shifting clan alliances traditionally contained within two national parties had not yet coalesced (Putzel, 1995).

Basic democratic freedoms of expression and access to information were guaranteed in the new constitution. The media regained its position as among the freest in the developing world, though important private media conglomerates continued to exercise considerable influence over editorial policy. The right to join independent associations, reaffirmed in the

Corazon Aquino and supporters, at a rally,
Fuente Osmena Plaza, 22 February 1986

constitution, was illustrated by the emergence of trade unions, farmers organizations and non-governmental organizations as significant forces within society. They combined a commitment to combating widespread poverty with an effort to influence public policy through both lobbying and mass mobilization.

President Ramos legalized the long banned Communist Party of the Philippines (CPP), demonstrating the self-confidence of the new democratic regime. At the same time the state was still opposed by the remnants of the CPP's underground New People's Army and the growing militancy of armed Islamic separatist organizations in the southern part of the country. Ramos also attempted haltingly to modernize the Armed Forces of the Philippines and bring an end to the arbitrary brutality that characterized military and police activities during the Marcos years.

Democratic restoration in comparative perspective

When President Marcos declared martial law in 1972, his stated intention of building a 'New Society' mirrored the earlier assertion of the 'New Order' by Indonesian generals. However, the fact that a liberal democratic form of government replaced Marcos rather than a military dictatorship was linked to several factors that have distinguished the Philippines from Indonesia.

First, under Marcos the military was relatively weak and dependent on the USA. It remained subordinate to the President and his cronies, never assuming the independence that the military in Indonesia had. A major distinction between the Suharto regime and the Marcos regime was that the abuse of power that was increasingly associated with patrimonialism in Indonesia was moderated by the existence of a strong military (even though officers shared in corruption), whereas no organization was capable of checking the corruption of the Marcos family and its close associates.

Second, the idea of democracy was much more firmly rooted in Philippine political history than in Indonesia. This was due to the introduction of elitist partial democracy under colonial rule, the reformist and largely peaceful character of the nationalist movement and the much longer period of liberal democratic rule after independence in the Philippines.

Third, in 1986 in the Philippines there was no threat that democracy would encourage separatist movements or endanger the integrity of the nation-state. The major threat to the state was posed by a growing communist movement that derived much of its legitimacy as an alternative to the corruption of the Marcos regime. It was widely believed that democratic restoration would undermine the movement. In Indonesia, the authoritarian regime had wiped out the communist movement, but, while making great strides in uniting the disparate ethnic and linguistic identities, it still faced a weakly integrated nation-state (especially in peripheral areas).

The liberal democratic restoration in the Philippines after 1986 remained fragile. This was demonstrated by repeated attempted *coups d'tat* during the Aquino government. The possibility for further consolidating or 'deepening' democracy was dependent on three interrelated processes of change still under way by the mid 1990s. First, the state was still very much penetrated by clan interests, and not yet able to function as an 'impersonal public authority'. Second, the institutions and organizations of civil society remained weak, reflecting a need for the strengthening of education, programmatic politics, citizens' associations and the independence of the media. Third, little had been accomplished in eliminating the dependency bred by extreme poverty and inequality (see the discussion in Putzel, 1995).

──────────────── *Summary of Section 10.3* ────────────────

- The events of 1986 led to the restoration of a liberal democratic regime in the Philippines, although this was largely an elite-dominated process.

- Several factors distinguished the Philippines from Indonesia and help to explain why the military did not take power in the wake of Marcos's decline: (a) the military was relatively weak and lacked independence from Marcos and his cronies, whereas in Indonesia the military was the strongest organization in the Suharto state; (b) democratic ideas were more firmly rooted in the Philippines; and (c) there was no threat that liberal democracy would lead to national disintegration in the Philippines as it might have done in Indonesia.

- Democratic restoration remained fragile in the Philippines due to the persistence of clan politics and widespread poverty.

10.4 Reflections on the process of democratization

No single factor can explain why liberal democracy has had greater success in the Philippines than in either Indonesia or Malaysia. Nor can any of the three theoretical approaches to the study of democracy alone account for this varied experience. However, my comparative discussion of political experience in the three countries, through the prism of the five explanatory factors employed here, suggests that a selective application of insights from all three approaches does shed light on both past experience and the potential for future democratization.

These explanatory factors were drawn together through a focus on the shifting grounds for regime legitimacy. The process of democratic transition and consolidation can best be understood as a battle over what constitutes legitimate government.

The structuralists' focus on historically constituted structures of power within and between state and society provided insight into the context in which political change occurred. The relative positions of power of the bureaucracy, military and elected officials within the state and their relationship with societal groups at different historical moments provided opportunities and barriers to would-be authoritarians and democrats in all three countries.

The modernization approach informed my examination of how differing degrees of national integration enabled or limited democratization. The threat of national disintegration was consistently used by authoritarian actors in Indonesia to justify their rule, as was the threat of ethnic violence in Malaysia, while in the Philippines at least the elite shared a sense of national identity.

Both the structuralist and the modernization approaches informed my discussion of the relationship between economic and political change, though I discounted any absolute correlation between either capitalism and democracy or particular classes and political inclinations. Nevertheless, positive economic performance was important to the maintenance of legitimacy of authoritarian rule in Indonesia and Malaysia, while economic crisis undermined the legitimacy of the Marcos regime among the elite as well as passive legitimacy among the population at large.

My discussion has indicated that the legacy of ideas inherited from colonial administrations and nationalist movements influenced the course of regime change. However, rather than seeing ideas as simply the reflection of structures of power in state and society, my interpretation is more in line with transition theorists' propositions about the historically specific character of ideas in choices taken by leaders and organizations.

Finally, political change in all three countries was influenced by international factors, most importantly the very shaping of the polities by colonial administrations, but also the active intervention of foreign powers in the post-colonial period (especially the US role in relation to Indonesia and the Philippines). However, in examining this dimension I have differed both from structuralist propositions that directly link regime types to functional requirements of the 'international system' and the modernization theorists' tendency to treat the developed democracies, especially the USA, as benign advocates of democratization.

The battle for legitimacy

The future possibilities for democratic transition in Indonesia and Malaysia, and for the consolidation of the newly restored democracy in the Philippines, depend very much on whether the 'idea of democracy' can become incorporated in the criteria by which regimes are judged legitimate.

In 1995, the military continued to regard itself as the guardian of the nation-state in Indonesia and, although less than in the late 1960s, retained enormous power within state organizations, while the organizations of society remained weak and parented by the state. Ethnic politics continued to underpin the organization of the Malaysian state and permeated most of the organizations of society. The success of both regimes in promoting economic development contributed enormously to the maintenance of legitimacy among the high- and middle-income groups and to securing at least the passive acquiescence of the society as a whole.

There is a tendency among some authors to view goals of securing economic growth and political stability as primarily valued by the elite or by domestic and international capitalists (Robison, 1993, pp.46, 62). However, authoritarian politics emerged to dominance in Indonesia and prominence in Malaysia and maintained that position in no small part due to the value that the ordinary citizen placed on political stability and economic growth. Memories of the violence and unrest characterizing Sukarno's rule and the turbulence of the 1969 racial riots in Malaysia have great staying power. Political stability itself could become the principal grounds for legitimacy even in the case of future economic decline. This is why both regimes often refer to the chaos that could erupt if Western forms of liberal democracy were promoted.

National integration represents a real stumbling block to democratic politics. Sub-national identities of a religious, ethnic, linguistic and even 'tribal' character have enormous staying power. Indonesian and Malaysian authorities point to separatist and ethnic divisions as a justification for the perpetuation of authoritarian rule. Ethnic peace and national unity have been important grounds for the legitimacy of both regimes. There is a genuine problem in introducing liberal democratic politics in a context of divergent visions of the very boundaries of the nation-state. It is not unimaginable that a quick transition to democratic politics could make Indonesia the Yugoslavia of Southeast Asia.

There is a uniform growth in the middle-income groups in all three countries and some reason to believe that they may be inclined to the pursuit of liberal democratic reforms. However, whether this group turns to and endorses such reforms, as they did during the 'people power' events in the Philippines, or turns towards the promotion of non-democratic alternatives, like students' involvement in Islamic revivalism in Malaysia in the early 1990s, will be determined largely by the battle of ideas. The same is true for the much more consequential role that can be played by the wider group that constitutes the poor.

Even with the decimation of the PKI in the late 1960s and the virtual collapse of the communist movement internationally, in 1995 the Indonesian regime was taking only the first tentative steps towards ceasing to label all opposition as 'communist'. By the early 1990s in Malaysia, to suggest that politics be conducted on a secular and multi-ethnic basis could be considered a seditious act punishable by imprisonment. In this context the battle of ideas will remain difficult to wage and the promotion of democratic principles as the grounds for regime legitimacy will not be easy.

References

Agoncillio, T.A. (1960) *Malolos: the Crisis of the Republic*, Quezon City, University of the Philippines.

Ahmad, Z.H. (1989) 'Malaysia: quasi democracy in a divided society' in Diamond *et al.* (eds) pp.347–82.

Alagappa, M. (ed.) (1995) *Political Legitimacy in Southeast Asia: the Quest for Moral Authority*, Stanford, Stanford University Press.

Anderson, B. (1983) 'Old state, new society: Indonesia's New Order in comparative perspective', *Journal of Asian Studies*, vol.42, pp.477–96 (also in Anderson, 1990, Chapter 3).

Anderson, B. (1990) *Language and Power: Exploring Political Cultures in Indonesia*, Ithaca, Cornell University Press.

Anderson, B. (1991) *Imagined Communities*, London, Verso.

Anek, L. (1992) *Business Associations and the New Political Economy of Thailand*, Oxford, Westview Press.

Colbert, E. (1977) *Southeast Asia in International Politics 1941–1956*, Ithaca, Cornell University Press.

Crouch, H. (1993) 'Malaysia: neither authoritarian nor democratic' in Hewison *et al.* (eds) pp.133–58.

Diamond, L., Linz, J.J. and Lipset, S.M. (eds) (1989) *Democracy in Developing Countries: Volume Three, Asia*, London, Adamantine Press.

Doronila, A. (1985) 'The transformation of patron–client relations and its political consequences in post-war Philippines', *Journal of Southeast Asian Studies*, vol.16, no.1, pp.99–116.

Francisco, L. and Fast, J. (1985) *Conspiracy for Empire: Big Business, Corruption and the Politics of Imperialism in America, 1876–1907*, Quezon City, Foundation for Nationalist Studies.

Hall, D.G.E. (1981) *A History of Southeast Asia* (4th edn), Basingstoke, Macmillan.

Held, D. (1989) *Political Theory and the Modern State*, Cambridge, Polity Press.

Hewison, K., Rodan, G. and Robison, R. (eds) (1993) *Southeast Asia in the 1990s: Authoritarianism, Democracy and Capitalism*, London, Allen and Unwin.

Institute for Popular Democracy (1992) *All in the Family: a Study of Elites and Power Relations in the Philippines*, Quezon City, Institute for Popular Democracy.

Jomo, K.S. (1988) *A Question of Class: Capital, the State, and Uneven Development in Malaya*, New York, Monthly Review Press.

Kahin, A. and Kahin, S. (1995) *Subversion as Foreign Policy*, New York, New Press.

Kerkvliet, B. (1977) *The Huk Rebellion: a Study of Peasant Revolt in the Philippines*, Berkeley, University of California Press.

Kolko, G. (1988) *Confronting the Third World: United States Foreign Policy, 1945–1980*, New York, Pantheon Books.

Legge, J.D. (1972) *Sukarno: a Political Biography*, Harmondsworth, Penguin.

Lipset, S.M. (1963) *Political Man: the Social Basis of Politics*, New York, Anchor.

Lloyd, C. (1986) *Explanation in Social History*, Oxford, Blackwell.

MacIntyre, A. (1990) *Business and Politics in Indonesia*, Sydney, Allen and Unwin.

Marchetti, V. and Marks, J.D. (1974) *The CIA and the Cult of Intelligence*, New York, Dell Publishing.

Means, G. (1991) *Malaysian Politics: the Second Generation*, Oxford, Oxford University Press.

Putzel, J. (1992) *A Captive Land: the Politics of Agrarian Reform in the Philippines*, London, New York and Manila, Catholic Institute for International Relations, Monthly Review Press and Ateneo University Press.

Putzel, J. (1995) 'Democratisation and clan politics: the 1992 Philippine elections', *Southeast Asia Research*, vol.3, no.1, pp.18–45.

Rivera, T.C. (1995) *Landlords and Capitalists: Class, Family and State in Philippine Manufacturing*, Quezon City, University of the Philippines Press.

Robison, R. (1986) *Indonesia: the Rise of Capital*, London, Unwin Hyman.

Robison, R. (1993) 'Indonesia: tensions in state and regime' in Hewison *et al.* (eds) pp.39–74.

Steinberg, J. (ed.) (1987) *In Search of Southeast Asia: a Modern History* (revised edn), Sydney, Allen and Unwin.

Sundhaussen, U. (1989) 'Indonesia: past and present encounters with democracy' in Diamond *et al.* (eds) pp.423–74.

World Bank (1993) *The East Asian Miracle*, Washington, World Bank.

Wurfel, D. (1988) *Filipino Politics: Development and Decay*, Ithaca, Cornell University Press.

I would like to thank Peter Carey, Irene Gedalof, John Harriss and John Sidel for criticisms and suggestions but absolve them from any responsibility for the final views expressed here.

Afterword

David Potter

Each chapter in this part has addressed a different question about democratization in either Latin America or Asia by engaging in *comparative analysis* framed by a distinctive *theoretical approach* and set of *explanatory factors* as introduced in Chapter 1. There are certain ideas and explanatory factors which figure importantly in several or all five of the chapters, and it is the purpose of this brief Afterword to note them.

One such idea, broadly linking two explanatory factors, is central to the structural theoretical approach. It concerns the relation between *state power* and *class divisions.* The literature using a structural theoretical approach suggests broadly that democratization is unlikely where the state is either excessively powerful in relation to social classes or is excessively dependent on powerful landed classes engaged in labour repressive agriculture; democratization is more likely where there is a rough balance of power between the state and relatively independent classes. What do the chapters on Latin America and Asia have to say about this?

Evidence from Chapters 6 and 9, in which the structural approach is particularly prominent, serves both to clarify and qualify these broad propositions about relative state power and democratization. For example, it does appear that democratization in Latin America struggled where *landed classes* were powerful in relation to the state. The analysis in Chapter 6 of the rural class structure and the power of the landed class in a number of authoritarian Latin American countries in the 1960s and 1970s broadly supports this proposition; also noteworthy is the fact that in Venezuela, one of the very few liberal democracies at that time, landed elites were comparatively weak. However, the rather striking evidence in Chapter 9 from South Korea and Taiwan qualifies this general proposition. In both these Asian countries, the large landlords were virtually wiped out as a class due to land reforms being pushed through in the late 1940s and early 1950s, yet democratization did not begin to occur until the late 1980s. Indeed, the reforms seem to have benefited the peasantry and stabilized the countryside, which helped (with other factors) to sustain authoritarian rule for the next 35 years. This experience underlines a quite fundamental point about historical changes in the balance of power between the state and rural class structures: such changes did not *by themselves* cause democratization at that time, but the choices and actions that propelled South Korea and Taiwan in a particular political direction 35 years later were unlikely to have been democratic if there had existed a powerful (anti-democratic) landlord class closely allied to the state. In other words, democratization occurred because of a *conjuncture* at a particular time of various factors, one of which was a propitious rural class structure which had changed to that propitious form many years previously.

The same general point can be made regarding the relations of power between the state and the *urban working class.* Structural approaches emphasize the growing importance, due to industrialization, of the urban working class as a major force pushing for greater democratization in society and extensions of the suffrage. Once again, however, the comparative evidence from Latin America and Asia suggests that this factor by itself cannot wholly explain democratization in particular countries. Chapter 9 suggests that the urban working class was far stronger and better organized in South Korea than in Taiwan, but both countries commenced democratization at about the same time; and Chapter 6 suggests that, although the urban working class had become a major force in Argentina and Brazil by the mid twentieth century, the potential power of this class in pushing for democratization was deflected by the forces of populism. Once again, the rise of a potentially pro-democratic social class need not by itself cause democratization.

Modernization and transition theoretical approaches pay less attention to class, more to the relative power of state and *civil society* – that set of uncoerced human associations and relations in society 'formed for the sake of family, faith, interests and ideology' (Chapter 1). The argument in these approaches is that the growth of civil society can assist democratization by gradually taming the excessive power of the state apparatus. Evidence for the importance of this explanatory factor is considered in Chapter 8 in the comparison made between India's comparatively lush civil society and China's comparatively weak and state-penetrated one. The general point is interestingly qualified in Chapter 7 in the author's analysis of the swing towards democratization across Latin America in the 1980s and early 1990s. The forms and dynamics of these democratization transitions appear to have been controlled largely by elites, although there is reference in the chapter also to pressure from civil society and the role of social movements. It seems in Latin America that the absence more or less of a rich assortment of uncoerced human association in civil society, particularly amongst the mass of the rural and urban poor, is not necessarily a barrier to the commencement of democratic transitions, but a weak civil society does appear to be one reason why the consolidation of liberal democracy has been difficult.

The ideas and explanatory factors already mentioned refer in part to relative state power, a very abstract concept indeed. The chapters in this part drawing on transition or modernization theories underline the importance of unpacking such abstractions when engaged in trying to explain democratization in particular countries. This unpacking exercise involves paying attention to such considerations as the relative importance of different *political institutions* within the state and the extent of consensus on basic policy orientations among state elites. For example, such considerations are part of the explanation given in Chapter 10 for the stronger impulse towards democratization in Malaysia and the Philippines, as compared to Indonesia. The analysis suggests that in Indonesia political elites have been fractious and the military as a political institution within the state has been very prominent as compared to Malaysia and the Philippines where there has tended to be more elite consensus within the state and a less dominant military presence relative to other political institutions.

The party system is regarded as one such political institution, although an unusual one. Political parties are concerned with occupying the state apparatus and using it to pursue their broad political project; but they are at the same time more or less grounded in, and representative of, parts of civil society. Chapters in this part refer to the varied nature of party systems when explaining democratization processes in different countries. Such a comparison, for example, is important in Chapter 8. Part of the explanation of India's liberal democracy rests on an analysis of the unusual character of the Indian National Congress, later the Congress Party, which had deep roots in rural civil society and helped to institutionalize democratic politics. China's different political trajectory is explained partly in terms of its different party system. The comparison in Chapter 7 of a number of Latin American countries suggests that the consolidation of liberal democracy can be difficult in those countries where party systems are weak.

All three theoretical approaches pay attention to *economic or capitalist development* as it affects the power of the state and political institutions within it. Structural approaches emphasize how capitalist development can change class structures. Transition and modernization approaches consider the effects of economic development on the character and growth of civil society. As a factor helping to explain democratization economic/capitalist development figures in all five chapters. Its direct bearing on democratization, however, is far from clear if one reflects on the Latin American and Asian countries considered in this part. For example, there seems to be no consistent association between levels of development and democratization. Countries in Latin America that experienced the most repressive dictatorships from the 1960s, including Argentina, Uruguay and Chile, were amongst the most developed in the region (Chapter 6); when the wave of democratization occurred in the 1980s it affected not only the wealthy countries but also some of the poorest, e.g. Ecuador, Peru and Bolivia (Chapter 7). In Asia, India sustained liberal democracy in the context of a low level of development (Chapter 8). Also, authoritarian regimes do not necessarily move towards democracy as they develop. Economic growth rates were impressive in China (Chapter 8) and Indonesia (Chapter 10) during the 1980s and early 1990s, but that did not by itself trigger democratization. Mexico remained a partial democracy during the latter part of the twentieth century despite impressive economic performance (Chapters 6 and 7). The comparative evidence is somewhat more supportive of the argument common in modernization theories that, once liberal democracy exists, the level of economic development is important to its survival. Economically poor democracies are more likely to be fragile; this is clearly suggested by analysis in Chapter 7 of problems with consolidation in Latin America in the 1980s and early 1990s. Liberal democracy is more likely to endure in more wealthy countries; Japan from 1950 onwards is an example.

The comparative evidence from Latin America and Asia points to a number of possible explanatory relationships between democratization and factors related to *international* contexts and relations including war. All three theoretical approaches pay attention to this factor. However, the extent to which such relationships can be relied on to explain democratization is uncertain. For example, the end of superpower confrontation and of the Cold War in the late 1980s appears to have been an important factor behind democratization in some Latin American and Asian countries, but the continued existence of authoritarian regimes in both regions also cautions us against making too much of this single factor. The collapse of an authoritarian regime in one country (e.g. the Philippines) can help to trigger democratization in some nearby countries (e.g. South Korea and Taiwan), but not in others (e.g. Indonesia). The Cuban revolution had knock-on effects in many Latin American countries, but not all in the same way. Democratic 'conditionalities' were laid down by the USA and Japanese governments, the World Bank and others prominent in the global capitalist system in the late 1980s and early 1990s in order to put democratization pressures on authoritarian regimes; but they appear to have had more of an effect on some countries (e.g. the Philippines) than others (e.g. Indonesia).

Latin American and Asian countries experienced colonial rule, a transnational structure of power which was the antithesis of democracy. That historical experience is important in explanations of different political trajectories, as the comparison in Chapter 8 between India and China suggests. But the comparative evidence suggests that the colonial experience did not leave common political legacies once the colonialists departed. For example, India, Pakistan, Ceylon/Sri Lanka, Burma/Myanmar and Malaya/Malaysia were all part of the British empire, yet three of them consolidated liberal or partial democracies after independence and two of them did not. It also appears that the importance of the colonial experience for subsequent political development can fade with time; there is little reference to nineteenth-century Spanish and Portuguese colonialisms in Latin America in the analysis of democratization there in the late twentieth century, whereas the significance of more recent colonial rules figures importantly in the analyses of Asian democratization.

War as a transnational event has also had varied political consequences. For example, all of Asia was involved in the Second World War in Asia (1941–45), directly or indirectly. India and Ceylon mobilized for the war but experienced it indirectly in the sense that they avoided military occupation by the Japanese. British colonial states continued to rule there throughout the war, with civilian control of the military within the apparatus of the state firmly maintained. India and Ceylon went on to establish liberal democracies after the war. Most of the other Asian countries experienced the war directly, and in many cases were occupied by the Japanese army. That experience strengthened the political position of the military in society and in the state, and in the absence of other countervailing forces that powerful military apparatus threatened the prospects for liberal democracy. But even in these cases some countries formed fragile democracies after the war (e.g. the Philippines, Indonesia and Malaysia), others formed communist authoritarian regimes (e.g. China and Vietnam).

In short, international factors constrain but do not determine the democratization outcomes in an absolute way. The point will be reinforced in the forthcoming discussion of sub-Saharan Africa in Part IV.

PART IV
Africa and the Middle East

Introduction   269

CHAPTER 11   The rise and fall and rise (and fall?) of   272
democracy in sub-Saharan Africa

CHAPTER 12   South Africa: democracy delayed   294

CHAPTER 13   Middle East exceptionalism – myth or   321
reality?

CHAPTER 14   Islam and democracy   345

CHAPTER 15   Israel: constraints on consolidation   367

Afterword   387

Introduction

Margaret Kiloh

Part IV moves on from Latin America and Asia to consider two new areas, the Middle East and Africa south of the Sahara. The exploration of democratization drawing on the explanatory framework in Chapter 1 considers the two regions generally, examines two case studies in some depth (Israel and South Africa), and assesses the role of Islam in the democratization process.

Africa south of the Sahara forms a single geographic entity which (with the addition of the island states of Madagascar and Mauritius) Chapter 11 takes as its area of study (see Map 11.1). Politically and culturally the situation is less clear and it is reasonable to question whether all of the countries in the region should be considered in the same category for the purposes of comparison. The borders of individual states were set, by and large, during the period of colonialism. They cut across linguistic and cultural boundaries and may be the subject of dispute. Nevertheless, they are generally accepted for the moment. Nearly a third of the world's independent states are located in sub-Saharan Africa. It is not surprising, therefore, that they exhibit considerable diversity, making comparison and generalization difficult. However, there are also important similarities. For example, with the partial exception of Liberia and Ethiopia, all African states share a common experience of colonialism (somewhat differentiated according to the characteristics of the colonizing power). They also tend to be poor and, most importantly for the purposes of the chapters in this part, their experience of democratization, whilst varied, also displays common characteristics.

The Middle East can be defined differently according to whether geo-political, socio-economic or religious and cultural factors are used. The term has been used to refer to the band of countries stretching from Morocco in North West Africa to Afghanistan and Pakistan in Asia. Much more narrowly it can describe the Arab East (the region between the Gulf, the Red Sea and the Mediterranean, including Egypt) or what used to be called the Near East, namely the Arab East and its immediate neighbours, Turkey and Iran. This is the definition used in Chapter 13 (see Map 13.1). Chapter 14, in contrast, uses a completely different perspective, taking as its starting point not the geo-political boundaries of the contemporary Middle East but the universalistic belief system of Islam and its many manifestations. It raises the question of how far the common culture of Islam *defines* Muslim countries and, in particular, whether this culture is responsible for the charge of 'exceptionalism' as regards those factors which elsewhere have fostered the advent of liberal democracy. Those states which claim to be Islamic display an enormous range of political regimes from absolutist monarchy in Saudi Arabia to republicanism in Iran. Therefore, whilst Islam is an important defining characteristic of the Middle East its relative importance for the process of democratization needs to be viewed alongside other characteristics.

The two case study countries in this part also raise questions of definition. South Africa (Chapter 12) is geographically defined by the borders confirmed by the Act of Union of 1910, but until the 'freedom election' of 1994 its *political* identity was that of a white racist enclave marked off from the rest of Africa. In the context of the Middle East Israel (Chapter 15) is also an odd country out. Its creation was the culmination of a period of intensive Jewish settlement in the British-administered League of Nations Mandate of Palestine. Jewish settlement led to bitter fighting with the Palestinian population who were defeated by the Zionist forces. In May 1948 the state of Israel was declared and in 1949 a series of Armistice agreements between Israel and the Arab states drew up the *de facto* borders of the new state. The creation of Israel made refugees of the Palestinians who fled from the areas controlled by the new government. Continuing conflict has led to the occupation of further territory making the boundaries of the state a contentious issue and calling into question its democratic legitimacy.

The approach of this part of the book is to proceed by means of different levels of comparison to try to tease out answers to a series of questions set up by the chapters. Chapters 11 and 13 are interested in finding answers to questions which are applicable across sub-Saharan Africa and the Middle East, respectively. Each chapter asks a pair of organizing questions. For Chapter 11 these are: why have liberal democratic regimes generally been so difficult to sustain in sub-Saharan Africa? and why was there a general trend in the region towards re-democratization at the beginning of the 1990s? For Chapter 13, is 'Middle Eastern exceptionalism' an acceptable explanation for the general lack of democratization in the region? and if not, what other general explanations can be found? In the course of this chapter the role of Islam is raised briefly as an issue. Chapter 14 explores this in depth through questions about the nature of Islam, how it relates to secular politics and how, in particular, it relates to democratization or the lack of it. Finally, Chapters 12 and 15 ask another kind of question. They are not so much concerned with general issues as they are with the specific conditions of democratization in South Africa and Israel. For Chapter 12 the key questions are: what brought about the end of apartheid in South Africa? and what were the significant features of the transition to liberal democracy? Chapter 15 asks why a liberal democratic system was introduced when the state of Israel was established and what the constraints on the consolidation of that democracy have been.

Within each of the chapters comparisons are made – either between the different states in a relatively wide area (sub-Saharan Africa, the Middle East, the Islamic world) or between a case study country and the rest of the region concerned (South Africa, Israel). At each level there are similarities which encourage comparison. For example, grouping sub-Saharan Africa and the Middle East together for the purposes of comparison has a certain logic. They are geographically adjacent and can even be said to merge into one another in areas such as Mauritania and the Sudan. There are also important historical and cultural links. Although economically the Middle East appears to be more 'developed' in both areas the presence or absence of natural resources such as oil has played an important role and politically both have been crucially affected by great power rivalry and the Cold War. Most importantly, until recently they shared the dubious reputation of providing possibly the most inhospitable conditions for – and the fewest examples of – successful democratization among all of the regions surveyed in this book (see the Appendix to Chapter 1).

When Chapters 11 and 13 examine the history of the failures of liberal democracy in their respective regions they come up with a similar pattern. In Africa there have been three different periods in the history of democratization – an early period of liberal democratic constitutions bequeathed by the colonial powers, a middle period of authoritarian or military rule and a late period of re-democratization which may or may not be consolidated. In the Middle East too there were limited post-independence experiments with liberal democratic politics which were swept away by authoritarian regimes, renewed pressures for democratization in the 1980s and 1990s and some tentative moves towards more democratic institutions.

Comparing the two case studies with each other and with the rest of their regions is also fruitful. Both Israel and South Africa are atypical of their region; both were new states founded by an ethnically cohesive immigrant group which achieved its security by monopolizing economic and political power at the expense of the indigenous people; both have a history of partial militarization and both have been significantly affected by the ramifications of international politics. As a result both have a troubled history as far as democratization is concerned and can supply us with evidence about the relative importance of different factors which can also be applied elsewhere.

In the course of their exploration of their questions and the comparisons which they make each of the chapters engages with the different theoretical approaches outlined in Chapter 1. What the theories have to offer for sub-Saharan Africa and the Middle East is brought to a conclusion in the Afterword for this part.

CHAPTER 11

The rise and fall and rise (and fall?) of democracy in sub-Saharan Africa

John A. Wiseman

Introduction

Even when operating within the framework of the limited model of *liberal democracy* the states of sub-Saharan Africa can scarcely be regarded as collectively representing a major exemplar of democratic forms of rule in the post-independence period. However, whilst popular stereotypes of post-independence African politics involving khaki-clad dictators and authoritarian single-party states are not without foundation, they do represent a less than complete view of African political life. The chronicle of democracy in Africa is partly concerned with its fragility, overthrow, and suppression but it is also concerned with its survival and revival and with the tenacity of the idea that democratic rule is what *ought* to exist. Through an examination of both the socio-economic structural foundations of African states and of the ways in which African political actors, especially political elites, have attempted to shape the political environments in which they operate, this chapter will attempt to shed some light on three key questions concerning the functioning of liberal democracy in Africa.

The first question relates to why it has proved so difficult to establish and consolidate democratic political systems in spite of the widespread, though not ubiquitous, belief amongst Africans that such systems are desirable. What are the major obstacles to the operation of democracy? The second question starts from the opposite direction by asking why, in spite of these difficulties and obstacles, democracy has survived on the African political agenda as a viable alternative to authoritarian rule. Thus, we need to explain both the absence and presence of democracy in the states of sub-Saharan Africa. Third, we have to recognize that the exercise of democracy in Africa is not a static phenomenon, but rather is subject to fluctuation over time. Although, in historical terms, the post-independence period in Africa is relatively brief it can easily be demonstrated that the relative presence or absence of democracy has varied considerably during that period. Particularly striking has been the movement away from authoritarianism and towards democracy in so many African states in the period since 1989. Why has this fluctuating change occurred?

Any attempt to understand these states has to incorporate both the differences between them and the commonalties which exist. Important differences exist in relation to many variables which impinge on political processes including population size, physical size, natural resource base, foreign influence, religion, culture, and so on. Equally they exhibit a diverse range of historical experiences, stretching back into the pre-colonial period.

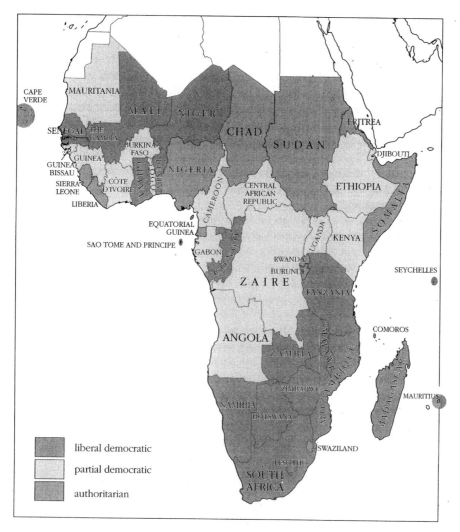

Map 11.1   Political map of Africa, 1995

However, whilst it is essential to recognize the differences between African states this should not be done at the expense of failing to recognize what they share in common. Broadly speaking these common features, in terms of social and economic conditions, tend not to be those normally associated in structural or modernization theory with the establishment of stable and consolidated liberal democracy. In spite of this the African experience suggests that it is possible to create democracy even in, what appear to be, unfavourable conditions.

11.1   The problems of cultural heterogeneity and economic underdevelopment

With the partial exceptions of Liberia and Ethiopia, the current territorial definition of African states has its origins in the partition of the continent by the major European colonial powers, Britain, France, Portugal, Belgium, and to a much lesser extent, Germany and Spain, in the late nineteenth century. The externally imposed nature of state boundaries, which resulted from a European balance of power, led to high levels of cultural and linguistic heterogeneity within the colonial and post-colonial state. For the most part these boundaries have been resolutely defended by the political elites of the post-independence period. However, in many cases the artificiality of the state, in traditional cultural terms, has produced a weak sense of national identity which has posed problems for the creation of political order. The problems of creating and sustaining democracy in conditions of cultural heterogeneity are not insurmountable (see Lijphart, 1969, 1977) but they are more demanding.

The economic conditions of most African states are non-supportive of democracy. Although the precise relationship between levels of economic development and the existence or non-existence of democratic rule is complex it is universally accepted that there is a strong statistical correlation between the two (Lipset, 1959; Lipset et al., 1993). Although some individual Africans are extremely wealthy (President Mobutu Sese Seko of Zaire, for example, is generally reckoned to be one of the wealthiest men in the world) most African states are amongst the least developed in the world and African peoples are among the poorest. In several African states average GNP per capita is less than $100 per year. In Angola and Mozambique one in three children who survive birth die before their fifth birthday. In the Central African Republic only one person in ten has access to safe drinking water. In a majority of African states less than half of the adult population possess functional literacy and in some the proportion is very much lower. In the main African women are far more disadvantaged than their male counterparts.

Whilst there can be no serious disagreement with the view that the economies of African states are significantly underdeveloped in comparison with the rest of the world, attempts to explain why this is the case, and even more to suggest remedies for the problem, have remained contentious issues among analysts. Rather than trying to identify a single cause of economic underdevelopment it is more useful to see the latter as the product of a range of factors and to recognize that the relative importance of these factors differs from one state to another.

One might begin by examining the 'natural causes' of economic underdevelopment. Certainly there are some African states which appear singularly lacking in natural resources. States which have no known mineral resources, suffer from extreme aridity and have poor soil quality are severely handicapped. Burkina Faso, in West Africa, and Lesotho, in Southern Africa, are instructive examples of states lacking any significant natural resource base and where labour migration, to Côte d'Ivoire and South Africa respectively, has traditionally provided the only possible route to even moderate economic viability. There are also states which have a potentially rich resource base but in which other factors, most notably extreme maladministration, have precluded positive economic development. Sierra Leone and Zaire, for example, enjoy abundant mineral resources, have rich soils and more than adequate rainfall, and yet remain seriously under-developed. Tropical Africa has more than its fair share of debilitating disease, to which AIDS has recently become a disastrous addition. On top of this most African populations are extremely vulnerable to the vagaries of drought, flood and insect infestation which tend to overwhelm poor underdeveloped states.

The position of Africa within the global economy is a further factor which merits consideration. For the most part Africa is non-industrialized and its global economic role is as a supplier of raw materials and a recipient of manufactured goods. The terms of trade, over which Africa has little control, tend to be distinctly unfavourable. Apart from a few states such as Botswana (diamonds), Gabon and Nigeria (oil), and Zambia (copper), the bedrock of African economies is agricultural production. The latter is mainly based on small-scale peasant farming rather than on the plantation agriculture which is more prominent in other parts of the Third World. For historical reasons plantation agriculture in Africa is most associated with those states, such as Kenya and Zimbabwe, which attracted large settler communities during the colonial period. In most of Africa the economic base of the state is constructed through the expropriation of a rurally produced surplus by an urban based political elite.

This raises the question of 'urban bias' which many scholars identify as an important component of explanations of underdevelopment. Broadly speaking it is possible to locate a divergence between the interests of rural producers and urban consumers with political power residing with the latter especially with urban elites. In the absence of structures of political accountability government policies reflect the perceived balance of power and act against the interests of the rural masses. This results not only in unequal allocation of national resources but ultimately to a partial loss of state control as exploited peasants seek to avoid the predatory state by refocusing their economic activities on the rapidly expanding informal sector of the economy. Urban elites have acted as an intermediary between the peasant producers and the global market through the mechanisms of government marketing boards and other bureaucratic structures. Such structures serve not only to siphon off the rural surplus but also provide immense scope for the organization of political patronage networks through which the senior political elites reward their clients in an attempt to ensure their continued support. The use of bureaucratic structures for such clientelist purposes resulted in the massive growth of large, non-productive, and frequently corrupt state machines which were detrimental to economic development.

11.2 Ideology, state and class

At the level of official state ideology the approaches to economic development in Africa appear to have been remarkably varied, ranging from Marxism–Leninism through African socialism (which emphasized the, supposedly, egalitarian communal values of 'traditional' African society) to an open espousal of free-market capitalism. What is striking in practice is not the diversity of government economic policy and behaviour but rather just how similar things have been across the ideological spectrum. In almost all cases the key feature was the attempt to impose the state as the key player in economic development. In states advocating leftist development models this was achieved through high levels of nationalization through which the state and parastatal institutions sought to control economic activity in order to move towards a 'transition to socialism'. In states espousing capitalist development models the reality of statist domination was not significantly different. Aspirant business entrepreneurs found themselves highly dependent on forms of state patronage and, hence, subject to state control. Free market rhetoric to the contrary the private economic sector was forced to establish close links with the functionaries of the state in order to obtain import and export licences, access to foreign exchange, government grants and contracts, and reasonable treatment in relation to the payment (or in many cases non-payment) of duties and taxes. Within this sort of 'crony capitalism' the linkages between business and political elites were structured largely through clientelist networks. In many cases it was precisely the political and bureaucratic elites who used their control of the state to develop their own business enterprises. To operate a successful economic enterprise it was necessary to hold an important position within the state or to acquire a patron who did. These crucial patron–client structures frequently exhibited personal, ethnic, and kinship dimensions.

In 'socialist' and 'capitalist' states alike it was the state which provided the main organizational mechanism for the development of the class system, and particularly a ruling class which has been alternatively identified as a 'state class', or a 'bureaucratic bourgeoisie'. The primary aspect of these conceptualizations is that it is the control of political power which precedes and makes possible the attainment of economic power through the control, but not necessarily the ownership, of the means of production and distribution. At the end of the colonial period there occurred the take-over of the (colonial) state by a political elite which at that point in time was of an ambiguous and unformed class character, but which then proceeded to use the mechanism of the state (and particularly the state control of the economy) to constitute itself into a type of ruling class.

In most African countries this state-based ruling class is far from secure: in none can it be said to have achieved hegemony. It suffers from a lack of cohesion and is often divided and unstable; sometimes violently so (see for example Graf, 1988). Divisions within the ruling class are based on competitive ethnicity, regionalism, religious and linguistic cleavages, and a highly personalized form of political manipulation in seeking domination. This emphasis on the personalized aspects of conflict within the ruling class raises the important element of 'personal rule' within African politics most clearly elaborated by Robert Jackson and Carl G. Rosberg (1982). They have argued that 'politics in most African states do not conform to an institutionalised system' but 'are most often a personal or factional struggle to control the national government or to influence it'. From this perspective although the focus is on the personal it is, at the same time, on the system. Within this type very great emphasis is placed on the role of patrimonialism and clientelism in conjunction with the political skill of the personal ruler in manipulating networks established on these patrimonialist and clientelist bases.

The above features can be seen as having contributed to the development of forms of political authoritarianism, institutionally the single-party state and military rule, in the post-independence period in most African states. With control of the state being regarded as vital for individual or group economic prosperity, and frequently for personal survival, the tolerance needed for the existence of legal and legitimate opposition, and of a vibrant and autonomous civil society, which are so fundamental for democracy, has been scarce. African political authoritarianism has had a negative effect on economic development. The model of the authoritarian developmental state, identified in such places as Taiwan, Singapore, Malaysia, and South Korea as occupying a key role in promoting economic growth (discussed in Chapter 9) is not replicated in Africa. One of the reasons for this is that in Africa the authoritarian state has generally been of an essentially weak and fragile character as opposed to the strong state character of the above Asian examples. For much of the post-independence period the bulk of African states have witnessed a combination of weak and fragile political authoritarianism and economic decay.

The preceding outline of the political economy of Africa, whilst inevitably being open to accusations of over generalization, clearly presents a set of circumstances and conditions which can only be seen – from the perspective of any of the available theories of democracy and democratization – as highly unpromising for the development of democracy.

——————————— *Summary of Sections 11.1 and 11.2* ———————————

- For historical reasons, associated with European imperialism, most African states exhibit high levels of cultural pluralism and a correspondingly weak sense of national identity.

- In social and economic terms African states are significantly underdeveloped with the rural areas being especially disadvantaged.

- The state–class relationships which developed after independence were not conducive to democracy, political order, or development.

11.3 Fluctuation and change: a periodization of African democracy

In the light of the above discussion one could argue that the really interesting question about the place of liberal democracy in Africa is not why it has experienced so many difficulties and setbacks (which it certainly has) but rather why it has survived on the African political agenda as a viable alternative to authoritarian rule (which it, equally certainly, has). To answer this question it is necessary to confront the evolving experience of African politics. In examining this experience it is useful to divide recent African political history into three major periods, each of which presents a different picture. The democracy-related periodization to be adopted is

- the *early period*, which incorporates the late colonial and very early post-colonial period;
- the *middle period*, which runs from around the mid-to-late 1960s to around the end of the 1980s; and
- the *late period* from around 1989.

Historical periodization is always open to argument, especially so when it involves so large a number of different states as it does here. However, it is not impossible to identify common trajectories among the, admittedly varied, experiences of specific African states.

The early period

From the late nineteenth century until over half way through the twentieth century the whole of Africa (with the exception of Ethiopia and Liberia) was under the control and administration of the European colonial powers, of which Britain and France were by far the most important. By its very nature colonialism is logically incompatible with democracy, based as it is on the political supremacy of an alien ruling elite whose ultimate accountability is to the government of the metropolitan power rather than to those being governed. African participation in national government was extremely limited until very late in the colonial period, and even then was largely non-existent in the Belgian and Portuguese territories. In settler colonies, such as Kenya and Zimbabwe, there was a higher degree of local control but this was restricted to the European settlers and excluded the indigenous African population. Two major sets of factors explain the demise of European colonialism in Africa. The first was the relative decline of the European powers in the global political system, which became evident after the Second World War and the emergence of the USA and the Soviet Union, both of which were hostile to European colonialism, as the major world superpowers. The second set of factors related to the simultaneous growth of African nationalism within Africa and the demand for the democratization and indigenization of political control.

Once the decision had been taken to terminate colonial rule in Africa the next question to be answered was precisely how this transfer of power was to be accomplished. Clearly power had to be transferred to indigenous African political leaders but which particular leaders should inherit control of the colonial state from the departing colonial power? The establishment of democratic political systems at the end of the colonial period was designed to answer this question. Across Anglophone and Francophone Africa the colonial authorities permitted the free formation of political parties, many of which were based on existing nationalist movements, to prepare for competitive elections which would decide who was to govern following imminent independence. It is important to stress that this form of competitive multi-party electoral democracy was by no means foisted off onto unwilling or incomprehending Africans. In most African countries nationalist leaders and their supporters had, for some time, been voicing demands for freedom of political association, a universal franchise, and the holding of free elections. Subsequently many of these leaders were to repudiate the idea of a legal and legitimate opposition and to claim that multi-partyism was divisive, destabilizing, and harmful to development, but their claims (designed to legitimate a new type of authoritarianism) that such systems had been imposed on them by the departing colonial authorities are not supported by the historical evidence. Whilst it is possible to argue that the new independence constitutions of African states, drawn up in a series of negotiations between the colonial authorities and nationalist leaders, were often too closely modelled on those of the departing colonial power and not carefully enough adapted to specific local circumstances, this can hardly be regarded as either explanation or justification for the large-scale dismantling of liberal democratic institutions which subsequently took place in many African states.

For most of Africa the movement towards independence occurred within a limited time span. With the exception of Guinea (independent in 1958) and the microstates of Comoros and Djibouti (independent in 1975 and 1977 respectively) the Francophone territories all achieved independence in 1960. The pattern in Anglophone Africa was not quite as uniform but most states became independent in the period between 1957 (Ghana) and 1968 (Swaziland) although the special circumstances existing in Zimbabwe delayed independence until 1980. In the Portuguese territories of Angola, Mozambique and Guinea-Bissau independence followed a period of armed anti-colonial struggle and was delayed until after the *coup d'état* in Lisbon in April 1974.

The later colonial period was marked by a massive upsurge in political party formation and campaigning which culminated in the pre-independence elections which were to determine the make-up of the first post-independence governments. In a few states this resulted in highly fragmented party systems: with an ethnically homogeneous population of around 3 million Somalia produced no less than 130 different political parties. At the other end of the scale there were a couple of states in which only one party of any significance emerged in this period: in the pre-independence elections in Nyasaland (Malawi) and Tanganyika (later Tanzania) only the Malawi Congress Party (MCP) and the Tanganyika African National Union (TANU) respectively enjoyed significant support. The vast majority of African states, however, produced party systems which fell between these extremes of party proliferation and *de facto* single-partyism and thereby offered their newly enfranchised electorates a manageable degree of choice. Across Africa in the late 1950s and early 1960s there were a large number of *Uhuru* (the KiSwahili word for 'freedom') elections held to prepare for independence. For the most part these elections, run by the colonial authorities, were free and fair and represented the first occasion on which most people had cast a vote. This is not to say that most traditional African political systems had been devoid of democratic content. It was the precise electoral mechanism embodying popular sovereignty and accountability which was new. As a result of these elections most of the governments which came to power at independence could plausibly claim to have gained a democratic mandate. A cause for concern in a number of states (e.g. Nigeria, Kenya and Uganda) was that the bases of party support patterns showed a rather ominous correlation with ethnic and regional lines of cleavage. This potential problem should not be over exaggerated. Most large parties represented fairly flexible ethnic coalitions grouped around important individual leaders rather than narrow sectionalist organizations seeking ethnic dominance. As part of the process of political competition it is common for African party leaders to present their own parties as representing the 'national interest' whilst condemning their opponents for being 'narrow tribalists'. How political leaders manipulate the cultural symbols of ethnic difference is more important than the simple fact of culture difference when one is explaining ethnic conflict. Cultural diversity is not, in itself, a serious political problem but it can certainly be made one. In Africa ethnic conflict has far more frequently resulted from authoritarian rule than it has from multi-party electoral competition.

The independence era in Africa was one of euphoric optimism. The end of colonial rule was seen as ushering in an age of democracy and development which would bring benefits of a material and non-material kind to the populations of the newly-independent states. For many African peoples the dream turned into a nightmare as most African states moved fairly rapidly towards a period of authoritarian rule and economic disappointment.

─────────────── *Summary of the early period* ───────────────

- At the end of the colonial period liberal democratic systems were established in most African states to facilitate the transfer of power to indigenous leaders.
- At the time most African nationalist leaders indicated their support for these democratic systems.
- In only a small minority of states was democratic competition hampered by either a proliferation of parties (too many) or by the non-emergence of a viable opposition (too few).

The middle period

This period stretched from shortly after independence until the end of the 1980s. During this period it is possible to discern three major features relating to the role of democracy in African politics. The clearest, and best known, feature was that for a significant majority of African states this period marked the dismantling of the, recently established, democratic structures and their replacement by more authoritarian systems of single-party and/or military rule. However, this retrenchment of democracy was not ubiquitous and even during this period one can point to the survival of the terminal colonial democratic structures, albeit in a very limited number of states. This dichotomous picture of widespread abandonment of liberal democracy combined with limited survival of democratic structures presents, however, an incomplete version of events because even in those states which moved to authoritarian rule one can witness the survival of democratic aspirations among significant sections of civil society and political counter-elites. In a number of cases this led to attempts, on the whole not very successful, to reconstruct liberal democratic political institutions even in this middle period. Furthermore, in spite of much bombast and rhetoric to the contrary, Africa's authoritarian political systems were insecurely constructed. Although they were often extremely oppressive and highly predatory in their relationship with their citizenry their authoritarianism was of a weak type which suffered an escalating crisis of legitimacy.

In many states the party which had won power in the pre-independence elections attempted to secure its long-term control of government through the introduction of a single-party state in which opposition parties were allowed no legal existence. In some cases some of the existing opposition elites were co-opted into the ruling party and offered a share in the spoils of office in return for abandoning their oppositional role. In many cases the transition was of a cruder character as opposition leaders were imprisoned, exiled, or simply killed. In an attempt to justify the introduction of the single-party state ruling party leaders accused opposition parties of being divisive and hindering the development of national unity.

In a few states a residue of democracy was retained by allowing limited competition between candidates of the same ruling party in national elections. Whilst the element of democratic choice for the electorate was not entirely absent from such elections it was highly circumscribed. All candidates belong to the same party, share the same policy platform, and have been chosen, or at least approved, by the same party elite. In practice such elections often became less competitive over time. Bavu (1989) demonstrates how in Tanzania it became more and more common for senior figures within the ruling party to be returned unopposed at elections. Potential alternative candidates were informed that it would be 'disrespectful' to oppose senior figures within the ruling party. Tanzanian presidential elections never had more than one candidate in this period. The case for 'single-party democracy' was most clearly argued by the Tanzanian President, Julius Nyerere, who by the mid 1980s was to become one of the most cogent critics of single-party rule.

In Tanzania the party (initially the Tanganyika African National Union, TANU, but redesigned in 1977 as Chama Cha Mapinduzi, CCM, 'Party of the Revolution') remained a well organized and lively body but in many single-party states the party, as a political organization, atrophied so that it became little more than a front for the domination of a small coterie of national leaders. In some cases the notion of party membership became meaningless. In Zaire, for example, all citizens were deemed to be members from birth of the Popular Movement of the Revolution (MPR). This was never more than a flimsy and unconvincing camouflage for the militaristic, highly personalized, and massively corrupt dictatorship of President Mobutu Sese Seko Kuku Ngbendu Wa Za Banga (see Young and Turner, 1985).

From the first military *coup d'état* in Togo in 1963 African armies became major players on the African political scene and during this middle period a high proportion of African states were ruled by overtly military regimes. (See Part III for comparison with Latin America.) A frequently repeated pattern was for the creation of a single-party state to be followed fairly quickly by the overthrow of civilian rule and the imposition of military rule. Rather than overturning democracy military intervention more often meant the substitution of one form of authoritarian rule by another. One frequently voiced justification of military intervention was the desire by the soldiers to 'restore democracy' to what had become undemocratically ruled states. Whilst this pro-democracy sentiment might have had some basis of reality as a motivation for some of the military it would be a little naive to regard this as a prime cause of military intervention. More persuasive are the interest-based explanations which focus on the corporate interests of the military and the sectionalist or personalist interests of those involved in planning and executing the *coup d'état* (for an excellent survey of the role of the African military see Luckham, 1994). Initial expressions of optimism by some observers that the armed forces would provide a strong stabilizing force which would promote development were soon shown to be inaccur- ate by the reality of high levels of factionalism and division which became evident. The result of this was that military rule did not usher in an era of stability and development. Just as the most common result of the declaration of the single-party state was the military coup, so the most common result of the coup was the counter-coup as different army factions struggled for the control of the state.

From a democratic perspective the above account of this period of African politics presents a thoroughly bleak picture. This picture is not inaccurate but it is incomplete. Seemingly against the odds a small handful of African states persisted with the liberal democratic multi-party systems erected at the end of the colonial period. The Gambia (independent in 1965), Botswana (1966), and Mauritius (1968) all maintained relatively democratic political systems during this middle period: it was a supreme irony that in July 1994, at a time when nearly all the other African states had moved to multi-partyism, the army in The Gambia staged a *coup d'état* and took the country into a period of military rule. This group of states is geographically dis- persed: The Gambia lies in West Africa, Botswana in Southern Africa, and Mauritius is an Indian Ocean state lying off the coast of East Africa. In spite of regular, relatively fair, elections contested by free opposition parties, the incumbent ruling parties, the Botswana Democratic Party (BDP) and the People's Progressive Party (PPP) in The Gambia, retained power throughout the period. In both cases opposition parties continued to hold a minority of parliamentary seats and in Botswana the opposition Botswana National Front (BNF) became the dominant party in the urban town councils. Only in Mauritius did political alternation occur at the national level. In a general election in June 1982 the Mauritius Labour Party (MLP) of Seewoosagur Ramgoolam, which had ruled the country since independence, lost power when it failed to win a single seat in parliament. The new ruling party, the Marxist-inclined Movement Militant Mauricien (MMM), enjoyed only a short period in office and in the election of June 1983 was voted out and replaced by a coalition of a revived MLP and the newly created Movement Socialist Militant (MSM).

Although it is not possible here to go into the details of the survival of democracy in these three states (see Wiseman, 1990) some points of comparison can be made. All three states have relatively small populations of between 1 and 1.5 million although the physical size of Botswana is hugely greater than the other two. One of the effects of having a small population is that the size of that group we would refer to as the political elite, including the counter-elite of the opposition, is correspondingly small. Leaving aside the problems associated with defining the membership of the political elite in these states it would be broadly accurate to say that in none of them would it number more than around 100 persons. In these circumstances it is not surprising that these people tend to know each other rather well and not infrequently are related through kinship ties. This has made compromise and conciliation, which are so important for the survival of democracy, very much easier to obtain than would be possible in larger societies. Although small size of population by no means guarantees democratic survival in Africa (Equatorial Guinea, for example, has a much smaller population but has witnessed nothing but brutal dictatorship in the post-independence period) it is probably true that the exceptionality of these three states is facilitated by small population size (for a wider discussion of the effects of this factor see Dahl and Tufte, 1973).

None of these three states could be described as exhibiting cultural homogeneity. In different ways all three exhibit various combinations of ethnic, religious, linguistic, and tribal heterogeneity: in Mauritius the situation is further complicated by racial diversity (Mauritius is unusual in having no historically indigenous population group and is currently peopled by descendants of settlers from India, China, Africa, and Europe). Although cultural diversity has impinged upon political life in all three states in a number of ways none have developed deep-seated communal cleavages of an intolerant type which endangers democracy. Part of the explanation for this, and indeed part of the broader explanation of democratic exceptionality, has been the style of political leadership particularly in relation to the 'fathers of the nation' figures who led their countries to independence. The roles played in supporting democracy by Seretse Khama, Dawda Jawara and Seewoosagur Ramgoolam, in Botswana, The Gambia and Mauritius respectively was crucial. Not only did all three have a personal commitment to democratic forms of rule but, at least as importantly, all had the level of political skill necessary to sustain democracy in divided societies in the crucial period after attaining independent statehood. At the beginning of the post-independence period the new institutions of government were inevitably weakly institutionalized, a factor which made the issue of political leadership especially important.

If we turn to the issue of economic development we see more of a divergence between these states. Botswana and Mauritius have been the most successful examples of rapid economic growth in the post-independence period. Over the past quarter of a century Botswana has had the fastest growing economy in the world, admittedly starting from a low base line, whilst Mauritius has enjoyed particular success in developing a manufacturing sector and becoming less reliant on the production of sugar cane. In terms of GNP per capita both are comfortably in the top five in Africa. In contrast to this The Gambia has remained relatively stagnant economically with an export economy based largely on peanuts. Whilst it is difficult to see the precise causal relationship between democracy and development in Botswana and Mauritius (development may be seen to aid democracy, or vice versa) the two features may be regarded as mutually supportive. Although democracy survived in The Gambia during this middle period its subsequent replacement by military rule may be partly explained by relative economic failure.

With the exceptions noted above (plus Zimbabwe which did not achieve independence until 1980) all other African states turned to single party and/or military rule at some time during this middle period. However, an important additional feature of this period was the attempt in many of these states to revive more democratic forms of rule. Most commonly these revivals occurred as part of a process of demilitarization of state power. In a manner which had very striking parallels with the late colonial period military governments created liberal democratic competitive structures to facilitate the transfer of power to civilian leaders (earlier the transfer had been from colonial to indigenous leaders). In at least some of these states a genuine democratic transition took place although consolidation proved to be altogether more problematic.

In Nigeria in 1979 the military regime of Olusegun Obasanjo went back to the barracks after organizing what were probably the fairest elections the country had ever experienced (this still remains the only occasion on which genuine demilitarization has occurred in Nigeria). The Second Republic of Nigeria cannot be considered a success. Although the government of President Shehu Shagari's National Party of Nigeria (NPN) could plausibly claim to have been democratically elected in 1979 its time in office was marred by corruption and inefficiency. For reasons only partly under government control the national economy went into decline and the regime was further delegitimized by the badly flawed elections of 1983 when, in contrast to 1979, serious electoral malpractice was evident. On 31 December 1983 a further *coup d'état* took place and Nigeria returned to military rule which has grown increasingly oppressive in recent years. Similar events took place in Ghana which had also experienced a competitive demilitarization election in 1979 which produced a corrupt and ineffective civilian government, under President Hilla Limann, which was deposed by a military coup led by Jerry Rawlings two years to the day earlier than its Nigerian counterpart.

During this middle period there were also attempts at democratic transitions as a part of the process of demilitarization in Uganda, Liberia, Sudan, Central African Republic, Burkina Faso, and (at local government level only) Mauritania, none of which met with long-term success. In this period the only state where a return to competitive democracy took place without any role being played by the military was Senegal (as will be shown below this pattern became very common after 1989). In a series of steps between 1974 and 1981 the Senegalese political system moved from single-partyism to a limited multi-partyism with tight restrictions on party formation and, eventually, to an unrestricted multi-partyism after President Abdou Diouf replaced the retiring President Leopold Senghor. In Senegal the staged transition may have produced a less than perfect liberal democracy but it is a democracy that has survived (for a recent discussion see Villalon, 1994).

The middle period can accurately be regarded as representing the nadir of democracy in post-colonial Africa. However, whilst the number of African states which could plausibly be regarded as operating a reasonably democratic system was small, and subject to fluctuation, it is important to recognize that, even then, at least some democratic systems continued to operate and in many parts of Africa the idea that democratic civilian rule was what 'ought' to exist exhibited a remarkable tenacity which might have appeared at odds with empirical reality.

————————————— *Summary of the middle period* —————————————

- In most states liberal democracy was replaced by single party and/or military rule.

- A small minority of states continued to operate liberal democratic systems and there were attempts to revive liberal democracy in several others, usually as part of a process of demilitarization.

The late period

From the end of the 1980s to the middle of the 1990s the political systems of African states underwent a remarkable transformation, the key element of which was the attempt to construct or reconstruct a more democratic form of politics. Whilst the essential dynamics of this process can be observed right across Africa political outcomes varied from state to state. On the credit side (from a democratic perspective) one could see that by 1995 pluralistic party systems were in place in more than three-quarters of African states and in thirteen of them (Benin, Burundi, Cape Verde, Central African Republic, Congo, Lesotho, Madagascar, Malawi, Mali, Namibia, Niger, Sao Tome and Principe, and Zambia) change of government through the ballot box had actually taken place. Whilst it would be wrong to imagine that only elections which change governments can be seen as democratic the fact that this occurred in so many states is important. By 1995 the classic single-party system, which had for so long been the most common form of civilian rule, could be observed nowhere in Africa.

On the debit side one could observe a number of less positive developments. Military governments remained in place in Nigeria, Sierra Leone and Sudan and, as previously noted, The Gambia succumbed to military rule for the first time in July 1994. In Uganda President Yoweri Museveni persisted with his own brand of 'no-party democracy' (in which electoral competition takes place without the involvement of political parties) whilst in Swaziland a rather authoritarian version of 'traditional' monarchy still dominated. In both of these states pro-democracy movements persisted with demands for change. In several countries (e.g. Liberia, Somalia, and Chad) the situation was one of state collapse where no government, democratic or otherwise, could be said to be exercising control over more than a portion of national territory (see Zartman, 1995). In such cases the question of democratization is irrelevant because there is no state to

*A woman casts her vote at a village polling station,
15 October 1994, in Botswana's seventh election
since independence in 1966*

democratize. In a fair number of states which had restored formally democratic multi-party systems the operation of the political system fell so far short of acceptable democratic practice that they might best be thought of as *partial democracies*, also referred to in the literature as façade democracies, quasi-democracies, or examples of liberalized authoritarianism (e.g. Kenya, Cameroon, and Burkina Faso). A further limitation was that even in those states which might plausibly be regarded as having experienced a demo-cratic *transition* the possibilities and prospects of democratic *consolidation* remained very uncertain.

The above comments certainly suggest that it is necessary to adopt a rather cautious approach to recent redemocratization in Africa and to avoid any temptation towards unwarranted euphoria. Nevertheless, it remains unarguable that, in general terms, Africa has made significant strides in the direction of democracy in the more recent period when compared with the position in the middle period. From this perspective the important question relates to why this occurred. Why did democracy occupy a more important and widespread place within African political life than it did ten years ago?

Analyses of recent political change in Africa invariably point to the conclusion that change has come about as a result of a combination of external and internal pressures. In assessing the relative importance of these two sets of factors there is a high, but not total, agreement among Africanist scholars that internal pressures have played the more important role in persuading authoritarian rulers and governments in Africa to restructure the political system along more democratic lines (see, for example, Bayart, 1993; Chazan, 1992; Clapham, 1993; Bratton and van de Walle, 1992; Joseph, 1991; Klein, 1992; Wiseman, 1995, 1996).

External pressures for change in Africa can be seen as a product of wider change within the global political environment, most notably the ending of the Cold War and the essentially bi-polar political competition which the latter had produced. During the Cold War period, which until the late 1980s had completely overlapped with the post-independence period in Africa, both superpowers had attempted to establish spheres of influence in Africa, and to prevent each other from so doing, as a part of the wider global conflict. In pursuance of this objective both the USA and the USSR had repeatedly shown themselves willing to offer economic and military support to 'friendly' African regimes irrespective of the manner in which such regimes treated their own citizens to oppression and predation. Within Africa many highly authoritarian political leaders had exploited this situation and had used the external environment as a resource for ensuring, or trying to ensure, regime survival. The end of the Cold War contributed to a new position of global strategic marginality for Africa which was enhanced by its global economic marginality. The Soviet Union, and subsequently its successor states, more or less completely disengaged from Africa. This disengagement removed the strategic importance of Africa for the USA and with American economic investment in Africa accounting for less than one half of one per cent of total America foreign investment (Michaels, 1993) the economic importance of Africa for the USA can be seen as extremely marginal. As a result of these changes authoritarian leaders in Africa were no longer able to market their strategic importance for outside support against domestic opponents.

From around the end of the 1980s many Western governments, as well as international financial institutions such as the World Bank and the International Monetary Fund (IMF), began to attach political 'conditionalities' to aid and investment in Africa such that regimes which denied human and civil rights to their citizens were to be denied outside funding (see Chapter 9). In some cases political conditionality was directly linked to democratization but in others it was linked to the more nebulous notion of 'good governance'. The reasoning behind political conditionality was partly economic in that it was argued that economic failure in Africa was in some measure due to the absence of democracy and political accountability and that without political change the imposition of economic conditionality, which had begun around a decade earlier and which had required economic reform as a precondition for aid and investment, would not produce the desired economic results. Democratic political change was also considered to be a desirable end in its own right. The question of the morality of imposing democracy from outside hardly arises as in no single case in Africa was political conditionality applied in advance of significant domestic pressure for democratization. In some cases the addition of outside pressure helped tip the balance as authoritarian leaders, who had been unwilling to give way to domestic pressure, reluctantly agreed to political liberalization. Kenya and Malawi provide examples of this phenomenon although the consequences varied. In Malawi the long-term authoritarian national leader, Hastings Kamuzu Banda, was voted out of office in a peaceful election in 1994, whilst in Kenya President Daniel arap Moi managed to retain power as a result of a combination of electoral malpractice and opposition fragmentation.

In addition to external pressures for democratization events in other parts of the world provided a series of external influences pointing in the same direction: whilst the imposition of political conditionalities was intended to produce particular results direct intent was lacking in relation to these other factors. The global political environment had changed over time as a result of what Samuel Huntington (1991) has referred to as the 'third wave of democratization' which had produced a replacement of authoritarian regimes by democratic ones in some 30 states of Southern Europe, Asia, and Latin America between 1974 and 1990. By the end of the 1980s Africa's single-party and military-ruled states were looking increasingly anachronistic. Of more immediate influence were the changes which took place in Eastern Europe in 1989 when mass-based popular uprising succeeded in dislodging unpopular authoritarian regimes which had previously been able to rely on outside (Soviet) support in suppressing pro-democracy movements. Events in Eastern Europe emboldened pro-democracy activists in Africa and weakened the confidence of many autocratic leaders: in the memorable phrase of President Omar Bongo of Gabon 'the winds from the East are shaking the coconut trees'.

During the 1980s Africa's authoritarian regimes faced an increasingly grave crisis of legitimacy. Partly this had been caused by political factors and the alienation of large sections of the population brought about by the long-term denial of human and civil rights under an oppressive form of rule. Equally crucial to this crisis of legitimacy was the record of economic failure which undermined regime claims that some diminution of open public political contestation was necessary to ensure economic growth and prosperity. Economic conditionalities exacerbated the problems of the political elites because, by enforcing some reductions in the economic role of the state, they undermined the existing political economy of the 'state class'. The latter had used their control over the economy to construct support coalitions of a largely clientelist type but it became increasingly difficult to maintain these clientelist structures. The ability to gain support through prebendalism declined as the number and importance of available prebends declined. At a sub-elite level bureaucratic retrenchment created further hostility towards governments and towards political patrons who had decreasing amounts of patronage to disburse to their clients.

These crises made Africa's authoritarian regimes increasingly vulnerable to the internal pressures for political reconstruction along democratic lines. Much of this pressure can be seen as arising from a resurgent *civil society* (for recent discussions see Diamond, 1994; Apter and Rosberg, 1994). Several different component groups of civil society were involved in pressures for democratization especially from the late 1980s and a, necessarily brief, examination of the character and activities of these groups is essential for an understanding of recent political change in Africa. These groups did not operate in isolation from each other: they frequently supported each other and often had overlapping personnel.

In many states churches and their leaders played a prominent role in applying pressure for democratization. Even in the period prior to recent liberalization churches often provided a critical voice in relation to authoritarian rule and were able to retain a degree of autonomy often denied to other societal groups. In highly religious African societies popular respect for church leaders gave them a status and influence which regimes found difficult to ignore. They exhibited an organizational strength stretching back to the pre-independence period and enjoyed the additional advantage of belonging to globally organized communities. In cases where governments enforced a ban on mass meetings other than those which they controlled, the church service and the 'political sermon' proved more difficult to control. A classic example of the crucial role played by the churches in recent democratization in Africa can be seen in Malawi which had previously been one of the most highly authoritarian states on the continent under its ageing leader Hastings Kamuzu Banda. In March 1992 Archbishop James Chiona and all the Catholic bishops of Malawi issued a pastoral letter which was read out at the same time in every Catholic church in the country. The letter provided an unprecedented public critique of all aspects of public life in the single-party state and called for an end to all restrictions on free political expression and association. Rapidly the leaders of the other Christian denominations announced their support for the message of the letter. Although the regime initially reacted in a very hostile manner to these developments the actions of the church leaders decisively opened up a new political space which could be exploited by others to bring about the ending of authoritarian rule in Malawi. The churches played a very significant role in exerting pressure for democratization in a large number of African states (see, for example, Gifford, 1995).

The activities of trade unions were crucial in many states and were enhanced by the use of the 'political strike' to put pressure on reluctant authoritarian regimes. Initially many of these strikes were related to industrial grievances (such as the late payment or non-payment of wages) against the government in its role as the main employer of labour but were quickly expanded into demands for political reform. Unions which had previously been controlled by the government asserted their autonomy and new unions sprang up to challenge authoritarian rule. In Zambia the main pro-democracy organization, the Movement for Multi-Party Democracy (MMD), drew a significant amount of its support and clout from the union movement and it was the leader of the Zambia Congress of Trade Unions

(ZCTU), Frederick Chiluba, who was the successful presidential candidate of the MMD in the 1991 elections which ousted President Kenneth Kaunda and his hitherto single ruling party the United National Independence Party (UNIP). Although lacking the mass membership of the trade unions, professional associations played a crucial role in many states in articulating demands for reform. These organizations of the educated elites of lawyers, medical doctors, academics and so on frequently allied themselves with, or in some cases took the lead in creating, a whole range of pro-democracy and human rights groups. University students gave such organizations a numerical strength which they might otherwise have lacked.

An important component in the pressure for democratization in Africa has been the expanded role of the indigenous independent (i.e. free from government control) media, especially the print media. In examining the role of the media it is necessary to see it as both a cause and effect of political liberalization. Pro-democracy newspapers and magazines help to create an opening up of political space and can then exploit such openings to exert further pressure on authoritarian regimes. The, not always successful, struggle for a free press has been inextricably linked with the search for democratic political restructuring. In states where authoritarian regimes have strenuously resisted pressures to democratize (e.g. Nigeria), writers and reporters have often been the most prominent victims of government suppression.

In recent years a crucial element in the pro-democracy struggle in Africa has been mass protest. In states across the continent vast crowds, numbering up to half a million, have taken to the streets to demand an end to autocratic rule. In many cases initial protests have been met with a violent reaction by the state and its security forces, often resulting in death and injury for significant numbers of demonstrators. It would be wrong to neglect the sheer bravery of so many pro-democracy activists in Africa at both elite and mass levels in opposing undemocratic rule.

The foregoing description of the internal aspects of the pressure for democracy in Africa reflects the observations of scholars analysing pro-democracy movements in other parts of the world. Writing about Latin America O'Donnell and Schmitter (1986) stress a similar 'popular upsurge' and the process of 'resurrecting civil society' and describe how 'trade unions, grass-roots movements, religious groups, intellectuals, artists, clergymen, defenders of human rights and professional associations all support each other's efforts towards democratization, and coalesce into a greater whole which identifies itself as the people'. Although the process of consolidation of democracy in Africa is likely to encounter greater obstacles than in Latin America the process of transition exhibits marked resemblances (see Chapter 7). Already the democratization of African political systems has been marked by a number of serious reverses and the future is far from certain (for an attempt to grade the prospects for consolidation for all the states of sub-Saharan Africa see Clapham and Wiseman, 1995).

--------------------------- *Summary of the late period* ---------------------------

- The single-party state was abandoned everywhere in Africa and examples of military rule significantly reduced in number.

- The systems which replaced them were a mixture of liberal democracies and partial democracies.

- Change was brought about by a combination of external pressures following the end of the Cold War, and internal pressures from opposition elites, civil society, and mass action.

Conclusion

In conclusion it will be useful to examine how the experience of Africa can be related to more general comparative theories of democracy and democratization. The African case, or more accurately cases, would support the contention advanced in Chapter 1 that no single theory or explanatory factor can adequately explain the complex processes involved. Different theoretical approaches and factors may be seen to shed light on different aspects of empirical reality. The account presented here of democracy in Africa suggests both continuities and discontinuities over time. We need to explain why things stay the same (why democratic transition and, even more, consolidation is so difficult in Africa) and why they change (how to account for the fluctuating role played by democracy in Africa's political systems over time).

It can be argued that different theories can shed light on the different questions posed. In accounting for the severe difficulties encountered in attempts to establish democratic political systems in Africa both *modernization* and *structural* approaches have much to offer. The existence of underdevelopment, poverty, lack of education, and cultural heterogeneity mean that the 'prerequisites' suggested by modernization theory are absent in Africa, at least to a significant extent. Equally, the class structures which developed in Africa are hardly those which structuralist theories suggest are most likely to produce consolidated democracy. The development, within varied ideological mediums, of a weakly established state class which was dependent for its existence on maintaining control of a statist economic structure made democratic contestation for public office a very unattractive proposition for incumbent elites. During the Cold War the perceived strategic need of the superpowers to maintain 'friendly' regimes in office offered a level of external support to authoritarian rulers which made them less vulnerable to domestic pressures. Conversely the end of the Cold War to a significant extent undermined the global structural relationships which had hitherto aided anti-democratic rulers and consequently made the latter more vulnerable to pre-existing and newly constructed domestic pressures for political reform.

An analysis of the operation of these domestic pressures for democracy relocates the debate into the context of areas emphasized more overtly by transition theorists in stressing the importance of human agency. The operation of human agency has occurred at different levels of society from elite to mass. Opposition elites espousing democracy have been able to use the negative performance records of authoritarian regimes to generate considerable open mass support for their goals. Also of crucial importance has been the intermediate level support of a resurgent civil society invigorated by the weakening of authoritarian rule.

It is clear that in recent years African political systems have moved considerably in the direction of becoming more democratic. By 1995 a significant number could be plausibly designated as liberal democratic, with perhaps a larger number operating varied forms of partial democracy: the boundary between the two types often appearing somewhat imprecise in practice. Unambiguously authoritarian regimes were very much the exception and were remarkably few in number. Although a considerable number of African democracies were in what Rustow refers to as the *habituation* phase, the continued obstacles to democracy in most African states made *consolidation* a less than inevitable long-term conclusion to the process.

References

Apter, D.E. and Rosberg, C.G. (eds) (1994) *Political Development and the New Realism in Sub-Saharan Africa*, Charlottesville, University Press of Virginia.

Bavu, I.K. (1989) 'Policy issues on the democraticeness of one-party elections in Tanzania' in Meynes, P. and Wadada Nabudere, D. (eds) *Democracy and the One-Party-State in Africa*, Hamburg, Institut für Afrika-Kunde, pp.91–110.

Bayart, J.-F. (1993) *The State in Africa: the Politics of the Belly*, London, Longman.

Bratton, M. and van de Walle, N. (1992) 'Popular protest and political reform in Africa', *Comparative Politics*, vol.24, no.4, pp.419–42.

Chazan, N. (1992) 'Africa's democratic challenge', *World Policy Journal*, vol.9, no.2, pp.279–307.

Clapham, C. (1993) 'Democratisation in Africa: obstacles and prospects', *Third World Quarterly*, vol.14, no.3.

Clapham, C. and Wiseman, J.A. (1995) 'Assessing the prospects for the consolidation of democracy in Africa' in Wiseman, J.A. (ed.).

Dahl, R.A. and Tufte, E.R. (1973) *Size and Democracy*, Stanford, Stanford University Press.

Diamond, L. (1994) 'Rethinking civil society: toward democratic consolidation', *Journal of Democracy*, vol.5, no.3, pp.4–17.

Gifford, P. (ed.) (1995) *The Christian Churches and the Democratisation of Africa*, Leiden, E.J. Brill.

Graf, W.D. (1988) *The Nigerian State: Political Economy, State Class and Political System in the Post-Colonial Era*, London, James Currey.

Huntington, S.P. (1991) *The Third Wave: Democratization in the Late Twentieth Century*, Norman, University of Oklahoma Press.

Jackson, R.H. and Rosberg, C.G. (1982) *Personal Rule in Black Africa: Prince, Autocrat, Prophet, Tyrant*, Berkeley, University of California Press.

Joseph, R.A. (1991) 'Africa: the rebirth of political freedom', *Journal of Democracy*, vol.2, no.4.

Klein, M.A. (1992) 'Back to democracy', *African Studies Review*, vol.35, no.3.

Lijphart, A. (1969) 'Consociational democracy', *World Politics*, vol.4, no.2, pp.207–25.

Lijphart, A. (1977) *Democracy in Plural Societies*, New Haven, Yale University Press.

Lipset, S.M. (1959) 'Some social requisites of democracy: economic development and political legitimacy', *American Political Science Review*, no.53, pp.69–105.

Lipset, S.M., Seong Kyoung-Ryung and Torres, J.C. (1993) 'A comparative analysis of the social requisites of democracy', *International Social Science Journal*, no.136, pp.155–75.

Luckham, R. (1994) 'The military, militarization and democratization in Africa: a survey of literature and ideas', *African Studies Review*, vol.37, no.2, pp.13–75.

Michaels, M. (1993) 'Retreat from Africa', *Foreign Affairs*, vol.72, no.1, pp.93–108.

O'Donnell, G. and Schmitter, P. (1986) *Transitions from Authoritarian Rule: Tentative Conclusions about Uncertain Democracies*, Baltimore, Johns Hopkins University Press.

Villalon, L.A. (1994) 'Democratizing a (quasi) democracy: the Senegalese elections of 1993', *African Affairs*, vol.93, no.371, pp.163–93.

Wiseman, J.A. (1990) *Democracy in Black Africa: Survival and Revival*, New York, Paragon House.

Wiseman, J.A. (ed.) (1995) *Democracy and Political Change in Sub-Saharan Africa*, London, Routledge.

Wiseman, J.A. (1996) *The New Struggle for Democracy in Africa*, Aldershot, Avebury.

Young, C. and Turner, T. (1985) *The Rise and Decline of the Zairian State*, Madison, University of Wisconsin Press.

Zartman, I.W. (ed.) (1995) *Collapsed States: the Disintegration and Restoration of Legitimate Authority*, Boulder, Lynne Rienner.

CHAPTER 12

South Africa: democracy delayed

Margaret Kiloh

Introduction

1989/90 saw fundamental changes in the configuration of world politics. In quick succession the two symbolic 'evil empires' which had ruled since the end of the Second World War both collapsed. In Eastern Europe the hegemony of the Soviet Union came to an end, and at the same time the apartheid regime of the Afrikaner National Party in South Africa began a process of democratization which was to lead to its own demise. The leader of the African National Congress (ANC), Nelson Mandela, was released after 27 years' imprisonment and South Africa's first non-racial democratic elections were held four years later. The ANC won a majority of the votes and an interim government of national unity was set up under the presidency of Mandela.

It seemed like a miracle but, unlike miracles, political processes are susceptible to analysis. For the purposes of analysis democratization can be divided into four stages: '(1) decay of authoritarian rule, (2) transition, (3) consolidation, and (4) the maturing of democratic political order' (Shin, 1994, p.143). This chapter analyses the process of democratization in South Africa by examining the first and second of these stages and asking two questions: what made the system of apartheid untenable and brought about the shift towards majority rule? and what were the significant features of the transition to liberal democracy?

Different theoretical approaches are appropriate for analysing these two different stages of democratization. The two theoretical approaches which are most useful in analysing the first stage are modernization and structural approaches whereas the approach most appropriate to the second stage is the transition approach. As Chapter 1 points out, modernization theories and structural theories have both been modified since their early development in the 1960s and there is now a degree of convergence between them. Both agree that there is no single factor which is necessary or sufficient for democratization and that this will result from a combination of factors which will be different in different countries. Certain explanatory factors, like economic or capitalist development are common to both approaches, although how they are handled and how they relate to other factors is rather different. Facilitators of democracy in both approaches can be divided into internal and external factors. Major internal factors deployed in this chapter are the legitimacy of authoritarian rule and the strengthening of civil society by the processes of economic or capitalist development. Major external factors in this chapter are direct (governmental and non-governmental) moral, economic, diplomatic and military pressures from other countries and the indirect influence of global economic relations and the diffusion or demonstration effect of events elsewhere. The main factors which *obstruct* the overthrow of authoritarian regimes deployed in this chapter are the use of state power, ethnic and cultural cleavages and international support for authoritarianism by powerful allies.

12.1 The breakdown of authoritarian rule

In this section I will be analysing the first stage of democratization in South Africa – the breakdown of authoritarian rule – by looking at the internal and external factors which facilitated or obstructed that process. In order to do that I need first to establish the specific nature of the South African state and the authoritarian regime which ran it.

The apartheid state

The greatest obstacle to democratization in South Africa was the existence of the racially and ethnically-based system of social, economic and political domination which we call apartheid. The chief characteristics of apartheid were the comprehensive classification of the population according to 'race', the establishment of separate legal rights and institutions for different groups and the use of state violence to crush opposition. Although South Africa had liberal democratic institutions, before April 1994 it was a sham democracy in which most of the population – some 30 million Africans – were denied citizenship. 87 per cent of the land and most other economic assets were monopolized by the white minority, and human rights were systematically abused.

The roots of the apartheid state lay in the model of the colonial state established in South Africa and other countries in sub-Saharan Africa in the nineteenth century. The main role of the colonial state was the provision of a legal framework for capitalist development backed up by military force and a legitimizing ideology of European culture and 'civilization' as opposed to black barbarism. Cheap labour was procured either by force, the use of indentured labour or the imposition of poll taxes and Native Reserves were created to provide reserve pools of migrant labour which preserved 'traditional' laws and life-style. The economy was an appendage of the global political economy and wealth was largely exported, apart from a proportion which was retained to maintain a small ruling expatriate elite. Onto this model were overlaid other features which stemmed from the specific nature of South African society as a settler society in which the majority of the settlers were of a different national origin to the colonizing power. Differences of interest developed between the Afrikaner descendants of the original Dutch settlers, who wanted to determine their own political and economic affairs, and the British administration established in 1809. These culminated in the second South African War of 1899–1902 and the Act of Union of 1910 whereby South Africa became a self-governing Dominion.

Under the Union a system of *internal colonialism* developed, with the state continuing to act as the agent of capital in the name of 'development' and European values. There was, however, an important difference between this and external colonialism in that in place of the typical expatriate ruling class there was a substantial indigenous white minority which was itself divided along ethnic and class lines. There was a contradiction between the role of whites as 'natural rulers' and the class competition between working-class whites and employers. This came to the surface in the 'Rand Revolt' of white miners in 1922. The immediate crisis was solved by the incorporation of the white working class into the ruling elite, bought with legislation which further deprived Africans of land, regulated their rights of residence and movement and reserved occupations for whites. In addition the limited property-based African franchise which had been retained in the 'liberal' Cape Province was abolished.

The result was a state in which blacks were simultaneously exploited by capitalism and dominated and controlled by whites but it was still not the apartheid state. This came into being only in 1948 when Afrikaner nationalism added new cultural and ideological dimensions.

Afrikaner nationalism originated in the nineteenth- and early twentieth-century conflicts between the original Calvinist Dutch settlers, the indigenous African population and the British administration. Following the Act of Union these differences were built upon by organizations such as the Broederbond which used religious ideology and cultural symbols such as the Afrikaans language to legitimize their claims to racial superiority, attack the continuing influence of the English-speaking community and gain support for the idea of an Afrikaner 'Volk'. Nationalism increased during the economic depression of the 1930s leading to the eventual defeat of the United Party government by the National Party (NP) in 1948. The NP came to power determined to implement its policy of apartheid (literally, apartness), which was ostensibly based on theories of cultural and racial difference. It immediately began to increase the power of the state to coerce and control the black population but also, specifically, to bolster the economic position of Afrikaners.

Detailed legislation was used to create separate racially-based systems in every sphere of public and private life (see Box 12.1). A cornerstone of apartheid was the physical separation of different 'races' which was considered necessary for both economic and cultural reasons. Black labour was required for the mining and manufacturing industries on which the South African economy was based but employers and government wanted to preserve a pool of cheap labour and avoid the social and political consequences of urbanization. The right of Africans to live in urban areas was therefore controlled by the use of passes which were tied to employment; migrant workers were segregated in tribally-based hostels, residential areas were strictly segregated according to race, skilled jobs were reserved for whites and the wages and right to organize of African and other non-European workers were controlled. By forcible removal and relocation of rural Africans a number of tribal 'homelands' (Bantustans) were established creating a state-dependent black elite of nominal rulers and an African population separated on ethnic lines. At the same time state intervention in the economy was used to counter-balance the existing English commercial domination, and state employment and state enterprises

Box 12.1 Apartheid legislation, 1948–63

1948   *Asiatic Laws Amendment Act*: withdrew parliamentary
        representation of Asians.
        Electoral Laws Amendment Act: tightened registration rules
        for Coloureds.

1949   *Prohibition of Mixed Marriages Act*: applied to white/non-
        white marriage.
        Asiatic Land Tenure Amendment Act: restricted rights of
        residence of Asians.
        Native Laws Amendment Act: created labour bureaux to
        control supply of African labour.

1950   *Population Registration Act*: established a racial register.
        Suppression of Communism Act: outlawed a variety of
        political activities.
        Immorality Amendment Act: prohibited white/non-white
        sexual intercourse.
        Group Areas Act: divided all land on a racial basis.

1951   *Separate Representation of Voters Act*: removed Coloured
        voters from the common roll.
        Bantu Authorities Act: established appointed Bantu
        Authorities in the Reserves and abolished the Natives'
        Representative Council.

1952   *Natives (Abolition of Passes and Co-ordination of Documents)
        Act*: consolidated passes into a reference book issued to all
        Africans.
        Native Laws Amendment Act: prohibited Africans to remain in
        urban areas for longer than 72 hours without a permit.

1953   *Bantu Education Act*: African education transferred to
        Department of Native Affairs.
        Reservation of Separate Amenities Act: permitted reservation
        of facilities for the exclusive use of any race.
        Native Labour (Settlement of Disputes) Act: outlawed strikes
        by African workers, set up separate disputes machinery.
        Criminal Law Amendment Act: prescribed severe penalties
        for political protest.
        Public Safety Act: provided for rule by decree in an
        emergency.

1954   *Natives Resettlement Act*: provided for forcible removal of
        Africans from designated areas.
        Riotous Assemblies and Suppression of Communism Act:
        increased penalties.

1955   *Departure from the Union Regulation Act*: empowered
        Minister of the Interior to withhold or withdraw passports.

Natives (Urban Areas) Amendment Act: further restricted rights of residence.

Criminal Procedure Act: gave immunity to police killing suspects.

1956   *Industrial Conciliation Act*: provided for splitting of trade unions on racial lines and for reservation of jobs on a racial basis.

Native Administration Amendment Act: permitted banning orders without notice.

Natives (Urban Areas) Amendment Act: allowed local authorities to expel any African.

1957   *Native Laws Amendment Act*: further limited rights of Africans to enter and remain in urban areas.

Group Areas Amendment Act: banned particular racial groups from public places without a permit.

1958   *Natives Taxation and Development Act*: increased rate of taxation.

1959   *Extension of University Education Act*: excluded Africans from 'open' universities and established separate ethnic colleges.

Promotion of Bantu Self Government Act: abolished African representation and established procedures for 'self government' in the Reserves.

1960   *Reservation of Separate Amenities Amendment Act (and others)*: further extended provision of separate facilities.

Unlawful Organisations Act: provided for the banning of the ANC and the Pan African Congress.

1961   *General Law Amendment Act*: detention without bail up to 12 days.

Urban Bantu Councils Act: replaced local authority advisory boards with new separate (partially elected) councils.

1962   *General Law Amendment Acts*: laying down penalties for political activity.

1963   *Better Administration of Designated Areas Act*: provided for mass removals of urban Africans.

General Law Amendment Act: provided detention without trial.

Bantu Laws Amendment Act: eliminated African urban residence rights.

Transkei Constitution Act: provided for 'self government' in Transkei.

Publications and Entertainments Act: provided for censorship.

(Adapted from Bunting, 1964.)

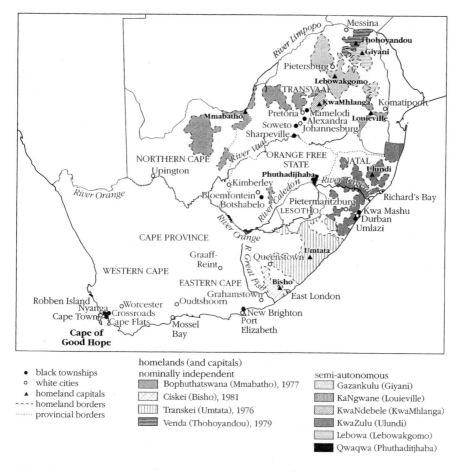

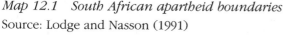

		homelands (and capitals)		
•	black townships	nominally independent		semi-autonomous
○	white cities	▨ Bophuthatswana (Mmabatho), 1977		▨ Gazankulu (Giyani)
▲	homeland capitals	▨ Ciskei (Bisho), 1981		▨ KaNgwane (Louieville)
- - - -	homeland borders	▨ Transkei (Umtata), 1976		▨ KwaNdebele (KwaMhlanga)
......	provincial borders	▨ Venda (Thohoyandou), 1979		▨ KwaZulu (Ulundi)
				▨ Lebowa (Lebowakgomo)
				■ Qwaqwa (Phuthaditjhaba)

Map 12.1 South African apartheid boundaries
Source: Lodge and Nasson (1991)

were greatly increased. This performed the dual function of providing what has been described as a vast employment and welfare agency for members of the Afrikaner community while simultaneously ensuring complete loyalty and commitment to apartheid in all spheres of public life. White unity supported the repressive machinery of the state which was used to ensure the continued provision of cheap labour for the economic production on which the whole edifice was based. The result was an 'apartheid state' which combined ethnic and cultural, economic and military instruments to form a formidable obstacle to democratization.

Challenges to the legitimacy of the state

The creation of institutionalized ethnic inequalities delayed the development of the African population and advantaged the white minority, allowing them to use their monopoly of economic and military power to suppress any challenge to their control. On the other hand, by the extremes of inequality which it created between the races, by the brutality and the universality of its implementation, apartheid succeeded in alienating international opinion and uniting Africans against it from many different backgrounds. The particular character and power of the apartheid state gave it an unparalleled capacity to resist demands for democratic reform but it also gave it a rigidity and inability to adapt to circumstances which made challenges to its legitimacy inevitable and led eventually to its breakdown (Legassick, 1985).

The challenge to the legitimacy of the regime began as soon as it was born, coming first from the black population most affected, then from sections of the international community and finally from within the regime itself. However, there were also countervailing forces which delayed and placed obstacles in the way of progress towards democracy.

The history of the breakdown of apartheid is one of intensifying state repression and increasing organized resistance to it. This can be divided into three periods: 1948–69, 1970–78 and 1978–90. In the first period opposition came primarily from political parties but in the second and third periods a major role was played by the organizations of *civil society*, in particular trade unions, the church and Civic Associations.

Black political opposition to white domination was as old as the Union itself: the ANC, then a group of moderate middle-class Africans, was formed in 1912 but it was not until the imposition of apartheid from 1948 on that effective mass action developed. In 1950 the Suppression of Communism Act classified virtually all political opponents as communists and brought together groups such as the ANC, the South African Communist Party (SACP), the Indian National Congress and the Coloured People's Congress – a process which culminated in the Congress Alliance and the drawing up of the Freedom Charter calling for a non-racial democratic South Africa.

To begin with the policy of the Alliance was one of Ghandian passive resistance but unlike the British in India the apartheid regime was prepared to use the maximum force of the state to protect its interests. On 21 March 1960, at Sharpeville, 67 African demonstrators were killed and 186 wounded when police opened fire on a peaceful crowd involved in a protest against the pass laws organized by the Pan African Congress (PAC), a radical off-shoot of the ANC. The ANC abandoned its policy of peaceful protest and joined the PAC in accepting the principle of armed struggle. A military wing, Umkhonto we Sizwe was formed but the African opposition was unable to match the violence of the state. Between 1961 and 1964 a series of General Laws Amendment Acts gave massive powers of repression to the government. Most of the national and regional leadership of the ANC and PAC (which also included most of the black trade union leadership) was arrested and imprisoned or banished, and remaining activists were forced into exile.

In the early 1970s internal opposition re-established itself. In the absence of legal parties a lead was taken by a re-grouped, ostensibly non-political trade union movement and by the Black Consciousness Movement which encompassed the South African Students' Organization, the Black People's Convention (BPC) and a number of community-based civic organizations. In 1973 a series of strikes which began in Natal involved thousands of workers, showing their potential to disrupt the economy. At the same time the BPC instigated a campaign against the cultural apartheid of the Bantu Education Act which provided an inferior education for the country's blacks. Young Africans demonstrated by boycotting their schools and on 16 June 1976, school children in Soweto rioted against the introduction of teaching in Afrikaans, beginning a period of unrest in the townships which was to lead to numerous deaths, including that in custody of the leader of the BPC, Steve Biko. Many young people fled into exile, swelling the ranks of the ANC which established schools in the frontline states and arranged scholarships for students to study in sympathetic countries.

Hector Peterson, the first child to be killed, is carried towards a nearby clinic, 16 June 1976

In 1978 the Prime Minister, John Vorster, was replaced by his former deputy, P.W. Botha. The change was to prove significant because although there can be no doubt that their final objectives were the same – that is to say, the preservation of the apartheid state – the route which Botha was prepared to take diverged considerably from that of Vorster and provided openings towards democratization. Botha's policy was to defend white economic and political superiority through the adaptation of apartheid. It was not an

abdication of white privilege but an attempt to entrench it in different ways –
by making new alliances and by attracting the support of new groups
through limited social reform while at the same time using the military to
crush opposition both within and without South Africa's borders.

In the next decade state institutions and legislation were harnessed to
this end. The constitutional changes which had begun with the declaration of
the 'independence' of the Transkei homeland in 1976 were followed up by
that of the Ciskei in 1977, Venda in 1989 and Bophuthatswana in 1981. The
1982 Black Local Authorities Act set up elected councils in the black
townships for the first time and in 1983 a whites-only referendum on
constitutional change resulted in the introduction, two years later, of a new
tricameral parliament with separate houses for whites, Asians and
Coloureds. Black trade unions were put on the same footing as white; a
number of 'petty apartheid' measures were abolished and a campaign to
upgrade township facilities was instituted. These measures, however, failed
to win allies for the government or to convince external observers of its
democratic intentions. Most Asians and Coloureds rejected the new
constitution because it still embodied the principles of apartheid: in the
first elections to the three houses of parliament only 14 per cent of the new
electorate voted. The newly 'independent' homelands were not recognized
by the international community as genuine self-governing states and their
leaders were seen as clients of the National Party, having to be maintained in
power by force. At the same time the continued exclusion of blacks from the
franchise (on the grounds that they were citizens of the newly independent
homelands) served only to increase the opposition which was growing in the
townships and the workplace.

This opposition had its basis in a strong, autonomous civil society which
had continued to thrive throughout the period of apartheid and now
combined to demand genuine democratization. Interest-based organizations such as the South African Council of Churches operated at local,
national and international level articulating the moral case against
government policy; township Civic Associations organized rent and
consumer boycotts and African trade unions joined together in a new
federation. At the same time, however, the ANC in exile retained the loyalty
of the majority of Africans and continued to influence events. Whilst it was
unable to mount a major invasion, Umkhonto we Sizwe's battles with South
African troops on the borders kept morale high and cadres were infiltrated
into the country to help with the organization of opposition. As a result what
started as relatively uncoordinated activity became increasingly organized
with the establishment in August 1983 of the umbrella United Democratic
Front (UDF) representing some 600–700 member organizations. This came
together with the Confederation of South African Trade Unions (COSATU),
founded in 1985, and the South African Students' Organization to form the
Mass Democratic Movement (MDM).

The MDM reached deep into the heart of the townships and the
workplace making the country effectively ungovernable. Between 1984 and
1986 strikes increased by over 90 per cent (Price, 1994); some 700,000 pupils
boycotted their schools and black local authorities were unable to function.

WE DEMAND TO BE HEARD

(Soweto Civic Association logo)

IN MAY 1986 THE PEOPLE DECIDED TO BOYCOTT RENT FOR THE FOLLOWING REASONS:

1. **High Rents which residents could not afford to pay.**
2. **High Electricity and Water Bills**
3. **Bad Services, Dirty Streets etc.**
4. **Demand for the Resignation of the Councillors who Represent their Own Interests.**
5. **Removal of Security Forces from Soweto and from Schools.**

* Instead of addressing the grievances of the People, a STATE OF EMERGENCY was declared and many of OUR PEOPLE WERE DETAINED, including the Executive Members of The Soweto Civic Association. The Soweto Council resorted to evictions, threats of Evictions, and cutting of electricity. Meetings to discuss our problems have been BANNED. In effect those in authority have chosen to simply ignore the VOICE OF THE PEOPLE OF SOWETO

Therefore.........

WE DEMAND TO BE HEARD

To Soweto Residents

All Residents of Soweto are hereby informed to that the
SOWETO CIVIC ASSOCIATION
has requested a meeting with NICO MALAN (but not with Councillors) to discuss grievances of the PEOPLE and to demand an end to Evictions

This Meeting with NICO MALAN was called for as a response to the failure to resolve the PEOPLES GRIEVANCES!

Issued by: S.C.A.

Globe

Government reaction was to adopt a 'total strategy' of state repression. From 1979 onwards the military exercised an increasing influence over foreign policy and internal security, frequently acting secretly and unaccountably. State machinery was reorganized to focus on security and total war – both internally and externally. Power was centralized in the hands of the Prime Minister with a new State Security Council dominated by the military and superior to the civilian cabinet. This put in place the National Security Management System which paralleled government structures at all levels and effectively controlled all aspects of the state throughout South Africa. Arms production and spending on the South African Defence Force and the South African Police Force were increased. In 1985 a state of emergency was declared; in the last six months of 1986 over 29,000 people were arrested and held without charge, and between September 1984 and December 1988 some 4,000 people died. Covert operations were conducted to assassinate black political leaders, infiltrate opposition groups and train homeland troops to be used against the ANC and UDF. Nevertheless, civil disobedience and the level of violence escalated.

The apartheid regime was forced to resort to increasingly severe measures, to the diversion of yet more funds into security and to the increasing militarization of the state machinery. A 'Third Force', later revealed to have been guided by senior members of the military and intelligence establishment, fomented ethnic and political rivalries in Natal and the townships of the Rand, supplying arms to the Inkatha Freedom Party, which had been established by Chief Buthelezi, the Chief Minister of the semi-autonomous KwaZulu homeland, for use against ANC supporters.

As a result of the breakdown in law and order international pressure for a negotiated settlement was put on the government. Starting in 1986, informal contacts were made between different parties including ANC exiles, Western and African diplomats, church leaders, South African businessmen, National Party representatives and Mandela in his prison cell. Botha and his military supporters resisted but when in 1989 his successor F.W. de Klerk was appointed the situation changed. de Klerk announced his willingness to talk, though not to relinquish power. He recognized that the moral authority of the ANC made it the only organization with which he could legitimately negotiate. Mandela was released, the exiled leadership of the ANC and the SACP (South African Communist Party) returned to South Africa and negotiations began.

———————————————— *Summary of Section 12.1* ————————————————

- Democratization in South Africa was obstructed by the nature of the apartheid state.
- Challenges to the legitimacy of apartheid led to a cycle of repression and resistance.
- Internal opposition by a strong autonomous civil society, and a military and diplomatic offensive by the ANC in exile opened avenues to democratization.

12.2   Explaining the breakdown of authoritarian rule

The breakdown of authoritarian rule can best be explained by looking at a combination of economic and international factors but there is no straightforward causal connection.

The role of economic development

Modernization and structural theorists have conflicting views on the role of economic development in democratization. For modernization theorists development creates the 'necessary' conditions for democratization such as literacy and the growth of civil society. For structuralists, it leads to democratization through a transformation of power structures. Capitalism allies itself with the repressive machinery of the state to break down existing social relations, create order, acquire cheap labour, so establishing optimum conditions for the generation of profit. In time the social changes brought about by industrialization, such as education and urbanization, give rise to a challenge to authoritarianism (Rueschemeyer *et al.*, 1992).

The South African evidence suggests that whilst neither of these two approaches accounts for the specific nature of South Africa's late democratization it is the structural approach which has more to offer. At the time when most of the impoverished colonies of Africa were receiving their independence and their brand-new constitutions, South Africa was the most economically developed country in sub-Saharan Africa. It also had the most urbanized society and the largest working class. According to modernization theorists the conditions prevailed for South Africa to become a stable liberal democracy; according to structural theorists the class conditions existed for a successful challenge to authoritarianism; but democratization did not happen. This suggests that the connection between economic development and democratization is by no means automatic and that other factors may intervene, either to distort and delay the process or to accelerate it. The South African case shows that when considering the effect of economic development it is important to look at not only the *level* and the *nature* of development but also the *control* of the economy and the *distribution* of resources. South Africa uniquely demonstrated that 'a dominant racial minority can perpetuate social rigidities and feudalistic traits on an advanced and expanding industrial base' (Simons and Simons, 1969, p.618). To understand this situation we need to look at the background to South Africa's economic development.

As I noted earlier, colonial economic development in South Africa was like that in other African colonies in that it was specifically geared to bolster the power of the white minority which was used to oppress and exclude the indigenous population from any share in decision making or in the wealth created. There were, however, some important differences between South Africa and other African colonies. The first, which had the effect of accelerating the pace and the *level* of socio-economic change, was scale. The discovery of gold and other minerals in the nineteenth century led to rapid development and the need for both skilled labour and a very large number of cheap, unskilled workers. Skilled workers were imported from Europe but the demand for unskilled labour had to be met through local recruitment. Increasing numbers of Africans and Asians were drawn into the wage economy on a semi-permanent basis and towns grew despite efforts to prevent the proletarianization of the indigenous population. The second difference, which influenced the *control* of the economy, was the level of European settlement. As was noted above, when political independence was granted in 1910 it was not to the African majority but to the white minority who instituted a system of *internal colonialism* under which growth depended on continued economic exploitation and political oppression of Africans by Europeans. The working class was divided on racial lines. The employment and wages of white workers were protected and they were incorporated into a racial ruling class while Africans were deprived of both land and employment rights.

From 1919 to 1939 the economy grew. Mining remained the chief source of employment and national income until 1939 but by 1945 manufacturing industry's share of GDP was greater, largely due to the growth of home production during the war (Lodge, 1996, p.188). The Second World War changed the nature of the South African economy and its patterns of employment. Increased production resulted in a larger black work-force. Africans provided two-thirds of the increase in the total labour force and African employment in manufacturing industries grew from 48.6 per cent of the total number in the sector in 1939 to 54.6 per cent in 1945. Economic development did not, however, automatically improve the lot of Africans or lead to a strengthening of the African working class. African workers were systematically discriminated against. Skilled jobs were reserved for whites, and white women rather than blacks were recruited and trained to meet shortages. By the end of 1948 Africans in industries in which wages were set by government wage determination formed 80.8 per cent of the unskilled labour force, 34.2 per cent of the semi-skilled and 5.8 per cent of those in skilled occupations. Black wages were approximately half the amount needed to meet the cost of living in towns (Luckhardt and Wall, 1980).

When the National Party came to power its policy was one of state control of key industries and import substitution fostered by protection of local manufacturing. The shortage of labour enhanced black bargaining power and encouraged demands for improvements. It was clear that the development of the economy provided the *potential* for increased black employment opportunities and greater economic and political freedom but the racial ideology of the state and the requirement for cheap labour were working in the opposite direction. Reporting in 1951 the Industrial Legislation Commission warned that if Africans were given parity of bargaining power 'they could not be restricted indefinitely to unskilled or even semi-skilled work but would get an increasing hold on skilled occupation' leading to 'complete social and political equality for all races' (South Africa, UG 62, 1951). The Commission recommended the recognition of strictly controlled and separated African trade unions but the subsequent Native Labour, Settlement of Disputes, Act (1953), although it did not make African trade unions illegal, denied them any recognized role in collective bargaining and outlawed strikes by African workers.

The apartheid policy was to retard the social changes which industrialization and economic development produced by continuing to restrict African rights to live in towns, segregating Africans from one another on ethnic lines in both rural and urban areas and restricting the growth of a unified trade union movement. Trade unions originated among the British immigrant miners of the 1880s and had a strong anti-capitalist tradition, demonstrated by the Rand Revolt of the 1920s, but they also had a deep vein of racism which had been effectively mined by the Nationalists who made common cause with white trade unionists against black workers. Attempts at large-scale African unions such as the 1920s' Industrial and Commercial Workers Union and the African Mine Workers Union, which organized a massive strike in 1946, had been suppressed. The post-war trade union movement was split on racial lines. Multi-racial unions were banned and there were two rival federations, the largely white Trade Union Council, formed in 1954, which supported government legislation and the South African Congress of Trade Unions (SACTU), formed in 1955 with the support of the SACP, which supported the ANC. SACTU and its affiliates suffered for their opposition. Mass imprisonment and bannings took place between 1961 and 1964, driving the remaining leaders into exile and setting back the development of effective African trade unions. Nevertheless, this was not for long.

Between 1948 and 1970 the economic trend which began during the Second World War continued. GDP grew at a rate of some 5 per cent per annum and the manufacturing sector, much of it financed by foreign (mainly British) investment, increased rapidly (Lewis, 1990). This trend accelerated in the 1960s when industry underwent a number of structural changes. There was a concentration of capital with production in the hands of either the state, foreign companies or the four to six industrial/mining conglomerates which dominated the Johannesburg Stock Exchange. Mass production and technological innovation increased and with them the size of workplaces and work-forces. Conditions were once again ripe for the growth of working-class organizations. Skilled labour was scarce and job reservation was increasingly ignored, enabling Africans to fill hitherto forbidden posts. African trade unions re-emerged, building their support on workplace bargaining and strong local organizations. When the world recession of the 1970s hit South Africa the unions were therefore in a position to respond effectively.

The fortunes of South Africa's economy were tied closely to those of the world economy. Growth had depended on state intervention and the attraction of foreign investment by a policy of cheap labour but low wages restricted the development of a home market. The downturn in the world economy from 1970 therefore had disastrous consequences. Despite short apparent recoveries, the South African economy was in a state of crisis from then onwards. Consumer prices increased by 10–16 per cent per annum with expenditure on essentials such as food, transport and clothing rising by 30 per cent between 1972 and 1973. Private investment fell and unemployment rose. Black wages rose hardly at all and 25–35 per cent of the economically active African population were engaged in the informal rather than the formal sector (Manzo, 1992; Legassick, 1985). A wave of strikes, involving some 61,000 workers, took place in Natal in 1973, followed by rolling strikes in the mines of the West Rand. These strengthened existing black unions and encouraged the formation of others which were to form the core of the struggle against apartheid in the 1980s.

Industrial unrest in the 1970s could not be dealt with in the same way as wartime unrest. The strikers were not unskilled migrants who could be returned to the reserves and replaced by raw immigrant labour but well organized members of a growing urban working class. Between 1970 and 1980 townships and illegal settlements expanded and the urban African population increased by 1.5 million. Large employers began to support institutionalized collective bargaining as a means of getting the labour mobility and supply of skilled labour which they thought necessary for the restoration of economic growth. The result was an end to the pact between employers, white labour and the state – which had been based on protectionism and cheap black labour – and the introduction of industrial reforms which played an important part in the breakdown of apartheid.

The aim of these reforms was to create a 'moderate' non-political trade union movement which would not threaten industrial peace or take part in anti-government activity but the result was quite different. The first reform, the Bantu Labour Relations Amendment Act (1973), legalized strikes by African workers and provided local industrial relations committees as a forum in which trade unions could gain experience and skills through discussions with management. Trade unions, whilst not legally recognized were accepted and in the late 1970s a new trade union federation, the Federation of South African Trade Unions (FOSATU) was formed. The next step of the government was to set up two Commissions of Inquiry, the first, the Wiehahn Commission (South Africa, RP 47, 1979), into the industrial relations system and the second, the Riekert Commission (South Africa, RP 32, 1979), into influx control and pass laws. The report of the Wiehahn Commission blamed industrial unrest not on apartheid but on multinational corporations which 'distorted' the economy by paying higher wages than South African companies. It nevertheless accepted the need for a system of collective bargaining which would ensure a common loyalty to both the system and the country. Privileges for white unions and formal job reservation for whites were therefore to be ended and registration extended to the formerly unrecognized black unions. The report of the Riekert Commission recommended certain changes in the pass laws but for most urban Africans influx control was to be more rigorously applied.

The aim of the two commissions was 'the intensification of state control over African workers and the development of a more streamlined divide-and-rule policy for the entire black population' (Luckhardt and Wall, 1980, p.461). Their objective was to legalize and co-opt black unions, controlling their activities through registration (which prohibited any political activity) and controlling the increase in the number of urban Africans through the pass laws. The proposals succeeded in causing a temporary split in the black trade union movement. FOSATU affiliated unions, which supported 'constructive engagement' with apartheid, favoured registration but those which supported the ANC were opposed. The government hoped for support from major multinational companies, such as Polaroid and General Motors, which had campaigned to normalize industrial relations since the beginning of the 1970s (Coker, 1981). These recognized, however, that a collective bargaining system required fewer restrictions on union activities. Many firms extended recognition to non-registered as well as to registered unions, and as a result unions were freed from many of the previous constraints. In 1984 FOSATU abandoned its non-political stance and in 1985 joined with pro-ANC unions to form COSATU (the Confederation of South African Trade Unions), which was to play a vital role in the demise of apartheid, using the concessions and new freedoms granted by the government as a lever to increase the political as well as the economic bargaining power of the African working class.

External factors

Transnational and international factors had initially a negative but later a positive effect on democratization. It has been argued (Manzo, 1992) that South African politics are historically the effect of global power relations originating with colonialism. Colonialism was, as Chapter 11 points out, profoundly anti-democratic. It was a system of economic exploitation and it was also the progenitor of powerful ideologies relating to identity, 'civilization' and 'freedom' which unavoidably influence colonized and colonizers alike. Within this general framework other transnational and international factors played a major role in both fostering and delaying the democratization of South Africa. The actions of the government and the African opposition, whilst not predetermined, took place within an international framework of ideas and politics which constrained and influenced their actions.

The Second World War was one important international factor. As has been noted above, the war led to changes in the economic structure of the country which encouraged the development of new classes. It also introduced new ideas. The defeat of Nazism brought, in rhetoric at least, an international emphasis on human rights and freedoms, expressed not only in the Cold War against the Soviet Union but also in demands for independence from European colonial empires. Black opposition was not, therefore, an isolated phenomenon but was part of, and gained impetus from, the global post-war shift towards decolonization.

The new generation of African leaders did not use the 'traditional' tribal discourse which had been espoused by colonial authorities but ideas of nation and freedom and arguments derived from a wide range of philosophies – from Christianity, liberal democracy, radical democracy and communism as well as from the Pan Africanism of the black writers who were an inspiration for both the Civil Rights movement in the USA and African nationalists. Mandela himself cites the principles of the Atlantic Charter signed between Churchill and Roosevelt in 1941 and argues that 'the principles they were fighting for in Europe were the same ones we were advocating at home' (Mandela, 1994).

At the same time, however, the development of the Cold War and South Africa's place in the world political and economic order reinforced the anti-democratic nature of the apartheid regime. The Afrikaner government was both a product of and a player in the geo-political game being fought out between the world's great powers and their supporting allies. Afrikaner ideology emphasized the defence of white Christian civilization against the forces of darkness reflecting a mainstream of colonial and imperialist thinking. South Africa's racial laws were themselves not unique. Similar laws existed in a number of African colonies and the southern USA practised overt racial discrimination until the 1960s. Despite a flirtation with fascism by some Afrikaner leaders, the Union fought on the side of the allies in the Second World War, and with the onset of the Cold War South Africa cast itself in the role of the champion of democratic freedom against the spread of totalitarian communism in Africa. It was accepted as such by the Western Alliance and the exclusion of those defined as unfit to vote by virtue of their race was ignored or even applauded as a bulwark against 'communist inspired' African nationalists.

Direct foreign investment in South Africa aligned the regime firmly with the West, reinforcing Afrikaner identification of their racial policies with the defence of European Christian civilization against black barbarism. There can be no doubt that, in South Africa as elsewhere, greater importance was given by the West to keeping the world free for capitalism than to the democratic rights of Africans: policy towards South Africa was shaped by calculations relating to Western political and economic interests in the region. Pressure for change from Western governments and the international organizations which they dominated did not lead but followed domestic pressure in South Africa and was always influenced by the individual interests of the countries concerned.

The Sharpeville massacre marked a turning point in the struggle against apartheid. The publicity given to the killings at Sharpeville brought international condemnation of the South African regime and the flight of foreign investment alarmed at the prospect of political instability. In 1962 the United Nations requested all members to break off diplomatic and most commercial relations with South Africa, and in 1963 the UN Security Council recommended a complete arms embargo. South Africa was isolated within the international community as the last bastion of legally institutionalized racism. It had already made a final break with Britain by leaving the Commonwealth and declaring itself a Republic. The response of Western governments was muted, however, by the adoption of the armed struggle by the ANC and by the close ties between the ANC, the SACP and the black trade union movement, which possessed the economic power to threaten Western investment. The two largest investors, Britain and the USA, opposed the use of economic sanctions and indirect Western support for apartheid continued until the late 1980s.

Nevertheless, from 1960 onwards there was a challenge to these policies from a number of directions – from liberal opinion and economic forces within the Western industrialized nations themselves, from a range of non-governmental organizations and from the large number of African states which gained their independence during the early 1960s – supported by the Soviet Union and the Eastern Bloc. In the USA, the Kennedy government recognized the campaign by the black Civil Rights movement for an end to discrimination and the extension of political representation in the South. Similarly, Harold Macmillan's 'wind of change' speech, delivered in South Africa a few months before the Sharpeville killings, was not a grand democratic vision but a pragmatic response to demands for self government by colonized peoples and the weakened state of post-war Britain. Post-Sharpeville, considerable influence was exerted by the Anti Apartheid Movement, the World Council of Churches, the international trade union movement and other pressure groups which used the international media to change the prevailing climate of opinion away from racism and towards the abolition of apartheid; they also collected funds to support the struggle inside South Africa. Britain and the USA were still concerned about the protection of their economic interests and the threat of communism in Southern Africa but both came finally to shift their policy from one of open support for apartheid to one of defending their political and economic investment in the area by encouraging political reform and negotiation.

At the same time the ANC received help from the 'non-aligned' states such as Sweden, from the Soviet bloc, which supplied money, arms and training, and from frontline African states as they became independent. First Zambia and Tanzania then Mozambique, Angola and Zimbabwe (all of which themselves suffered from South African military or economic domination and aggression) were host to large numbers of exiles, including the wave of students which left South Africa following the Soweto riots of 1976 and the schools rebellion of the 1980s. They provided office accommodation for the ANC and bases for its military wing, Umkhonto we Sizwe, and even, in the case of Zimbabwe and Angola, joined forces with Umkhonto we Sizwe to fight the South African army.

Much of the war against apartheid took place, quite literally, in the international arena as Pretoria took steps to persuade or to force neighbouring states to acquiesce in South Africa's political and economic objectives. Special units were set up to raid neighbouring territories, and surrogate forces trained and led by the South African Defence Force were established to undermine the legitimate governments of states considered to be unfriendly. At the same time the threat of economic sanctions was used to bring reluctant countries into line. Between 1980 and 1983 South Africa engaged in a campaign of regional destabilization which included a major invasion of Angola, the use of surrogate forces in Lesotho, Mozambique, Zambia and Zimbabwe and widespread sabotage and assassination throughout the region. The ANC retaliated by joining forces with Cuban troops in Angola where South African troops suffered some significant defeats. International disquiet was aroused, especially from the USA which feared that its economic interests in the region would be damaged.

In 1984 Botha sought to placate international opinion by negotiating non-aggression pacts with Angola and Mozambique. In 1986 attacks on both countries resumed but it was becoming increasingly clear that South Africa needed the support of the West which the West was only prepared to give if internal concessions allowed the economy to stabilize. It was at this point that the collapse of the Soviet Union and the end of the Cold War changed the situation, removing both South Africa's bargaining strength as a surrogate for the USA in the fight against communism in Southern Africa and USSR financial support for and supply of arms to the ANC. International factors were therefore closely involved in the final decision by both sides to come to the negotiating table.

─────────────── *Summary of Section 12.2* ───────────────

- The democratization in South Africa was the result of a combination of economic and international influences which eventually overcame the obstacle of the apartheid institutions of the state.

- Economic development did not automatically lead to democratization but produced an urban working class with the power to challenge the systematic discrimination of apartheid.

- International factors had initially a negative but later a positive effect on democratization.

12.3 The transition to liberal democracy

The breakdown of authoritarian rule is the first stage in the democratization process but until authoritarianism has been replaced by democratic institutions the process cannot be said to be complete. Authoritarian regimes may be overthrown by force or mass mobilization but, according to transition theorists, this is unlikely to result in their replacement by stable liberal democratic regimes and the new government is likely to regress into or be replaced by new forms of authoritarianism (Huntington, 1991; Karl and Schmitter, 1991). A successful transition to democracy is more likely to occur, it is argued, through a process of negotiation and pacts between the incumbent elite and the new challenging elite, in particular, between 'softline' reformers in the ruling party and moderate opposition leaders (O'Donnell *et al.*, 1988). By its nature this kind of transition process emphasizes the role of leadership and excludes mass participation. Outcomes are not dependent on structural factors, it is claimed, because there is an element of choice in terms of constitutional settlements or electoral systems. At the same time, however, choice is constrained by the need to make trade-offs, to compromise and in particular to protect the property rights of the bourgeoisie and the interests of the armed forces without whose agreement the transition cannot take place. The result is likely to be a minimalist democracy which is essentially procedural and conservative rather than one which undertakes a fundamental transformation of society.

Transition theories advance general arguments which are relevant to democratization in South Africa (Shapiro, 1993). As we shall see in this section, despite the long period of struggle against apartheid, authoritarianism was not defeated by force of arms and there was a long process of negotiation before the agreement was reached which led to the 1994 election. Indeed, South Africa could almost be taken as a text book example of the classic situation described by Huntington in which the conflicting sides 'can neither do without each other nor unilaterally impose their preferred solution on each other if they are to satisfy their respective divergent interests' (Huntington, 1991, pp.141–2). The result of the negotiations was not a majoritarian democracy but a power-sharing agreement which preserved many of the institutions of the former regime and left the distribution of resources untouched. On the other hand, it could be argued that South Africa's experience has *not* exactly conformed to what might have been expected and that structural factors have played a more important part than transition theories would allow for.

The negotiating phase of the transition to liberal democracy in South Africa was in three stages. First, there was a period of discussion on the form which negotiations should take. Second, there followed the abortive all-party Convention for a Democratic South Africa (CODESA) in 1991 and 1992. Third, the Multi-Party Negotiating Forum eventually agreed the Interim Constitution and Bill of Rights on which the 1994 elections were based.

The first stage of the negotiations bears witness to the limitations of the transition approach in analysing a situation as complex as that pertaining in South Africa. Transition theorists present a simplified picture of clearly identifiable elites who, whilst approaching the issue from different directions, have a mutual interest in democratization. In South Africa, however, the situation in 1990 was far from being so clear. The organization of the apartheid state and the deep divisions which split society meant that there was a complex configuration of different interests. In place of ruling and oppositional elites contending for power there was a collection of actors, incapable of building effective coalitions for whom both internal and external relations were equally difficult and acrimonious (Ottaway, 1993). The main actors, the NP and the ANC, had not come together from choice but were what might be termed 'reluctant reconcilers' (Friedman, 1993a, 1993b). They had been forced to the negotiating table by economic and international pressures but neither side fully accepted the need to compromise on the means of negotiation (multi-party conference or constituent assembly) or the model of democracy to be pursued (a power-sharing consociational/ federal or centralized majoritarian state). (See Horowitz, 1991 for a discussion of consociational proposals.) The NP believed that the balance of power was still on its side and that it could use negotiations to control the pace and limit the scope of democratization. The ANC believed that it could force the government to relinquish power without making any concessions in return. The commitment to democracy on both sides was limited, the NP aiming to hold on to the vestiges of power for as long as possible while the ANC's primary objective was an end to white rule.

It took almost two years from the initial talks between de Klerk and Mandela in 1990 before all-party constitutional talks began. During this time the level of violence within the country – primarily 'black on black' – reached unprecedented heights. ANC supporters in Natal and the townships of the Rand were attacked by (mainly rural and migrant) supporters of Chief Buthelezi's Inkatha Freedom Party, which had been formed with the financial backing of the NP, ostensibly as a Zulu cultural organization but in reality as a vehicle for opposition to the ANC. In response 'Self Defence Units' were formed which took revenge on supposed collaborators and members of Inkatha. There was also a high level of criminal violence which capitalized on the lack of legitimacy of the police force and the easy availability of firearms. Violence was a persistent backdrop to the transition process as protagonists on all sides manipulated the force (legal and illegal) available to them in order to impede or to influence the outcome of negotiations.

In contrast to the behaviour of 'typical' transitional elites described in Chapter 1 relations between the NP and the ANC continued to be adversarial and competitive and in May 1991 discussions on the terms for negotiation were broken off, Mandela blaming de Klerk for failing to control anti-ANC violence. For talks to begin again it was necessary to reduce the level of violence and this could only be done by the two principal negotiators agreeing to the inclusion of other interest groups – in particular the Inkatha Freedom Party which was responsible for most of the attacks. In September 1991 the National Peace Accord was signed, all major parties agreeing to work together to end violence. All sides also demanded representation in the negotiations, and the inclusive principle was finally adopted by the national executive of the ANC as the basis for an all-party conference to agree the terms of the transition to democracy.

The second stage of the negotiations, the Convention for a Democratic South Africa (CODESA) which met for the first time on 20 December 1991, demonstrated yet again how far South Africa was from the ideal of a transition pact by elites. The convention divided into five working groups to consider the constitutional details of the transition to democracy. Working group negotiations continued for the next five months but became, in the words of one commentator, 'impenetrably complex' and never seemed likely to reach agreement. In March 1992 a whites-only referendum gave de Klerk a 69 per cent majority in favour of his policy but public impatience grew and communal violence continued to escalate. In May 1992 the working groups met in plenary once again to make progress reports on their deliberations but it was no surprise when the convention finally collapsed in a welter of mutual recriminations. One of the main reasons for the breakdown to talks was the influence of the institutions of apartheid. The ethnic divisions which had characterized apartheid were reflected in the negotiations and had a profound effect on the outcome. Almost all of the parties concerned fielded multi-racial negotiating teams and during the course of the negotiations alliances were forged between different racial and ethnic groups. Nevertheless, the interests which were represented were ethnically-based and had been specifically constructed by the working of apartheid (see Box 12.2).

The third and final stage of the negotiations, by the Multi-Party Negotiating Forum, appears to conform most closely to the idea of a pact between old and new elites but raises the question of to what extent the outcome of the final agreement was a matter of leadership choice, how far it was influenced by mass action (a factor discounted by most transition theories) and how far it was influenced by structural factors. Following the collapse of CODESA an ANC national conference met. Rank and file members, led by members of COSATU, were dissatisfied with the lack of progress by negotiators and adopted a policy of rolling mass action which pushed the leadership into a more militant stance. The campaign began with mass stay-aways on 16 June 1992, the anniversary of the 1976 Soweto riots. The following day, in a raid later proved to have been aided by the police, an Inkatha hit squad massacred ANC supporters living in Boipatong township. The raid was a calculated move by the right to derail negotiations, and five days later Mandela formally suspended talks with the government, putting forward a list of fourteen demands to be met before negotiations could

> **Box 12.2 Principal bodies involved in the negotiations**
>
> – The National Party (NP)
>
> – The African National Congress (ANC) and its allies in the Tripartite Alliance: the South African Communist Party (SACP) and the Confederation of South African Trade Unions (COSATU)
>
> – The Concerned South African Group, later calling itself the Freedom Front: a loose alliance of the right-wing Conservative Party, the Zulu based Inkatha Freedom Party and representatives of the homeland governments of Ciskei, Transkei, Venda and Bophuthatswana
>
> – The Democratic Party
>
> – Two minority 'Africanist' parties: the Pan African Congress (PAC) and the Azanian Peoples' Organization.

resume. The next three months were a period of acrimonious accusation and counter-accusation against a background of continuing violence culminating in the shooting of ANC marchers at Bisho, the capital of Ciskei. Finally, however, on 26 September the ANC and NP signed a Record of Understanding, laying out the ground for the resumption of negotiations.

The reasons for the rapprochement were twofold. The most immediate factor was the belated acceptance by the ANC and NP of the classic 'transitional calculation' – that the situation was one in which neither side could be sure of winning. Conditions inside the country convinced both the NP and the ANC that they could no longer maintain their inflexible negotiating position and that it was necessary to reach a bilateral agreement which could be used as a framework to constrain the disruptive potential of the other interest groups. Consequently, although other interest groups were included in the new discussions, this was on the basis of a settlement which had already been reached between the NP and ANC which they now had to defend against all comers.

The Record of Understanding was indeed a classic example of a transitional pact but it was not a pact freely arrived at simply as a matter of choices made by the leadership of two sides. On the contrary, the decision was constrained by structural factors, stemming from South Africa's role in the global and regional economy. The extent of foreign investment in South Africa gave rise to fears that if a revolutionary situation was allowed to develop these interests (and others in Southern Africa) would be under threat. International pressure was brought on both the NP and the ANC and a UN mission of some 40 observers, headed by former US Secretary of State Cyrus Vance, was despatched to the country to make it clear that the economic position would not improve until agreement had been reached. Internally the economic crisis was affecting business interests and employees alike leading to a temporary alliance between employers and COSATU which also put pressure on their respective sides.

The influence of mass action at this point in the negotiations is open to debate. Adler and Webster (1995, p.77) have argued that in place of an elite-centred approach to democratization should be a recognition of the importance of the labour movement in South Africa not only in creating the conditions which led to the transition but also in shaping its form and content. Most transition theories are inherently conservative in that they suggest that a precondition for elite-pacted democratization is the preservation of capitalist institutions by the suppression of radicals and 'extremists' and the incorporation of the leadership of social movements which might disturb the balance of such an agreement (see Przeworski, 1991; Shain and Linz, 1995). In South Africa, in contrast, the SACP and COSATU played a leading role in negotiations and it was mass action not elite agreements which provided the vital impetus which pushed the NP to return to the table in 1993.

On the other hand, the nature of South Africa's involvement in the world economy severely constrained the ability of radical elements to bring about a significant shift in economic power relations. To provide the conditions for the increases in wages and employment which COSATU demanded and expected it was necessary that the economy should grow and that businesses should not pull out at the prospect of majority rule. To this end came the unlikely spectacle of cadres of the SACP meeting and socializing with Afrikaner businessmen and representatives of foreign companies in order to reassure them of the nature of the economic reforms which might be expected to follow an ANC victory at the polls. Plans for large-scale nationalization and redistribution of resources were abandoned and more moderate liberalization of the highly protected South African economy substituted. This was considered necessary not only to encourage private investors but also to attract the Western aid which would be central to the success of the projected Reconstruction and Development Programme to redress the social and economic inequalities of apartheid once the political inequalities were abolished by the new constitution. The weapon of mass protest was used judiciously in support of the liberal democratic proposals rather than of the radical demands of populist leaders and supporters of a more participatory form of democracy (represented by the leadership of militant Civic Associations) which were increasingly marginalized.

Despite their agreement it proved impossible for the ANC and NP to impose their terms on the other interest groups involved in the negotiations. On 5 March 1993 a new Multi-Party Negotiating Forum began its deliberations. A Transitional Executive Council, with representatives of 20 of the 26 delegations involved in the Forum was set up to oversee government and discussions began on the details of a system that would allow all parties winning 20 per cent of the total vote to a share of executive power in an Interim (5 year) Government. Nevertheless, there remained serious obstacles in the way of a successful transition. For a pact to be successful it is necessary for the parties to it to guarantee the support of their followers by buying-off or disciplining their extremist wings. In South Africa this was not possible as opposition to the agreement came form those excluded by it who had already spun out of the control of the two main protagonists. Attempts to undermine the process began almost immediately.

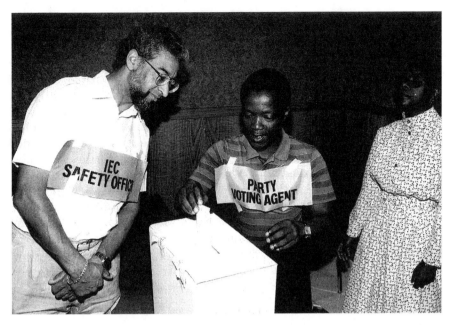

Volunteers oversee a voter education workshop hosted by the Institute for a Democratic South Africa in preparation for the 1994 election

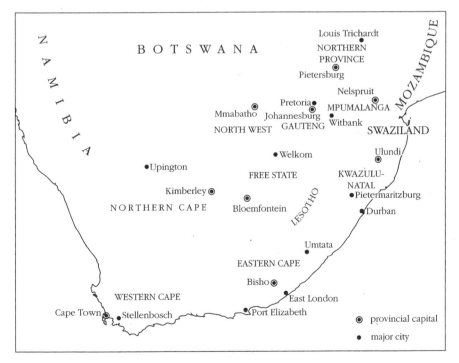

Map 12.2   South African Provinces, 1996

First, the country was disrupted by the assassination of the popular ANC and SACP leader Chris Hani, who had given his support to the pact and had been instrumental in holding in check militant elements in Umkhonto we Sizwe. Second, in a rival pact, members of the Freedom Front (formerly the Concerned South Africa Group) attempted to unstitch the agreement and replace it by another whereby a confederal constitution would give virtual independence to the new provinces. By acting in concert the ANC and NP were able to contain the violence and avoid the breakdown of talks and an election date was set for one year hence, but the Freedom Front threatened to undermine the legitimacy of the elections by refusing to take part unless their demands were met. As the date of the election drew nearer more concessions were wrung from the ANC and NP, including increased provincial powers, special constitutional status for KwaZulu Natal and a commission to consider the setting up of an Afrikaner homeland (Volkstaat) and it was not until the last minute that a combination of international intervention and mass action to overthrow their governments by the people of Bophuthatswana, Ciskei and Venda persuaded most of the boycotters to participate and enabled the elections to take place.

———————————— *Summary of Section 12.3* ————————————

- The democratic settlement in South Africa was achieved by negotiation not force.
- The process was not a straightforward accommodation between elites.
- Institutionalized interests which had been fostered by apartheid obstructed and influenced the negotiations.
- Economic structures restricted the scope of the agreement to introduce change.

Conclusion

By 1994 South Africa had completed two of the four stages of democratization identified in the Introduction to this chapter. During both stages a combination of different factors facilitated or obstructed the process. This chapter has argued that democracy was delayed because the factors which might have facilitated the necessary breakdown in authoritarian rule, in particular economic modernization and the formation of social classes, were constrained by the structural pressures of apartheid. The first stage was drawn out for some 40 years during which time a combination of economic development, structural change in both social and economic terms (the power of black workers and consumers), external political and economic pressure, urban unrest and the wars on South Africa's borders eventually brought about the conditions under which negotiations could begin.

In order to understand the outcome of the negotiation process it is useful to use both structural and transitional theories. Without social change the basis for elite negotiations does not exist (Stedman, 1994). On the other hand, the process of transition is not automatic. It has to be guided and it can be guided in one direction or another. In comparing South Africa's transition with that of Rwanda and Burundi Lemarchand (1994) has argued that structural factors were important but not decisive. They may have limited the range of options open to negotiators but the critical variable was leadership. To this extent transition theories, which emphasize the element of choice and the role of elite leadership, appear convincing. On the other hand, it is possible to argue that the constraints put upon agreement by structural factors inherited from the period of apartheid were responsible for delaying and distorting democratization in a way which was to a large extent beyond the control of the main participants.

The delay in reaching a settlement and the nature of the final settlement itself were caused by the inability of the different interest groups to move beyond their fixed positions, by the culture of violence fostered by apartheid and by attempts to recreate the ethnic divisions of apartheid in the new constitution. Further delays and distortions were caused by the entrenched power of the apartheid bureaucracy and security establishment, which not only succeeded in protecting its own interests by using the NP to extract guarantees of job security and freedom from prosecution but also intervened actively to derail negotiations through assassinations, plots and the fomenting of 'black on black' violence.

As a result, negotiations were dragged out for four years during which time many innocent lives were lost. The Interim Constitution was a complex mix of new institutions which, while it institutionalized liberal democracy, left many issues unsettled and failed to make difficult economic choices (Sisk, 1994; Friedman, 1994). How firm a basis this will be for the consolidation stage of democracy remains to be seen.

References

Adler, G. and Webster, E. (1995) 'Challenging transition theory: the Labour movement, radical reform, and transition to democracy in South Africa', *Politics and Society*, vol.23, no.1, pp.75–106.

Bunting, B. (1964) *The Rise of the South African Reich*, Harmondsworth, Penguin.

Coker, C. (1981) 'Collective bargaining as an internal sanction: the role of U.S. corporations in South Africa', *Journal of Modern African Studies*, vol.19, no.4, pp.647–66.

Friedman, S. (1993a) 'South Africa's reluctant transition', *Journal of Democracy*, vol.4, no.2, pp.56–69.

Friedman, S. (1993b) *The Long Journey: South Africa's Quest for a Negotiated Settlement*, Johannesburg, Raven.

Friedman, S. (1994) *Yesterday's Pact: Power Sharing and Legitimate Governance in Post Settlement South Africa*, Johannesburg, Centre for Policy Studies.

Horowitz, D.L. (1991) *A Democratic South Africa? Consociational Engineering in a Divided Society*, Berkeley, University of California Press.

Huntington, S.P. (1991) *The Third Wave. Democratization in the Late Twentieth Century*, Norman, University of Oklahoma Press.

Karl, T.L. and Schmitter, P. (1991) 'Models of transition in Latin America, Southern and Eastern Europe', *International Social Science Journal*, no.138.

Legassick, M. (1985) 'South Africa in crisis: what route to democracy?', *African Affairs*, vol.84, pp.587–603.

Lemarchand, R. (1994) 'Managing transitional anarchies: Rwanda, Burundi and South Africa in comparative perspective', *Journal of Modern African Studies*, vol.32, no.4, pp.581–604.

Lewis, S. (1990) *The Economics of Apartheid*, New York, Council of Foreign Relations.

Lodge, T. (1996) 'South Africa: democracy and development in a post-apartheid society' in Leftwich, A. (ed.) *Democracy and Development: Theory and Practice*, Cambridge, Polity Press.

Lodge, T. and Nasson, B. (1991) *All, Here, and Now: Black Politics in South Africa in the 1980s*, London, Hurst and Co.

Luckhardt, K. and Wall, B. (1980) *Organise or Starve! The History of the South African Congress of Trade Unions*, London, Lawrence and Wishart.

Mandela, N. (1994) *Long Walk to Freedom*, London, Little, Brown.

Manzo, K.A. (1992) *Domination, Resistance and Social Change in South Africa*, London, Praeger.

O'Donnell, G., Schmitter, P. and Whitehead, L. (1988) *Transitions from Authoritarian Rule. Vol.5: Conclusions about Uncertain Democracies*, Baltimore, Johns Hopkins University Press.

Ottaway, M. (1993) *South Africa: the Struggle for a New Order*, Washington, Brookings Institution.

Price, R.M. (1994) '*South Africa, the Political Economy of Growth and Democracy*' in Stedman, S.J. (ed.).

Przeworski, A. (1991) *Democracy and the Market*, Cambridge, Cambridge University Press.

Rueschemeyer, D., Stephens, E. and Stephens, J. (1992) *Capitalist Development and Democracy*, Cambridge, Polity Press.

Shain, Y. and Linz, J. (1995) *Between States: Interim Governments and Democratic Transition*, Cambridge, Cambridge University Press.

Shapiro, I. (1993) 'Democratic innovation: South Africa in comparative context', *World Politics*, vol.46, pp.121–50.

Shin, Doh Chull (1994) 'On the Third Wave of democratization', *World Politics*, vol.47, pp.135–70.

Simons, H.J. and Simons, R.E. (1969) *Class and Colour in South Africa, 1850–1950*, Harmondsworth, Penguin.

Sisk, T.D. (1994) 'Perspectives on South Africa's transition: implications for democratic consolidation', *Politikon*, vol.21, no.1, pp.66–75.

South Africa, RP 32 (1979) *Report of the Commission of Inquiry into Legislation affecting the Utilization of Manpower*, Government Publication.

South Africa, RP 47 (1979) *Report of the Commission of Inquiry into Labour Legislation*, Government Publication.

South Africa, UG 62 (1951) *Report of the Industrial Legislation Commission*, Government Publication.

Stedman, S.J. (1994) 'South Africa: transition and transformation' in Stedman, S.J. (ed.) pp.7–27.

Stedman, S.J. (ed.) (1994) *South Africa: the Political Economy of Transformation*, Boulder, Lynne Rienner.

CHAPTER 13

Middle East exceptionalism – myth or reality?

Simon Bromley

13.1 Patterns of political development

As the Introduction to Part IV has already suggested, the range of countries comprising the Middle East is to some extent a matter of convention and there is considerable unevenness among the countries of the region, however defined. Here I concentrate on the Arab East (Egypt, Iraq, Jordan, Lebanon, Syria and Saudi Arabia and the Gulf States, i.e. Bahrain, Kuwait, Oman, Qatar and the United Arab Emirates), as well as their large and important non-Arab but Islamic neighbours, Iran and Turkey. But even within this relatively small group of states there are marked differences of historical experience, socio-economic development, and political and cultural inheritance. In addition, the important role of oil income and wealth in the region makes generalization about levels of economic development difficult, not only in that some states have lots of oil (Saudi Arabia) and others none (Jordan), but also in that access to oil wealth does not itself necessarily give rise to more general development. In the light of this diversity, it will be useful to operate with some sub-divisions in what follows. There are at least three ways to distinguish between the countries of the Middle East: by reference to their social structures at the outset of the formation of the modern state; in terms of the history of their entanglements with outside powers; and by whether or not they have been major oil producers in the post-Second World War period. Other differences abound, but these three have been especially important in shaping the political trajectories of the region (see Table 13.1). This classification is based on an application of a structural approach to the Middle East, and thus categorizes the states in terms of their inherited social structure, the impact of international determinants and the resources available to the state. This chapter will argue that these are the most important factors in explaining different patterns of political development in the region. I will also suggest that once the political development of the Middle East is interpreted through the framework of structural theories, its alleged exceptionalism, its apparent failure to fit into more general patterns of democratization in the developing world, is largely mythical.

Oversimplifying matters greatly (and somewhat anticipating the argument to come), on the basis of this classification we can distinguish three patterns of political development among the states of the Middle East in the post-independence period. These patterns are the historical outcomes of complex interactions between changing social structures (especially class structures), the international constraints and opportunities faced by the state and the kinds of resources available to the state.

Table 13.1 Classification of states

	Social structure	External powers	Major oil producer
Turkey	Small- and medium-scale land-owning and merchant class	Independent of direct or indirect control of a European power; informal US influence after 1945	No
Iran	Small- and medium-scale land-owning class, nomadic tribes, strong urban merchants, strong independent clergy	Indirect influence of Britain and Russia in nineteenth and twentieth centuries; informal US influence 1945–79	Yes
Egypt	Presence of strong, urban-based land-owning and merchant class	Part of Ottoman Empire in nineteenth century; British protectorate 1914–22; informal British influence until 1952; independent; US influence after 1971	No, but significant earnings after mid 1970s
Syria	Presence of strong, urban-based land-owning and especially merchant class	Part of Ottoman Empire in nineteenth century; French protectorate 1920–43, some autonomy from 1930; independent; allied to Soviet Union after early 1970s	No, but significant earnings after mid 1970s
Iraq	Presence of strong, urban-based land-owning and merchant class	Part of Ottoman Empire in nineteenth century; British influence 1918–58; formally independent 1932; allied to Soviet Union after early 1970s	Yes
Jordan	Small- and medium-scale landed class, merchant class, and nomadic tribes	Part of Ottoman Empire in nineteenth century; British control; independent, but informal British influence, 1922–58	No
Lebanon	Large Christian population, presence of urban merchant class, small- and medium-scale land-owning class	Part of Ottoman Empire in nineteenth century; French influence; protectorate 1920–43; independent; 1975 civil war followed by Syrian and Israeli influence	No
Saudi Arabia	Nomadic tribal forms, trade-based merchants	Informal British influence in nineteenth and early twentieth century; US influence after 1945	Yes
Kuwait	Strong, trade-based merchant class, tribes	Informal British influence in nineteenth century; 1899–1971 informal British influence; independent since 1961; US influence after 1971	Yes

First, there are the revolutionary nationalist, modernizing, authoritarian regimes of Egypt, Iraq and Syria, which followed, in different circumstances and for different reasons, the paths pioneered by Turkey and Iran in the years between the First and Second World Wars. These authoritarian regimes were based on nationalist development led by the state, aimed at overthrowing old social classes and foreign influence. Within this broad and general category of authoritarian–modernizing regimes, there are important variations. In the first place, different social structures and different relations to the international system characterized the Arab states of Egypt, Syria and Iraq, on the one hand, and Turkey and Iran, on the other. In the former cases large-scale, urban-based, landed classes were present, whereas the pattern of land ownership in Turkey and Iran was more fragmented. Also, the Arab states experienced a greater degree of European colonial control and influence. A second, cross-cutting, variation was the presence or absence of large-scale oil wealth: Turkey, and Egypt and Syria (at least until the 1970s and 1980s), lacked oil wealth, while Iran and Iraq had it in abundance.

A second broad pattern of political development is shown by the small states of Jordan and Lebanon, lacking both significant landed classes and access to oil wealth. In these cases, the more limited role of the state in promoting development, mobilizing resources and controlling society has allowed a greater degree of pluralism in the political sphere. Though neither state has approached liberal democratic rule, both have some experience of partial democracy, Jordan through a monarchical system and Lebanon by means of consociationalism.

Third, there are the relatively pure 'rentier states' (small states not based on agrarian development but with access to oil wealth) of Saudi Arabia and the Gulf States, which lacked landed classes, indeed lacked any significant socio-economic forces prior to the formation of the modern state, and developed almost solely on the basis of oil rents and indirect external support. The limited social basis of these regimes and the fact that the state appropriates virtually all its resources from external sources has meant that there has been very little space for the emergence of forms of independent political representation. Ruling tribes have been turned into monarchies and authoritarian monarchical rule is the norm.

Although this diversity makes generalization about the Middle East difficult, many have argued that not only has there been little democracy and democratization in the Middle East, but also that this distinguishes the region from much of the rest of the developing world. For example, Ellis Goldberg and others have remarked that: 'When mentioned in the same sentence, the words "democracy" and the "Middle East" usually elicit a sense of deep suspicion, if not outright disbelief' (Goldberg *et al.*, 1993, p.3); and John Waterbury has stated that, 'the Arab Middle East is exceptional in its resistance to political liberalization, respect for human rights, and formal democratic practice' (Waterbury, 1994, p.23). Why should this be so? What is it that explains the comparative record of democracy and democratization in the Middle East? Does the Middle East constitute an exception to more general processes at work elsewhere in the developing world?

In order to address these questions, about democracy in the Middle East and its alleged exceptionalism, the rest of this chapter will be divided into

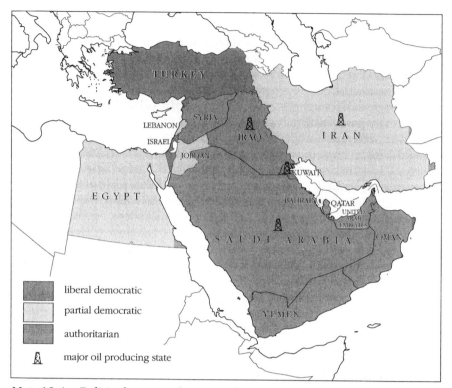

Map 13.1   Political map and major oil producing states of the Middle East, 1995

three main sections. In Section 13.2 I briefly review the fortunes of liberal democratic politics in the region after independence, in the nationalist period of the 1950s to the 1970s and in the era of economic liberalization since the 1980s and in the 1990s. Then in Section 13.3 I consider some of the work that has tried to explain the problematic nature of democratic politics in the Middle East, focusing on the search for socio-economic prerequisites for liberal democracy and the role of political culture. I argue that these approaches, primarily based on a modernization approach, are not very successful. In Section 13.4 I challenge the alleged 'exceptional' nature of Middle East politics and suggest that structural accounts, including those that focus on international factors, provide a better explanation for the relative absence of liberal democracy and democratization in the region. I also argue that structural accounts, and to a lesser extent international factors, provide the means to account for the differentiation *within* the Middle East. And finally, I conclude by drawing the threads of the argument together and assess the explanatory powers of the different approaches to the study of democracy in the Middle East.

─────────────── *Summary of Section 13.1* ───────────────

- In this chapter I concentrate on the countries of the Arab East and its immediate neighbours, Turkey and Iran.

- The Middle East comprises states at very different levels of development. Outside the oil sector, however, there are significant similarities.

- The countries of the region can be differentiated by social structure, the influence of external powers and the role of oil.

- Despite these differences, there is a general consensus that the Middle East has witnessed limited democratization and contains few, if any, liberal democracies, and that this differentiates it from much of the rest of the developing world.

13.2   The fortunes of democratic politics

Both during and after the colonial period some limited forms of democratic participation were to be found in the Middle East. During the mandate period of the years between the First and Second World Wars the colonial powers, Britain and France, established assemblies and elections of various kinds and these persisted for a time after independence. As David Pool has pointed out: 'Although kings, presidents and prime ministers followed the colonial precedent of rigging elections and banning communist and radical nationalist parties, and there were occasional military interventions, parliaments played a significant political role from 1946–54 and 1961–3 in Syria, 1932–58 in Iraq, 1936–52 in Egypt and 1946–75 in Lebanon' (Pool, 1994, p.206). In addition, in both republican Turkey and monarchical (and post-revolutionary) Iran, assemblies have existed throughout the post-war period, notwithstanding periodic military intervention (Turkey) and monarchical and clerical rule (Iran). Similarly, monarchical Jordan and Morocco have some limited experience of assemblies and elections.

The original experience of partial democracy in the Middle East was based on a very limited constituency of support. In those countries (Egypt, Iraq and Syria) where the post-independence state was combined with strong urban-based, land-owning and merchant classes, and often combined with the continuing indirect influence from the colonial powers, political and economic power was largely in the hands of 'notables'. These 'notables' who were urban-based, absentee landlords, with links to tribal chiefs and merchants, dominated political life and conducted a politics of clientelism in which patrons (notables) operated in the state in order to deliver benefits to themselves and their clients (tribes, peasants, urban workers). In return, clients performed labour services and provided political support for their patrons. This meant that where elected assemblies existed they were dominated by notables or their representatives, and that executive power, which in any case was nowhere effectively answerable to a legislature, also embodied notable power. Notable dominance, electoral malpractice and a population that was largely rural and illiterate made the organization of liberal democratic politics exceptionally difficult (Owen, 1993). Before the Second World War the typical pattern was a combination of male suffrage and two-stage elections which provided ample scope for notable manipulation. After the war, however, there were some significant extensions of liberal democratic practice, encompassing, for example, female suffrage, the abolition of special privileges for minorities and the introduction of secret ballots. Despite these advances, organized political activity remained limited. Party organization was minimal: parties existed largely only at election time, they were urban based, and they had little internal organization or democracy.

Even in those countries where notable dominance was weaker or absent, and which escaped European colonial control, as in Turkey and Iran, strong nationalist leaders, basing themselves on the control of the armed forces, quickly came to dominate the political scene in a more or less authoritarian manner. Turkey and Iran were thus pushed into modernization by powerful autocratic military leaders, Kemal Ataturk and Reza Shah, respectively. Jordan pursued a precarious balancing act as the monarchy based its power on the armed forces with external backing and internal support from tribal groupings. In Lebanon a unique consociational constitutional settlement based on religious–confessional representation was developed, but the impact of consociational forms of representation was limited by notable agreement across the religious communities to limit the power and role of the state. (Lebanese consociationalism involved the allocation of seats to the legislature as well as the distribution of political office on the basis of quotas for the main religious communities.) And in the Arabian peninsula, in Saudi Arabia and the Gulf States, the presence of oil wealth and external support allowed the new rulers to buy off the power and influence of local merchants and to offer welfare without representation.

Thus such trappings of liberal democratic practice as existed either reflected notable dominance of the political scene, or were limited by monarchical rule or confessional differences, or blunted by oil wealth. In all cases, democratic practices were poorly institutionalized in the political system. In Egypt, Iraq and Syria, it was not long before the emergence of new middle strata, especially as organized and represented in the armed forces, began to contest their relative exclusion from the political system. Notable rule was also seen as weak in the face of the still potent remnants of European imperial power and control over many economic and strategic assets. Nationalist forces concerned with independent programmes of state-led development came to the fore, sweeping notable power away through programmes of land reform, military control of the state, the replacement of parliamentary politics by a mixture of populist mobilization and corporatist forms, and the elaboration of bureaucratic mechanisms of control orchestrated from above by the state–party apparatus. In these circumstances, the overriding priorities of the new states were the consolidation of their rule over and against alternative sites of authority and the mobilization of economic resources for projects of national development. Where it continued to exist, party organization was subordinated to these twin demands and thus remained under control of the army and the state. Electoral politics were perceived and portrayed as nationally divisive, contributing to a weakening both of the development effort and of resistance to the legacies of imperialism.

In these circumstances, populist-inclusive ideologies of nation-building overseen by a benign but authoritarian leadership won considerable support. To this extent, the post-independence course of Egypt, Iraq and Syria can be seen as following that taken by Turkey and Iran in the inter-war years. (For more on populism see Chapter 6.) In all of these cases, the attitude to liberal or representative democracy was well expressed by the greatest of the Arab nationalist leaders, the ruler of Egypt after the 1952 revolution, Gamal Abdel Nasser:

> Can I ask you a question: what is democracy? We were supposed to have a democratic system during the period 1923 to 1953. But what good was this democracy to our people? I will tell you. Landowners and Pashas ruled our people. They used this kind of a democracy as an easy tool for the benefits of the feudal system. You have seen the feudalists gathering the peasants together and driving them to the polling booths. There the peasants would cast their votes according to the instructions of their masters. ... I want to liberate the peasants and the workers, both socially and economically, so that they can say 'yes'. I want the peasants and the workers to be able to say 'yes' and 'no' without this in any way affecting their livelihood and their daily bread. This in my view is the basis of freedom and democracy.

> (President Nasser of Egypt, interview with an Indian newspaper editor, March 1957, quoted in Owen, 1993, p.21)

In the 1950s and 1960s nationalist mobilization embodying much of the thinking outlined by Nasser swept across the Middle East, ending or restricting electoral and competitive democracy wherever it existed. The formal institutions remained in place in Lebanon, parts of the Gulf and Jordan, as also in Turkey and Iran. But in all of these cases the scope of electoral politics was severely circumscribed by state- and army-imposed restrictions. In Egypt, Iraq and Syria openly authoritarian regimes replaced the partial democracies.

In the 1970s and 1980s, however, a number of previously authoritarian regimes undertook experiments in political and economic liberalization. In Egypt, President Sadat introduced a degree of multi-party elections, allowed a freer press to develop and recognized a real measure of independence for the judiciary. Though an emergency law remains in place, as do formal electoral restrictions and widespread informal improprieties (including arbitrary detention and torture), these limited openings have been maintained by President Mubarak, notwithstanding militant Islamic opposition to the state. In the late 1980s and early 1990s, King Hussain of Jordan started a programme of political liberalization based on new elections and the negotiation of a National Pact. Following unification in 1990, Yemen had elections but the resulting government split and again civil war was the result. In Iraq there had been no political liberalization, and in Syria very little by the mid 1990s. The Gulf States and Saudi Arabia saw pressures for more accountability in the 1990s and a very limited form of accountability was reintroduced into Kuwait after the Gulf War. Turkey returned to a restricted form of liberal democracy after the 1980 military coup and even post-revolutionary Iran conducted elections, though the latter were strictly controlled and of limited effect. Finally, in Lebanon the consociational system collapsed into civil war in 1975/76 under pressures from an urbanizing and modernizing society and the influx of Palestinians from the Arab–Israeli dispute. In the 1990s, order was only restored in exchange for *de facto* Syrian and Israeli influence.

It is difficult to generalize about the reasons for these moves towards greater liberal democracy, let alone to account for the relative successes and failures. But a number of analysts have pointed to the connections between the need for economic liberalization, often in response to large public debts, especially owed to foreign creditors, and the advent of political liberalization (Harik and Sullivan, 1992; Niblock and Murphy, 1993; Owen, 1993; Pool, 1994). From the point of view of incumbent rulers, it might seem that expanding the scope for political participation would enhance the legitimacy of the regime as well as facilitate the devolution of responsibility for difficult policy choices to groups and forces outside the state. Thus limited steps towards liberal democracy might be attractive for authoritarian rulers (see Chapter 14, Section 14.4 for further discussion). Demonstration effects from democratization elsewhere in the international system and the collapse of the party–state model of command socialism in the Eastern bloc no doubt added to these economic pressures. More generally, there is a widespread sense that the nationalist–authoritarian model of development has run its course and is no longer able to offer convincing solutions to the economic, social and political problems that the countries of the Middle East face: 'the scope of failure is so broad that few rulers today have pockets deep enough or jails large enough to cope with the problem in traditional ways' (Norton, 1993, p.206).

Against this association of economic and political liberalization, some analysts have argued that authoritarian regimes may prove effective economic liberalizers without relaxing political control and that political liberalization may make economic reform harder to pursue, since it allows the mobilization of opposition to painful reforms. Equally, some have suggested that the lessons of the collapse of communism in the Eastern bloc for authoritarian leaders is that economic reform must be accomplished *prior to* political liberalization, otherwise the state risks a serious dissolution of its authority. President Assad's reforms in Syria in the late 1980s and early 1990s are sometimes presented in this light (Heydemann, 1993), as are some of President Mubarak's pronouncements in Egypt.

Now, if we set this post-war record – from notable rule legitimated by restricted democracy, through the nationalist–authoritarian phase, to limited political liberalization – in a comparative context, then the Middle East has many similarities with the rest of the developing world. Not only were there some democratic beginnings in the Middle East after independence, but also the ending of these experiments in the authoritarian–nationalist politics of the 1950s–1970s had much in common with developments in Asia, Africa and Latin America. Across much of the developing world, authoritarian rule of one kind or another rapidly became the norm after independence. As Waterbury (1994, p.25) reminds us: 'Until the 1980s, the Middle East was not exceptional'. Indeed, one might press the case a little further. Given the renewal of a limited democratic politics in Egypt under Presidents Sadat and Mubarak and the more recent experience of elections in Jordan and the unified Yemen, as well as the continuing presence of a qualified electoral democracy in Turkey, elections in post-revolutionary Iran and the development of consultative councils in the Gulf and Saudi Arabia, the alleged exceptionalism of the Middle East may better be understood as one of degree rather than as one of kind. Perhaps the process of democratization is just slower and more uneven in the Middle East than elsewhere. After all, feeble beginnings, stalled transitions to democracy and regressions to authoritarian rule are not unique to the Middle East, and we must therefore beware of allowing a focus on relatively short periods of history to direct us into misleading comparative generalizations. Augustus Richard Norton sums up this view well when he suggests that: 'The evidence is still mixed, but there is sufficient evidence to suggest that the time has come to stop talking about Middle Eastern exceptionalism when we discuss global trends' (Norton, 1993, p.216).

----------------------------- *Summary of Section 13.2* -----------------------------

- The conventional view is both that democracy and democratization are strangers to the Middle East.

- The limited post-independence experiments with democratic politics did not survive the rise of nationalist forces seeking modernization and independence, or were thwarted by monarchical rule and oil wealth.

- Beginning in the 1970s, and especially in the 1980s and 1990s, there were renewed pressures for democratization.

- Seen in comparative perspective, the Middle East may be only exceptional in the timing and fragility of its democratization, rather than constituting a wholesale departure from patterns found elsewhere.

13.3 Explaining the absence of liberal democracy

In order to begin to make sense of the question as to whether or not the Middle East constitutes an exception to global trends towards liberal democracy, we now turn to an examination of some different theories of democracy in the region. Broadly speaking, most attempts to explain the pattern of (democratic) politics in the Middle East fall into one of three schools depending on whether they give primary emphasis to the presence or absence of relevant socio-economic preconditions, to questions of political culture, or to the influence of certain international factors. Questions of socio-economic preconditions and political culture are the home ground of modernization theory. We will see that after the failure of a simple application of modernization theory based on the socio-economic requisites of liberal democracy, most of these accounts of Middle East politics have seen the primary analytical task as explaining its exceptional character as viewed in comparative perspective. In particular, it has been argued that, given its level of socio-economic development, the Middle East has been peculiarly resistant to patterns of democratization and has provided a less than fertile soil for democracy. The answer to this conundrum is usually sought in the region's political culture. Let us begin then with the socio-economic version of modernization theory.

In the general comparative literature on democratization a number of developments associated with the modernization of society have been seen as conducive to the establishment and maintenance of liberal democratic politics. Typical phenomena include economic growth and rising incomes, the decline of agriculture and the rise of industry, an increasingly urbanized population, improved levels of literacy and education, and high levels of social mobility. The advance of these indicators is held to promote liberal democracy. Based on an empirical study of attitudes and beliefs, Daniel Lerner applied these arguments directly to the Middle East, asserting that: 'the Western model of modernization exhibits certain components and sequences whose relevance is global. Everywhere ... increasing urbanization has tended to raise literacy; rising literacy has tended to increase media exposure; increasing media exposure has "gone with" wider economic participation ... and political participation' (Lerner, 1958, p.45). (See Chapters 1, 3 and 6 for further discussion of modernization theories.)

While few would dispute that other things being equal indicators of socio-economic modernization are relevant for understanding the propensity to liberal democracy, there are (admittedly a few) significant examples of democracies that do not score well on indicators of modernization and there are many more authoritarian states that have high levels of modernization. In the case of the Middle East, Turkey moved towards a fairly high degree of democratic politics before reaching the level of modernization many had thought necessary. Turkish democracy was in *advance* of Turkey's level of modernization, while others (especially the oil-rich Gulf States and Saudi Arabia) have long passed the appropriate levels without any significant democratization. (Turkey, as Chapter 1 indicates, provided one of Rustow's examples for the focus on elite-led transitions to democracy.) Clearly, then, there is no simple relationship between socio-economic modernization and the development of liberal democracy in the Middle East.

Notwithstanding these difficulties, it has often been argued that the modernization of Turkey does basically fit the model. To be sure, the origins of Turkish democracy lay in a period (1945–50) when the country was still largely agrarian, rural and illiterate and lacking in economic development, and its subsequent history has been plagued by military intervention (in 1960, 1971 and 1980), but progress in raising living standards, improving literacy and education, and fostering social mobility have been claimed as the reasons for Turkey's relative success with liberal democratic politics (Rustow, 1988). Other observers, noting the continued restrictions placed on party formation, the role of the military in national politics (including emergency rule in the Kurdish south-east of the country), the outstanding issue of the place of Islam in the state and long-standing economic problems, are less confident (Kedourie, 1992).

The difficulties in assessing these competing claims are several. In the first instance, the causal mechanisms held to be at work are often obscure. It is one thing to note a statistical correlation between levels of development and the propensity to stable democratic rule, but it is another to explain this connection. Second, as noted above, the 'leads' and 'lags' in the process seem to make it very difficult to establish robust correlations in any case. Without a clearer specification of the actual patterns of influence which translate socio-economic modernization into political democracy, the explanatory power of this perspective is difficult to assess. In the general literature, two kinds of causal mechanism have been put forward as plausible candidates: first, economic growth may reduce inequalities of wealth and power as well as leading to a more differentiated and complex society, thereby expanding the social basis for political participation as well as the resources of non-state actors; and second, a more educated and socially mobile population may be less susceptible to traditional, paternalistic forms of legitimation and better able to hold political leaders to account for their actions. Both of these mechanisms seem to have been at work in the Turkish case, and these general processes are arguably having a more diffuse effect across the region as a whole.

For the Middle East, however, the problem remains that the indicators of socio-economic development have been ascending 'for some time ... Yet, to

A supporter of Turkey's Islamist Welfare Party prays for his party's success during a campaign rally for nation-wide elections in December 1995

date, this ... has had no unambiguous "democratic pay-off"' (Waterbury, 1994, p.24). This state of affairs might be interpreted in several different ways. We might conclude that Turkey's early shift to a partial democracy, combined with the absence of liberal democracy in such 'developed' countries as Saudi Arabia, shows that modernization theories based on socio-economic prerequisites are false. Alternatively, we might see Turkish democracy as a confirmation of the theory and seek to retain the connection between socio-economic modernization and the advance of political democracy. We might then argue that other factors, not included in the theory, render the Middle East exceptional in relation to the rest of the developing world. (In this latter case, Turkey constitutes an exception in relation to the rest of the Middle East, but not in comparison with other parts of the Third World.)

It is in this context of a deficit of democracy as predicted by the socio-economic factors that the question of political culture has achieved its particular salience in writings on the Middle East. Positing the existence of an intransigent and anti-democratic political culture becomes the means by which the lag between the advancing socio-economic indicators and the slow and uneven arrival of liberal democracy is explained. And the issue of political culture has been posed very largely in relation to the region's religious culture and institutions, in terms of the vexed question of Islam and democracy. (You will find an extended discussion of this question in the next chapter but it is necessary to summarize some of the main arguments here.) Many analysts have argued that as a system of belief Islam is based on a revealed text embodying quasi-legal ordinances, and that, as such, it is incompatible with democratic politics. Though complex, the reasons for this are essentially twofold: on the one hand, it is argued that Islam rejects the idea of the nation-state and with this the modern, secular conceptions of nationalism (Vatikiotis, 1987); at the same time, it is claimed that Islam neither recognizes a separation of temporal and spiritual power and authority nor permits intermediate institutions between the religious-political leader and the individual believer (Kedourie, 1992). In Islamic societies, therefore, it is impossible to generate legitimacy either for the existence of a national state or for the conduct of organized democratic politics within it. Evidence for these claims is to be found both in the problematic fortunes of liberal democratic politics in countries where a majority of the population are Muslim and in the practices of so called Islamic governments in, for example, Iran.

Other analysts have questioned this pessimistic view of the relation (or rather lack of it) between Islam and democracy. To begin with, it has been pointed out that Islamic political thought and religious teaching have in fact taken a wide variety of forms depending on the social and historical context (Ayubi, 1991; Esposito, 1991). John Esposito, for example, has shown that there is a great diversity of positions among groups defining their politics in Islamic terms and that, in practice and in some instances, there has been a significant accommodation to the notion of the nation-state and even to some aspects of liberal democratic government. Another set of objections to the strong thesis that Islam and democracy are incompatible draws on the empirical record of democracy in Turkey, as well as the more limited experiences of democratic politics elsewhere in the Islamic world. Going even further, still others have argued that in some respects Islam is ideally suited as a belief system for modern industrial societies. Most notably, Ernest Gellner has argued that 'by various obvious criteria – universalism, scripturalism, spiritual egalitarianism, the extension of full participation in the sacred community not to one, or some, but to *all*, and the rational systematisation of social life – Islam is, of the three great Western monotheisms, the one closest to modernity' (Gellner, 1981, p.7). And finally, the very idea that religious belief can operate as an insuperable obstacle to a particular kind of politics, democracy, has been challenged on the grounds that all religions require *interpretation* to give them meaning in specific contexts. In this sense, religious belief is socially and politically *contingent*, it does not and cannot determine or prescribe a particular kind of politics (Zubaida, 1988).

The issue of Islam has also been discussed in relation to questions of patriarchy and the entry of women into the political system. Leila Ahmed's brilliant study of *Women and Gender in Islam* argues that: 'In establishment Islamic thought, women, like minorities, are defined as different from and, in their legal rights, lesser than, Muslim men. Unlike non-Muslim men, who might join the master-class by converting, women's differentness and inferiority within this system are immutable' (Ahmed, 1992, p.7). Such a posture is scarcely conducive to political equality. However, Ahmed also notes that 'Islam's ethical vision ... is stubbornly egalitarian, including with respect to the sexes' (ibid., p.63). This ethical vision is clearly in some tension with, indeed is subversive of, the institutionalized form of Islam. Whereas institutional Islam has been conservative and patriarchal seeking to restrict women's access to civil and political rights, its ethical vision has provided a basis for claims for equal treatment. And, in fact, where civil and political rights have been secured in the Middle East, women have often achieved a significant degree of formal equality.

In assessing these debates we would perhaps do well to remind ourselves that in the 1950s and 1960s the traditional Catholic culture of Spain was held to account for the persistence of dictatorship under General Franco. Scarcely a generation later these arguments seem a poor guide to reality. The point here is both empirical and theoretical. Empirically speaking, it is just a fact that cultures, even religious cultures, can and do change over time. The pattern of institutionalization of religion is not given by the character of belief, let alone by words in a book (the Bible or the Koran). Theoretically, the point is to remember that cultures are always interpreted and understood by particular groups, in particular contexts, and with particular interests. That is to say, the institutionalization of religious belief is interest- and context-dependent. If Islamic beliefs as understood by specific communities in particular contexts are anti-democratic (or patriarchal) in theory and practice, then this in itself is in need of explanation – it does not constitute evidence for the timeless incompatibility of Islam and democracy.

Moving beyond modernization theories on to the terrain of structural theories, a quite different starting point from both of the above accounts – focusing respectively on socio-economic prerequisites and political culture – is adopted by analysts who focus on the international and military obstacles to democracy in the Middle East. Here the concern is with the place of Middle East states within the international system, with the pressures coming from the world economy and the nation-states system. Once again, however, the starting point is often taken to be that the socio-economic requisites approach to explaining liberal democracy is largely sound, but that it does not apply to the Middle East for other (international and military) reasons. These arguments focus on the role of oil, the implications of the Arab–Israeli dispute and the entanglement of the region in superpower military rivalry.

In the first instance, many Middle East states are said to be 'rentier' states, deriving a large part of their national income, state revenue and foreign exchange from sales of oil on the international market. In addition, the geopolitical importance of the Middle East (itself largely a reflection of the region's huge oil reserves) has brought with it large amounts of economic and military aid from the superpowers. This state of affairs, where much of the income available to the state is not generated by the productive activity of the population, indeed is not in any real sense produced within the territory of the state, is said to imply very different patterns of representation and legitimation to those cases where the state must tax the productive activities of its citizens in order to obtain revenue. If there can be 'no taxation without representation', then perhaps states which do not need to tax do not need to develop representative institutions.

A second set of international determinants which have been seen as hostile to the development of liberal democracy in the Middle East stem from the Arab–Israeli conflict and the more general impact of superpower competition in the region during the Cold War. The Arab–Israeli conflict, and with it the support of the USA for Israel and of the former Soviet Union for the radical Arab powers, contributed to a high level of military competition in the Middle East. In turn, this militarization of Middle East politics had the effect both of strengthening the state in relation to other groups in society and of reinforcing the power of the military in the institutions of the state. This prominent role for the military in Middle East politics has blocked pressures for more democratic political systems.

Finally, the effects of the region's oil and the Arab–Israeli dispute have been further augmented by the specific interests of the superpowers: on the one hand, the Soviet Union encouraged its allies to adopt the single party, command economy model of the communist world; and on the other, the USA opposed reformist and nationalist movements for fear of compromising the West's influence and access to oil on favourable terms. The overall result has been a powerful set of international pressures reinforcing authoritarian rule.

At first glance, empirical support for these observations is easy to find. Elizabeth Picard has pointed out that 'military intervention in politics had become commonplace in many Arab states, actually with a much higher frequency than in most Third World countries during the 1950s and 1960s' (Picard, 1990, p.190). In Turkey also the military played an important role in national politics, as did the Shah's coercive forces in Iran. From the early 1970s through to the mid 1990s, the share of military expenditure in national income was nearly twice as high in the Middle East as the next most militarized region (the former Warsaw Pact) and over three times the world average.

However, at the same time, the proportion of states under military control in the Middle East was on a par with Latin America (just below the developing world average), and as Chapter 11, Section 11.3 shows, much less than in South Asia, the Far East and Africa (Tilly, 1990). Indeed, prior to the Iran–Iraq War of 1980–88 and the Gulf War (1990–91) the Middle East was a safer place in which to live than much of Africa. The main source of conflict was within states, concerned with the pacification and repression of domestic populations. Seen in a comparative perspective, then, what differentiates the Middle East is not the scope of military rule, nor even the scale of conflict, but the quantity of resources devoted to the military. But the explanation of this is obvious: the enormous incomes derived from oil after the major price increases in the 1970s. Thus it is no accident that the biggest military spenders have been major oil producers, Iran, Iraq and Saudi Arabia, not the so called frontline states in the Arab–Israeli conflict, Egypt, Jordan and Syria.

Thus, we might conclude that access to oil rents mitigates the pressure to develop representative institutions; that the Arab–Israeli dispute, together with the regional involvement of the superpowers, has contributed to the militarization of the Middle East and its politics; and that the scale of resources devoted to military ends is accounted for by oil wealth; but that the role of the military in Middle East politics is not qualitatively greater than elsewhere in the developing world, even though the level of military expenditure is quantitatively higher. This is certainly not to argue that international causes have not proved inimical to democratic advance in the Middle East, clearly they have, but simply to put this observation into context by reference to the more general phenomenon of military rule in developing countries.

The burden of my argument so far, then, is that attempts to account for the deficit of liberal democracy in the Middle East, as highlighted by the predictions of socio-economic modernization theory, either in terms of political culture or by reference to international factors, are not on the whole successful. In the case of political culture, such arguments underestimate the fluidity of culture. And in the case of more structural attention to international factors, such attempts are only partly successful because they fail to take sufficient notice of the fact that the features and processes adduced to explain the exceptional character of the region are also present elsewhere in the developing world. It is therefore difficult to argue that these features and processes can account for the exceptional nature of democracy in the Middle East. If this is so, then there are two possible ways in which we might proceed. We can retain a general endorsement of modernization theory as socio-economic requisites and look to other factors for the causes of the lack of democracy in the Middle East, trying to identify some other features which are specific to the region and which are not shared by the rest of the developing world. Alternatively, we could conclude that the problem lies in modernization theory itself. If the modernization perspective is not well founded, then the disparity between levels of socio-economic modernization and the degree of political democracy may tell us more about the deficient nature of the theory than about the resistance of the Middle East to democracy.

------------------ *Summary of Section 13.3* ------------------

- The Middle East can either be seen as falsifying modernization theory (Turkey becoming democratic too early, Saudi Arabia too late) or as corroborating it (modernization has consolidated Turkish democracy, whatever its origins), with the rest of the region then seen as exceptional.

- If Turkey is taken as a confirmation of the modernization approach, then other factors not included in the theory must be called upon to account for the failure of the approach elsewhere in the region. Other factors are the region's dominant religion, Islam, and the place of the Middle East in the international system, especially the role of oil, the Arab–Israeli conflict and the superpower rivalry.

- If modernization theory is rejected, then we need to see if there is another approach which can explain the relative absence of democracy and democratization in the region, without invoking the existence of factors that somehow operate in the Middle East but not elsewhere in the developing world.

13.4   Structural and historical approaches

Is there, then, an approach which can account for the comparative absence of democratization and liberal democracy in the Middle East, or at least its late and hesitant development, without arguing that different factors are at work in the region as compared with the rest of the Third World? Let us see if structural theories can meet these demands. A number of theorists have indeed contested the alleged peculiarities of the Middle East (e.g. Halliday and Alavi, 1988; Owen, 1992; Zubaida, 1988). These analysts have argued that politics in the Middle East, including the absence or presence of liberal democracy, can best be approached as particular examples of general political processes common to the developing world. The Middle East is different, but so are all regions of the developing world. For example, the authoritarian-nationalist regimes of the Middle East are fairly easily assimilated into more general patterns of development. Roger Owen has presented this case with some force, arguing that since nationalist opposition to colonial powers did not guarantee domestic legitimacy, and since the authority of the post-independence states was not assured at the outset, it is only natural that:

> the difficulties experienced in the first post-independent decades do not seem markedly different from those to be observed elsewhere in the Third World ... political instability was overcome largely as a result of the general process of the expansion of the power of the central bureaucracy and of the security forces

> (Owen, 1992, p.26)

Within the context given by this general expansion and centralization of the state institutions, socio-economic development was in many cases frustrated by the power of the urban, notable classes, and thus opposition forces increasingly turned towards the military. During the subsequent period, the post-independence states of urban-based, land-owning classes were overthrown by military-backed coups or revolutions and replaced with new authoritarian polities.

I will argue that this kind of approach can be extended to the other patterns of political development in the Middle East. (You should look again at Table 13.1 at the start of this chapter before reading any further.) Also, these general processes at work in the political development of the region, I will suggest, can best be understood by reference to structural theories. These theories focus on historical change, consider the relations among the major social classes and their relations to the state, as well as looking at the international pressures on the state, in order to assess the forces ranged in favour of and against democratization and to explain the scope for political pluralism in relation to the basic socio-economic processes of development. In explanatory terms, we will see that structural approaches to the question of democracy in the Middle East enable us to do two things. In the first place, structural and historical approaches allow us to explain the relative absence of liberal democracy in the Middle East, and the tentative nature of its democratization, without invoking factors that are peculiar to the region such as Islamic culture or the Arab–Israeli dispute (though, of course, even Islamic culture is not unique to the Middle East). Second, structural factors also give us the means of accounting for the differences of democratic performance within the Middle East.

Indeed, once the Middle East is placed in the context of the patterns of state formation and social development after independence, it seems natural to apply structural theories to the problems of democratization and democracy. This is the approach adopted by Haim Gerber in his study of *The Social Origins of the Modern Middle East* (1987). The title of this work is a deliberate echo of Barrington Moore's seminal work on the *Social Origins of Dictatorship and Democracy* (1966) and Gerber's work is an attempt to apply the same approach to the modern Middle East. Gerber argues that the pattern of democratic politics in, say, Turkey and Lebanon, on the one hand, compared with that of authoritarian rule in, say, Egypt, Iraq and Syria, on the other, is accounted for by the absence of a large-scale landed class in Turkey and Lebanon at the time of the formation of the modern, independent state and its presence in Egypt, Iraq and Syria. Following Barrington Moore, Gerber maintains that it is the need for a repressive and authoritarian state by landowners dependent on large-scale peasant labour that accounts for the distribution of dictatorship across the region.

Not only did Turkey and Lebanon enter the modern period without large-scale landlords dependent on peasant labour, but by the same token they also avoided the anti-landlord revolutions conducted by military-led, nationalist forces that occurred in Egypt, Iraq and Syria. Of course, there were mobilizations for national independence in the former cases, signified by the Kemalist movement in Republican Turkey in the 1920s and the Lebanese National Pact of 1943, but these did not involve the removal of an existing dominant economic class and its replacement by the state. Thus despite Turkey's adoption of state-led policies of import-substitution and indus-trialization in the inter-war years, the role of the state in the economy was much greater in the cases of Egypt, Iraq and Syria. In addition, the more radical anti-landlord nature of political mobilization in these latter cases made the nationalist leaders there more sympathetic to Soviet models of planned development. For very different reasons the state also played a central role in economic development in Iran, Saudi Arabia and the Gulf States: economic development was based very largely on oil incomes accruing to rentier states.

These considerations suggest the need for a modification or an addition to Gerber's account, for the issue is not simply whether a landed class is present or absent. Just as Moore neglected to analyse the actual route taken to liberal democracy and the role played by the modern social classes of industrial capitalism in the process, so Gerber similarly fails to consider the form of the post-independence state and the role of the bourgeoisie and the working class in his case studies. This neglect has the effect of antedating the origins of democracy, as if a certain kind of agrarian class structure in the past could by itself prescribe future democratic rule, and of ignoring the actual course of the conflicts and struggles which helped to establish and consolidate democratic procedures. Although it does not consider the Middle East as such, the comparative study of *Capitalist Development and Democracy* by Dietrich Rueschemeyer *et al.* sets out these points with particular force:

> [There is] a first minimal condition of democracy: democracy is possible only if there exists a fairly strong institutional separation ... of the realm of politics from the overall system of inequality in society ... We retain ... in our theoretical framework Moore's emphasis on agrarian class relations and on landlord–bourgeoisie–state coalitions; but we combine this emphasis with an equally strong focus on the role of the subordinate classes in the new capitalist order. ... Capitalist development is associated with the rise of democracy primarily because of two structural effects: it strengthens the working class as well as other subordinate classes, and it weakens large landowners
>
> (Rueschemeyer *et al.*, 1992, pp.41, 58)

If we apply these considerations to the Middle East, then a rather more complex picture emerges than that drawn by Gerber (Bromley, 1994). In the Turkish and, especially, the Lebanese cases, the absence of a large landed class was complemented by a pattern of state formation in which the state did not dominate economic development. Equally, in both cases the absence of radical anti-landlord mobilization meant that there was little or no ideological support for Soviet-type models of planned socio-economic development. And finally, neither Turkey nor Lebanon had oil reserves and they therefore avoided the tendency of rentier states towards underdeveloped representative institutions. The result was that there was a significant degree of separation between the political system and the control of economic resources and thus some social space for political and ideological mobilization independently of the state. A degree of democratic politics proved possible under these circumstances.

In the cases of Egypt, Iraq and Syria, powerful anti-landlord revolutions placed the state centre stage in the subsequent projects of economic development. At the same time, the more radical political mobilization involved against landlord and foreign interests led to a much tighter control over the political system by the revolutionary leadership, including the adoption of significant elements of the Soviet model. Moreover, Soviet influence in these countries gave further support to this state-led, authoritarian model of development. Directly in the Iraqi case and indirectly in the cases of Egypt and Syria oil rents provided a significant source of state revenues. For these reasons, therefore, the separation of economic resources from the control of the state has been very limited and the corresponding social space for independent organization and contestation has been similarly restricted. Movement towards the Turkish pattern has been most pronounced in Egypt and least successful in Iraq, but in all cases the state-elite maintains a strong hold over the political system.

Finally, in Iran, Saudi Arabia and the Gulf States, while there were no landed, notable classes to overthrow, and hence no nationalist revolutions during the 1950s and 1960s, the presence of the state in the economy has been very significant due to the oil-based character of economic development. These states come closer to the model of rentier states than any others in the Middle East or elsewhere, and the scope for liberal democratic politics is accordingly limited. In Iran a longer history of independence and development partly mitigated the impact of the rentier state and some groups in society (particularly merchants and the clergy) were able to maintain a degree of independence from the state, though this was never translated into democratic arrangements, but in the Gulf States and Saudi Arabia the scope for organizational freedom of manoeuvre has been minimal. In all these cases (at least prior to the Iranian revolution in 1979), the existing patterns of authoritarian rule were supported by the West, especially the USA, in order to safeguard oil and other strategic interests.

To return to the comparison offered by Gerber, what distinguishes the Turkish case is not simply the class structure of its agrarian origins, though this was clearly important, but also the degree of political independence achieved by the bourgeoisie and the working class. By contrast, in both Egypt and Iraq, for example, the state sector remains the dominant player in the economy, thereby blocking the development of relatively independent organizations (e.g. chambers of commerce, employers' federations, trade unions) outside the state. In part this is a result of the greater degree of social transformation involved in the Egyptian and Iraqi revolutions as compared with the Kemalist coup in Turkey, but it is also due to the anti-imperialist character of these revolutions, dictated by the significant foreign penetration of the economies and polities of Egypt and Iraq, and the subsequent influence of the Soviet model in these cases. And in the Iraqi case, there is also 'the important additional fact that the country is a major oil producer.

In sum, in those instances where a degree of capitalist development has occurred outside the direct control of the state and has facilitated the beginnings of independent organization by the bourgeoisie and the working class, in short where a civil society has begun to develop, some liberalization and controlled experiments in popular participation have emerged – Turkey most obviously, to a more limited extent Egypt and even Iran. By contrast, where the state has maintained control and has blocked the organization of independent classes and forces, where there has been no opportunity for the emergence of civil society, then the scope for popular initiative has been more limited – the limit cases being Iraq and Saudi Arabia.

What about the position of women in relation to civil and political rights in those Middle East countries that have established a degree of constitutional and representative government? As noted in Section 13.3, formal civil and political equality with men, as well as access to education, has often been won by Middle East women. Indeed, it is sometimes suggested that Islam provides a more secure basis for political equality than much of the Christian West, since Islamic law allows women to own property in their own right. However, women's access to property was largely through inheritance and gift and they were essentially excluded from areas of the economy in which wealth might be productively acquired – unless they could buy themselves into these areas. Thus Ahmed concludes that: 'The number of women owning property substantial enough to render them financially independent of male relatives must always have been minute' (Ahmed, 1992, p.112). Moreover, Islamic family law, 'the cornerstone of the system of male privilege set up by establishment Islam ... is still preserved almost intact' (ibid., p.242). Thus the formal rights won by women in the Middle East have often been severely limited by a structure of patriarchal power based, not on formal exclusion from the 'public' sphere, but on legally sanctioned male control over the 'private' sphere. In this respect, then, as in many others, the history of democratization and democracy in the Middle East has much in common with the rest of the world.

―――――――――――――――― *Summary of Section 13.4* ――――――――――――――――

- I argued that a structural approach to the question of democracy in the Middle East focuses on the historical patterns of state and class formation.

- Substantively, I suggested that where the pattern of political and economic development allowed a degree of separation of the state and the economy, and with this the space for a degree of independent social organization in civil society, there was some scope for limited constitutional rule and democratic accountability.

- I also suggested that the structural approach not only explains the fortunes of democratization and democracy in the Middle East, but also its varied scope between different kinds of regime.

- The fact that women could own property in Islamic law has not made much difference to the restriction on their real civil and political equality, since legally sanctioned patriarchal structures of power persist in the 'private' sphere.

Conclusion

Explaining the pattern of democratization in the Middle East is a complex business. I have argued that a modernization approach based on the socio-economic requisites of liberal democracy is inadequate, and that attempts to remedy the predictive failure of this framework by reference to an anti-

democratic (Islamic) political culture fail to address the basic issues. A focus
on the international limits to democratization in the region is only partly
successful in explaining the gap between levels of socio-economic
development and actual democratization, since many such constraints exist
elsewhere in the developing world and hence cannot account for the
peculiarity of the Middle East. Given the problems with these popular
approaches, I turned to structural theory. One test of this latter approach is as
follows: if the above application of structural theory to the question of
democracy in the Middle East is cogent, then it should be able to clarify the
difficulties I encountered in applying the modernization approach and to
incorporate the valid insights of the focus on international constraints.

We saw in Section 13.3 that Turkey played a somewhat ambiguous role in
theories of democracy in the Middle East. For some the precocity of Turkish
democracy undermined the prerequisites approach, while for others the
subsequent modernization of Turkish society accounted for the consolidation of democratic rule. Equally, for many, Turkey appears to provide
evidence that Islam does not constitute a barrier to democracy, while others
point to the unresolved issues of secularization in contemporary Turkish
political affairs. I have argued in Section 13.4 that Turkey has moved further
towards consolidated constitutional and liberal representative government
than any other state in the Middle East not because of its *levels* of development
or its *culture*, but because its pattern of post-independence development has
facilitated a significant separation of the state from surplus extraction and
thereby allowed some organizational development of modern social classes.
Combined with the absence of a large landed class and the non-existence of
the rentier aspects of an oil state, this inheritance has created a relative
favourable condition for liberal democracy in Turkey. Finally, Turkey's pro-
Western international alignment (through NATO and, later, association with
the European Union) has strengthened democratic forces. Turkey is, then,
something of an exception, not because of its level of socio-economic
development or the character of its Islamic culture, but because of the
historical patterns involved in the development of the structure of the state
and social classes, together with its international position.

These points may be generalized, for we have also seen in Section 13.4
that other states in the region may be usefully compared with Turkey along
these dimensions of state and class formation, international position and the
role played by oil. In each case we saw that what mattered for the course of
democratization was not the level of development as such (nor the religious
culture, since all were Islamic), but rather the qualitative character of
development, in particular the degree of institutional separation of the state
from the economy and the scope for independent organization in civil
society. Where the pattern of state and class development, together with the
international alignment, facilitated such a separation and a space for actors
in civil society, then a degree of democratization was compatible with low
levels of development. Where such features were absent, or more
accurately, where the pattern of development pushed the state into a
major and central role in the economy, then there was little separation of
economic and political power, little scope for independent organization and
hence limited opportunities for democratization, even at high levels of

development. These considerations give rise to a complex picture which is difficult to summarize, but we can identify the following paired causal chains at work:

(a) Abundant oil
      → rentier state
      → underdeveloped
         representative institutions

(a*) No oil
      → state must raise resources
         internally
      → tendency to develop
         representative institutions

(b) Large-scale landed classes based
      on subordinated peasantry
      → strong impulse for nationalist
         revolutions with high social
         content
      → large role for state in
         development and consequent
         domination of political sphere

(b*) Small- and medium-scale landed
      classes
      → weak/medium impulse for
         nationalist revolution with
         limited social content
      → limited role for state in
         development and consequent
         domination of the political
         sphere

(c) Imperialist influence
      → anti-imperialist (and often
         Soviet support)
      → strong role for state in
         economic and political
         development

(c*) Weak foreign influence
      → nationalist independence
         more pro-Western
      → small impetus for state
         involvement in economic and
         political development

(d) Strong role for state in economic
      development
      → limited separation of
         economic and political power
      → economic dominance requires
         control of the state
      → limited opportunity for
         democratization

(d*) Limited role for state in economic
      development
      → relative separation of
         economic and political power
      → economic dominance does
         not depend on direct political
         control of state
      → possible space for
         democratization

(e) Strong role for state in economic
      and political development
      → limited scope for civil society
      → actors favouring democracy
         cannot organize

(e*) Limited role for state in economic
      and political development
      → significant scope for civil
         society
      → actors favouring democracy
         can organize

My argument has been that a combination of (a) + (b) + (c) will tend to produce (d) and (e), and that, by contrast (a*) + (b*) + (c*) will result in (d*) and (e*). Thus I might crudely summarize the patterns outlined above by saying that there are two limiting cases, with Iraq and Turkey as exemplars: Iraq = (a), (b), (c), (d), (e); and Turkey = (a*), (b*), (c*), (d*), (e*); many other combinations are possible, with more varied implications for the fortunes of democracy. (You might try to rank the other countries in the light of the discussion in Section 13.4 and compare the results.) It is these kinds of causal chains and their interactions which are highlighted by structural theories and I have argued that they are the key to understanding the patterns of democratization in the Middle East. On balance, then, I conclude that structural approaches, focusing on state and class formation, international pressures and the balance of social forces, seem to provide the best explanation of the patterns I have described.

References

Ahmed, L. (1992) *Women and Gender in Islam*, New Haven, Yale University Press.

Ayubi, N. (1991) *Political Islam*, London, Routledge.

Bromley, S. (1994) *Rethinking Middle East Politics*, Cambridge, Polity Press.

Esposito, J. (1991) *Islam and Politics*, Syracuse, Syracuse University Press.

Gellner, E. (1981) *Muslim Society*, Cambridge, Cambridge University Press.

Gerber, H. (1987) *The Social Origins of the Modern Middle East*, Boulder, Lynne Rienner.

Goldberg, E., Kasaba, R. and Migdal, J. (eds) (1993) *Rules and Rights in the Middle East*, Seattle, University of Washington Press.

Halliday, F. and Alavi, H. (eds) (1988) *State and Ideology in the Middle East and Pakistan*, London, Macmillan.

Harik, I. and Sullivan, D. (eds) (1992) *Privatization and Liberalization in the Middle East*, Bloomington, Indiana University Press.

Heydemann, S. (1993) 'Taxation without representation: authoritarianism and economic liberalization in Syria' in Goldberg, E. *et al.* (eds).

Kedourie, E. (1992) *Politics in the Middle East*, Oxford, Oxford University Press.

Lerner, D. (1958) *The Passing of Traditional Society*, New York, Free Press.

Moore, B. (1966) *Social Origins of Dictatorship and Democracy: Lord and Peasant in the Making of the Modern World*, Boston, Beacon Press.

Niblock, T. and Murphy, E. (eds) (1993) *Economic and Political Liberalization in the Middle East*, London, British Academic Press.

Norton, A. (1993) 'The future of civil society in the Middle East', *The Middle East Journal*, vol.47, no.2.

Owen, R. (1992) *State, Power and Politics in the Making of the Modern Middle East*, London, Routledge.

Owen, R. (1993) 'The practice of electoral democracy in the Arab East and North Africa: some lessons from nearly a century's experience' in Goldberg, E. *et al.* (eds).

Picard, E. (1990) 'Arab military in politics' in Luciani, G. (ed.) *The Arab State*, London, Routledge.

Pool, D. (1994) 'Staying at home with the wife: democratization and its limits in the Middle East' in Parry, G. and Moran, M. (eds) *Democracy and Democratization*, London, Routledge.

Rueschemeyer, D., Stephens, E. and Stephens, J. (1992) *Capitalist Development and Democracy*, Cambridge, Polity Press.

Rustow, D. (1988) 'Transition to democracy' in Heper, M. and Evin, A. (eds) *State, Democracy and the Military: Turkey in the 1980s*, Berlin, W. de Gruyter.

Tilly, C. (1990) *Coercion, Capital and European States, AD 990–1990*, Oxford, Blackwell.

Vatikiotis, P. (1987) *Islam and the State*, London, Routledge.

Waterbury, J. (1994) 'Democracy without democrats?, the potential for political liberalization in the Middle East' in Salame, G. (ed.) *Democracy Without Democrats?*, London, I.B. Tauris.

Zubaida, S. (1988) *Islam, the People and the State*, London, Routledge.

CHAPTER 14

Islam and democracy

Nazih N. Ayubi

Introduction

During a recent visit to Algeria the renowned Egyptian Islamist Yusif al-Qardawi was surprised at how often he was questioned on the subject of the relationship between democracy and the absence of belief in God. In 1948, during the revolt against Imam Yahya, the despotic ruler of Yemen, the rebellion was described as a 'sell-out to the Christians' that would lead to the loss of 'home, wife and religion' because it called for a 'constitution'. And in Egyptian elections on the eve of the First World War, the Liberal candidate, Ahmad Lutfi al-Sayyid, was challenged on the grounds that he was a suspected 'democrat' (democrats being those who would allow women full equality with men and even the right to marry four men at once) (cf. Huwaidi, 1993, pp.97–102, 134ff.).

These diverting examples should be sufficient to remind us that the term 'democracy' – and the concepts associated with it such as constitutionalism and political rights – are European in their derivation and connotation, and therefore are, or have until recently been, alien to, and barely understood by, the majority of people in non-Western countries. Furthermore, given the long history of competition between Europe and the Muslim world in particular, complete with memories of the incursion into Muslim lands of the Crusades and of the recent colonial encounter, it is understandable that 'Islam' can sometimes function as a kind of 'defensive nationalism' that renders Muslims particularly suspicious of, and even resistant to, the hegemonic potential of all Western concepts, 'democracy' included. Indeed many orientalists and other 'culturalists' (including some modernization theorists) go to the extreme of arguing that Islam and democracy are utterly incompatible (Kedourie, 1994). However, a more nuanced discussion is needed if one is to understand properly the complexities of this intricate subject of the relationship between Islam and democracy.

I structure this chapter along the following lines. First, since the main 'variable' in this chapter is a belief system (Islam), I will look first at the doctrinal implications of this system, in terms both of its juridic theory, sponsored in particular by the 'religious scholars', and of the opinions and views of contemporary Islamic writers with regard to democracy. Second, I will move to a more general study of political practice in Muslim countries, and I will look at two issues: the position of religious minorities and the position of women. Third, I will consider the implications for democracy of having the *Islamists* – who are to be distinguished from just Muslims – either in government or in opposition. Finally, I will aim for a more focused answer, in light of the foregoing discussions, to the question of why democracy has been rather delayed in most Muslim countries.

You will probably find this chapter somewhat different from the others in this book. Not only does it deal with a very extensive historical span of some thirteen centuries but it also discusses a number of theological and juridic concepts that you may find unfamiliar or that may not have an equivalent in the European languages. Take for example the case of the radical Islamists. These are people who believe that Islam offers a total and comprehensive model of life whose adoption in our time is not only possible or desirable but also mandatory. Such people have been labelled 'fundamentalists' in English-speaking countries (a term derived from the Protestant experience) and '*intégristes*' in French-speaking countries (a term derived from the Catholic experience). The English and the French terms do not actually mean the same thing and yet they are both used to describe the same phenomenon of the contemporary rise in radical Islamism – an indication that they cannot really carry an accurate connotation of that same phenomenon. Although I have reduced foreign terms to a minimum there are still some which are either inevitable (because of the impossibility or inaccuracy of any attempt at translation), or else useful to know (because they are extremely important for understanding the distinctive character-istics of the cultural system called Islam). Such terms appear in italics and are briefly explained in the text or in the Glossary at the end of this chapter, and reference should be made to them whenever necessary.

14.1 Islamic doctrine and democracy

Islam means literally 'submission' (to the will of God, that is). Islam is the most monotheistic of the monotheist religions: no minor deities, and no 'Trinity' or other semblance of multiplicity in the essence of eternal omnipotence. The credo starts with the witness that "There is no god but God". This is known as the doctrine of *tawhid* (oneness, unification, monotheism) and is regarded by many modern Islamists as the pivotal or defining concept of Islam. Although it cannot be proven empirically, some commentators suggest that such an unrelenting doctrine of exclusive divine omnipotence has gradually led to an implicit doctrine of the exclusive power of the ruler in his capacity as successor on earth first to Prophet Muhammad, then to God himself.

From the start Muslims have had to innovate, to borrow and to improvise in developing their political systems, in view of the limited nature of *political* (as distinct from moral and social) stipulation contained in the major textual sources of their religion: the Quran and the *Hadith* (sayings of the Prophet). In this process of development they have been inspired first by the *shari'a* as represented in the Quran and the *Sunna* (traditions of the Prophet including his Hadith); second by Arabian tribal traditions; and third by the political heritage of the lands that they conquered, most particularly the traditions of Persia and Byzantium. The influence of the first of these sources was more evident during the era of the first four *Rashidun* (or rightly-guided) *caliphs*, the influence of the second during the *Umayyad* dynasty, and that of the third during the *Abbasid* and *Ottoman* dynasties.

Bases of legitimacy

One of the main propositions of the juristic theory of the *caliphate* concerned the issue of 'legitimacy'. Initially Abu Bakr and Umar, the first two 'rightly-guided caliphs', had emphasized the aspect of 'legitimacy' by resorting as often as possible to the nomadic-inspired tripartite principle of *shura* (inner-circle consultation), *'aqd* (ruler-ruled contract), and *bay'a* (oath of allegiance). This was a kind of 'direct democracy' that was also applied when appointing their successor Uthman. Gradually, however, *shura* was abandoned, and then, when the *Umayyads* established a hereditary semi-aristocratic monarchy, *'aqd* and *bay'a* were also discarded.

From then on the emphasis in jurisprudence (*fiqh*) focused on the authority of the leader (caliph) as a political symbol, and on the unity of the 'community' (*jam'a* or *umma*) as a human base (Al-Sayyid, 1984, pp.122–41), and the writings of classical scholars such as Al-Mawardi illustrate this. Still later, when the authority of the leader and the unity of the community had ceased to be intact and absolute, the emphasis, as the writings of Ibn Taimiya make clear, shifted to *shari'a* as a basis for ideological unity since political and human unity were no longer achievable. Under the *Abbasids*, writings on the caliphate by the jurists were mainly concerned with the caliph himself – his qualifications and his traits. Rights were mainly classified into those of the leader (*imam*) and those of the community, and there was scarcely any trace of the rights of the individual. Even Ibn Taimiya, who gave one of his major works the subtitle *On the Rights of the Ruler and the Subjects*, spoke only of civil individual rights over one's life and possessions, and made no mention of any sort of public or political rights. The subject of individual rights and the related subject of liberty received very little attention from the jurists (cf. Watt, 1968, p.96ff.).

The 'official' *Sunna* theory, which reached its peak under the *Abbasids* and subsequent dynasties, had thus ended up with the translation of a proclaimed religious authority emanating from God into a pure political authority for the caliph. The original religious concept of *tawhid* was gradually transformed into a concept of unique, supreme and absolute power for the ruler (cf. Hanafi, 1988, pp.7–8). The concept of leadership as depicted in traditional Islamic writing was also so personalized that any delegation of power was seen as encroaching on and diminishing the position of the caliph, the one and only source of real political power (cf. Al-Sayyid, 1984, p.91). Such glorification of political leadership was to remain a characteristic feature of Islamic political thought right up to the modern period, as is illustrated by the reference to concepts of the 'benevolent despot' in the writings of Afghani, Abduh and others in the nineteenth and twentieth centuries.

Political authority was understood as the instrument through which the application of the main tenets of the divine message could be supervised, so that sovereignty was thus not for the ruler or for the clergy (let alone for the 'people') but was for the Word of God as embodied in the *shari'a*. The Islamic State was therefore neither an autocracy nor a theocracy but rather was a nomocracy (Rule of rules), and the state was perceived simply as a vehicle for achieving security and order in ways that would assist Muslims to attend to their religious duties of advocating good and preventing evil. Legislation was not really a function of the State, for the (divine) law *preceded* the State and was not one of its products, and the legal process was restricted to deducing detailed rules and judgements from the broader tenets of the *shari'a*. A certain element of equilibrium and balance was presumed among three powers: the caliph, as a guardian of the community and the faith; the *ulama* or religious scholars, involved in the task of furnishing religio-legal advice (*fatwa*); and the judges, who settled disputes according to religious laws.

Why did the historical Islamic State then turn gradually into a despotic state? The answer to this question cannot be found exclusively within the doctrinal sources and one has to look into the socio-economic conditions of the region where Islam was to spread first (cf. Ayubi, 1991, Ch.1, 1995a, Ch.2 and refs cited). Ecological factors, the bureaucratic traditions of several of the conquered peoples, as well as certain strategic decisions taken by Umar and other leaders in the early decades of the empire (particularly in relation to the non-distribution of conquered lands and the maintaining of an ethnic division of labour), all pointed in the direction of a state with a dominant role to play in the economic and social affairs of its society (for details see Ayubi, 1991, Ch.1). By degrees an 'Islamic' political theory was elaborated, mainly premised on the principle of obedience to the ruler and the need to avoid civil strife; a theory that owed less and less to the nomadic egalitarian ethos, while becoming more and more 'orientalized' under the impact of traditions of the neighbouring civilizations. The concept of a whole cosmology was borrowed, from the Iranian culture in particular, in which everything was arranged in a certain order, and governed by a universal principle of hierarchy: a hierarchy of things, of 'organs' of individuals and groups. Everyone had his proper station and rank in a stable and happy system, with the caliph/king standing at the top of the social pyramid. His authority was made to sound almost divine (he was eventually described as the successor on earth of God, not of Muhammad), and opposition to him, bringing strife to the Islamic community, was declared tantamount to outright blasphemy.

The role of the ulama

We have already seen that much of Islamic jurisprudence, especially that of the mainstream *Sunni* tradition, was related to a doctrine of civil obedience. The *ulama* (religious scholars) often taught that the caliph – or in reality anyone in effective possession of political power – had to be obeyed, since even an unjust ruler was still better for the community than civil strife. In that capacity, activist opposition to the historical Islamic State (as, for example, by the *Kharijites* – 'deviants', 'exiters'), or disgruntled withdrawal from public affairs (as, for example, by the *Sufis* – 'mystics', 'gnostics'), were both dealt with severely by the state as being heresies against the religion itself. Yet the historical Islamic State was not as monolithic a polity as some scholars claim. Not only did *fiqh* develop into a multiplicity of 'legal schools' with a certain degree of freedom and independence, but the important institution of *awqaf* (charitable endowments usually run by the clerics) was also to bestow on the community a certain degree of financial and organizational autonomy from the ruler, who otherwise controlled most of the means of production and all the means of coercion.

The work of the *ulama* had helped to fulfil two major functions within the Islamic State: to justify the government of the day while at the same time making sure that the clerics (as judges, advisers, scribes, officials, teachers, etc.) had a political and social role to play. As members of a 'middle class' of the intelligentsia, they often assumed a mediatory function between the caliph on the one hand and the various social forces (notably the merchants and the urban 'masses') on the other. The *ulama* thus carved out a certain niche for themselves as a moral authority and an intellectual elite, and at various times enjoyed a certain degree of autonomy *vis-à-vis* the ruler. However, in the final analysis the autonomy of the *ulama*, who were mainly state employees, was bound to be limited, normally evident only in emergency situations. The rulers employed various manoeuvres to contain or to constrain the autonomous function of the *ulama*, such as the tradition initiated by the *Mamluks* of appointing representatives of the four juristic *Sunni* schools. Although this might have allowed an element of intellectual pluralism it did in the meantime enhance the ruler's power of manipulation as the jurists usually disagreed with each other and the ruler could always obtain a *fatwa* (religio-legal counsel) legitimizing whatever he wanted to do.

Contemporary Islamic views on democracy

In this section I consider the views of contemporary Islamic writers on contemporary politics and modern democracy. 'Islamic' here does not mean simply Muslim, but people who claim to be particularly inspired by theological and juridic Islamic teachings. Islam can play many intellectual roles. It may be used politically either to justify the status quo or to change it, and in doing this or that in the name of Islam, there is no single formula that is recommended by all contemporary scholars and believers. In terms of the degree of political control and participation (that is, democracy), there are some, such as Shaikh Mutawalli al-Sha'rawi, who believe that Islamic government is not about participation but is about devotion to God and wisdom in decision making, and that the Muslim ruler is not obliged to take into consideration the advice and opinions (*shura*) that are given to him by others. There are, on the other hand, those who believe that the Islamic principle of *shura* is roughly equivalent to the term 'democracy' in its modern connotations. As the Egyptian thinker Khalid Muhammad Khalid puts it, "*shura* in Islam is the democracy that gives people the right to choose their rulers and their deputies and representatives, as well as the right to practise freedom of thought, opinion and opposition" (interview in *Mayu*, Cairo, 8 March 1982; for further discussion of this view see Abd al-Karim, 1995, Ch.6; Imara, 1995, Ch.2).

Although most Islamic literature appears to be unfavourable towards unlimited hereditary systems (that is, monarchical rule), the position of contemporary Islamists is ambivalent with regard to 'republican' systems if they imply fixed terms of office for the ruler. Thus, for example, literature of the Islamic Liberation Party of Jordan/Palestine stipulates that, "The system of Islam is not that of a republic but of a caliphate, for Islam prevents the specification of a certain period for the head of state; he continues for life as long as he is committed to the application of the Book of God and the way of His prophet, and is capable of shouldering the burdens of government". Recently too, certain Afghan religious scholars have also issued an edict stating that it was not Islamic to specify a period of tenure for the head of state.

The subject of political parties is also controversial (cf. Al-Ghanushi, 1993, Ch.VI, Section 5; Huwaidi, 1993, Chs.1 and 2). Among many contemporary Islamists there is a strong tendency towards rejecting the idea of political parties and the concept of 'opposition' altogether. A philological problem may be involved here, since the Quranic term *azhab* is used to describe modern political parties. The catch is that the Quran speaks of only two parties in contradiction: the 'Party of God' (*Hizbullah*) and the 'Party of Satan'. Conventional tracts by the Muslim Brothers of Egypt (established 1928) and the Jamaat-i-Islami of Pakistan (established 1941) discourage political parties. Thus the influential Mawdudi of Pakistan says in the late 1930s that the 'Islamic Consultation Council' in an Islamic State should not be divided by groups or parties, but its members should express their opinions in their individual capacity. Likewise in the 'fundamentals of an Islamic constitution' approved by an assembly of *ulama* from the Indian subcontinent in the early 1950s, there is reference to freedom of belief, worship, opinion, movement and assembly, but no reference to the idea of political pluralism or institutionalized parties (cf. Huwaidi, 1993, pp.64–74). The Syrian Islamic leader Sa'id Hawwa is also against loyalty to any 'non-Godly' party. However, the Muslim Brothers of Egypt and Jamaat-i-Islami of Pakistan have both recently agreed to participate, in the context of multipartism, in the political life of their respective countries. The contemporary radical Islamist Jihad organization in Egypt rejects multi-partism as being contrary to Islam, but the National Islamic Front of Sudan, Al-Nahda Islamic Party of Tunisia (in the early 1980s), and the Islamic Liberation Party of Jordan/Palestine (as early as the 1960s) all accept the principle of multipartism.

A majority of mainstream Islamists have come to accept that the contemporary concept of political parties is different from the original 'theological' notion and that it represents a level of plurality which is far more complex than the conventionally-understood differences between the various juridic schools. This is because modern political parties are based on concepts pertaining to the interests (*masalih*) of the community and the possible ways of action and reform, and are as such very useful for conducting the affairs of a Muslim society (see Tamimi, 1993).

──────────────── *Summary of Section 14.1* ────────────────

- Classical Islamic jurisprudence was primarily a theory of supreme caliphatic power and civil obedience.

- Religious scholars provided both a rationalization of authoritarian polities and an ideological and practical source of dissent.

- Contemporary Islamic thought has both endorsed this heritage and challenged it, interpreting Islamic scriptures in a democratic manner.

14.2 Islamic practice and democracy

To what extent have the practices of states with Muslim majorities, both historically and in the contemporary period, been favourable or unfavourable to democracy? I will deal with three topics in an attempt to answer this question. To start with I consider the position of two groups which raise 'special questions' with regard to Muslim societies and polities: religious minorities and women. I then look at some contemporary countries that are taken to be Islamic States (and not simply countries with Muslim majorities) to see how democratic or undemocratic they are.

predominantly Muslim

significant outlying Muslim communities

Map 14.1   Predominantly Muslim states

The position of religious minorities

Although the historical Islamic State could not tolerate a high degree of difference within the Islamic doctrine itself (as manifested by the long hostility between the *Sunnis* and the *Shi'is*), it could – by contrast – tolerate and even recognize the institutional presence of other monotheistic religions within the state. Indeed the Islamic State had developed various interesting methods of quasi-consociational aggregation of communities that were quite advanced and sophisticated by the standards of their time. Following the precepts of the Quran and *Hadith*, those 'people of the Book' (*ahl al-kitab* – mainly Jews and Christians) who lived within the Islamic dominion were normally accorded their freedom of belief and security of life and possessions in return for paying a sort of 'poll tax' or *jizya*. A juridic disagreement eventually emerged as to whether the *jizya* was to be levied as a means of pressure to induce more people to convert to Islam, or whether it was enforced in return for the non-Muslims not being required, because of their sensitive position, to participate in the activities of war (i.e. that it was payment in return for their being protected and exempted from the military duties of *jihad*). The Christians and Jews (and Sabaeans and Magi) were subsequently categorized by the jurists as *dhimmis*, implying that they were, by accord (*'ahd*), under the protection of the Muslims. Their conditions varied from ruler to ruler but on the whole, given prevailing standards, they were treated with tolerance and many of them did assume fairly influential posts in the service of the State. Historically they were also on occasion exempt from paying the *jizya* if the State failed to protect them or if they were recruited for military service (Ayubi, 1992).

However, it is still a controversial matter among Muslim jurists as to whether the *dhimmis* could be considered as 'citizens' of the Islamic state or whether they counted legally as 'permanent residents'. As members of *dar al-Islam* (the Household of Islam) they were citizens of the State to be treated differently from other 'foreign' Christians and Jews belonging to *dar al-harb* (the Household of War). Even so, the category into which their 'citizenship' fell was of a 'second class' nature (indeed it does not even reach that level, according to some contemporary Islamists), since they were not expected by jurists to occupy positions of military, political or even administrative leadership. The medieval jurist Al-Mawardi, for example, thought that they could be 'ministers of execution' but not 'ministers of delegation' and that they could not adjudicate in cases involving Muslims. It is also important to remember that a Christian or a Jew did not enjoy as an individual whatever rights he did have – rather he enjoyed them *as a member of his community*: if he deserted his church, for example, he lost his 'legal' status and the rights and duties that went with it.

The religious communities therefore represented part of the general pattern of 'unity in diversity', as the historical Islamic State was perhaps almost as much corporatist as it was integrative. Under the Ottomans this semi-consociationalist formula was further developed into the system of *millets*, which enjoyed a high degree of social and cultural autonomy within the state. Even today religious minorities are often subject to their 'own' religious laws with regard to 'personal status' and family matters. Politically too there is also some continuity, not only in Lebanon (the archetypal consociational polity) but also in countries such as Egypt and Jordan, where a certain number of seats is usually set aside for Christians in the parliament and in the cabinet.

Within the Islamic State, the religious minorities are often professionally distinct from the majority of Muslims. From the early days of the Muslim State there was always a certain element of 'ethno-religious division of labour', a situation that continued for many centuries and some features of which can be detected to this day. Not only do non-Muslims often engage in activities prohibited by Islam (such as the practice of usury and the making of wines), but they have tended historically to be highly represented in professions carrying lower social status.

The ethno-religious division of labour was eventually to be somewhat reversed, and to work for the benefit of the religious minorities when, from the eighteenth – and especially from the nineteenth – century, European colonialism was opening up the Ottoman empire, Egypt and North Africa to the world capitalist market. Christians and Jews were preferred as commercial agents, possible because of religious affinity with the Europeans but more importantly because of their commercial and financial expertise as well as their greater proficiency in foreign languages. An exceptionally high percentage of all people involved in business, commerce and finance in Turkey and most parts of the Arab world were normally from among the non-Muslim communities. This sometimes led to a Muslim backlash against the minorities once 'national' independence had been gained, even though the Christians, in particular, had played a prominent role in the nationalist movements of several countries (Egypt, Syria, Palestine).

What are the implications of ethno-religious plurality for the prospects of democratization? It has been argued that the shift from the traditional *millet* system to Western-style regimes in societies that were not adequately integrated on the social and cultural level, has resulted among other things in an automatic transfer of ethnic minorities into political minorities – if majorities and minorities are taken to be permanent and fixed quantities, politics is likely to reflect the 'force of numbers' and turn ethnic communities into minorities that cannot enjoy actual equality within the political system (cf. Kedourie, 1988, pp.25–31).

The contemporary Middle Eastern state, secular and Islamic, has not succeeded in dealing with its communal problems. In Iraq, the Shi'i–Sunni split is not a divisive one in terms of the social culture; yet the Shi'is – who constitute a numerical majority of the population – are still politically excluded, *in spite of* the secularist slogans. In Iran the religious minorities (mainly Jews, Christians and Zoroastrians) enjoy a measure of tolerance and protection in the conventional Islamic way – no more and no less. But precisely *because of* the ideological (religious) nature of the state in Iran, some religious sects are being persecuted (the Baha'is), and non-Shi'i Muslim sects are seriously under-represented.

There is no effective solution to the communal problem in the contemporary state that can be derived literally and ready-made from conventional jurisprudence of the early Islamic State. The *ahl al-dhimma* formula that was so noble and progressive ten centuries ago is hardly suitable after the centuries of human and constitutional progress that have affected all societies. One can quite understand the alarm with which the Christians' of Egypt, for example, receive the incessant calls for a full application of the *shari'a* (which is often taken to mean conventional jurisprudence). Nor is there any provision in the conventional jurisprudence for the position of 'other' Muslim sects within an Islamic State (cf. Ayubi, 1992).

Improvisation and innovation are therefore required, and it is refreshing to observe a few attempts by contemporary Islamic writers to address such issues in an enlightened way. One of the most explicit has been Fahmi Huwaidi, who has put a persuasive case for the full 'citizenship' of non-Muslims in a contemporary Islamic state. He derives his argument from Islam's humanitarian inclination, from the shared monotheism of the three major Middle Eastern religions, from the 'Madina Constitution', and from the Prophet Muhammad's ruling about *ahl al-kitab*: "To them what is due to us, and from them what is due on us". Huwaidi reminds his fellow-Muslims that the *dhimmi* categorization was a juridic device (not necessarily purely Islamic) which is no longer appropriate for the conditions and requirements of the modern State. Thus in application, for example, if non-Muslims share with their fellow Muslims the task of defending the fatherland, the extraction of the *jizya* poll-tax from them ceases to be mandatory (Huwaidi, 1985, pp.128–45).

Such improvisation would still fall within the general tradition of Islamic jurisprudence. What could well continue to be more problematic in a truly Islamic State would be the position of 'other' Muslim or near Muslim sects. The persecution of Qadyanis in Pakistan and of Baha'is in Iran would attest to that, not to speak, of course, of the under-representation of Shi'is in Sunni states and the under-representation of Sunnis in Shi'i states. The problem is even more complex with communities that cannot be classified as either Muslims or 'people of the Book' (e.g. Hindus, Confucians, Buddhists, or even 'the most dangerous': atheists). Muslim rulers and intellectuals may need to go beyond, and even outside, conventional Islamic jurisprudence in order to deal with this issue in a humane and effective way.

The position of women

The subject of gender is a complex one and does not fall wholly within the theme of democracy; but a few passages in this connection would be in order. In its modern, individualistic Western form, democracy assumes formal equality in rights, regardless of most differences including those of gender. In the original texts of Islam (as in Judaism and Christianity) there are, however, strong indications that women are considered less equal than men. The most obvious example in Islam is that women are generally entitled to inherit only half the amount allotted to men. This is not to doubt that Islam had considerably improved women's status in comparison with the pre-Islamic period: it abolished female infanticide, emphasized the contractual rather than the proprietary nature of marriage, allowed women to retain their property and their maiden names after marriage, and so on.

But verses in the Quran assign to a woman's testimony half the value of a man's, permit men to divorce their wives unilaterally and appear to sanction polygyny. Although modesty in dress is required, there appears to be no requirement in Islam for the comprehensive veiling and seclusion that tended to develop in certain Muslim societies, especially in the urban centres. This was probably more the outcome of ecological and cultural influences than of religious commandment.

Supporters of women's rights are able to quote several cases from the early 'golden age' of Islam of women assuming important positions as advisors, market controllers, judges and even military leaders (not to speak of poets, artists and cultural patrons). It is a fact, however, that up to the early twentieth century women were secluded and confined in most urban centres of the Muslim world. While there are serious indications that women enjoyed, and continue to enjoy, a significant degree of 'informal' influence within the family and the community, attempts to change personal status laws in the direction of more formal equality started only in the second decade of the twentieth century and in some cases they continue to unfold slowly. Often introduced under the influence of colonial or semi-colonial administrations and with initiative from Western-educated elites, these were part of a 'modernization' drive that was partly coercive and partly emulative. Given the long history of competition and hostility between 'Christian' Europe and the 'Islamic' Middle East, such modernization was seen as little more than Westernization and it smacked of colonial or neo-colonial 'designs' that needed to be resisted.

Personal status matters, subject as they are to centuries of conservative patriarchal control, have proved more resistant to reform than matters pertaining to the public sphere. Even so, there have been a few of the former, such as reforms making polygynous marriages impossible or more difficult (e.g. in Turkey, Tunisia, Syria), or making divorce more legally or judicially controlled. In the public sphere, female education has expanded everywhere under state auspices and there is a fair degree of formal and often real equality with regard to employment opportunities, especially in the public sector (cf. Hijab, 1988). Women are also enfranchised in most Muslim countries, with a few islands of resistance – such as in the Gulf region – but even here the possibility of women's participation in elections was raised in the case of Kuwait. Women's associations and organizations do also exist in most Muslim countries and some of these are sponsored by Islamist organizations, most notably the Muslim women's organization headed in Egypt since the 1930s by Zainab al-Ghazali.

In some respects, 'state feminism' is ahead of the society at large. A number of ruling parties have women's groups affiliated to them, women have been appointed as cabinet ministers in several countries (Egypt, Syria, Iraq, Algeria), and they have won municipal and parliamentary seats in most others, while in some cases (Egypt, Jordan) a certain number of seats are reserved for women in the parliament. In the non-Arab Muslim world, women in 1995 occupy the prime ministerial post in Turkey, Pakistan and Bangladesh (where the leader of the main opposition party is also a woman). Conservative attitudes towards women pertain more to familial/private than to political/public matters, and these examples show that Muslim-majority countries are fully able, and willing, to elect women to lead them politically.

In the last two decades, women have supported or even joined the radical Islamist movements in noticeable numbers and many have taken *voluntarily* to wearing the veil. This act, which is automatically taken in the West to mean oppression, is found psychologically liberating and socially empowering by some Muslim women, creating a positive self-image of piety and authenticity and providing unimpeded physical mobility in public space and in professional life. It is also arguable that veiling represents an ambivalent mix of protest and accommodation, of resistance and acqui-escence (Macleod, 1991). Women take the veil partly as a politico-moral statement against a social order that they have come to detest. But in protesting against that order, they have resorted to an instrument that society regards as a hallmark of conservatism and acquiescence and that men have conventionally used (and may re-use) as a mechanism for sexual and social control. Re-veiling is therefore a kind of 'passive revolution' that can only be a 'one-off' occurrence and one which cannot be escalated or developed (Ayubi, 1995b).

Islam as government

The few contemporary polities that call themselves, or are taken to be, Islamic (rather than simply 'Muslim') States are very different from each other in their most important *political* aspects including the levels of pluralization and democratization. Such countries may be similar in terms of applying so-called Islamic penalties (*hudud*) or of trying to avoid the receiving or giving of banking interest (taken to be forbidden usury, *riba*), yet they are very different from each other with regard to their political forms and constitutional arrangements. Nor do they usually have mutual recognition of each other as being Islamic states (Ayubi, 1995c).

Saudi Arabia is taken to be the earliest contemporary Islamic State, its history dating at least to the early 1930s. It is a monarchy – a form that is considered by many to be un- or even anti-Islamic. It does not have a constitution (the Quran being its fundamental law), nor does it have a parliament or political parties, although it has a modern-looking cabinet and bureaucracy. The crucial role played officially by the *ulama* and the 'moral police' ensures that the country is socially conservative, though in terms of employment and services it has been a generous welfare state. Though different in most respects, Morocco has sometimes been likened to Saudi Arabia in being an 'Islamic monarchy'. The state is constitutional with a certain measure of pluralism represented by the political parties and other unions and associations. The constitution is unambiguous, however, about describing Morocco as an 'Islamic State' and in describing the king as the Commander of the Believers and the Protector of the Religion.

Islamic Iran, on the other hand, is a republic with a constitution, a president, a parliament and political parties, as well as the cabinet, bureaucracy and courts; none of these institutions is particularly 'Islamic'. The current state owes its existence to a multi-class popular revolution

within which the religious wing, led by the Shi'i *ulama*, was able to assume
the upper hand. Islam played a mobilizational role and the discourse of
Ayatollah Khomeini made it possible to combine social conservatism with
political radicalism and to construct a basically *étatiste* economy in post-
revolutionary Iran. The distinct features of such a regime have been the
supreme role of the jurisconsult as 'Leader of the Islamic Republic', the high
representation of clerics in the parliament (*majlis*) and the key part they
perform in the Council of Guardians and Assembly of Experts, and the
important role played by the Islamic Republican Party (until its dissolution in
1987) and by the Islamic Revolutionary Guards. Although by no means a
'democratic paradise' by Western standards, it can certainly be argued that
Islamic Iran is more democratic on several counts than was Iran under the
Shah.

Yet another variety of regime claiming to construct an Islamic state may
have its origins in a military *coup d'état*. Pakistan under Zia-ul-Haq (1977–88)
is one such example, where the process was initiated in 1980 by the issuing of
an 'Islamic' legal code, to be applied through *shari'a* courts. Such moves
were halted by Zia's death in a plane crash in 1988 but the Islamization trend
has continued. The government of Nawaz Sharif was brought to power in
1990 with a coalition including the Islamic parties, and Sharif introduced his
own *shari'a* bill for Islamizing the state which was duly given the vote of
approval by the National Assembly. Thus the process of Islamizing the state
which was initiated under military rule has been continued by a government
brought to power by elections.

It should be clear from these cases that although so-called Islamic states
may adopt similar practices with regard to moral and social issues there is
hardly any similarity in the *political* features of such states or even in their
socio-economic orientation. There is perhaps a tendency among 'Islamic
states' not to allow or tolerate parties that adopt different ideologies. But this
is a widespread trait of most regimes in underdeveloped countries, and is not
only confined to Islamic ones.

—————————————— *Summary of Section 14.2* ——————————————

- Pre-modern Islamic states did not tolerate major differences within
  Islam but set historically high standards for the humane treatment of
  ethnic and religious minorities. However, it is not clear that the same
  theological arguments can be translated into a theory of equal
  citizenship.

- Islam's initial impact on women was both positive and negative.
  Despite depicting women as inferior to men, particularly in economic
  terms, it abolished a number of patriarchal tribal practices. In the
  contemporary Muslim world, Islamic thought has provided the
  rationale for both 'state feminism', and the promotion of women's
  interest as well as for more regressive practices.

- Contemporary states that claim to be Islamic display an enormous
  variety of political regimes from absolutist monarchy in Saudi Arabia,
  to the military dictatorship in Pakistan, to republican Iran.

14.3   Islam in opposition

Having looked briefly at some of the regimes that are taken to represent Islamic States, I now look at the way in which secularist governments on the one hand and Islamist groups on the other, have interacted with each other in countries where the majority of the population is *Muslim* but where the government cannot be described as being specifically *Islamic*, with a view to considering the democratic implications of such an interaction. But rather than discussing democracy (or the lack of it) in the abstract, it would be more useful here to think in terms of democratization as a process of transition (and possibly of counter-transitions), and rather than talking about full-fledged participation, representation and contestation, one should perhaps think in terms of an inclusion/exclusion scale or continuum (Ayubi, 1995a, Chs.1 and 11). The possible variants include the following.

1   Full and forced exclusion: as in the case of Syria with regard to its Muslim Brothers, or the lesser cases of Iraq, Tunisia, Libya and, more recently Algeria since the December 1991 *coup d'état*. This is usually accomplished at huge moral and human cost and may possibly involve organizational and political costs too – as in the extensive arrests of Islamists leading to the assassination of President Sadat of Egypt by an Islamist in 1981.

2   Marginalization: this strategy aims at building some kind of political consensus (through, for example, a pact or a national alliance) that attaches to the Islamists a recognized, but reduced and controlled, space. This method has been tried in Jordan and Yemen, where Islamist groups have been allowed to compete in elections and enter parliaments. The policy has been tried in Egypt by allowing the Muslim Brothers to stand in elections in the list of other parties (since they are not themselves recognized as a legal party), and to some extent in Tunisia and Morocco. In Tunisia, following the removal of President Bourguiba in 1987 by Zain Al-Abidin Ben Ali, an initially 'inclusionary' national pact was subsequently used to weaken opposition to the ruling party, especially that emanating from the Islamists, and then to suppress the opposition movement altogether by depriving it of any serious representation at national or local levels.

3   Pre-emption: another middle-of-the-road method is to try to deprive the Islamists of their main weapons by adopting these in some form as part of the government's own repertoire. By making a claim to exceptional Islamic authority, the governments of Saudi Arabia, Iran, Morocco and Sudan can, and often do, rob their radical Islamic movements of part of their claim to the higher moral ground. This is not a guaranteed solution, however, as countries such as Saudi Arabia, Morocco and even Iran have had their own Islamic oppositions. More populist forms of radical Islam may eventually gain more popularity in Morocco, and more puritanical forms of political Islam have already expressed themselves in Saudi Arabia during the takeover of the Mecca Grand Mosque in 1979 and in the emergence of the Committee for the Defence of Legitimate Islamic Rights in the 1990s.

4   Limited accommodation: this can be employed with or without some use
     and/or threat of coercion, but often involves some divisionary tactics that
     are aimed at splitting the relatively milder Islamist elements from the
     more militant, radical ones. This method has been used – not without
     difficulty – in Egypt where the more established Muslim Brothers are al-
     lowed to stand in elections on the list of other parties (in other words, in
     electoral alliances), whereas the more 'extreme' Islamist organizations
     (*jama'at*) are singled out for more consistent police action. This aims
     at forcing mainstream Islamic associations to compete openly with other
     (possibly secular) political parties, and should ideally – if the latter are
     adequately rewarded – force an ever-widening gap between them and
     the extremists, thereby ultimately marginalizing the more radical organ-
     izations that want to wreck the system altogether. Shades of this method
     have also been tried in Jordan and Kuwait, with some degree of success.

5   Full inclusion: this is an imaginary scenario (apart from the special Iranian
     case where various Islamic and some 'less-Islamic' forces can compete in
     elections). It is possible to imagine such a scenario in a country with rela-
     tively 'fixed' democratic procedures, provided that one is prepared to
     believe that the Islamists will not abolish the democratic process once
     they become supreme in power (such as Lebanon and Turkey). It ap-
     peared viable in Algeria in the period from October 1988 to December
     1991, but since has given way to exactly the opposite effect.

Given the 'non-democratic' way in which current regimes in the Middle
East have come to power, one can understand their apprehension about the
possible outcomes of full inclusion and the likelihood of their being
removed from power altogether, which most will strongly resist. However, it
must be starting to become increasingly clear even to the most stubborn of
rulers that limited accommodation may be the best option for most regimes,
ideally as a transition phase towards full inclusion of all those parties
(Islamists included) that are prepared to play according to the liberal–
pluralist rules of the game (Hudson, 1995).

Whatever the case may be, it is clear that Islamists in 1995 form the main
opposition groups in most Arab societies and the largest opposition group in
most of the parliaments that allow opposition representation (Esposito and
Piscatori, 1991). Since democracy is not only about representation and
participation but is also about opposition or formal contestation, the
Islamists in many Arab countries have become, both in practice and in
objective terms, part of the democratization process itself, as a brief review of
the Arab countries in particular should illustrate (cf. Ayubi, 1995a).

In Egypt the Muslim Brothers, in alliance with the Wafd Party, won
twelve seats in 1984, and in alliance with Labour, won 36 seats in 1987, but
they boycotted the November 1990 elections as a way of protesting against
government restrictions. In Jordan the Muslim Brothers won 22 seats in the
November 1989 elections, and twelve more went to other Islamists.
Subsequently they also gained in several local elections. The Speaker of
the Parliament was a member of the Muslim Brothers and in January 1991 the
Brothers were given five cabinet posts (although some were excluded later
on). The 1993 elections reduced the number of Islamists in the parliament

but not significantly: it brought in sixteen 'organized' and ten independent Islamists who together represented more or less a quarter of the total number of deputies.

In Tunisia the MTI (Mouvement de la Tendance Islamique, later called Al-Nahda) participated in the parliamentary elections of April 1989. Islamist candidates won 14 per cent of the country's vote and about 30 per cent in important cities such as Tunis, Sousse and Gabes, but failed to win any seats in parliament. Consequently no Islamists stood in the 1994 elections, which resulted in the (secular) opposition and independents gaining only nineteen out of the 163 parliamentary seats. In Northern Yemen, Islamists won 32 out of 128 parliamentary seats in 1988, and in unified Yemen the two Islamic parties, Al-Islah and Al-Haqq, gained respectively 62 and two out of 301 parliamentary seats in 1993.

In Algeria the events were particularly dramatic (cf. Mortimer, 1991). In the municipal elections in June 1990 the FIS (Front Islamique du Salut) won an incisive victory, taking 54 per cent of the vote (against 34 per cent for the ruling FLN – Front de Libération Nationale) and predominating in 32 out of the 48 governorates, including Algiers, and in 853 out of 1,539 local councils (with the FLN taking only 487). Carried away by this altogether unexpected triumph (which was perhaps more a vote against the FLN than a vote for the FIS), the Islamists then took to the streets to demand the bringing forward of the general parliamentary elections and the amending of the election laws. Not only were their slogans often openly anti-democratic, but they subsequently engaged with the police in vicious skirmishes. The regime appears to have assumed that the anti-democratic inclinations of the Islamists revealed by this display of violence and destruction would have been all too obvious to the public, and that their popularity with the

Algerian municipal elections, June 1990: counting votes at Kouba

electorate would thus have been reduced. The parliamentary elections duly went ahead in December 1991, but the level of apathy was high, and the majority of potential FLN-supporters or FIS-opposers did not vote. This produced the stunning result that the FIS won 188 out of 231 seats, with 28 seats being left for a second round of voting which was to have been held on 1 January 1992 but which was forestalled by a military-backed 'palace coup' taking over power.

What is the significance of all these cases? It is possible, broadly speaking, to interpret the rise of Islamism as a contest with the State over public space. The post-independence state has tended to impart a distinctly *economic* meaning to public space (and hence the indigenization and nationalization of firms and the creation of many 'public' enterprises). Politics was turned into economics, and the state encroached on the civil society via the public economic sector. It was the failure or exhaustion of this model, and the ensuing exclusion and marginalization of some of the upwardly-mobile segments of the society, that resulted in the rise of radical Islamic movements in many Arab societies. The Islamists struck back at the state by imparting to the public space a distinctly *moralist* colouring. They invoked ethics as the substance of politics, and struck out at the State with the scourge of public morality.

In the immediate instance, most 'fundamentalist' groupings act as a counter-democratic force: they frighten regimes away from initiating further liberalizations while pushing them increasingly towards adopting parts of the Islamists' (anti-secularist and anti-humanist) platform. Yet it is also important to note, with Hudson, that in the most recent cases in which the Islamists were allowed to participate in elections, the "Islamist vote is significant but modest. In no case does it approach a majority, and in several cases it constitutes a plurality ... Inclusionary strategies seem, therefore, to work" (Hudson, 1995, p.244). But what about the longer term? Is it completely beyond the bounds of the possible that radical Islamism may eventually become a force for long-term democratization by virtue of the fact that it currently acts as one of the few effective anti-state forces in several Muslim societies? This is an important question that only time can answer.

——————————— *Summary of Section 14.3* ———————————

- Contemporary Islamic movements in the Middle East are often the main opposition force to the state and ruling elites. Their degree of political incorporation is a measure of democratization.

- States vary widely in their treatment of Islamists from coercively-backed repression, through marginalization to semi-incorporation.

- The outlook of Islamic movements has been broadly undemocratic but their rise, especially in Algeria, has displayed the equally undemocratic attitudes of rulers in the region.

- The rise of these movements is less to do with the content of Islamic theology and more to do with the total occupation of economic and political life by the state. Islamists have sought to carve out territory for themselves in the domain of morals and values.

14.4 Towards an explanation

Is democracy at all possible in the Middle East, or is the Middle East, and the Muslim world at large, governed by a vicious exceptionalism that renders it immune to the infective influences of democracy (Ayubi, 1993; Waterbury, 1994, p.25ff.)? Careful examination of the evidence would suggest that Islamic culture contains elements that can be both congenial and uncongenial towards democracy, depending on the particular society and on the historical circumstances. But be this as it may, it is interesting to note that in reality only two of the 37 countries in the world having Muslim majorities (between 1981 and 1990) were ever rated 'free' by Freedom House's annual survey (The Gambia for two years and Northern Cyprus for four). Moreover, whereas opposition movements in other regions almost unanimously embraced, or at least declared, Western-style democratic values throughout the 1980s, in authoritarian Muslim societies those movements that campaigned explicitly for democratic politics were relatively weak, and – by contrast – the most powerful opposition came from 'Islamic fundamentalists'. Many of these groups are openly anti-democratic, and it is impossible, with regard to those that are not, to know whether they would relinquish power voluntarily once they had achieved it. In the meantime, many Middle Eastern countries have been forced by the intensely Islamic character of the opposition to adopt some of its policies or slogans by way of pre-emption and self-defence. Since the commitment of the Islamic radicals to democracy has remained questionable such countries have tended to become more wary of the liberalization process generally.

Yet it might also be argued that the prerequisites for a democratic transformation are not available in the majority of Middle Eastern countries because they are not advanced capitalist societies. There have been attempts to determine a certain economic or developmental threshold beyond which democracy will become possible, or probable. The idea is that processes of economic development involving significant industrialization lead to a more diverse and a more complex class structure, which becomes increasingly difficult for authoritarian regimes to control. A country's involvement in the world economy creates non-governmental sources of wealth and influence, and opens that society to the impact of the democratic ideas prevailing in the industrialized world (Huntington, 1991, pp.65–7). However, oil-based economies may represent a different case. Dependence on oil revenues leads to the development of a 'rentier state', with weakened extractive, regulatory and distributive powers, which appears superficially strong and autonomous but which is not really able to mediate and arbitrate effectively among the various 'raw' interests developing in the society (Ayubi, 1995a, especially Ch.7; and see Bromley's Chapter 13).

Whatever limited democratization might have occurred in the Middle East has probably been the indirect outcome of two factors: the financial crisis of the state, and globalization. The fiscal and structural exhaustion of the state has led to regimes sanctioning a certain degree of plurality, partly by way of reducing the financial and organizational overload, and partly by way of increasing the numbers of those who would share the blame for the expected austerity measures that are required by international financial agencies and prospective foreign investors. Liberalization can thus be seen at least partly as a mechanism for system maintenance. But this was unlikely by itself to prevent some of the Islamic forces in the society from making use of the few political 'openings' that began to emerge within the political system as a result. This in turn has frightened the existing authoritarian regimes and has led to a slowing down of their already uncertain democratization initiatives.

Democratization in the Muslim world is not completely absent but is more delayed than it is in other parts of the world. Democracy in the Middle East is in some respects more delayed than it is in the rest of the Muslim world. I say 'delayed' because there are indeed signs of growing pluralization if not of full democratization in many of these countries (Ayubi, 1995a; Deegan, 1993). To what extent is Islam – as a cultural system – exactly responsible for this delay? This is a difficult question to answer with precision, for one often uses 'culture' as a residual variable to explain all that cannot be explained by other factors. However, it would be possible to say that inasmuch as people are influenced in their everyday life by the Islamic heritage, that heritage – both in terms of its jurisprudence and in terms of its historical practice – has been more favourable to stability of government than to freedom of opposition, to political obedience than to social rebellion. This is particularly true of what has become the mainstream *Sunni* tradition, although one can of course quote writings, movements and regimes that were more libertarian or revolutionary.

But what is more important than an imagined essence of Islam is its political and social significance in various contexts. For one thing, Islam in the Middle East is difficult to disentangle from a long history of competition and hostility between Europe and the Levant. Inasmuch as democracy can be a 'political technique' that may be borrowed and transferred, Middle Eastern countries have been rather apprehensive that modernization, including democratization, might end up being little more than Westernization, and Islam has sometimes functioned as a proto-nationalist defensive shield against a potentially hegemonic Westernization. What appeared to the elites to be a more urgent task than democratization was to confront imperial European colonialism, and its successor Zionist 'settler colonialism' in Palestine. European colonialism was comparatively late and partial in the Middle East: it framed rather than penetrated these societies and was thus not able to impart some of its democratic devices on these societies over a long period (as happened in India and the West Indies). After independence, the populist policies of some Arab systems and the rentier income accruing to others from their oil resources have given these systems a period of grace and a lease of time through which they could distract their citizenry away from specifically political (that is democratic) concerns and demands. But as the financial resources get scarcer so will legitimacy be put to the test, and more rights and freedoms will have to be conceded.

On the other hand, the appropriation by the Middle Eastern State of most 'economic capital' in the society has left the opposition with no alternative but to try to appropriate 'moral capital' (Islam) for itself. In turn, the fact that the main opposition to the existing regimes is of a religious nature makes the ruling elites even more apprehensive about further liberalization, especially in view of the fact that the long-term democratic intentions of the Islamists remain in doubt. The West, for its part, is also hostile to the Islamic trend and apprehensive about its hyper-nationalist potential. Both the authoritarian elites and the Western powers, as the Algerian events of the 1990s have tragically shown, are willing to sacrifice democratization in order to stop the Islamists reaching power. Indeed Western support for oppressive regimes (US support for the Shah in Iran, French for the junta in Algeria) often enables the Islamic movements – whose grievances are originally against their own native states – to acquire the added strength of becoming a nationalist movement against 'foreign domination' as well.

One may therefore be able to assume (and, as with most things cultural, *only* assume) that Islamic traditions, with their hypersensitivity against civil discord, might have some impact on the delay of democratic transformation in the Muslim world (particularly its Middle Eastern core). But as we have seen in this chapter, what is more important is not our concept of an essentialist Islam, but the various contingencies and conjunctures that give Islam its variable social and political roles. Whereas some of the factors that explain the delay of democratization in the Middle East are purely economic or technological, rather than religious and cultural, there is little doubt that the refusal by ruling elites to allow an element of participation for Islamic movements is an added cause for the slow pace of democratization in many Muslim societies.

Glossary

Abbasids – dynasty of caliphs ruling from Baghdad from AD 750 to AD 1258, although with very little power after AD 945.

awqaf (sing. *Waqf*) – religiously-endowed property, entrusted to clerics to manage for charitable purposes.

caliphate (Arabic *khilafa*) – the institution of Islamic government (and its theory) after Muhammad. The caliph (*khalifa*) was the 'successor' to the Prophet Muhammad. The last caliphate was abolished by the Turkish Republic in 1924.

dawla – originally 'turn' or 'cycle', subsequently 'dynasty'; currently 'State' (in the European sense).

dhimmis – 'protected subjects', the term jurists eventually gave to *ahl al-kitab* (people of the Book): mainly Jews and Christians who live under protected status within the Islamic Dominion.

fiqh – jurisprudence; a highly autonomous body of knowledge based on a strictly textual methodology which analyses the relationship between words and their meaning and applies opinion only by way of deduction and analogy.

Hadith – sayings attributed to the Prophet Muhammad.

Integrists – the Anglicized form of the French word *intégristes*. English uses the term 'fundamentalists' which has recently been translated directly into Arabic as *al-usuliyyun*. However, the French term *intégrisme* expresses more accurately than 'fundamentalism' the holistic comprehensive notion of Islam that is preferred by the contemporary Islamists.

Kharijites (Arabic *Khawarij*) – 'exiters' or 'seceders', deviating from the 'consensus of the community'. Originally rebellious ultra-zealous religio-political movements that disagreed with and revolted against Ali and subsequent Muslim rulers.

Mamluks – one of the ethnic/military regional dynasties which, with the Ayyubids, ruled mainly in Egypt and Syria following the disintegration of the Islamic dominion from the twelfth century AD.

millet – from *milla*, religion or sect, a system of religious and social autonomy for the Christian and Jewish communities within the Ottoman state.

Ottomans – a Turkish dynasty claiming to have inherited the caliphate from the Abbasids, they ruled the Muslim empire and parts of South East Europe, using Istanbul as their capital after AD 1453, until overthrown by the Turkish Republican movement in 1924.

Rashidun – the 'wise' and rightly-guided first four caliphs to succeed Muhammad (Abu Bakr, Umar, Uthman and Ali). Ruled from AD 632 to AD 661. Their era is regarded as the 'Golden Age' of Islam from a *religious* point of view.

shari'a, also *shar'* (adj. *shar'i*) – originally 'path' or 'way'; subsequently the 'legislative' part of religion as stipulated in the Quran and Hadith.

Shi'is (*Shi'a*; adj. *Shi'i*) – members of 'the party of Ali', who believe that after Muhammad the leadership of the Muslim community should have gone to Ali (the Prophet's cousin and son-in-law) and his family.

shura – usually unbinding consultation sought by the ruler from colleagues or scholars (or, in modern interpretations, from the 'people').

Sufis – 'mystics'.

Sunni – the noun *Sunna* is, strictly, the sayings, ways and 'traditions' of Prophet Muhammad; by extension, the adjective *Sunni* is used to distinguish the mainstream majority Muslim 'sect' (*Sunnis*) from the *Shi'a*, or 'the party of Ali'.

tawhid – 'oneness', 'unification'; strictly signifying monotheism, but taken by some to signify a holistic world view or even, on occasion, used to urge for an integrated orderly community.

ulama (sing. *Alim*) – 'scholars' or people trained in the religious 'sciences'.

umma – community, either in an ethno-cultural, or, more frequently, in a religious sense.

Umayyads – dynasty of caliphs ruling from Damascus from AD 661 to AD 750.

References

Abd al-Karim, K. (1995) *Al-Islam bain al-dawla al-diniyya wa al-dawla al-madaniyya* [Islam Between the Religious and the Secular State], Cairo, Sina.

Ayubi, N.N. (1991, 1993) *Political Islam: Religion and Politics in the Arab World*, London, Routledge.

Ayubi, N.N. (1992) 'State Islam and communal plurality', *Annals of the American Academy of Political and Social Science*, special issue 'Political Islam', vol.524, November, pp.79–91.

Ayubi, N.N. (1993) 'Is democracy possible in the Middle East?', *European Consortium for Political Research*, Joint Sessions, Leiden, April.

Ayubi, N.N. (1995a) *Over-Stating the Arab State: Politics and Society in the Middle East*, London, I.B. Tauris.

Ayubi, N.N. (1995b) 'Rethinking the public/private dichotomy: radical Islamism and civil society in the Middle East', *Contention*, vol.4, no.3, pp.79–105.

Ayubi, N.N. (1995c) 'The Islamic state', entry in Esposito, J.L. (ed.) *The Encyclopaedia of the Modern Islamic World, Vol.2*, New York, Oxford University Press.

Deegan, H. (1993) *The Middle East and Problems of Democracy*, Buckingham, Open University Press.

Esposito, J.L. and Piscatori, J. (1991) 'Democratization and Islam', *Middle East Journal*, vol.45, no.3.

Al-Ghanushi, R. (1993) *Al-Hurriyyat al-'amma* ... [Public Liberties in Islam], Beirut, Centre for Arab Unity Studies.

Hanafi, H. (1988) *Min al-'aqida ila al-thawra* ... [From Faith to Revolution; Vol. 1: Theoretical Introduction], Cairo, Madbuli.

Hijab, N. (1988) *Womanpower: the Arab Debate on Women at Work*, Cambridge, Cambridge University Press.

Hudson, M. (1995) 'Arab regimes and democratization: responses to the challenge of political Islam' in Guazzone, L. (ed.) *The Islamist Dilemma in the Arab World: National, Regional and International Dimensions*, Reading, Ithaca Press.

Huntington, S.P. (1991) *The Third Wave: Democratization in the Late Twentieth Century*, Norman, University of Oklahoma Press.

Huwaidi, F. (1985) *Muwatinun la dhimmiyyun* [Citizens, Not Protected Subjects], Beirut, Dar al-Shuruq.

Huwaidi, F. (1993) *Al-Islam wa al-dimuqratiyya* [Islam and Democracy], Cairo, Al-Ahram.

Imara, M. (1995) *Hal al-Islam huwa al-hall?* [Is Islam the Solution?], Cairo, Dar al-Shuruq.

Kedourie, E. (1988) 'Ethnicity, majority, and minority in the Middle East' in Esman, M.J. and Rabinovich, I. (eds) *Ethnicity, Pluralism, and the State in the Middle East*, Ithaca, Cornell University Press.

Kedourie, E. (1994) *Democracy and Arab Political Culture*, London, Frank Cass.

Macleod, A.E. (1991) *Accommodating Protest: Working Woman, the New Veiling and Change in Cairo*, New York, Columbia University Press.

Mortimer, R. (1991) 'Islam and multiparty politics in Algeria', *Middle East Journal*, vol.45, no.4.

Al-Sayyid, R. (1984) *Al-Umma wa al-jama'a wa al-sulta* [Community, Group and Authority], Beirut, Dar al-Iqra.

Tamimi, A. (ed.) (1993) *Power-Sharing Islam*, London, Liberty for the Muslim World.

Waterbury, J. (1994) 'Democracy without democrats? The potential for political liberalization in the Middle East' in Salamé, G. (ed.) *Democracy Without Democrats? The Renewal of Politics in the Muslim World*, London, I.B. Tauris.

Watt, W.M. (1968) *Islamic Political Thought: the Basic Concepts*, Islamic Surveys, no.6, Edinburgh, Edinburgh University Press.

CHAPTER 15

Israel: constraints on consolidation

Michael Dumper

Introduction

Unlike the other chapters in this part of the book, this chapter is concerned not only with the initial establishment of liberal democratic structures but also with the consolidation phase of democratization identified by transition theorists as being essential if democracy is to become entrenched. It studies democratization in Israel by asking two questions. First, what were the factors which led to the setting up of a liberal democratic system in 1948? Second, what have been the constraints on the consolidation of that democracy?

The dilemma of Israeli democracy is the tension which exists between the democratic aspirations of the founders of the state and the ethnically exclusive basis of Zionism. Present day Israel is the result of the process of nation building which began once the decision had been made to establish a nation-state to provide a homeland free of anti-semitism in which Jews would control their own destiny. This process had two requirements, internal stability and commitment of all citizens to the ideal of the Jewish state and freedom from external aggression. The first of these led to the creation of a broad inclusive liberal democratic system constructed so as to neutralize social divisions, incorporate all shades of Jewish opinion and cement allegiance to the state; the second to the expulsion of the majority of the Palestinians within the borders of the 1948 state, a series of territorial wars between Israel and its Arab neighbours and the increasing militarization of Israeli society (see Box 15.1).

Section 15.1 approaches the democratization of Israel by pointing out that it needs to be viewed in the context of two important conditioning factors – on the one hand the history of the experience of the persecution of Jews in Europe; on the other, the resistance of the indigenous Palestinian Arabs. Through an examination of one of the key institutions in the state-building process established during the British Mandate for Palestine between 1922 and 1948, the Zionist trade union federation known as the Histadrut, it shows how democratic means were used to accommodate the interests of different groups and to consolidate immigrants from diverse origins into a single Jewish community. At the same time however, it is pointed out that this accommodation took place purely within the framework of the establishment of a Zionist Jewish state. No attempt was made to reach agreement with non-Jewish parties or groupings which opposed the foundation of such a state and the future status of the indigenous Arab population was left unclear.

Section 15.2 continues this theme by discussing how, following the partition of Palestine in 1947, liberal democracy was used in support of Zionism, which was the dominant ideology of the new Israeli state. The immigrant nature of Israeli society and the rapid growth of the population

Box 15.1 Arab–Israeli conflict, 1948–96

1948–49   Effective partition of Palestine. Israel established on coastal plain, Galilee and Negev Desert. 'West Bank' incorporated into Jordan, Gaza Strip administered by Egypt.

1956   Israel invades Gaza Strip and Egypt up to Suez Canal. Forced to withdraw by the USA.

1967   June war of 1967. Israel occupies Gaza Strip, Sinai Desert, West Bank and Golan Heights. Armies of Egypt, Jordan and Syria defeated. Rise of the Palestine Liberation Organization (PLO).

1973   October war of 1973. Armies of Syria and Egypt poised to defeat Israel but ultimately forced to withdraw. New armistice lines drawn in Sinai peninsula and Golan Heights.

1977   President Sadat of Egypt visits Jerusalem marking the start of peace negotiations which culminate in Camp David Agreements.

1982   Israel invasion of Lebanon. 'Control region' established up to 50 km from Israeli border; Israelis withdraw to smaller 'security zone'.

1987–90   Palestinian uprising in West Bank and Gaza Strip against Israeli rule. Start of peace negotiations between Arab states, Palestinians and Israel in Madrid.

1993–96   Secret negotiations between PLO and Israel accelerate agreement which leads to partial Israeli withdrawal from Gaza Strip and West Bank.

through incorporation of Jews of different national origins presented problems of cohesion. Liberal democratic institutions were used to mediate these different interests and to bring about the flexibility and unity of purpose that was necessary in the face of the hostility of neighbouring Arab states and militant refugee organizations. The procedures which were developed (in particular the extreme form of proportional representation which was adopted), were inclusive for the Jewish majority but they marginalized the remaining Palestinian population by placing obstacles in the way of ethnic and regional representation which would have allowed them a voice.

Section 15.3 sees the continuing influence of Zionism, the continuing dispute over the territory of Israel and the continuing exclusion of Palestinians from any form of power as one of two major constraints on the consolidation of Israeli democracy in the period between 1948 and 1995 – the other being the prolonged domination of middle-class Ashkenazim Jews of European and North American origin and the growth of ethnic tensions between these and the poorer Mizrachi Jews from Asian and North African countries. It shows that although the integration of the Mizrachi Jews into the

Israeli polity has been a gradual process accompanied by social and political upheaval the liberal democratic system, operating within the framework of the Jewish state, has been able to mitigate the destabilizing effects of this social division. In contrast, the nature of Israel as a Jewish state has stood in the way of the democratic solution of the dilemma of the role of the Arab minority who cannot be absorbed or accommodated because they are non-Jewish.

In examining the nature of Israeli democracy and the constraints on its consolidation three explanatory factors are shown to be of particular relevance. In analysing Israeli democratization and the constraints on its consolidation particular use is made of three of the six explanatory factors outlined in Chapter 1.

Social divisions in Palestine before the creation of the state and after 1948 as Israel, particularly those of ethnicity and religion, have moulded the form and content of Israeli democracy. A state founded by Jews for Jews was bound to marginalize non-Jewish groups and qualify the extent of the democratization process. This tendency was reinforced by a *political culture* based on the ideology of Zionism – a national movement of the Jewish people. Nevertheless, to focus simply on the impact of Zionism upon non-Jewish inhabitants of Israel would be to also overlook a political culture committed to democratic procedures most notably in the form of electoral compromise and coalition-building among the mainstream Jewish Zionist parties.

The third explanatory factor to be considered, *international engagements including war,* has had a forceful impact in a contradictory way. The close cultural ties between the Israeli Ashkenazi elite and the West has led to the integration of the Israeli economy in the economies of the West, the provision of extensive US aid in the form of loans, grants, technological expertise and sophisticated military equipment. This has encouraged the pursuit of democratic procedures and a degree of openness in the Israeli political system. Conversely, the establishment of Israel on what its Arab neighbours have consistently perceived as Arab land has created a militarization of Israeli society which has undermined the practice of democracy through the imposition of military rule over many parts of Israel itself and areas it acquired after 1967.

15.1 State building and democratization

This section will focus on the growth of Jewish political institutions during the era of the British Mandate for Palestine. Reference will be made to the Palestinian Arab community, but because the 1948 war between the two communities resulted in the destruction of Palestinian religious and political institutions, tracing the inception of the dominant Jewish political institutions is more relevant to our study of the evolution of Israeli democracy. The section will examine the impact of the social divisions in Mandatory Palestine maintained as a result of mutually exclusive political cultures of the Palestinian Arab population and the Zionist settlers. It is here that the explanatory factor of political culture in the form of the ideology and practice of Zionism greatly helps us to appreciate the exclusive character of Israeli democracy. One can see how the ideological foundations of that democracy concerned itself with the Jewish community and left the future status of the Palestinian Arabs unclear.

The specific features of Israeli democracy have been shaped both by the experience of Jews in post-Enlightenment Europe and the political conditions in which the settler community grew during the British Mandate for Palestine from 1922 to 1948. The development of secularism and the notion of the nation-state during the nineteenth century enhanced the role of individual citizens and provided greater opportunities for minority religious groups to integrate into the social and political culture of the nation. However, the progress of political integration and cultural assimilation was often marked by the spasmodic rejection of minority groups by the dominant population group. In the case of the Jewish community in Europe and Russia, the uneven progress of integration was illustrated by waves of anti-semitism, highlighted by the Dreyfuss case (false imprisonment of a Jewish army officer) in France during the 1890s and pogroms in Russia, Poland and other parts of Eastern Europe.

In response to what was perceived as a European intransigence to Jewish integration and assimilation, Jewish intellectuals, such as Theodore Herzl, proposed the creation of a Jewish state. The state was to be culturally Jewish, but secular, and was to provide a haven for persecuted Jews from all over the world. Discussion on this project coalesced into an international movement and the proponents of a Jewish state became known as Zionists. In 1897, the World Zionist Organisation was set up and in 1898, the first Zionist Congress was held in Basle.

Zionist leaders began to negotiate with the imperial powers of the day as to the possibility of obtaining land for Jewish settlement in their colonies and under their initial protection. While Palestine had its attraction as the biblical homeland for Jews, its control by the Ottoman Empire made its feasibility as a goal of the Zionist endeavour initially unlikely. Plans were made for Zionist colonies in Uganda, Argentina and Palestine. It was not until the prospect of the British control over Palestine surfaced during the 1914–18 war that Zionist attention focused in a more determined manner on Palestine. Jewish leaders in Britain persuaded Lord Balfour in 1917 to make his famous declaration that Britain 'would view with favour' the establishment of a Jewish homeland in Palestine. In order not to antagonize Britain's erstwhile Arab allies it was left unclear what would constitute a 'homeland' although for the Zionist movement it was clear that it would form the basis for a Jewish state following a British withdrawal.

The inter-war period saw the rapid growth of the Jewish community, or the Yishuv as it became known, in Palestine, both in demographic and political terms. The Jewish population increased from approximately 93,360 in 1922 to 599,922 in 1946 comprised 11.4 per cent and 31 per cent of the total population (McCarthy, 1990, pp.35–6). The biggest increases in population came in the mid 1930s following the rise of fascism in Europe and its accompanying anti-Semitic policies. These policies culminated in the slaughter of Jews in the Nazi Holocaust during the early 1940s and led ever greater numbers of Jews to seek refuge in Palestine. The overwhelming majority of these immigrants came from Eastern Europe and were intellectuals, professionals or skilled workers and not well-suited to the demands of the primitive settler communities they were encouraged to settle in. At the same time, many adapted and great strides were made with British assistance in introducing a basic infrastructure for a modern state.

For its part the Palestinian Arab community was a largely rural population living within a feudal land-owning structure. The urban population was small, dominated by the large aristocratic families of Palestine. The educated class was also small, predominantly Christian, and employed by the British Mandatory authorities. Politically active Palestinians were drawn from the latter two groups and political parties were not large or of great consequence in Palestinian politics during the Mandate period.

The interests of the various sections of Palestinian society were expressed by the large families acting, sometimes in concert, sometimes in competition, in bodies such as the Higher Executive Committee, which later became the Arab Higher Committee, and the Supreme Muslim Council. The former two were the main interlocutors with the British authorities and the Zionist leadership but were riven by a split between the two major clans. The main aims of the Palestinian leadership were to persuade the British government to drop its commitment to a Jewish national home in Palestine and to resist continued Zionist settlement. Some individual Palestinian leaders explored the possibility of an accommodation with the Zionist movement which would include curbs on future Jewish immigration but these came to nought and did not correspond with the general Palestinian determination to create their own state.

The increasing numbers of Jewish settlers had a knock-on effect, projecting the Zionist leaders into key players in Mandate politics. Formal British support for the Jewish national home policy gave political recognition to the activities of the Yishuv. There was a flourishing of Zionist para-state organizations which provided a framework through which the demands of the community could be mediated with the British authorities and the Palestinian Arab opposition. In the absence of an agreement for elections to a joint Legislative Council for Palestine comprising Palestinian Arabs and Jews, the British encouraged the settlers to establish the Va'ad Leumi, a representative council for the Yishuv. Organizations such as the Jewish Agency, the Jewish National Fund and the Settlement Department of the World Zionist Organization and the trade union federation, the Histadrut, all contributed to the embryonic structures of the proposed Jewish state and gave an opportunity for groups and individuals to acquire logistic and leadership skills.

The formal recognition of Jewish representative bodies by the British authorities combined with the Zionist emphasis on separaté development and produced a 'state within a state' on the eve of the British departure in 1948. There was a separate Jewish educational system, a separate postal system and virtually a separate economy with Jewish entrepreneurs, the Histadrut and Jewish settlements attempting to employ only Jewish labour. There was also a land acquisition policy which tried to establish, consolidate and extend Jewish enclaves in different parts of Palestine and, finally, the creation of an illegal militia to defend the gains of the Yishuv.

A passer-by reads a Hebrew Legion poster in London, 28 January 1948. The Legion's founder, Samuel Weiser, said that he is using the posters to recruit a brigade of men who will set sail for Palestine to 'fight for the rights of the Jews'

At this juncture, it is important to note that while there was considerable overlap in the doctrine, strategy and goals of the various Zionist, non-Zionist and other Jewish groups in Palestine, by no means did they act as a monolithic bloc. This was partly due to their different ethnic, religious and class origins. Ethnically, there was a division between the Ashkenazi Jews of West and Central European origin and the Sephardi Jews, that is, Jews who lived throughout the Mediterranean. Prior to the waves of immigration in the twentieth century, the Jewish presence in Palestine had largely consisted of Sephardi Jews and had been given formal recognition as a religious community by the Ottoman state. The waves of immigration at the end of the nineteenth century and during the British Mandate period comprised mostly Ashkenazi Jews whose numbers eventually swamped those of the Sephardis and created lasting animosities. A second division was that between the religious and more secular-oriented Jews. While Zionism as an ideology did not exclude traditional and orthodox Judaism, the main organizers and political leaders tended to have a secular outlook who frequently clashed with the demands of religious Jewry for strict adherence to dietary laws, Sabbath regulations and other religious injunctions for the Yishuv. As the numbers of settlers increased, particularly in the 1930s, the secular–religious divide increased. Secular leaders, such as David Ben Gurion of the Histadrut, with their greater access to funds, to political influence in Palestine and Europe, to a sympathetic public opinion in Europe, to a greater reservoir of potential immigrants, began to dominate the decision-making processes of the Yishuv and monopolize the contacts and negotiations with the British authorities and Palestinian Arab leaders. Their dominance was an important factor in the decision to establish Israel as a democracy and not a theocracy. Finally, there were, of course, divisions amongst the secular settler groups and it is here that, as one might expect, we find class conflicts the most salient.

By examining the political developments in a key institution dominated by secular settlers, the Histadrut, it is possible to see not only how such conflicts played out but also how they were framed within the wider Zionist goals shared by all the political groups which were laid over these social divisions. The general trade union federation, the Histadrut, was founded in 1920 and became one of the most important state-building institutions in the Yishuv. It became much more than a mere trade union. As well as representing the interests of its members it set up a wide range of enterprises in construction, manufacturing and even banking. It also provided services such as labour exchanges and a comprehensive health-care system to all its members and affiliates. As a result of these roles and the bureaucracy that was created to administer its operations, by 1948, the Histadrut was the largest employer of Jewish labour in Palestine and was in a position to constitute the public sector of the projected state. The question of who controlled the Histadrut was an important feature of Jewish Zionist politics during the Mandate period.

The Mapai Party, led by David Ben Gurion, was in a position of dominance in the Histadrut. Mapai realized that if the Histadrut was to succeed in being the vehicle for establishing the state it was of vital importance to include rival groups on the left and on the right of the Zionist spectrum and from the religious parties. Ben Gurion, therefore, proceeded to either co-opt or marginalize rival groups. Hashomer Hatza'ir, its rivals on the left, was given access to Histadrut funds for its *kibbutzim* and its members obtained employment in the Histadrut's bureaucracy. In return the party supported Mapai at Histadrut meetings and in elections in the World Zionist Organization.

Similarly, the National Religious Party (NRP), an amalgam of smaller religious parties also entered into a voting pact with Mapai in the Histadrut and World Zionist Organization. It agreed to accept that the public sector was the key instrument for the implementation of the Zionist goal of a state and would be given preferential treatment over the private sector and that the land acquired by the Jewish National Fund would be nationalized. Furthermore the NRP dropped its demands that the future state would be administered by traditional rabbinic laws. In return for these agreements, the NRP was granted access to the health system and labour exchanges of the Histadrut, and was given an agreed number of seats in the World Zionist Organization bureaucracy. The Histadrut also agreed to introduce Sabbath and religious dietary restrictions in all its organizations. Thus both adversaries to the Mapai Party were co-opted into the socialist-syndicalist approach to Zionism.

In contrast, the Revisionist or Herut Party as it was later called, founded by Vladimir Jabotinsky failed to come to an agreement with Mapai. Herut, although well known for proposing an extreme version of Zionism in which the expulsion of the native Palestinian Arab population was seen as inevitable and desirable, was largely the party of the *petite bourgeoisie*, the small traders and business people. It saw itself as the defenders of free enterprise in the

Zionist movement and strongly opposed the dominance of the socialist wing. It remained outside the coalition created by Mapai which at times led to violent disputes between them.

What is significant in any discussion of the foundations of Israeli democracy is the complete absence of political agreements or alignments between the Zionist parties and Palestinian Arab elites, parties or groupings. While accommodation and compromise were achieved between the Zionist elites and there was a paring down of the multiplicity of parties, this was being carried out within the framework of establishing a Zionist and Jewish state. Some Jewish leaders, particularly those in the Communist Party and a small party called Brit Shalom did argue that conflict with the Palestinians and Arabs could only be avoided in a bi-national state, but they had little influence over the main thrust of the Zionist movement. There is no evidence of any significant class alignment between the two national camps and although there were some tentative attempts at elite bargaining these consistently collapsed over issues such as the Zionist demand for the unlimited immigration of Jews.

────────────────── *Summary of Section 15.1* ──────────────────

- Anti-semitism in Europe combined with the opportunities provided by European imperialism made the Zionist project of a Jewish state feasible.

- Zionist colonization in Palestine was in the main designed to establish an exclusive Jewish state.

- The coalition politics of the Histadrut established a broad ideological consensus which established the foundations of the Israeli state based on Zionism.

- There was little basis for elite compromise across the ethnic divide and the status of the Palestinian Arabs in the projected Jewish state was uncertain.

15.2   The consolidation of Israeli democracy

This section examines the particular forms that Israeli democracy has taken. In doing so it attempts to show how those forms are closely linked to the specific circumstances of the creation of the state and its social and ethnic make-up. The section starts with an examination of questions of territoriality and citizenship which help illustrate the nature of the Israeli polity. It then follows with the presentation of some basic data in order to indicate the complexity of Israeli society and to explain the subsequent strains encountered by the state and its democratic processes. The section concludes with a discussion of the structures adopted and of the Israeli political system in practice.

The case of Israel raises important general issues about the constraints on the consolidation of democracy. These should be borne in mind in any examination of Israeli democracy and encompass subsidiary but important questions about the nature of citizenship, the legitimacy of a state's sovereignty over territory acquired through conflict and the extent to which defence strategies override civil and political liberties.

Two sets of questions relating to the question of democracy and Israel arise from these issues. The first is, what is the territory of the Israeli state? It is important to establish a clear understanding of the territory involved, the extent to which the state's authority is recognized and how that authority is applied. These specific Israeli issues introduce more general questions as to whether a democratic state can maintain martial law indefinitely over certain areas and sections of the population and still remain democratic.

It is now widely accepted by the international community that the territory of Israel extends to the Armistice lines of 1949 (see Map 15.1) but it has not accepted Israel's claims to the Golan Heights or to those parts of the West Bank which fall within an extended Israeli Municipality of Jerusalem. The evolution of Israeli democracy has been as much affected by the uncertainty of the extent of Israeli sovereignty and Palestinian and Arab resistance to the claimed borders as it has been by other internal structural causes.

The second question is closely connected to the first: who are the citizens of the Israeli state? The dual Zionist and democratic nature of the Israeli state highlights the role of the non-Jewish minority, the Palestinian Arabs, which remained in Israel after 1948 and of the inhabitants of the occupied territories. There is a tension between the notion of a state which was set up on behalf of persecuted Jews, with Jewish cultural and religious trappings, and the inclusion of non-Jews as equals. That is between an ethno-cultural nationalism such as Zionism and the idea and practice of democracy which includes the protection of minority groups. In laying out these sets of questions one can clearly see how the nature of democracy in Israel is shaped by the Zionist ideals of the dominant Jewish community and is intrinsically tied up with the conflict with its neighbours and minorities.

Finally, there is the issue of what civil and political liberties a democratic state may legitimately restrict when it is under external threat. Clearly the imposition of security and preventative measures has an impact on the functioning and development of democracy. The fact that some security measures are justified needs to be balanced by the knowledge that they can be applied selectively against a minority and constrain their participation in the political life of the state. In the case of Israel one has to consider carefully those practices and policies which can be attributed to security measures and those which can be attributed to the pursuance of its ethno-cultural nationalism, and, importantly, what are the causal links between them.

There is no doubt that a formal democracy was introduced in Israel in 1948 and despite certain exclusive aspects, it was strengthened and deepened in the years after the creation of the state. That it took place despite the difficulties in absorbing huge numbers of new immigrants, integrating a heterogeneous population and the military footing on which much of the domestic politics of the country was played out, is a testimony to the commitment to democracy of its founders.

Between 1948 and the early 1950s, the Jewish population of the new state increased from just under half a million to two million. This meant that three-quarters of the new state comprised recently arrived immigrants. By the late 1980s, 45 out of every 100 Israelis were new immigrants and following the

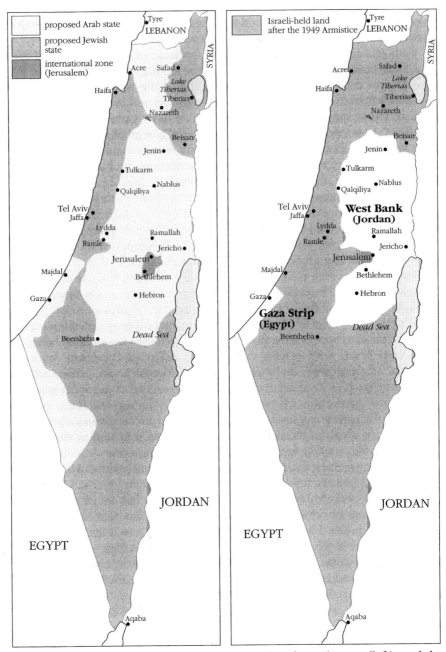

*Map 15.1   United Nations' 1947 partition plan for Palestine (left) and the
1949 Armistice demarcation (right)*

influx of Soviet Jews from 1989 onwards, immigrants once again became a
majority of the population. This 'newness' and the fact that at any given time
the majority of the population was in some stage of absorption and
orientation has meant one of the key components of democratization, the
emergence of new classes and their conflict with each other, has been
obscured (Smooha, 1993a, p.315). Quite clearly, Israel is a state of

newcomers and the drain on resources in providing housing, employment, schools and orientation has been quite considerable.

However, the aspect of this feature which is of most interest to this topic is the lack of homogeneity in the population profile of the state. There are linguistic, cultural, religious, dietary cleavages not only between Palestinians and Jews, but between Jews of Western European, Eastern European, Slavic, Middle Eastern, North African, North American and Asian origin. There are, in fact, Jews from at least 52 ethnic origins in Israel. When one adds to these divisive pressures the 'normal' divisiveness one finds in a modern industrializing society of class, wealth, employment and religious belief, one has a heterogeneous mix of a potentially explosive sort.

The fact that Israel has not gone through a regime instability of the South American pattern as a result of these cleavages is noteworthy. As I have already discussed, this has much to do with the dominance of Zionism as the state ideology and the cultural consensus built round this. Partly as a result of the impact of the successful Zionist project on the Arab world and the conflict it generated, it has also produced a social cohesion within the country where cleavages are submerged. But it is also to do with the type of democratic procedures which are, on the one hand, inclusive for the Jewish majority and, on the other, place obstacles in the way of ethnic and regional representation.

The setting up of the Israeli government was laid down by provisions in the 1947 UN resolution on the partition of Palestine into a Jewish and an Arab state. The Jewish settler elites, however, decided that a provisional council comprising members of the Va'ad Leumi, that is the National Council of the Jewish Community, and members of the Zionist executive would elect the provisional government.

This meant that the broad coalition of groups that formed the Zionist mainstream continued to dominate the transitional and early state structures. The ultra-orthodox Jews, the Communist and the Revisionist groups which had boycotted the Yishuv elections were not included in the provisional bodies, although they were included at a later date. It also meant that non-Jews, the Palestinians, were not included. The transitional structures very clearly incorporated the ideology of Zionism and set the scene for the problems of consolidation which were to come. This can be seen in the way references in the early drafts of the Israel declaration of independence, which explicitly stated that 'the Jewish state would be democratic', were replaced with more general commitments to the 'full social and political equality of all its citizens without distinction of race, creed or sex' (Medding, 1990, pp.14–15).

While there was broad agreement on the governmental structures of the transitional period, there was little agreement over the constitutional foundations of the state. The religious content of the state, its final borders, the identification of Jewishness were all definitions which required a renewed consensus which went beyond the pragmatic one that had built up round resistance to the Palestinian Arabs and the British during the Mandate period. Ultimately, the issue of a written constitution was side-stepped and a number of 'Basic Laws' were and continue to be introduced every few years which cover many of the main electoral procedures and relationships between the executive, legislative and judiciary.

The formal democratic system in Israel is a liberal representative system with both majoritarian features, such as a strong executive which dominates the legislative, and consensual features, such as proportional representation. During the course of its lifetime it has been argued that while the structures of the founding period have remained the same, in practice there has been a gradual shift towards a more consensual system of representative democracy (Medding, 1990, p.6). What, then, are the main features of Israeli democracy?

In the first place, it comprises a single legislative chamber elected by proportional representation every four years. The electorate is universal and extends, therefore, to the Palestinian Arab population within the 1949 Armistice lines also. The apparent conflict between this fact and the argument that Israel is a partial democracy is dealt with in greater detail in the next section. The Knesset, as the legislative chamber is called, has 120 members and elects the Prime Minister who then selects the cabinet.

The real power in Israeli politics lies with the cabinet where the state's resources are divided up amongst the different ministries. Due to the tradition of Israeli governments being made up of broad coalitions, Israeli cabinets tend to be overlarge. Each party and each faction within a party demands a reward for its commitment to the coalition in the form of ministerial or deputy ministerial appointments and cabinets up to 30 members are not unusual. This is an unwieldy number for speedy decision making and as a result there is often a *de facto* 'inner' or 'kitchen' cabinet where policies of the dominant party are thrashed out and key defence and foreign affairs decisions are made (Beillin, 1991, pp.61–2).

The Knesset itself is relatively impotent once the coalition bargains have been struck and Knesset debates on detailed legislation are often poorly attended. A recent innovation along the Westminster model of Standing Committees in which cabinet decisions are scrutinized has reinvigorated the role of the Knesset member to some extent, but the committees themselves have no constitutional authority to overturn cabinet decisions. Their influence is derived from the threat of bad publicity and exposure. As a result of what is regarded by many constitutional experts as excessive power in the hands of the executive, there has been frequent resort to the Israeli Supreme Court to challenge cabinet decisions. Great attention is also given to the views of the State Comptroller who conducts a national audit on the government and whose annual reports are often scathing at ministerial inefficiencies.

The electoral system in Israel is regarded as an unusually pure form of proportional representation. Until the 1992 elections, any party receiving as little as 1 per cent of the votes cast would obtain a seat and it only required the support of 750 signatories before a candidate was eligible to stand for national elections. Such a low threshold usually requires an extremely stable democratic regime to offset the instability of coalition government.

In Israel there were two effects of this low threshold which tended to balance each other out. First, there was a proliferation of small parties obtaining a small number of seats but who, as a totality, were able to deny the larger parties a working majority. Since 1948, governments have been formed by the larger parties coaxing the smaller parties into broad coalitions in order to form a majority. Not only did this blunt the policies of the dominant party

Box 15.2 Gender and Israeli democracy

Despite the media attention devoted to the female units in the Israeli army, gender equality in the Israeli democracy is no more advanced or institutionalized than in any other democracy. The presence of Golda Meir as the Israeli Prime Minister during and after the 1967 war and the influential role exercised by the Israeli State Comptroller, Miriam Ben-Porat, do not reflect any measure of added integration of women into the political decision-making processes of the country. Despite being 48 per cent of the electorate, only 6.8 per cent of the total number of members of Knesset elected since 1948 have been women. The total proportion of women in any single Knesset has never reached 10 per cent. Representation of women in the executive has been similarly low. Between 1948 and 1992 only four women have served in the cabinet (Pope, 1993, pp.202–3). Indeed, in the army itself, female conscription is only two thirds of men's; they are denied any combat role, and 40 per cent of women conscripts are to be found in clerical and servicing roles.

but it also gave disproportionate influence to minor members of the coalition in terms of ministerial seats and budgetary allocations.

This has particularly been the case for the small religious parties which have succeeded in obtaining significant changes in social matters, such as Rabbinical control over marriage, abortion, autopsy, dietary and Sabbath regulations, and in the allocation of budgets for the religious ministries and religious education system and, finally, military service exemptions. These concessions have not been supported by the more secular majority and have exacerbated the religious–secular divide.

A second, more positive effect of the low threshold was that it served to include minor sectoral interests in a heterogeneous population and political culture. Certainly a tyranny of the majority has been avoided which would have been destabilizing in face of the strains of state building and war. It is interesting to note, however, that this inclusivity has not as yet extended to the Palestinian Arab population. Parties with Jewish leadership but with a predominantly Palestinian membership and support, such as the New Israeli Communist Party and the Progressive List for Peace, have not once been part of a ruling government coalition.

A further counter-balance to the instability which can accompany such a low electoral threshold is the fact that Israel votes as a single constituency. Electors vote for a party list, not for individual members and the amount of votes cast for a party determines how many members on that list become parliamentary deputies. If there is a death or a resignation the gap is replaced by the next name on the list. In this way no relationship is built up between the voters and the Knesset members. It is the party which determines who should be on the list and at what level. In order to garner as wide a cross-section of support as possible parties work hard to elicit the support of community leaders to scatter amongst their lists of party candidates.

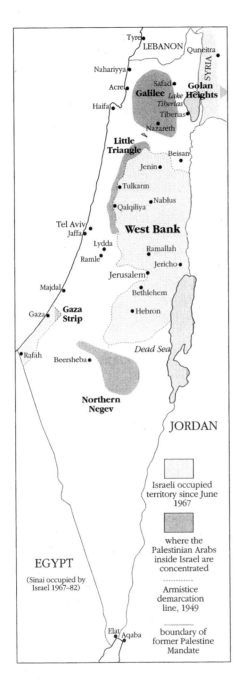

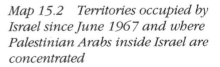

Map 15.2   Territories occupied by Israel since June 1967 and where Palestinian Arabs inside Israel are concentrated

The combination of the absence of voter identification with individuals and the ability of large parties to co-opt potential leadership figures has been to deter ethnic or regional representation. It has only been since the 1980s when disillusion with the two main blocs, the leftist Labour Alignment and the rightist Likud Party, was so severe that disaffected ethnic and religious communities began to organize electorally and parties such the Tami Party

(Moroccan, now defunct), Shas (Mizrachi and orthodox), and the Arab Democratic Party (Palestinian) were created. In 1992, the low threshold was raised to 1.5 per cent with the result that some of the more extreme parties were excluded and the number of parties elected was reduced from fifteen to ten.

The single constituency system as a deterrent against regional represen-tation has been particularly effective against the Palestinian minority in Israel. One only has to consider the overwhelming demographic dominance that Palestinians have had in the Galilee region of northern Israel to see how, if Israel had been divided into small constituencies, the Galilee constituencies would return Palestinian Knesset members with solid majorities. Co-ordination between those Knesset members promoting regional interests would raise the prospect of autonomy demands, and possibly secessionist ones at a later stage, which would undermine a Jewish-dominated Israel. Also Israeli feminists have argued that the large single constituency disadvantages women's participation. Nominations are made by central party activists who have the time to lobby away from home, by-passing women who may participate in grassroot political activity but because of their family responsibilities are more tied to their locality.

------------------------ *Summary of Section 15.2* ------------------------

- Uncertainty over the territory of the state raises questions of citizenship and the application of democracy to areas under martial law.
- The democratic system of Israel gives considerable power both to the party and to the cabinet.
- Extreme proportional representation has produced unstable coalition government but regime stability.
- Despite active participation in the army, female participation in higher political posts is not significantly greater than in other democracies.

15.3 Ethnicity and nationalism: twin challenges to Israeli democracy

Given both the extraordinary circumstance surrounding the birth of Israel and the formidable external pressures it has been subjected to, the resilience and extent of Israeli democracy is remarkable. Here was a state initially equipped with only the most rudimentary resources, absorbing nearly two million new immigrants, fending off military attacks from all directions and trying to provide extensive infrastructure to the undeveloped areas it had acquired, and, at the same time, obliging itself to introduce sufficient democratic procedures to keep its leaders accountable to the burgeoning Jewish population and interest groups both in Israel and its supporters abroad. It was, one could argue, inevitable that short cuts and compromises were made in the assembling of Israeli democracy challenging its very nature. This section will examine two key challenges to Israeli democracy: ethnic divisions within the Jewish community, and, Palestinian nationalism.

In Israel, Mizrachi Jews – Jews from Asian and African countries – constitute the poor and working classes while Ashkenazi Jews, from Europe and North America, dominate the middle, upper and elite classes. The explanations for this stratification along ethnic lines are numerous. Part of the reason has been the constraints placed on social mobility in a society where family and cultural divisions remain strong.

The Ashkenazim have been accused of discouraging the advance of Mizrachi Jews to protect their own position. Welfare and educational programmes introduced by the new state were effective in containing poverty but not in reducing inequalities (Smooha, 1993b, pp.162–5). More specifically, Mizrachi immigrants were directed to development towns in remote areas of the country where the housing, social facilities and employment prospects were poor; Mizrachi youth were pushed into vocational rather than higher education courses, and the land and quotas available to Mizrachi agricultural co-operatives (*moshavim*) were inferior to those acquired by the Ashkenazi (*kibbutzim*).

The sense of grievance this treatment engendered was to produce an electoral backlash against the Ashkenazi-dominated Mapai, subsequently known as the Labour Party. In 1977, Mizrachi Jews voted overwhelmingly against the ruling Labour coalition and for the right-wing Likud Party which took over the government. It was a political upheaval of cataclysmic proportions and shattered the old socialist and Ashkenazi dominance of the Israeli establishment. There has been, subsequently, a significant improvement in Mizrachi and Sephardi representation in the Israeli polity: there has been a Mizrachi state president, deputy prime minister, minister for foreign affairs, army chief of staff, secretary general of the Histadrut and treasurer of the Jewish Agency.

Nevertheless, Ashkenazim still maintain a monopoly in the economic sphere. They dominate the government ministries and corporations, the industrial complex of the Histadrut and the political bodies of the private sector, such as the Industrialists' Union. Social unrest has not continued at the same intensity, but the increasing independence of Mizrachi factions within both the Likud Party and the breaking away of the Mizrachi faction in the ultra-orthodox party, Agudat Torah, to form the successful and numerically superior Shas Party, reveal the continued existence of ethnic issues as a factor in Israeli politics.

One fear often expressed by (Ashkenazim?) scholars of the Israeli scene is that the lack of a democratic background in the Mizrachim's countries of origin makes their commitment to democracy fragile. To which Mizrachi leaders rather acidly reply that the democratic background of the Ashkenazim did not preclude the introduction of anti-democratic and discriminatory policies to consolidate their dominance of the political structures of society.

We turn now to the second major challenge to democracy in Israel. It is important to remember that from the perspective of the Palestinian minority in Israel, the virtues of the democracy introduced by the dominant Jewish population were not obvious. This was a community that prior to 1948 formed the majority of the population and who owned the vast majority of the land of Palestine. Following the British withdrawal and the outbreak of hostilities between the two national groups, the greater part of the Palestinian population fled and became refugees in Lebanon, Syria, Jordan and Egypt. Of the total of 900,000 Palestinian Arabs who had lived before 1948 on those areas of Palestine which became the Israeli state, only 120,000 remained (Abu-Lughod, 1971, pp.153–6).

Military rule was imposed over areas of Palestinian residence in Israel. The scene these Palestinians witnessed in 1948 was desperate. They experienced the division of families, the loss of land, the destruction of communal patterns, the exile of their political and religious leadership and what was perceived as an abandonment by the Arab world, the United Nations and world opinion. They were a physically and psychologically broken community.

Despite military rule, formal democratic procedures were extended to the Palestinian minority. They were made citizens of the state and given the right to vote. In addition, the government invested in roads, schools and other welfare services in Palestinian areas. To a large extent these moves were taken to pre-empt their affiliation to any other political entity. The predominantly Palestinian areas were those outside of the borders recommended by the UN and by introducing citizenship and the right to vote the government was consolidating its hold over the area. If it had denied them citizenship, it would have added to the uncertainty of the status of those areas (Peretz, 1991, pp.84–5). However, the continuation of military rule for eighteen years and the much greater proportion of government investment in the Jewish sector than in the Arab sector points to a practice which negated the theoretical inclusion of Palestinian political participation in the new state.

In addition to the imposition of military rule there are two other Israeli government policies which are relevant to our discussion. The first was the refusal by the government to consider the return of Palestinian refugees to their homes on what had become Israel. In 1948 there were 700,000 Jews in Israel and 120,000 Palestinians. Approximately 780,000 Palestinians had fled the fighting and were now refugees. Clearly to have accepted the return of all of them would have altered the demographic balance of Israel to the extent that Israel would have become a bi-national state. Even if only half wanted to return their numbers would have questioned the dominance of the Jewish community and nothing would have been gained by the fighting. Instead the government preferred to place the onus of their departure on the policies of the Arab states and was prepared to accept the prevailing hostile relations with them in order to prevent the return of the refugees.

The second policy is closely connected to the first. Much of the land of Mandatory Palestine was not owned by Jewish institutions or individuals prior to 1948. Some had been acquired by the British government, some was owned by the churches, but the great majority was owned by Palestinians and Arabs (Reudy, 1971, pp.132–3). In order to both consolidate its territorial base and in order to provide space for the new immigrants which were beginning to arrive, the government had to acquire this land and make it available for development. Accordingly, the government passed a series of laws, most notably the Absentee Property Law of 1950, which succeeded in transferring the land and property of the Palestinian refugees to Jewish municipal councils, agricultural settlements, such as the *kibbutzim* and *moshavim*, the

THE ARAB NIGHTMARE   **ISRAEL'S NIGHTMARE**

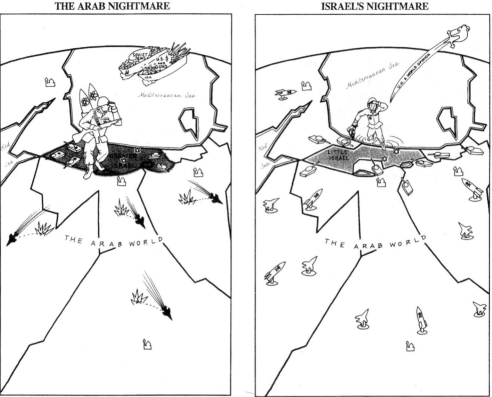

Jewish National Fund and to the state itself. Thus the perpetuation of Palestinians as refugees was essential to maintain the demographic superiority, to maintain the territorial integrity of the state and to provide space for its new citizens.

As a result of these and other laws which favoured the settlement of new Jewish immigrants and investment in a supportive infrastructure for their absorption, the Palestinian Arab community in Israel has remained largely marginalized in Israeli politics. Palestinians were barred from joining the Labour Party until 1970 (Beillin, 1991, p.176). Not until the 1990s was a wholly Palestinian Arab party allowed to function in Israel. The role of a non-Jewish minority in a Jewish state remains the central dilemma of Israeli democracy.

Associated with this dilemma has been the occupation by Israel of the remaining areas of Palestine, the West Bank and Gaza Strip, and part of Syria, the Golan Heights. This has added to the militarization of Israeli society already frequently on a war footing as a result of the conflict with the Arab states. Fears of the impact of prolonged military rule over Palestinians and Syrians on civil and political liberties in Israel itself are remarkably similar to those fears expressed by many liberals in the UK over the spillover effect of the Northern Ireland problem into the UK, particularly infringements on civil liberties, such as the Prevention of Terrorism Act and detention.

The Israeli government has directly intervened to constrain Palestinian political expression there, through censorship, severe policing practices, prolonged incarceration of leaders and activists as well as a military rule which had permeated every aspect of Palestinian life. In addition, the prolonging of an unaccountable military administration has led to the appearance of vested interests and corruption in the Israeli administration itself. Finally, the ambiguity in Israeli political circles over the ultimate fate of these territories and the extension of Israeli legal jurisdiction over Jewish enclaves there threw the majority of Palestinian inhabitants into a legal and political grey area.

─────────────────── *Summary of Section 15.3* ───────────────────

- The integration of Mizrachi Jews into the Ashkenazi dominated Israeli polity was a gradual process accompanied by social and political upheaval.

- Despite continued Ashkenazi dominance in key economic sectors, Mizrachi influence and representation has been sufficient to mitigate the more destabilizing aspects of this social division.

- While formal democratic rights were extended to the Palestinian Arab majority, legal and political restrictions have prevented the full exercise of those rights.

- Israeli democracy has not solved the dilemma of the role of a non-Jewish minority in a Jewish, albeit democratic state.

Conclusion

The evolution of the Israeli form of democracy can be traced back to the days of early Jewish settlement in Palestine. While anti-semitism in Europe provided the initial impetus for the Zionist movement its political development was as much influenced by democratic ideas and practices as it was by the inclusive pragmatism of the founders of Israel. The necessary bargains that had to be struck between disparate ideological groups to create a cohesive front against both the British Mandatory government and the Palestinian Arabs laid strong foundations for the liberal democratic institutions which were to follow later. The result was a vibrant democracy for the Jewish community in Israel. There were regular elections, a form of proportional representation which allowed for the political expression of minority views and a state whose structures were permeated with a Judaic ethos and ambience. For the defeated Palestinian Arabs that remained in Israel after 1948, however, Israel was a democracy circumscribed by security and ethnic restrictions.

This chapter has sought to explain the particular evolution in form and content of Israeli democracy by drawing attention to the importance of three explanatory factors. It argued that of the social divisions in Israel, it was those of ethnicity and nationalism which not only gave Israeli democracy its specific form, but also qualified it for non-Jews. The role of an Israeli political culture which reinforced the centrality of Jewishness in the state served to justify security concerns on ideological grounds. Finally the overwhelming presence of conflict and war has both kept the Jewish community cohesive and increased the marginalization of the Palestinian Arab minority. The combination of these three factors help to explain the constraints on the consolidation of Israeli democracy.

At the time of writing, Israel is going through a period of such enormous change that any definite conclusions and speculation of whether a deepening of democracy in Israel is in the offing has to be very tentative. Great demands are being placed on the Israeli economy by the absorption of nearly half a million new immigrants in the early 1990s, by the urgent requirement that Israel enters the world market and that it has some access to the economies of the Middle East. Current trends in the Middle East indicate that the combination of US security guarantees, aid and political pressure will lead to an agreement between Israeli leaders and Arab elites. The road to Israeli integration in the Middle East is being smoothed by external agencies.

However, while the success of Israel's current policies towards the Palestinians and its Arab neighbours may provide it with the means to integrate itself into the region, it will not resolve the dilemma of Israeli democracy: as a Jewish state how will it deal with the non-Jewish minority in territory under its control? In this way, a peace agreement with the Arab states and with the Palestinians will also require a re-examination of Zionism in its current form and practice. As a vehicle for establishing a homeland for the Jewish people, and for providing the social and political cohesion for the state in its formative stages it has been extraordinarily successful. But as an ideology which places a glass ceiling over Palestinian participation in the state's structures and decision-making processes, it can be argued that Zionism will hamper the evolution of Israel as a democratic society.

References

Abu-Lughod, J. (ed.) (1971) *The Transformation of Palestine*, Evanston, North-Western University Press.

Beillin, Y. (1991) *Israel: a Concise Political History*, London, Weidenfield and Nicholson.

Kyle, K. and Peters, J. (eds) (1993) *Whither Israel? The Domestic Challenges*, London, Royal Institute of International Affairs and I.B. Tauris.

McCarthy, C. (1990) *The Population of Palestine*, New York, Columbia University Press.

Medding, P. (1990) *The Founding of Israeli Democracy, 1948–1967*, Oxford, Oxford University Press.

Peretz, D. (1991) 'Early state policy towards the Arab population, 1948–1955' in Silberstein, L. (ed.) *New Perspectives on Israeli History: the Early Years of the State*, New York, New York University Press.

Pope, J.J. (1993) 'The place of women in Israeli society' in Kyle, K. and Peters, J. (eds).

Reudy, J. (1971) 'The dynamics of land alienation' in Abu-Lughod, J. (ed.).

Smooha, S. (1993a) 'Class, ethnic and national cleavages and democracy in Israel' in Srinzak, E. and Diamond, L. (eds) *Israeli Democracy Under Stress*, London, Lynne Rienner.

Smooha, S. (1993b) 'Jewish ethnicity in Israel' in Kyle, K. and Peters, J. (eds).

Afterword

Margaret Kiloh

Part IV has looked at democratization in sub-Saharan Africa and the Middle East. The arguments put forward in the chapters present a body of material structured by the explanatory factors and theoretical approaches introduced in Chapter 1. Apart from Chapter 13, which expresses a clear preference for structural theory, all of the chapters draw on more than one theoretical approach. They also use the explanatory factors in an eclectic manner, demonstrating that at certain historical points one variable may be important and at others different factors may come into play. Comparison between sub-Saharan Africa and the Middle East and between the case studies of South Africa and Israel emphasizes the conclusion that whereas there is a common framework within which democratization can be considered – colonialism, economic development, globalization – the specificity of the experience of each country means that it is difficult to find any one theoretical approach which can account for the processes which are taking place. Partly for this reason, the main argument in each chapter, with the exception of Chapter 13, is advanced primarily in terms of explanatory factors.

Economic development features as an explanatory factor in each of the five chapters but each uses it in a different way. Chapter 11 identifies lack of economic development as a common feature of African states which is usually held to be unconducive to democratization. The evidence which is produced suggests that in the period between the mid 1960s and the late 1980s, when authoritarian regimes held sway, there appears to be a correlation between economic underdevelopment and the undemocratic nature of most African states. In contradiction to this, however, there was no improvement in economic performance to account for the wave of democratization which took place in the following period from the late 1980s to 1995. (Nor, for that matter, were African nations any less poor when they gained their first democratic constitutions in the post-colonial hand over of power.) Of the three African countries which managed to retain democratic forms of government after independence the success of two (Botswana and Mauritius) might be said to owe something to a relatively high level of economic development. However, other countries which are well endowed with natural resources, such as Nigeria, have constantly succumbed to military coups and corruption. Also, as Chapter 12 points out, South Africa, which is the most industrially advanced country in sub-Saharan Africa, did not hold a democratic election until 1994.

This paradox is repeated in the case of the Middle East, where Chapter 13 can discover 'no simple relationship between socio-economic modernization and the development of liberal democracy' (Section 13.3). Indeed, it almost appears as if the *reverse* is true. Turkey achieved a form of democracy when it was still lacking in economic development and the oil-rich Gulf States and Saudi Arabia continued to maintain non-democratic systems despite their great wealth. In Israel too, economic development had little to do with the decision to introduce liberal democratic institutions when the state was founded.

Thus, whilst each of the chapters acknowledges that the level of economic development is an important factor in the process of democratization it is clear if we compare the evidence from Africa and the Middle East that this cannot stand alone as a general explanation for the presence or absence of liberal democracy. The experience of the countries discussed in this part of the book appears, rather, to confirm Barrington Moore's observation that economic development may lead *either* to democratization *or* to an intensification of authoritarian rule. To understand the path which particular countries take other factors need to be considered which may interact with economic development in different ways.

One of these factors is the level and nature of *international influences* on different regions or individual states within those regions. Both Africa and the Middle East have been influenced by Western colonialism and the Cold War in terms of their political systems and economic development. In the Middle East income from oil sales and foreign aid reinforced authoritarian Arab governments and insulated them from popular demands for increased participation. Internal productive forces were underdeveloped and the growth of new social groups was retarded. At the same time the Arab–Israeli conflict led to increased militarization and the strengthening of the state against other forces in society. The support of the USA for Israel perpetuated the problem of the Palestinian refugees while the Soviet Union encouraged its allies to adopt its own centralized control model of government. In Africa the specific geo-political circumstances were different but a similar overall pattern is discernible. Colonialism exploited Africa's natural resources and locked newly independent countries into an unequal trading relationship with the West. White settler regimes were supported but elsewhere power was handed over to a nationalist elite who were provided with economic and military aid even when they abandoned their post-independence democratic constitutions. Cold War rivalries divided the continent, and caused civil wars, the breakdown of the social order, famine and destruction in many states.

It may seem that international influences have been all negative but it is also possible to trace the more recent pressures for democratization in Africa and the Middle East to international influences, both direct and indirect. The evidence from South Africa illustrates how multinational companies and non-governmental organizations have spread their activities in ways which have helped to facilitate the growth of work- and interest-based organizations. These developments can promote democratic pluralism. At the same time diplomatic and economic pressure has been put on authoritarian regimes to liberalize their political systems.

All five chapters identify the nature of the *state and political institutions* as important factors in relation to the influence of economic development on democratization. In Africa, until recently, governments of all ideological complexions (including the white racist regime in South Africa) relied almost exclusively on the state as the key instrument in implementing economic policy. State control of the economy created a ruling 'bureaucratic bourgeoisie' which monopolized both political power and the fruits of economic activity, access being controlled by a system of 'clientelism' and patronage. The result of 'statist' systems, it is suggested, is both to limit development and, where development does occur, to limit the distribution of the benefits of development which might foster democratization to a very narrow section of the population. This conclusion is reinforced by Chapter 13 which draws a distinction between those countries such as Iraq, Syria, Egypt, the Gulf States and Saudi Arabia, where a state-elite has maintained a strong hold over the political and economic system, and Turkey (and to a more limited extent Iran) where capitalist development has taken place outside the direct control of the state and has allowed a degree of liberalization of the political system which has not occurred elsewhere.

The nature of the state both reflects and helps to create the kinds of *social divisions* which exist in society. Gender inequalities exist in all of the countries discussed in this part but these divisions come to the fore particularly in Islamic states where the extent to which both formal and effective civil and political rights have been extended to women can be seen as one measure of democratization. As Chapters 13 and 14 point out, however, state 'feminism' which recognizes women's political equality is often in advance of the views of Islamic societies as a whole and the formal rights extended to women have often been limited by the patriarchal basis of the 'private' domestic sphere. It is perhaps significant that in countries such as Iran and Algeria issues such as the role and control of women have become a major battleground between liberalizers and fundamentalists who reject democracy as an alien and un-Islamic philosophy.

Class divisions are also universal, although they are not all of the same kind. The Middle Eastern states discussed in Chapter 13 are divided into those with strong land owning and/or merchant classes which monopolized political and economic power and those without. In Africa, on the other hand, traditional societies were largely (though not exclusively) 'stateless' with no land-owning class, no centralized political control, communal ownership of land and economies based on subsistence and simple exchange. Colonial rule created states which provided a legal framework for the introduction of capitalism, wage labour and a class system based on race and the ownership of the means of production. When the colonial powers retreated they maintained control of the means of production and handed over political power to a nationalist elite 'which then proceeded to use the mechanism of the state (and particularly the state control of the economy) to constitute itself into a type of ruling class' (Chapter 11, Section 11.2). In South Africa, power was transferred to European settlers who used their control over the state machinery to bolster their own position by continuing to pursue a policy of white domination. Ruling class monopoly of state power is shown to be a fearsome obstacle to democratization. There is also evidence, however, of the importance of the role of other classes produced by economic development, in particular the organized working class. In Africa (especially South Africa) the trade union movement has played a major role in democratization. In the Middle East too, it is not only the presence or absence of a large-scale landed ruling class, but also the way subordinate classes relate to this which creates the distinction between authoritarian states and those in which some measure of democratization has occurred.

Control of the state once achieved can also affect social divisions based on ethnicity. This tendency has been particularly marked in the two case studies, South Africa and Israel, but it also shows itself in other African countries where the boundaries imposed by colonial powers created states in which ethnic divisions were strong and a sense of national identity was weak. The chapters in this part suggest that ethnic divisions *need not* lead to authoritarianism; as Chapter 11 points out, the three African states which managed to maintain their democratic systems in the period when others were falling apart all displayed considerable ethnic conflict.

Civil society has played a different role in Africa and the Middle East. In the Middle East, with the exception of Israel, the growth of civil society has been constrained not only by authoritarian political regimes but also by political culture and a tendency within Islam towards 'an implicit doctrine of the exclusive power of the ruler in his capacity as successor on earth first to Prophet Muhammad, then to God himself' (Chapter 14, Section 14.1). This is not to say that civil society is entirely absent. For example, in Turkey and Egypt, liberalization has led to the development of civil society to a certain extent. In other Islamist states, forms of non-Islamic organizations are frowned upon and discouraged, meaning that the basis for any impetus towards democratization originating in civil society is non-existent. In Israel the situation is somewhat different. The state of Israel had its base in the strong non-governmental Jewish organizations (such as the Histadrut) which were established during the period of the British Mandate. Since 1948, however, these have been largely incorporated and the same national-ist political culture which harnessed them for the creation of the Israeli state has frequently led them to see their role as supporting the government in the struggle between Jews and Palestinians.

In Africa, in contrast to the Middle East, the evidence is that the church, trade unions, civic associations and other grassroots organizations not only provided an important focus for opposition to the undemocratic rule of colonial powers but have also continued to play this role in the post-colonial period. In the middle period identified in Chapter 11 many of these organizations were either incorporated or disbanded by the post-colonial state and their leaderships imprisoned. Nevertheless, the 1980s saw a resurgence in the strength and vitality of civil society and its claim to occupy the political space which was empty of effective political parties. How important this has been in the process of re-democratization is difficult to judge, although Chapter 11 allocates it a major role. There is certainly evidence that in South Africa the part played by civic associations and trade unions in the 1980s was in many ways a decisive one in bringing an end to apartheid, and many observers allocate to civil society a crucial role in the consolidation of democracy in that country.

The issue of *political culture* is a connected one. As Chapters 11 and 12 point out, the power of political ideas, in particular the idea that democratization is what *ought* to happen, should not be underestimated. But liberal democratic ideas are not the only ones which may exercise an influence as Chapter 14 on Islam amply demonstrates. Belief systems and ideologies, whether they be religious or political, can challenge liberal democracy and obstruct its development.

To sum up the lessons of Part IV an awareness of the explanatory factors and how they can be used is clearly important. Their systematic deployment which takes into account the interplay between them and the nature of the particular society concerned is needed when trying to explain democratization in sub-Saharan Africa and the Middle East.

PART V
Communist and post-communist countries

Introduction   393

CHAPTER 16   Democratization in Eastern Europe   399

CHAPTER 17   Russia's troubled transition   421

CHAPTER 18   Political participation in post-communist democracies   443

CHAPTER 19   Nationalism, community and democratic transition in Czechoslovakia and Yugoslavia   466

CHAPTER 20   Political change in Vietnam   490

Afterword   513

Introduction

Paul Lewis

The collapse of communism, at least in its original European variant, was one of the major events in late twentieth century world politics. If the end of the 'long nineteenth century' (Chapter 2) was marked by the outbreak of the First World War in 1914, the close of the 'short twentieth' can be dated by the ending of communism in Eastern Europe in 1989. Whether or not it signalled an 'end of history' was debatable (Held, 1996); it certainly, however, spelt the end of a political system that had exercised a powerful influence over the political history of twentieth century Europe. In so doing, it also uncovered prospects of democratization in parts of the world long deprived of them. It is with such fundamental changes that Part V of the book is concerned. Unlike the previous parts, this one directs attention not so much to democratization in a particular region of the world as to processes of political change under an authoritarian regime – that is, communist rule – and subsequent developments in countries where it had come to an end. The emphasis in this section is placed on democratization in Eastern Europe and the former Soviet Union, with Vietnam presented as a case of political change within an established communist state.

As a result of the end of communist rule many democracies were established, although definition of the precise form of democracy that came into existence was often hazardous and – at the end of 1995 – could only be tentative on the basis of just six years of systemic change. On the basis of current information, the situation in the formerly communist countries of Eastern Europe and the Soviet Union could be summed up as in Table V.1

Table V.1

Liberal democracies	Partial democracies	Authoritarian regimes
Bulgaria	Albania	Azerbaijan
Czech Republic	Armenia	Kazakhstan
Estonia	Belarus	Tajikistan
Hungary	Bosnia	Turkmenistan
Latvia	Croatia	Uzbekistan
Lithuania	Georgia	
Poland	Kirgizistan	
Slovenia	Macedonia	
	Moldova	
	Romania	
	Russia	
	Serbia-Montenegro	
	Slovakia	
	Ukraine	

While the political condition of many individual states was open to considerable doubt, it was clearly the case that the process of democratization had made considerable progress over the region as a whole and that the situation of liberal democracy was much stronger than it had been before 1989 (it could hardly, after all, be otherwise). Some post-communist states seemed to have established themselves quite securely in the group of liberal democracies, while others had clearly failed to disentangle themselves from authoritarian practices. Yet more, which represented the largest group, fell into the category of partial democracies and often appeared to hover between democratic and non-democratic patterns of liberal-democratic behaviour.

The democratization of formerly communist societies certainly comes towards the end of the overall story of the progress of the democratic idea and its associated practices. While the influence of democratic ideas and even elements of established liberal constitutional practice were by no means absent from Eastern Europe and the lands of the former Russian empire, it was only in inter-war Czechoslovakia that an effective liberal democracy operated for a reasonable length of time (this experience was surveyed in

Chapter 3 and is examined further in Chapter 19). Unlike the countries of Western Europe, where democratization took root at an early stage of modern political development and the features of liberal democracy emerged more clearly than in most other parts of the world (processes outlined in Chapter 2), the democracies established after the First World War in states on the lands of the Ottoman (Turkish), Austro-Hungarian and Russian empires were mostly partial and politically unstable. The majority of them fell prey to the rise of the authoritarian dictatorship that engulfed much of Europe between the two world wars, whilst the relatively successful liberal democracy of Czechoslovakia was an early victim of Nazi expansionism. Democratic tendencies in Russia itself were even weaker. With the consolidation of Soviet power after the revolution of 1917 and civil war from 1918 to 1921, there were no real signs of liberal-democratic development at all and, after the colonial experience common to the region, maintained the practices of authoritarian communist rule.

The origins of democratization in formerly communist countries have been correspondingly varied although, if we take the case of Russia and Eastern Europe, they can be divided into two broad categories. One fundamental problem concerned the running of a modern economy on the basis of central planning or, more concretely, through processes of state administration. Communism, particularly in relatively under-developed countries, proved capable initially of producing high rates of economic growth but found it increasingly difficult to sustain them. Failure to sustain early rates of economic growth and fulfil the promise of material plenty compounded the political problems associated with authoritarian rule and exacerbated the legitimacy problem that many communist regimes experienced. In the absence of satisfactory living standards for much of the population, the loss of national independence and absence of the civic rights associated with liberal democracy were also more difficult to tolerate for the inhabitants of communist countries, although this was more keenly felt in some countries than others. Throughout the region economic slowdown affected living standards, weakened the capacity of the communist authorities to satisfy the material expectations of the citizenry and demonstrated the failure of the communist systems to keep up with Western economies.

Another, related problem, was that technological innovation also lagged way behind that seen in developed Western countries and, despite the priority accorded to the military sector, the Soviet Union was unable to respond to new moves within the framework of Cold War competition like the Strategic Defence Initiative of the USA undertaken in the early 1980s. The question of reform (primarily economic, but also political and social) thus occupied an important place on the agenda of leaders in Eastern Europe and the Soviet Union from an early stage, and gained increasing prominence over time. The decision to confront this problem head on and to contemplate a more radical solution was a further major factor in the unfolding of the democratization process. This change occurred following the accession of Mikhail Gorbachev to the leading position in the Soviet political elite in March 1985. While he clearly recognized the need for major reform at the outset, it took some years before the extent of the reform that might be necessary and the scale of the reform that the Soviet communist leader might deem to be acceptable became clear.

Of particular importance for democratization in Eastern Europe was the decision of the Soviet leadership to let the countries of Eastern Europe go their own way, and not to continue with the imposition of the preferred Soviet model on its East European satellites. It had in this way both limited their national independence since the establishment of Soviet dominance over the region after the Second World War and held back any possibility of democratization. As the central decision-making powers in the region rested in Moscow with the Soviet leadership (which its decisive response to successive reform moves in Hungary, Czechoslovakia and Poland between 1956 and 1981 clearly showed), it took a major shift in the outlook of the Soviet leadership to change matters in this area within the region as a whole. The consequences of this change are examined in Chapter 16.

In this part, as in others, the discussion of democratization across a range of countries is structured by a series of questions. In Chapter 16 the questions addressed are: 'Why did communism collapse throughout Eastern Europe in 1989?' and 'Why did different patterns of democratization subsequently emerge in the countries concerned?' Chapter 17 asks 'What are the factors that have facilitated and those that have obstructed democratization in Russia?' Following chapters switch the focus away from individual countries or groups of countries and turn to consider comparative topics. In Chapter 18 the questions addressed are 'What forms of political participation have emerged in the post-communist countries?' and 'How may these developments be accounted for?'. Chapter 19 examines the issue of nationalism and asks 'What are the conditions for a successful transition to democracy in a multiethnic context?'. Finally, Chapter 20 considers political change in a country which has retained structures of communist rule and confronts the question 'What exactly did political liberalization in Vietnam entail?'.

The democratization seen in communist countries was marked by a number of particular characteristics. It involved, firstly, political change but was also part of at least a dual transition in that the structures of a market economy also had to be established alongside those of liberal democracy and conditions established for capitalist development. In some cases there was even a triple transition in that the framework of an independent state also had to be constructed. All these processes affected democratization in diverse and often fundamental ways, and the complex relations between these different aspects of change frame much of the analysis in the chapters that follow this Introduction.

It was, secondly, also a process strongly marked by diverse international influences, probably to a greater extent than in previous cases of democratization. The reform measures initially adopted by Gorbachev were primarily designed to enhance the economic performance of the Soviet Union in relation to the USA and other Western powers as it had become increasingly clear that the Soviet Union had, in military and economic terms, effectively lost the Cold War. Gorbachev and much of the final generation of communist leaders throughout the region were keenly aware that the isolation of the communist countries from broader and more dynamic development processes bore much of the responsibility for the failure of communism. They were strongly disposed to encourage the influence of the international environment both on the liberalization of the communist system and on post-communist democratization. The global context of technological development and innovation, the role of international and transnational economic institutions, and the significance of capitalist models all combined to exert an extremely strong influence on the central processes of post-communist development.

A third feature of this democratization, whose implications stood in some contrast to the point just made, was the strength of nationalism and the domestic tendencies to ethnic activism that arose, a factor closely related to the break up of formerly communist-dominated federations and the establishment of new states. This concerned both Czechoslovakia and Yugoslavia in Eastern Europe (as well as influencing the formation of an enlarged Germany), and the move to greater independence and sovereignty on the part of former Soviet republics and of different ethnic areas within them (like that of Chechnya within the Russian Federation). A fourth factor that played an important part was the critical nature of relations between the state with civil society, a further domestic counterbalance to the significant role played by international and transnational influences. Communist authoritarianism assigned a strongly dominant role to political forces associated with the state – thus giving considerable significance to tendencies in civil society as the main vehicles of opposition and leading forces of democratization. The role played by these four factors is examined in each of the chapters in this part.

Post-communist democratization and associated processes of political change are approached in this part, as in the others, comparatively. The basic forms of comparison in contemporary comparative politics can be divided, as outlined in Chapter 1, into approaches that are variable-oriented or case-oriented. The variable-oriented approach begins with some theory or idea of likely explanatory factors and looks for explanations about democratization in one or more particular cases in those terms; the case-oriented approach seeks to understand democratization in light of the relatively full – and complex – reality of one or more empirical cases. In practice, as will now be obvious, political scientists often tend to use these methods in combination.

This is certainly the case with Chapter 16, where the process of democratization in Eastern Europe as a whole is investigated and different forms of explanation then applied to account for the differences in democratic development that can be identified in the region. Chapters 17 and 20, on the other hand, look at the single cases of Russia and Vietnam but set them in a comparative context that permits the role of explanatory factors or particular theories to be examined. Chapter 19 conducts a case-oriented comparison of two countries and directs attention to developments in Czechoslovakia and Yugoslavia in the attempt to establish conditions under which a multi-ethnic political community can be formed and examines the relationship of nationalism to democratization. Chapter 18 also employs more of a combined approach and surveys a range of post-communist countries in an attempt to define and account for the forms of democratic participation that have developed there. While the strategies of comparison in this part might vary, though, all seek to explain processes of democratization and major political developments associated with them.

Reference

Held, D. (1996) *Models of Democracy* (2nd edn) Cambridge, Polity Press.

CHAPTER **16**

Democratization in Eastern Europe

Paul Lewis

Introduction

In 1989 the 'third wave' of democracy identified by Huntington (see Chapter 1) gained further strength with the collapse of communism in Eastern Europe and the gathering pace of political change in the Soviet Union. This had particular significance in signalling the end of the major twentieth-century challenge to liberal democracy in its European variant, a development that had further repercussions in terms of its effects on Soviet client states elsewhere in the world. In this context the collapse of the Soviet Union was undoubtedly the most important single event, but the swift termination of communist rule and the onset of democratization within Eastern Europe as a whole also holds particular interest in terms of comparative analysis. For a number of countries which had for decades existed within a common framework of political, economic and social development suddenly found the central structures of that framework removed as they embarked on a process of democratization which, while naturally sharing a number of major features, also soon began to show some important differences. This chapter addresses firstly, then, the question of why communism collapsed at this time throughout the region and, secondly, why the different patterns of democratization emerged in the countries concerned.

Eastern Europe, in this context, refers to the countries that came under Soviet control after the Second World War and remained under Soviet domination until the collapse of communist rule in 1989. The group was made up of six countries: Bulgaria, Czechoslovakia, the German Democratic Republic (East Germany), Hungary, Poland and Romania (Yugoslavia and Albania were communist states but remained mostly outside the sphere of Soviet influence). Between April 1989, when Polish Solidarity representatives reached an agreement with the communist authorities about the re-legalization of the independent trade union, and December of the same year (when the tyrannical Ceauşescu regime in Romania was overthrown) communist systems throughout the region suddenly began to fall apart. But this represented only the beginnings of a democratization process, and both the pace of political change and the solidity of democratic achievement varied across the region. In the following sections the main factors involved in the end of communism and the origins of democratization in Eastern Europe will be outlined, and basic features of the process of post-communist change identified. The rest of the chapter will seek to explain why the pattern of democratization has varied across Eastern Europe and how the differences may best be explained. Particular attention will be paid here

Map 16.1   Eastern Europe, 1945–89

to perspectives emphasizing modernization and accounts which focus on the role of elite factors in democratic transition.

16.1   The end of communism in Eastern Europe

There are at least two major aspects to any account of the origins of democratization in Eastern Europe – on one side the causes of the collapse of authoritarian communist rule and, on the other, the roots of the political changes that sustain changes leading to the development of a liberal democratic order. The two components are by no means fully separate, but they contribute different elements of an overall explanation for the process as a whole. In terms of the collapse of communist rule in Eastern Europe, major elements of the explanation lie outside the countries actually under scrutiny. The starting point for any answer must refer to changes in Soviet regional policy under the leadership of Mikhail Gorbachev and the abandonment of the Brezhnev Doctrine of limited sovereignty (the justification for the Soviet invasion of Czechoslovakia in 1968 promulgated by Leonid Brezhnev, which articulated the view that the socialist states allied with the Soviet Union did not have powers of autonomous decision and that the Soviet Union, as the leading socialist power, had a veto over acts and policies it considered non-socialist). It was clear that national political authority and domestic sources of legitimacy were not enough to sustain communist rule in Eastern Europe, so the shift in Soviet policy and Gorbachev's decision not to maintain communism in Eastern Europe by force was a major condition of its collapse and the movement of the region towards democratization.

It is, however, important not to over-personalize the policy shift. It was a change linked with a broader reappraisal of the role and capacity of military power, both on the part of the Soviet Union (primarily as the concrete underpinning of the Brezhnev doctrine) and as a component of communist rule within the East European countries themselves. With respect to the Soviet Union, the invasion of Afghanistan and the problems the Soviet army found itself confronted with there provided a salutary lesson concerning the limitations of military power. The Soviet experience in Afghanistan warned against further military intervention in Eastern Europe on the pattern of the earlier invasions of Hungary and Czechoslovakia in 1956 and 1968 respectively. Under Brezhnev the Soviet leadership had decided not to intervene militarily in Poland to restore socialist order during the Solidarity period (1980–81). But it was only after Gorbachev's accession to power that a full redefinition of security was conducted in the Soviet Union which reflected a recognition that the country's interests were not best achieved by a continual build-up of military resources and the constant threat of their use.

A further military factor underlying the shift in Soviet attitudes was the pressure of Cold War competition on the Soviet economy and the growing inability of the Soviet Union to meet the American challenge. Even on the basis of relatively optimistic calculations, Soviet GNP was no more than half that of the USA for much of the post-war period while the level of Soviet military expenditure approached that of the USA during the 1970s. In the 1980s the US Central Intelligence Agency estimated that the Soviet Union was spending 50 per cent more in real terms on defence. President Reagan's escalation of US military expenditure far outstripped Soviet capacity to maintain any pretence of keeping pace in terms of technology and the development of military resources. On both a global and regional basis, the Gorbachev leadership came to the conclusion that military power should have less prominence in Soviet foreign policy.

Equivalent developments could be detected within the political systems of the East European countries themselves, and the declining effectiveness of military and coercive power was apparent within most of them. Polish party leader Gierek's need to maintain close political and economic relations with the West due to the country's high level of indebtedness dissuaded him first from clamping down on opposition groups and dissidents during the 1970s and then from forcibly breaking the 1980 strikes that gave birth to Solidarity. Coercion could be more easily applied in Czechoslovakia, East Germany and Romania, but even the enormous effort of post-1968 'normalization' in Czechoslovakia following the Soviet invasion and the pervasiveness of the East German security organization were unable to prevent the development and survival of core opposition groups which were ultimately able to attract much more extensive support. Political repression eventually failed also in Romania, while its maintenance throughout the 1980s had been accompanied by and associated with the wide-spread impoverishment of society and the great mass of the population. Even more eloquent of the limitations of coercive power was the limited success of post-1981 martial law in Poland and the semi-militarized regime that succeeded it.

While less associated with the burden of military expenditure than in the Soviet Union, the problems of economic stagnation and relative economic failure were also pronounced in Eastern Europe. Romanian society was particularly impoverished but great problems were apparent in more developed countries like Hungary and Poland, both of which had accumulated massive foreign debts during the 1970s which they found impossible to pay-off owing to their poor economic performance. Party leader Janos Kádár's attempt to create a socially acceptable form of communism in Hungary involved securing popular acquiescence by providing reasonable living standards and maintaining a steady level of economic growth. In 1968 a New Economic Mechanism, relatively radical in its reform measures in the East European context, was introduced but by 1985 it was admitted that both real wages and the standard of living were declining. Economic growth and recovery after the Solidarity period were equally sluggish in Poland, and by 1988 per capita national income was still some way off the level reached ten years earlier. The critical shift in Soviet policy towards Eastern Europe was thus accompanied by significant changes in domestic policy within the countries of the region.

In a situation of economic stagnation and relative decline it was understandable that increasing attention was paid to economic reform, particularly as the maintenance of communist rule through coercion and the activity of security organizations was either becoming less effective or was deemed to be less appropriate. In the first half of the 1980s partial measures were taken in Hungary, which included the break-up of some large monopoly enterprises, measures to sub-contract work to groups of employees and a reform of the banking system. From 1987, 'when the writing appeared on the wall' in terms of the future of the communist system, these new opportunities were increasingly taken advantage of by party officials and state bureaucrats to convert their existing power into resources more appropriate to a market economy or liberal democracy (Hankiss, 1990, p.26).

An equivalent move towards privatization was made during the same year in Poland, and small steps towards change were also taken in Bulgaria and East Germany. Particularly significant were the measures taken towards the very end of the communist period in 1988 and 1989 to privatize state enterprises in Hungary and Poland through joint ventures, the sale of state assets to foreign purchasers and the increasing granting of property rights to public officials and managers of state enterprises. By taking these steps communist leaders in both countries were showing a clear willingness to qualify the monopoly of economic power they had previously claimed and to move decisively away from the practices of the command economy, which had been a major pillar of communist rule. While differentiated and inconclusive in many areas, there were indications that the communist state was prepared to withdraw from some areas of the East European economy.

There were also signs of political liberalization, again most obviously in Hungary and Poland (analogous processes in Latin America are discussed in Chapter 7). In Poland, following an endorsement from Gorbachev at the congress of the Polish United Workers' Party in 1986, Jaruzelski released all political prisoners. Even more significant was the offer in 1988, after further rounds of industrial strikes, to negotiate with Solidarity representatives over prospects for trade union pluralism, which promised to reinstate the free trade union in Polish public life. The resilience of the opposition had meanwhile been strengthened by the continuing resistance of the Catholic Church to communist power and its contribution to the preservation of major areas of social and intellectual autonomy, as well as the survival of several influential human rights groups since the mid 1970s. In 1985 the Hungarian regime also responded to a strong public demand to allow independent candidates to run for office in forthcoming parliamentary elections. The activities of opposition and independent political groups became more prominent in 1987 without attracting any significant official disapproval. While Kádár, too, showed little inclination to yield any power or make concessions to the growing number of critics both within and without the party, younger members of the party leadership resisted his attempts to marginalize them and strengthened links with broader reformist forces. Most significantly, the Soviet leadership made no attempt to prevent the removal of Kádár as party leader in 1988 and left the Hungarian party with a free hand to choose his replacement.

Regardless of the stance of party leaders and policies of the communist authorities, social forces in Eastern Europe showed a growing capacity for self organization and an increasing ability to challenge state power. Starting in the late 1970s they took a different form in each country (predominantly independent political party formation in Hungary, trade unions in Poland, protestant churches in East Germany, artists and intellectuals in Czechoslovakia) but nevertheless jointly reflected the emergence of a comparable civil society in several countries of Eastern Europe. The strength of such movements showed considerable differences throughout the regime, the establishment of Solidarity in Poland during 1980 being an early major achievement in this context. The response of the communist authorities also differed significantly among the countries concerned, Hungary and Poland (despite the ultimate resort to martial law in 1981) being more receptive to the changes. Such developments had a significant transnational component which had a direct influence on the different types of regime transition that occurred in Eastern Europe, the marked weakness of civil society development in Romania and the absence of transnational links being directly linked with the violent overthrow of the Ceauşescu leadership and the authoritarian character of the original successor regime in that country.

Strong internal pressures thus accompanied the shift in Soviet policy towards Eastern Europe and created domestic conditions for the rapid collapse of communist rule throughout the region. The coercion that had characterized the early phase of Soviet-imposed authoritarianism became less appropriate as the circumstances of communist rule changed, while growing economic crisis indicated the overall failure of communist policy in this critical area. Early progress along the path to democratization was signalled by measures of economic and political change which reflected the growing willingness of communist leaders to tolerate reduced state control of the economy and assign a greater role for autonomous political activity. The greater prominence of independent social movements strengthened the currents of official political change and demonstrated an increasing capacity for social self-organization.

Critical weaknesses were, therefore, evident in East European communism well before the accession of Gorbachev to the Soviet leadership although, as the period of martial law in Poland during the early 1980s showed, coercive measures could still be taken which maintained communist rule so long as the Soviet Union stood by its established policy of regional dominance. The end of orthodox communist rule was signalled, at least in Hungary and Poland, by measures of political liberalization and economic reform that went considerably further than the anodyne measures previously permitted. The first communist regime actually to collapse was that in Poland. Although the communist authorities had sought to preserve their dominance by permitting free elections to only 35 per cent of parliamentary seats in June 1989, the arrangement unravelled due to the combination of a surprisingly high level of popular support for the opposition, defection of previously subservient parliamentary allies and sheer miscalculation on the part of the communist establishment. Gorbachev reaffirmed his decision that communism would no longer be sustained in Eastern Europe by force and Tadeusz Mazowiecki was installed as a Solidarity-sponsored prime minister in September 1989.

Already far advanced down the path of political liberalization, the Hungarian leadership also now held round-table talks with the opposition and planned the immediate introduction of a liberal democratic, parliamentary system. A rather more restricted path of change was followed in Bulgaria, where a palace coup dismissed the incumbent leader and a reformist communist group assumed power. It took extensive demonstrations and the sudden eruption of popular opposition to accelerate the process of change in the more firmly entrenched communist leadership in East Germany and Czechoslovakia, but once this had begun the established regime rapidly crumbled in those countries, too. Less susceptible to Soviet pressure and having maintained its power by a bitter and long-lasting period of political repression, the Ceauşescu dictatorship held out until the end of December 1989 when it was overthrown by an ambiguous combination of excluded communist politicians, popular opposition and the military establishment.

────────────── *Summary of Section 16.1* ──────────────

The main factors in the ending of communist rule in Eastern Europe are as follows.

- Gorbachev's reformulation of Soviet regional policy in the light of growing economic and military problems.

- Similar problems in Eastern Europe which, in the case of Hungary and Poland, were accompanied by growing movements of social opposition.

- An accelerating process of political liberalization which soon moved beyond the parameters of communist rule in Poland and Hungary, and provided a model for democratization within the other countries of the region.

16.2   Patterns of democratization in Eastern Europe

With the collapse of communist rule throughout the region, the Eastern Europe shaped by the Soviet Union shortly after the Second World War disappeared. It did not take long for a quite different configuration of states and political forces to emerge in the region and the lands that bordered it.

While all claimed democratic credentials, though, there were major differences in the position they occupied in the democratization process and the degree to which they implemented liberal democratic principles. A 'democratic transition' can be defined quite precisely (Pridham and Vanhanen, 1994, p.2) as 'a stage of regime change commencing at the point when the previous totalitarian/authoritarian system begins to collapse, leading to a situation when, with a new constitution in place, the democratic structures become routinized and the political elites adjust their behaviour to liberal democratic norms'. But what may appear to be a simple definition gains in complexity when attempts are made to operationalize it comparatively. It is not easy to decide, for example, whether structures are 'routinized' or how far elites really have adjusted their behaviour to liberal democratic norms. Despite the fact that they had shared a common framework of communist rule, too, it soon became clear that the countries of Eastern Europe showed a differentiated pattern of democratic development.

The fate of East Germany was a wholly unique one, as the early phase of post-communist change led directly to unification with the Federal Republic (West Germany), and further democratization of the former GDR took place within a framework dominated by the vastly more powerful liberal democratic, capitalist portion of the previously divided country. The ruling Socialist Unity Party (communist) adopted the title of the Party of Democratic Socialism in December 1989 and was divested of its monopolistic political role in the constitution at the beginning of the same month. Free elections were held in March 1990 and an overwhelming victory was won by the Christian Democratic Union, which had existed in East Germany in attenuated form as a submissive partner of the communist party but which soon became a branch of the dominant West German version of the party. Internal developments were, however, totally dominated by the impetus for

Map 16.2   Eastern Europe, 1995

unification strongly pressed by West German Chancellor Kohl and impatiently anticipated by the great majority of East Germans. Currency union was implemented from 1 July 1990 on terms favourable to the East and political unification completed the takeover at midnight on 2/3 October.

Democratization in Eastern Europe thus combined some factors that were common to all the countries involved and others that were specific to one or only a few cases. The shared framework of communist rule that made them a highly appropriate subject for comparative study in fact saw the development of a range of democratic transitions. I have already identified the background of economic reform and political liberalization that enabled Hungary and Poland to lead the process of democratic change. Further distinctions can be made according to whether the initial stage of transition was negotiated (Poland) or evolutionary (Hungary), whether change involved an implosion or collapse followed by transition (East Germany and Czechoslovakia), where it was accompanied by moderate violence (Romania), or took the initial form of a palace coup (Bulgaria). It also seemed to be the case that some modes of transition and extrication from communist rule favoured a more rapid and less troubled form of democratization. A number of variables can be used to define the extent of democratic change that has occurred, and an extensive list can include as many as thirteen major issues of conflict resolution that have to be faced in the process of transition (Welsh, 1994, pp.381–2). In terms of a brief survey of the pattern of democratization in Eastern Europe three key factors might be identified:

- resignation of the communist party from its monopolistic ruling position;
- constitutional amendments introduced to establish liberal democracy;
- free elections and the establishment of a parliamentary democratic legislature.

Such landmarks were reached at different times in the various countries of Eastern Europe. In terms of the initial criterion, the first country to abolish its orthodox monopolistic communist party was Hungary in early October 1989, when the Hungarian Socialist Workers' Party (established during the Soviet invasion in 1956) was recreated as the Hungarian Socialist Party under reformist leadership – although a rump HSWP was recreated by disgruntled hardliners in December 1989. This organization, however, now existed as a relatively minor component of a multi-party system. The equivalent Polish communist party was wound up soon after, in January 1990. The Bulgarian Communist Party followed only a little later, and renamed itself the Socialist Party (accompanied by complaints from existing social democrats) in April 1990 following a referendum amongst its members. The Romanian communist party took even longer and retitled itself the Socialist Labour Party in November 1990. Only the Czechoslovak party remained as a self-proclaimed communist body, a decision which seemed to do it little harm in the eyes of the electorate, as it still came second (although way behind the Civic Forum based on the former opposition) in the June 1990 elections.

In terms of constitutional change, the agreements reached at the Polish round-table negotiations between the communist authorities and Solidarity representatives concerning the establishment of a new bicameral parliament and the powers of the presidency were passed by the existing parliament in April 1989 at the same time as laws guaranteeing the right of free association. The leading role of the communist party was abolished once a new government under a Solidarity prime minister was installed in September 1989 and, just before the end of the year, Poland formally ceased to be a People's Republic. Hungary changed its name to an independent Republic even earlier on 23 October, the anniversary of the outbreak of the 1956 revolution, and numerous other changes agreed at the Hungarian round-table negotiations were given constitutional effect the same month. Despite the slower pace of events in Czechoslovakia constitutional amendments to adopt a pluralist political system had already been passed by the end of November 1989. But attempts to frame a new constitution as a whole proved to be far more difficult (not least due to the country's multinational character and the problematic federal structure of the state) and threatened to paralyse government activity altogether.

New constitutions were introduced somewhat later in Bulgaria (July 1991) and Romania (December 1991). Such changes did not, however, resolve all constitutional conflicts and countries like Poland and Hungary, which had introduced amendments at an early stage to abolish the leading role of the communist party and open the way to competitive elections, were not so successful in producing wholly new constitutions. The basis of the existing Czechoslovak state also soon disappeared as the country divided and a separate Slovakia and Czech Republic came into existence at the beginning of 1993. Wrangles over the role and powers of the presidency continued in Poland, for example, for the whole five years of Lech Wałęsa's incumbency in that post and were still unresolved when the second presidential election of the post-communist period was held in November 1995 and Wałęsa lost the presidency.

The record in terms of holding free elections and forming a democratic legislature was broadly similar, and Poland here paid the price for holding the first round-table negotiations and paving the way to regional democratization. Only 35 per cent of seats in the main legislative chamber were open to free competition in the election of June 1989, although due to the failure of virtually all communist candidates to secure election on the first round of voting and various misjudgements on the part of the authorities it later proved possible to form a coalition government under a Solidarity representative. Clearly a post-communist government, then (and one which proceeded to implement a radical liberal programme of economic stabilization and transformation), it became more so in its composition as time elapsed. But it was nevertheless not one that arose from free or fully competitive elections. This was a development for which Poland had to wait until October 1991. Fully competitive elections were, however, held in East Germany in March 1990 and in Hungary during March and April. Elections were then held in Romania in May 1990, and in Czechoslovakia and Bulgaria during June of that year.

In distinction to the outcome in Poland, East Germany, Hungary and Czechoslovakia, though, it was the reconstituted communist party (BSP) that won the election in Bulgaria. In Romania it was the National Salvation Front that gained an overwhelming victory and both the presidency and government were dominated by ex-communists. There were growing suspicions that the break with communist rule had by no means been a complete one, doubts that were strengthened by the arrival of crowds of miners in Bucharest summoned to attack and disperse demonstrators and protesters against the result of the election and the way it had been conducted. Government hesitancy to pursue price liberalization and resistance to the introduction of radical economic reform further fed such doubts as to its post-communist status.

After a relatively short period of time, then, it became possible to identify two groups of post-communist states by their apparent level of democratization in terms of such indicators:

Group 1   Czech Republic, Hungary and Poland.

Group 2   Bulgaria, some way ahead of Slovakia and Romania by the end of 1995.

Group 1 countries had relatively rapidly established a reasonably viable constitutional order and multi-party system, having held free elections, seen unequivocal changes of government and generally established basic civil liberties. Group 2 countries saw a more protracted extrication from communist rule, although Slovakia is something of a special case as the split from the Czech Republic placed a general question mark over its status in terms of its democratic performance under ex-communist Vladimir Mečiar. Civil liberties, the smooth transfer of government power and the prevalence of non-authoritarian practices were all less evident in Group 2 countries. Nevertheless, it should be noted that the difference was one of degree and doubts about the authenticity of the regime change in Romania and Bulgaria were relatively quickly dissolved. Note, as a further complicating factor, that both Hungary, Poland and Bulgaria also later saw a return to government power of post-communist socialist forces, although there was little reason to doubt their democratic credentials.

In seeking to account for these differences in the pattern of democratization a number of factors can be readily identified that may contribute to an explanation, among them:

1 cultural differences and background historical factors, notably the Ottoman (Turkish) tradition in most Group 2 countries in distinction to an Austro-Hungarian or North European influence;

2 higher levels of socio-economic development in Group 1;

3 the stability of communist rule in most Group 2 countries in distinction to the prevalence of political instability, ideological revisionism, communist reformism and a rejection of orthodoxy in Group 1;

4 linked with this factor, the relative strength of civil society and its influence in Group 1 countries;

5 following on from this, the modes of exit from communist rule which involved social movements or major counter-elite influences in Group 1, rather than the prominence of establishment-dominated change in Group 2.

Amongst these factors some, for example (1) referring to historical and cultural factors, appear to be largely *sui generis* and thus difficult to link with more general explanations and those of a theoretical character. Reference to and apparent correlations of democratic outcomes with levels of socio-economic development (2), however, suggest a close link with the modernization theories outlined in Chapter 1, while references to the constellation of elite forces, links with social movements and the different modes of exit from communist rule (3, 4 and 5) prompt further consideration of transition theories and elements of strategic choice.

––––––––––––––––– *Summary of Section 16.2* –––––––––––––––––

The pattern of democratization in Eastern Europe can, therefore, be:

• Defined by such factors as the speed with ruling communist parties reformed themselves, the nature of constitutional changes, and the organization and outcome of competitive elections.

• Differentiated according to the pace and nature of the process of post-communist change.

• Subject to different interpretations and is likely to be open to contrasting explanations.

16.3 Democratization and socio-economic development

We now turn to possible explanations for the pattern of democratization that has developed in Eastern Europe. It certainly appears to be the case that it was the more highly developed East European countries that democratized more rapidly. Table 16.1 presents some basic indicators of the comparative picture.

Table 16.1: Indicators of democratization and socio-economic development

	Democracy rating, 1994[1]	$GDP per capita ($) 1992[2]	UN Index of human develop-ment[3]	Percentage of labour force in agricul-ture, 1973[4]	Ownership of TV sets per 1,000 of the popula-tion, 1987[5]	Students per 1,000 of the popula-tion, 1989–90[6]
E. Germany	–	–	–	10	754	–
Czech Republic	82	2,450	89.2[7]	11[7]	285[7]	119[7]
Hungary	82	2,970	88.7	17	402	96
Poland	75	1,910	83.1	32	263	143
Slovakia	72	1,930	89.2[7]	11[7]	285[7]	119[7]
Bulgaria	51	1,330	85.4	36	189	176
Romania	37	1,130	70.9	40	173	71

Sources: [1]Beetham (1994); [2]*Almanach Swiata, Warsaw* (1994); [3]*Economist: World in Figures* (1995); [4]Mason (1992); [5]*Times Guide to Eastern Europe*, London (1990); [6]*Rocznik Statystyczny*, Warsaw (1992); [7]Data for former Czechoslovakia.

The association of democratization with higher levels of socio-economic development in Eastern Europe suggests that the modernization approach outlined in Chapter 1 might well play a part in explaining the nature of political change in post-communist Europe. But it is difficult to identify any clear theory within the terms of the modernization perspective or to isolate a specific explanation of democratization. As in the earlier literature, current accounts leave the translation of economic forces into democratic political institutions largely unexplained. The correlation is a persuasive one on an intuitive and broad empirical basis but it remains imprecise in its more specific implications, throwing little light on why modernization seems to encourage democratization in some – indeed most – cases but fails to do so in others (for example Germany in the early twentieth century: see discussion in Chapter 3).

Moreover, to the extent that modernization has any explanatory capacity even its proponents admit that this is less strong once the 'first wave' of democratization (1828–1926) ceases to be a primary object of attention.

Huntington (1991) suggested that it was during the first wave of democratization that the modernization dynamic was at its strongest:

> economic development, industrialization, urbanization, the emergence of the bourgeoisie and of a middle class, the development of a working class and its early organization, and the gradual decrease in economic inequality all seem to have played some role in the movements towards democratization in northern European countries in the nineteenth century.
>
> (Huntington, 1991, p.39)

The pattern for the third wave (1974–90), of which the initial phase of East European democratization was a part, seemed to be considerably more complex and less reducible to socio-economic factors, although one factor noted (Huntington, 1991, p.45) was the unprecedented global economic growth of the 1960s 'which raised living standards, increased education, and greatly expanded the urban middle class in many countries'. The declining legitimacy of many authoritarian regimes during the 1960s and 1970s was also directly linked with their poor economic performance, and often associated with their inability to cope with the oil price rises and various debt crises. This occurred to a limited extent in the case of the East European countries but with immediate consequences that were less critical: 'It did not become a factor promoting democratization in those countries until the Soviet Union allowed that to happen' (ibid., p.54). Eastern Europe, like other middle-income countries such as those in Latin America, seemed to reside very much in a 'zone of choice' where political change was dependent on many factors and where economic stagnation and popular frustration could undermine any kind of regime (Misztal, 1992, p.156).

Another problem in seeking an explanation of democratization in these terms lies with the very broadness of the concept of modernization and the nature of the process of development at issue. There are many different paths of modernization and it should not be forgotten that the process of change initiated by the Russian Revolution was itself seen as a means of catching up with the West and a project of modernization in its own right. When transferred to Eastern Europe, the model carried less conviction, although it was by no means lacking in relevance to the dominantly agricultural countries of the Balkans. Even Hungary and Poland had been regarded as semi-developed countries, and the programme of socialist industrialization launched in the late 1940s was welcomed by many as a means of reducing unemployment and rural over-population.

But the situation in East Germany and Czechoslovakia was different and, if the beginning of the key economic transition in Hungary and Poland (the time when fewer than 50 per cent of the population belong to the primary sector) can be dated from 1951 and 1957 respectively, the start of modernization in Germany and the Czech Lands can be traced back as far as 1876 and 1900 (Musil, 1993, p.481). It is not just that modernization was more advanced in those countries but that a different model of development could be identified. This, it has been suggested, can be linked with specific cultural configurations in terms of Czech conceptions of democracy and their particular stress on the role of the individual, and is reflected amongst other things in the strength of Czech views on the role of private property and the desirability of returning communist assets to their former owners. The formation of such a modern political culture characteristic of developed urban-industrial society has been thought to have facilitated the rapid democratization seen in the Czech Republic since 1989, while the relatively high level of socio-economic development in communist Czechoslovakia (in the absence, it should be noted, of the high levels of foreign debt seen in Hungary and Poland) smoothed the course of subsequent economic transformation and cushioned the social impact of the transition to a market economy which might otherwise have thrown up impediments to democratization.

While, too, events in Poland during 1989 were critical for the whole process of regional democratization, the key development that governed much of the political and social response in that country to Gorbachev's opening to political change lay some years in the past with the rise of the Solidarity movement in 1980. This was by far the largest independent workers' movement seen in communist Eastern Europe which created an unprecedented form of dual power within the communist system that lasted some fifteen months, although the conditions overall were not there for this to give rise to a coherent process of either national or regional democratization. It was the specific course of socio-economic development seen in Poland and the particular form social modernization took under communist rule that played an important part in shaping the social force that was central to these events. We shall note the character of these structural developments to suggest how a specific aspect of modernization affected the general course of democratization. The rapid growth of an industrial working class has generally been associated with the emergence of extensive social conflict, although its implications for democratization remain a matter of some dispute. This has equally been the case in Eastern Europe.

The working class there grew rapidly as a result of the socialist industrialization drive, and by around 1970 a majority of industrial workers in Romania, Bulgaria and Hungary had been born into peasant families. The hereditary working class remained in a slight majority in Poland but the new working class was still very numerous, the total of non-agricultural workers having grown from 2.7 million in 1950 to 6.3 million in 1970. A major influence on the emerging social structure in Poland was the persistently high birth rate during the early years of communist rule – 29 per thousand inhabitants in 1948 and 26 in 1958 (contrasting at this stage with 17 per thousand in Czechoslovakia and 16 in Hungary and East Germany). As a result of this high rate of growth 6 million young people entered the Polish work-force during the 1970s. Together with the survival of individual peasant farming (which tended to keep people on the land), the high rate of internal growth accounts for the relatively limited extent to which the communist working class in Poland was swamped by rural emigrants. Conditions in Poland were therefore more favourable for the transmission of an established working-class culture and the survival of a more integrated social group. Workers had been highly active in opposition movements during 1956 in both Poland and Hungary, but it was only in Poland that they showed their continuing capacity for resistance to communist rule in the later period.

By 1980 the communist system in Eastern Europe had produced a large working class which no longer had the opportunities for social mobility and occupational advancement available to the first generation of socialist workers. In Poland it was a young group with an unusually high number of members who were seeking their own housing, that scarce commodity which communist systems had a particularly poor record of providing. Expectations of material improvement there were, moreover, relatively high following Gierek's espousal of a policy of rapid growth (albeit one fuelled by foreign loans) in the early 1970s although their satisfaction was increasingly unlikely as real incomes fell in both 1978 and 1979. The younger portion of the working class was also a group that was far better educated than the older generation. As a Polish sociologist presciently observed in May 1980, the younger generation of workers emerged as a social force with an unusually high potential which had yet to find any application in terms of occupational or social activity. Finally, a large part of this young working class was excluded from the informal mechanisms of participation and interest-articulation evolved by more established employees and found itself at a greater social distance from the increasingly in-bred, technocratic management that had come to dominate communist industry. These conditions fostered a stronger labour identity that cut across lines of internal class segmentation and opened the way to more decisive collective action than had been possible in the strikes that had broken out ten years earlier at the end of 1970.

All in all, the intensifying economic and political crisis of the late 1970s was linked with changes in the Polish working class that recalled the dynamics of a critical period in British political life that opened the way for the emergence of modern liberal democracy. There, too, the economic crisis which clearly affected Britain in the 1880s placed increased pressure on the working class (or classes), enforced a higher level of internal integration, encouraged greater collective activism, movement towards a 'new unionism' and, ultimately, the campaign for parliamentary representation that opened the way to the establishment of a modern liberal democracy. The Solidarity period in Poland that followed the strike movement of 1980 was, however, curtailed by the imposition of martial law at the end of 1981. So long as the Soviet Union maintained its commitment to the continuity of communist rule in Eastern Europe, the very partial solution to Poland's continuing economic, political and social crisis that martial law represented seemed just about sufficient. Once Gorbachev signalled his abandonment of the Soviet commitment, the legacy of Solidarity and the worker activism of 1980 returned.

It was the experience of the suspended social movement that helped push forward the limits of the reform programme offered by the communist leadership in 1989 in the direction of more substantial democratization, which in turn opened the way to major political change in the region as a whole. The Solidarity interlude had created an authoritative worker-intelligentsia elite which, although excluded from political life with the imposition of martial law and the subsequent communist 'normalization', remained available for participation in round-table negotiations at the end of the decade and the formation of non-communist government after the elections. Although an intellectual counter-elite existed in Hungary, as well as (to a rather lesser extent) Czechoslovakia and East Germany, in no other country did it have the broader social links formed by Solidarity or the experience of organized political opposition that extended as far back as 1980.

––––––––––––––––– *Summary of Section 16.3* –––––––––––––––––

- It was the more socially and economically developed countries in Eastern Europe that democratized more rapidly.
- It is nevertheless difficult to identify any 'modernization theory' that actually explains this.
- The nature of the social structures formed by particular modes of socio-economic development help explain specific tendencies of democratization.

16.4 Elite strategy and leadership choice in the democratization process

As the above discussion suggests, it is difficult to avoid questions of elite strategy and leadership response to the demands of the political, socio-economic and international environment when seeking to account for democratization and the different forms it has taken in Eastern Europe. However, the transition theory which directs particular attention to these factors is derived from the experience of democratization in Southern Europe and Latin America, and the very feasibility of explaining East European democratization at all within such a framework has been questioned. Unlike the original cases, East European democratization got under way in a situation characterized at least in part by elements of totalitarianism rather than just authoritarian rule, which seems to some to exclude the interplay between state and social forces that governs much of the early dynamic of democratization. Major parts of the dynamics of the situation and former limitations on democratization in Eastern Europe were externally imposed and did not rest on domestic forces in the way that Southern European and Latin American transitions are understood to have done. Post-communist democratization was critically bound up with processes of fundamental economic change and the structural transform-ation of the communist command economy, which suggests that democratization may not really be susceptible to analysis as a discrete process. Unlike the cases in Southern Europe and Latin America, too, links with earlier periods of democratic rule in Eastern Europe were either located in the very distant past or completely absent.

There are telling comparative points which reflect reasonable methodological doubts about the extension of the comparative enterprise to quite a different region. But the differences between Eastern Europe on the one hand and Southern Europe and Latin America on the other are not necessarily so marked as to rule out from the outset the application of transition theories. The undoubted significance of Soviet influence for example, as we have seen, did not exclude a significant part being played by domestic factors. Neither was the level of totalitarianization such as to marginalize the role of social forces or exclude the possibility of differential relations developing between state and society in Eastern Europe. East Germany, Hungary, Czechoslovakia and Poland had all experienced major instances of popular unrest and opposition. In Poland a strong and relatively independent Catholic Church survived and helped extend the political space in which social forces could operate.

The issue was not just one of conflict between popular forces and the communist leadership, but major differences of approach and policy within the elite were also involved. The possibility of contrasting patterns of elite–mass relations, also emerged. In the southern countries the situation was, however, different. The dictatorial regime in Romania was strongly repressive to the end and tolerated neither popular opposition nor elite dissent. After an instance of elite conflict in the 1960s, the Bulgarian leadership was also resolutely orthodox and firmly entrenched. The mode of exit from communist rule also showed significant differences in terms of the influence of counter-elites and social movements in the more advanced countries.

In Poland and Hungary respectively, therefore, Solidarity representatives and groups centring around the Hungarian Democratic Forum and the Alliance of Free Democrats exerted a strong influence in the round-table negotiations that opened the way to free (or, in the case of Poland, partially free) elections. At a later date, a broad popular movement rapidly developed around Civic Forum and Public Against Violence in Czechoslovakia and also dominated both the round-table talks and subsequent elections. Elsewhere, in Romania and Bulgaria, the move away from communist orthodoxy took the form rather of a palace coup or rearrangement of elite forces than a sharp break from the communist regime and its characteristic practices or personnel. To this extent, in those countries the exit from communism was gradual and more qualified, and the pace of democratization correspondingly reduced.

All the major crises of communist Eastern Europe occurred in the more developed countries of the northern tier and were intimately linked with questions of economic strategy and reform. These issues forced themselves on to the political agenda as the inadequacies of the communist model, developed and originally applied with some success in the considerably more backward Soviet Union, became increasingly evident in Eastern Europe. The problems of applying the principles of the Soviet-inspired command economy in such a context contributed in a major way to the central conflicts that emerged in the communist political system both in the elite and mass dimension. The most serious crises of the communist period occurred when these dimensions coincided. Such problems not only underlay the regular outbursts of popular dissatisfaction and opposition but also provided the grounds for fundamental rifts within the communist elite and the party-state leadership (recall here the typology of political actors in transitions presented in Chapter 1). Political hardliners, counting on Soviet support to help cope with popular dissent, were generally opposed to the introduction of market principles and reform of the economic mechanism that others thought necessary if economic performance was to be improved. Reformers, both in economic and political spheres, were more sensitive to domestic social pressures, inclined to reduce central control overall and were generally identified with a softline tendency.

Differences between nationally-oriented groups and those with a stronger allegiance to the Kremlin had also emerged in the very early days of communist rule in Eastern Europe and factional politics was never really absent from the ruling communist parties, being most pronounced in Poland where (for a variety of reasons) rigorous political control was difficult to impose not just on society but also within the leading organs of the party. The tensions that arose in the 1980s with the looming failure of the East European communist order as a whole thus developed on the basis of established differences between conservatives and reformers, hardliners and liberals, ardent Muscovites and nationalists, etc. In Poland and Hungary in particular, where the need for urgent action was most clearly apparent, major divisions were evident in the elite at an early stage and critical shifts in the internal balance of power, including changing relations with emerging counter-elites, were evident well before 1989. This certainly follows the pattern of democratic transition drawn by O'Donnell and Schmitter (1986, p.19), who point out that, 'there is no transition whose beginning is not the consequence – direct or indirect – of important divisions within the authoritarian regime itself, principally along the fluctuating cleavage between hardliners and softliners'.

In both countries, then, major splits within the elite could be seen which opened the way to negotiations, the conclusion of political pacts and emergence of broad reformist coalitions which promised to set both Hungary and Poland on the path to post-communist democratization, although it has been argued that only the Hungarian transition fitted the model formulated by O'Donnell and Schmitter in terms of a clear division between hardliners and softliners that opened a clear path to liberalization (Jenkins, 1992). Important divisions within the opposition and counter-elite were also evident. In Hungary this concerned the degree to which opposition forces should collaborate with the communist establishment and traditional distinctions between populist and more intellectual orientations, whereas in Poland divisions within Solidarity dated back to 1981 while some opposition groups also stood out against Solidarity's domination of the opposition side in the qualified contest offered by the 1989 elections. To this extent elements of political liberalization at elite level and signs of incipient pluralism were present in Poland and Hungary on both sides of the political divide. This gave some prominence to political competition before a final agreement was reached on the opening up of the system as a whole to mass participation, the establishment of a range of political parties and the holding of general elections, thus providing a firmer base for subsequent democratization. Poland and Hungary thus showed more signs of following the pattern outlined by Dahl (1971, p.36) whereby opportunities for liberalization precede inclusiveness (the opening of decision-making centres to broader participation), and are therefore more likely to introduce and sustain liberal democracy. This helps to account for the more rapid pace of democratization in those countries.

Such elements of intra-elite competition, liberalization, openness to alternative leadership strategies and the co-operation of establishment groups with competing counter-elites were, indeed, less in evidence in places where the process of democratization advanced more slowly. Some elements of counter-elite development could be seen in Czechoslovakia and East Germany, although their influence was considerably more restricted. The communist establishment in those countries was far less disposed to take account of it as an alternative political force due to the limited reach of the opposition movement and the weakness of the challenge offered to the communist state by any emerging civil society. It was, however, a weakness that was to some extent compensated for by the relatively strong transnational links that were developed.

While there were signs of growing division within the communist establishment, mostly concerning economic policy in Czechoslovakia and over the extent to which opposition groups could be controlled by outright repression in East Germany, these were far less prominent than in Poland and Hungary. Evidence for the existence of divisions within the establishment or the emergence of any autonomous counter-elite was even less strong in Romania and Bulgaria; in the latter country, indeed, it has been argued that the communist party leadership was faced with a clear choice between the slow disintegration of the former ruling body into two or more parties or the creation of a distinct, but amenable, opposition which could involve some of its former supporters.

In the countries with experience of more stable communist rule and orthodox leadership practices broad establishment solidarity was maintained, with any critical rupture associated with regime change occurring some time after the initial break had been made in Poland and Hungary. Nevertheless the apparent lack of elite conflict, absence of developed strategies for elite-led change or moves towards the conclusion of pacts with competing forces does not seem to have provided much of an obstacle to the relatively rapid democratization seen in Czechoslovakia in terms of the swift abnegation of the communist party from its leading role, the establishment of a multiparty system and the holding of competitive elections marking a distinct break from the former system. A number of factors are likely to have played a part here, including the quality of the country's leaders (amongst whom was Václav Havel, opposition leader turned President), democratic traditions deriving from the pre-Second World War legacy as well as more recent experience of the liberalization that preceded the Soviet invasion of 1968.

The advanced level of socio-economic development of, particularly, the Czech Republic probably exercised a significant influence on this development too. The cultural aspects of modernization in this respect have already been noted. The early beginnings of industrialization in the Czech Lands had also established a network of many enterprises located in small- or medium-sized towns which maintained the link between work-place and residence that was largely lacking in areas that had the communist model of industrialization imposed on them. This sustained a higher level of social homogeneity than was possible under the conditions of insufficient urbanization characteristic of communist outcomes, in which many workers commuted from the countryside to their new place of employment. Jenkins (1992, p.138) points to the importance of 'pre-existing organizational networks' characteristic of such a society which were able to mobilize rapidly to form an umbrella organization which could then channel and represent the newly evident popular discontent. The influence of the small opposition groups was magnified by the concentration of power and population in Prague as a well-developed capital city in a relatively small country. Slovak sociologists have also contrasted the alacrity with which the Czech 'islands of positive deviation' transformed themselves into a revolutionary political elite with the slower-moving pace of change in their own country (Bútora and Bútorová, 1993, p.76).

In Bulgaria and Romania, on the other hand, different tendencies or reform currents within the communist elite were largely absent and there were few alternative forces which might have pointed the way to an alternative path of political change. Bulgarian party leader Zhivkov introduced a pale copy of Gorbachev's *perestroika* policy in 1987, although few changes were made in the operation of the political system. It did, however, encourage some intellectuals to band together to press for more effective change. In contrast to the actions of leaders in Poland and Hungary, though, Zhivkov resorted to repressive measures rather than attempting to incorporate them with a view to introducing a programme of party-led reform. Even more isolated from the current of reform that eventually flowed throughout the region, Romania remained subject to the strict dictatorship of the Ceaușescus until the very end of 1989 and was faced with virtually no organized opposition from any quarter.

The overthrow of the dictatorship was finally sparked off by demonstrations and violent reprisals after an attempt to arrest a local priest in the Hungarian-settled north-west of the country. Even at this stage the impetus for change came from the margins of Romanian society and from a group with ethnic ties to a country in the forefront of regional political change. In both countries there was a clear association of conditions of largely uncontested leadership with a slower rate of democratization and a less sharp break with the institutions and practices of communist rule. Counter-elites and a mobilized social opposition were lacking overall in the Balkan countries, although even in the countries where reformist strategies did emerge and pacts were struck with representatives of alternative political forces the level of social mobilization was rather limited.

Summary of Section 16.4

- Transition theory does seem to be applicable to East European democratization and useful for explaining the process.
- In Hungary and Poland divisions within the political elite were of major importance as they had been in earlier cases of democratic transition.

- Such splits were much less in evidence in Czechoslovakia, and the subsequent rapid pace of democratization is more likely to be explained in that country by the high level of modernization.
- The absence both of elite divisions and social movements in Bulgaria and Romania was in line with the slower pace of democratization.

Conclusion

The leading factor that opened the way to democratization in Eastern Europe was the situation of growing crisis in the Soviet Union, increasing awareness of the failure of the communist modernization project and Gorbachev's response to it. Abandonment of the Brezhnev doctrine and the decision not to maintain communist rule by force were the critical changes made with respect to Eastern Europe. Communist rule came to an end in different ways throughout Eastern Europe, however, and democratization advanced faster in some countries than others. On the basis of the above discussion, an analysis which focuses on elite strategy and leadership choice helps considerably in constructing an explanation for the rapid pace of democratization shown by Hungary and Poland. In both cases there were major splits within the elite which prepared the way for negotiations and the conclusion of political pacts, developments which have both been identified from the investigation of earlier cases of democratization as critical steps in the transition to democracy. Civil society was also more strongly developed in those countries and the activities of social forces were important in redefining the political space and limiting the power of the communist party-state leadership. Such forces were significant in their own right in helping to counter the influence of the communist authorities, but they also served to strengthen the position of counter-elites and the softliners in the political establishment who were more committed to pressing for liberalization, modifying the character of the existing regime and creating a liberal democratic order.

The situation was however different in Czechoslovakia and its successor states, where the regime remained authoritarian to the end, splits within the elite were largely absent and there were few signs of opposition within the broader society. Groups like Charter 77 were indeed important, but they did not have many supporters and their political influence both on the leadership and the population as a whole was rather limited. Nevertheless Czechoslovakia, and particularly (since the beginning of 1993) the Czech republic, certainly moved forward after 1989 in terms of democratization no less successfully than Hungary and Poland. Czechoslovakia's pre-war record of democratic practice and its more recent experience of the reform movement prior to the Soviet invasion of 1968 is likely to have played a part in this. Modernization and the country's high level of socio-economic development also made a major contribution here in terms of the public's perception of the changing political situation, its capacity to mobilize and a readiness to adapt to the practices of a developing liberal democratic order. The form that socio-economic development took in Poland and the nature of the modern social structure that emerged, particularly with respect to the changing nature of the working class, also contributed to the early challenge to communist rule that emerged with the formation of Solidarity.

On the basis of this evidence, then, the modernization thesis also seems to carry some explanatory value in the East European context, although precisely how processes of socio-economic development were linked with political outcomes and the dynamics of democratization remains unclear. While, too, modernization may well account for the rapid pace of democratization once it was under way in Czechoslovakia (and perhaps East Germany, although the dynamics of further change there were quite unique) it was evidently not a sufficient condition to ensure that the critical steps were taken to initiate the process in the domestic context. The elite perspective offered by transition theories provides a surer guide to the processes involved in the critical move from authoritarian rule towards the introduction of democratic practices. The slower pace of democratization in Bulgaria and Romania, on the other hand, could equally well be accounted for by elite factors or by their lower level of modernization. Both showed lower indices of socio-economic development as well as having a history of more repressive authoritarian rule than Hungary and Poland, particularly in the closing years of communist rule.

References

Beetham, D. (1994) 'Are we really free?', *New Statesman*.

Bútora, M. and Bútorová, Z. (1993) 'Slovakia after the split', *Journal of Democracy*, vol.4, pp.71–83.

Dahl, R. (1971) *Polyarchy*, New Haven, CT, Yale University Press.

Hankiss, E. (1990) 'What the Hungarians saw first' in Prins, G. (ed.) *Spring in Winter: the 1989 Revolutions*, Manchester, Manchester University Press.

Huntington, S.P. (1991) *The Third Wave*, Norman, OK, University of Oklahoma Press.

Jenkins, R.M. (1992) 'Society and regime transition in east-central Europe' in Szoboszlai, G. (ed.) *Flying Blind: Emerging Democracies in East-Central Europe*, Budapest, Hungarian Political Science Association.

Mason, D. (1992) *Revolution in East Central Europe*, Boulder, Westview Press.

Misztal, B.A. (1992) 'Must Eastern Europe follow the Latin American way?', *Archives Européens de Sociologie*, vol.33.

Musil, J. (1993) 'Czech and Slovak society', *Government and Opposition*, vol.28, pp.479–95.

O'Donnell, G. and Schmitter, P.C. (1986) *Transitions from Authoritarian Rule: Tentative Conclusions about Uncertain Democracies*, Baltimore, MD, Johns Hopkins University Press.

Pridham, G. and Vanhanen, T. (eds) (1994) *Democratization in Eastern Europe: Domestic and International Perspectives*, London, Routledge.

Welsh, H. (1994) 'Political transition processes in central and eastern Europe', *Comparative Politics*, vol.26, no.4, pp.379–94.

CHAPTER 17

Russia's troubled transition

Stephen White

Introduction

The Union of Soviet Socialist Republics (USSR), the world's largest state, covered a sixth of its land surface and stretched across eleven time zones. It was one of the world's nuclear superpowers, and had one of its largest economies. Above all, for the purposes of this book, it was the world's leading model of communist rule, with a Marxist–Leninist party which had firmly held political power since 1917. It was a party with a leadership that had faced no legitimate challenge, and which was sustained (in the last resort) by an army, police force and security service that were among the most powerful in the world. Not only that: the USSR supported the East European state system and a wider network of communist parties. The transition to post-communist rule that took place in other countries at the end of the 1980s would have been impossible if the Soviet leadership, under Mikhail Gorbachev, had not agreed to replace the Brezhnev doctrine with the 'Sinatra doctrine' (that the East European states, discussed in the last chapter, could do it 'their way').

Just as the October revolution in 1917 was a landmark in world history so, too, the end of communist rule in its country of origin was a turning-point, and not just for Russia. But how did a system that had been a going concern for 70 years collapse so suddenly? What were the forces that had sustained communist rule throughout those years, and what were the factors that had brought about its end? What weight should be attached to long-term factors such as 'modernization', and what to particular and much more short-term circumstances including Western pressure and the choices of the Soviet leadership itself? What, indeed, had 'collapsed' and what had continued after the end of Soviet rule? Had an authoritarian system continued under a different leadership, or had a form of democratic rule come into being in just a few years? And were these the only choices?

In this chapter I consider, in Section 17.1, the transition itself, from the reforms that took place under Gorbachev to the collapse of communist rule at the end of 1991, by which time the USSR had already become a multiparty state with an alternative press, freedom of conscience and competitive elections. In Section 17.2 I look at some of the explanations social scientists have offered for the stability of the Soviet system over more than 70 years, including the notion of a 'social contract' between regime and society, before considering the sources of long-term decline and in particular the impact of social change or 'modernization' and of particular elite choices in the late 1980s. And finally, in Section 17.3, I consider how far Russia's system of government in 1995 resembled that of a liberal democracy. What are the forces that help to sustain democracy, and those that undermine it? The USSR was for many years a model communist system; the Russian experience of democratization offers an equally instructive example of a state attempting to modify its form of government in a society with weak democratic traditions while at the same time attempting an unprecedented move from state planning to private enterprise.

17.1   Russia and democratic transition

Unlike Eastern Europe, communism in Russia was indigenous. Lenin was the son of a provincial schools inspector, his brother was a part of the populist movement that had attempted to overthrow tsarist rule in the late nineteenth century (and was condemned to death for his participation). The Bolsheviks, led by Lenin after a split with the more moderate Mensheviks, never won a popular majority at a competitive election. But when elections were held to a Constituent Assembly in November 1917, just after they had taken power, the Bolsheviks alone took about a quarter of the vote and socialist parties of various kinds won over three-quarters. Later, after Soviet rule had hardened into a repressive dictatorship, the Bolsheviks were back in the front line: more than 27 million Russians lost their lives during the Second World War, more than any major country had lost in any war, and more than three million of the dead were party members. There was a reconciliation with the church; and later, a period of post-war reconstruction followed by a sustained growth in living standards under Khrushchev and Brezhnev (party leaders respectively from 1953 to 1964 and from 1964 to 1982).

There were no more competitive elections, up to the end of the 1980s, and there was only one legal party. But as first Khrushchev, and then Gorbachev gradually extended the boundaries of debate and public contestation, there was the beginnings of what later came to be called 'socialist pluralism'. Journals and newspapers began to express mildly divergent points of view. The rule of law was strengthened, and the law codes themselves were liberalized. Groups and associations began to express a view on public issues, and to exercise some influence. The mass public had no choice of candidate, but they could write to the newspapers, or contact their local deputy, or comment on the legislation that was published for national discussion, or even (occasionally) take to the streets: as when the Georgian capital, Tbilisi, saw a successful protest against plans to drop the native language in favour of Russian in the new republican constitution. In 'high politics', to use Bialer's distinction, public influence was minimal and sanctions could be severe; but in 'low politics' – on matters like local transport or housing – public opinion was regularly consulted and it could sometimes be decisive (Bialer, 1980, pp.166–7).

Popular influence advanced once more under Mikhail Gorbachev, who was General Secretary of the Communist Party of the Soviet Union (CPSU) from March 1985 until just after the attempted coup of 1991. Gorbachev, according to his wife, had not expected the nomination and spent some time deciding whether to accept: all that was clear was (in a famous phrase) 'We just can't go on like this' (Gorbacheva, 1991, p.14). The key issue, in the early months of his administration, was the economy: an acceleration of economic growth, in particular, was the 'key to all our problems, immediate and long-term, economic and social, political and ideological, domestic and foreign' (*Materialy*, 1986, p.22). But the emphasis gradually shifted from *uskorenie* (economic acceleration) to the more radical policy of *demokratizatsiya* (democratization, or within-system political reform), and on to a complex of changes that had taken the Communist Party, by the end of its period of rule, to an almost social democratic position: not only accepting but approving a mixed economy, a multiparty system, the rule of law, freedom of conscience, and a co-operative rather than a confrontational relationship with the outside world.

Of all the policies that were promoted by the Gorbachev leadership, *glasnost* was perhaps the most distinctive and the one that had been pressed furthest by the end of communist rule (for a fuller account of the reform process as a whole see Sakwa, 1990; White, 1994; Brown, 1996). *Glasnost*, usually translated as openness or publicity, was not the same as freedom of the press or the right to information; nor was it original to Gorbachev (it figured, for instance, in the 1977 Brezhnev Constitution). It did, however, reflect the new General Secretary's belief that without a greater awareness of the real state of affairs and of the considerations that had led to particular decisions there would be no willingness on the part of the Soviet people to commit themselves to his programme of *perestroika* (or 'restructuring'). Existing policies were in any case ineffectual and sometimes counterproductive. The newspaper *Sovetskaya Rossiya* reported the case of Mr Polyakov of Kaluga, a well-read man who followed the newspapers and never missed the evening news. He knew a lot about what was happening in various African countries, Polyakov complained, but had 'only a very rough idea what was happening in his own city'. In late 1985, another reader complained, there had been a major earthquake in Tajikistan in Soviet Central Asia, but no details were made known other than that 'lives had been lost'. At about the same time there had been an earthquake in Mexico and a volcanic eruption in Colombia, both covered extensively with full details of the casualties. Was Tajikistan really further from Moscow than Latin America?

Influenced by considerations such as these, the Gorbachev leadership made steady and sometimes dramatic progress in removing taboos from the discussion of public affairs and exposing both the Soviet past and present to critical scrutiny. The Brezhnev era was one of the earliest targets. It had been a time, Gorbachev told the 27th Party Congress in 1986, when a 'curious psychology – how to change things without really changing anything' – had been dominant. A number of its leading representatives had been openly corrupt, and some (such as Brezhnev's son-in-law, Yuri Churbanov) were brought to trial and imprisoned for serious state crimes. More generally, it had been a period of 'stagnation', of wasted opportunities, when party and government leaders had lagged behind the needs of the times.

The Stalin question was more difficult, and Gorbachev, to begin with, was reluctant even to concede there was a question (Stalinism, he told the French press, was a 'notion made up by enemies of communism'). By early 1987, however, Gorbachev was insisting that there must be 'no forgotten names, no blank spots' in Soviet literature and history, and by November of that year, when he came to give his address on the seventieth anniversary of the revolution, he was ready to condemn the 'wanton repressive measures' of the 1930s, 'real crimes' in which 'many thousands of people inside and outside the party' had suffered. Several of the most prominent victims of the past, such as the former *Pravda* editor Nikolai Bukharin, were posthumously pardoned; later, whole categories of victims were restored to respectability, while a discussion continued on the number that had been arrested or lost their lives during the period.

Glasnost led to further changes in the quality of Soviet public life, from literature and the arts to statistics and a wide-ranging discussion on the future of Soviet socialism. Public information began to improve with the publication of official figures on abortions, suicides and other 'dark sides of Soviet life'. Subjects that had been taboo during the Brezhnev years, such as violent crime, drugs and prostitution, began to receive extensive and even sensational treatment. Some of the disasters of earlier years, such as a devastating earthquake that had taken place in Ashkhabad in 1948 and a nuclear accident in the Urals in 1957, were belatedly acknowledged. Figures for defence spending and foreign debt were revealed to the Congress of People's Deputies for the first time in 1989; figures for capital punishment followed in 1991. The Congress itself was televised in full and followed avidly throughout the USSR; so too were Central Committee plenums and Supreme Soviet Committee hearings. (Note: the Congress of People's Deputies and Supreme Soviet were part of the Soviet government structure. The Central Committee was a leading organ of the Communist Party. The main features of the party structure are outlined in Box 17.1.) Still more remarkably, the Soviet media were opened up to foreign journalists and politicians, and even (in a few cases) to émigrés and open opponents of Soviet socialism. Opinion polls suggested that *glasnost*, for all its limitations, was the change in Soviet life that was most apparent to ordinary people and the one that they most valued.

The 'democratization' of Soviet political life was an associated change, and was similarly intended to release the human energies that, for Gorbachev, had been choked off by the bureaucratic centralism of the Stalin and Brezhnev years. The Soviet Union, he told the 19th Party Conference in the summer of 1988, had pioneered the idea of a workers' state and of workers' control, the right to work and equality of rights for women and all national groups. The political system established by the October revolution, however, had undergone 'serious deformations', leading to the development of a 'command-administrative system' which had extinguished the democratic potential of the elected soviets. The role of party and state officialdom had increased out of all proportion, and this 'bloated administrative apparatus' had begun to dictate its will in political and economic matters. Nearly a third of the adult population were regularly elected to the soviets, but most of them had little influence over the conduct of government. Social life as a whole had become unduly politicized, and ordinary working people had become 'alienated' from the system that was supposed to represent their interests. It was this 'ossified system of government, with its command-and-pressure mechanism', that was now the main obstacle to *perestroika*.

> **Box 17.1 Terminology of Communist Party life**
>
> 1   *Central Committee* – The Communist Party implemented party
> decisions through the Central Committee; the Central
> Committee elected the Political Bureau (or Politburo), which
> was the highest policy-making body of the party.
>
> 2   *National Party Congress* – Party Congresses were traditionally
> held once every five years. They were the most important
> event in the political calendar at which personnel changes in
> the Central Committee and the Politburo took place, and
> policy directions over the next five years were set out. Party
> conferences were held less regularly to discuss matters of major
> political importance.
>
> 3   *Democratic centralism* – Community Party organization was
> formally based on the principle of democratic centralism,
> whereby decisions made by the Central Committee and
> Politburo had to be obeyed and implemented by lower level
> party organizations. Party members were permitted to express
> their views freely during party meetings but once a decision
> was made they were not supposed to oppose it.

The Conference duly approved the notion of a 'radical reform' of the political system, and this led to a series of constitutional and other changes from 1988 onwards. An entirely new election law, for instance, approved in December 1988, broke new ground in providing for (though not specifically requiring) a choice of candidate at elections to local and national assemblies. A new state structure was established, incorporating a relatively small working parliament for the first time in modern Soviet political history and (from 1990) a powerful executive Presidency. A constitutional review committee, similar to a constitutional court, was set up as part of a move to what Gorbachev called a 'socialist system of checks and balances'. Judges were to be elected for longer periods of time, and given greater guarantees of independence in their work. And ordinary members of the CPSU were to be given much greater powers, although in practice the changes were less far-reaching than in other parts of the political system and in the end were not sufficient to preserve the party's authority. Leading officials, it was agreed, should be elected by competitive ballot for a maximum of two consecutive terms; members of the Central Committee should be involved much more directly in the work of the leadership; and there should be much more information about all aspects of the party's work, from its finances to the operation of its decision-making bodies.

Together with these changes, for Gorbachev, there had to be a 'radical reform' of the Soviet economy. Levels of growth had been declining since at least the 1950s (see Table 17.1). In the late 1970s they reached the lowest levels in Soviet peacetime history, and may altogether have ceased per head of population. Indeed, as Gorbachev explained in early 1988, if the sale of alcoholic drink and of Soviet oil on foreign markets were excluded, there had been no increase in national wealth for at least the previous 15 years. Growth, at least for many reforming economists, could not be an end in itself: what was important was the satisfaction of real social needs. But it was equally apparent that without some improvement in living standards there would be no popular commitment to *perestroika*, and no prospect that socialism would recover its appeal to other nations as a means by which ordinary working people could live their lives in dignity and sufficiency.

Table 17.1 Soviet economic growth, 1951–85 (average annual increase, percentages)

	National income produced	Industrial output	Real income per head
1951–55	11.4	13.2	7.3
1956–60	9.2	10.4	5.7
1960–65	6.5	8.6	3.6
1966–70	7.8	8.5	5.9
1971–75	5.7	7.4	4.4
1976–80	4.3	4.4	3.4
1981–85	3.6	3.7	2.1

Source: Soviet official data

Radical reform, as Gorbachev explained to the 27th Party Congress and to an important Central Committee meeting in the summer of 1987, involved a set of related measures. One of the most important was a greater degree of decentralization of economic decision making, leaving broad guidance of the economy in the hands of the State Planning Committee (Gosplan) but allowing factories and farms throughout the USSR more freedom to determine their own priorities. They should be guided in making such decisions by a wide range of 'market' indicators, including the orders they received from other enterprises and the profits they made on their production. Under the Law on the State Enterprise, adopted in 1987, enterprises that persistently failed to pay their way under these conditions could be liquidated. The state sector, more generally, would gradually be reduced in size, and co-operative or even private economic activity would be expanded in its place. Gorbachev described these changes, which were brought into effect from 1987 onwards, as the most radical to have taken place in Soviet economic life since the adoption of the New Economic Policy in the early 1920s.

Nor were these merely words. At the 1989 elections to the new Soviet parliament, about three-quarters of the seats were contested: there were more deputies who were members of the CPSU than ever before (over 80 per cent), but about 40 regional party leaders were defeated, and in Leningrad a candidate member of the ruling Politburo lost his seat (he was dropped from the Politburo shortly afterwards). Meanwhile Boris Yeltsin, forced out of the Moscow party leadership and into the political wilderness, bounced back

Рис. В. БОГОРАДА.

A voter in the new Russian democracy begins to
feel mugged by ballot boxes.
Izvestiya, 1995

with over 89 per cent of the vote in Moscow – and a majority so large it entered
the *Guinness Book of Records*. In 1990, in elections to the Russian and other
republican parliaments, Yeltsin won again and was shortly afterwards
elected parliamentary chairman. Other radicals won the elections for mayor
of Moscow and mayor of Leningrad (it became St Petersburg again later in
the year), and in the three Baltic republics nationalist candidates won
substantial majorities and (in Lithuania) declared their independence.
Nationalist candidates were also successful in Georgia and Armenia. The
Communist Party, meanwhile, had abandoned Article 6 of the Constitution,
which guaranteed its political monopoly; it was amended in March 1990 to
acknowledge the existence of 'other political parties, as well as trade union,
youth and other public organizations and mass movements'. And in October
1990 the USSR officially became a multiparty state with the adoption of a
new law on parties and other public associations; by early 1991 there were
about 20 of them, with several hundred more loosely defined 'movements'.

There were further reforms in the mass media, and in freedom of conscience. The new law on the media, which was approved in June 1990, established the right of all citizens to 'express opinions and beliefs and to seek, select, receive and disseminate information and ideas in any form'; and it outlawed censorship (previously even the existence of censorship had been censored). A new law on religion, adopted in October 1990, was similarly unqualified in its commitment to the right of all citizens to 'decide and express their attitude towards religion' and to the 'unhindered confession of a religion and the performance of religious rites'. The law made it clear that parents could bring up their children within a religious faith, it dropped the prohibition on religious ceremonies being performed on state occasions, it allowed religious schools to be set up alongside the state system, and the churches were given much broader rights than in the past to engage in charitable work and to publish their literature. The first priests, meanwhile, had been elected to the Soviet parliament, and the Communist Party dropped its requirement that members be committed atheists (for these and other developments see Anderson, 1994).

Communist rule, accordingly, had greatly changed – it could be argued that it had effectively ended – even before the events of late 1991 that led to the suspension and then suppression of the CPSU and then the breakup of the USSR itself. The crucial event was the attempted coup of 19–21 August 1991, led by a group of party hardliners determined to prevent any further loosening of the Soviet state (the outcome was in fact to accelerate its disintegration). The conspirators included the Vice-President, Gennadii Yanaev; the Prime Minister, Valentin Pavlov; the KGB Chairman, Vladimir Kryuchkov; the Defence Minister, Dmitrii Yazov; and the Interior Minister (who commanded the police), Boris Pugo. Gorbachev, on holiday in the Crimea, was placed under house arrest; but the coup was resisted by Boris Yeltsin and the Russian parliament, it was denounced by most of the world community, and within a few days it had collapsed and the conspirators were under arrest. Yeltsin took this opportunity to suspend and then (in November 1991) suppress the Communist Party; and in early December, at a hunting lodge in Belorussia, he agreed with the Ukrainian president and the Belorussian parliamentary chairman to found a new interstate union in place of the USSR, the Commonwealth of Independent States. By the end of 1991 Gorbachev had resigned as President of a state that no longer existed, and the post-communist era had begun.

———————————— *Summary of Section 17.1* ————————————

The late Soviet period accordingly saw several developments:

- A broadening of patterns of consultation within what was still a single party system.
- The introduction of a programme of political and economic reform (*perestroika*) under the Gorbachev leadership after 1985.
- The breakdown of communist rule under the impact of the attempted coup of August 1991, but also reflecting a steady loss of party and state authority in the face of nationalist and oppositional forces.

17.2 Social science, communism and transition

The collapse of Soviet rule was a surprise to the outside world, and indeed to its own citizens. There were many, certainly, for whom there had been few prospects of a change in communist rule during the 1980s, not only in the USSR but throughout Eastern Europe. For Samuel Huntington, writing in 1984, the likelihood of democratic development in Eastern Europe was 'virtually nil' (Huntington, 1984, p.217). For Jerry Hough, as late as 1990, Soviet difficulties had been 'grossly exaggerate[d]'; the real story of that year had been the 'further consolidation of Gorbachev's political position', and he was 'almost certain to remain in power at least until the 1995 presidential election' (Hough, 1990, pp.642, 669). Gorbachev's position, Hough wrote a year later, would be 'very strong in the mid 1990s', and the Communist Party through which he ruled had an 'excellent chance to become a dominant electoral party in the Slavic areas on the model of Mexico's Institutional Revolutionary Party ... [for] the rest of this century' (Hough, 1991, p.106).

There were few who argued that governments of the Soviet type had secured the active approval of those who nominally elected them. But there was, it appeared, a basis for stability in the implicit 'social contract' that had been concluded between the authorities and the society over which they ruled, based upon an exchange of political rights for a stable and assured standard of living (Cook, 1993). Many gained real advantages from Soviet rule. Levels of higher education, per head of population, trebled in the Brezhnev years. Career opportunities improved enormously, particularly in the white collar professions and in science (the USSR had a third of all the world's scientific manpower). There were measurable improvements in the Soviet diet, and in dress and appearance. The USSR was a major sporting power, and the leader in space exploration. And at the same time prices had been kept low for basic necessities. The rents for public housing, for instance, had remained at the same level since 1928; foodstuffs were heavily subsidized; and public transport was extremely cheap (for decades the standard fare on the Moscow underground had been five kopeks, about six US cents at the rate of exchange of the time).

There were more specific advantages for women from a system of the Soviet kind. Women, certainly, were under-represented in political life (see Table 17.2 on p.430). Their earnings were less than those of men, because they were concentrated in less well paid occupations. They had to work a 'double shift', as their partners took little responsibility for shopping, child care, or other domestic tasks. But women, all the same, were better represented in political life than they were in other countries (there were more women in the Soviet parliament than in the British, American, French and Italian put together). Women were steadily increasing their presence in public life, with the largest ever share of the Central Committee membership in 1990 (8 per cent) and the first member of the Politburo for many years (she was also a member of the powerful Secretariat). Women, under the Constitution, were guaranteed equal educational and professional opportunities, an equal right to participate in political life, and equal pay; a series of more particular measures provided for paid leave for expectant mothers and for women with young children, including a gradual reduction in the working day.

Table 17.2 Women in Soviet society and their representation in political bodies (1970s, percentages)

Women in total population	Communist Party	Central Committee	Politburo	Local Soviets	Council of Ministers
53.5	24.7	4.0	0.0	49.0	1.0

Source: Soviet official data and party statistics

For many, indeed, this was a system that was securely established. It suited an authoritarian culture, it had earned the support of the Soviet people when it led the resistance to Nazi occupation during the war, and it provided a secure and steadily improving standard of living for all its citizens. For some, its longevity was in itself a source of stability. Once a regime had been in existence for two or three generations, it was suggested, it became the predominant influence upon the political memories of its adult population and would increasingly be taken for granted by those who reached adult years under its auspices (Rose, 1971, p.35). The Soviet system, by the late 1980s, abundantly satisfied these criteria. It had been in existence for more than 70 years and more than 90 per cent of the population had been born since its establishment, nearly 70 per cent of them since the Second World War (*Itogi,* 1992); it should gradually have gained acceptance, on this basis, as those with a conscious recollection of the pre-revolutionary order became a small and steadily diminishing proportion of the population as a whole.

Views of this kind, however, were far from universally accepted. And from at least the 1960s there were very different suggestions, for instance that the 'new class was divided' between party officials and a more adaptable group of technocrats (Parry, 1966). Another influential interpretation was that there would be 'convergence' between the Soviet system and its Western counterparts as both were influenced by the requirements of industrial society (Johnson, 1970); a trotskyist variation on this theme was that the bureaucracy was 'breeding its own gravediggers', as education and social change overwhelmed the centralized structures that had been inherited from late Stalinism (Deutscher, 1967, pp.59–60). By the late 1970s, as economic growth slowed down, the emphasis shifted away from the pluralizing consequences of a maturing society to a deepening tension between the ruling group and the wider population; and by the early 1980s, when growth per head of population had fallen to virtually zero, the prognoses had become extremely bleak. For Goldman (1983), the USSR was 'in crisis'; for Richard Pipes, it already fitted Lenin's description of a 'revolutionary situation' (Pipes, 1984, p.50). For Martin Malia, writing rather later in a celebrated article that appeared under the pseudonym 'Z', there was no prospect of a viable reform under Gorbachev because the internal contradictions of the system were 'simply too overwhelming' (Malia, 1990, p.295).

For most of these writers, and for many others, the weakness of Soviet rule was more than a matter of short-term difficulties: it was much more the product of a fundamental contradiction between communist authoritarianism and the open and bargaining culture that corresponded to its economic maturity. Perhaps the most influential exponent of this view was Talcott Parsons, a sociologist – and member of the Russian Research Center at Harvard University – who drew his inspiration from Darwin and much older theories of social change. All states, for Parsons, had to develop a range of capacities or 'evolutionary universals' that would allow them to adapt to the requirements of modern society, among them a 'democratic association with elective leadership and fully enfranchised membership' (Parsons, 1964a, pp.340–1). The communist states, in Parsons' view, would be unable to offer a convincing alternative to liberal-democratic systems in the long run, and would be compelled to make adjustments in the direction of electoral democracy and a plural party system if they were to survive (ibid., p.356). As a result of their own internal dynamics, Parsons wrote, the communist states would therefore be bound to develop towards the 'restoration – or where it has not yet existed, the institution – of political democracy' (Parsons, 1964b, pp.396–8).

A more developed version of this theory took the form of political modernization: the view, as Robert Dahl put it, that 'because of its inherent requirements, an advanced economy and its supporting social structures automatically distributes political resources and political skills to a vast variety of individuals, groups and organisations' (Dahl, 1971, p.77). The monopoly of political power enjoyed by communist leaders, according to Dahl, was therefore being undermined by the programmes of social and economic development that they themselves had sponsored. The more communist leaders succeeded in transforming the social and economic structures of the countries over which they ruled, the more their political skills were threatened by obsolescence; but if they sought to retain their dominance by force alone they would be confronted by the enormous costs of managing a modern society in this anachronistic way. The change from Stalinism to the post-Stalinism, Dahl suggested, was already a 'profound step towards liberalization'; further steps were inescapable as a centrally dominated political system became increasingly difficult to reconcile with the pluralistic pressures of a modern economy and society (ibid., pp.64–5, 76–9, 218).

Dahl was not the only scholar in the 1970s and 1980s to point to an 'iron law of pluralism'. The Soviet historian and commentator Roy Medvedev spoke of democratization as an 'inevitable tendency'; Ghita Ionescu suggested that 'pluralization and institutionalization' were an 'inevitable trend' which accompanied the 'process of economic, social and political development'; and Karl Deutsch identified an 'automatic trend towards pluralization and disintegration' (cited in White, 1978, pp.105-6). Gabriel Almond, in perhaps the most far-reaching of such prognoses, spoke of the 'pluralistic pressures of a modern economy and society' and of a 'secular trend in the direction of decentralization and pluralism'. As their societies and economies developed, Almond suggested, communist systems would face the 'inevitable demands of a healthy, educated, affluent society' for both more material and what he called 'spiritual consumer goods' (such as a share in the decision-making process). Already, Almond wrote, 'Russian success in science, education, technology, economic productivity and national security have produced some decentralization of the political process. I fail to see how these decentralizing, pluralistic tendencies can be reversed, or how their spread can be prevented' (Almond, 1970, pp.27, 318–9).

There was little evidence, as the Prague Spring was crushed and dissidents were incarcerated in mental hospitals, that pluralistic pressures were exerting the influence that had been so widely expected, but as economic growth slowed down in the late 1970s and early 1980s, the prevailing Western interpretation became an increasingly bleak and uncompromising one. For Tucker (1981), Brezhnev's Russia was a 'spent state and a swollen society'; for Bialer (1986), it was 'external expansion, internal decline'. There was an environmental crisis (Komarov, 1980), and a widening gap between rich and poor (Matthews, 1986); there was also a widening network of privilege and corruption (Matthews, 1978; Simis, 1982; Clarke, 1983). Indeed for some the changes that took place in the late 1980s were evidence that modernization theories had been right all along, as the East European systems found themselves unable to resist the pressures that sprang from the diversity that was a result of economic development, as well as the spread of international and electronic communications. For Lucian Pye, these were nothing less than 'inevitable forces of history' (Pye, 1990, p.6); for Moshe Lewin, similarly, the changes of the 1980s were evidence that Soviet society needed a state that could 'match its complexity' (Lewin, 1988, p.146).

Soviet society, on this interpretation, had outgrown its political system: centralized, authoritarian communist rule was simply disfunctional to the requirements of a modern and technologically advanced society. But while modernization theories of this kind were persuasive, at least in retrospect, they raised almost as many questions as they answered. There were states more economically advanced than the USSR that had retained a form of authoritarian politics – for instance, in Southeast Asia (cases already discussed in Part III). There were poorer states that had sustained democracy – for example, in India. The transition from communist rule, arguably, represented a step towards *more* authoritarian forms of politics, not more democratic practices, in the Central Asian republics: they had been obliged to implement the Gorbachev reforms, with all their limitations, but were free (after 1991) to ban opposition parties, instal their presidents for lengthy periods of office and muzzle the local press. Modernization theories gave little sense of threshold – how much economic development was needed to sustain a pluralist politics? – and they were deterministic, in that they made little allowance for the influence of history and culture in shaping the politics of democracy in different ways in different countries, and assumed a universal progress towards (in practice) the political forms of Western liberal democracy.

Rather different accounts have been given by those employing *transition theory*. As the sociologists have suggested, we need to consider 'agency' (human choices and actions) as well as 'structure' (the wider context within which human choices and actions take place). In the long run, a process of social change was taking place in the communist-ruled countries that would almost certainly have led to a broadening of their forms of popular consultation and eventually, perhaps, to a form of 'socialist pluralism'. But in the short term, it was elite choices that were decisive. Gorbachev, when he spoke to the Politburo meeting that agreed to nominate him to the leadership, told them there was 'no need to change [their] policies' (*Istochnik*, 1993, p.74); and when he addressed the Central Committee after his election he called for no more than the 'acceleration of socio-economic development and the perfection of all aspects of social life', a formulation that was thoroughly Brezhnevite. But his agenda broadened as it developed: into arms agreements with the West, an accommodation with the church, political rather than a more limited 'socialist' pluralism, and (decisively) a different relationship with Eastern Europe which allowed those countries to replace their communist governments and withdraw from the Soviet sphere of influence. This carried a distinctly 'softline' connotation (see Chapter 1).

It is still far from clear that Gorbachev and the reformers generally 'had' to undertake such changes because of the requirements of a mature society and economy. Economic growth in the early Gorbachev years was a respectable 3 per cent. There is little reason to doubt the opinion polls of 1989 or early 1990 which indicated that the Communist Party enjoyed substantial support, and that Gorbachev personally would have won a presidential election against any other candidate. The experience of China showed that it was possible to sustain a high level of economic growth while at the same time maintaining a single-party communist government.

Many of the reformers, looking back with the benefit of hindsight, believe that policy misjudgements were at least as important as wider systemic factors in the slow-down in Soviet growth that took place in the late 1980s, followed by an absolute decline. The anti-alcohol campaign that was launched in 1985, for instance, led to a serious shortfall in public revenues and had no lasting impact on consumption (White, 1996). It was also suggested that the reforms should have started, as did the Chinese, with agriculture, and only then moved on to industry. There were some wholly 'random' factors, such as the Chernobyl explosion in April 1986 and the Armenian earthquake in December 1988. Any adequate social scientific explanation of the end of communist rule in the USSR must take account of these short-term circumstances, and of particular elite choices, as well as of the longer-term requirements of system change and adaptation.

And it must take account of the wider international context, not just of domestic Soviet developments. Unlike most of the East European countries, the USSR was not particularly dependent on foreign trade (no more than 5–6 per cent of national income). Its currency was insulated from global monetary flows because it could not be converted. It could veto decisions in the UN Security Council, and had the means of enforcing its own decisions inside the USSR and in Eastern Europe more generally. But it had to compete with the Western nations in military terms, a competition that grew more difficult to sustain as new generations of weapons – like anti-ballistic missile systems and later the Strategic Defense Initiative – were developed and deployed. It had to compete for influence in the developing world, and had to spend heavily to retain its foreign allies (like Cuba and Vietnam). Its own society was increasingly permeated by Western pop music, youth culture, religions, drinks, fashions of all kinds. Gorbachev's diplomacy, in these circumstances, was essentially a 'diplomacy of decline' (Sestanovich, 1988), ending expensive commitments abroad and making unilateral concessions in arms negotiations. It was the West that 'won' the Cold War; and its greater economic strength helped to create an environment in which the USSR was always seeking to reduce its defence costs, raise its level of economic growth, and develop forms of consultation that would satisfy a population increasingly exposed to Western sources of information and a very different world outlook.

─────────────── *Summary of Section 17.2* ───────────────

Social scientists, accordingly, have explored a number of different perspectives in accounting for the collapse of Soviet socialism:

- Soviet economic performance, in the 1950s and 1960s, sustained a steady improvement in living standards and particular groups, such as women, enjoyed a wide range of social benefits.

- Theories of political modernization none the less suggested that this economic advance would of itself generate pressures for a more open and pluralistic form of politics.

- Such theories need to be combined with a focus on elite decisions, which (at least in the short term) were the key to political change.

- The global context must also be considered, and the pressures that it imposed upon successive Soviet leaders.

17.3 The friends and foes of democratization

As I suggested in the first part of this chapter, the Russian transition may best be seen as an extended process that began in the late Gorbachev era, but there was no doubt that it had been taken further in the early years of post-communist rule. Nevertheless, the leadership was still largely composed of former communists: Boris Yeltsin had been a member for 30 years and a member of the ruling CPSU Politburo; Prime Minister Viktor Chernomyrdin had been a member of the Central Committee. Former members of the communist *nomenklatura* (i.e. politically vetted occupants of important posts) accounted for about three-quarters of Yeltsin's top leadership, and for more than 80 per cent of leading officials in the Russian regions (Kryshtanovskaya and White, 1996). The KGB (security police) disappeared, but a new Federal Security Bureau took its place with similar powers. The central government was even larger than the old Communist Party apparatus. Most Russians, in the summer of 1994, thought the communists were 'still in power' (*Argumenty i fakty*, 1994, no.23, p.2). And had the defeat of the attempted coup in 1991 led to an 'end of the communist regime?' A year later, 41 per cent agreed but 41 per cent took the opposite view; two years later the jury was still out, with 43 per cent in agreement but 45 per cent unconvinced (*Izvestiya*, 20 August 1993, p.4).

Formally, at least, the new constitution of December 1993 marked a step forward. It was a constitution that committed the new state to 'ideological pluralism', to 'political diversity' and a multiparty system; and there could be no 'compulsory ideology' (Article 13). A whole chapter dealt with the rights and freedoms of the individual, including equality before the law, and equal rights for men and women. There were guarantees of personal inviolability and privacy. There was a freedom of information provision, allowing citizens to discover whatever was held about them by any organ of government. There was freedom of movement, within the country and across national boundaries. There was freedom of conscience, of thought and speech, and of association and assembly. Press freedom was guaranteed, and censorship was abolished. And there were economic guarantees: private ownership was explicitly recognized, and the right of citizens to engage in business. All these rights were entrenched: in other words, they could not be amended without a complicated procedure involving a constitutional conference and (normally) a referendum.

The old Soviet constitution had recognized a number of these rights, including freedom of speech, association and assembly. But they had been severely qualified in practice by their subordination to the 'interests of socialism'. The new Russian constitution reflected an emerging democratic reality. Property, for a start, was more widely diffused. Under a scheme launched in late 1991, vouchers or 'privatization cheques' were distributed to all members of the population, including children and Russian citizens living abroad. 'We need millions of property owners, not just a handful of millionaires', as President Yeltsin declared in a television interview. 'The more property owners there are in Russia ... the sooner prosperity will come to Russia, and the more likely its future will be in safe hands' (*Izvestiya*, 20 August, 1992, pp.1–2).

There were all kinds of problems. Vouchers were counterfeited or stolen; they were sold for vodka, or eau de cologne; in a case that was reported in Yaroslavl they were accepted as advance payment for funerals. Several large-scale swindles were organized: in the largest of these, three investment companies in St Petersburg simply disappeared together with the vouchers of about 400,000 of the local population. By the mid 1990s, none the less, a substantial redistribution of property had taken place. At least 110,000 enterprises had been privatized by the end of 1994, most of them in the service sector (*Sotsial'no*, 1995, pp.79–83); and within the labour force, over 37 million – or 55 per cent of the total – worked in the non-state sector, co-operative as well as private (*Rossiiskii*, 1995, p.9). By 1994, again, 62 per cent of GNP originated in the non-state sector, of which 25 per cent was in the private sector (*Sotsial'no*, 1995, p.5). For Barrington Moore, one of the conditions of a democracy was a reasonable diffusion of private property. Privatization had no obvious effect on economic performance, but it did serve the more political purpose of extending a form of individual owner-ship to large numbers of Russians, and in this sense it helped to sustain the post-communist order (Moore, 1989, p.20).

But there were powerful factors working against the emergence of a consolidated democracy, and by the mid 1990s they seemed to be gaining ground. Russia was still a democracy, in the sense that there were competitive elections and a wide range of civil liberties, but several of the institutions of a functioning democracy were very weak, among them political parties. Parties and movements of all kinds had been legalized in the late Soviet period by the law of October 1990, and by the summer of 1992 there were at least 1,200

Рис. В. БОГОРАДА.

'Your attitude to opinion polls?'

Izvestiya, January 1994.

operating on a Russia-wide basis. The largest of them was the Communist Party, banned in November 1991 but then allowed to reconstitute itself in early 1993. The party claimed about 500,000 members, making it by far the largest of the new formations although far short of the 19 million members that the CPSU had been able to claim at the height of its influence in the last years of the USSR. Several other parties fought the 1993 and then the 1995 parliamentary elections, among them Vladimir Zhirinovsky's nationalist Liberal Democrats, an Agrarian Party based on state-run rather than private agriculture, and the pro-Yeltsin movement known as Russia's Choice (it registered as a party in 1994).

There was, in fact, a party to reflect most political preferences, including greens, monarchists, beer-drinkers and gays, but they suffered from a number of serious weaknesses. Apart from the communists, none had a significant national membership. They split repeatedly, and they had little support from ordinary Russians. Opinion surveys, certainly, found that political parties were the least trusted of all political institutions. A Russia-wide investigation in December 1992, for instance, asked respondents if there were any parties to which they were 'ideologically close' or which 'represented the interests of people like you'. An overwhelming 78 per cent responded that there was no such party. Some 40 per cent agreed that political parties had 'no relevance to ordinary people', and more than half (52 per cent) thought all the new parties were 'founded by people who are greedy for power' (for some, the new party activists were just 'misfits with nothing better to do'). And asked about the new parties that were active in the early post-communist years, none had a positive rating of more than 18 per cent; negative assessments were much more common, but most common of all – as high as 80 per cent – was to have no opinion at all (White *et al.*, 1995, pp.188–90).

What about human rights more specifically? Just 13 per cent, in a Eurobarometer survey that appeared in 1996, thought they were broadly respected in post-communist Russia; more than five times as many (85 per cent) thought they were not. Former Soviet republics, including Russia, were the most likely of all the post-communist countries to believe there had been no fundamental improvement in their human rights, and they were the most likely to express dissatisfaction with the development of democracy in their own country. Russians were the most dissatisfied of all, with only 6 per cent taking a positive view *(Central and Eastern Eurobarometer,* 1996). Russians, again, were generally the most likely to take a positive view of the society they had left, and the most jaundiced view of the present and immediate future. Some 72 per cent, in a survey conducted by the Public Opinion Research Centre in early 1996, took a positive view of their economic system 'before the start of *perestroika*'; only 22 per cent took a positive view of the post-communist system, and no more than 40 per cent thought they would have a better system in five years' time (Rose, 1996, pp.22–4). The communist-era political system, similarly, was rated positively by 59 per cent; just 28 per cent approved of the system of governing as it stood in the mid 1990s, and no more than 43 per cent thought they would take a more positive view in five years' time (ibid., pp.47–50).

There was no stronger commitment, in the mid 1990s, to any other system of government. One-third were in favour of a return to communist rule, but two-thirds were against. Very few thought the army should rule (10 per cent were in favour but 90 per cent against). Even fewer wanted a return to the Tsar (6 per cent were in favour, 93 per cent against). But there was strong support for the idea that 'important decisions about the economy should be made by experts and not the government and parliament' (77 per cent were in favour and just 23 per cent against) (Rose, 1996, p.57). Many were prepared to see parliament suspended, and the President rule by decree; 42 per cent said they would approve if political parties were suspended (ibid., p.53). Just 9 per cent 'often' or 'sometimes' took part in public life; those who did so, in the view of ordinary Russians, were likely to be 'manipulating things to help themselves' or 'dishonest' (Rose, 1995, pp.40–1). Fewer Russians, as compared with the late 1980s, said they were interested in politics, and fewer, certainly, had been voting. The first competitive elections, in 1989, attracted 90 per cent; 75 per cent turned out in the Russian presidential elections of 1991; but no more than 54 per cent exercised their democratic rights in December 1993, and not many more – 64 per cent – did so in December 1995.

Few social institutions, in fact, enjoyed the support of ordinary Russians. The President, personally, was increasingly unpopular, with 71 per cent negatively disposed towards him in early 1996 and just 14 per cent positive, but virtually all institutions were distrusted, with the partial exceptions of collective farms, the armed forces and the various churches. Just over half (53 per cent) of Russians trusted collective farms, and 43 per cent trusted the army (36 per cent were more doubtful). Virtually every other public institution was negatively rated by about two-thirds of Russians, including private enterprise (72 per cent negative), political parties (67 per cent), parliament (68 per cent), the trade unions (63 per cent), the police (67 per cent), the civil service (74 per cent) the courts (60 per cent) and the President himself (75 per cent) (Rose, 1996, pp.51–4).

Opinion polls were a relatively new development in Russia, and there was some controversy about their validity (Shlapentokh, 1994; Gibson, 1994; White, 1995; Miller *et al.*, 1996). There was some doubt that a properly representative national sample had been constructed, with urban areas much more likely to be reached than the deep countryside. The old communist tradition of telling people in authority what it was thought they wanted to hear continued to apply; there was unusually extensive migration, which made it difficult to use the census or residents' lists as a sampling frame, and the increase in crime made Russians more reluctant than most to open their front doors. Fewer than half had a telephone, outside the major cities, and this limited the use of another well-developed method of inquiry. The survey results, nonetheless, tended to show low levels of support for democratic institutions for their own sake; levels were generally falling; and they were generally lower than in the post-communist states of Eastern Europe.

Women voting in Moscow, December 1995

All of this, moreover, was in a context of economic collapse. The late communist period had seen a slow-down, and then – for the first time in 1990 – a fall in officially recorded economic activity. Thereafter levels of output fell sharply, by perhaps as much as a half over the five years from 1990: a greater relative decline than any major country had suffered at any time outside war. And unlike some of the East European countries, where growth resumed after a couple of years, in Russia, in the mid 1990s, the decline was continuing. In 1994, gross national product was 15 per cent down on the year before; industrial output was down by 21 per cent, agricultural output by 9 per cent, services by 36 per cent; real incomes were up, on the average, but they were much more unequally distributed and over 36 million were living – according to official statistics – below subsistence minimum (*Sotsial'no*, 1995, pp.3–4). And there were worrying indicators at a more human level: life expectancy, for instance, was falling (for urban men to 59), several serious diseases were reappearing, and there were fewer live births – indeed for the first time since the war the Russian population, after 1992, was actually falling.

There has been a long and inconclusive debate about the extent to which support for democratic values is a cause of democracy, or a consequence of the performance of regimes that are governed by competitive elections (Barry, 1970). Russians, certainly, were prepared to support many democratic values in the abstract – equality before the law, a multiparty system, freedom of speech. But they were less likely to believe that they had priority over public order, or social justice, or national unity. Russia, in addition, had been ruled in an authoritarian manner for most of its history: there were no parliamentary institutions until the early twentieth century, the franchise was very restricted by the European standards of the time, and there was a close association between the state, the church, and popular beliefs in general (White, 1979). The experience of Spain, and some of the other Mediterranean countries, showed that an authoritarian past could be overcome under favourable circumstances. Equally, the experience of China suggested that even communist rule could sustain itself if it was accompanied by a rise in living standards and – particularly – an adequate food supply (these cases have been discussed in Parts II and III). In early post-communist Russia those wider circumstances were unlikely to strengthen popular support for democratic rule; and the Russian tradition was one in which that support had in any case always been weaker than in Eastern Europe.

The outcome was certainly a form of liberal democracy, in that there were competitive elections, the courts were formally independent, government could be criticized, and there was a choice of parties. But it was a very partial democracy, in the terms that have been defined in this volume: parliament had little control over the government, political parties were weak, the courts were heavily influenced by government, and government itself, particularly at local level, was based upon the former communist *nomenklatura* and sometimes upon a criminalized mafia. If there is a more general lesson from the Russian experience, it may be that just as there was no single 'transition to democracy' in the formerly communist world there was no single 'post-communism' but a variety of experiences ranging from a successful capitalism in the Czech republic to more strongly statist forms of politics further east, sometimes headed by re-elected former communists. And at least in

Russia, it was less a transition to democracy than to a hybrid with many features of the old regime as well as some more pluralist elements. This was the end, at least in Europe, of the monopolistic rule of Marxist-Leninist parties; but for the societies concerned it was the beginning and not the end of a new form of history, the history of post-communism.

────────────────── *Summary of Section 17.3* ──────────────────

- While there was considerable continuity with the communist period, democratization made significant progress after the collapse of the Soviet Union.

- Obstacles to further democratization were nevertheless considerable, major factors being the restitution of the Communist Party and the weak development of alternative parties.

- Public opinion was lukewarm about all new parties, the condition of post-communist democracy and political life in general.

- Indices of economic performance and social conditions continued to decline, and the outlook for the further development of liberal democracy in Russia was uncertain.

Conclusion

The collapse of Soviet communism, accordingly, suggests a more general conclusion about the process of democratization. Just as the starting point could be very varied, from societies that had already democratized (and were *re*democratizing) to those with a traditional and often authoritarian culture, so too the destination could be very different. There could be a 'benign' outcome, often in more developed societies with an earlier history of democracy (as in the Baltic). But there could also be 'malign' outcomes, as in Russia and still more so in Central Asia, in societies that were generally less prosperous and in which democratic traditions were less securely established. The model, in these instances, was less the pluralistic democracy of the developed West, and rather more the limited and rather formal liberal democracies of Latin America (see Chapter 7) with their strong personalist rule, weak representative institutions, ineffective courts, criminalized parties, wide social divisions and passive citizenries. In an influential study of Italian civic traditions, Robert Putnam has suggested that Palermo might be the 'future of Moscow' (Putnam, 1993, p.183). It may be that parallels should be sought in the larger, less developed countries of Africa, Asia and Latin America; and there was every indication, despite the hopes that had been entertained in the early days of post-communism, that it was a form of politics that would be nasty, brutal and rather extended.

References

Almond, G. (1970) *Political Development*, Boston, Little, Brown.

Anderson, J. (1994) *Religion, State and Politics in the Soviet Union and Successor States*, Cambridge, Cambridge University Press.

Barry, B. (1970) *Sociologists, Economists and Democracy*, London, Collier-Macmillan.

Bialer, S. (1980) *Stalin's Successors. Leadership, Stability, and Change in the Soviet Union*, Cambridge, Cambridge University Press.

Bialer, S. (1986) *The Soviet Paradox: External Expansion, Internal Decline*, New York, Knopf.

Boeva, I. and Viacheslav S. (1992) *Russians Between State and Market: the Generations Compared*, Glasgow, Centre for the Study of Public Policy, University of Strathclyde.

Brown, A. (1996) *The Gorbachev Factor*, Oxford, Oxford University Press.

Central and Eastern Eurobarometer (1996) no.6, March, Annex figures 6 and 7.

Clarke, M. (ed.) (1983) *Corruption*, London, Pinter.

Cook, L.J. (1993) *The Soviet Social Contract and Why it Failed*, Cambridge, MA, Harvard University Press.

Dahl, R.A. (1971) *Polyarchy*, New Haven, Yale University Press.

Deutscher, I. (1967) *The Unfinished Revolution: Russia 1917–1967*, Oxford, Oxford University Press.

Gibson, J.L. (1994) 'Survey research in the past and future USSR', *Research in Micropolitics*, vol.4, pp.87–114.

Goldman, M. (1983) *The USSR in Crisis*, New York, Norton.

Gorbacheva, R.M. (1991) *Ya nadeyus'...*, Moscow, Novosti.

Hankiss, E. (1990) *East European Alternatives*, Oxford, Clarendon Press.

Hough, J.F. (1990) 'Gorbachev's endgame', *World Policy Journal*, vol.7, no.4, pp.639–72.

Hough, J.F. (1991) 'Understanding Gorbachev: the importance of politics', *Soviet Economy*, vol.7, no.2, pp.89–109.

Huntington, S. (1984) 'Will more countries become democratic?', *Political Science Quarterly*, vol.99, no.2, pp.193–218.

Itogi (1992) Itogi Vsesoyuznoi perepisi naseleniya 1989 goda, Tom II, chast' 1, Minneapolis, EastView.

Johnson, C. (ed.) (1970) *Change in Communist Systems*, Stanford CA, Stanford University Press.

Komarov, B. (1980) *The Destruction of Nature in the Soviet Union*, London, Pluto.

Kryshtanovskaya, O. and White, S. (1996) 'From Soviet nomenklatura to Russian elite', *Europe-Asia Studies*, vol.43, no.5, pp.711–33.

Lewin, M. (1988) *The Gorbachev Phenomenon*, London, Radius.

Malia, M. ['Z'] (1990) 'To the Stalin mausoleum', *Daedalus*, vol.119, no.1, pp.295–344.

Materialy (1986) *Materialy XXVII s"ezda KPSS*, Moscow, Izdatel'stvo politicheskoi literatury.

Matthews, M. (1978) *Privilege in the Soviet Union*, London, Allen and Unwin.

Matthews, M. (1986) *Poverty in the Soviet Union*, Cambridge, Cambridge University Press.

Miller, W.L., White, S. and Heywood, P. (1996) 'Twenty-five days to go: measuring and interpreting trends in public opinion during the 1993 Russian election campaign', *Public Opinion Quarterly*, vol.60, no.1 (Spring), pp.106–27.

Moore, B. Jr. (1989) *Liberal Prospects under Soviet Socialism: A Comparative Historical Perspective*, New York, Harriman Institute, Columbia University.

Parry, A. (1966) *The New Class Divided: Science and Technology versus Communism*, New York, Macmillan.

Parsons, T. (1964a) 'Evolutionary universals in society', *American Sociological Review*, vol.29, no.3, pp.339–57.

Parsons, T. (1964b) 'Communism and the West' in Etzioni, A. and Etzioni, E. (eds) *Social Change*, New York, Basic Books.

Pipes, R. (1984) 'Can the Soviet Union reform?', *Foreign Affairs*, vol.63 (Autumn), pp.47–61.

Putnam, R.D. (1993) *Making Democracy Work: Civic Traditions in Modern Italy*, Princeton NJ, Princeton University Press.

Pye, L. (1990) 'Political science and the crisis of authoritarianism', *American Political Science Review*, vol.84, no.1, pp.3–19.

Rose, R. (1971) *Governing Without Consensus*, London, Faber.

Rose, R. (1995) *New Russia Barometer IV: Between Two Elections*, Glasgow, Centre for the Study of Public Policy, University of Strathclyde.

Rose, R. (1996) *New Russia Barometer V: The Results*, Glasgow, Centre for the Study of Public Policy, University of Strathclyde.

Rossiiskii statisticheskii ezhegodnik 1995 (1995) Moscow, Goskomstat Rossii.

Sakwa, R. (1990) *Gorbachev and his Reforms 1985–1990*, Hemel Hempstead, Philip Allan.

Sestanovich, S. (1988) 'Gorbachev's foreign policy: a diplomacy of decline', *Problems of Communism*, vol.37, no.1, pp.1–15.

Shlapentokh, V. (1994) 'The 1993 Russian election polls', *Public Opinion Quarterly*, vol.58, pp.579–602.

Simis, K. (1982) *Secrets of a Corrupt Society*, London, Dent.

Sotsial'no-ekonomicheskoe polozhenie Rossii 1994 g. (1995) Moscow, Gosudarstvennyi komitet Rossiiskoi Federatsii po statistike.

Tucker, R.C. (1981) 'Swollen state, spent society: Stalin's legacy to Brezhnev's Russia', *Foreign Affairs*, vol.60, no.2 (Winter), pp.414–35.

White, S. (1978) 'Communist systems and the "iron law of pluralism"', *British Journal of Political Science*, vol.8, no.1, pp.101–17.

White, S. (1979) *Political Culture and Soviet Politics*, London, Macmillan.

White, S. (1994) *After Gorbachev*, (4th edn), Cambridge, Cambridge University Press.

White, S. (1995) 'Public opinion and political science in post-communist Russia', *European Journal of Political Research*, vol.27, no.4 (June), pp.507–26.

White, S. (1996) *Russia Goes Dry: Alcohol, the State and Society*, Cambridge, Cambridge University Press.

White, S., Wyman, M. and Kryshtanovskaya, O. (1995) 'Parties and politics in post-communist Russia', *Communist and Post-Communist Studies*, vol.28, no.2, pp.183–202.

CHAPTER 18

Political participation in post-communist democracies

Paul Lewis

Introduction

Participation has a close relation with the very idea of democracy in both theoretical and empirical terms. The extension of participation thus emerges as a major component of democratization. But its role in modern politics emerges as an ambiguous one, and this is no less true of the recently established democracies of Eastern Europe and the former Soviet Union. Their experience of participation casts a critical light on the form and quality of the democratic systems they are engaged in constructing. The role of social movements and high levels of popular engagement in some cases of democratic transition seemed to promise a new form of participatory democracy different from established liberal democracies, where participation is generally restrictive and largely formalized. Any such hopes soon proved to be illusory, and post-communist democracy turned out to show distinct similarities to established Western practice – and seemed, if anything, to be rather less participant in certain key respects. The focus in this chapter is therefore directed less to the process of democratization in Russia and Eastern Europe as such, a topic that has been covered at some length in Chapters 16 and 17, than to an examination of the nature of the democracy that was created there in terms of one of its critical dimensions. The main questions addressed are: 'What forms of political participation have emerged in the post-communist democracies?' and 'How may these developments be accounted for?'

The issue of participation occupied a particular place in the political doctrine of the former communist regimes and emerged as a central feature in the transition from authoritarian communism. These experiences also influenced the practices of post-communist democracy. While in this book the communist political system is regarded as a form of authoritarianism, such a view does not accord with the image projected by the former communist regimes. They promoted a doctrine of socialist democracy in which mass participation was claimed to play an important role. This chapter outlines the theory and practice of participation under the former regime before turning to consider the patterns of participation that characterized the beginnings of the transition to democracy. The dissolution there of formerly prominent social movements and the rapid shift of focus to parliamentary forms of politics was not followed by the formation of a range of parties that offered alternative channels of participation and effective means of influencing decision makers. An institutional structure to sustain new democratic practices was in the process of emerging, and existing patterns of participation were marked by these and other such recent experiences.

Considering further the post-communist situation, the chapter notes how voting in elections between competing parties is by far the most prevalent form of participation in established democracies and that this, too, emerged as the leading mode of participation in post-communist democracies. But voter turnout was not always high, and the post-communist democracies did not emerge as particularly participant ones. Patterns of participation differed amongst social groups and women were not generally advantaged in the process of post-communist change. The rigours of radical economic change bore, too, on prospects for the persistence and development of a civil society, which many have seen as critical to the full development and consolidation of political democracy.

Previously identified explanatory factors like economic development and the development of civil society thus emerge as strong influences on patterns of participation and part of any account of its role in democratization. The importance of international agencies in the transformation has also been such that participation in domestic political activities was often perceived to be ineffective. The rather low rates of participation seen in established liberal democracies seemed to be generally replicated in the new post-communist democracies, with some additional barriers to participation being imposed by the conditions of rapid political and economic change. The context of modernization helps to account for some aspects of this process, although precisely why some groups and social categories were more participant than others is not readily explicable. The links between transition theories, processes of participation and institutional development seem to be more strongly established, and the chapter sets out to define the nature of democratization in Eastern Europe more closely in these terms.

18.1 Participation and democratization

Political participation is one of the prime components of democracy in its classical conception and one of the main constitutuents of modern democracy as an operative form of political regime. Dahl's notion of an effective liberal democracy, for example, involves two broad characteristics of citizenship: that citizenship is extended to a relatively high proportion of adults – thus providing the possibility of extensive participation – and that its rights include the opportunity to oppose and remove from office high government officials, which make that participation politically effective (Dahl, 1989, p.220). The extension of rights of meaningful participation to a large proportion of the population is thus an important aspect of democratization. Emphasis on the centrality of participation is a thread that runs through the entire history of democracy, although the way in which participation is understood and the view that is taken of it has varied considerably. Athenian democracy, for example, rested on a concept of citizenship which involved those concerned participating *directly* in the affairs of state. For many contemporary theorists of political development more generally the form of participation and the conditions under which it occurs are also of great importance.

In practice, the levels of participation in established Western democracies fall short not only of the classic Athenian ideal (not least for highly practical reasons) but also of the participant civic culture supportive of democracy that is associated with modern pluralist society. The notion of participation covers a range of political activities which Birch, for example, lists under eleven headings (Birch, 1993, p.81). Heading the list are items like voting in elections, canvassing, and party membership, although activities not associated with elections and party politics are also included. Relevant here might be pressure group membership, involvement in political demonstrations, strikes with political objectives, forms of civil disobedience, membership of consumer councils for publicly owned industries, and various forms of community action. Citizen involvement in such activities is limited in liberal democracies and empirical work on Britain, which does not seem to be very different from other Western countries, suggests that in terms of participation it is a very 'thin' democracy. Only 10 per cent of the population were found to have contacted their MP over a five year period, while 11 per cent had been involved in an organized group. 15 per cent had once attended a protest meeting and 5 per cent gone on a protest march, while 3.5 per cent had canvassed for a political party (Council of Europe, 1994, p.134). It is only elections that involve a large proportion of the population. Standard texts note the high rate of voter participation in general elections in countries like Italy (around 90 per cent) and Britain (80 per cent), but a lower turn-out (58 per cent and often lower) in the USA, despite its status as the leading Western democracy. Participation in local elections is considerably lower across the board.

Whether participation actually has any effect on the nature of political processes and the quality of the democratic order is another question. Evidence from the USA seemed to suggest that participation did indeed make a difference in terms of individual attitudes and behaviour, the quality of representation and on policy outcomes. Relatively high levels of satisfaction with the outcome of their activity were also reported by those politically active in a wide-ranging study of political participation in Britain. Evidence on the role of participation in modern democracies is therefore ambiguous. Actual levels of participation in the longer established democracies of Western Europe and North America are generally rather low and suggest a considerable discrepancy between political practice and any notion of participatory democracy. But participation emerges as an important component of democratization and is a significant feature in the institutionalization of democracy, as well as a source of satisfaction and effective means of exercising political influence for those who do take part.

How this contrast can be explained and why people actually do participate has often been regarded as something of a puzzle in comparative politics. Modernization seems to offer a plausible explanation in that more tightly integrated forms of political community emerge, education broadens the horizon of social awareness, communication skills are enhanced and more resources are available to make participation possible. And, indeed, higher levels of education and greater affluence are generally closely correlated with greater participation in any given Western democracy. But like other attempts to explain cases of democratic behaviour and democratization within the framework, modernization does not take us very far in terms of causal processes or the linkage of general conditions with specific outcomes. Levels of electoral participation do not correlate at all well with levels of affluence, for example. Structural accounts, too, may explain why certain groups are excluded from the political space or find their path to political participation relatively open, but they do not shed much light on the question of why certain segments of the population are more inclined to participate than others.

In terms of explanation at the individual level, rational choice theory has been the dominant approach for some decades. It is a form of analysis that seeks to establish the conditions of individuals' participation in politics in terms of their calculation of the likely costs and benefits of any particular form of political involvement. Instead of seeking to establish why people were often so apathetic, this perspective pointed to the low probability that any one person's involvement would make any difference to a political outcome. The general conclusion drawn in this case was that it was generally just not rational for people to participate in any given political activity (Downs, 1957). Against this view, though, it has been argued both that the benefits of participation are highly subjective and not subject to rational calculation or that the 'cost' of, for example, casting a vote is so low that it is virtually irrelevant.

Analysis of the institutions that link the individual with the centres of political power and provide opportunities for participation offer other perspectives on such activities. Accounts of participation in institutional terms promise to avoid problems both of excessive generality and of reducing all political explanation to the level of the individual. It is institutions, for example, that provide individuals with structured opportunities for participation and make that participation effective in collective terms. The institutional characteristics both of the communist regime and the situation that its collapse has created may help to explain also the nature of participation in post-communist states.

─────────────── *Summary of Section 18.1* ───────────────

- Participation is a prime component of both classical and contemporary conceptions of democracy.

- In practice, established liberal democracies show quite low levels of participation.

- The explanation of differing levels of participation is generally seen as problematic.

18.2   Participation and political change under communist rule

Democracy was hardly a concept that had been absent from the public realm of the countries which have recently set out on the course of post-communist democratization. Their political systems might generally have been defined by Western political scientists in terms of authoritarianism or totalitarian dictatorship, but the official self-description of the communist political order

– based on a carefully formulated ideology derived (at least in the Soviet Union and most countries of Eastern Europe) from a Soviet version of Marxism – was that of socialist democracy. It was a political doctrine that placed a strong emphasis on the importance of participation in political life, and may be associated with the category of direct democracy outlined in Chapter 1 (see also Held, 1996, Chapter 4). Contrasts between the empirical analysis of political behaviour and its interpretation in terms of different varieties of political theory are therefore marked in this context. The Soviet version was well summarized in an official regime publication during the period when the publication of all material had, of course, to be sanctioned by the political authorities:

> The fundamental difference of socialist democracy lies in the fact that for the first time in history it spelled government by the toiling majority, the multi-million masses ... we do call Soviet socialist democracy genuine democracy. For we judge it by the extent to which the masses take part in the running of production, the state and public affairs.

(Novosti Press, 1981)

The Soviet Union, therefore, claimed to practice not only 'socialist democracy' but, in distinction to that characteristic of the West, a 'genuine democracy'. The chief difference between Soviet democracy and bourgeois democracy, according to one Soviet guide, was that the first was democracy in deed while the second was democracy in word only. Following Lenin's view that under socialism the mass of the population would take an independent part not only in voting and elections but also in everyday administration of the state, it was further held that non-Marxist theories shunned this criterion of 'mass participation in running the country, which makes for continuous growth of creative activity by the population in all spheres of public life' (Babiy and Zabigailo, 1979).

Participation, then, was certainly not absent from the dominant theory of established communist systems nor wholly irrelevant to their political practice. Some obvious examples of the latter attracted the attention of Western political scientists, who often contrasted it with the low levels of participation certainly seen in the USA and other Western democracies. Some 99 per cent of those eligible in the Soviet Union were claimed to vote in every election, approximately twenty million were members of public organizations in local communities, fourteen million were members of the communist party and even more were members of other organizations. It was even concluded by one American political scientist that 'both the American and Soviet political systems are participant systems, with the Soviet somewhat more so than the American ... The stark differences between the political systems of the two countries lie not so much in their participatory mechanisms as in the characteristics of the systems themselves' (Little, 1976, p.455). Others were critical of this judgement and directed attention both to the importance of whether participation had a voluntary or compulsory basis, and to the idea that participation implied some influence on decision making (recall here the discussion in Chapter 17).

The nature of political participation in communist systems was, however, considerably more than just a theoretical conundrum. It also reflected a major contradiction and area of uncertainty in the operation of communist politics. The citizens of communist states were sent contradictory messages about the role they were expected to play as political participants. Their initiative and active enthusiasm were regularly invoked by the authorities, but the roles they were supposed to play were strictly prescribed for them both in public and private life. Activism practised in opposition to the regime was, of course, rigorously suppressed. The major crises that erupted in several East European regimes (Hungary 1956, Czechoslovakia 1968, Poland 1970 and 1980) involved issues of participation both in the conditions that gave rise to the crisis and as part of the package of measures applied to rectify the situation once the crisis had run its immediate course. Most crises in Leninist regimes, for example, 'were engendered or exacerbated by demands for participatory expansion in societies characterized by high levels of social mobilization but low levels of meaningful participation' (Taras, 1990, p.4). Reformed participatory mechanisms were emphasized as a way out of such crises by communist leaders in Eastern Europe, but the patterns advocated also involved manipulation and principles of selection that eventually increased public demands for more meaningful participation.

Attempts to confront the contradictions that were embedded in official doctrines of participation in communist states lay at the heart of the collapse of the European communist regimes between 1989 and 1991. The stabilization of the Polish political system after the application of martial law in 1981 involved an *ad hoc* institutional pluralism and form of state corporatism based on a new trade union organization and broad patriotic front. Such forms of officially sponsored association proved to be highly vulnerable to sudden collapse when civil society created spheres of authentic popular participation. As outlined in Chapter 16, in Hungary and Poland – if not elsewhere – the communist leadership attempted to strengthen its support base by engaging in discussion with opposition representatives and extending the possibility of constrained participation without losing overall political control.

But even in those countries the extent and speed of communist collapse was a surprise not just to the incumbent leadership. Solidarity leaders had considerable doubts as to whether society could be sufficiently mobilized under the conditions of established communism to take effective advantage of the electoral opening offered by the outcome of the round-table agreement made by the communist authorities with the political opposition. Neither should the extent of the political mobilization that was achieved be exaggerated. Even at the height of its popularity in 1989 Solidarity commanded the active support of only two-fifths of Poland's adult population. It is a proportion that seems to reflect considerably less than overwhelming support, but one that was nevertheless achieved on the basis of voluntary participation in marked distinction to the patterns of participation seen during the previous decades of communist rule.

But the anti-communist opposition in Poland at least had the experience of the Solidarity movement that had arisen nearly a decade earlier to build on. The new informal associations that sprang up in the Soviet Union during 1987 and 1988 under the new conditions of *glasnost* set in place by Gorbachev had less secure foundations and were more diverse. Some groups developed around issues that formed natural clusters (those fostering demands for ethnic-national sovereignty and movements focusing on the interests of labour, for example) while others were cross cutting, which meant that the followings of different movements were independent of one another. Unfortunately for the progenitor of the drive for Soviet political reform, though, the new politics of mass participation that had begun to arise mobilized far more political activity around national causes than on the restructuring of socialism within the Union. As Gorbachev had been shifting his political base from the party to the federal state in response to the growing unpopularity of the party, this placed him in an increasingly difficult position.

The immediate context of the East European transitions was, as pointed out in Chapter 16, largely elite centred. This was equally true of the democratization process in Russia. The mass mobilization of Polish society in anything other than an electoral sense had occurred during 1980 and 1981, a considerable time before the fundamental change of 1989. The major steps in the Hungarian transformation were also taken by reformist forces within the party leadership in conjunction with leading groups of the increasingly well-organized political opposition. This was based almost exclusively on Hungary's intellectual elite, which largely drew on the population of the capital, Budapest. While popular demonstrations and mass participation in the collapse of the communist regimes were prominent in East Germany, Czechoslovakia and Romania, they were also involved in the first two cases with established if numerically limited movements of protest involving groups of intellectuals and other dissidents. Yet the context in which elite negotiations were conducted was in most cases strongly influenced by more extensive patterns of participation and the support opposition representatives derived from broader social strata.

The transition thus saw different modes of extrication from the former regime and contrasting patterns of participation: some involving negotiation and extensive elite activity, others highlighting the role of mass protest, and in some cases a mixture of different factors. In the Polish case the partially free election of 1989 was a critical factor in the collapse of the old regime. These varied transitions reflected individual regime histories, differing patterns of elite–mass relations, and specific configurations of social and political forces in processes of change which had their own implications for subsequent patterns of participation.

—————————— *Summary of Section 18.2* ——————————

- The former communist regimes claimed to implement principles of socialist democracy in which mass participation was a central feature.

- Questions of participation were involved both in successive crises of the communist regimes and in the measures taken to reform them.

- While often elite-centred, East European modes of transition generally involved significant mass or social participation.

18.3 Participation in post-communist states

The evident tensions that surrounded the issue of participation during the communist period, and the general impetus often shown towards patterns of wider popular participation during the transition, have been followed by a mixed and somewhat surprising picture in terms of participation in post-communist political processes. Opportunities for greater participation have not generally been seized. While political parties have been established (often in great number) most have remained organizationally weak and attracted few members; parties have fragmented and reformed frequently, it has appeared, on the apparent whim and inclination of their leaders and a few ambitious members. The sharply defined social cleavages that gave rise to labour and conservative (capitalist), clerical and secular parties in Western Europe have been lacking in the post-communist East. Politics there has tended to remain elitist, its centre of gravity isolated and distant from much of the population, most of whom have viewed politics with some distaste and its practitioners with considerable suspicion. Mass participation, when it did emerge, generally took a very different form from the united expression of social solidarity and democratic sentiment seen in most cases of transition.

Some of the most striking cases of participation in the early post-communist period were spontaneous, bitter and even violent, although the form they took varied considerably – from the mass strike and demonstrations in Budapest against oil price rises following the Iraqi invasion of Kuwait in 1990 to the government-inspired intervention of coal miners in Romania to oppose and intimidate liberal critics of the regime during the same year. Other forms of participation and spontaneous political expression, were also significant throughout the region, some involving

Hungarian taxi drivers protest against a 65 per cent increase in petrol prices

marginal groups (like skinheads and groups of disaffected young people) in extremist and racist actions of an anti-democratic character. A general pattern of participation is, therefore, not easy to establish and what empirical material there is does not paint a clear picture. One survey showed a wide variation across East European countries in terms of participation in a wide range of political actions. Broadly speaking, participation was reported to have been higher where popular action had played an important part in bringing down the former communist regime, with East Germany and Czechoslovakia leading in this respect. Thus only 17 per cent of respondents in East Germany and 34 per cent in Czechoslovakia said that they had not taken part in any kind of political activity, compared with 48 per cent in Bulgaria, 66 per cent in Slovenia, 67 per cent in Russia, 69 per cent in Estonia, 72 per cent in Poland and 84 per cent in Hungary (Mason, 1995, p.396). A further striking finding was that 57 per cent of respondents in post-communist states overall stated that they had not participated in any kind of political activity at all, compared with only 26 per cent in a selection of Western states.

Another series of surveys, conducted at a later date in a slightly different set of countries and on a somewhat altered basis, both confirmed and qualified these findings. Participatory activities like protest participation and petition signing were in this case differentiated, although together they seemed to cover the range of activities examined in the earlier study. The Czech Republic and Slovakia again came out as the most participant countries (East Germany not being included on this occasion), with 50 per cent of respondents reporting participation in protest activities and 38 per cent in petition signing in the Czech case, and 36 per cent and 30 per cent

Pro-government miners wielding clubs converge on anti-government demonstrators in Bucharest

respectively in Slovakia (Gigli, 1995). The ordering then was different from that deriving from the earlier study, with Estonia emerging as the next most participant country on both scores and Bulgaria, Poland and Russia coming lower down but being ranked differently (though not far apart) on the two scales. No obvious general conclusion emerges from these findings, although the high levels of participation in Slovakia and the Czech Republic in both investigations is surely significant.

Electoral activity and voter participation provide further pointers to the levels of participation in different countries. While only one form of citizen involvement in politics, voting in elections occupies a central place – as noted earlier – both in patterns of participation in Western political systems and in related studies in contemporary political science. Electoral participation and activities surrounding the membership and organization of political parties are one of the main spheres in which contemporary civic participation is made effective. Most would accept that, for better or for worse, voting is the main, and for a large proportion of citizens the only, means by which their attitudes and judgement impinge directly on the political sphere. It occupies a central place both in democratic politics and in the comparative study of political participation. Voting participation is, as one leading writer on democracy states, 'a unique dimension of involvement, more frequently performed, less related to other forms of political activity, than most other types of citizen action' (Powell, 1982, pp.111–12). It does, however, reflect a very limited form of participation which involves a 'cost' to the individual which is so low that it involves a very minimal form of political commitment, while the importance of international determinents of post-communist transformation make the effect of domestic political involvement on key issues of post-communist policy that much less significant.

Table 18.1 presents information on turnout in various elections and referendums that have been held in the former communist countries of Eastern Europe and the Soviet Union. The picture is a mixed one, showing

Table 18.1 Electoral turnout as a percentage of registered electorate (L = local election)

	1989	1990	1991	1992	1993	1994	1995
Bulgaria		91	84	75		74	55 L
Czechoslovakia		96		90	Slovakia	76	
		74 L			Czech Rep.	62 L	
East Germany		93					
Hungary		63				69	
		40 L				43 L	
Poland	62	61	43		52	34 L	68
Romania		86		75			
Russia	90		75		54		63

high levels of voter participation (90 per cent plus) in early elections like those held in Bulgaria, Czechoslovakia and East Germany, which tended to decline on successive occasions, and moderate to low levels of participation (dipping to 43 per cent in the 1991 Polish election) in other countries, where turnout nevertheless tended to stabilize or even rise over time. The experience of yet other countries was between the two extremes, although the general trend was often towards lower voter participation, while low turnout levels in local elections were generally seen throughout the region. Turnout has been lowest in Poland, but also showed a downward tendency in Russia and Romania. After several years experience of democratization voter participation in major elections settled around the West European norm, slightly below the level seen in most British general elections but higher than turnout in comparable US ballots. Voter participation in post-communist countries, in fact, reflected patterns of behaviour apparently little different from those seen in many established democracies. A certain reluctance to become involved politically may have surprised Western observers who anticipated a more dramatic public response to the change of regime, but the more nuanced pattern of participation that emerged is unlikely in itself to provide any great shock to the political analyst.

The most striking levels of abstention in post-communist societies were those in Poland, where the turnout during the 1991 election was particularly low. Not surprisingly, electoral abstention and political passivity during the range of events that took place during the 1989–91 period were found to be associated with a low level of education, low wages and income per household member, but also less frequent religious practice and general indifference towards religion. Overall, it was regarded as remarkable how similar the apathetic citizen of the post-communist country was 'to the passive prototype who inhabits the countries characterized by stable democracy' (Markowski, 1992, p.59). But particular features of the Polish context were also involved. While the turnout in the 1991 election was higher in districts with more highly educated inhabitants and reduced where unemployment was higher and personal income lower, participation rates were also positively associated (and quite strongly at that), with the organized presence of the Catholic Church. A specific institutional factor in this case emerged as a major factor in participation. The critical factors affecting the turnout were therefore church influence and, negatively, the level of unemployment. Somewhat surprisingly, the level of income and private sector employment were, as individual factors, also found to be negatively related to voting turnout in this study.

In Russia conventional political participation (in which voting plays a major part) was found to be linked with high levels of overall political interest and, again, benefits derived from regular employment, as was membership of a higher age bracket – particularly between the years of 1952 and 1966 (McAllister and White, 1994, p.610). In both cases the phenomenon of abstention was understood to have considerable political significance: the high level of abstention in Poland during 1991 was fed by people disillusioned above all by the direction and results of the transformation of the preceding couple of years which, particularly as it involved a silent majority rather than just a minority, was felt to contain a major explosive potential. Abstention in Russia was also felt to carry a certain menace, as it was motivated as much by opposition to the regime as by apathy. The strong link between economic dissatisfaction and the likelihood of protest could become more significant as the dislocation of the former Soviet economy progressed (unemployment levels when the survey was conducted in early 1992 were quite low, for example), and it is difficult in this context to accept the argument that has often been made by Western political scientists that abstention and non-participation help support the political process and contribute to the consolidation of democracy (see, for example, the discussion of competitive elitism in Held, 1996).

In Eastern Europe there were also some important historical factors involved in the developing pattern of participation, and the means by which the immediate transition from communist rule was secured seemed to have considerable significance. Unlike the overall pattern of democratization charted in Chapter 16, levels of participation did not show any obvious association with the degree of modernization as measured by the obvious socio-economic indices. Links were however stronger with the recent experience of the collapse of communist rule and the way in which the transition to the democratic regime had begun. Participation in terms of engagement in a range of broadly conceived protest activities was, as noted by Mason, high in countries where communist governments had been brought down in situations marked by popular demonstrations and the prominence of crowd activity (Mason, 1995, p.396).

A similar association could be detected in terms of high levels of participation in early post-communist elections. The context of economic transformation and wide-spread social crisis was a major condition throughout the region and had a direct effect, through such factors as unemployment, on participation processes. The economic changes that had accompanied democratization often discouraged involvement and any commitment to further change. Voting against the communist regime, which had also been partly motivated by its failure to fulfil the most rudimentary economic commitments, had only brought about a worsening of people's material conditions and few saw in political activity any means of protecting their interests.

The global context of post-communist change added a further dimension to political responses. The strong international pressure exerted by institutions like the European Union and the International Monetary Fund was a major dynamic of rapid economic transformation, but any identifiable centres of decision making associated with them were wholly inaccessible to citizens of the post-communist states. Virtually all governments and major political forces in Eastern Europe acquiesced (with varying degrees of alacrity and enthusiasm) in the pressures these international agencies exerted and endorsed the direction of change they favoured. The greater freedom offered by a competitive electoral system did not, therefore, seem to offer much real choice for the voter who rejected this path of development or some of its particular features. The high levels of abstention seen in some countries seemed to some, then, to suggest not so much apathy – and even less passivity induced by overall contentment – as a rapidly created crisis of democratic representation (Gowan, 1992, p.20).

While smaller rates of decline had provoked demonstrations and rebellion during the communist years, the response in the post-communist period was mostly one of quiescence, involving a retreat from political action and re-emphasis on the private sphere. Disappointment and mistrust of the consequences of market reforms also affected voting patterns in providing unexpectedly high levels of support for parties based on the former communist parties. Such socialist parties were returned to government first in Lithuania and then in Poland, Hungary and Bulgaria between 1992 and 1995. As Chapter 17 made clear, a strong nostalgia for the former system also developed rapidly in Russia.

———————————— *Summary of Section 18.3* ————————————

- Participation has been varied across the post-communist countries, but has generally been quite low.

- Levels of participation in the early stage of democratization were closely associated with the form taken by the process of democratic transition.

- Abstention from voting has been most strongly associated with unemployment and low income.

18.4   Institutional dimensions of participation and democratic change

In terms of the low level of political participation in post-communist countries overall particular importance was ascribed to the relatively weak and partial development of political parties. They play a major role in organizing political activity, channeling participation and providing the means to make it effective in established democracies – although it should be recognized that where it does exist this outcome is the result of a lengthy, complicated and uncertain process that took decades during earlier periods of democratic development. Despite their manifest shortcomings, frequent warnings of their imminent demise and the considerable criticism made of the way they tend to operate, professionally organized parties seem to be essential to the establishment and continuity of a liberal democracy. In most practical senses, 'democracy in the modern world is representative democracy, and the contribution made by political parties is central' (Burnell, 1994, p.3).

Whilst social movements had often acted as the prime vehicle for popular mobilization during the key period of political transition from the old regime (Solidarity in Poland, Civic Forum and Public Against Violence in Czechoslovakia, New Forum in East Germany), they did not maintain their unity or prove able to withstand the diverse challenges and stresses of rapid political change in Eastern Europe. They did not generally survive to provide the means for participation in the developing post-communist democracies and failed to provide ready material for the construction of a select range of viable parties. The coherence of these broad movements and their apparent firmness of purpose owed much, it transpired, to the strength and unified character of the communist regimes they opposed, features of the movements that did not long survive the disappearance of their communist opponents. In this the experience of the social movements showed marked similarities with those in the West, where mass movements and the mobilization of certain groups also failed to have the political impact that many anticipated in the 1980s. In Eastern Europe, however, there were few established institutions to sustain the new political processes of the post-communist period.

Some gifted leaders did emerge from the social movements but the development of a select range of effective parties did not necessarily follow. The disintegration of Solidarity was followed by the foundation of a broad range of small and mostly ineffective parties in Poland which, in association with the application of a fully proportional electoral law in 1991, produced a highly fragmented parliament and created great obstacles to the formation of a viable coalition government. Even when an apparently effective and coherent multiparty system did emerge in Hungary and provided the basis for the rapid formation of coalition government following the election of 1990,

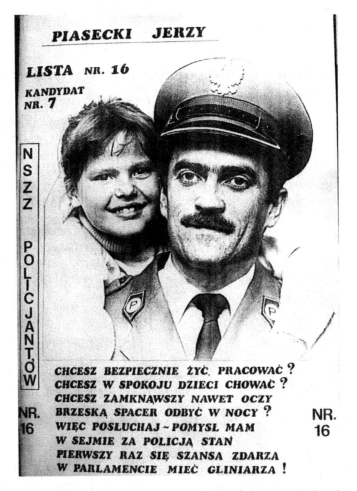

Even the police union presented candidates in Poland:
'Your chance to have a cop in parliament'

the parliament then formed soon became the arena of extensive party fragmentation and the kind of institutional flux seen in other less stable political systems of Eastern Europe. A more successful party, however, was established by Václav Klaus in Czechoslovakia on the basis of the Civic Forum in the form of the Civic Democratic Alliance.

It was perhaps significant that it was in Poland among the more developed countries of Eastern Europe, where the most extensive and inclusive social movement emerged (9.5 million members mobilized in a matter of weeks in 1980), that the party system faced extensive problems of development, parliaments were particularly fragmented and levels of voter participation strikingly low. The fact that the heyday of Solidarity was nearly ten years before the end of communist rule, and was then repressed for a lengthy period, and the experience of Poland as the first post-communist country to implement a policy of economic transformation (one which was, moreover, quite radical in its provisions) were also likely to be of considerable importance in helping to explain the low levels of participation during early years of post-communist transition.

The informal associations that formed spontaneously and cases of social self-organization seen under communism often failed to survive. Many of the smaller movements and pressure groups that had started their activities towards the end of the communist period in Poland and Hungary were shunted to the political sidelines under the new conditions, their members and activists often finding that new demands were put on their time and personal resources. Green movements in Hungary, for example, were directly marginalized by shifting public priorities as individuals and families sought to defend their material situation (Hajba, 1994, p.188). Some green associations active during the communist period were also really broad anti-system movements that lost much of their *raison d'être* with the change of regime.

Such factors contribute to an understanding of the nature of democratization in Eastern Europe in the light of comparative experience drawn on by transition theorists. Developments in Latin America and Southern Europe examined in Parts II and III provide some instructive contrasts and pointers to conditions for the development of effective institutions that support the process of democratization. Amongst several factors that helped to explain the more solid start of the South European transitions in relation to those in Latin America, one as Schmitter notes was the different configuration of civil society in the two regions and its greater strength in Southern Europe. Democratization was stronger where communities existed independently of the state and groups had some capacity to act autonomously in pursuit of their interests; more relevant to the concerns of this chapter, interests had to be organized for action and participation accomplished in large part 'through political parties which compete to win electoral majorities, ally with others in dominant coalitions, or enter into consociational arrangements' (Schmitter, 1986, p.6). In the light of this observation it was tentatively suggested that the higher level of institutionalized participation seen in the stronger party systems of Southern Europe was associated with the more effective consolidation of liberal democracy in that region. It helped to limit the role of personality in a developing liberal democracy and reduce the likelihood of leadership cults with their attendant dangers of political destabilization emerging.

It seems equally reasonable to propose in this context that the low levels of participation and the weakness of party development seen so far in post-communist Russia and Eastern Europe also point to problematic areas in the democratization process and the obstacles likely to be encountered in the consolidation phase. Such factors have been associated with the major role played by individuals in the politics of the post-communist states whose relation to particular interests or the aspirations of concrete groups has been, at best, highly ambiguous. Major areas of the political space have been dominated by the activities of people like Boris Yeltsin in Russia, Lech Walesa in Poland, Vladimir Mečiar in Slovakia or István Csurka in Hungary whose influence has often run counter to that of the developing democratic institutions which help to organize mass participation in politics and mediate between the individual and perceived collective interests. While not necessarily antithetic to democracy in a general sense, their influence has nevertheless strengthened tendencies to populism and majoritarian democracy which conflict with the institutional procedures of liberal democracy and the possibilities of its consolidation.

An equivalent weakness in terms of the institutionalization of participation and organizational mobilization can be seen at micro level, and correspondingly weak patterns of participation emerge in terms of party membership. A broad overview has suggested that 4 per cent of the population were members of a political party in the Czech Republic, 2 per cent in Hungary, and 1.3 per cent in Poland during the early to mid 1990s. Around 1.8 per cent of the population of the former East Germany were also members of a party. This is certainly less than the equivalent levels of 16.4 and 15.4 per cent seen in Austria and Sweden, but not strikingly low in comparison with measures of 2.1 and 2.5 per cent in the Netherlands and the United Kingdom (see Lewis, 1996). In this, as in other respects, established democracies show marked differences between themselves in terms of political behaviour and participation. While party membership was low in the post-communist countries (as is the level of participation in a number of countries), it was not that low in comparison with some Western democracies.

But in the case of the new democracies in Eastern Europe, other established channels of political participation were also generally lacking. Mass participation in liberal democracies, even in terms of organized activity, is by no means restricted to political parties. Political participation can also be effected through such diverse means as active membership of a pressure group or industrial action undertaken for political objectives. The overall pace of political change, economic transformation and social upheaval in Eastern Europe, however, has meant that effective channels of participation through local government, pressure groups and other forms of political association were also not available.

One form of institutional affiliation that is often more wide spread for citizens of modern democracies than membership of political parties is that of trade unions. While membership in Eastern Europe was extensive under the former communist regimes, the unions themselves formed a central part of the old power structure and their status was drastically reduced by the process of democratization. While new unions did emerge, the conditions for their activity were less favourable than had been the case for their communist predecessors and overall union membership declined significantly throughout the region, this process being most pronounced in countries generally leading the process of democratic change like Poland, Hungary, Lithuania and the Czech Republic. A common feature of post-communist countries during the early years of democratic transition was the claim of high levels of union membership deriving from the virtually automatic (and obligatory) membership that pertained during the years of communist rule. Statistics from the early 1990s, for example, suggested that the official trade union centre in Bulgaria still covered 100 per cent of employees, while the rival *Podkrepa* organized just over 10 per cent. In Czechoslovakia the established union organization claimed 80 per cent coverage, and in Hungary an equivalent 70 per cent was recorded (with just 3 per cent for an independent union). In Poland unions established by the old regime claimed to cover 57 per cent, leaving just 20 per cent for Solidarity (Myant and Waller, 1994, p.173).

Whatever the situation with regard to formal membership, surveys of worker experience showed a low level of actual participation in the activities of both old and new unions. No more than 16 per cent of Russian workers in a range of towns claimed to take part in the activities of the old unions, and only 9 per cent in those of the new unions (Baglione and Clark, 1995, p.223). To the extent that citizens of the post-communist democracies did participate through membership of political or para-political organizations, then, it was often effected through institutions inherited from the communist period whose effectiveness under the new conditions might well be doubted. The combined impact of political and economic change was one that often weakened or eliminated existing institutions and local organizations without putting anything in their place or providing the conditions for replacement channels of participation to develop to any great extent. The independent social organizations and co-operative spheres of social autonomy that had emerged were generally weakened by the rising public emphasis on individual activity, the prominence of the profit motive and the spread of market relations.

In some cases the impact of economic change on movements and the public outlook that had sustained them was a direct one, with institutions dissolving and people disengaging from political activity as individuals reviewed their material situation and reassessed their personal priorities. Some institutions and sectors of East European society were more resilient to this process, like the Church in Poland and the areas of Czech society that had a strong civic tradition, but in general civil society was weakened by processes of economic transformation and the spread of market relations. The role of civil society in post-communist political change was therefore an ambiguous one. It has often been argued that a developed free-market system is necessary to underwrite civil freedoms and enable competitive democracy to work effectively as a procedure for the arbitration and reconciliation of interests. The process of constructing the market and establishing capitalist structures nevertheless had the effect of dissolving and weakening the elements of civil society that were already in place (Offe, 1991, pp.875–6). This in turn has meant that public participation in politics was likely to become endangered or less effective as the social channels through which it might occur were themselves weak or developing under unfavourable conditions. Democratization itself would thus also be obstructed in its development and slowed down – or even halted altogether.

───────────────── **Summary of Section 18.4** ─────────────────

- Low levels of participation were associated with a weak process of party development.
- The social movements that had often featured in the early stages of democratic transition generally failed to provide a basis for institutional development.
- Alternative channels of political participation were also lacking and civil society was correspondingly weakened.

18.5 Gender differences in participation

Participation varies not only between the different post-communist countries but also across different groups within them. Generally, in view of the close relationship that holds between democracy and participation, it would seem reasonable to expect levels of elective participation to increase under the conditions of post-communist change. This, however, was by no means always the case, and the existence of particular groups whose participation did not increase either absolutely or in relation to that of others directs attention to critical areas of the democratization process and prompts further consideration of the nature of the post-communist political order in comparison with the system that preceded it. The role of women in post-communist politics in particular initially appeared to be a highly limited one, and it has been argued that after the events of 1989 and 1990 'women seemed to disappear from view' (Corrin, 1993, p.196). A number of factors may be involved here: the devaluation of political activity during the communist period did not motivate people (and, perhaps, women in particular) to participate once the compulsion to do so was removed; the abolition of the quota system applied by communist authorities to secure the formal representation of major social groups in leading political bodies; the struggle to survive under conditions of rapid socio-economic change and, in many cases, growing material shortage made it more difficult for women in particular to participate politically; cultural barriers to female participation remained in place; and the patriarchal attitudes that had persisted through the communist period were still prominent after 1989.

Whatever the particular reasons, some dimensions of women's formal participation showed certainly a significant decline. For example the representation of women in parliament fell quite drastically in some cases (see Table 18.2). The most dramatic drops in the number of women parliamentary representatives were seen in Romania and Albania, the two countries with the lowest standard of living (and thus where the strains of economic transition may have been even more rigorous than elsewhere) and most oppressive forms of dictatorship (where both cultural and practical barriers to participation may have remained more difficult to overcome). Otherwise the proportion of women involved in parliamentary politics in post-communist countries after the decline was closer to that seen in Western democracies like Britain and France, but now far short of the participation rates in Sweden and Iceland.

Table 18.2 Percentage of women holding seats in parliament, 1988–91

	January 1988	June 1989	June 1991
Albania	28.8	28.8	3.6
Bulgaria	21.0	21.0	8.5
Czechoslovakia	29.5	29.5	8.7
East Germany	32.2	32.2	20.4
Hungary	20.9	20.9	7.0
Poland	20.2	13.5	13.5
Romania	34.4	34.4	3.6
Soviet Union	31.1	15.3	15.3

Source: Corrin (1993)

From whatever perspective the fall is viewed, it was clear that the implicit promise of democratization in its early phase was not delivered in terms of female political participation in this area. If the key component of post-communist change in this respect was the enhancement of the role of the individual in society, the changes seen in the years after 1989 suggested that this objective was not being achieved for women as a whole. In terms of ideological principle, democratization was a process in which class reductionism (the formulation and implementation of public policy according to class criteria) was being replaced by a market reductionism in which the concept of profit prevailed. This shift did not provide better conditions for women's participation or overcome any existing reluctance to participate. For one thing, women were poorly motivated to participate in politics and approximately half as many women as men in post-communist countries declared themselves to be very interested in politics (Gigli, 1995). Interest in politics rose markedly among those with higher education, though, and the disparity between men and women narrowed considerably (particularly in Eastern Europe) when this was taken into account. Moreover, in terms of political activity the gender difference was less evident and women's voting rate, for example, was close to that of men – and in some cases (Slovakia, Russia, Estonia, Lithuania) actually higher. An aggregate index of political participation nevertheless (including voting, signing a petition, protest marching and joining a party) showed women to be rather less participant (Table 18.3).

Table 18.3 Political participation index (percentages)

	All men	*All women*	*Men with higher education*	*Women with higher education*
Poland	28	24	42	39
Czech Republic	48	38	68	60
Slovakia	41	36	56	62
Romania	30	26	39	42
Bulgaria	34	30	52	54
Russia	24	23	33	31
Estonia	27	26	42	36
Lithuania	38	35	57	52

Source: Gigli (1995)

The implications of democratization for the political role of women were, therefore, by no means clearly positive and their position was often little better than under the political system that had preceded it. In certain concrete areas (the collapse or weakening of welfare provision, less child care and fewer facilities for the elderly, restricted abortion rights in Poland) their situation was generally worse. The record of the communist regime with regard to women's rights showed that the claims of socialist democracy were by no means wholly false in that particular area. But the communist experience also showed marked ambiguities. Although some significant gains had been made by women under the former system (particularly in more traditional societies like Russia or China), they, too, were limited in their range to those compatible with the revolutionary programmes of the regimes and their realization was constrained by political objectives as well as more traditional attitudes.

Amongst the employed population in the Soviet Union as a whole, for example, women became better educated and the rise in their level of educational achievement continued to be greater than that of men: between 1979 and 1989 the number of men with secondary and higher education increased by 13 per cent and that of women by 19 per cent. Yet gender separation remained at high levels and was particularly strict in some occupations like the higher echelons of the power structure, foreign affairs and high technology industries, for example (Rimashevskaia, 1992, p.15).

Not surprisingly, the response of women to the changes that began towards the end of the communist period was also mixed and, while not conservative in a blanket sense (as some observers suggested), numerous women in the former Soviet Union certainly showed a number of anti-reform attitudes. The growing emphasis on market forces and material incentives carried little promise of improvement in their position. Opposition to change in that situation was, therefore, not so much the reflection of a conservative ideology as a rational assessment of the restraints and prospects inherent in the system. Women in these countries took this position precisely because 'little in the proposed democratic reforms suggests a better life for women' (Hesli and Miller, 1993, p.526). 'Conservatism' and scepticism with regard to reforms that made up the democratization package were therefore by no means reducible to resistance to change overall. To the extent, too, that women were more likely than men to cast their vote in Russia, Lithuania and the Ukraine, rational choice theory might help on this occasion to explain not why people are non-participant but why women in those countries where collective benefits were particularly under threat might have sought to defend their rights by participating in the electoral process.

─────────────── *Summary of Section 18.5* ───────────────

- The political participation of women declined in key areas after communism.

- Women's attitudes and responses to post-communist change were particularly mixed.

- Conditions for women deteriorated in certain specific areas during democratization.

Conclusion

The process of post-communist democratization did see the emergence of relatively novel forms of mass participation and political organization in the form of the broad social movements which, in slightly different ways, prepared the way in several countries for the collapse of the communist regimes and provided the framework for subsequent political development and the personnel for successor governments. They proved, however, to be short lived and did not fulfil the expectations of many that Eastern Europe might see the development of distinctively new forms of democracy. Based on the broad movements of anti-communist opposition and involving new forms of popular participation, it was hoped that new institutions and practices would avoid both the unpopular practices of communist authoritarianism and the professionalized machine politics of Western democracies which were seen as similarly distant from the concerns and activities of the great majority of citizens. But the movements soon disintegrated and institutions like political parties that would have served as alternative channels of political participation were slow to develop. Where it had been high during the early phase of post-communist transition, participation as reflected in voter turnout showed a definite tendency to decline – and in some cases it had been low from the very start.

But it was by no means clear that such indices pointed to a basic failure of participation processes or crisis of democratic representation as a number of observers suggested. Low voting rates in some countries showed a tendency to rise, and participation in the post-communist countries as a whole was generally sufficient to validate new democratic procedures and legitimize the post-communist political systems. Turnout in local elections, where non-participation was most apparent, is invariably low in Western democracies and post-communist countries did not show a very distinctive pattern of participation in that respect. While not delivering on some early hopes of new forms of popular participation, post-communist countries certainly saw a higher level of procedural democracy than under the former regime (including the holding of competitive elections and the relatively effective application of constitutional provisions), and they were by no means always less effective in that respect than either developing or established liberal democracies elsewhere.

In terms of explaining these outcomes, the modernization approach provides some useful pointers in terms of linking participation with indices of socio-economic development like income and education. Rational choice theory, too, suggests why non-participation makes sense in some areas of the post-communist situation and why 'anti-reform' sentiments, conversely, provide a relatively strong motivation for women to participate in some countries. Strong links may also be drawn between the different ways in which communist rule was brought to an end and subsequent levels of political participation, as well as the role played by particular institutions in the early stages of post-communist political development.

References

Babiy, B. and Zabigailo, V. (1979) 'Popular participation in government as a criterion of democracy' in *Political Systems: Development Trends*, Moscow, USSR Academy of Sciences.

Baglione, L.A. and Clark, C.L. (1995) 'Participation and the success of economic and political reforms: a lesson from the 1993 Russian parliamentary elections', *Journal of Communist Studies and Transition Politics*, vol.11, no.3, pp.215–48.

Birch, A.H. (1993) *The Concepts and Theories of Modern Democracy*, London, Routledge.

Burnell, P. (1994) 'Democratization and economic change worldwide – can societies cope?', *Democratization*, vol.1.

Corrin, C. (1993) 'People and politics' in White, S., Batt, J. and Lewis, P.G. (eds) *Developments in East European Politics*, London, Macmillan.

Council of Europe (1994) *Disillusionment with Democracy: Political Parties, Participation and Non-Participation in Democratic Institutions in Europe*, London, Council of Europe.

Dahl, R. (1989) *Democracy and Its Critics*, New Haven, Yale University Press.

Downs, A. (1957) *An Economic Theory of Democracy*, New York, Harper and Row.

Gigli, S. (1995) 'Towards increased participation in the political process', *Transition*, vol.1, pp.18–21.

Gowan, P. (1992), 'The European Community and East-Central Europe 1989–1991', *Labour Focus on Eastern Europe*, no.43.

Hajba, E. (1994) 'The rise and fall of the Hungarian greens', *Journal of Communist Studies and Transition Politics*, vol.10, no.3, pp.180–91.

Held, D. (1996) *Models of Democracy* (2nd edn), Cambridge, Polity Press.

Hesli, V. and Miller, A. (1993) 'The gender base of institutional support in Lithuania, Ukraine and Russia', *Europe-Asia Studies*, vol.45, no.3, pp.505–32.

Lewis, P.G. (ed.) (1996) *Party Structure and Organization in East-Central Europe*, Aldershot, Edward Elgar.

Little, R.D. (1976) 'Mass political participation in the US and the USSR', *Comparative Political Studies*, vol.8, no.4.

McAllister, I. and White, S. (1994) 'Political participation in post-communist Russia: voting, activism and the potential for mass protest', *Political Studies*, vol.42, pp.593–615.

Markowski, R. (1992) 'Absencja wyborcza i biernosc polityczna', *Krytyka*, no.38.

Mason, D.S. (1995) 'Attitudes toward the market and political participation in the post-communist states', *Slavic Review*, vol.54, no.2., pp.385–406.

Myant, M. and Waller, M. (1994) 'Parties and trade unions in Eastern Europe: the shifting distribution of political and economic power' in Waller, M. and Myant, M. (eds) *Parties, Trade Unions and Society in East-Central Europe*, London, Frank Cass.

Novosti Press (1981) *Socialism: Theory and Practice*, Moscow, Novosti Press.

Offe, C. (1991) 'Capitalism by democratic design? Democratic theory facing the triple transition in east-central Europe', *Social Research*, vol.58, no.4.

Powell, G.B. (1982) *Contemporary Democracies*, Cambridge, Mass., Harvard University Press.

Rimashevskaia, N. (1992) '*Perestroika* and the status of women in the Soviet Union' in Rai, S., Pilkington, H. and Phhizacklea, A. (eds) *Women in the Face of Change*, London, Routledge.

Schmitter, P.C. (1986) 'An introduction to Southern European transitions from authoritarian rule', *Transitions from Authoritarian Rule*, vol.1.

Taras, R. (1990) 'The crises of East European communism: the grand failure of manipulated participation', *Journal of Communist Studies*, vol.6, no.3, pp.1–21.

CHAPTER **19**

Nationalism, community and democratic transition in Czechoslovakia and Yugoslavia

Peter Ferdinand

Introduction

Democratization in post-communist countries has, as we have seen, encountered a number of obstacles. One of the most intractable problems has been the greater salience of nationalism which, in some of its more aggressive forms, has not just obstructed the development of liberal democratic institutions and practices but also undermined the stability of some of the federal states in which it has arisen. In this chapter I examine the role of nationalism in Czechoslovakia and Yugoslavia, countries which split up early on in the process of post-communist transition under the pressure of ethnic tensions. The issue of multi-ethnicity and democratization has already been examined in Chapters 3, 5 and 10. We will be concerned here with the processes through which a viable political community becomes established, and will seek to answer the question: What are the conditions for a successful transition to democracy in a multi-ethnic context?

A democracy is built upon the principle of rule by the people and for the people, but who are 'the people'? Are they the same as the nation? In states which are ethnically homogeneous the answer is relatively simple. In ethnically mixed societies the answer is conceptually and practically more difficult. Such questions need to be answered and an identifiable political community established before any form of democratic representation can be contemplated. Transition theorists like Rustow identify the existence of national unity – and thus a resolution of this basic problem – as a precondition for any democratization, while a modernization approach similarly pre-supposes the existence of such a community; a historical structural account like that of Moore tends to build in some ideas of national development within its overall narrative. None of these approaches confronts directly the very basic question of how a political community comes into existence or specifies the conditions of its survival in the modern world. Such issues have, however, proved to be critical during post-communist democratization.

One of the most serious threats to the establishment of some degree of trust and mutual respect between nationalities, and therefore to the development of liberal democracy, is ethnic antagonism based upon nationalism. At the least, this leads to prejudice, discrimination and a centrifugal political system. At its most extreme it leads to genocide. Political science offers a way of understanding these problems and identifying the means for coping with them in terms of the idea of 'consociational democracy'. This is a political arrangement that seeks to overcome the problems of forming a political community in states where the population is ethnically divided or shows other forms of deep cultural division. The concept (already introduced in Chapter 13) specifies a form of democratic rule especially suitable for societies which are divided along deep ethnic, linguistic, religious, or ideological lines, and where therefore majority rule of a more traditional kind might be ineffective or have polarizing effects. It involves a role for political institutions in binding together diverse communities at the top, but it also assumes flexibility in the structure of liberal-democratic rule, with a high degree of autonomy for each separate community. Thus the state, even if fragile, has some internal basis for integration. The approach is based upon the apparent success of a number of states in structuring their political arrangements to cope with such diversity, e.g. Belgium (divided between Flemings and Walloons, as discussed in Chapter 4), Holland (with deep religious cleavages) and Austria (characterized by sharp antagonism between anti-clerical socialists and a Catholic bourgeoisie).

Consociational democracy itself can be defined in terms of two basic principles and two secondary ones. The primary principles are firstly, executive power sharing or a grand coalition of parties covering most of the spectrum of political views found in that country, and secondly a high degree of autonomy for the various ethnic communities. The secondary principles are proportionality, i.e. the distribution of public offices between different ethnic communities in proportion to their share of the population as a whole, and the veto right of any minority. Proponents of this theory have also suggested nine preconditions which would favour a successful consociational democracy (see Box 19.1). It might be hypothesized that these preconditions would apply to any viable multi-ethnic political system, whether or not it sought to use the mechanisms of consociationalism. In

---

Box 19.1 The nine preconditions of consociational democracy

- the absence of a single dominating ethnic group;
- ethnic communities of roughly the same size;
- a relatively small number of ethnic communities, ideally between three and five;
- a relatively small total population;
- foreign threats that are perceived as a common danger;
- overarching loyalties which counterbalance the centrifugal effects of individual ethnic loyalties;
- the absence of large socio-economic inequalities;
- the geographical compactness of individual ethnic communities;
- pre-existing traditions of political accommodation.

Source: Bogdanor, V. (1991)

this chapter I shall investigate how far these conditions were fulfilled in the cases of Czechoslovakia and Yugoslavia.

To examine these issues, this chapter will assess the role played by nationalism in the collapse of the former communist countries. It will ask why it reappeared with such force in communist systems which claimed to be practising a fundamentally anti-nationalist creed and which, like the pre-Second World War states, had adopted policies which sought (with varying degrees of success) to mitigate the effects of ethnic division. It will first provide a brief survey of the region's historical legacy and the long-term conditions that provided grounds for the emergence of modern nationalism.

19.1   The legacy of history and the neurosis of national survival

To begin with, it is important to be clear about the definition of nationalism. According to Ignatieff:

> As a political doctrine, nationalism is the belief that the world's peoples are divided into nations, and that each of these nations has the right of self-determination, either as self-governing units within existing nation-states or as nation-states of their own.

> As a cultural ideal, nationalism is the claim that while men and women have many identities, it is the nation which provides them with their primary form of belonging. As a moral ideal, nationalism is an ethic of heroic sacrifice, justifying the use of violence in the defence of one's nation against enemies, internal or external.

(Ignatieff, 1993, p.3)

Ignatieff, along with others, then goes on to identify two kinds of nationalism: civic and ethnic. For him, civic nationalism:

> ... maintains that the nation should be composed of all those – regardless of race, colour, creed, gender, language or ethnicity – who subscribe to the nation's political creed. This nationalism is called civic because it envisages the nation as a community of equal, rights-bearing citizens, united in patriotic attachment to a shared set of political practices and values. This nationalism is necessarily democratic since it vests sovereignty in all of the people.

(ibid., p.3)

It should be noted that this kind of nationalism tended to develop at a relatively early stage in established West European states. By contrast 'ethnic nationalism ... claims that an individual's deepest attachments are inherited, not chosen. It is the national community which defines the individual, not the individuals who define the national community' (Ignatieff, 1993).

One of the reasons for directing attention to this distinction is that, as we shall see, communism and its downfall in Czechoslovakia was associated with nationalism of the more civic kind, whilst in Yugoslavia it was inherited traditions of ethnic nationalism which contributed both to the collapse of communism and the state that had encompassed it since 1945. It would be wrong, however, to insist upon a black-and-white distinction between the two. Rather, it would be better to conceptualize a continuum of nationalism, with civic and ethnic varieties at either end. Again, as we shall see later, countries and movements zigzag between these two poles and have been subject to different influences throughout the centuries.

It is, therefore, impossible to understand the force of nationalism in Eastern and Central Europe without some appreciation of the region's history and geography, for history is keenly felt and plays a vital part in the political consciousness of the inhabitants. For centuries the region has been occupied, colonized and subjugated. Before the twentieth century Serbs looked back 500 years to their last time of independence, Croats and Slovaks over 800 years. The peoples who live there are all relatively small in numbers and most are Slav. They have suffered for centuries. In the fifteenth century the combined populations of Serbia, Bosnia, Dalmatia, Croatia and Slovenia (see Map 19.2) were larger than that of England, which had three million inhabitants. By the twentieth century the population of Great Britain was several times larger, and that was despite continual emigration to the British Empire and the USA.

State boundaries have been drawn and redrawn in the past at the behest of larger neighbours, chiefly non-Slavs: Austria, Hungary, Germany, Russia and Turkey. Rupnik reminds us:

> Eastern and Central European borders are relatively new and they do not coincide with ethnolinguistic dividing lines. Less than a quarter of them predate the nineteenth century, about a quarter had been established around the time of WWI (1910–22), and about one third emerged in the aftermath of WWII. Well over half of all European borders are twentieth-century creations. European borders are more recent than African borders.

(Rupnik, 1994, p.98)

The rivalries and struggles for control caused repeated migrations and 'ethnic cleansings'. According to Kovačević, 'everyone in the Balkans is escaping from somewhere and wishes to find somewhere to get out of the way'. This enforced nomadic history led peoples of the region to long for 'homelands' and safe areas and strive for their creation. Colonizers, further, suppressed the ethnic identity of local inhabitants. For example, in the Hungarian-dominated part of the Hapsburg Empire, which included Croatia and Slovakia, the common language of administration was Latin until 1867, when the government embarked upon an aggressive policy of magyarization, which forced minorities to learn Hungarian in schools. At the beginning of the twentieth century there was, indeed, a widespread view that the Slovak nation was on the verge of extinction under the pressure of Magyarization and that it might well have disappeared in another generation (Seton-Watson, 1943).

Local identities were kept alive with folk history and myths, embellished with generations of telling. On the other hand, the life experience of most individuals and groups was limited to their villages and districts. This was the boundary of their primary loyalties. So these 'nations' very much exemplify Anderson's concept of nations as 'imagined communities', in the sense that they created an image of community in their minds, even though on a personal level most of them were strangers to each other (Anderson, 1991).

But if the history of Central and Eastern Europe was one of repeated colonization, it was also marked by numerous and prolonged struggles for national liberation. In that respect this region of Europe demonstrated similarities with the experience of post-colonial states since the Second World War. Issues of ethnic security and survival could still be easily manipulated by political leaders and 'ethnic entrepreneurs' (Akhavan, 1995). Because the history of the region was one which did not provide much of a basis for the development of civic nationalism, it was the ethnic variant that tended to prevail and major groups remained available for political mobilization by leaders through diverse appeals made on ethnic grounds.

─────────────── *Summary of Section 19.1* ───────────────

- Two variants of nationalism may usefully be distinguished: civic and ethnic.

- The political identity of ethnic groups in Central and Eastern Europe has been subject to considerable uncertainty.

- This has tended to encourage sentiments of ethnic rather than civic nationalism.

19.2 The first attempt at political communities: Czechoslovakia and Yugoslavia between 1919 and 1945

Both Czechoslovakia and Yugoslavia were created out of the sudden collapse of the Austro-Hungarian Empire and the peace treaties concluded at the end of the First World War (see Chapter 3). They took their shape from the decisions of the Great Powers following the collapse of the Austro-Hungarian Empire.

Their inhabitants had lived apart for centuries. Though the chief constituent parts of Czechoslovakia – Bohemia, Moravia, and Slovakia (see Map 19.1) – had all been incorporated into the Austro-Hungarian Empire, they had actually been in different parts of it. Bohemia and Moravia had been ruled from Vienna (and in 1848 had been invited to send representatives to the Frankfurt Congress which attempted to 'unify' *German* states), whilst Slovakia had been ruled from Budapest. Protestantism was a national tradition in Bohemia and Moravia, Roman Catholicism in Slovakia. And there were also major differences in living standards, with the Czech lands already possessing significant industry, whilst Slovakia remained predominantly agricultural.

In Yugoslavia the differences were even greater. Serbia had been ruled by the Ottoman Empire for 500 years until 1878. Croatia and Slovenia had been part of the Austro-Hungarian Empire, so they were Catholic. Although their languages were somewhat different in grammar, at least they used the Latin alphabet. Serbs, however, were Orthodox Christian, and although their language was very similar in grammar to Croat, it used the Cyrillic alphabet. In the First World War Serbs and Croats had fought on opposite sides. In

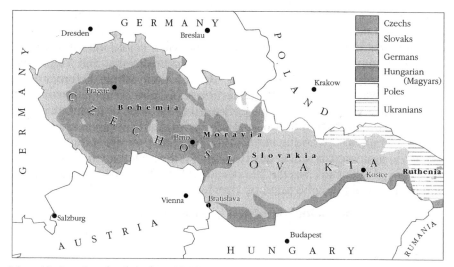

Map 19.1   Czechoslovakia 1919

addition, in Bosnia there was a significant community of Slav Muslims, who had been converted from Christianity during Ottoman rule, whilst further south, in Kosovo and Macedonia, there were sizeable numbers of non-Slav, Albanian Muslims. Thus the linguistic and confessional differences were greater than in Czechoslovakia, as were the variations in the levels of economic development, Croatia and Slovenia being much more indus-trialized than Serbia.

These various nationalities were united into new states by the conscious efforts of elites, rather than by pressure from below. Although this was a fragile basis for a new state, there were three reasons for hope that these states would form viable political communities and prosper. Firstly, they were all free from outside domination for the first time in centuries. Independence itself bred optimism. Secondly, there was hope that Slavs, left to themselves, would find new ways of co-operation. Some were sympathetic to pan-Slavism, i.e. the belief that Slavs as a whole constituted the 'nation', and that each distinct 'language' was really only a dialect, spoken by a separate 'tribe' (Tudjman, 1970). Thirdly, there was the fear of colonists returning if the local peoples could not co-operate. The first President of Czechoslovakia, T.G. Masaryk, believed that Czechs and Slovaks needed each other to avoid recolonization by Germans and Hungarians.

Moreover, if we consider Czechoslovakia and Yugoslavia according to the nine preconditions for viable consociational democracy listed above, they scored positively on several of them. Both lacked a dominant majority nationality. They had relatively small populations by world standards, although not by comparison with other consociational democracies (see Table 19.1). They had at least the memory of a foreign threat, even if it was less immediate than in the past. In addition Czechoslovakia had a relatively small number of ethnic communities, which were also geographically concen-trated. The weaknesses of the two states lay in the lack of pre-existing traditions of political accommodation, of overarching loyalties which transcended ethnic ones, and in significant regional inequalities.

The most important priority was to establish a viable state framework, and since unity was a high priority, both Czechoslovakia and Yugoslavia were established as unitary systems, despite their ethnic heterogeneity. Centralism was also deemed to be necessary because some nationalities in each country were relatively too backward to be able, at least initially, to make a full contribution to national life. In 1918, for instance, there were 12,447 civil servants working in the Slovak counties, mostly Hungarians, but only 35 volunteered to stay behind to work for the new state there. Only one judge stayed out of 464. For the first decade at least, the gaps in public service in Slovakia could only be filled by Czechs.

Table 19.1 Some major identified groups by ethnicity (1921)

	Number	Percentage
Czechoslovakia		
Czechoslovak	8,760,937	65.51
German	3,123,568	23.36
Magyar	745,431	5.57
Total population:	13,374,364	
Yugoslavia		
Serbs (incl Montenegrins)	5,154,000	43.0
Croats	2,757,000	23.0
Slovenes	1,019,000	8.5
Total population:	11,986,000	

Czechs and Slovaks were combined in the census (as, indeed, were Croats and Serbs in the original version). To give a general indication of the situation in Czechoslovakia, though, 73.4 per cent of the country's population lived in Czech provinces and 22 per cent in Slovakia.

Source: Rothschild (1974), pp.89, 202–3

In Yugoslavia, too, the new state had the former Kingdom of Serbia as its core, although it was initially rechristened the Kingdom of Serbs, Croats and Slovenes in deference to the two other main Slav nationalities. Serbs and Czechs both tended to assert national leadership within their respective states. Although neither constituted a majority of all the citizens, each felt that it was basically 'their' state. This was most clearly reflected in the composition of the officer corps in the armed forces. As late as September 1938 only one general out of 139 in the entire Czechoslovak army was a Slovak. The picture was very similar for the Yugoslav army, which in 1941, on the eve of the Second World War, had 165 generals. Of these, two were Croats, two Slovenes and the rest were Serbs.

What proved particularly difficult, however, was the creation of a common inter-ethnic identity: 'Czechoslovakism' or 'Yugoslavism'. However hopeful people might have been about the ease with which some kind of Slav solidarity might be created, reality proved more obdurate. Partly this was the result of the leading role which Czechs and Serbs assigned to themselves. They were reluctant to relinquish this privileged position after other

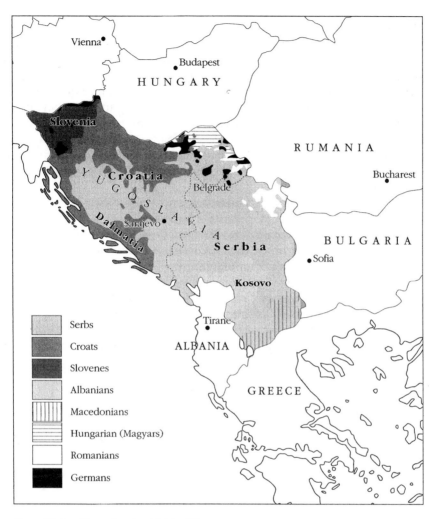

Map 19.2   Yugoslavia 1919–45

nationalities had begun to produce more and better qualified public servants of their own.

Long-term reductions in inequality were also difficult to achieve. Both countries carried out land reform in the early 1920s, partly as a way of dispossessing colonial 'collaborators'. They managed to prosper in the 1920s, but the Depression hit the more backward parts of each country – Serbia and the southern regions of Yugoslavia, and Slovakia. By the 1930s the most prosperous parts of the two countries were the same as they had been in 1914: the Czech lands, and Croatia and Slovenia. Economic conditions did not, therefore, create overarching solidarities which could bind the state together. Linguistic divisions also remained a problem. Czech and the Serbian version of Serbo-Croat remained dominant, and the other minorities continued to complain of inferior treatment.

The new institutions of liberal democracy compounded rather than eased the problems. Both new states introduced multiparty, parliamentary democracies with proportional representation to ensure that minorities could make their views known. So a wide range of parties won seats. None was able to achieve a majority or form a government on its own. More damagingly, large numbers of voters voted for 'their' ethnic parties rather than supranational ones, especially in Yugoslavia. In order to become viable, government therefore depended upon enough parties co-operating in a spirit of equality, whether or not they had equal numbers of seats in parliament. In political science terms, these states needed to establish the practices of a consociational democracy.

Here the experiences of Czechoslovakia and Yugoslavia diverged. In Yugoslavia what made ethnic co-operation impossible was the failure of the political system to accommodate demands from Croats for formal autonomy. And since the main Croat party, the Croat Peasant Party (CPP), was large enough regularly to frustrate government business, it antagonized everyone else and was scarcely ever invited into government. This graphically exemplified the fact that there was and could be no minority veto, such as a consociational system would enshrine. There was and could be no grand coalition which included the two main parties. In the end passions ran so high that in 1928 a Montenegrin deputy fatally wounded the leader of the CPP on the floor of parliament. This ended parliamentary democracy. The Serbian monarchy then headed an authoritarian government during the 1930s, which never won the support of the Croats.

The first decade of Czechoslovakia's existence was more successful. Though most parties were elected on an ethnic basis, the tendency was not as pronounced as in Yugoslavia. Moreover the leaders of the ruling parties established an informal consociational-type practice of informal consultation as a way of providing leadership which the cabinet and therefore parliament could not give. Known as the 'petka' (quintet) because it involved the leaders of the five largest parties, it operated on the principle that 'We have agreed that we will agree' (Crampton, 1994). Though not a grand coalition in the full sense of the term, it came closer than Yugoslavia to establishing consociational procedures that expressed the mutual respect of all ethnic communities in Czechoslovakia. Thus the Czechoslovak politicians did attempt to practise civic rather than ethnic nationalism, as Ignatieff defined the different variants.

The success of the Czechoslovak system in the 1920s can be seen in the fact that the nationality which was most opposed to the new state at the outset, the Sudeten Germans, did not maintain a Croat-type intransigence, but instead were gradually won over to participate in politics and abide by democratically taken decisions. In the 1930s, however, this was all changed by the Depression, for it hit the Sudeten Germans and the Slovaks much harder than the Czechs. The Germans became more receptive to revanchist calls from Nazi Germany, and the Slovaks began demanding much greater autonomy and economic control over their affairs. Yet democracy did survive until German dismemberment of Czechoslovakia in 1938, unlike every other state in Central and Eastern Europe in the inter-war period.

In the end both states collapsed because of invasion by Germany in 1938 and 1941, but they had been gravely weakened before that, and neither had solved the problem of the appropriate degree of autonomy for significant minorities. They were both to some extent caught in a vicious circle. Being relatively new states, their peoples had not had the time to develop the habit of inter-ethnic co-operation. But the fact that they had not done so kept them fragile.

During the Second World War Germany dismembered both Czechoslovakia and Yugoslavia and it offered the disaffected second-largest nationalities, the Slovaks and the Croats, the opportunity to establish their own 'independent' states, under Axis tutelage. Since this was the first time for nearly 1,000 years that either nationality had enjoyed any kind of statehood, it proved very attractive to the ethnic nationalists among them, though neither was able to exercise significant autonomy. Czechs and Serbs, however, regarded it as treachery.

Yet there was a vital difference between the quisling Slovak and Croat states, and it has exercised an impact upon the dissolution of both Czechoslovakia and Yugoslavia in the 1990s. Whilst both puppet states were required to implement Nazi policies of anti-semitism, the Slovaks did not practise genocide against other minorities. And in 1944 they 'redeemed' themselves with an uprising which swept the fascists aside, even if only briefly. The Croat state did practice genocide. It set out systematically to cleanse itself of the previously dominant Serbs by forcing them to convert from Orthodoxy to Catholicism, and by expelling or killing them. Hundreds of thousands suffered each fate – estimates vary widely between 200,000 and 700,000. Whatever the actual numbers, this left an enduring conviction among Serbs that their kin should never again be left at the mercy of Croats, hence their defence of Serb self-rule in Croatia after 1991.

Summary of Section 19.2

- Major social divisions were apparent within post-First World War Czechoslovakia and Yugoslavia.

- Certain factors of their situation provided preconditions for the consociational model but the record was a mixed one.

- Relations between the different ethnic parties were more conducive to consociational democracy in Czechoslovakia than in Yugoslavia.

19.3 Czechoslovakia and Yugoslavia under communist rule

Czechoslovakia and Yugoslavia were resurrected by the Great Powers within almost the same borders after the Second World War. Once again there were reasons for hope that they would prove durable. For one thing their peoples could see the sufferings which disunity had caused, so they had an incentive to make supra-ethnic concerns paramount. To some extent population movements during the war and after led to the greater geographical concentration of ethnic groups. In Czechoslovakia one cause of instability, the Sudeten Germans, numbering over two million, had been expelled at the end of the war. And whilst Yugoslavia still had more nationalities than Czechoslovakia, the trauma of inter-ethnic killing which had taken place during the war, where 10 per cent of the population had died, offered grounds for hope that everyone would recognize the need for ethnic tolerance. It was true that the regional inequalities in both countries were as great as ever, but everyone was poorer as a result of the war, and it could be presumed that all would co-operate to build a better future. The advent of the Cold War resurrected the spectre of a foreign threat to their survival – another reason for co-operation.

The primary tasks were again to establish the core of the new state and to create a new value system which would overcome ethnic fragmentation. After their take-over in Czechoslovakia during 1948 communist parties ruled in both political systems. This gave their central leadership great power as the core of the new regimes. They attempted to rebuild the state on the basis of class, i.e. proletarian, rather than ethnic, solidarity. To transform those parts of each country which were still agricultural and poor the regimes embarked on crash programmes of industrialization, intended to lay the economic and social basis of socialism and eliminate inequalities. Economists have estimated that at various periods after 1948 between 2.5 and 5 per cent of the national income of the Czech lands (Bohemia and Moravia) was transferred to Slovakia.

Both regimes therefore began constructing a fairly similar model for political and economic development borrowed from the Soviet experience. In 1948, however, Yugoslavia was suddenly expelled from the Soviet camp. After that the paths of Yugoslavia and Czechoslovakia diverged for 40 years until the regimes ultimately disintegrated within a year of each other. In explaining how and why this occurred, it will be necessary to outline the process for each country separately.

Czechoslovakia

At the outset there was one fundamental difference between the communist regime in Czechoslovakia and that in Yugoslavia. The Yugoslav Communist Party had come to power largely through its own efforts in organizing resistance to Axis occupation in the Second World War, and thus gained considerable legitimacy. The Czechoslovak Communist Party (CPCz), on the other hand, came to power at Soviet instigation in 1948. It was never able to generate widespread domestic legitimacy and maintain close relations with Moscow at the same time. Led by Alexander Dubček, it did make one attempt to realize the two simultaneously in the form of the 'Prague Spring' of 1968, when it tried to create a new form of communist rule, i.e. 'socialism with a human face'. Ultimately, however, the Soviet leadership became convinced that Dubček had lost control of events and was being pushed aside by anti-Soviet forces. So on 20 and 21 August 1968, troops from several Warsaw Pact countries under Soviet leadership invaded Czechoslovakia to 'preserve the gains of socialism'.

Only one major reform from the 1968 programme survived – federalization – which was implemented on 1 January 1969, though even its importance was eroded as the government then pared back the economic autonomy of the Czech and Slovak governments.

The regime was forced once again to give relations with Moscow greater priority than domestic legitimacy. Opposition to the regime took on a nationalist character, though it did also protest human rights abuses in general – the Charter 77 group formed in 1977 informed Western nations about repression inside Czechoslovakia and aimed to bring Czechoslovakia's performance on human rights up to the level of developed capitalist countries. Thus although nationalism – the demand for Czechoslovakia to be free from Russian domination – was a fundamental source of opposition, it was civic rather than ethnic nationalism in Ignatieff's terms. It was akin – and deliberately so – to Western liberalism. It did not attempt to establish separate rights for Czechs or Slovaks.

The irony, however, was that even if the objectives of the opposition were not aimed at benefitting one ethnic community, the members of the opposition were confined to the Czechs. Partly because a Slovak, Gustav Husák, was President, the government's economic policies led to more rapid development for Slovaks. Indeed by the end of the 1980s Slovaks had caught up to the level of development of Czechs for the first time in their history according to a whole series of social and economic indicators. Thus on the eve of its demise communism in Czechoslovakia finally removed the last obstacle to the creation of a viable multi-ethnic state in Czechoslovakia. Of the nine preconditions listed in the first section of this chapter which consociational theory required, that of inter-ethnic inequality was now fulfilled. Yet one consequence of this change was decreasing job mobility between the Czech lands and Slovakia, and in terms of personal contacts they were growing apart (Musil, 1995).

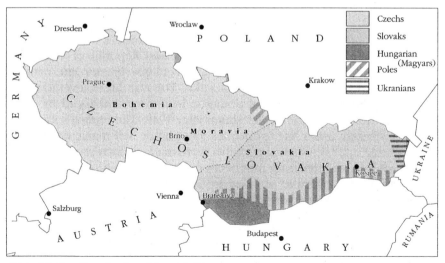

Map 19.3   Czechoslovakia, 1945

It would be untrue to say that Slovaks were actively enthusiastic about the communist regime. Nevertheless very few Slovaks joined the human rights opposition, or indeed any kind of opposition at all, at least until a large peaceful demonstration by Catholics in Bratislava in March 1988. The number of Slovaks who signed petitions of protest was minuscule compared to that of Czechs. By the end of the late 1980s the regime had achieved a grim equilibrium based upon internal realpolitik. The state could prevent overthrow from below but it could not eliminate opposition, still less widespread political apathy. Dissidents could meet in small groups in private, but could not bring the regime down.

The fundamental cause of the regime's collapse was the Soviet Union (see Chapter 16). Moscow had ensured that Czechoslovakia was dependent upon it in 1968. Now its regime paid the price. Once Gorbachev had emerged as Soviet leader, his willingness to contemplate increasingly radical reforms at home set him apart from his predecessors. Having embarked upon reforms, he found that he was following in the footsteps of the Czech reformers of 1968. This obviously undermined Husák's position. Although Gorbachev did not openly disavow the now conservative leaders of Eastern Europe, he let it be known that he did not sympathize with their domestic predicaments. And he implied that the maintenance of Soviet control over Eastern Europe was no longer essential to the USSR's security relations with the West.

The catalyst for the collapse of communism in Czechoslovakia was a series of student demonstrations in Prague in October and November 1989, which were only half-heartedly suppressed, and which therefore swelled in size. On 21 November a demonstration of over 200,000 gathered on Wenceslas Square in Prague. By 26 November a general strike had been called. On 3 December the CPCz leadership had resigned as the government, and within a week so too had President Husák.

Yugoslavia

Given the bloody civil war which accompanied its demise, it was ironical that, for almost all of its existence, the Federal Socialist Republic of Yugoslavia apparently enjoyed greater domestic, and certainly greater international support, than did communist Czechoslovakia. This was due to several factors. There was the regime's original domestic legitimacy, enhanced by Tito's success in holding off the Soviet Union after 1948. The regime's model of socialism based upon the principles of worker self-management had considerable appeal. Gradual attempts were made to increase democracy, or at least involve increasing numbers of citizens in decision-making fora, even though the principle of one-party dominance of society was never abandoned. The regime was relatively open and allowed its citizens to go abroad if they wished. Prosperity increased on the basis of quite rapid economic development. And there was also the apparent success in solving the country's ethnic problems, symbolized by the multi-ethnic character of the party and government, where all major nationalities were represented at the highest levels.

In 1945 the new regime created three new federal republics – Macedonia, Montenegro and Bosnia-Hercegovina – which had previously been incorporated into Serbia or Croatia. The languages of all the nationalities after whom federal republics were named became those of administration within their respective republic, as well as becoming established as the languages of inter-republic communication. Over time these rights grew. Even smaller nationalities were entitled to have their children educated in the native tongue if the local commune agreed. In addition to the official languages of the republics and autonomous provinces, full elementary education was to be provided in a further seven languages (Bulgarian, Czech, Italian, Romanian, Ruthenian, Slovak and Turkish). In secondary schools an application by fifteen pupils would be enough to guarantee instruction in the language of the nationality involved, whilst the same was true for higher education if a class of 30 students applied.

In addition the state seriously undertook to reduce the wide economic disparities which divided Slovenia in the north-west from Macedonia and Kosovo in the south. Initially this was done through the central plan, but later, after directive planning was abandoned, a federal fund was established to aid

Map 19.4   Yugoslavia, 1945

underdeveloped regions. It managed to gather over 2 per cent of GDP for redistribution between 1966 and 1986. Though this was less than half of what the Czech lands transferred to Slovakia, it was still double the figure which developed nations set aside to aid the developing world (*NIN*, 21 September 1990; Lydall, 1984). Thus the poorer republics and provinces were able to attract greater subsidies and investment from the rest of Yugoslavia than they would have done if they had been independent states.

A further change after the split with the Soviet Union was a gradual increase in the powers of the republics *vis-à-vis* the centre, initially as a reaction against the over-centralized Soviet model. It culminated in constitutional amendments in 1974 which established that sovereign rights lay with the republics rather than the federation, and that autonomous provinces had almost the same rights. This reflected an approach based upon civic rather than ethnic nationalism, for the right was granted to the constitutional unit rather than specific nationalities. To the anger of Serbia, this meant that 'their' autonomous province of Kosovo was now almost treated as a constitutional equal with a right of veto over national policy.

Moreover, unlike other communist regimes where decentralization within the state apparatus was not matched in the ruling party, the Yugoslav party became as federalized as the state. Partly to symbolize the change it was renamed the League of Communists of Yugoslavia (LCY), rather than the Yugoslav Communist Party. So although the refusal to contemplate a multiparty system necessarily precluded a consociational 'grand coalition' of dominant parties as such, the LCY effectively practised a grand coalition on a territorial basis.

For all these reasons, then, it seemed as though the regime had solved, or at least had made substantial progress towards solving, the nationalities question in Yugoslavia. Members of ethnic communities lived, worked and played together on an individual basis without being preoccupied by each other's nationality. Intermarriage (by 1981 one in seven marriages were between people of different nationalities) and social mobility led people to move around the country and settle in different areas. In all it has been estimated that over ten million inhabitants moved from one settlement to another inside Yugoslavia between 1947 and 1991, and of these, three million had moved from one republic to another. In some regions nationalities became even more intermingled. By 1981 one-fifth of all children born in Yugoslavia since 1945 came from ethnically mixed marriages. In the census in 1981 5.6 per cent of the population classed themselves as 'Yugoslavs' rather than Serbs, Croats, etc. In 1971 the equivalent figure had been 1.4 per cent (Šuvar, 1995).

It seemed that habits of trust and co-operation had taken root, unlike the inter-war period, although it was perhaps disturbing that the proportion of 'Yugoslavs' among party officials from all republics was lower than in the population as a whole. Ethnic criteria proved to have some significance for political advancement (Mirić, 1985). Overall, however, developments under communism had provided quite favourable conditions for the establishment of consociational democracy.——

The situation began to change in 1980, though. In that year President Tito died and no-one could step into his shoes. Since 1948 he had been obsessed with parallels with the USSR under Lenin and Stalin. He wanted to ensure that no Stalin figure would emerge as the 'grave-digger' of the Yugoslav revolution. So he established collective presidencies of the party and of the state, where chairmen rotated every year between representatives from each of the republics. Their practice was to make decisions on the basis of 'consensus', i.e. unanimity. The consequence of this, however, was that no-one had the authority to impose tough decisions when the need arose, except Tito.

The regime therefore became increasingly fragmented after his death. This showed up most clearly in the economy. Individual republics increasingly pursued their own strategies for economic development and penalized 'imports' from other republics. There was a decline in economic integration. The value of goods and services delivered from one republic or province to another fell as a proportion of total trade in Yugoslavia from around 40 per cent in 1970 to a little over 32 per cent in 1978 (*Treći Program Radio Beograda*, 1982). Few enterprises developed production facilities in more than one republic, in case the 'foreign' workers expropriated the investment. Nevertheless at this time it was the individual republics, rather than individual nationalities, which were growing in importance. Civic nationalism still predominated over ethnic.

There were two consequences of this 'federalization' of the economy. The first was increasing regional inequality. For all the efforts at redistribution of resources, by the 1980s the gap between the south and the north, between the two extremes of Slovenia and Kosovo, was greater than ever (Mihailović, 1981). The second was inflation, as each republic printed money and manufactured credit to support 'its' enterprises. Inflation rose from an annual rate of 30 per cent in 1982 to nearly 1,000 per cent in 1989, despite repeated central government programmes to bring it under control. This led to increasing public frustration. Everyone felt that they were losers, whatever their nationality. These economic travails undermined the sense of security and comfort which had been built up over the previous 30 years. They began to create an anxiety about the future. They were, moreover, compounded by renewed ethnic frictions.

Above all these concerned Kosovo. This had been the site of Serbia's 'golden age', a kingdom which included Macedonia and Thessalonika in Greece, until it was overwhelmed by the Ottoman Turks in 1389. The place where that defeat occurred, Kosovo Polje, is still regarded as a vital piece of Serbian territory, even though by the 1980s most Serbs had left it to the Albanians, who had gradually grown more self-confident and had begun to question the province's constitutional status. Some wanted full equality with the other republics of Yugoslavia. Others wanted to go further and demanded full independence. The League of Communists in Kosovo was dominated by Albanians and could no longer be regarded as an automatic bulwark against secession. In 1986 the claim surfaced that Serbs in Kosovo were facing genocide and that this was the most serious threat to Serbs in general since their revolt against the Turks. More ominously it alleged that Serbs in Croatia were also now under the greatest threat since their oppression by the Ustashe government in the Second World War (Silber and Little, 1995). Thus it extended concern to the Yugoslav level. This was not civic but ethnic nationalism, and of a primitive kind.

The mounting malaise caused by economic difficulties and apparent government powerlessness created an opportunity for someone who could take the initiative. In April 1987 Slobodan Milošević, a previously colourless communist politician, visited Kosovo and made an impromptu defence of Serbian interests, condemning heavy-handed treatment of Serb demonstrations by the police. He suddenly aroused public adulation and established himself as the spokesman for impatient Serbs. He accused others in the party of wanting or acquiescing in the allegedly Titoist policy of keeping Serbia weak as a precondition for a strong Yugoslavia. Instead, he declared, a strong Yugoslavia was inconceivable without a strong Serbia.

Matters came to a head in the Serbian Central Committee in September 1987 when the then party boss, Ivan Stambolić, warned of the threat which Milošević was posing and appealed to the spirit of civic nationalism which had previously prevailed within the party. In this situation Milošević challenged Stambolić for the Serbian party leadership and won the vote easily. In July and August 1988 Serb demonstrations in the province of Vojvodina, instigated from Kosovo, protested resistance by their leadership to greater control from Belgrade.

Then the demonstrations spread to Montenegro. There, too, groups of Serbs were mobilized to protest the republican leadership's coolness towards Milošević and its general ineffectiveness. Faced with the threat of escalating demonstrations and criticism from Belgrade for trying to stop them, the leadership resigned. This was an ominous development. Milošević had now brought down the leadership of another federal republic. The aggressive, nationalist communism which Milošević preached seemed to point towards a confrontation with popular aspirations for greater democracy throughout the country, while providing Milošević with a powerful political base at a time when traditional communism held few attractions.

The tensions were felt particularly keenly in Slovenia, which in the 1980s had seen a great flowering of civil society that the local party leadership had come to accept. Slovenes became concerned about the fate of their democracy if Milošević should become national leader. Thus nationalism from Serbia provoked a nationalist response, albeit still of a civic kind, in defence of democracy. Although all the other leaders recognized the implicit challenge of autumn 1989, their responses varied. The leadership in Macedonia kept a low profile because their republic had had to declare bankruptcy in 1987 and so it was heavily dependent upon the federal government in Belgrade, whoever controlled it. The leadership in Bosnia-Hercegovina tried quiet diplomacy. But Slovenia and Croatia carried their disagreements with Serbia into the highest levels of the League of Yugoslav Communists as well as the state. They insisted upon even greater autonomy for their own party organizations, as well as for their state, as a check upon pressures from Belgrade.

Their resolve was stiffened by the contemporaneous collapse of communism in Eastern and Central Europe. In January 1990 an emergency congress of the LCY was held, but the Slovenian delegation walked out in protest at being consistently outvoted, and the Croatian delegation refused to allow the Congress to continue in their absence. It was adjourned and never recalled. Attempts to drum up popular support, however, backfired on the communist parties. In Slovenia the party leader, Milan Kučan, was able to win the election for President, but the League of Slovenian Communists, now renamed the Party of Democratic Renewal, lost and a non-communist government was elected. In Croatia not even the post of President was won by the communists. There it was Franjo Tudjman who won the election with his Croatian Democratic Union (HDZ).

After that there was no prospect of Yugoslavia surviving. Disagreements between the republics had escalated to a point where the state presidency included both communists and non-communists. As already mentioned, the basic operating principle there had been unanimity. Tudjman and Milošević could never agree on any policy, except the most basic. Very quickly all Yugoslav-wide institutions, except the army, were paralysed by disputes. In Spring 1991 Slovenia and Croatia declared independence, and the country degenerated into civil war. Milošević was prepared to let Slovenia go, but he fought to prevent Serbs in Croatia being left at the mercy of an 'Ustashe' government in Zagreb. Once fighting had begun and the sense of security had been destroyed throughout the country, the only type of nationalism which could survive was ethnic rather than civic.

Though individual villages, towns and even cities such as Sarajevo attempted to resist it and preserve the cosmopolitan harmony which had been built up over decades, hardliners from various nationalities stirred up trouble and provoked confrontation. This spread terror and a sense of the need for ethnic unity to withstand it. There were demands for boundaries to be redrawn so as to form compact, ethnically homogeneous states, even if this was in practice impossible without partition or ethnic cleansing. Ethnic nationalism took over and ensured not only that the old Yugoslavia disintegrated, but also that there would be no return to it or nostalgia for it. By 1995 rudimentary estimates suggested that at least 150,000 people had been killed, 250,000 wounded, two and a half million people had been forced to move, and perhaps half a million had emigrated. This was out of a population of almost 24 million in mid 1991 (Šuvar, 1995). And although the old Yugoslavia was dead, the borders of Slovenia, Serbia and Croatia were almost exactly where they had been at the outset. Only Bosnia-Hercegovina had been radically changed – and it had not originally been involved in the conflict.

_____ *Summary of Section 19.3* _____

- The modernizing communist regime in Czechoslovakia helped strengthen prospects for consociational democracy by reducing socio-economic inequalities between ethnic groups.

- Nationalist opposition to Soviet control grew, but it remained essentially civic in character.

- Developments in Yugoslavia under Tito were also relatively favourable for the creation of conditions conducive to consociational democracy.

- The institutions he had devised to preserve ethnic balance proved to be less effective after his death and weakened the economy of the country as a whole.

- Popular discontent combined with growing dissatisfaction in Serbia to increase sentiments of ethnic nationalism.

- This was used by Milošević in ways that soon led to the break-up of the Yugoslav state.

19.4 The disintegration of Czechoslovakia

If the Yugoslav socialist system collapsed together with the state, in Czechoslovakia communism collapsed first. The subsequent demise of the state during 1992 came as much as a surprise to its own citizens as it did to outsiders. The new political system had been intended to introduce western liberal democratic norms; and in the new President, Václav Havel, it had indeed a leader with a long and distinguished record of support for human rights.

Two factors, however, undermined its viability in the eyes of Slovaks. The first was the effect of market reforms and the privatization of state enterprises. Partly as a result of the very efforts of the previous system to give priority to investments there, Slovakia was particularly well endowed with large, state-subsidized factories which faced particular difficulties in adapting to the world market. Although the whole of the Czechoslovak economy went into recession because of the reforms, the Slovak part suffered worse. This was compounded by the early decision of President Havel to stop arms sales when most of the arms factories were in Slovakia. The Czech Finance Minister in charge of reforms (and later prime minister) Václav Klaus showed little sympathy for calls for state assistance to ease the transition.

To Slovaks this reawakened suspicions that Czechs were returning to the old high-handed treatment of which they had complained in previous decades. This was the second factor which undermined for Slovaks the attractiveness of union. It suggested that the centuries-old stereotypes of each other held by Czechs and Slovaks had still not been overcome, even if economic inequalities had. Slovaks remained extremely sensitive to what they regarded as Czechs' sense of natural superiority. Czechs, on the other hand, pictured Slovaks as excitable, emotional and suffering from an inferiority complex (Musil, 1995).

This rekindled ambitions for the greater economic autonomy of Slovakia. Slovaks feared that all the gains of the previous decades were about to be sacrificed, whilst the Czech republic forged ahead again. Thus it was not regional inequality which contributed to the downfall of Czechoslovakia as much as the fear of its return. On the other hand, Czechs became exasperated by Slovak calls for a slowdown in reform. Czechs wanted the old system replaced as quickly as possible, for they felt that it had cost them a good deal. Slovaks retained a certain nostalgia for features of the old system (Musil, 1995).

Yet although tension mounted, public opinion polls in both the Czech lands and Slovakia in the first half of 1992 still showed that a majority in both regions wanted to preserve union and believed that separation would bring more harm than good. The new political system was extremely volatile. Czech and Slovak leaders were engaged in negotiations over economic reforms, and in the process each pushed his position very hard to extract the best deal. The Slovak prime minister, Mečiar, began to threaten the break-up of the state if the Czechs did not accept his proposals. Whether or not this was bluff, it increased distrust on both sides. Some Slovak leaders began to talk of full independence for Slovakia within the European Union.

By even introducing such questions into public debate they legitimized the search for solutions of this far-reaching nature. It antagonized Czechs and co-operation broke down. Finally, in the summer of 1992, leaders from the two sides agreed that the Czech Republic and Slovakia would each assume full independence from January 1993. But at least when this happened, it took place without the acrimony, let alone the violence, of the disintegration of Yugoslavia.

One very important cause of this was the different memory of the Second World War in Czechoslovakia from that in Yugoslavia. Serbs could still remember the genocide which had been inflicted upon them by the Croat *Ustashe* regime and Milošević wanted at all costs to prevent Serbs in Croatia in the 1990s from being subjected to the same fate. He attempted to redraw the boundaries of Croatia, so that Serb settlements there could be incorporated into a 'Greater Serbia'. Czech memories of their treatment by the Slovak fascist state during the war were not so extreme and therefore they did not harbour the same grudges. The separation in 1992 was eased by the fact that neither side expressed territorial claims against the other. And the 300,000 Slovaks living in the Czech lands expressed no qualms about their status there, nor any demands for their interests to be 'protected' by Slovakia. Nor did the 59,000 Czechs in Slovakia (Rupnik, 1994; Musil, 1995). To that extent, in both halves of the former Czechoslovakia the principle of civic rather than ethnic nationalism still prevailed.

───────────────── *Summary of Section 19.4* ─────────────────

- It was primarily the issue of post-communist economic reform that aroused the suspicions of Slovaks, although this did not give rise to major popular demands for separation.

- The break-up of the federal state involved nationalist sentiments which were essentially civic in nature.

Conclusion

The cases of Czechoslovakia and Yugoslavia provide a graphic demonstration of the obstacles to post-communist democratization in multi-ethnic states. While democratization progressed in the Czech Republic and Slovenia, the development of liberal democracy was more partial in Slovakia and the other states formed from the republics of former Yugoslavia. Wars fought in parts of Croatia and virtually throughout the whole of Bosnia destroyed both peace and any idea of an ordered political life in the countries affected. Their conduct exerted a profound influence on the domestic politics of Serbia and Croatia and had a decidedly negative effect on the development of liberal democracy in those countries. In neither case did the federal state structure in place throughout the communist period survive, and any stable prospects for democratization in the areas affected seemed to be premised on the abandonment of the idea of a multi-ethnic political community.

Neither Czechoslovakia nor Yugoslavia, then, provide clear guidance as to what the conditions for a successful transition to democracy in a multi-ethnic context might be, as they were clearly absent in these two countries. Their experience does, nevertheless, demonstrate the effects that different kinds of nationalism have on democratization. Civic nationalism, based on the idea of the nation as a community of citizens with equal rights, is essentially democratic in its implications and fosters practices that are by no means inimical to democratization.

Ethnic nationalism, however, rests on a conception of inherited characteristics that necessarily excludes some individuals and groups from any multi-ethnic community and offers no real prospect of effective democratization. The dominance of civic nationalism in Czechoslovakia helped explain the greater progress of democratization in that country and the peaceful way in which the federal state was divided. The prevalence of ethnic nationalism in Yugoslavia prepared the way for the bloody breakup of the state and the restricted prospects for liberal democracy associated with it (with Slovenia, a compact, economically developed and ethnically homogeneous country which escaped much of the hostilities, providing a singular exception).

Certain kinds of political arrangements have also been identified as being conducive to the formation of a political community capable of sustaining a multi-ethnic liberal democracy. The model of a consociational democracy was proposed as a form of liberal democracy effective in societies characterized by deep ethnic or other forms of cultural division. The history of Czechoslovakia and Yugoslavia since their establishment as multi-ethnic states after the First World War was therefore examined to determine how far and in which ways their experience between the wars provided conditions under which the consociational model might operate. The picture was mixed, with some factors conducive to consociationalism being identified at the outset accompanying others which were clearly less favourable.

In general terms, internal divisions were more pronounced in Yugoslavia than Czechoslovakia. The creation of a common inter-ethnic identity proved to be a particularly difficult task. This was compounded in Yugoslavia by the dissatisfaction of the Croat minority with its status, and the eventual undermining of liberal democratic procedures. The main principles of the consociational model were never applied and democracy thus ended in Yugoslavia well before its destruction as an independent state with the German invasion of 1941. The record of consociational democracy was a stronger one in Czechoslovakia, although it was put under increasing pressure by the growing dissatisfaction of the Slovak and German minorities after the onset of the Depression. The latter group in particular were associated with the crisis of the inter-war democratic state, but it was the pressure of Nazi Germany that brought about its destruction.

The establishment of communist states after 1945 provided a fresh set of conditions for the development of consociational practices – if not in a liberal-democratic form. The legitimacy of the Czechoslovak communist state was a problem from the outset, and only worsened after the Soviet invasion of 1968. It fed strengthening currents of nationalist opposition, although these were essentially civic rather than ethnic in nature and did not have a deleterious effect on future prospects of democracy. Developments in the economy were unambiguously favourable for consociationalism and helped reduce ethnic inequality. In Yugoslavia under Tito the consociational model seemed to become even more· strongly established and, while progress towards the reduction of inter-ethnic inequality was equally noticeable, problems of domestic legitimacy were also less pronounced. Although there was Serbian dissatisfaction with their reduced status, this was largely containable within the procedures of the federal communist state.

The situation changed radically after Tito's death in 1980, when the institutional arrangements devised to promote ethnic balance also turned out to impede the adoption of policies favourable to integrated economic development. This produced conditions favourable to the development of ethnic nationalism in Serbia, which was increasingly used both to undermine existing forms of consociationalism and the structures of the federal state. The way in which communist rule came to an end in Yugoslavia thus offered very limited prospects of democratization.

The situation was again different in Czechoslovakia. A post-communist liberal democracy was established on what seemed to be a relatively firm footing. But economic factors were once more critical and the rigours of post-communist economic change bore harder on Slovakia than on Czech areas, the effects being more keenly felt because they were often the result of policies followed by Czech politicians. The dissolution of the state, when it came in 1992, was nevertheless carefully handled by political methods and nationalist pressures restricted to the civic rather than ethnic variant. The end of communist rule in Czechoslovakia and subsequent political developments in the country were therefore considerably more conducive to democratization.

The form taken by nationalist developments and the way in which they impinged on the preconditions for consociational democracy and the principles of its operation (although these could hardly be fully applied in the context of communist rule) thus explained much of the pattern of democratization (or its absence) in Czechoslovakia and Yugoslavia. While we have not discussed these developments in terms of the theoretical approaches, the role of the explanatory factors presented throughout this book does emerge very strongly in the above account.

The whole notion of consociational democracy is, firstly, based on the existence of major *social divisions* in a society. The particular institutional arrangements it proposes are associated with a form of *state* organization and the establishment of a set of *institutions* designed to cope with politically significant ethnic divisions. But such divisions may also provide a basis for the development of aggressive sentiments that take the form of nationalism which may come to exert a determining influence on the *political culture* of the society. They, while clearly national in form, have invariably been a response to the pressure of different forms of *international and transnational engagement* which have critically affected the position and outlook of particular groups, which in this case were predominantly ethnically based. The model of consociational democracy thus engages very closely with our set of explanatory factors in establishing the conditions favourable (or, in this case generally unfavourable) to democratization in a multi-ethnic context.

References

Akhavan, P. (ed.) (1995) *Yugoslavia, the Former and Future*, Washington, DC, The United Nations Research Institute for Social Development.

Anderson, B. (1991) *Imagined Communities* (2nd edn), London, Verso.

Bogdanor, V. (ed.) (1991) *The Blackwell Encyclopaedia of Political Science*, Oxford, Blackwell.

Carter, A. (1982) *Democratic Reform in Yugoslavia: the Changing Role of the Party*, London, Pinter.

Crampton, R.J. (1994) *Eastern Europe in the Twentieth Century*, London, Routledge.

Glenny, M. (1992) *The Fall of Yugoslavia*, Harmondsworth, Penguin.

Ignatieff, M. (1993) *Blood and Belonging*, London, BBC Books and Chatto & Windus.

Korbel, J. (1977) *Twentieth-Century Czechoslovakia*, New York, Columbia University Press.

Kovačević, D. (1991) 'Jugoslavija: Osvajanje ili Gubitak Istorije' in *Raspad Jugoslavije: Produzetak ili Kraj Agonije*, Belgrade, Institut za Evropske Studije, pp.11–19.

Leff, C.S. (1988) *National Conflict in Czechoslovakia: the Making and Remaking of a State, 1918–1987*, Princeton, NJ, Princeton University Press.

Lydall, H. (1984) *Yugoslav Socialism: Theory and Practice*, Oxford, Clarendon Press.

Mihailović, K. (1981) *Ekonomska Stvarnost Jugoslavije*, Belgrade, Ekonomika.

Mirić, J. (1985) *Sistem i Kriza*, Zagreb, CKD.

Morgenthau, H.J. (1957) 'The paradoxes of nationalism', *Yale Review*, vol.46, no.4, June, pp.481–96.

Musil, J. (ed.) (1995) *The End of Czechoslovakia*, Budapest, Central European University Press.

Ramet, S.P. (1994) 'The re-emergence of Slovakia', *Nationalities Papers*, vol.22, no.1, pp.99–117.

Rothschild, J. (1974) *East Central Europe Between the Two World Wars*, Seattle, Washington University Press.

Rupnik, J. (1994) 'Europe's new frontiers', *Daedalus*, no.3, pp.91–114.

Seton-Watson, R.W. (1943) *A History of the Czechs and Slovaks*, London, Hutchinson.

Silber, L. and Little, A. (1995) *The Death of Yugoslavia*, Harmondsworth, Penguin.

Šuvar, S. (1995) 'The demographic balance of the second Yugoslavia (1945–92) and demographic aspects of the future development of the successor states', *Balkan Forum*, vol.3(4), no.13, pp.137–52.

Treći Program Radio Beograda (1982) no.52, p.64.

Tudjman, F. (1970) *Velike Ideje i Mali Narodi*, Zagreb, Matica Hrvatska.

CHAPTER 20

Political change in Vietnam

Martin Gainsborough

Introduction

Compared with changes in Eastern Europe, or in South Korea or Taiwan in the late 1980s and early 1990s, democratization tendencies in Vietnam were quite limited. This is not to say they were insignificant – on the contrary – but there was no dramatic break with the past as witnessed in the Eastern European countries, and no clear shift to democratization as seen in South Korea and Taiwan (see Chapter 9). Instead, what got under way in Vietnam was a process of political liberalization overseen exclusively by the Communist Party of Vietnam (CPV), which had held power in the country as a whole since 1975, set against the backdrop of a market-oriented economic reform programme. The primary questions addressed in this chapter are: What exactly did political liberalization in Vietnam entail? Why did it get under way in the first place? and Why did it remain a limited process of change, falling some way short of democratization? Box 20.1 gives some information about the historical background of Vietnam (refer also to the map of Asia in the Introduction to Part III).

What characterized the process of political liberalization from 1986 to 1995? I understand liberalization as 'an attempt to maintain the existing political configuration while accommodating new forces' (refer here to the use of the term in Chapter 7 and subsequent discussion in Chapter 16). This can be distinguished from democratic reform, which opens the political system to 'any change in personnel, policies or structure that is supported by the public' (Womack, 1993, pp.290–1). Unlike liberalization, such reform involves a broader process of democratization which also permits the establishment and operation of independent organizations and at least a degree of political contestation. Although it is useful to distinguish between liberalization and democratic reform, the distinction should not be overdrawn. To some extent the tactics of a ruling elite can be mixed. The clear democratizing tendencies of liberalization should be recognized, although, as Womack notes, such changes are not supported by deeper institutional changes and liberalization can always be aborted by a return to more repressive measures.

The limited scope of political change involved in liberalization means that the theoretical approaches used to explain democratization do not have much to offer in this context. Theories which consider the subject of democratization generally look to the point at which one-party authoritarian governments give way to a multiparty system in which the right to hold

Box 20.1 Historical background to Vietnam

1   Vietnam's history has been dominated by struggles against outside powers. China, its huge northern neighbour, ruled Vietnam for several hundred years to AD 937 and again from 1407 to 1427. A high degree of mistrust characterizes relations with China to this day.

2   A process of territorial acquisitiveness during the fourteenth and fifteenth century and struggles between rival families led to the renunciation of the country under the Nguyen dynasty in 1802.

3   French missionaries appeared on the scene from the seventeenth century, leading to the progressive colonialization of the country between 1858 and 1883.

4   Ho Chi Minh declared Vietnam independent in 1945. His communist and nationalist Viet Minh led an anti-colonial struggle against the French, resulting in the historic defeat of the colonial power at the battle of Dien Bien Phu in 1954.

5   The Geneva agreements signed in the same year resulted in the partition of the country into North and South Vietnam pending nationwide elections scheduled for 1956. The northern Democratic Republic of Vietnam was led by Ho Chi Minh.

6   The elections anticipated by the Geneva agreements were never held which led to the decision by the communists to wage armed struggle against the Southern regime in 1959, and the commencement of what came to be known in the West as the 'Vietnam War'.

7   In its desire to prevent the spread of communism, the USA increasingly came to the aid of the South, including heavy bombing of the North and the large-scale deployment of US combat troops. By 1968, it had over half a million soldiers in Vietnam.

8   Northern resilience, changing realpolitik, and US domestic opposition to the war led to a decision by Washington to 'disengage', and the subsequent communist victory over the South in 1975. Formal reunification of the country as the Socialist Republic of Vietnam took place in 1976.

political office is contested at the ballot box. Rustow goes a step further, focusing on how democratic rules and norms gain widespread acceptance among major political actors. While theories of this kind provide insights as to how Vietnam might evolve one day, in other respects they jump the gun as far as the time period being considered here is concerned. If one considers the time which elapsed between economic take-off in South Korea and Taiwan and the point at which they completed the first stage of the democratic transition, then many years could elapse between the liberalization outlined here and a similar transition in Vietnam. Rustow's 'historical moment' or Lijphart's 'overarching co-operation at the elite level' (Lijphart, 1968) involved in the development of consociational democracy as discussed in Chapter 19 looked a distant prospect in the early 1990s.

To explore these issues further in the context of political change in Vietnam, I shall, firstly, consider the changes that took place under the umbrella of political liberalization from the late 1980s to the mid 1990s. Secondly, I explain why they took place, ask how they should best be interpreted and seek to cast light on the factors which led to such changes taking place at all. Thirdly, I offer an explanation of why democratization tendencies were not more radical and engage in some comparative analysis with Eastern Europe.

20.1 Political liberalization and its limits

The aim of this section is to explore both the extent and the limits of what has actually taken place in Vietnam. Consideration of possible explanations of why events happened as they did will follow in the next two sections.

Vietnamese conceptions of democracy

Although political systems dominated by a single party have proved to be vulnerable to abuse, we should not be too hasty in dismissing one-party conceptions of democracy as a contradiction in terms – not least because recognition of their existence is crucial to understanding the nature of political change in Vietnam. Central to Vietnamese conceptions of democracy is the idea of mass participation (see also Chapter 18). Although parallels can be drawn with Marxist–Leninist theory, this style of political organization owes its existence mostly to techniques of popular mobilization developed during the wars against the French and the USA. Traditionally, the mass organizations which involved broad segments of the population and represented all major social groupings such as the labour unions, women, youth, peasants, intellectuals and religious groups, were regarded as one of the main arms of the political system. Although the role of the mass organizations was to persuade their constituents to support official policy, they were also regarded as a way in which the CPV could keep in touch with its citizens. More often than not, when the Vietnamese elite use the word 'democracy', they were thinking of it in this mass-mobilizing sense. Consider, for instance, the comment of the director of the Central Committee's Propaganda and Training Department, Tran Trong Tan, in 1988:

> 'Broadening democracy means to ... mobilise various positive forces in society to participate in renovation.'

(Quoted in Turley, 1993, pp.262–3)

The other sense in which the elite used the word 'democracy' was to call for an increase in internal party democracy. However, again, the key point to note is that this was 'democracy' rooted in a one-party context.

On the other hand, it would be a mistake to see Vietnam's conception of democracy as something static, or entirely distinct from rival conceptions. Marx and Engels, for instance, regarded the liberal democratic struggle for political equality as a major step forward even if they went a stage further,

> ## Box 20.2 Leadership generations in Vietnamese political life
>
> 'Generations' – communist leaders are commonly classified on generational lines determined by the point at which they joined the party. In Vietnam, the first generation had their formative political experiences in 1925–35, remaining politically active often into the 1980s. The so-called 'one and a half' generation of slightly younger revolutionaries joined the party in the late 1930s, some of whom still held top offices in the mid 1990s. The second generation was recruited from the hundreds of thousands who joined patriotic groups in 1945. Although many died in battle or were purged in the 1950s, they became the vital middle echelon of the party, state and military hierarchies, remaining dominant until the 1980s. A third generation was recruited during the mobilization drives of the early 1950s. In the late 1980s/early 1990s, this generation commonly managed state-owned enterprises and held senior positions in the military.
>
> In other respects Vietnamese political life was largely conducted within the structures outlined in Chapter 17.

stressing the importance of democratization in the economic sphere. Moreover, the Vietnamese leadership had to face up to the failings of the political system, which involved drawing on diverse resources. Although one should not lose sight of the mass-mobilizing tradition, the reforms of the late 1980s and early 1990s embodied at least the beginnings of what may prove to be a gradual move towards recognizing the importance of a number of what may be regarded as classically liberal ideas, such as a representative elected assembly; freedom of expression; and the principle of the limited state and a separation between the public and private spheres (Beetham, 1993, pp.56–7).

One example will suffice here to illustrate the way in which rival conceptions of democracy were beginning to be superimposd on one another in Vietnam. Writing in the CPV's journal, *Tap Chi Cong San* (*Communist Review*) in January 1989, theoretician Nguyen Dang Quang called for a reassessment of 'bourgeois democracy', including freedoms of speech, press, and assembly. Vietnam's concept of socialism, Quang wrote: 'must include achievements scored by the modern bourgeois state, including the systemization of democracy, law, and human rights' (quoted in Porter, 1993, p.97). (There is no question that Quang was thinking of democracy in anything other than the one-party sense.)

The rejection of multipartyism

Given my comments so far, it should be clear that by classifying political changes in Vietnam up to the mid 1990s under the umbrella of liberalization, there is little room for a discussion of multipartyism. Indeed, my understanding of liberalization – as distinct from democratic reform – leaves *no* room for it. This is not to suggest that there were no calls for multiparty politics. There were, with the deputy editor of the party daily newspaper *Nhan Dan*, Colonel Bui Tin, now living in France, among the most prominent. Similar views have also been widely attributed to politburo member Tran Xuan Bach, who was dismissed from his post in March 1990. However, such voices were generally rare. Like Bach, they were quickly sidelined, and their calls not heeded. Thus, to emphasize, there is no sense in which the liberalization process was extended to incorporate change along multiparty lines.

Defending the old system

The first officially instituted move towards 'economic reform' can be linked to the decision taken at the sixth plenum of the Fourth Central Committee in August 1979. By way of a *post facto* response to what was already beginning to take place, peasant households were permitted to sell output produced above the amount agreed with the co-operative on the open market, and there were concessions to industry and foreign trade.

As part of a gradual shift towards recognizing the private household as the key agricultural producing unit, the decisions taken at this time have had profound political consequences (discussed below). However, official moves of an overtly political nature (i.e. recognizing the need for changes to how political life is structured) were not evident until some time later. Indeed, the essentially conservative nature of these early changes – concessions to defend the core elements of the central plan and existing institutions – should be stressed: 'In reality, conservatism drove this program in the early 1980s, with continued Stalinization of everyday life (restricting contacts with foreigners, limiting access to information etc.) and thinly disguised hostility to the free market and the private sector' (Fforde, 1993, p.301).

In delineating the change process in Vietnam there should not be too much emphasis placed on defining moments. Change tended to be evolutionary, and there was never a 'Damascus road' style conversion on the part of the leadership. One event attributed such landmark status is the Sixth Party Congress in December 1986, when *doi moi* (renovation) is regarded as having been launched. However, it is doubtful that the actual content of *doi moi* was known at the time of the Congress, with some crucial decisions not made until 1988.

The first steps towards political liberalization

Notwithstanding this caveat, it is difficult, when considering overt *political* change, to date its emergence much before the Sixth Party Congress. In May 1986, politburo member Le Duc Tho published an article in which he highlighted CPV shortcomings, writing of the existence of corruption at all levels. However, this was only seven months before the Congress opened, and quite unprecedented.

At the Sixth Congress, this line was nevertheless sustained. The political report issued at the meeting stated unequivocally that there had been a failure of party leadership. Although there was to be no diminution of the CPV's leading role, the report argued that party committees should no longer 'run the whole show' (Communist Party of Vietnam, 1987). Consequently, the Sixth Party Congress set in train a number of changes, which have come to characterize the liberalization process. These included:

Economic reforms have brought US, Japanese and Korean firms to Vietnam as the country seeks 'most favoured nation' trading status with the USA

- improving party leadership, and clamping down on the abuse of power;
- more clearly separating the tasks of the party from the government, including at the local level:
- revitalizing the mass-organizations;
- affording a greater role to the National Assembly, the country's parliament, thereby strengthening the rule of law; and
- encouraging greater openness in the media and public debate.

Let us briefly consider these issues.

Reinvigorating the party

Following the official criticism of the party which emerged in 1986, the leadership launched a campaign against corruption and incompetence in its ranks, with citizens encouraged to highlight abuses of power. The numbers affected by the campaign were not insignificant, with 127,800 party members disciplined, of whom 78,200 were expelled between 1987 and 1991. If in less dramatic form, the essence of the campaign – to ensure that party cadres operate within the law – was sustained into the 1990s. Another element to party reform included attempts to increase internal party democracy. Greater competition for posts was encouraged. At the Seventh Party Congress in 1991, the procedure for electing party officials was altered with the traditional show of hands replaced by a secret ballot.

Party–government relations

Recognition of the fact that the party had come to 'control the whole show' in a way which was unhealthy led to efforts to more clearly distinguish between the role of the party and the government, both centrally and locally. This was emphasized at the Sixth Party Congress, while the constitution, which was redrafted in 1992, described the party as the 'force assuming leadership of the state and society' (Socialist Republic of Vietnam 1992, Article 4). Previously, it was described as the 'only force'. The reforms also stressed that the party was supposed to set broad policy goals, while the state was responsible for day-to-day administration and policy application. In 1989, steps were taken to reform the People's Councils and People's Committees. They were originally intended to institutionalize popular participation in local government, but had become dominated by party chapters. Specifically, the reforms sought to increase the power of the directly elected councils in relation to their standing executive bodies, the committees.

Revitalizing the mass organizations

Following the Sixth Congress, the operating of the mass organizations was criticized as being undemocratic and bureaucratic. This prompted efforts to make them more responsive to their memberships. In 1988, a congress of the Vietnamese General Confederation of Trade Unions voted to replace around 70 per cent of those on its executive committee. Also in 1988, the Vietnam Collective Peasant's Association (now Vietnam Peasants' Union) held its first ever national congress.

Strengthening the National Assembly

Another dimension to efforts to more clearly delineate the roles of the party and the government was the emergence of the popularly elected National Assembly as a body scrutinizing the activities and policies of the government. By the early 1990s, debate was frequently heated, and it was commonplace for government legislation to be subjected to major revision. Via the Constituent Delegation System, the assembly was also more in touch with the grass-roots. This revitalization was also evident in the election of assembly deputies. Although all candidates had to be approved by the Vietnam Fatherland Front (the umbrella mass organization), the process became more open, deputies were younger and better educated, and the concept of 'independent' candidates (i.e. non-party members) began to emerge. In the 1992 election all posts were contested.

Encouraging public debate

As part of the party's attempts to tackle the abuse of power within its ranks, the press has been permitted to be more critical of the established order. An early pioneer included the newspaper, *Tuoi Tre* (Youth), which opened a complaints department with reporters assigned to investigate readers' problems. One author has written of the 'effective destalinization of everyday life', which took place from 1986, reflected in greater access to information, easier contact with foreigners, and a relaxation of party control of the media, culture and entertainment (Williams, 1992, pp.27–9). Also evident was a more tolerant party approach towards religion. Overall, therefore, new thoughts, whether home-bred or imported, had a greater chance of being heard and reflected on.

Liberalization's limits

When considering the changes detailed above, it is, however, important to be aware of their limitations. Something similar to a formal versus substantive definition of democracy is helpful in this regard. Thus even though the CPV instigated the introduction of some changes designed to increase partici- pation, representation, and accountability – including the institutional development to match – the party continued to impose limits on this process. There were also occasions when the party, fearing where change might be leading, applied the brakes. Such a clampdown took place in the latter part of 1989 when those deemed too critical were arrested, editors were dismissed, periodicals closed, and associations exhibiting too much autonomy given a party relaunch.

The Seventh Congress incorporated a similar 'drawing a line in the sand', when the party asserted its opposition to multiparty politics, and its right to retain monopoly power:

> There can be no democracy without centralism, without State discipline and order, without civic responsibility. Democracy must go hand in hand with the law ... In the context of this country, there is no objective need to establish a pluralistic political mechanism, a multiparty system with opposition parties. Recognition of a multiparty system with opposition parties means facilitating the immediate and lawful surfacing of the forces of reaction and revenge living in the country or returning from abroad to act against our homeland, our people, our regime. This is something that our people will never accept.

> (Communist Party of Vietnam, 1991, pp.22–3)

Examples of the limitations of liberalization with the party continuing to 'lead' and the government 'implementing' were easily found. Nearly all cabinet members, for instance, continued to sit on the CPV central committee, and in excess of 90 per cent of National Assembly delegates were party members. Also, of the 36 self-nominated 'independent' candidates, who applied to stand in the parliamentary elections in 1992, only two qualified for the final voting, neither of whom were elected.

Co-optation or imprisonment

One should also note limits to the degree to which new forces were 'accommodated'. Prevalent was a desire by the party to group all social organizations under the umbrella of the Vietnam Fatherland Front. Those, which exhibited or demanded too much autonomy, were not tolerated. For example, one outspoken group, the Club of Former Resistance Fighters, which was formed in 1986 (although some sources say 1983) in Ho Chi Minh City calling for the serious implementation of reform (not, it should be stressed, multiparty politics), was relaunched in 1990 as the Veterans Associations under the VFF umbrella. The party was also frequently in conflict with the United Buddhist Church (UBC), which resisted incorporation in the officially sponsored Vietnam Buddhist Church, leading to the detention of UBC leaders.

––––––––––––––––– *Summary of Section 20.1* –––––––––––––––––

- There was no sense in which liberalization was extended during the first half of the 1990s to incorporate change on multiparty lines.
- Overt political reforms emerged from 1986.
- A key theme was that the Communist Party should no longer 'run the whole show'.
- More internal party democracy, revitalized mass organizations, a strengthened National Assembly, and greater public debate were other prominent features.
- However, the party sought to limit liberalization through co-optation and arrests.

20.2 Explaining liberalization

In considering how tendencies for liberalization are best explained, it is important to make a distinction between:

1   factors which are conducive to the existence of democracy; and

2   why and how such conditions emerge, or do not emerge.

By identifying the importance of a balance between state and societal forces, a strong party system, vigorous legislatures and judiciaries, modernization theorists, like Diamond, perform well on the first point (Diamond *et al.*, 1989). However, they shed much less light on the second. For instance, how and why does a country develop a strong party system, a vigorous legislature and so on?

More enlightening on this second – and arguably more important – point are the transition theorists, with the elaboration of Rustow's writing by Mainwaring, O'Donnell and Valenzuela particularly helpful (Mainwaring *et al.*, 1992). Although the Latin American origins of this latter work gives their analysis a 'dramatic content' which was not evident in Vietnam, their emphasis on the choices and actions of political elites, on differences between elites, and on liberalization triggered by crisis, all ring true. They also do not lose sight of the fact that decisions by agents are influenced by structures.

For guidance on the structural context, we can also usefully consider the findings of Rueschemeyer *et al.* (1992). Their focus on transnational factors and the role of the state, along with their review of the attitude of different classes to democratization are helpful. In particular, their suggestions that historically the peasantry have generally been a weak force for democratization, and that the role of the urban bourgeoisie and the salaried and professional middle classes has been somewhat ambiguous would appear to be worth pursuing in the Vietnamese context.

While emphasizing the crucial role played by political elites, we should not, however, lose sight of the fact that such elites – prompted to begin liberalization in a context of crisis – may in part be responding to pressures 'from below'. As will become clear, such an observation is applicable in the Vietnamese case. The key distinction to make, however, is between elites *choosing* to make adjustments in light of such pressures, and elites being forced to make changes far beyond their wishes in face of popular pressure.

Capitalism and democracy

Some of the explanatory factors used to account for democratization seem to be particularly relevant to the Vietnamese situation as well as occupying a prominent place in several theoretical approaches. Most theories considering issues of democratization posit a link between capitalist economic development and democracy, which, as long as the relationship is not viewed in a deterministic way, is legitimate. Diamond, thinking particularly of South Korea, talks of the 'pressures and props' for democracy which derive from a higher level of socio-economic development. He particularly notes an increase in political participation resulting from higher income and education (Diamond *et al.*, 1989, pp.33–5).

Rueschemeyer, meanwhile, writes of capitalist-induced urbanization, improved means of communication and levels of literacy furthering the growth of 'civil society'. This, in turn, establishes a 'counterweight to state power', which is conducive to democracy (Rueschemeyer *et al.*, 1992, p.6). Writing on Indonesia, Robison argues that the state gradually came under pressure from increasingly powerful middle and capital-owning classes, who began to object to the economic and social controls imposed by the government. This led to a weakening of the 'pact of domination' between the military bureaucratic state and leading capitalists, with positive implications for democracy (Robison, 1988, pp.52–74). Whether by reference to the historical emergence of democracy in the West, or to the experiences of Taiwan or South Korea, scholars advancing these kinds of argument generally recognize – quite rightly – that it can be many years before such capitalism-induced developments effect the ordering of political life.

Redefining civil society

Where the existing theoretical literature offers less guidance is in 'unpacking' what precisely is going on during these long years – when capitalist productive relations are in full swing but there is no move towards democracy. Part of the answer lies with the fact that other factors can intervene to prevent democratization (i.e. there is no deterministic link between capitalism and democracy). Also, it takes time before middle and

The widening financial gap between peasantry and the urban bourgeoisie: an old peasant begs for money in Ho Chi Minh City

capital-owning classes are strong enough to press for political change. The role of another of our explanatory factors – that of civil society – here gains particular significance and repays quite careful study.

As will be seen with reference to Vietnam, something *resembling* 'civil society' groups start to emerge quite quickly once market-oriented reforms are introduced – even if we must be careful to define their characteristics precisely. Their existence prompts the question: 'How are such groups relating to the state if they are not pressing for democratic change?' Scholars such as Diamond *et al.*, Rueschemeyer *et al.*, and Robison do not address this. However, an answer is necessary if the dynamics of the liberalization process in Vietnam are to be more clearly laid out.

Theoretical clarification on this issue is available in writing on China, which has much in the way of insights of relevance to Vietnam. Here, civil society – in the sense of a separation between state and society, a distinct public and private sphere, or autonomous social organizations – has been detected only in the most embryonic of forms. Instead, the impetus for the formation of new social organizations, such as groups representing private business, labourers, consumers, etc. (i.e. many derived from the expansion of capitalist activity) is seen largely as coming from *above*.

Consequently, such organizations embody contradictory elements (White, 1993, pp.85–6):

1   They incorporate a mixture of public and private in which the public is predominant.

2   They have a limited degree of autonomy, although they cannot be described as independent.

3   They are not entirely subordinate to their bureaucratic 'minders', although they cannot be described as pressure or interest groups.

4   Membership cannot be described as voluntary, although there are voluntary elements.

Two additional points can be made. First, these organizations are largely non-political (at least in the short term). Second, they are quite different from old-style mass organizations, which often were mere links in 'a chain of hierarchical statist controls'. With reference to China, White is therefore doubtful about theories that afford civil society – in the traditional sense mentioned above – special prominence among factors driving democratization at the outset. Civil society, he argues, has only a minor role to play during the liberalization process. Similar doubts have been expressed in writing on Eastern Europe about the significance of the role of civil society in undermining communist rule (see Chapter 16).

When considering the factors which led to change, it is useful to break the question down. First, what factors prompted the move towards political liberalization? Second, what does the leadership see liberalization as achieving (i.e. why does it regard it as necessary)?

When considering the first, one might focus on domestic crises, pressures on the leadership stemming from intra- and extra-party differences, and on international factors, such as the crisis of international communism. With regard to the second, the focus is more on the outlook and philosophy of the ruling elite, in particular their sense of the need to reverse the loss of faith in the CPV both within its own ranks and among the population at large.

I would like, however, to continue my discussion of why political liberalization emerged by relating it to the decisions, touched on briefly, to introduce limited economic changes from the late 1970s. That this is not the only entry point – pressure for political change was also justified in its own right – will become apparent. However, it is an appropriate starting point.

Change prompted by crisis

The idea of a crisis prompting the adoption of initial economic adjustments was very evident in the Vietnamese case. Against a backdrop of an already dire economic performance, one can point to such factors as the weather-induced crop failures of the late 1970s; the legacy of decades of war; renewed war with the Khmer Rouge and China; and the loss of Soviet aid in the 1980s. The USA had maintained an economic blockade of the country since the failure of its intervention in the mid 1970s, so the subsequent loss of Soviet aid was a particularly important blow. Also important was the way in which the early changes represented a response to 'pressures from below' – that is the breakdown of agricultural co-operatives, and the so-called 'fence breaking' of state-owned enterprises (SOEs), which started to develop relations with suppliers and customers outside the central plan, including direct links with foreign markets.

However, we can be more specific about where this 'pressure from below' was coming from, namely that it was the lower echelons of the *state*, including SOE managers, who 'fence broke' (Beresford, 1995, p.9). Even if they were in part responding to grass-root discontent, there was a clear sense in which pressure on the party at the centre was coming from *within* its own ranks. Many of those managing SOEs were recruited as a 'third generation' of party members in the early 1950s.

Political change prompted by economic factors

What, then, is the link between this and the adoption of political liberalization? Initially, as has been emphasized, there was no link. Remember Fforde's comment that to begin with the 'Stalinization of everyday life' continued. However, by the Sixth Congress in 1986 (possibly earlier), many in the leadership recognized that economic changes could not be carried out without some political adjustments. For instance, creating a legal framework necessary for a market-oriented economy – particularly one in which foreign investors were to participate – required upgrading the law-making authority of the National Assembly, which in turn required subjecting the CPV to the rule of law, and distinguishing more clearly between the role of party and the government. A particularly explicit statement of the need for political adjustments to accompany economic reforms was contained in the fifth plenum resolution of 1988, which noted the impossibility of: 'effect[ing] renovation in the economic, social, security and national defence fields without reforming the political system. The outstanding problem here is to distinguish the party's function of leadership from the state's function of management'. The resolution, it should be emphasized, only called for political adjustments of a limited kind. There was no suggestion that because Vietnam has shifted to a multisectoral economy, it should allow pluralism in political parties and ideology as well, although some within the party possibly did believe this.

Political change for its own sake

The need for political change was also justified in its own right – namely that it was necessary to reverse the loss of faith in the party. In 1989, CPV General Secretary Nguyen Van Linh lamented the scepticism in party ranks about the usefulness of Marxism–Leninism itself. Moreover, popular disaffection was evident in declining rates of party recruitment, with membership of the Ho Chi Minh Communist Youth Union – commonly a first step to party membership – down to below 2 million in 1992, from 4.7 million five years earlier. According to official figures, there was a big increase in party recruitment proper in 1994, when 60,000 new members joined, compared with 37,500 in 1992 and 48,000 in 1993. This emphasis on elite decision making is crucial. Although economic renovation had certain spontaneous features, on the political side it was initiated entirely by the top echelons of the party.

This is not to say that senior leaders were immune to outside influences. Pressure for political change can clearly be seen coming from beyond the immediate ranks of the senior leadership. Two questions are important here: First, where precisely was this pressure coming from? Second, what impact did it have on the ruling elite's decision making?

Responding to elite pressures

On the question of where pressure for political change has come from, it is again appropriate to stress its elite origins. In Vietnam, there was nothing resembling the 'broad social movements' evident in Eastern Europe from the late 1980s and discussed in Chapter 16. Instead, pressure predominantly came from within party ranks, and from that other elite group, intellectuals, many of whom were also party members or former party members. Earlier, the criticisms of the former deputy editor of *Nhan Dan*, Bui Tin were mentioned. Also noted were the Club of Former Resistance Fighters, whose criticisms should particularly be regarded as coming from within the party.

Other critics included: intellectual and party member Nguyen Khac Vien, who criticized the party's interference in state affairs, and pressed for greater freedom of the press, thought and assembly. Other major figures were: writer and party member (until she was expelled) Duong Thu Huong, who wrote of how war veterans were disillusioned after the long years of struggle as they were now living in an unfree and poor society (a common theme in Vietnamese literature of this period), and former party activist and southern intellectual Lu Phuong, who questioned whether the party had to adhere to Marxism-Leninism simply because it was introduced by its founding father Ho Chi Minh.

As noted earlier, the statements of critics were generally moderate – rarely calling for the overthrow of socialism or for multiparty democracy. Rather, they pressed for greater internal party democracy, more personal freedom, making the existing system work better, and so on. However, no one ever threatened to leave the party taking a faction with them, like Boris Yeltsin in the then Soviet Union.

Given that much discussion went on behind closed doors, the precise impact criticism had on elite decision making is hard to gauge. There was certainly a sense in which criticism demanded a response by the party, although the degree of influence critics have had to a large extent was determined by the nature of their message and the way in which it has been delivered. Public exhortations of a more radical nature broadcast on the BBC World Service by Bui Tin tended to be dismissed out of hand. Arguably, more moderate criticism delivered less publicly by someone like Nguyen Khac Vien had a significant effect. That said, there is little evidence to suggest that the party leadership was pushed to make decisions in the political sphere it did not wish to.

The crisis of international communism

The other area which deserves consideration at this juncture in terms of factors influencing political liberalization are developments on the international stage. A number of authors have emphasized the shock which events in Eastern Europe and the Soviet Union caused the Vietnamese leadership, and the onus it placed on it to explain why Vietnam was different (Williams, 1992, pp.66, 85). Others have stressed the way in which events in Eastern Europe and the Soviet Union – notably Mikhail Gorbachev's emergence – led to ideological doubt in Vietnam and created openings for political dissent.

At the same time, reform in Vietnam (both economic and political) predated the turmoil within European communism of the late 1980s/early 1990s – underlining the importance of domestic dynamics. That said, it was no coincidence that the party's application of the brakes in terms of curbing the (relative) climate of outspokenness which had developed by 1989 came hot on the heels of events in Europe, and also in neighbouring China, where in June 1989 the Chinese Communist Party had opened fire at Tienanmen Square on student and other demonstrators pressing for political change. The rejection of multiparty democracy which emerged so strongly at the Seventh Congress in 1991 can also be related to conclusions drawn by the party about events in other formerly communist party-led countries.

However, this line of argument should not be pursued too far. In many respects, turmoil affecting once fraternal parties merely reinforced already deeply held political beliefs of the Vietnamese leadership. Indeed, the 'late 1989 clampdown' can be seen getting underway before the key events in Eastern Europe and China, notably with the dismissal in 1988 of the editor of *Van Nghe* (Literature and Art), Nguyen Ngoc, following his publication of politically risque short stories by writer Nguyen Huy Thiep.

─────────────────── *Summary of Section 20.2* ───────────────────

- Writings on civil society in China may have something to offer with reference to Vietnam.
- Political liberalization in Vietnam emerged against a backdrop of economic crisis, demanding in the party's view a limited political response.
- Liberalization was also designed to reverse the loss of faith in the party.
- Although change was initiated entirely from the top with spontaneity or pressure from broad social movements absent, the ruling elite was not immune to 'outside' influences.
- However, pressure for change predominantly comes from other elites, generally within the party.
- International factors strengthened the leadership's conviction that limited political reform was the right approach.

20.3 How far can political change go?

That Vietnam followed a markedly different route to Eastern European communist regimes is worth reflecting on. In the context of seeking to explain tendencies towards democratization, consideration of this issue should help us highlight some of the factors limiting democratization in Vietnam. After the focus on the role of the agent in the last section, here the emphasis will shift more towards longer term structural factors. However, as I think is appropriate, the agent's contribution will never be far away.

One explanation (among many) offered as to why Vietnam pursued a more limited liberalization process concerns the fact that after Ho Chi Minh's death in 1969, the country relied on a 'collective leadership' with no single leader inheriting his mantle of authority (Williams, 1992, p.24). In addition, the hold of the first generation of CPV leaders on power was only just breaking by the end of the 1980s as they grew old and died. However, many still exercised substantial influence, with the so-called 'one and a half' generations who had been with the revolution since the 1930s stepping into their shoes.

In addition, those in command had a profound sense of what they had fought for, which translated into a conservative approach to change. This can be contrasted with Eastern Europe where individual leaderships, with its heightened risk of elite-based crises, were commonplace, and where second or third generation leaders were running the show. In this section, I would like to consider four other issues, which go some way to offering an answer as to why democratization was more limited in Vietnam than Eastern Europe: the route to power; political culture; the approach to reform; and, something which we have touched on already, the international context.

The nationalist road to power

The key distinguishing factor between Vietnam and the Eastern European countries on this issue is that the CPV came to power after a 40 year nationalist struggle, which although it received assistance from China and the Soviet Union was essentially achieved by its own efforts. The regimes in Eastern Europe, on the other hand, were to a great extent established on the basis of Soviet military presence, and therefore lacked the same depth of support and legitimacy (although a sense of 'external imposition' was to some extent valid in the south of Vietnam: Womack, 1993).

Possibly more significant – once the CPV's revolutionary mantle became frayed – was the way in which during the long years of struggle alternative political forces in Vietnam had been eliminated either by the French, or by the communists. Remnants of the Vietnam Quoc Dan Dang (Vietnamese Nationalist Party), who were largely shattered by colonial repression in 1930, were further discredited when they entered Vietnam with Chinese nationalist troops after the Japanese surrender in 1945 (Porter, 1993, pp.7–13).

Political culture fashioned by conflict

Arguments about culture as a constraining (or enabling) factor for democratization need to be made cautiously. After all, we can argue that Western European countries lacked a democratic tradition – if we look far enough back – and yet they developed democracy. Moreover, arguments suggesting that Confucianism (see Chapter 8) with its emphasis on harmony and respect for elders works to perpetuate undemocratic political systems are problematic. How, then, does one explain the success of the communist movement founded by young men who believed in smashing the old order?

What one can say is that the legacy of centuries of struggle, notably against the Chinese, has created a praetorian quality to the organization of society, which is inimical to democracy (Pike, 1994, pp.2–5). Such tendencies have been reinforced by more recent wars. A state resting on this kind of social basis involves a form of politics that is weakly institutionalized and where shifting power resources impinge directly on the form and structure of political relations. However, like any other factor, the existence of a particular cultural trait is not determinative. A contrast with Eastern Europe on this issue, while to some extent valid, should not be overdone. Prior to 1945, only Czechoslovakia had anything resembling democracy.

A pragmatic approach to reform

In a speech to the National Assembly in December 1989, one senior leader argued that Eastern European regimes had collapsed because they had adapted too slowly to the information explosion; violated the principles of 'socialist democracy' (i.e. sought wider support on pluralist rather than on mobilizational principles); and clung too long to an outmoded economic model. There were errors, he said, that Vietnam would not commit. With reference to Eastern Europe, it is certainly possible to point to events like the Hungarian revolution of 1956 and the 'Prague Spring' of 1968, and note the way in which repression and inaction by communist leaderships radicalized reformers and created pent-up forces, which led to rapid political change in the late 1980s.

In Vietnam, by contrast, the struggle to unify the country hid the system's structural flaws and delayed the emergence of reformist sentiment (and hence the need for its containment). It is also striking how the generally moderate tone of internal party critics in Vietnam up to the mid 1990s – favourable to the continuation of a leading role for the party – had similarities with voices raised in Eastern Europe in the 1950s and 1960s (Womack, 1993, pp.278–9).

It is also worth emphasizing the way in which the central plan in Vietnam deviated from the classic Soviet model. The plan was never imposed in a straightforward 'top down' way but rather emerged as the result of negotiation between groups with differing interests. This relative *decentralization* can be related to the fact that in the centuries-long struggle against foreign invaders a certain amount of authority had always to be devolved to lower levels (Beresford, 1995, pp.5–6). However, it gave the system a certain flexibility, and in time made change easier.

The Southeast Asia 'model'

A contrast with the Eastern European communist regimes can be drawn in terms of regional context. Whereas the East European regimes were situated next to economically successful Western liberal democracies, the Vietnamese communist party existed in a regional environment where the one-party model had recently been the predominant one. Yet these countries were also flourishing economically. Vietnam's membership of the Association of Southeast Asian Nations (ASEAN) in July 1995 further strengthened its association with a group of countries where one-party rule was still sanctioned, or had been until relatively recently.

The instability of political liberalization

While liberalization may represent a limited form of political change it may carry the seeds of further transformation within itself. As a process, liberalization – accommodating new forces while maintaining the existing political configuration – is inherently unstable and embodies contradictory elements. It is worth considering, for example; how far the CPV really could be subject to the rule of law, and where the party's relationship with the government, the mass organizations, and the National Assembly was actually leading?

With all these institutions, the reforms emphasized the importance of the party affording them greater autonomy. Although there was considerable overlap between the party and these bodies during the period under examination, the relationship between the party and the National Assembly could no longer be captured in a strict one-way hierarchical notion of communication. Moreover, debate in the Assembly was beginning to reflect differences within the party, *beyond the control of democratic centralism*. In this sense, a process of institutionalization conducive to future democratization was underway.

Implications of the development of 'civil society'

Some societal changes evident in the early 1990s, which might ultimately lead to pressure for democratization in the multiparty sense, could also be related to contradictions arising from capitalist-style economic development, namely the emergence of new classes and the implications this had for the development of civil society. It was earlier argued that although the assertions made by Diamond *et al.*, Rueschemeyer *et al.*, and Robison about the relationship between capitalism and democracy must be accepted, the 'process' could be unpacked more. When considering how new classes which emerged with the capitalist mode of production *were* relating to the state – if they were not pushing for democracy – a typology which argued that civil society in the sense of social organizations with distinct autonomy from the state was rare to non-existent. was presented. Instead, it was emphasized that such organizations embodied contradictory elements, and, at least initially, were not overtly political.

Vietnamese women sit in front of a row of newly-built houses in Hanoi

This approach has much to recommend it with reference to Vietnam. By the early 1990s, new classes were emerging on the back of market-oriented economic reform and social processes were clearly marked by the influence of international agencies like the IMF and closer engagement with global economic processes. As one scholar wrote in 1993:

> Phenomena such as peasant households, private industries, service activities, growing foreign investments, decentralised contacts with foreign firms, Western aid, and the information flow that these structures generate, are all bound to have effects on the class character of the society and lead to the formation of diversified interest groups. Peasant associations, chambers of commerce, bar associations, and other coalitions of interest will demand to be allowed to have a voice or express dissent.

(Ljunggren, 1993, p.373)

Although emphasizing the weakness of extra-bureaucratic forces, others have noted the emergence of 'new entrepreneurial classes', mainly, although not exclusively, in the commercial centre around Ho Chi Minh City during the 1990s.

A broadening of social space

In association with these developments it is indisputable that in the early 1990s new social space was emerging. We noted how a group like the chambers of commerce was qualitatively different from the old-style mass organizations. Also, there is a sense in which extra-bureaucratic business interests were exercising increasing influence, although it is hard to provide substantive evidence. Furthermore, while the party's influence remained strong, it was no longer the only route to success and status. Employment with a foreign company offered, for example, an alternative.

Also relevant as one considers factors constraining or enabling democratization in Vietnam was the youthfulness of Vietnam's population. In 1994, some 39 per cent were under the age of fifteen. Thus, by the mid 1990s, there had emerged a new generation with little or no memory of the Stalinization of everyday life, and whose values were very different from their parents. Increasingly, one could expect them to take present-day liberties for granted, and possibly expect more.

Mass mobilization in the new era

Until now, I have focused on the emergence of new social forces but it is also possible to point to changes within the mass organizations, which were granted greater organizational independence from the party under liberalization. With reference to China in the early 1990s, White (1993, p.74) argues that mass organizations were exploring new roles, and seeking greater independence. This was partly a reflection of the more permissive reform environment but it also represented a response to the impact of rapid socio-economic changes on mass organizations constituencies. A good example would be organized labour, which it is worth recalling played a significant role in East Asian democratization.

In early 1990s Vietnam, it is difficult to identify substantive differences between labour unions and the government. However, with infinitely more complex labour relations in the reform era, some commentators were beginning to argue that the potential was there. In 1995, for instance, the government hesitated before eventually conceding to union calls for a raising of the minimum wage payable by foreign companies.

The 'political' social organizations

However, when considering democratization tendencies. It is important to emphasize the largely non-political nature of these groups in this period. Consider, for instance, a group like the chambers of commerce. In 1995, there were six such groups in Vietnam in Hanoi, Ho Chi Minh City, Danang, Vung Tau, and Can Tho, although only the first two were officially regarded as 'fully fledged'. Moreover, membership was small, with little over one thousand members nationwide, of which the majority represented 'state' companies. In addition, in keeping with the typology mapped out above, chambers of commerce were established by the state. They cannot be described as independent, or as pressure groups but rather they acted more as an information and advice centre. Nevertheless, they represented something different from old-style mass organizations, and were not mere links in a state-dominated, hierarchical chain of command (Gainsborough, 1995).

Similarly, however, it is inappropriate to see Vietnam's up-and-coming urban bourgeoisie, or the salaried and professional middle classes in the early 1990s – who Rueschemeyer *et al.*, note as historically having been ambivalent towards democracy – as overtly pushing for democratization. To advance such an argument would be to underestimate both the extent to which the party was still pervasive, and the central role played by 'state' in the economy – notwithstanding recent changes. Advancement was still highly dependent on who you knew. Thus, for a private business people seeking licences to operate or diversify, access to export quotas or raw materials, cultivating contacts with the authorities was essential (Gainsborough, 1995).

—————————————— *Summary of Section 20.3* ——————————————

- Vietnam's collective leadership has reduced the risk of elite crises associated with personal leadership structures.

- The nationalist struggle gave the party a legitimacy that even post-1975 failings did not wipe out.

- A largely pragmatic approach to economic reform has prevented the build-up of discontent, or the radicalization of critics.

- Vietnam is able to draw comfort from the popularity of the one-party model among fellow elites in Southeast Asia.

- The limitations of liberalization as a form of change were not necessarily impenetrable.

- Continuing economic development carried implications for the development of civil society and further, although still limited, forms of political change.

Conclusion

Liberalization in Vietnam was a form of political change that involved greater account being taken by power holders of the population's interests and demands but stopped short of institutional transformation. It was very much an elite based form of change and reflected the leadership's response to a range of changes in economic and political conditions. Several features of Vietnamese communism helped maintain the limitations of liberalization as a form of political change, although the implications of capitalist development for the strengthening of civil society seemed likely to broaden the scope of political change. Throughout this chapter, I have emphasized the essentially limited nature of political change in Vietnam in the late 1980s and early 1990s – liberalization rather than democratization. Drawing on Mainwaring *et al.*, I have also emphasized the elite origins of political change with any pressure from broad social movements being largely absent (although there was some spontaneity with regard to economic change – the so-called 'fence-breaking'). While the ruling elite was not immune to 'outside' influences, the key point is that pressure for change predominantly came from other elites, generally within the party.

The appropriateness of the transition approach of Mainwaring *et al.*, to the Vietnamese case should not be overemphasized however. For instance, the focus of these authors on the interplay between regime and opposition forces, including hardliners and softliners within the ruling elite, and opportunists, moderates, and maximalists in the opposition, may be of limited relevance. First, talk of an opposition is rooted in the Latin American experience in a way which was inapplicable to Vietnam up to the mid 1990s. Second, distinctions between hard and softliners are overly simplistic, with the same individual quite likely to be 'hard' on one issue and 'soft' on another (Dang Phong, 1995, p.21).

A range of factors go some way to explaining why developments in Vietnam did not go further, such as the route to power; political culture; the approach to reform; and the international context. Also, given the peasantry's historical reputation as a weak force for democratization, the predominantly rural nature of Vietnamese society points to a further constraint on democratization. Reference to the 'late softening' of authoritarianism in Taiwan (or South Korea) long after economic take-off and the point at which living standards began to rise represents a precedent which may also be relevant in explaining the Vietnamese case (Wade, 1990, pp.253–4).

Throughout this chapter, I have emphasized that any sort of 'historical moment' where the party 'bites the bullet' of multiparty politics looked a distant prospect in Vietnam in the mid 1990s – not least because for historical reasons alternative political forces were hardly in evidence. However, we have noted the tolerance at this time of *approved* non-party members as National Assembly candidates, and how the Assembly came to reflect party differences beyond the control of democratic centralism. Some authors not unreasonably have seen these changes as potentially laying the foundations for political pluralism. On the other hand, it is more appropriate to stress the obstacles to the emergence of new political parties at this time, with repression by the party guaranteed for any group which aspired to such status.

Even if – in the future – the party adopted a more permissive attitude, any aspiring political group would find it hard to counter the CPV's nationalist credentials reinforced – by the early 1990s – by a not unimpressive economic record.

The process of political change in Vietnam thus emerges as a distinctive one, its path of liberalization different from the democratization seen both in the former communist states of Eastern Europe and in neighbouring Asian countries. A number of factors were associated with this. In relation to the Eastern European regimes Vietnam had a different structure of communist rule (it had been less subject to direct Soviet influence although economic ties had been very important) and it had not seen the development of social movements which articulated currents of political opposition. In distinction to some other countries the process of market-oriented economic development in Vietnam was belated and less advanced. It already had some form of socialist (although not liberal) democracy and a political regime which had considerable reserves of legitimacy. Further political change (probably of a more radical nature) is certainly likely to occur in Vietnam, but it may continue to be introduced gradually and is likely to be strongly marked by the characteristics of its domestic environment.

References

Beetham, D. (1993) 'Liberal democracy and the limits of democratization' in Held, D. (ed.) *Prospects for Democracy: North, South, East, West*, Cambridge, Polity Press.

Beresford, M. (1995) 'Interpretation of the Vietnamese economic reforms 1979–85' in *Researching the Vietnamese Economic Reforms: 1979–86*, Australia–Vietnam Research Project, Monograph series, no.1, January.

Chao, L. and Myers R.H. (1994) 'The first Chinese democracy: political development of the Republic of China on Taiwan, 1986–1994', *Asian Survey*, vol.34, no.3, March.

Communist Party of Vietnam (1987) *Sixth National Congress of the Communist Party of Vietnam: Documents*, Hanoi, Foreign Languages Publishing House.

Communist Party of Vietnam (1991) *Seventh National Congress of the Communist Party of Vietnam: Documents*, Hanoi, Foreign Languages Publishing House.

Dang Phong (1995) 'Viewing the decade 1976–86 in Vietnam vertically and horizontally' in *Researching the Vietnamese Economic Reforms: 1979–86*, Australia–Vietnam Research Project, Monograph series, no.1, January.

Diamond., Linz, J.J. and Lipset, S.M. (1989) *Democracy in Developing Countries, Vol.3, Asia*, Boulder, Lynne Rienner.

Economist Intelligence Unit (1995) *Vietnam*, Country Report, first quarter.

Emmerson, D.K. (1995) 'Region and recalcitrance: rethinking democracy through South-east Asia', *The Pacific Review*, vol.8, no.2.

Fforde, A. (1993) 'The political economy of "reform" in Vietnam – some reflections' in Ljunggren, B. (ed.) *The Challenge of Reform in Indochina*, Harvard, Institute for International Development.

Gainsborough, M. (1995) Interviews carried out in Hanoi, Ho Chi Minh City, and Tay Ninh with government officials, diplomats and businessmen, including a representative from the Chamber of Commerce and Industry of Vietnam, Ho Chi Minh City branch, March–April. Unpublished.

Lijphart, A. (1968) 'Typologies of democratic system', *Comparative Political Studies*, no.1.

Ljunggren, B. (1993) 'Concluding remarks: key issues in the reform process' in Ljunggren, B. (ed.) *The Challenge of Reform in Indochina*, Harvard, Institute for International Development.

Mainwaring, S., O'Donnell, G. and Valenzuela, J.S. (eds) (1992) *Issues in Democratic Consolidation: the New South American Democracies in Comparative Perspective*, Notre Dame, IN, University of Notre Dame Press.

Pike, D. (1994) 'Vietnam: its durability and its direction', paper presented at the international workshop on the durability and direction of China, Vietnam, Cuba and North Korea, organized by the Korean Association of International Studies and the Research Institute for National Unification, Seoul, South Korea, May.

Porter, G. (1993) *Vietnam: the Politics of Bureaucratic Socialism*, Ithaca, NY, Cornell University Press.

Robison, R. (1988) 'Authoritarian states, capital-owning classes, and the politics of newly industrialising countries: the case of Indonesia', *World Politics*, no.26.

Rueschemeyer, D., Stephens, E. and Stephens, J. (1992) *Capitalist Development and Democracy*, Cambridge, Polity Press.

Socialist Republic of Vietnam (1992) *Constitution of the Socialist Republic of Vietnam*, Hanoi, Foreign Languages Publishing House.

Thompson, M.R. (1993) 'The limits of democratisation in ASEAN', *Third World Quarterly*, vol.14, no.3.

Turley, W.S. (1993) 'Party, state, and people: political structure and economic prospects' in Turley, W.S. and Selden, M. (eds).

Turley, W.S. and Selden, M. (eds) (1993) *Reinventing Vietnamese Socialism: Doi Moi in Comparative Perspective*, Boulder, Westview Press.

Wade, R. (1990) *Governing the Market: Economic Theory and the Role of Government in East Asian Industrialisation*, Princeton, NJ, Princeton University Press.

White, G. (1993) 'Prospects for civil society in China: a case study of Xiaoshan City', *The Australian Journal of Chinese Studies*, no.29, January.

Williams, M.C. (1992) *Vietnam at the Crossroads*, Royal Institute of International Affairs, London, Pinter Publishers.

Womack, B. (1987) 'The party and the people: revolutionary and post-revolutionary politics in China and Vietnam', *World Politics*, vol.39, no.4.

Womack, B. (1993) 'Political reform and political change in communist countries: implications for Vietnam' in Turley, W.S. and Selden, M. (eds).

The author acknowledges the assistance of John Sidel from SOAS for his help and useful comments in preparing the first draft of this chapter.

Afterword

Paul Lewis

Part V has examined democratization in communist and post-communist countries, and each chapter has posed questions about particular aspects of the process. What kind of answers have been delivered? How far have they really answered the questions? This Afterword briefly surveys the last five chapters from this angle and casts an eye over the role played both by the theoretical approaches introduced in Chapter 1 and the explanatory factors deployed throughout the book. The point of this brief discussion, it should be emphasized, is to reconsider the main points of the last five chapters as a whole and draw a few links between the chapters rather than to provide an exhaustive recapitulation of the arguments presented.

The way in which democratization came on to the political agenda in Russia and Eastern Europe, and the main features of democratic change there, give clear indications of the theoretical framework within which explanations of post-communist democratization have tended to be approached. Communist revolution was intimately concerned with ideas of *modernization* and a guiding light of communist policy was the attempt, as successive Soviet leaders intimated, 'to catch up and overtake the West'. Communist achievements in this area were, however, mixed and it was the relative failure of the communist system to match the economic performance of developed capitalist countries and keep up with the accelerating pace of technological and military development that initially prompted Gorbachev to contemplate a broadening programme of economic and political change. Yet it was also the formation of a relatively modernized society that helped provide the conditions for a rapid transition to liberal democracy in at least some of the communist countries.

But the salience of the issue of modernization did not necessarily mean that post-communist democratization was best explained within the context of the modernization approach. The precise contribution that the modernization approach makes to our understanding of democratization in Russia and Eastern Europe was examined in Chapters 16, 17 and 18. Levels of modernization certainly showed an association with democratization (Chapter 16 and, more ambiguously, Chapter 17) but the links between the two processes in general terms were imprecise. A firmer grasp on the relationship between modernization and democratization could be reached when the form that modernization took in particular societies was examined and the impact, say, of economic development on class structure was examined more closely (as in Poland). Some links could be drawn (Chapter 18) between the effects of modernization and some aspects of political participation (education and voting, for example) but, once more, modernization failed to provide a convincing explanation of this aspect of democratization.

A feature of post-communist democratization that does suggest a strong link with another of the theoretical approaches employed in this book is the part played by political elites and the importance of choices made by particular leaders or leadership groups. The communist countries developed markedly hierarchical and elitist forms of rule and, in the absence of any significant decision-making input from the mass of the population or major system breakdown, there was generally no alternative source for political initiatives to come from. Elite strategy and the choices made by particular leaders were therefore of primary importance. It is difficult, for example, to imagine what the course of European communist history might have been like without the person of Gorbachev and the policies he developed and pursued during the 1980s. It is significant that the experience of communist regimes with respect to democratization in parts of the world less susceptible to direct Soviet decision-making influences, like Asia (especially China) and Latin America (Cuba), was considerably different. In this part, therefore, the *transition approach* received considerable attention in Chapters 16, 17 and 20, while characteristics of elite composition and political strategy were central to the discussion in Chapter 19.

Transition theory drawing on Latin American experience and focusing on the critical split between hardliners and reformist softliners had considerable resonance in the context of Hungary and Poland and helped explain the strong impetus and democratization in those countries (Chapter 16). In Russia, too, central decision making and elite choice were decisive and accounted for many of the processes that led to the collapse of the Soviet Union (Chapter 17) – although their contribution to any understanding of subsequent processes of democratization was (like any other one factor) rather limited. Political liberalization in Vietnam (Chapter 20) was also a process best understood in terms of changing elite attitudes and shifting leadership conceptions. But, while helping to explain much of the dynamics of change in communist systems, all such perspectives directed attention to short-term factors and elements of strategy and choice in situations formed by processes of long-term change. Their contribution to any explanation of democratization was, to this extent, also a qualified one.

The other main theoretical perspective used in the book, the *structural approach*, directing attention to long-term historical shifts in structures of power, received less attention in this part. The reason for this is largely self-evident and follows on from the observations made above: democratization in former communist states has so far been a short-term affair and was in large measure shaped by changes in elite strategy and driven by factors of leadership choice. That is not to say that structural change had not taken place in communist countries or that power relations remained static prior to democratization. The developments taken account of within the modernization approach themselves involve elements of structural change, while elite strategies similarly did not shift arbitrarily but did so in response to changing structures of power both nationally and internationally. Such factors have also been taken into account in the chapters in this part and links made between the different approaches where relevant. Historical perspectives were also not neglected, and the roots of nationalism and historical conditions for the emergence of 'consociational democracy' in the former Czechoslovakia and Yugoslavia were examined in Chapter 19.

None of the theoretical approaches used, therefore, gave a fully satisfactory answer to the questions posed in this part although, in combination, they often explained the major dynamics of democratization. In seeking to answer specific questions, too, one or more of the explanatory factors outlined in Chapter 1 proved useful in helping to construct an answer about democratization. The relative part played by different explanatory factors often emerges quite clearly from the overall characteristics of post-communist democratization identified above and indications of the theoretical perspectives discussed earlier in this Afterword. In terms of Russia and Eastern Europe (Chapters 16 and 17) the *international context* was of prime importance in terms of Soviet perceptions of its relative weakness and poor performance in areas of economics and technology. As a condition for this sharpening perception, the Cold War had dominated world politics to varying degrees since the late 1940s and remained a major determinant of communist policy until the 1980s. In Vietnam (Chapter 20) international pressures were also significant, although the foundations of the communist order were not undermined to the extent that measures were taken to create a liberal democracy. The nature and form of the subsequent democratization process was also strongly affected by international factors as communist and post-communist countries became further enmeshed in the global economy and the social consequences of economic restructuring impinged on political attitudes and activities (Chapter 18).

On a different plane, the development of *civil society* exerted an important domestic influence on democratization in some East European states (Chapter 16) and encouraged elements of liberalization within existing authoritarian regimes that generally opened the way to subsequent processes of democratization – although this further development was not apparent in Vietnam (Chapter 20). The existence of developed civil society has also proved to be a significant factor in sustaining and fostering the development of various liberal democratic practices and institutions through which democratic participation could be made effective (Chapter 18). *Political culture* was a closely related factor that influenced the kind of civil society that developed and the particular ideas and policies it articulated. The role of nationalism thus proved to be important in a number of countries (Chapter 19), and elements of national culture like religious sentiment and practice also proved to be highly significant, affecting for example patterns of electoral participation in Poland (Chapter 18).

Economic development was a major issue in terms of the overall modernization of communist systems although, in ways rather similar to the implications of the modernization approach (pointed out in Chapter 17), its impact on democratization in communist countries was a highly ambiguous one. While incomplete and in many areas unsatisfactory in terms of its achievements, it nevertheless contributed to the formation of a social structure in most communist countries that included groups whose position and outlook inclined them to activities that encouraged democratization. The role of an organized working class and independent minded intelligentsia can be singled out for attention here (Chapters 16 and 20). While somewhat stretching the idea of development, trajectories of development malformation and economic crisis have been more prominent in the dynamics of democratization and the ending of communist authoritarianism. To varying degrees they occupy a central position in explaining all the cases of liberalization and democratization discussed in this part, and also impinged directly on the rise of nationalism in Yugoslavia and Czechoslovakia (Chapter 19). Economic development, under contemporary conditions, is also closely bound up with the complex of factors associated with transnational and international engagement and others associated – both positively and negatively (see Chapter 18) with the development of a civil society.

Aspects of economic development and modernization are also closely associated with the kind of social divisions that develop within a particular society and their capacity to sustain the kind of activity and opposition to authoritarian regimes that harbour and promote tendencies of democratization. The development of a particular kind of working class was highly significant for developments in some countries of Eastern Europe (Chapter 16), while gender divisions emerged as an important factor in patterns of post-communist political participation (Chapter 18). Ethnic divisions were of great importance for Czechoslovakia and Yugoslavia although, as argued in Chapter 19, their implications for the development of the post-communist state and democratization could differ markedly according to the leadership strategies pursued and the institutional context within which the ethnic divisions received political expression.

Such factors lead naturally to consideration of the role of the *state* and the part played by *political institutions* more generally. The nature of the state was of particular importance for democratization in Russia and Eastern Europe and could hardly be otherwise in view of the massive role it played in conjunction with the wide range of institutions it controlled in countries subject to communist rule. Under the communist regime, however, state dominance took a very particular form in that overall control was exercised by the communist party and this had its own, highly specific way of operating. Democratization was, therefore, in large measure a process concerned with opposing and transforming the political order associated with the communist party-state regime (Chapters 16 and 17), while liberalization was a related process whose roots were more closely tied to the party-state elite (Chapter 20). Nevertheless, even within the communist state, significant institutional variation was possible, as the differing consociational arrangements developed in Czechoslovakia and Yugoslavia clearly showed (Chapter 19). During later stages of democratization, the role of the state has been more prominent in its absence from important areas of post-communist society (parts of the economy or welfare network, for example). In this context more specialized political institutions become important and a more diverse, pluralistic institutional structure becomes necessary to sustain democratization and support key processes like participation (Chapter 18).

PART VI
Conclusion

CHAPTER 21

From democratization to democratic consolidation

Adrian Leftwich

Introduction

Comparison has always been at the core of efforts in social science to build general explanatory theories about political development. Within this tradition, comparative politics has been at its most challenging when exploring large and complex political processes over a range of different societies at different times and in different contexts. This was the objective of many of the great nineteenth-century social and political theorists, culminating in the works of Marx and Weber. More recently, the appeal of Barrington Moore's comparative treatise on the origins of dictatorship and democracy (1966) or that of Theda Skocpol in her study of revolutions (1979) are illustrative modern examples of this; as is the analysis of *Capitalist Development and Democracy* (Rueschemeyer *et al.*, 1992) which has been referred to frequently in the preceding chapters.

The focus of this book has also been on one of the major political phenomena of modern history, and its comparative range has been world-wide: the patterns of democratization and the different explanatory traditions which have been developed to interpret and explain them (see the Preface and Chapter 1). Accordingly, there has throughout been a concern to balance historical depth with theoretical understanding and to integrate empirical detail with interpretative analysis. This necessary and mutual intimacy between evidence and explanation is fundamental to the craft of comparative politics (Lane and Ersson, 1994, pp. 1–10). For without reliable evidence there is no basis for comparison, nor for generating or testing explanatory theory. And without explanatory theory, or frameworks of explanatory factors, the search for evidence becomes arbitrary and random.

Given the richness of the detail and the arguments presented thus far, this concluding chapter will stand back from the immediacy of the material about countries or groups of countries and also from the implicit debate between the three major theoretical approaches (see especially Chapters 1 and 2). It will offer a retrospective overview of the explanatory implications of this comparative exercise and will go on to explore further aspects of democratization which have been raised but not investigated thus far. The first section therefore deals with the issues of evidence and explanation in comparative politics as refracted through the patterns of democratization. The second section focuses more sharply than has been possible in most chapters on the conditions for the *consolidation* of democracy (but see Chapters 3, 4 and especially Chapters 6 and 7 on this point); that is, on the conditions which appear to sustain democracies, once established. In a book which has covered so much, that might seem enough. But it would not be wise to conclude before raising in the third and final section some paradoxes about the political character of consolidated democracies.

21.1 Evidence and explanation in the analysis of democratization

Routes to democracy: the evidence

The evidence from the previous chapters makes very clear that the routes by which different societies have reached democracy have varied greatly. This was a central theme of Barrington Moore's thesis and other structuralist theorists since him (Therborn, 1977; Mann, 1993; Rueschemeyer *et al.*, 1992) as discussed in Chapters 1 and 2. The *doyen* of transition theory, Dankwart Rustow, made a similar point when arguing that 'there may be many roads to democracy' (Rustow, 1970, p.345).

In some societies democratization has been largely a matter of *internal* development (though never exclusively so, nor without external factors, such as the effect of war as discussed in Chapter 2). Britain is the prime example and illustrates what Huntington has described as the 'linear model' of a 'stately progression from civic rights to political rights to social rights, gradual development of parliamentary supremacy, cabinet government and incremental expansion of the suffrage over the course of a century' (Huntington, 1984, pp.210–11). Other examples include Switzerland, Australia and New Zealand.

Elsewhere, overt and powerful *external* factors have been influential, if not decisive, commonly after defeat in war. This was true in many states in Europe after 1918 (see Chapter 3) and also in Japan after 1945 where democratic institutions and processes were largely imposed by the USA (Eccleston, 1989, pp.15–19). However, even without defeat in war, many African states in the 1990s became democratic (Malawi is an obvious example) largely as a result of external pressures (see Chapter 11), without which it is highly unlikely that democratization would have occurred, at least not for some time (Holmquist and Ford, 1994; Chalker, 1994).

In other societies, top-level negotiations between elites appear to have been far more salient than such direct external pressure (though it has been present), as in Latin America from the 1980s (see Chapter 7). Such negotiations, before coming out into the public domain, have often also been highly secretive and hence closed to scholarly scrutiny. The case of South Africa (see Chapter 12) is illustrative of this since it has provided us with a fascinating insight into these processes of private and subsequent public negotiations. For although the substantive discussions, in open forum, about South Africa's future political and constitutional structure only commenced after 1990, we are now much more aware of the importance of the secret discussions between Nelson Mandela (and others in the ANC abroad) and officials and ministers in the South African government, between 1986 and 1990, remarkably while Mandela was still in prison (Sparks, 1995). But, again, one should never forget the powerful role played by internal resistance, external war and socio-economic and political isolation which made such negotiations both possible and desirable by slowly and steadily reducing the benefits and increasing the costs of maintaining non-democratic white rule. Negotiation was also important in Eastern Europe (see Chapter 16 and the Afterword to Part V), but the onset of democratization there was utterly contingent on the Soviet Union relinquishing its grip on the area.

Elsewhere, a combination of very different kinds of socio-economic modernization and ensuing change in social structures eroded the basis, necessity and determination of previously inflexible authoritarian regimes, as in South Korea and Taiwan (see Chapter 9). This was, arguably, the deeper process at work in South Africa too. A similar combination of economic modernization – and especially its requirements for greater pluralism and decentralization of decision making – plus social-structural change, seems to have played a part in the collapse and break-up of the communist Soviet Union and the emergence of partial and liberal democracies there (see Table 1.2 and Chapter 17). But, here again, many contingent factors spurred the process: international pressures and competition, escalating military costs, regional and national pressures and sudden changes in leadership.

In short, the comparative evidence makes clear that the major forces and agents of democratization have sometimes been solely or largely endogenous, that is mainly internal in origin and action. In other cases they have been primarily external, and commonly there have been both internal and external factors in a varying mix. In some, the internal pressures have come mainly from below, in others from above. In each case there is a different mixture of the 'explanatory factors' outlined in Chapter 1: economic development, social divisions, state and political institutions, civil society, political culture and ideas, and transnational and international engagements including war. The patterns of democratization, and the various forms of democracy which have resulted, it could be argued, have always been the product of the particular ways in which these factors (which we might also call the variables of democratization) have combined and interacted, with different factors, or groups of factors, having primacy in different instances. Moreover, the forms of democratic institutions and the extent of democratic practices in each vary greatly, yielding liberal or partially democratic political systems, each with different prospects for survival and consolidation, as will emerge later.

Many of the *non-political* characteristics of these new democracies also differ dramatically. Some are highly industrialized (Taiwan), some remain primarily agricultural (Tanzania); by comparison with each other, some have relatively even distributions of income (South Korea), some have highly unequal ones (Brazil). Some are more rather than less homogeneous in terms of their cultural, ethnic or religious structures (Chile); others are very much more divided by sharp cleavages (Mozambique). Some have complex, established and robust class structures (Argentina); others have systems of class stratification which are more fluid and evolving and which are intensely complex because they overlap with other systems of stratification, such as caste in India, 'race' or colour in South Africa, or ethnicity in Central America and many parts of Africa (see Chapters 6, 7, 8, 11 and 12). However, although the combinations and patterns of the democratization variables have varied, although their routes to democracy have differed and although their institutional, social-structural and ethno-cultural features display sharp variations, they all are now liberal or partial democracies (see Appendix to Chapter 1).

This diversity of evidential detail, timing and pace in the democratic trajectory of the individual cases would seem to defy theoretical or explanatory generalization of any kind. Yet, as has been patent throughout, the craft of comparative politics as an analytic approach requires a framework, that is some set of more or less explicit criteria or explanatory factors which can be tested, evaluated, compared with others and modified or merged where necessary. What, then, in the light of this comparative evidence can be said about the explanatory capacities of the three broad theoretical approaches outlined in the first chapter? And is there scope for a synthesis which is not an artificial or forced one?

Routes to democracy: the explanations

For present purposes only the core elements of the three explanatory approaches discussed in Chapters 1 and 2 need to be restated here. The *modernization approach*, which is associated historically with the work of S.M. Lipset (1960, 1992, 1993, 1994), focused mainly on the deep processes of *economic development and change* and the social consequences these processes generated in the form of 'requisites' for democracy. The approach stressed that these 'requisites' were closely associated, or correlated, with existing democratic polities. The *structural approach*, having its formal debut in the work of Barrington Moore (1966), has placed explanatory primacy on the varieties and shifts in the *structures of class and power* in different societies. Finally, the *transition approach*, originating in the work of Dankwart Rustow (1970) and developed later by others, particularly those with a specialist interest in Latin America, emphasized the role of *elite choice, bargaining and negotiation* as central to the essentially political processes of transition to democracy. There are a number of important points to make about these explanatory traditions.

In the first place, it is clear from the evidence above that none of these approaches, on its own, can claim explanatory universality with respect to all the cases of democratization discussed in the book.

In the case of modernization theory, there are many historical anomalies. Turkey is one (see Chapter 13), but perhaps the most obvious ones are Germany and India. Germany from the 1920s represented one of the most modern or developed societies in the world, in terms of the typical indices used by Lipset and others in their work on the social requisites of democracy. Yet democracy did not last long there (see Chapter 3). By contrast (see Chapter 8 and the Afterword to Part III), an explanation for the origins of Indian democracy cannot be easily deployed using the typical indicators and expressions of modernization and development, but has to draw on factors normally found beyond it. These include the role of imperial rule and its interaction with indigenous political culture (which shaped the particular form which civil society took in India) as well as the long dominance of the Indian Congress Party, at least until relatively recently. Moreover, modernization does not explain the continued (if increasingly shaky) endurance of democracy in India, which has lasted much longer than did German democracy in the inter-war years. Moreover, by contrast with Germany in 1920, India in 1947 was one of the poorest and least 'developed' societies in the world, with some very deep social divisions. That remains the case for almost half its people today. Over 50 per cent remain illiterate (World Bank, 1995, p.162), while about 40 per cent are sunk in absolute poverty (UNDP, 1995, pp.179, 223). Yet it remains the world's largest democracy, though not without increasing regional and religious tensions. An explanation for both the birth and continuing life of Indian democracy is not easily mobilized solely from within a narrowly modernization frame of analysis. The same is true for the flurry of democratizations in Africa (excluding South Africa) which occurred after 1990, and whose origins have much more to do with a mixture of internal political processes and choices and external pressures (see Chapter 11), neither of which are central explanatory categories associated with the modernization school.

To be fair, theorists working within the modernization tradition agree that the recent emergence of democracies in very poor countries will radically reduce the previously quite strong correlation between economic wealth and democratization (Lipset *et al.*, 1993, p.156), at least for the present. But if, as many analysts expect, new democracies fail in very poor countries (as in sub-Saharan Africa), then the correlation between economic wealth and democracy may once again become strong, especially in the context of the conditions which sustain democracies, an issue to which I will return later (ibid., p.171).

Limitations and shortcomings may also be identified in the other explanatory approaches. Structuralism, for example, is not helpful in the sub-Saharan African context where class formation generally remains far more feeble than in East Asia or Latin America largely in consequence of the low and slow states of economic growth and diversification. Furthermore, Chapter 9 showed that the focus on the choices and actions of elites in transition theory was important in explaining South Korean and Taiwanese democratization. But such an explanation would be both shallow and misleading if it did not take account of the deeper and prior changes in socio-economic structure, such as land reform which had occurred in the 1950s under US auspices, and which had established at least some of the conditions for democratic choices made in the late 1980s.

The important point here is that when theory meets history, that is when concrete explanatory accounts are required, many of the chapters show that at least two of the broad approaches, and sometimes all three, are needed to account for different aspects, phases or moments in the complex and varied patterns of democratization over time and space.

A second main point is that while each approach differs in terms of its emphasis and the features which it highlights, it is both easy and tempting – but wrong – to exaggerate the differences or to over-estimate the confidence or claims of each. A careful reading of the literature illustrates quite clearly that the major theorists who have been referred to in this book offer accounts of their own positions which are far less certain and far more probabilistic, far less confident theoretically and far more tentative and cautious in their predictions than might at first appear to be the case. Moreover, there is much overlap between them.

Lipset's account of the importance of the social requisites for democracy (not pre-requisites, he stresses), for example, is not a causal account. 'Socio-economic correlations are merely associational, and do not necessarily indicate cause', he argues (Lipset, 1994, p.16). They 'point to probabilities' (Lipset *et al.*, 1993, p.158). Moreover, although the evidence from *before* the 1990s does suggest 'interconnections between democratic structures and rising levels of income ... *economic growth does not determine political democracy itself*' (ibid., pp.156, 170). Finally, in a manner that sounds more like a transition theorist than a modernization theorist, he argued that: 'Whether democracy succeeds or fails continues to depend significantly on the choices, behaviours and decisions of political leaders and groups' (Lipset, 1994, p.18). In short, the theory is associational and probabilistic, not causal or deterministic. In its refinements, there are clear echoes of other approaches for it obviously recognizes the salience of human agency. Lipset's classic summary of the modernization position not only makes this clear but also reminds one that he was not talking so much about the causes or conditions of democratization as the *conditions for its survival*: 'the more well-to-do a nation, the *greater the chances* that it will *sustain* democracy' (Lipset, 1960, p.31).

Structuralists are equally tentative about prediction or certainty, 'not only because of the limits of our theoretical understanding but even more so because of our limited ability to anticipate structural developments at the national or international levels' (Rueschemeyer *et al.*, 1992, p.292). There are even echoes here of the modernization approach for while the structuralist position has as its focus 'the economic power base of elites, the strength of civil society, the balance of class power and the political articulation of civil society', they recognize that 'these factors were originally shaped by the *structure of the economy and the state*' (ibid., p.159, my emphasis) in which industrialization has played a critical part (ibid., p.215). In short, while stressing the centrality of class and state power as key macro-political determinants of the prospects for democratization, the structural persuasion is well aware that such structures, and especially changes in them, do not occur in a vacuum. They are the direct result of economic development and social change which, for instance, 'enlarges the size of the working class and ... increases the organizational power of subordinate classes generally [and] erodes the size and the power of the most anti-democratic force – the large landowning classes' (ibid., p.76).

Furthermore, all the major approaches are sensitive to two other important explanatory considerations. The first is the importance of *historical uniqueness* and contingency (chance events) and hence the timing and context of democratization in individual societies. Second, all the approaches recognize how the pace and form of democratization in each society is influenced by *international economic and political factors*.

Bearing these continuities and overlaps in mind, is it possible to suggest an explanatory synthesis between the main approaches? One fruitful way (but certainly not the only one) is to think about each of the main approaches as representing a different *level of explanation* and – for preliminary purposes, at least – to regard these levels as connected to each other in a broader and looser explanatory framework. Thus modernization theory is concerned with the *economic structure* and its social consequences, but without suggesting or demonstrating a necessary causal link between these and democracy. Structuralism moves up a level and has as its focus the *relations of class and power* which flow from the economic structure in different societies and the broad macro-political consequences of this. Finally, transition theory may be thought of as moving up yet another level, for it is very much concerned with the politics that arises out of these prior conditions. It thus operates at a level where there is a sharper *micro-political focus*, giving attention to the bargains, choices and negotiations of elites. And at each of these three levels (economy, socio-political structure and concrete human agency), the role and extent of external factors varies in form and intensity.

It does not follow, however, that all democratizations can be traced through these levels, from bottom to top, as we have seen. Some democratizations appear to have short-circuited some of these phases or levels entirely, especially where external pressures have been decisive in forcing the pace. Whatever the democratization route, the critical question which follows is sharp: what conditions will sustain the new democracies? In short, we must shift the focus of attention from the *processes of democratization* to the *conditions for its consolidation*. That is the subject of the next section.

─────────────────── ***Summary of Section 21.1*** ───────────────────

- The comparative method is at the heart of the social science effort to generate explanatory theory.

- Persuasive accounts in comparative politics are characterized by a close and plausible fit between evidence and explanation.

- There have been and remain a variety of routes to democracy.

- Despite significant differences in focus and emphasis between the three main approaches, a careful reading of each does not reveal certainty, confident prediction or sharp differentiation in the positions, but caution, probabilism and overlap in these explanatory accounts, both in general terms and in practical analysis of concrete cases.

- One way of viewing the different explanatory approaches is therefore perhaps not to see them as exclusive of each other, but rather as operating at different levels of analysis, with each level being vulnerable to both historical contingencies as well as external influences and interactions.

21.2   From democratic transition to democratic consolidation

Background

The starting point for this section is the distinction between the transition to democracy, on the one hand, and 'democratic consolidation' on the other (Mainwaring *et al.*, 1992, p.3). For it is one thing for a democratic transition to take place; but it is altogether another matter for democracy to survive. As Chapters 6 and 7 show, this concern with consolidation has been primarily associated with transition approaches (Rustow, 1970, pp.346, 339) and with studies of Latin America in particular, largely because democracy has so often come, and gone, in that continent before the onset of the present 'third wave'. But all the other main approaches acknowledge this explanatory distinction, too. The structuralists, Rueschemeyer *et al.*, suggest: 'one must be prepared to distinguish the causal conditions of the first installation of democracy from those that maintain it after consolidation' (Rueschemeyer *et al.*, 1992, p.76), while Lipset argues that 'New democracies must be institutionalized, consolidated and become legitimate' (Lipset, 1994, p.7). And there are enough examples of both new and born-again democracies which have failed to make this an important distinction.

But what is to count as 'consolidation'? The most obvious single defining feature of a consolidated democracy is where 'all major political actors take for granted the fact that democratic processes dictate government renewal' (Mainwaring *et al.*, 1992, p.3). To elaborate, with the help of Schumpeter's renowned definition, the politics of liberal democracy may be said to be consolidated where people, political parties and groups pursue their interests according to peaceful, rule-based competition, negotiation and co-operation within an 'institutional arrangement for arriving at political decisions in which individuals acquire the power to decide by means of a competitive struggle for the people's vote' (Schumpeter, 1965, p.269; Held, 1996, Chapter 5).

One of the important concluding points to emerge from Chapter 3 is that in both the USA and the UK, liberal democracy *did* survive through the 1930s despite the battering its institutional arrangements received from the economic crisis and socio-political distress of that decade. But such survival was rare when compared with the widespread collapse of democracy in Europe in the inter-war years, the chronic instability of democracy in much of Latin America in the twentieth century, and the general pattern of democratic demise after 1960 in many former colonies which were granted independence on a democratic basis in Huntington's 'second wave' from the end of the Second World War (Huntington, 1991). And there have already been reversals of the 'third wave' of democratization. For instance, by the end of 1995, democracy had already failed in sub-Saharan Africa in Nigeria, Sierra Leone, The Gambia and Niger, while in Algeria democratization was suspended in the middle of the electoral process at the end of 1991.

So it is clear that the establishment of democratic political systems in the past has in no way meant that they will become consolidated. It is appropriate therefore to ask: will recently established democracies survive? I offer a set of five conditions which the comparative evidence suggests are necessary for democratic consolidation to take hold.

Five conditions for democratic survival

Legitimacy

Legitimacy is a notoriously difficult concept to define and measure, especially in authoritarian societies (see Held, 1996, Chapter 5). Elusive as the concept is, its most simple meaning is *acceptability*. But as David Held points out, people may accept a political system – or, rather, not challenge it, which is different – for many reasons. They may acquiesce out of fear or as a result of traditional compliance; or they may give only resigned acceptance or conditional agreement. For instance (see Chapter 10) it has been argued that the ability of the Indonesian government after 1966 to promote economic growth and distribute its benefits widely has been one of the factors which has secured its legitimacy despite its sternly authoritarian rule. What has been described as widespread legitimacy, even popularity, of Suharto's New Order in Indonesia (Liddle, 1992, p.450) has been said to be conditional upon sustained economic growth. Held suggests that it is probably quite rare that positive informed acceptance is the basis of legitimacy (Held, 1996).

Despite these problems with the concept it is clear that no democratic polity can survive for long, that is it cannot consolidate unless it enjoys some form of legitimacy, whether of the passive acceptance kind or whether of the more unusual positive kind. However, the concept of legitimacy might be better understood and operationalized if it is broken down into three components: geographical, constitutional and political legitimacy.

Geographical legitimacy means that those who live within the state accept its territorial definition and the appropriateness of their place within it or, at least, they do not positively oppose it, except by constitutional means. Where, for instance, people do not consider the state is legitimate in this respect, democratic politics comes under threat. In the extreme case, the threat might take the form of a secessionist or irredentist movement, where a group or region wishes to break away and establish its own state or join another. Where people have no political means for achieving secession from the state, they are unlikely to abide by democratic processes and violence is almost inevitable. Democratic politics (at the very least in the disputed region, and often beyond it) is very difficult, if not improbable. This has been the case in the Basque region of northern Spain; it was the case in Eritrea which was formerly part of Ethiopia; it is the case in northern Sri Lanka where the Tamil community has been fighting for an independent state; and it has been dramatically illustrated in the mid 1990s by the struggle of Chechnya for independence from the new post-Soviet Russian Federation.

Constitutional legitimacy refers to acceptance of the constitution – that is the formal structure of rules whereby political power is competed for, organized and distributed – though again the range of possible kinds of acceptance needs to be borne in mind. One of the toughest parts of the process of democratization lies precisely in establishing such a constitution, as the complex negotiations in the case of South Africa between 1990 and 1994 illustrate (see Chapter 12). As democracies emerge from the political darkness of authoritarian rule, a whole range of interests erupt into the more open but *less predictable* political space or stand exposed in it. Some may be powerful or rich and fear change; some may be poor and hitherto weak and demand change. They may be economic interests (landowners), political or institutional interests (political parties and legislatures), functional interests (bureaucracies or armies, especially in Latin America), class interests (organized workers, as in Brazil), 'ethnic' interests (Afrikaners in South Africa or Indians in Fiji), regional interests (a province or sub-national area) or a mix of some of them. Each will want to have a shrewd idea how the new distribution of power in the constitution will affect it, and each will want to ensure that their interests will be protected. To some extent constitutions can do that (Przeworski, 1986, p.60), which is why negotiation and bargaining is normally so tough as groups seek to influence the shape of the constitution and what goes in it. Will it be a parliamentary or presidential system? If the latter, how powerful will the presidency be in relation to the legislature, and what will the role of political parties be? How will the army be controlled? What powers will be reserved to the centre (in a federal structure, for instance) and how much power – and resources – will the regions or sub-national regional governments have? Will there be a Bill of Rights? What will go in it? How difficult will it be to change it? For instance, will private property be protected as in the new 1996 South African constitution? If so, then the constitution places immediate and far-reaching constraints on government options in aspects of, say, economic policy.

Even in established and long-consolidated democracies (such as the United Kingdom or in the somewhat younger and less consolidated case of India), regional or ethnic interests can intensify over time and put pressure on the central state for constitutional reform: unsatisfied, this can extend into violence. In Britain, the debate about devolution of power to Scotland and Wales – which has waxed and waned – is a good example (Nairn, 1977). In India, demands for greater autonomy for the Punjab, even independence, have placed considerable stress on the Indian state (Singh, 1993). So, assuming people regard the geographical definition of the state as legitimate, they must also regard the formal constitution as legitimate for consolidation to have a chance.

Finally, there is *political legitimacy*. This refers to the extent to which the electorate (or, more realistically, organized parties in it, or other institutions like the army) regards the government in power as being entitled, procedurally, to be there. That is to say, for present purposes a government may be said to be politically legitimate where the outcome of the election reflects voting preferences according to the rules and that the results have not been rigged. In Haiti, for instance, there has been persistent and widespread rigging of the votes and violence in elections since the mid 1980s after the overthrow of the Duvalier regime, coupled with army intervention to cancel the democratic result. These have been just some of the factors which have reduced the political legitimacy and status of democracy in that country to such a low point. In Kenya, after the first multi-party election in 1992, many members of the opposition parties (which lost) claimed that there had been wide-spread irregularities and that the outcome of the election – and hence the new democracy itself – was in jeopardy (Holmquist and Ford, 1994). But the chairperson of the Commonwealth election observer mission concluded that 'we believe the results in many instances directly reflect, however imperfectly, the will of the people' (*Africa Report*, March/April 1993, p.3). In the event, it was accepted but an uneasiness has remained. Confidence in the *process* and confidence in the *outcome* of democratic electoral politics is crucial for democratic consolidation.

But the central point here is that, for all the difficulties with the concept, *geographical, constitutional* and *political forms of legitimacy*, are necessary conditions for a democratic polity to survive, although they are not sufficient conditions. However, these basic conditions are not easy to obtain in many of the new democracies where legacies of hate, mistrust and conflict remain.

Consensus about the rules of the game

For democracies to survive, there needs to be agreement or acquiescence about the rules of the political game and loyalty to those rules, that is to the democratic process itself, especially amongst political elites (Mainwaring, 1992, p.309). The political scientist, Adam Przeworski, has theorized democratization as: 'a process of institutionalizing uncertainty, of subjecting all interests to uncertainty' (Przeworski, 1986, p.58, 1988). By this he means that because democratic politics involves open competition for power, no group can be certain of winning. Indeed, the shift from authoritarian rule to democracy means precisely that the group which has held power (such as the military in Latin America, the Party in the former communist bloc or whites in South Africa) abandons effective control over outcomes and thus has to embrace 'uncertainty' (Przeworski, 1986, p.58). This uncertainty has at least two dimensions, both understandably threatening to the group which is giving up control: (a) that it may not win the election and hence would lose power, and (b) that the policy changes introduced by a new government would damage its interests – a point I shall return to shortly.

But, assuming that the constitution is agreed by the major political groups, even in the most limited and conditional sense, and assuming that an election has been judged to have taken place according to the rules, then for democracy to work the *losers* must abide by the result, and thereby show commitment to the democratic process itself. *Winners*, on the other hand, must know that they are not in power for ever and will have to compete again and put their record to the test in the next election, which they cannot suspend.

The 'losers' might be the party which represents the former authoritarian regime or it might be one of the groups which has fought for democracy and was suppressed by that regime. In both Myanmar and Nigeria in the early 1990s the military regimes refused to accept that 'their' parties had lost and cancelled the result of the elections. In Algeria, in late 1991, for somewhat different and more complex reasons, the government suspended the democratic electoral process when it became clear that the fundamentalist Islamic Front was about to win and might itself abandon democratic procedures (see Chapter 14). In Angola, one of the main political parties (UNITA) which had been engaged in a long civil war with the governing party (MPLA) immediately took up arms after losing the election, claiming that the ballot was rigged. In all these instances, democracy was simply overturned.

By contrast, in both Zambia and Malawi, the leadership of the old regimes (of Presidents Kaunda and Banda) went quietly when they lost, as did communist parties in many parts of Eastern Europe and the former Soviet Union (see Chapters 16, 17 and 18).

Where democracy emerges (or re-emerges) from right-wing authoritarianism (as in much of Latin America, the Philippines and South Korea), the political forces associated with the old regime must commit themselves to democratic practices. Crudely, the troops must return to the barracks and stay there. If and when democracy returns to Myanmar and Algeria, this will have to happen there too. But equally, groups on the left (such as the former ANC guerrillas in South Africa or the Nicaraguan Sandinistas) have to commit themselves to effective demobilization, the ballot box and committee rooms in their struggle for power or for influence over policy.

Policy restraint by winning parties

However, it is unlikely that any group or party would accept the rules of the electoral game if losing meant that it or the interests it represented would lose *too* much. It follows that while losers must accept the outcome, winners must also accept that there are significant limits to what they can do with their newly won power. This third condition means that democratic consolidation also depends on victorious parties exercising policy restraint when in government, although the temptation (and sometimes need) is often to re-write the policy book. That is to say, new or born-again democracies are more likely to consolidate and prosper if the new government does not pursue highly contentious policies too far or too fast, especially where these policies seriously threaten other major interests (see the discussion on democracy in Europe, 1945–89, in Chapter 4).

Indeed such limits on policy change are often established *before* democratic transition is completed, in the course of negotiations, whether secret or otherwise, and are thus part of that process itself (Huntington, 1991/92, pp.609–15). This shows that while the distinction between democratic transition and consolidation is conceptually important, there are also very important continuities between them. In short, what happens in the course of democratization has important consequences for what happens afterwards.

The case of Venezuela sharply illustrates the long-term salience of this principle of policy self-restraint as a condition for democratic consolidation, precisely because it has sustained democratic governance since 1958 – completely against the run of politics in Latin America (see Chapters 6 and 7). In 1958 two extraordinary pacts were agreed in Venezuela (McCoy, 1988). The first was a Worker–Owner Accord by which, in effect, 'capitalists accepted democratic institutions as a means for workers to make effective claims to improve their material conditions, while workers accepted private appropriation of profit by capitalists as an institution in expectation of further gains from production' (ibid., p.86). What this meant was that 'workers accepted capitalism and capitalists accepted democracy *each foregoing a more militant alternative*' (ibid.). It is the final point that is central here. The second agreement was the so-called Pact of Punto Fijo, signed by the three major political parties (but excluding the Communist Party). According to the pact, the three dominant parties would each have a share of government posts, irrespective of who won in the elections; they would pursue agreed national development goals and would keep the communists out (McCoy, 1988, p.88; Przeworski, 1992, p.124). Venezuela has of course been fortunate in having a steady stream of oil revenues to help fund the politics of these pacts by paying for social and economic reform (see Chapter 6). But the central point is that these pacts framed the limits of policy change and effectively tied the major parties into the democratic process by guaranteeing that they would all have a stake in the government and that neither they nor their supporters would ever lose too much.

Another good recent illustration of this comes from South Africa where the African National Congress (ANC) government since 1994 has thus far been extremely careful not to threaten white economic interests or the interests of capital more generally (Lodge, 1995). And in Mauritius, in a highly plural society consisting of Christians, Muslims and Hindus, where there has been a bewildering pattern of fusion and fission in party alliances, democratic consolidation has also been secured by comparable means. In the Mauritian case, however, this has largely been due to the acceptance by all parties that government can only be by coalition and because 'on core values (religious and linguistic toleration, parliamentary democracy ... and ... a development strategy based on a mixed economy but with concern for all) there has been a national consensus' (Bowman, 1991, p.101).

There is, however, at least one major problem which makes achieving such agreements about policy constraint so difficult in post-transitional politics. This is that the followers of some newly elected democratic regimes not unreasonably expect rapid and often radical policies of redistribution. After all, they might argue, have they not fought for this for many years? Yet the new government is likely to find that it cannot meet their demands (which may be for jobs, better wages, houses, health care, land reform), at least not immediately and at least not until sustained economic growth has generated the resources to pay for this. Also, for all the reasons given above, the government dare not dispossess the wealthy if they wish to sustain the political agreements that will keep the new democracy going. This is especially the case if there has been some form of 'pact' between the elites on the limits of policy change under the new democratic auspices: these may even have been written into the constitution. It is also especially the case if the new government seeks not only goodwill but also foreign aid and investment from major Western institutions and companies. Such assistance might be threatened if government policies were thought to be too radical or unfriendly to the operation of free markets, a feature of new democracies which illustrates the continuing salience of external factors even after democratization has been completed.

But if the new government does *not* satisfy the demands of its militant followers it is possible that they will use their newly-won democratic rights to the full in the political space now provided by democracy. How far they go will vary from place to place. They may turn against 'their' government, take to the streets, organize demonstrations, strikes, go-slows and perhaps even more violent forms of protest as have occurred in many parts of Latin America since the new democracies have been established. If these escalate, the danger is obvious. Not only may this destabilize democracy (hence tempting the army to storm out of the barracks again to re-impose 'order', or more), but it may undermine the economy and hence damage the new government's strategy for growth.

In short, while policy restraint by winners appears to be an important operational condition of democratic consolidation, it is not something that all new democratic regimes can willingly, easily or always ensure, given their domestic political situations and also external demands, conditions and expectations.

Poverty as an obstacle to democratic consolidation

Until the most recent phase of the 'third wave' of democratization, that is after about 1990, consolidated democracies have seldom been found in really poor societies. On the contrary, there has been a strong positive correlation between the wealth of a country and democracy (Huntington, 1984, pp.198–9; Lipset *et al.*, 1993, p.156), though India has remained the most important exception among liberal democracies. This is not to say that more wealthy societies will *automatically* be able to consolidate democracy, as the more deterministic interpretations of modernization theory suggest. The evidence of the Middle Eastern countries analysed in Chapters 13 and 14 shows that this is simply not the case. Wealth is not a sufficient condition for democracy.

None the less, most societies in the developing world with a per capita income of less than $600 per annum today (World Bank, 1995) have not been successful in consolidating liberal democracy before 1990. There are, of course, a few exceptions such as The Gambia (until 1994, at least) and especially India (allowing for its state of emergency between 1975 and 1977), though a few more have attained the status of partial democracy as the notion is used in this book (see Chapter 1 and its Appendix). Pakistan and Egypt are both intermittent and borderline cases in point. By contrast, it has generally been the case that those developing countries (India apart) which have consolidated liberal or partially democratic politics since the 1950s (such as Venezuela, Costa Rica, Jamaica, Botswana, Mauritius, Singapore and Malaysia) have for some time achieved per capita incomes in excess of $600 per annum.

One reason why serious poverty seems to restrain democratic consolidation is that in profoundly poor countries, the struggle for scarce resources, and the enormous advantages which permanent control of the state may bring to a party or faction, makes democracy very unlikely. Incumbents holding state power will be reluctant to engage in compromise and will be very unwilling to lose control. Suspending democracy is a good way of staying in power. This has been very much the case in sub-Saharan Africa (see Chapter 11), where poverty has given rise to a situation which has been described as the 'politics of the belly' (Bayart, 1993). Moreover, poverty is often accompanied by relatively low levels of literacy, formal education and communication, none of which have historically been associated with stable democracy.

While a large number of very poor countries have recently democratized, and hence have considerably eroded the positive correlation between wealth and democracy, the issue is not closed by any means. For if they fail to consolidate into the twenty-first century, this particular correlation will, again, be strong. But if this most recent *tranche* of especially poor countries are able to consolidate their democracies, the salience of this point will be greatly diminished.

Ethnic, cultural or religious cleavages as constraints on democracy

As Chapter 19 so graphically shows, sharp 'national', ethnic, cultural or religious differences (especially where they overlap with material inequalities between the groups) make *both* transition and consolidation difficult. Of course, they are not impossible to overcome in consolidating democracies, as in Switzerland, Canada, Mauritius and Trinidad. Carefully crafted constitutions, or inter-elite pacts can keep democracies going by binding or buying groups into the institutional structures of democracy. But without such countervailing conditions, divisions of this kind have never made it easy to sustain democracy, and Chapter 3 illustrates some of the problems which conflicting national and ethnic groups in Europe posed for democracy between the wars.

There are many other more recent illustrations of this. Severe conflict between the Chinese and Malays in Malaysia in the 1960s and in Fiji between native Fijians and Indians in the late 1980s both ended with the suspension of democracy. The African continent provides some of the sharpest modern examples of such ethno-cultural conflicts, as in the continuing instability in Nigeria, Angola and Sudan, not to mention the recent (but not new) bloodshed in Rwanda. Closer to Western Europe, the grim spectacle of Yugoslavian disintegration, with its special contribution of 'ethnic cleansing', illustrates the point graphically (see Chapter 19).

Elsewhere, intense religious conflict can erode the prospects of a consensual basis for democratic politics. This is best illustrated by the increasingly hostile and sometimes violent confrontations within Islam, as in Algeria, Egypt and even Bangladesh; by the rise of Hindu fundamentalism in India (Chapter 8) or Jewish fundamentalism in Israel (Chapter 15). In India, over the last 20 years, democracy has looked increasingly shaky as it has been threatened by first regional tensions and, more recently, by mounting religious conflict and Hindu fundamentalism (Kaviraj, 1995).

In all these examples, ethnic or religious differences become the contours along which political mobilization flows, often with uncompromising and therefore anti-democratic consequences. Perhaps not until the salience, that is the pull, of ethnic, religious or cultural loyalty is confined to the private sphere and hence disarmed and dispersed in favour of a widespread commitment to a common, public and above all secular citizenship will democratic political processes be consolidated. It certainly seems to be the case in Islamic countries that the strongest supporters of democratic processes come from the more secular sections of the societies, as in Turkey, Egypt and Algeria (see Chapter 13). And in Israel, those most determined to undermine the democratic traditions and who are least likely to accept the legitimacy of the state may be found amongst Jewish fundamentalists.

─────────── *Summary of Section 21.2* ───────────

- The transition to democracy can be regarded as conceptually distinct from the subsequent consolidation of democracy though there is continuity between these processes.

- Democratic consolidations seem more likely when certain conditions are present. These conditions are: (a) when the polity has geographical, constitutional and political legitimacy; (b) where there is agreement about the rules of the political game and the parties abide by them; (c) where opposing groups agree on policy restraint; (d) where there are low or declining levels of poverty; (e) and where ethnic, cultural and religious cleavages are not deep and uncompromising.

Conclusion

There are three main points to make here. First, the historical and comparative record suggests that the presence of only one of these conditions is unlikely to ensure democratic consolidation, while the presence of all will make it much more probable, provided contingent factors beyond the control of the regime do not intervene. The absence of some conditions may also be compensated for by the effectiveness of others. For instance, the effects of sharp ethnic or cultural cleavages may be mitigated by careful constitutional design, by policy restraint or broadly-based coalition-building. The problem however, is that most of the new democracies appear to have few of these conditions. As a consequence, the prognosis for widespread consolidation is not good and it would therefore be prudent to expect many democratic reversals over the next decade into the twenty-first century.

Second, historically-speaking it has been largely from within a Western perspective that democracy has been assumed to be a good thing. For instance, in the late 1950s, Lipset wrote that 'democracy is not only or even primarily a means through which different groups can attain their ends or seek the good society; *it is the good society itself in operation*' (Lipset, 1960, p.403, my emphasis). And although it is true that today there are voices and groups demanding democracy in almost every country, it is important to remember that this is not a view which is universally held. Some traditional elites within parts of Islam (see Chapters 13 and 14), hold that democracy is a Western institution and hence inappropriate for a non-Western society. Such views can also be found in the South Pacific where a *Fiji Times* editorial in 1992 described democracy as a 'foreign flower', unlikely to take root in Fijian soil (Larmour, 1995, p.230). Elsewhere, determined modernizing elites have argued that democracy can hinder the urgent tasks of economic transformation and that it would be both 'premature' and dangerous to allow liberal democracy to flourish in the volatile conditions of rapid economic change. Germany under Bismarck in the late nineteenth century, Japan after the Meiji 'revolution' of 1867, South Korea after 1960 and the People's Republic of China since 1980 are good examples of this. Indeed, both the Cuban and Chinese governments have regarded the post-Soviet Russian experiment (of combining political democracy with economic liberalization) with undisguised horror. Both Cuba and China have themselves embarked upon wide-ranging programmes of economic liberalization, but have done so under strictly non-democratic conditions. And the point raises a complex paradox about liberal democracies especially.

This paradox is that liberal democracies may be thought of typically as simultaneously radical *and* conservative. Democracies can be considered as 'radical' in that no other political systems have promoted and protected individual *political rights and civil liberties to the same extent* (Gastil, 1986; Humana, 1987). In their struggles to define, win or protect such rights in the political domain, countless millions of people have died or suffered appallingly at the hands of authoritarian regimes. These are the human dramas which illustrate so powerfully the 'narrative' of the struggle for democratization in the nineteenth and twentieth centuries which frames the central concerns of this book (see the Preface and Chapter 1).

But radical as they are in these respects, liberal democracies may be considered 'conservative' in other respects. They have not been able to the same extent to institutionalize social and economic rights, such as job security, minimum incomes and access to health and welfare systems (although their record in these matters is often better than authoritarian regimes). Chapter 5 on the USA illustrates this sharply for the industrial world. Moreover, poverty and socio-economic inequality remain profound and divisive in most of the consolidated Third World democracies (World Bank, 1995, p.220, Table 30). Of course, many liberal democrats would argue that these provisions (what the Chinese describe as subsistence rights), desirable as they may be, are not rights but the products of economic growth which democracy will promote. And without growth, they are simply undeliverable by any regime.

Democracy may be considered 'conservative' in another sense, too, that is in the difficulties it faces in taking rapid and far-reaching steps to reduce inherited structural inequalities (which may also be necessary for growth), for all the reasons given in Section 21.2. For although new democratic governments (like the ANC in South Africa) or older ones (as in India) may be committed to poverty reduction and promoting the welfare of the masses, it is often the case that radical and essentially *non-consensual* steps are necessary for this. The difficulty is that such steps could easily breach the formal or informal 'pacts' which may have helped to bring democratization about in the first place.

Land reform is a good example, since it is widely recognized that this can be an important condition for agricultural and rural development, for the economic and social welfare of rural people and hence for democratic stability. But landowners in general do not consent to land reform! And democratic Third World governments have seldom been effective in overcoming such vested rural interests to achieve the restructuring of rural wealth and power which land reform is designed to bring about. Indian democracy, for instance, has had very little success in pushing through land reforms; landlessness and appalling rural poverty remain, though some state governments in India, as in Kerala, have been more successful. Moreover, at a more general level of re-distributive policy and practice, there has been 'hardly any significant taxation of agricultural income and wealth' (Bardhan,

1984, p.46, Ch.6). And in Pakistan, even during its democratic phases, land reform has proved impossible, for instance under the Bhutto regime (Herring, 1979).

It may be that as and when the new democracies consolidate they will accumulate the political means and capacities for a slow and steady reduction in such inequalities of access to economic resources and opportunities. This has been the secular trend in most of Western Europe as some social and economic rights have been added to political and civic ones during the present century (Marshall, 1950). But it has often been a slow and commonly uneven process, sometimes moving forward and sometimes back – all of which illustrates why the politics of policy change in democratic polities is sometimes thought of as 'conservative', involving accommodation, compromise, agreement and incrementalism. For many that is its virtue; for others, its vice. But the paradox is that such changes may be too slow for democratic consolidation to occur, especially where democracy is being attempted 'on top of a minefield of social apartheid' (Francisco Weffort, cited in Lipset, 1994, p.17).

What all this suggests, finally, is that there are many goals of development or of progress, of which democracy, economic growth and greater equality are commonly regarded as the main ones (Huntington, 1987). But it may be that these goals cannot be attained simultaneously and that there are thus complex trade-offs between them, involving difficult choices at each step. Making these choices within democratic politics has never been a simple matter, but then no one ever said that democracy was easy.

References

Bardhan, P. (1984) *The Political Economy of Development in India*, Oxford, Blackwell.

Bayart, J.F. (1993) *The State in Africa: the Politics of the Belly*, London, Longman.

Bowman, L.W. (1991) *Mauritius: Democracy and Development in the Indian Ocean*, London, Dartmouth.

Chalker, L. (1994) *Good Government: Putting Policy into Practice*, London, Overseas Development Administration.

Eccleston, B. (1989) *State and Society in Post War Japan*, Cambridge, Polity Press.

Gastil, R.G. (1986) *Freedom in the World, 1985–6*, New York, Greenwood Press.

Held, D. (1996) *Models of Democracy* (2nd edn), Cambridge, Polity Press.

Herring, R. (1979) 'Zulfiqar Ali Bhutto and the "eradication of feudalism" in Pakistan', *Comparative Studies in Society and History*, vol.21, no.4.

Holmquist, F. and Ford, M. (1994) 'Kenya: state and civil society. The first year after the election', *Africa Today*, 4th Quarter, pp.5–25.

Humana, C. (1987) *World Human Rights Guide*, London, Pan.

Huntington, S.P. (1984) 'Will more countries become democratic?', *Political Science Quarterly*, vol.99, no.2, pp.193–218.

Huntington, S.P. (1987) 'The goals of development' in Weiner, M. and Huntington, S.P. (eds) *Understanding Political Development*, Boston, Little, Brown, pp.3–32.

Huntington, S.P. (1991) *The Third Wave: Democratization in the Late Twentieth Century*, Norman, University of Oklahoma Press.

Huntington, S.P. (1991/92) 'How countries democratize', *Political Science Quarterly*, vol.106, no.4, pp.579–616.

Kaviraj, S. (1995) 'Dilemmas of democratic development in India' in Leftwich, A. (ed.) pp.114–38.

Lane, J.E. and Ersson, S. (1994) *Comparative Politics. An Introduction and New Approach*, Cambridge, Polity Press.

Larmour, P. (1995) 'Democracy without development in the South Pacific' in Leftwich, A. (ed.) pp.230–47.

Leftwich, A. (ed.) (1995) *Democracy and Development. Theory and Practice*, Cambridge, Polity Press.

Liddle, R.W. (1992) 'Indonesia's democratic past and future', *Comparative Politics*, vol.24, no.4, pp.443–62.

Lipset, S.M. (1960) *Political Man*, London, Heinemann.

Lipset, S.M. (1992) 'Conditions of the democratic order and social change: a comparative discussion' in Eisenstadt, S.N. (ed.) *Studies in Human Society: Democracy and Modernity*, New York, E.J. Brill, pp.2–14.

Lipset, S.M. (1994) 'The social requisites of democracy revisited', *American Sociological Review*, vol.59, pp.1–22.

Lipset, S.M. *et al.* (1993) 'A comparative analysis of the social requisites of democracy', *International Social Science Journal*, vol.136, pp.155–75.

Lodge, T. (1995) 'South Africa: democracy and development in a post-apartheid society' in Leftwich, A. (ed.) pp.188–209.

McCoy, J. (1988) 'The state and democratic compromise in Venezuela', *Journal of Developing Societies*, vol.IV, pp.85–104.

Mainwaring, S. (1992) 'Transitions to democracy and democratic consolidation: theoretical and comparative issues' in Mainwaring, S. *et al.* (eds) pp.294–341.

Mainwaring, S. *et al.* (eds) (1992) 'Introduction' in Mainwaring, S. *et al.* (eds) pp.1–16.

Mainwaring, S. *et al.* (eds) (1992) *Issues in Democratic Consolidation. The New South American Democracies in Comparative Perspective*, Notre Dame, University of Notre Dame Press.

Mann, M. (1993) *The Rise of Classes and Nation-States, 1760–1914. The Sources of Social Power, Vol.II*, Cambridge, Cambridge University Press.

Marshall, T.H. (1950) *Citizenship and Social Class*, Cambridge, Cambridge University Press.

Moore, B. (1966) *Social Origins of Dictatorship and Democracy*, Boston, Beacon Press.

Nairn, T. (1977) *The Break-Up of Britain*, London, Verso.

Przeworski, A. (1986) 'Some problems in the study of the transition to democracy' in O'Donnell, G. *et al.* (eds) *Transition from Authoritarian Rule. Comparative Perspectives*, Baltimore, Johns Hopkins Press, pp.47–63.

Przeworski, A. (1988) 'Democracy as a contingent outcome of conflicts' in Elster, J. and Slagstad, R. (eds) *Constitutionalism and Democracy,* Cambridge, Cambridge University Press, pp.59–80.

Przeworski, A. (1992) 'The games of transition' in Mainwaring, S. *et al.* (eds) pp.105–52.

Rueschemeyer, D., Stephens, E. and Stephens, J. (1992) *Capitalist Development and Democracy,* Cambridge, Polity Press.

Rustow, D. (1970) 'Transitions to democracy', *Comparative Politics,* vol.2, pp.337–63.

Schumpeter, J.A. (1965) *Capitalism, Socialism and Democracy,* London, Unwin.

Singh, G. (1993) 'Ethnic conflict in India: a case study of Punjab' in McGarry, J. and O'Leary, B. (eds) *The Politics of Ethnic Conflict Regulation,* London, Routledge, pp.84–105.

Skocpol, T. (1979) *States and Social Revolutions,* Cambridge, Cambridge University Press.

Sparks, A. (1995) *Tomorrow is Another Country. The Inside Story of South Africa's Negotiated Revolution,* London, Heinemann.

Therborn, G. (1977) 'The rule of capital and the rise of democracy', *New Left Review,* vol.103.

UNDP (United Nations Development Programme) (1995) *Human Development Report 1995,* New York, Oxford University Press.

World Bank (1995) *World Development Report 1995,* New York, Oxford University Press.

Acknowledgements

Grateful acknowledgement is made to the following sources for permission to reproduce material in this book:

Tables
Table 18.2: Corrin, C. (1993) 'People and politics' in White, S., Batt, J. and Lewis, P.G. (eds) *Developments in East European Politics*, Macmillan Press Ltd, adapted from Inter-Parliamentary Union (1991) *Women in Parliament*; Table 18.3: Gigli, S. (1995) 'Towards increased participation in the political process', *Transition*, vol. 1 (16), Open Media Research Institute.

Maps
Map 5.1: adapted from Gilbert, M. (1993) *The Dent Atlas of American History*, 3rd edn, Dent, © 1968, 1985 and 1993 by Martin Gilbert by permission of Routledge; Map 12.1: Lodge, T., Nasson, B., Mufson, S., Shubane, K. and Sithole, N. (1992) *All, Here and Now: Black Politics in South Africa in the 1980s*, Hurst and Company, London, © Copyright 1991 by the Ford Foundation; Map 12.2: Courtesy of the South African High Commission; Maps 15.1 and 15.2: McDowall, D. (1994) *The Palestinians: The Road to Nationhood*, Minority Rights Group; Maps 19.1, 19.2, 19.3 and 19.4: based on maps in: *Atlas de Peuples d'Europe Centrale*, Jean et André Sellier, cartographie de Anne Le Fur © La Decouvert, Paris 1995 (new edition).

Photographs/Illustrations
p.8: Penny Tweedie/Panos; p.30: Greenpeace; p.52: Mansell Collection; p.53: Bildarchiv Preussischer Kulturbesitz; pp.78, 331: Popperfoto; pp.83, 108, 164, 372: Hulton Getty; p.130: Charles Moore/Black Star/Colorific!; p.167: Burt Glinn/Magnum; pp.183, 258, 286, 450, 495, 500, 507: Popperfoto/Reuter; p.199: Stuart Franklin/Magnum; p.208: Oriental and India Office Library and Records; p.229: AP/Wide World Photos; pp.301, 451: Associated Press; p.303: Soweto Civic Association; p.317: Photo Henner Frankenfeld/Southlight Photo Agency; p.360: Abbas/Magnum; p.384: Illustrations by Janet Stoeke; p.438: Jon Spaull; p.456: Courtesy of Paul Lewis.

Cartoons
pp.427, 436: *Izvestiya*.

Index

accountability of government 4, 5, 6, 41, 327
actors, political 15, 45, 415–16
Afghanistan 17, 37–8, 270, 401
Africa 269–320
    political map (1995) 273 Map 11.1
    sub-Saharan 272–93
African democracy 277–91
African-Americans in the USA 118, 120, 123, 124–7, 136
    (1940–60) 128 Map 5.1
African National Congress 294, 300, 302, 311, 313–16, 528–9, 533
Afrikaner 295–6
agency 15, 291–2, 432–3, 498, 522
agrarian societies 19–20, 519
agricultural associations 222, 224–5
agriculture,
    commercialization of see commercialization of agriculture
    labour-repressive 55, 56, 57
    plantation 21, 275
Al-Nahda Islamic Party (Tunisia) 350
Albania 87, 98, 399, 460, 473
Alfonsin, President 184
Algeria 102, 360–1, 524, 527, 531
Allende, S. 170
Alliance of Free Democrats (Hungary) 415
American Revolution 48
Amnesty 30
Angola 37–8, 108, 274, 311, 527–8, 531
anti-semitism 367, 370, 385, 475
apartheid state 294, 295–9, 318–19
    challenges to legitimacy of 299–304, 390
    legislation (1948–63) 296–8 Box 12.1
Aquino, Corazon 257, 259
Arab East 270, 321
Arab–Israeli conflict (1948–96) 334–5, 368 Box 15.1, 386, 388
Argentina 38, 146, 157, 160, 168, 174–6, 178, 180–92, 265–6, 370, 519
aristocracy see landed upper classes/landowners
Armed Forces Movement (Portugal) 108
Armenia 38, 427
ASEAN 506
Ashkenazi Jews 368, 369, 372, 382
Asia 145, 147–51, 195–263
    political boundaries (1995) 148–9 Map III.1
    political regimes (1975 and 1995) 150 Fig. III.2
Asian 'democracy' 253–4, 254
Asian 'tigers' 219
Assad, President Havez al- 328
Assam 7
Ataturk, Kemal 326
Attlee government 100
Australia 37–8, 44, 46, 60, 68, 518
Austria 37–8, 46, 59, 68, 75, 96, 458, 467
Austro-Hungarian Empire 62, 395, 470
'authoritarian (liberalizing)' 174–5
authoritarian regimes,

in Indonesia, Malaysia and the Philippines 250–3
listed by country 37, 38
in Middle East 323
in post-communist states 394 Table V.1
see also communist rule; dictatorships; military rule; single-party state
authoritarianism (definition of 4–5), 3, 7, 10, 54, 56, 144, 328
    breakdown of 295–304 (explanation 304–12)
    forms of 277
    and international community 256–7
    in Southern Europe 107–12
autonomy, associational 4, 5, 6, 176, 459, 500–1, 507
Azerbaijan 38

Bahrain 37–8, 321
Baldwin, S. 90
Balfour, Lord 370
Bangladesh 37–8, 355, 531
Barisan Nasional 252
Batista, F. 156
Beijing Workers' Autonomous Federation 214
Belarus 37–8, 428
Belgium 26, 37–8, 69, 116, 274, 467
belief systems, and democracy 270, 333, 345–66, 390–1
Ben Gurion, David 372–3
Benin 37–8, 285
Bharatiya Janata Party 205
Bhutan 37–8
Biko, Steve 301
Bill of Rights (USA) 122
Bismark, Otto von 53, 64
Black consciousness movement 300
'black economy' 35
Bohemia 470
Bolivia 152, 156, 160, 174–6, 180, 182–3, 187, 191–2
Bosnia 38, 471, 478, 482–3
Botha, P. 301, 304
Botswana 38, 226, 275, 282–4, 387, 530
    Democratic Party 282
    National Front 282
bourgeois democracy 447, 493
bourgeois revolution 54, 55–6
bourgeoisie 55–6, 65–6, 338, 339
    bureaucratic 276, 388–9
    urban 21, 499, 509
Bourguiba, President Habib 358
Branco, General H. 157, 169
Brazil 26, 157, 166, 174–9, 181–3, 185–7, 189–92, 265, 519, 526
Brazilian Labour Party 164, 169
Brezhnev, Leonid 400–1, 419, 422, 429
Britain 7, 35, 42, 54, 64, 88, 98, 99, 445, 458, 518, 524, 526
    (1919–39) 89–91
    ambiguous attitude to apartheid 310–11

as a liberal democracy 6–7, 116
nineteenth century democratization 50–1, 66
and Palestine 370–1
post-war 100–1
British Empire 95, 196, 202–3, 205–6
Brown v. Board of Education 131
Brunei 37–8
Bukharin, N. 424
Bulgaria 98–9, 399, 404, 406–8, 410, 417–8, 420
Bulgarian Communist Party 407
bureaucracy 41, 44, 116, 225
Burkina Faso 37–8, 274, 286
Burma 37, 147 see also Myanmar
Burundi 37–8, 285, 319
Buthelezi, Chief 304, 313

Caldera, President 189
caliphs 347–8, 364
Cambodia 17, 37–8
Cameroon 37–8, 286
Canada 37–8, 44, 46, 59, 531
Cape Verde 37–8, 285
capitalism 41, 44, 159, 221, 255, 276, 304–5, 310, 389, 459
capitalist development 21, 22, 338–9, 389, 396
as an explanatory factor 24–5, 115, 266, 499
late 219, 221
and liberal democracy 69–70
in Vietnam 507–8, 510
Cardenas, President L. 162, 164
Caribbean 20
Carter, Jimmy 133
case-oriented approach 32–3, 34, 36, 397
caste system 204–5, 520
Castro, Fidel 156, 167
Catalans 89, 111
Catholic Christian Democrats (Portugal) 109
Catholicism 29, 103, 110, 246, 403, 415, 453, 470
causal complexity 12–13, 25, 34–5, 330, 342
Ceaușescu, President 403–4, 418
Central African Republic 37–8, 274, 285
Central Committee (Soviet Union) 424–6, 429, 439
Central Intelligence Agency (USA) 401
central planned economy 395
centralism, democratic 197–8, 213, 217, 425, 472, 497, 507
centralization 116
Ceylon 147, 267
Chad 37–8, 285
chaebols in Korea 224, 227, 229, 230–1
chains-of-causation 25, 342
Chama Cha Mapinduzi (Tanzania) 281
Charter 77 Group 419, 477
Chartist movement 50
Chernobyl explosion 433, 476
Chernomyrdin, Viktor 434
Chiang Ching-Kuo, President 227–9, 233–4
Chiang Kai-shek 212, 224, 227
Chile 146, 152, 157, 169–70, 174–6, 180–2, 185–92, 266, 519
Chilean Communist Party 170
Chilean Socialist Party 170
Chilean Supreme Court 185
China 19, 148, 195–203, 208–14, 265–6, 491, 500, 501, 503–5, 514, 532–3

political history dates 210 Box 8.2
Chinese Communist Party 197, 208, 213
Chosŏn state 220
Christian Democrat Party (France) 102
Christian Democrats (Chile) 170
Christian Democrats (Germany) 105
Christian Democrats (Venezuela) 189
Christianity 143, 309
Chun Doo Hwan, General 227–31
churches 41, 111, 129, 289, 302, 390, 428
citizenship 4–5, 444, 531
and territorial issues 374, 375–81
Civic Forum (Czechoslovakia) 415, 455
civic nationalism 468, 477, 486
Civil Rights Movement, US 44, 45, 118, 120, 127–32, 137, 309, 310
civil society (definition of 4), 21, 141, 203, 457
as an explanatory factor 28, 390, 519
China 213–14
definition, Rueschemeyer's 206–7
development of 339–40, 341, 403, 419, 444, 507–8, 515
India 206–7
redefining 499–501
relationship with the state 4, 41, 265, 397
relative strength of 27, 226, 403, 409, 459–60, 510
resurgent 289–90, 292
role in breakdown of authoritarian rule 300–2, 501
Civil War (USA) 33, 48, 57, 61, 120, 125
class,
and democracy 42, 65–7, 255–6
ideology and the state 275–7
see also bourgeoisie; landed upper classes/landlords; middle class; peasantry; working class
class alliances 42, 54, 62–3, 67–8, 141–2, 202–3, 230–2
class divisions 25–6, 82–6, 219, 264, 389
class power (definition of 20), 522
class reductionism, defined 461
class relations, agrarian 55–7, 65, 222, 224–5, 275, 337–8
class structures 62–3, 202–3, 235, 519, 520
economic power and 54–7, 153–4
class struggle, re Lipset 12–13
class system, in Africa 276, 288, 291
classes, emergence of new entrepreneurial 507–8
clientelism 275–6, 288, 325, 389
definition 197
Clinton, Bill 133
coalition politics 106, 127, 369, 373–4, 377–9, 416, 456, 467, 480
Cold War 99–100, 141, 212–13, 266, 291, 309, 334, 388, 395, 401, 434, 476, 515
Collor, President 189
Colombia 154, 167, 176–7, 185, 187, 191, 193
colonial rule 13, 241, 260, 269, 278, 395, 469–70
British in India 205–6, 216
Japanese in China 211–13, 220–3
South African model 295, 309
colonialism,
internal 295–6, 305–6
in the Middle East 325, 353, 363, 387, 388

combined approach 33–4, 397–8, 523
command economy 402, 414, 415
commercialization of agriculture 19, 20, 55, 56, 154
Commonwealth of Independent States 428
communism 43, 85, 159, 197, 211, 309, 482
    collapse in Eastern Europe 393, 399, 400–5, 475–84
    crisis of international 393–6, 440, 503–4
    social science and transition 429–34
    Vietnamese 510, 511
Communist Party,
    China 213–14, 504
    in Eastern Europe 407, 476
    loss of faith in Vietnamese 490, 496, 502, 502–4
    Soviet 423, 425 Box 17.1; 427–8, 429, 436
Communist Party (France) 102
Committees for National Liberation (Italy) 103
Communist Party (Italy) 103
Communist Party of Indonesia 243, 248, 251
Communist Party of the Philippines 252, 258
Communist Party of the Soviet Union 422–3, 425–6, 433, 436
Communist Party of Vietnam 490, 492, 494, 497, 502, 504–6, 511
communist revolution 20, 513
communist rule 393, 421, 516
    in Czechoslovakia and Yugoslavia 99, 475–84
    in Russia 421–34
Comoros 37–8, 279
comparability 35
comparative methods 31–6, 264, 397, 518–23
    doubts about 414
comparative politics 3, 22–4, 517–20
conditionalities,
    democratic 267
    political to aid and investment 287–8
Confederation of South African Trade Unions 302, 308
Confucianism 29, 208, 209, 211, 216, 220, 505
Congo 37–8
Congress (USA) 122, 127, 131
Congress Alliance (South Africa) 300
Congress of People's Deputies (Soviet Union) 424
Congress Party (India) 196, 207–8, 266, 521
conjunctural causes (definition of 34), 264
consensus, and democratic survival 527–8
conservatism 165, 356, 357, 416, 463, 494, 533–4
Conservative Party (Britain) 60, 90, 100
consociational democracy 313, 323, 326, 353, 471, 486–8, 492, 514
    definition 466–7
    preconditions for 467 Box 19.1
consolidation of democracy 15, 17, 44, 518, 524–32
    in Africa 272, 286, 290, 292
    constraints in Israel 367–86
    defining feature 524
    in Europe 115–16, 139–40, 144
    problems in Latin America 183–93, 266
constitution 184, 186–7, 196, 279, 302, 313, 319, 356, 377, 407–8, 425, 429, 525–6, 531
    Russian 434–5

USA 119, 121–2
contingent factors, and structural factors 74–89, 158, 333, 522
corporatism, state 159, 163–4, 326, 448
correlations 12–13, 330, 409
corruption 104, 107, 190–1, 197, 231, 275, 385, 387, 423, 494, 496
Costa Rica 146, 152, 157, 170–1, 174, 176–7, 187, 530–1
Côte d'Ivoire 37–8, 274
counter-elites 409, 414, 416, 417, 419
Croat Peasant Party 474
Croatia 38, 87–8, 98, 469–75, 478, 481–3, 485–6
Cuba 156, 160, 174, 176–7, 186–7, 311, 433, 514, 532–3
cultural heterogeneity 283, 291, 295, 299–300, 531
    and economic underdevelopment 273–5
'Cultural Revolution' in China 197, 215
cultural symbols 280, 296
Cyprus 362
Czech Republic 409–10, 412, 417–18, 419, 484–5, 487
Czechoslovak Communist Party 476, 478
Czechoslovakia 75, 87–8, 96, 399, 406, 408–9, 411–12, 414–15, 420, 466–89, 514–16
    (1919) 471 Map 19.1
    (1945) 477 Map 19.3
    communist rule in 99, 400–1, 404, 407, 475–8
    ethnic divisions in 88, 397, 472–5, 486–7
    political community in 470–5
    see also Czech Republic; Slovakia

Dahl, Robert 3, 4–5, 431, 444
Dawda Jawara 283
De Gaule, Charles 98, 101
de Klerk, F. 17, 304, 314
debt crises 161, 411
decentralization 426, 431–2, 506
Declaration of Independence (USA) 121
decolonization 101, 102, 109, 248, 309
defeat, democracy by 58, 59
deinstitutionalization, political 197
demilitarization 183–7, 284
democracy,
    ambivalence of Western support for 248–9
    conditions for survival 525–31
    crisis in USA 119, 132–6
    delayed 294–320, 345, 363–4
    failure of 91–3, 521, 524
    habituation phase of 140, 292
    and liberal democracy 5–6
    models of 6
    requisites for 12–13, 291, 520, 522
    reversals of 532–4
    Therborn's preconditions for 58–61, 66
    use of term 345
    Vietnamese conceptions of 492–3
    Western views of 532
Democratic Party (USA) 90, 120, 125–6, 134
Democratic Progressive Party (Taiwan) 229, 233
democratic centralism 425
democratization (definition of 3), 6, 8, 174
    evidence and explanation 518–23

explanations of 54–70; summary 66 Table
2.1
pace in Eastern Europe 417–18, 420
stages in 294
theorization of 527
democratization, waves of see waves of
democratization
Deng Xiaoping 199, 213
Denmark 37–8, 60, 68, 98
dependency 22, 153–4, 221–2, 259
development, Lipset's indices of 11 Table 1.3
developmental states,
authoritarian 277
definition 225–6
Diamond, L. 24, 27, 28, 498, 499
Diaz, P. 162
dictatorships 43, 337, 395, 418
in Latin America 152–73, 159
direct democracy (definition of 6), 3, 444, 447
Disraeli, Benjamin 60
Djibouti 37–8, 279
doi moi 494
Dominican Republic 37–8, 175
Dreyfuss case 370
Dubček, Alexander 476

Eastern Europe 95, 96, 98, 99, 115, 399–420
(1945–89) 400 Map 16.1
(1995) 406 Map 16.2
indicators of democratization and socio-
economic development 410 Table 16.1
patterns of democratization in 405–9
economic change 246–7, 520
and political change 255–6, 260, 502
structural effects of 77–82, 142
economic crisis 24
and collapse of communism 402, 404
effects of 77–82, 89–91
post-communist 439
economic Depression (1920s and 1930s) 42,
160–3, 473, 474
economic development 120, 283–4, 515–16, 522
as an explanatory factor 24–5, 140, 141–2,
181, 200, 266, 387–8, 519, 520
role in breakdown of authoritarian rule
304–9
see also underdevelopment
economic growth 330–2, 522
communism and 395
in Europe 115–16
Soviet (1951–85) 422–3, 426 Table 17.1
economic liberalization 200, 213–14, 317, 324,
327–8
and political democracy 532–3
economic reform 395–6, 402, 404, 484
Soviet 425–7
in Vietnam 490, 494, 506
economic sanctions, threat of 311
Ecuador 37–8, 152, 157, 175, 180, 266
education 11, 13, 29, 291, 301, 445
women and 461, 462
Egypt 359, 390, 530–1
El Salvador 7, 37–8, 167, 175, 180
elections 4, 5, 6, 253–4, 327, 407, 408, 416, 417,
445
faith in, and political legitimacy 526–7

Israeli 378–81, 385
Soviet 421, 427, 439
turnout 444, 463
turnout in Eastern Europe and the Soviet
Union 452 Table 18.1
voting behaviour 444–5, 452–3
elite choices/strategies 45, 171, 280, 312, 314,
319, 330, 411, 413–19, 421, 432–3, 449, 490,
498–9, 502–3, 510, 513–14, 516, 520, 523, 534
elite divisions 60–1, 415, 416–17, 419
elites,
expatriate 295
nationalist 389
pacts between 154, 312–18, 318–19, 416,
419, 531, see also negotiations
party-state 328, 516
political 14, 15, 42, 45, 165, 170–1, 225, 265,
283, 288, 471
Engels, F. 492
England 19, 58
Equatorial Guinea 37–8, 283
Eritrea 37–8, 524
Estonia 38, 75, 451–2
Ethiopia 37–8, 269, 273
'ethnic cleansing' 469, 483, 531
ethnic divisions 13, 26, 246, 249, 280, 295, 299–
300, 314, 390, 487–8, 516
as constraints on democracy 26, 531
and Israeli democracy 369, 372, 377, 381–5
tensions in Czechoslovakia and Yugoslavia
88, 466–89
ethnic groups, in Czechoslovakia and
Yugoslavia 472 Table 19.1
ethnic nationalism 468, 483, 486, 487
ethnicity 44, 520
Europe, democratization in
(1871–1919) 49 Map 2.1
(1919–39) 72 Map 3.1
(1945–88) 97 Map 4.1
Europe, see also Eastern Europe; Southern
Europe
European Community 16, 341
European democracy, the quality of 115–16
exceptionalism,
Middle Eastern 270, 321–44
of USA 119, 124–32, 137–8
explanatory factors (definition of 24), 24–31, 294,
387, 397, 488, 515, 517, 519
for China's communist rule 208–14
for constraints on consolidation of
democracy in Israel 369–86
in European and US democratization 119–
24, 140–3
in Latin America and Asia 180–2, 204–14,
240–61, 264
export-oriented development 160–1, 165
external factors,
in democratization 287–8, 518, 523
role in breakdown of authoritarian rule
294–5, 309–11
extremists (definition of 15)

farmers 60, 63, 85
fascism 20, 103, 104–5
faulty data 35
federal republics, in Yugoslavia 478–81

federal system of government 122, 134, 143, 243, 244, 449, 486
federalization 476–81
Federation of Korean Industries 231
feminism, 'state' 355–6, 389
feudalism 209, 371
Fifth Republic (France) 102
Finland 37–8, 59, 75
First World War, consequences of 42, 59, 73, 74–7, 141, 393, 470–1
foco theory of revolution 167
Ford, Gerald 133
France 19, 46, 54, 57, 96, 98, 99, 370
    (1919–39) 89–91
    labour movement 64–5
    nineteenth century democratization 51–2, 66
    post-war 101–2
Franco, Francisco 71, 89, 98, 110
Franco-Prussian War 59, 60
Frei, Eduardo 170
French Revolution 2, 41, 46, 51
Frondizi, President 169
Front de Liberation Nationale (Algeria) 360
Front Islamique du Salut (Algeria) 360
Fujimori, President 189, 193
Fukuyama, F. 115
fundamentalism, religious 346, 362, 531

Gabon 37–8, 275
Gambia, The 38, 282–4, 285, 530
Gandhi, M.K. 212
gender,
    and democracy 354
    inequalities 26, 389
    and political participation in Eastern Europe and USSR 462 Table 18.3, 516
    see also women
Geneva Agreement (Vietnam) 491
Geneva Convention 185
genocide 466, 475, 485
geo-political relationships, as an explanatory factor 22, 43, 141, 219, 226, 227, 228, 235–6
Georgia 38, 427
German Communist Party 84, 100, 104
German Democratic Party 80
German Socialist Unity Party 104
German Socialist Party 104
Germany 19, 33, 56, 73–4, 89, 95, 96, 98, 99–100, 115, 116, 520–1, 532
    East (German Democratic Republic) 104, 399, 404, 405–6, 408, 410, 411, 412, 414, 417
    nineteenth century 52–3, 64, 66
    post-war 104–5
    unification of 54, 405–6
    Weimar Republic 75, 76, 79–81, 84, 85
    West (Federal Republic) 100, 105, 107
Ghana 37–8, 279
Giddens, Anthony 18
glasnost 423, 424, 448–9
global economy 159, 166, 172, 236, 275, 307, 411, 508
globalization 362, 387
Golkar 7, 253
Gorbachev, Mikhail 395–6, 400–1, 413, 418–19, 421–30, 432–3, 448–9, 478, 503, 513

Gosplan 426
Goulart, President 154, 169
Government of India Act 1935 196
governments, distinguished from regimes 4
Great Leap Forward 215
Greece 95, 98, 99
green politics 457
Greenland 37–8
Greenpeace 30
gridlock 133, 134, 141
group divisions 26
Guatemala 37–8, 167, 181
Guevara, 'Che' 167
'Guided Democracy' (Indonesia) 242, 251
Guinea 37–8, 108, 278
Guinea-Bissau 37–8, 279
Gulf War 327

Haiti 37–8, 178, 180, 526
Habsburg and Hohenzollern Empires 71, 75
Hani, Chris 318
hardliners (definition of 15), 180, 228, 234, 415–16, 428, 510, 514
Hastings Banda 288–9
Havel, Václav 417, 484
Held, D. 3, 4, 6
Hinduism 204–5, 216, 531
Histadrut 367, 371, 373, 382, 390
Hitler, A. 45, 71, 84, 90
Ho Chi Minh 491, 503–4
Honduras 37–8, 180
Hong Kong 147
House of Commons 27, 50
House of Lords 50
House of Representatives 122
Hu Yaobang 199
Huk rebellion 247
human rights 181, 182, 184–5, 287, 295, 403, 437, 477
Hume, D. 121
Hungarian Democratic Forum 415
Hungarian Socialist Party 407
Hungary 84, 399, 402–3, 404, 406–8, 410, 412, 414–16, 419, 456–7, 514
Huntington, Samuel 9, 31, 288, 312, 411, 429, 518
Husak, Gustav 477–8
Hussein, King of Jordan 327
hyper-inflation 77–9
hyper-pluralism 134, 135, 138, 141

Iceland 37–8, 98
ideas,
    legacy of in Indonesia, Malaysia and the Philippines 247–8
    role in democratization 28–9, 143, 241, 259, 260, 261, 309, 390–1, 394
    Vietnamese democratic 492–3
identity,
    ethnic and religious 241, 249
    inter-ethnic 472, 486
    linguistic 246, 473
    political 270
    see also national identity
ideology 4, 5, 188, 326, 391, 447
    bourgeois 55, 197, 198

dominant state 227, 275–7, 367–8, 369–70, 372, 375, 377, 385–6
    racial 138, 306, 309
    religious 296
    secular 44, 247, 253, 254
'imagined community' 245, 469–70
IMF 186, 287, 454
immigrants, to Israel 367–8, 370–1, 372, 375–6, 386
imperialism 196, 208–10, 212, 216, 520–1, *see also* colonial rule
independent states 269, 279, 396
India 7, 19, 20, 26, 195–218, 265, 432, 520–1, 526, 530–31, 533
    emergence of democracy 204–8
    political history dates 206 Box 8.1
Indian National Congress 196, 207–8, 212, 266
indigenization of political control, in Africa 278–80
individualism 411–12, 459
Indonesia 7–8, 240–63, 265, 527, 531
    authoritarian regime 251
    patterns of national integration and identity 245–6
Indonesian Nationalist Party 243
industrial action *see* strikes
industrialization 11, 19–20, 144, 306–7, 417–18, 476, 519, 522
    socialist 411, 412–13
inequality, socio-economic 26, 299, 389, 533–4
information, access to 254, 423, 424, 435
Inkatha Freedom Party 313–14
institutional unity 182
Institutionalized Party of the Revolution (Mexico) 157, 189, 429
institutions 41, 446, 487
    definition 27
    participation and democratic change 455–60
    see also political institutions; state
intelligentsia 290, 413–14, 515
interest groups 4, 312–18, 319
interests 155–6, 171, 225, 313
    minority 379
    organized 134–5, 457–8
    of superpowers 334
    vested rural 533
interim government, types of 16–17
internal development, democracy by 58, 60–1, 518
internal pressures 289–90, 294, 403–4, 519
    from above 54, 56, 500, 519
    from below 54, 57, 181, 338–9, 499, 501, 519
    from within the state 501, 502–3
international agencies 444
International Confederation of Trade Unions 30
international relations 182, 219, 235–6, 260, 309–11, 369, 396–7, 488, 515, 522
    as an explanatory factor 20, 29–31, 266, 388, 519
    context for Soviet transition 433
    and the Middle East 321, 322, 324, 329, 333–5
    pressures 260, 388, 454
    support for authoritarianism 256–7, 295, 310–11
intervening variables 24, 155

Iran 270, 321, 354, 356–7
Iraq 7, 321–3, 450
Ireland 37–8, 62, 98
Islam 29, 204, 248, 390, 531
    contemporary views on democracy 349–50, 532
    and democracy 332–3, 341, 345–66
    doctrine 346–50
    in opposition 358–61, 362
    role of 270
Islamic Liberation Party (Jordan/Palestine) 349–50
Islamic Republican Party (Iran) 357
Islamic states 356–7
Islamists, radical 345, 361, 362, 364
Islamist Welfare Party (Turkey) 331
Israel 38, 270, 367–87, 390, 531
    constraints on consolidation 367–86
Israeli democracy, features of 378–81
Israeli Supreme Court 378
Italy 35, 59, 75, 83–4, 88–9, 95–6, 98–9, 102–4, 106, 107, 115, 445

Jackson, A. (USA) 123
Jamaica 38, 530
Jammat-i-Islami (Pakistan) 350
Japan 9, 32, 38, 44, 148, 196, 212, 219–23, 236, 243, 257, 266, 518, 532
Jefferson, Thomas 121, 124
Jewish community 367–86
    in Palestine (Yishuv) 370–1
Johnson, Lyndon 133
Jommu and Kashmir 7
Jordan 321, 359–60
Juan Carlos, King 111
Judaism 372
judiciary (USA) 122, 131
judiciary, role of 48, 122, 131, 143, 425
juridic theory, Islamic 345, 347–8, 354

Kádár, Janos 402–3
Kaiser 53, 79
Kaunda, President K. 290
Kazakhstan 38
Kennedy, President John 310
Kenya 275, 288, 526
KGB 434
Khmer Rouge 501
Khomeini, Ayatollah 357
Kim Dae Jung 229
Kim Young Sam, President 229
King, Martin Luther 129
Kirgizistan 38
Klaus, Vaclav 457
Knesset 378–9
Kohl, Chancellor Helmut 406
Koran *see* Quran
Korean War 223
Kosovo 471, 479–82, 486
Kruschev, N. 422
Kubitschek, President 168
Kuomintang Party 210, 224
Kuwait 37–8 321, 327, 359, 450
Kwangju 227, 230–1

Labour Party (Britain) 100

Labour Party (Israel) 382, 384
Labour Party (Taiwan) 233
labour, ethno-religious division of 353
labour movements 60, 63–4, 127, 144, 314, 316,
   318, *see also* unions
land ownership, in Israel 383–4
land reform 222, 223–4, 232, 237–8, 326, 473,
   521, 533–4
landed upper classes/landowners 20, 41, 55, 56,
   57, 65, 222, 264, 522
      dependent on peasant labour 337
      urban-based absentee Middle Eastern *see*
         'notables'
Laos 37–8
Latin America 145–7, 152–94
      democratization (1980–95) 8–10, 174–94
      dictatorship (1930–80) 152–73
      political map (1975) 153 Map 6.1; (1995)
         175 Map 7.1
      political regimes (1930–79) 158 Fig. 6.1;
         (1970–90) 176 Fig. 7.1; (1975 and 1995)
         147 Fig. III.1
Latvia 38, 75
Le Duc Tho 494
leadership 154, 155, 172, 312, 314, 319, 326,
   339, 400
      collective 481, 483, 504–5
      cults 276, 458
      failure of 494
      generations in Vietnam 493 Box 20.2
      Islamic concept of 347–8
      Palestinian 371, 372
      Soviet 395–6, 421, 434
leadership choice *see* elite choices/strategies
League of Communists of Yugoslavia 480, 482–
   3
League of Nations 79
Lee Teng-hui, President 234
legitimacy 138, 181, 240, 332, 411, 476, 511
      battle for 242, 261–2
      challenges to in South Africa 299–304
      constitutional 525–6
      crisis of 281, 288
      definition 241
      and democratic survival 525–7
      geographical 270, 525
      of Islam 347–8
      passive 242, 249, 254
      political 115–16
      political, defined 526–7
      of post-war democracies 249–50
      problem of communist regimes 395
      regime 241–2, 260
      religious 204
Lenin, V. 422, 481
Lesotho 37–8, 274, 285
Liang Qichao 210
liberal democracy (definition of 4), 3, 5, 6–7, 272
      and capitalist development 69–70
      explaining its absence in Middle East 329–
         36
      failure of 44
      listed by country 37–8
      paradox of 533–4
      in post-communist states 394 Table V.1
      prerequisites for 324, 329–32, 341

      survival of 524
Liberal Party (Britain) 90
liberalization,
      explaining 498–504
      political 174, 180, 236, 290, 339–40, 362–3,
         390, 397
      in Eastern Europe 403–4
      instability of 506–7
      and its limits 492–8
      in Vietnam 490–2, 510–11, 514
      see also economic liberalization
Liberia 37–8, 269, 273
Libya 37–8, 358
Likud Party 381–2
linearity 12, 13, 518
linguistic divisions 246, 473
Linz, J. 15–17, 23, 24, 154, 172
Lipset, S.M. 11–13, 23, 24, 25, 32, 201, 241, 520,
   524, 532
literacy 41, 126, 130, 143, 197, 201, 215, 234,
   274, 330, 521, 530
Lithuania 38, 75, 427, 455
Locke, J. 121
Luxembourg 37–8

MacDonald, R. 90
Macedonia 38, 87, 473, 478–9
Macmillan, Harold 310
Madagascar 37–8, 269, 285
Madero, F. 162
Magyarization 469
Mahathir bin Mohamed, Dr 251–3
Mainwaring, Scott 15, 23, 498, 510
Malawi 37–8, 278–9, 285, 518, 528
Malawi Congress Party 279
Malaya 147, 267
Malaysia 240–63, 265, 530–1
      authoritarian regime 251–2
      patterns of national integration and identity
         246
Malaysian Communist Party 244, 248
Maldives 37–8
Malta 37–8
Mandela, Nelson 294, 304, 314–15, 518
Mann, Michael 61–5, 66
Mao Tse-tung 198–9, 211, 215
Marcos, Ferdinand 235, 242, 252, 255
market economy 24, 396, 459, 502, 508
Marshall plan 99
Marx, K. 492, 517
Marxism 447
Marxist–Leninist 211, 213, 275, 421, 440, 517
Masaryk, T. G. 471
Mass Democratic Movement (South Africa) 302
'mass line' 199
Mauritania 37–8, 271
Mauritius 38, 269, 282–4, 387, 529–31
Mauritius Labour Party 282
media 28, 190, 198, 257, 290, 330, 421, 424, 428,
   495, 497
Mencius 209
Menem, President 184, 189, 193
Mečiar, Vladimir 458, 483
methodological convergence 33–4
Mexico 7, 157, 162, 166, 176–7, 179, 187–90,
   192–3, 266

middle class, professional 21, 499, 509
Middle East 321–67
  definitions 270
  exceptionalism 270, 321–44
  political map and major oil producing states (1995) 324 Map 13.1
  small states in the 323
migration 120, 438
militarization 212, 334–5, 369, 384, 388
military 27, 43, 180
  politicization of the 250–1
  relative strength or weakness of 259, 401
  within the state apparatus 21, 326
military expenditure 184, 186, 334–5, 401
military rule 157, 277, 281–2, 285
  over Palestinians in Israel 383–5
Milošević, Slobodaban 482–5
minority groups,
  integration and assimilation in Israel 370–1, 375–81, 386
  and proportional representation 474
  veto rights of 467
Mizrachi Jews 368–9, 382
mobilization 42, 338–9, 418, 419, 448, 492, 508–9
  definition 59
Mobutu Sese Seko, President 274, 281
moderates (definition of 15), 180, 312
modernity 44, 333
modernization,
  communist concept of 411–12, 419, 513
  and democracy 444, 445–6
modernization approach (definition of 11–13), 10, 498, 513, 520–1, 523
  to Africa 291
  to Eastern Europe 409, 410–14, 417–18, 419–20, 466
  to Europe and USA 44–5
  to India and China 200–2
  to Latin America 152–3, 178
  to the Middle East 329–32, 335, 340
  to South Africa 294, 304
  to Southeast Asia 219–20, 260, 519
  to the Soviet Union 431–2, 464, 519
Moldova 38
monarchy 41, 270, 323, 326, 356, 474
monetary system 18
Mongolia 37–8
Montenegro 478, 482
Montesguieu 121
Moore, Barrington 19–20, 23, 24, 25, 27, 32–3, 154, 161, 202–3, 205, 214, 337, 388, 435, 517, 520
  political routes to democratization 54–8, 66, 518
Morocco 356
Morovia 470
Movement for Multi-Party Democracy (Zambia) 289
Movement Socialist Militant (Mauritius) 282
Mozambique 37–8, 108, 274, 316, 519
Mubarak, President 327–8
multiculturalism 124
multinational companies 166, 388
multiparty systems 408, 417, 421, 427, 434, 456, 474

  and Islam 350
  rejection in Vietnam 493–4, 497
Muslim Brothers (Egypt) 359
Muslim states, predominantly 351 Map 14.1
Mussolini, Benito 71, 83, 96, 98, 103
Myanmar 38, 267, 527–8 *see also* Burma

Namibia 17, 37–8, 285
Napoleon Bonaparte 51
Napoleon III 51, 64
Napoleonic War 50, 60
Nasser, Gamal Abdel 327
nation-states 41, 44, 370
  and Islam 332
National Action Party (Mexico) 165
National Assembly (Pakistan) 357
National Assembly (South Korea) 230
National Assembly (Taiwan) 228, 234
National Assembly (Vietnam) 495
National Democratic Union (Brazil) 165
National Islamic Front (Sudan) 350
National Party (South Africa) 296, 302, 306, 313–16
National Party Congress (Soviet Union) 425
National People's Congress (China) 198
National Religious Party (Israel) 373
National Rifle Association (USA) 135–6
National Salvation Front (Romania) 408
National Socialism 85
national identity 245–6, 390
national integration 241, 245–6, 259, 261, 466
national interest 4, 156, 280
national mobilization, democracy by 58, 59
national question, and democratization 62, 67
national security 168–9, 303–4
nationalism 101, 143, 247–8, 326–7, 332, 514, 515
  African 278, 309
  Afrikaner 296
  authoritarian 198
  in Czechoslovakia and Yugoslavia 397, 466–89
  'defensive' 345, 364
  definitions 468–9
  and Israeli democracy 381–5
  and political change 505
  see also civic nationalism; ethnic nationalism
nationalisms, conflicting 86–9
NATO 16, 99, 341
Nawaz Sharif (Pakistan) 357
Nazi Holocaust 370
Nazi Party 81, 85
Nazism 73, 76, 85, 90, 395, 474–5, 487
negotiations 312–19, 406, 416, 419, 449, 518–19, 520
Nehru, Jawaharlal 206
Nepal 37–8, 148
Netherlands 37–8, 53, 458, 467
New Economic Policy (Soviet Union) 426
New Israeli Communist Party 379
'New Order' (Indonesia) 251, 258
New Zealand 2, 37–8, 44, 46, 60, 68, 518
newly industrializing countries (NICs) 116, 226
Nicaragua 156, 167, 175, 177, 181, 187
Niger 37–8, 285, 524
Nigeria 26, 275, 284, 290, 387, 524, 527, 531

Nixon, Richard 133
nomenklatura 434, 439
nomocracy 347–8
non-governmental organizations 30, 256, 310, 388
North Korea 26, 37–8, 223
Northern Ireland 384
Norway 37–8, 96, 98
'notables' 325–6, 336

O'Donnell, G. 15, 17, 23, 24, 28
oil, role of 321, 322, 323, 326, 334, 339, 340, 362, 363, 388, 411
oligarchy 159, 244–5, 252
Oman 37–8, 321
Omar Bongo, President 288
opportunists (definition of 15)
opposition 5, 180, 281, 282, 510
    anti-communist 401–2, 415, 416, 463, 487
    to white political domination, black 118, 120, 127–32, 300–4
    Islam in 358–61, 362
Ottoman Empire 470
Oxfam 30

pacts, inter-elite *see* elites, pacts between
Pakistan 204, 267, 357, 530, 534
palace coups 406, 415
Palestinian Arabs 270, 367, 369, 371, 375, 381, 383–4, 385, 386
Palestinians 327
Panama 37–8, 175, 180
Pan African Congress 300
pan-Africanism 309
pan-Slavism 471
'Pancho' Villa, F. 162
pancasila democracy 247, 253, 254
Papua New Guinea 38
Paraguay 37–8
Paris Commune of 1871 44, 51
Park Chung Hee, General 226–7
parliament 42, 302, 407, 425, 443, 474
    women in Eastern Europe and Soviet Union 460–1, 461 Table 18.2
partial democracy (definition of 5), 3, 7, 286
    '(hybrid)' 175
    listed by country 37, 38
    in post-communist states 394 Table V.1
participation,
    and democratization 443–65
    gender differences in 460–3
    levels in Western democracies 445
    mass 443, 447–8, 492
    in post-communist states 450–5
    under communist rule 446–9
participatory democracy (definition of 5–6), 3, 443
party systems 187–90, 265–6, 445
    pluralist 284, 285
    see also single-party state
patriarchy 333, 340, 389, 460
patronage politics 244, 249, 251, 253, 275, 276, 288, 389
peasantry 21, 222, 499, 510
    revolt 54, 57, 209–10, 216, 338–9
People's Consultative Assembly (Indonesia) 7

People's Council (Malaysia) 254
People's Progressive Party (The Gambia) 282
'people', the 26, 466
perestroika 418, 423, 424, 426
Perez, President 193
Perón, Jaun 163–4
Peru 37–8, 152, 157, 160, 175, 180, 266
petite bourgeoisie 373–4
Philippines 240–63, 265, 528
    authoritarian regime 252–3
    democratic restoration in the 257–9
    legislature 257
    patterns of national integration and identity 246
Pilsudski 71, 79
Pinochet, General A. 157, 170, 192
pluralism 232–3, 388, 422, 431–3, 434, 448, 516
    ethno-religious 353–4
    social 204–5, 216
Poland 16, 87, 96, 99, 370, 399, 448, 453, 456–7, 513–15
    pattern of democratization in 401, 402, 403, 404, 406–8, 410, 412–14, 415, 416, 419–20
Polish United Workers' Party 403
Politburo 426, 429, 433
political change,
    and economic change 260
    under communist rule 446–9
    in Vietnam 490–2, 494–8
political community 4, 236, 445
    in Czechoslovakia and Yugoslavia 466–89
political culture 13, 191, 202, 390–1, 488, 505, 515
    as an explanatory factor 28–9, 143, 519
    China 209–11
    in Eastern Europe 412
    India 204–5
    in the Middle East 324, 329, 332–3
    and state structure, USA 120–3
    Zionism and 369–70, 375–81, 385
political development, patterns in Middle East 321–5
political institutions (definition of 27–8), 13, 44, 172, 219, 388–9, 516
    as an explanatory factor 27–8, 142–3, 265, 519
political order, as an explanatory factor 181
political participation *see* participation
political parties 4, 21, 27
    and Islam 350
    in Latin America 187–90
    party fragmentation 134, 138
    policy restraint by winning 528–30
    in post-communist Russia 435–7
    weak 450, 455, 458
political projects 155–6, 171
political reform 190–1, 395–6, 490
political regime (definition of 3, 4, 6)
    classification by country 37–8
    types 3–6 Table 1.1
polyarchy 4
polygyny 355
Popular Movement of the Revolution (Zaire) 281
population factors 412, 508

populism 120, 122–3, 163–6, 172, 265, 326, 363, 458
Portugal 7, 16, 95, 98
 democratic revolution in 107–10, 112
Portuguese Communist Party 16, 109
Portuguese Scoialist Party 109
post-communist states 393–516
 democratization and 434–40
 democratization levels 408–9, 464
 political participation in 450–5
 types of regime 394 Table V.1
post-war democracies 242–50
poverty 138, 192, 194, 197, 215, 259, 266, 269, 291, 521, 533
 as an obstacle to democratic consolidation 274, 530–1
Prague Spring 432
presidencies, collective 481, 483
pressure groups 445, 457, 458
private sphere 340, 455, 531
privatization 191, 402, 435, 484
 of politics 134–5, 138
profit motive 459, 461
proletariat, industrial see working class
proportional representation 378–9, 385, 386, 474
proportionality 467
Protestantism 29, 403, 470
protests 290, 451, 454, 478
Prussia 52
public opinion 422, 437–8, 485
public space 361
Punjab 7
puppet states 475

Qatar 37–8, 321
Qing Dynasty 209, 211, 213, 220
Quadros, President 168
quantitative data 12, 13, 35, 200–1
Quran (Koran) 347, 350, 352, 355–6

race 44, 295, 520
 politics of in USA 44, 124–32
racial segregation, USA 118, 125–7
Radical Party (Argentina) 168
radicals 180, 357, 533
Ramos, Fidel 257
rational choice theory 446, 463, 464
Reagan, Ronald 133, 401
Realpolitik 478
 definition 185
Red Army 98–9
Red Cross 30
redemocratization 154–5, 174, 257–9
 in Africa 286–91, 390
Reform Act 1867 50, 60
reform see economic reform; political reform; social reform
regime change, and economic change 255–6
regional factors 158, 280
Reichstag 53
religion, institutionalization of 29, 333
religious differences,
 as constraints on democracy 345, 351–4, 531
 and Israeli democracy 369, 372, 377, 381–5
rent-seeking 247, 249

'rentier states' 323, 334, 338, 339, 362, 363
reporting systems 215
representation 4, 6, 62, 67, 116, 133, 187–90
 crisis of democratic 454
Republican Party (USA) 90, 125–6, 134
republicanism 270
revolution,
 in Cuba 166–71
 democratic in Southern Europe 107–14
 French 42
 from above 54, 56
 from below 54, 57, 338–9
 Russian (1917) 42, 395, 421, 424
 social 156, 162
 theories of 167
 see also bourgeois revolution; communist revolution
rights,
 civil and political 4, 5, 6, 41, 287, 395, 408–9, 434–5, 533 see also Civil Rights Movement, US
 of religious minorities in Islamic states 352–3
 religious in Soviet Union 428
 social and economic 533–4
 subsistence 533
 of women 340
Roh Tae Woo, General 229, 232
Romania 20–8, 95, 98–9, 399, 402–3, 406–8, 410, 415, 417–18, 420, 460, 473
Roosevelt, F. D. 90, 127
Roxas, Manuel 245
Rueschemeyer, D. 20–8, 30, 33, 172, 179, 206–7, 237, 338, 499, 517, 522, 524
ruling class, state-based 276, 288, 291, 389
Russia 19, 77, 83, 370, 421–42, 453–4
Russo-Japanese War (1904–5) 220
Rustow, D. 13–15, 23–4, 26, 33, 171, 292, 330, 491, 498, 518, 520, 524
Rwanda 37–8, 319, 531

Sadat, President 327, 358
Salazar, A. 71, 98, 107
Salinas, President 190
Sandinista National Liberation Front 156
Sandinistas 528
Sao Tome and Principe 37–8, 285
Saudi Arabia 270, 356
security apparatus of the state 3–4, 5, 21
Second World War, 43, 96–9, 141, 306, 309, 422, 475, 485
 in Asia (1941–45) 220, 223–4, 267
Seewoosagur Ramgoolam 283
Sendero Luminoso 185
Senegal 284–5
Sephardi Jews 372
Serbia 469–73, 475, 478, 482–3, 485–6
Serbia-Montenegro 37–8, 87
Seretse Khama 283
settler society 295, 363, 388, 389
Seventh Party Congress (Vietnam) 496–7, 504
Seychelles 37–8
Shah of Iran 334, 357
Shain, Y. 15–17, 23
sharecropping 55
Sierra Leone 37–8, 274, 524

Singapore 35, 37–8, 246, 530
single-party state 6, 277, 281–2
    model in Southeast Asia 492, 506
Sino-Japanese War 1894–5 211, 220
Sixth Party Congress (Vietnam) 494–6, 502
slavery 44, 118, 120, 125–6, 137
Slovakia 98, 409, 451, 469–75, 477–8, 484–5, 487
Slovenia 38, 87, 451, 470–3, 476, 479, 481–3
social change 44, 200, 522
'social contract' 421, 429
social debt 191–3
Social Democrats (Germany) 90
social divisions 450, 487, 516
    as an explanatory factor 25–6, 82–6, 141–2,
        389–90, 519
    and Israeli democracy 369, 370–3, 385
    in USA 119, 124–32
social and economic indicators, India and China
    (1992) 201 Table 8.1
social movements 45, 191–3, 233, 265, 404, 409,
    443, 455–6, 463
social organizations, new 'political' 500–1, 509
social reform 170–1, 395–6
social science 36
    communism and transition 429–34
social space 508
socialism 106, 409, 422, 426, 432–3, 447, 476,
    478, 493
    African 275–6
    party-state model of command 328
Socialist Labour Party (Romania) 407
Socialist Party (France) 102
socialist democracy 199, 443, 447, 462, 506, 511
socio-economic development see modernization
    approach
softliners (definition of 15), 180, 229, 234, 312,
    416, 419, 433, 510, 514
Solidarity (in Poland) 214, 399, 402–3, 407, 412–
    14, 415, 416, 420, 448, 456, 457
Somalia 37–8, 278–9
Somoza, A. 156, 181
South Africa 294–320, 387, 390, 519–20, 525–7,
    529
    apartheid boundaries 299 Map 12.1
    provinces (1996) 317 Map 12.2
South African Communist Party 300
South African Council of Churches 302
South Korea 26, 219–39, 257, 264, 519, 528, 532
Southern Christian Leadership Conference
    (USA) 129
Southern Europe, democratic revolutions in
    107–14
sovereignty,
    Brezhnev doctrine of limited 400–1
    of consumers 24–5
    popular 26, 71
Soviet democracy 447
Soviet Union see USSR
soviets 424
Spain 7, 81–2, 84, 89, 95, 98, 116, 146, 524
    democratic revolution in 110–13
Spanish Civil War 71
Spanish Communist Party 112
Spanish Socialist Party 112
Spinola, General 109
Sri Lanka 38, 267, 524

Stalin, Josef 98, 481
Stalinism 430–1
state (definition of 3–4)
    as an explanatory factor 27–8, 219, 388–9,
        516, 519
    and class formation 203, 275–7, 338–9, 341
    financial crisis of the 362–3
    relationship with civil society 4, 41, 265, 397
    and the representative question 62, 67, 116
    role in the economy 337–40, 341, 388–9
    Weber's definition 3–4
state boundaries 26, 249, 269, 270, 274, 375, 469
state building 367, 369–74
state class 276, 288, 291
state collapse 285–6
state power 21, 295, 522
    changing patterns of 242–5
    and class divisions 264
    demilitarization of 284
    relative 265
state repression 303–4
state structure, as an explanatory factor 44, 61–
    2, 67, 142–3, 425
state-led development 163, 339, 389
state-owned enterprises (SOEs), 'fence
    breaking' by 501
states,
    classification of Middle Eastern 322 Table
        13.1
    'non-aligned' 311
Stepan, A. 154
Strategic Defence Initiative 433
strikes 83, 289–90, 307–8, 450, 458
Stroessner, A. (Paraguay) 156
structural approach (definition of 18–22), 10, 45,
    139, 514, 520–3, 524
    to Africa 291, 294
    to Eastern Europe 412–14
    to India and China 202–3
    to Latin America 154–5, 171, 172–3, 179
    to Middle East 321, 322, 333–5, 336–40, 341–
        2
    to post-communist countries 446, 498–9,
        504–9
    to South Africa 304–5, 314–18, 318–19
    to Southeast Asia 234–7, 240, 260
    to Southern Europe 112–13
    to Western Europe 74–89, 105–6
structural factors, and contingent factors 74–89
structure,
    and agency 432–3, 522
    and choice 154–5
structures of power (definition of 18–22), 520
student protest movements 199–200, 214, 256,
    290, 478, 504
Suárez Gonzáles, Adolfo 110–11
subordinate/subaltern classes, role of 46–7, 338
Sudan 37–8, 271, 531
suffrage 41, 42, 59, 64, 67
    female 59, 68–9, 85–6, 115, 120, 144, 355
    late arrival in USA 118, 119, 137
    universal 58, 133, 253–4
Suharto, President 7, 251, 253, 259, 525
Sukarno, President 242, 247, 251
Sun Yat-Sen 198, 210
Supreme Court (USA) 131

Supreme Soviet 424
Swaziland 37–8, 219
Sweden 14, 37–8, 59, 60, 64, 68, 98, 311, 458
Switzerland 26, 37–38, 46, 60, 69, 98, 518, 531
Syngman Rhee, President 223, 225
Syria 37–8, 321–3

Taiping Rebellion 211
Taiwan 32, 219–39, 264, 519, 521
Tajikistan 38, 423
Tanganyika African National Union 279
tangwai candidates in Taiwan 228, 230, 233
Tanzania 279, 281, 518
technological development 395, 397
territorial questions 62, 67, 116, 270, 374–6
Thailand 37–8, 148
Thatcher government 7
theoretical approaches (definition of 10), 1, 10–24, 44–5, 139–40, 178–9, 264, 517
Therborn, Göran 58–61, 66
Third Republic (France) 60, 64, 90
'third wave' *see* waves of democratization
Tiananmen Square 199, 214
Tito 478, 480, 483, 487
Togo 37–8, 281
totalitarianism 414
trade 55, 160, 275
trade unions *see* unions
transition, definition of 'democratic' 405
transition approach (definition of 13–18), 10, 45, 520–3, 524
    and political participation 444
    to Africa 290, 291–2
    to Eastern Europe 414–15, 420, 457, 466
    to Latin America 179–82, 194, 290, 457
    to the Middle East 358–61, 367
    to post-communist countries 510, 513–14
    to South Africa 312–19
    to Southeast Asia 220, 237, 498, 510
    to Southern Europe 113–14, 457
    to the Soviet system 422–8, 429–34
    to the USA 140
    to Western Europe 106–7, 139–40
transnational corporations 166
transnational relations 21–2, 309–11, 488, 499
    as an explanatory factor 20, 29–31, 519
Trinidad 38, 531
Truman Doctrine 99
Tudjman, Franjo 483
Tunisia 358, 360
Tunku, Abdul Rahman 244, 248
Turkey 14, 38, 321, 330–1, 341, 387, 390, 520
Turkmenistan 38

Uganda 37–8, 279, 285, 370
UK *see* Britain
Ukraine 38, 98, 428
ulama 348–9, 350, 356, 357, 365
UMNO (Indonesia) 244, 252, 254
UN (United Nations) 17, 29, 223, 310, 433
underdevelopment 24, 178, 273–5, 291
unemployment 453
Union of the Democratic Centre (Spain) 112
unions 289, 403, 413, 458–9, 508–9
    unions, in South Africa 300–2, 306–8, 389, 390

United Arab Emirates 37–8, 321
United Kingdom *see* Britain
United Nations *see* UN
universals 12, 13, 431
urbanization 11, 161, 201, 330, 499
Uruguay 37–8, 146, 152, 157, 175, 180, 266
USA 54, 95, 98, 99, 146, 168, 182, 223, 248, 266, 445, 491, 501, 518, 524, 533
    (1919–39) 81, 89–91
    ambiguous attitude to apartheid 310–11
    democracy (since 1945) 118–38
    nineteenth century democratization 48–50, 66
    support for democracy, ambivalence of 248–9, 287
USSR 1, 10, 28, 37, 95, 96, 98, 99, 287, 399, 401, 421, 478, 480, 505, 513–16, 519, 528
    see also Commonwealth of Independent States; Russia
Uzbekistan 38

Vargas, G. 164, 166
variable-oriented approach 32, 34, 35, 397
variables 12, 13, 272, 406–7, 519
varna see caste system
Venezuela 146, 152, 170, 176–7, 187–90, 192, 433, 528–9
Versailles Treaty 76
Veterans Associations (Vietnam) 498
Vichy Republic 96, 98
Viet Minh 491
Vietnam 6, 32, 37–8, 490–512, 514–15
    historical background 491 Box 20.1
Vietnam Buddhist Church 498
Vietnam Fatherland Front 498
Vietnam Peasants' Union 496
Vietnam War 491
violence 313, 319, 406, 525
Von Hindenburgh, P. 76
Vorster, John 301

Wafd Party (Egypt) 359
Walesa, Lech 408, 458
war 43, 219, 369, 501
    as an explanatory factor 20, 29–31, 58, 67–8, 140, 141, 266, 267, 386, 519
    and liberal democracy 22
warfare, industrialized 41–2, 59, 115
Warsaw Pact 99
waves of democratization 8–10, 13, 387
    'first wave' 410–11
    'second wave' 524
    'third wave' 8–10, 399, 411, 524, 530
    'third wave', in Africa 288
    'third wave', in Asia 150–1
    'third wave', in Latin America 174–82
Weber, Max 3–4, 517
Weimar constitution 53
Weimar Republic 75–6, 79, 85
welfare, and democracy 138, 533–4
Westernization 355, 363
Wilson, President Woodrow 71
women,
    in Indian society 215
    and Israeli democracy 379 Box 15.2, 381
    political participation 460–3, 464

position in Islam 333, 340, 345, 354–6, 389
in Soviet system 429–30 Table 17.2
women's suffrage 68–9
working class 20, 60, 66–7, 338, 339, 412–13
organized 515, 516, 522
urban 21, 264–5, 305–8
World Bank 16, 29, 31, 186, 256, 266, 287
World Council of Churches 32
World War I *see* First World War
World War II see Second World War

yangban class, Korea 220, 221, 222
Yeltsin, Boris 426–7, 428, 434, 435
Yemen 37–8, 327, 358
Yishuv *see* Jewish community in Palestine

Yugoslav Communist Party 476, 480
Yugoslavia 87–8, 95, 98, 99, 397, 399, 466–89, 514–16
(1919–45) 473 Map 19.2
communist rule in 475–6, 478–83
political community in 470–5
(post 1945) 479 Map 19.4

Zaire 37–8, 274
Zambia 289–90, 311, 528
Zambia Congress of Trade Unions 289
Zapata, E. 162
Zia-ul-Haq (Pakistan) 357
Zimbabwe 37–8, 275, 311
Zionism 367–72, 374–5, 377, 385, 386